I0010662

# OpenStack End User Guide

## SUSE OpenStack Cloud 7

# OpenStack End User Guide

SUSE OpenStack Cloud 7

ABSTRACT

OpenStack is an open-source cloud computing platform for public and private clouds. A series of interrelated projects deliver a cloud infrastructure solution. This guide shows OpenStack end users how to create and manage resources in an OpenStack cloud with the OpenStack dashboard and OpenStack client commands.

This guide documents OpenStack Ocata, Newton and Mitaka releases.

Publication Date: 08/04/2017

SUSE LLC
10 Canal Park Drive
Suite 200
Cambridge MA 02141
USA
https://www.suse.com/documentation

# Contents

# 1 Documentation Conventions

The following notices and typographical conventions are used in this documentation:

### Warning

Vital information you must be aware of before proceeding. Warns you about security issues, potential loss of data, damage to hardware, or physical hazards.

### Important

Important information you should be aware of before proceeding.

### Note

Additional information, for example about differences in software versions.

### Tip

Helpful information, like a guideline or a piece of practical advice.

```
tux > command
```

Commands than can be run by any user, including the `root` user.

```
root # command
```

Commands that must be run with `root` privileges. Often you can also prefix these commands with the **`sudo`** command to run them.

# 2 How can I use an OpenStack cloud?

As an OpenStack cloud end user, you can provision your own resources within the limits set by cloud administrators.

The examples in this guide show you how to perform tasks by using the following methods:

- OpenStack dashboard: Use this web-based graphical interface, code named horizon (https://git.openstack.org/cgit/openstack/horizon) ↗, to view, create, and manage resources.
- OpenStack command-line clients: Each core OpenStack project has a command-line client that you can use to run simple commands to view, create, and manage resources in a cloud and automate tasks by using scripts.

You can modify these examples for your specific use cases.

In addition to these ways of interacting with a cloud, you can access the OpenStack APIs directly or indirectly through cURL (http://curl.haxx.se) ↗ commands or open SDKs. You can automate access or build tools to manage resources and services by using the native OpenStack APIs or the EC2 compatibility API.

To use the OpenStack APIs, it helps to be familiar with HTTP/1.1, RESTful web services, the OpenStack services, and JSON or XML data serialization formats.

## 2.1 Who should read this book?

This book is written for anyone who uses virtual machines and cloud resources to develop software or perform research. You should have years of experience with Linux-based tool sets and be comfortable using both GUI and CLI based tools. While this book includes some information about using Python to create and manage cloud resources, Python knowledge is not a pre-requisite for reading this book.

# 3 OpenStack dashboard

As a cloud end user, you can use the OpenStack dashboard to provision your own resources within the limits set by administrators. You can modify the examples provided in this section to create other types and sizes of server instances.

## 3.1 Log in to the dashboard

The dashboard is generally installed on the controller node.

1. Ask the cloud operator for the host name or public IP address from which you can access the dashboard, and for your user name and password. If the cloud supports multi-domain model, you also need to ask for your domain name.

2. Open a web browser that has JavaScript and cookies enabled.

Note

To use the Virtual Network Computing (VNC) client for the dashboard, your browser must support HTML5 Canvas and HTML5 WebSockets. The VNC client is based on noVNC. For details, see noVNC: HTML5 VNC Client (https://github.com/kanaka/noVNC/blob/master/README.md). For a list of supported browsers, see Browser support (https://github.com/kanaka/noVNC/wiki/Browser-support).

3. In the address bar, enter the host name or IP address for the dashboard, for example, `https://ipAddressOrHostName/`.

Note

If a certificate warning appears when you try to access the URL for the first time, a self-signed certificate is in use, which is not considered trustworthy by default. Verify the certificate or add an exception in the browser to bypass the warning.

4. On the *Log In* page, enter your user name and password, and click *Sign In*. If the cloud supports multi-domain model, you also need to enter your domain name.
The top of the window displays your user name. You can also access the *Settings* tab (*Section 3.1.4, "OpenStack dashboard — Settings tab"*) or sign out of the dashboard.

The visible tabs and functions in the dashboard depend on the access permissions, or roles, of the user you are logged in as.

- If you are logged in as an end user, the ***Project*** tab (*Section 3.1.1, "OpenStack dashboard — Project tab"*) and ***Identity*** tab (*Section 3.1.3, "OpenStack dashboard — Identity tab"*) are displayed.
- If you are logged in as an administrator, the ***Project*** tab (*Section 3.1.1, "OpenStack dashboard — Project tab"*) and ***Admin*** tab (*Section 3.1.2, "OpenStack dashboard — Admin tab"*) and ***Identity*** tab (*Section 3.1.3, "OpenStack dashboard — Identity tab"*) are displayed.

Note

Some tabs, such as *Orchestration* and *Firewalls*, only appear on the dashboard if they are properly configured.

### 3.1.1 OpenStack dashboard — *Project* tab

Projects are organizational units in the cloud and are also known as tenants or accounts. Each user is a member of one or more projects. Within a project, a user creates and manages instances.

From the *Project* tab, you can view and manage the resources in a selected project, including instances and images. You can select the project from the drop-down menu at the top left. If the cloud supports multi-domain model, you can also select the domain from this menu.

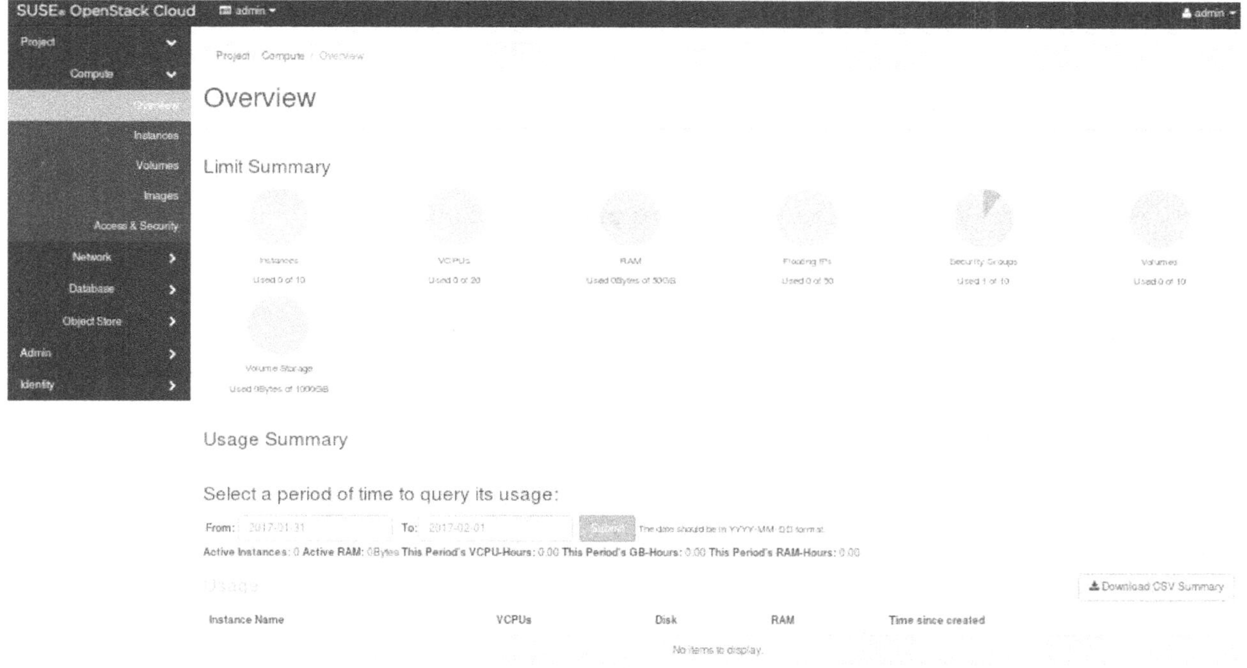


FIGURE 3.1: FIGURE: PROJECT TAB

From the *Project* tab, you can access the following categories:

### 3.1.1.1 *Compute* tab

- *Overview*: View reports for the project.
- *Instances*: View, launch, create a snapshot from, stop, pause, or reboot instances, or connect to them through VNC.
- *Volumes*: Use the following tabs to complete these tasks:
  - *Volumes*: View, create, edit, and delete volumes.
  - *Volume Snapshots*: View, create, edit, and delete volume snapshots.
- *Images*: View images and instance snapshots created by project users, plus any images that are publicly available. Create, edit, and delete images, and launch instances from images and snapshots.

- *Access & Security*: Use the following tabs to complete these tasks:
    - *Security Groups*: View, create, edit, and delete security groups and security group rules.
    - *Key Pairs*: View, create, edit, import, and delete key pairs.
    - *Floating IPs*: Allocate an IP address to or release it from a project.
    - *API Access*: View API endpoints.
- *Shares*: Use the following tabs to complete these tasks:
    - *Shares*: View, create, manage, and delete shares.
    - *Snapshots*: View, manage, and delete volume snapshots.
    - *Share Networks*: View, manage, and delete share networks.
    - *Security Services*: View, manage, and delete security services.

#### 3.1.1.2 *Network* tab

- *Network Topology*: View the network topology.
- *Networks*: Create and manage public and private networks.
- *Routers*: Create and manage routers.
- *Load Balancers*: Create and manage load balancers.
    - *Pools*: Add and manage pools.
    - *Members*: Add and manage members.
    - *Monitors*: Add and manage monitors.
- *Firewalls*: Create and manage firewalls.
    - *Firewalls*: Create and manage firewalls.
    - *Firewall Policies*: Add and manage firewall policies.
    - *Firewall Rules*: Add and manage firewall rules.

#### 3.1.1.3 *Orchestration* tab

- *Stacks*: Use the REST API to orchestrate multiple composite cloud applications.
- *Resource Types*: Show a list of all the supported resource types for HOT templates.

#### 3.1.1.4 *Object Store* tab

- *Containers*: Create and manage containers and objects.

### 3.1.2 OpenStack dashboard — *Admin* tab

Administrative users can use the *Admin* tab to view usage and to manage instances, volumes, flavors, images, networks, and so on.

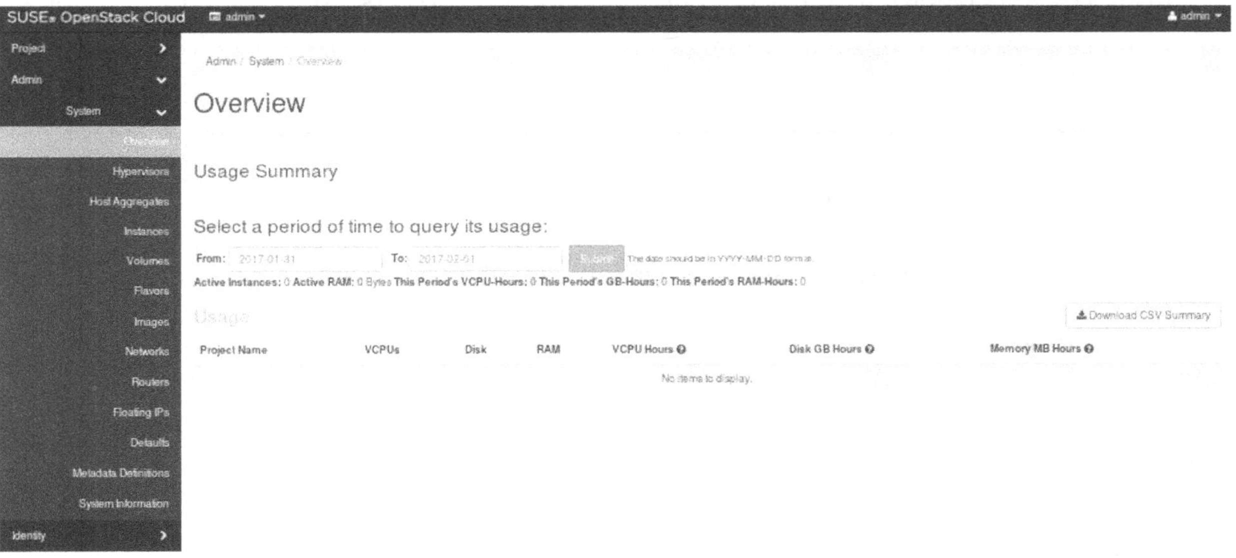


FIGURE 3.2: FIGURE: ADMIN TAB

From the *Admin* tab, you can access the following category to complete these tasks:

#### 3.1.2.1 *System* tab

- *Overview*: View basic reports.
- *Resource Usage*: Use the following tabs to view the following usages:
    - *Usage Report*: View the usage report.
    - *Stats*: View the statistics of all resources.
- *Hypervisors*: View the hypervisor summary.
- *Host Aggregates*: View, create, and edit host aggregates. View the list of availability zones.
- *Instances*: View, pause, resume, suspend, migrate, soft or hard reboot, and delete running instances that belong to users of some, but not all, projects. Also, view the log for an instance or access an instance through VNC.
- *Volumes*: Use the following tabs to complete these tasks:
    - *Volumes*: View, create, manage, and delete volumes.
    - *Volume Types*: View, create, manage, and delete volume types.
    - *Volume Snapshots*: View, manage, and delete volume snapshots.
- *Flavors*: View, create, edit, view extra specifications for, and delete flavors. A flavor is the size of an instance.
- *Images*: View, create, edit properties for, and delete custom images.
- *Networks*: View, create, edit properties for, and delete networks.
- *Routers*: View, create, edit properties for, and delete routers.
- *Defaults*: View default quota values. Quotas are hard-coded in OpenStack Compute and define the maximum allowable size and number of resources.
- *Metadata Definitions*: Import namespace and view the metadata information.

- *System Information*: Use the following tabs to view the service information:
    - *Services*: View a list of the services.
    - *Compute Services*: View a list of all Compute services.
    - *Block Storage Services*: View a list of all Block Storage services.
    - *Network Agents*: View the network agents.
    - *Orchestration Services*: View a list of all Orchestration services.
- *Shares*: Use the following tabs to complete these tasks:
    - *Shares*: View, create, manage, and delete shares.
    - *Snapshots*: View, manage, and delete volume snapshots.
    - *Share Networks*: View, manage, and delete share networks.
    - *Security Services*: View, manage, and delete security services.
    - *Share Types*: View, create, manage, and delete share types.
    - *Share Servers*: View, manage, and delete share servers.

### 3.1.3 OpenStack dashboard — *Identity* tab

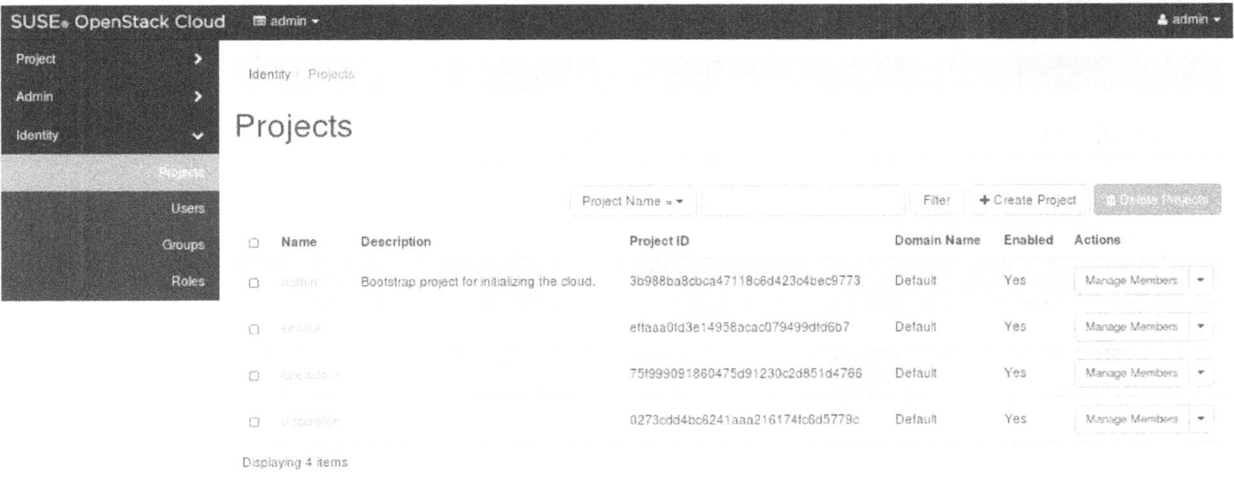


FIGURE 3.3: FIGURE:IDENTITY TAB

- *Projects*: View, create, assign users to, remove users from, and delete projects.
- *Users*: View, create, enable, disable, and delete users.

### 3.1.4 OpenStack dashboard — *Settings* tab

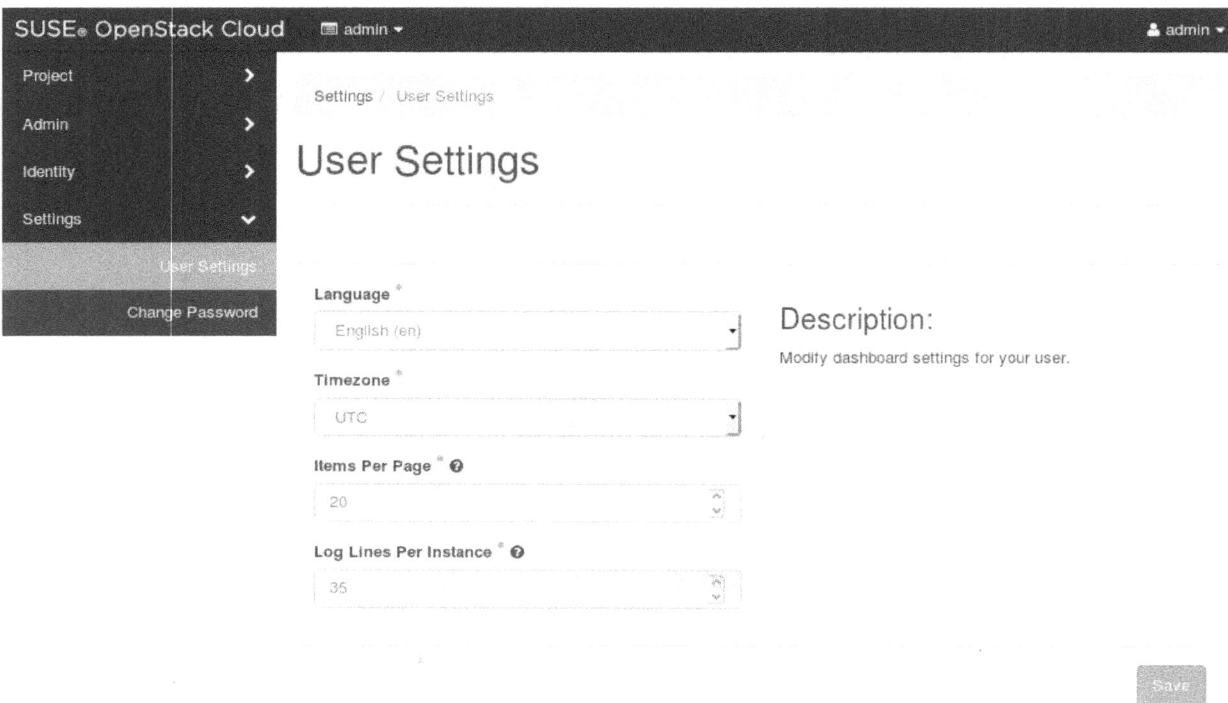


FIGURE 3.4: FIGURE:SETTINGS TAB

Click the *Settings* button from the user drop down menu at the top right of any page, you will see the *Settings* tab.

- *User Settings*: View and manage dashboard settings.
- *Change Password*: Change the password of the user.

## 3.2 Upload and manage images

A virtual machine image, referred to in this document simply as an image, is a single file that contains a virtual disk that has a bootable operating system installed on it. Images are used to create virtual machine instances within the cloud. For information about creating image files, see the OpenStack Virtual Machine Image Guide (https://docs.openstack.org/image-guide/) ↗.

Depending on your role, you may have permission to upload and manage virtual machine images. Operators might restrict the upload and management of images to cloud administrators or operators only. If you have the appropriate privileges, you can use the dashboard to upload and manage images in the admin project.

Note

You can also use the **openstack** and **glance** command-line clients or the Image service to manage images. For more information see .

### 3.2.1 Upload an image

Follow this procedure to upload an image to a project:

1. Log in to the dashboard.
2. Select the appropriate project from the drop down menu at the top left.
3. On the *Project* tab, open the *Compute* tab and click *Images* category.
4. Click *Create Image*.
   The *Create An Image* dialog box appears.

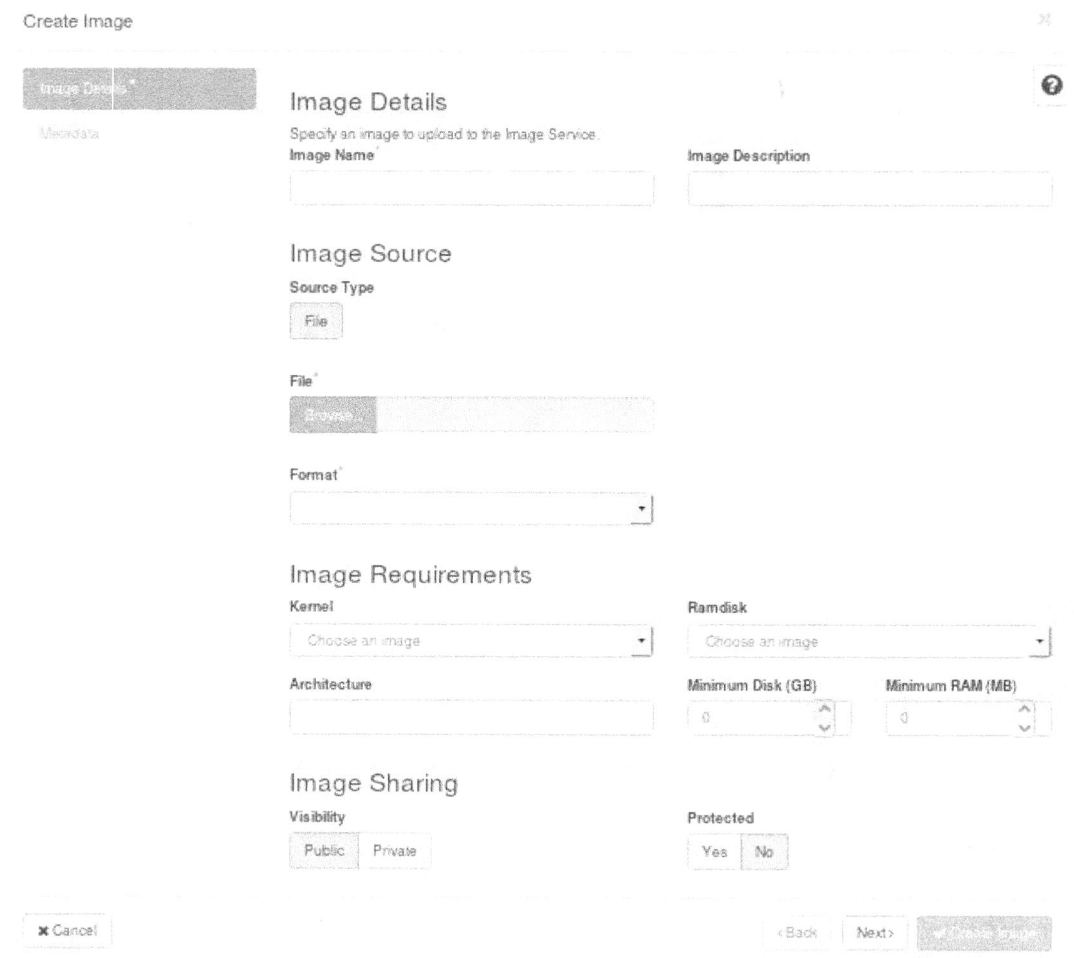


FIGURE 3.5: DASHBOARD — CREATE IMAGE

5. Enter the following values:

| | |
|---|---|
| *Image Name* | Enter a name for the image. |
| *Image Description* | Enter a brief description of the image. |
| *Image Source* | Choose the image source from the dropdown list. Your choices are *Image Location* and *Image File*. |

| | |
|---|---|
| *Image File* or *Image Location* | Based on your selection for *Image Source*, you either enter the location URL of the image in the *Image Location* field, or browse for the image file on your file system and add it. |
| *Format* | Select the image format (for example, QCOW2) for the image. |
| *Architecture* | Specify the architecture. For example, `i386` for a 32-bit architecture or `x86_64` for a 64-bit architecture. |
| *Minimum Disk (GB)* | Leave this field empty. |
| *Minimum RAM (MB)* | Leave this field empty. |
| *Copy Data* | Specify this option to copy image data to the Image service. |
| *Visibility* | The access permission for the image. `Public` or `Private`. |
| *Protected* | Select this check box to ensure that only users with permissions can delete the image. `Yes` or `No`. |
| *Image Metadata* | Specify this option to add resource metadata. The glance Metadata Catalog provides a list of metadata image definitions. (Note: Not all cloud providers enable this feature.) |

6. Click *Create Image*.
   The image is queued to be uploaded. It might take some time before the status changes from Queued to Active.

### 3.2.2 Update an image

Follow this procedure to update an existing image.

1. Log in to the dashboard.
2. Select the appropriate project from the drop down menu at the top left.
3. Select the image that you want to edit.
4. In the *Actions* column, click the menu button and then select *Edit Image* from the list.
5. In the *Edit Image* dialog box, you can perform various actions. For example:
   - Change the name of the image.
   - Select the *Public* check box to make the image public.
   - Clear the *Public* check box to make the image private.
6. Click *Edit Image*.

### 3.2.3 Delete an image

Deletion of images is permanent and **cannot** be reversed. Only users with the appropriate permissions can delete images.

1. Log in to the dashboard.
2. Select the appropriate project from the drop down menu at the top left.
3. On the *Project* tab, open the *Compute* tab and click *Images* category.
4. Select the images that you want to delete.
5. Click *Delete Images*.
6. In the *Confirm Delete Images* dialog box, click *Delete Images* to confirm the deletion.

## 3.3 Configure access and security for instances

Before you launch an instance, you should add security group rules to enable users to ping and use SSH to connect to the instance. Security groups are sets of IP filter rules that define networking access and are applied to all instances within a project. To do so, you either add rules to the default security group *Section 3.3.1, "Add a rule to the default security group"* or add a new security group with rules.

Key pairs are SSH credentials that are injected into an instance when it is launched. To use key pair injection, the image that the instance is based on must contain the `cloud-init` package. Each project should have at least one key pair. For more information, see the section *Section 3.3.2, "Add a key pair"*.

If you have generated a key pair with an external tool, you can import it into OpenStack. The key pair can be used for multiple instances that belong to a project. For more information, see the section *Section 3.3.3, "Import a key pair"*.

### Note

A key pair belongs to an individual user, not to a project. To share a key pair across multiple users, each user needs to import that key pair.

When an instance is created in OpenStack, it is automatically assigned a fixed IP address in the network to which the instance is assigned. This IP address is permanently associated with the instance until the instance is terminated. However, in addition to the fixed IP address, a floating IP address can also be attached to an instance. Unlike fixed IP addresses, floating IP addresses are able to have their associations modified at any time, regardless of the state of the instances involved.

### 3.3.1 Add a rule to the default security group

This procedure enables SSH and ICMP (ping) access to instances. The rules apply to all instances within a given project, and should be set for every project unless there is a reason to prohibit SSH or ICMP access to the instances.

This procedure can be adjusted as necessary to add additional security group rules to a project, if your cloud requires them.

Note

When adding a rule, you must specify the protocol used with the destination port or source port.

1. Log in to the dashboard.
2. Select the appropriate project from the drop down menu at the top left.
3. On the *Project* tab, open the *Compute* tab and click *Access & Security* category. The *Security Groups* tab shows the security groups that are available for this project.
4. Select the default security group and click *Manage Rules*.
5. To allow SSH access, click *Add Rule*.
6. In the *Add Rule* dialog box, enter the following values:
   - **Rule:** `SSH`
   - **Remote:** `CIDR`
   - **CIDR:** `0.0.0.0/0`

   Note

   To accept requests from a particular range of IP addresses, specify the IP address block in the *CIDR* box.

7. Click *Add*.
   Instances will now have SSH port 22 open for requests from any IP address.
8. To add an ICMP rule, click *Add Rule*.
9. In the *Add Rule* dialog box, enter the following values:
   - **Rule:** `All ICMP`
   - **Direction:** `Ingress`
   - **Remote:** `CIDR`
   - **CIDR:** `0.0.0.0/0`

10. Click *Add*.
    Instances will now accept all incoming ICMP packets.

### 3.3.2 Add a key pair

Create at least one key pair for each project.

1. Log in to the dashboard.
2. Select the appropriate project from the drop down menu at the top left.
3. On the *Project* tab, open the *Compute* tab and click *Access & Security* category.
4. Click the *Key Pairs* tab, which shows the key pairs that are available for this project.
5. Click *Create Key Pair*.
6. In the *Create Key Pair* dialog box, enter a name for your key pair, and click *Create Key Pair*.
7. Respond to the prompt to download the key pair.

### 3.3.3 Import a key pair

1. Log in to the dashboard.
2. Select the appropriate project from the drop down menu at the top left.
3. On the *Project* tab, open the *Compute* tab and click *Access & Security* category.
4. Click the *Key Pairs* tab, which shows the key pairs that are available for this project.
5. Click *Import Key Pair*.
6. In the *Import Key Pair* dialog box, enter the name of your key pair, copy the public key into the *Public Key* box, and then click *Import Key Pair*.
7. Save the `*.pem` file locally.
8. To change its permissions so that only you can read and write to the file, run the following command:

```
$ chmod 0600 yourPrivateKey.pem
```

Note

If you are using the Dashboard from a Windows computer, use PuTTYgen to load the `*.pem` file and convert and save it as `*.ppk`. For more information see the WinSCP web page for PuTTYgen (http://winscp.net/eng/docs/ui_puttygen).

9. To make the key pair known to SSH, run the **`ssh-add`** command.

```
$ ssh-add yourPrivateKey.pem
```

The Compute database registers the public key of the key pair.

The Dashboard lists the key pair on the *Access & Security* tab.

### 3.3.4 Allocate a floating IP address to an instance

When an instance is created in OpenStack, it is automatically assigned a fixed IP address in the network to which the instance is assigned. This IP address is permanently associated with the instance until the instance is terminated.

However, in addition to the fixed IP address, a floating IP address can also be attached to an instance. Unlike fixed IP addresses, floating IP addresses can have their associations modified at any time, regardless of the state of the instances involved. This procedure details the reservation of a floating IP address from an existing pool of addresses and the association of that address with a specific instance.

1. Log in to the dashboard.
2. Select the appropriate project from the drop down menu at the top left.
3. On the *Project* tab, open the *Compute* tab and click *Access & Security* category.
4. Click the *Floating IPs* tab, which shows the floating IP addresses allocated to instances.
5. Click *Allocate IP To Project.*
6. Choose the pool from which to pick the IP address.
7. Click *Allocate IP.*
8. In the *Floating IPs* list, click *Associate.*

9. In the *Manage Floating IP Associations* dialog box, choose the following options:

    - The *IP Address* field is filled automatically, but you can add a new IP address by clicking the + button.
    - In the *Port to be associated* field, select a port from the list.
      The list shows all the instances with their fixed IP addresses.

10. Click *Associate*.

Note

To disassociate an IP address from an instance, click the *Disassociate* button.

To release the floating IP address back into the floating IP pool, click the *Release Floating IP* option in the *Actions* column.

## 3.4 Launch and manage instances

Instances are virtual machines that run inside the cloud. You can launch an instance from the following sources:

- Images uploaded to the Image service.
- Image that you have copied to a persistent volume. The instance launches from the volume, which is provided by the `cinder-volume` API through iSCSI.
- Instance snapshot that you took.

### 3.4.1 Launch an instance

1. Log in to the dashboard.
2. Select the appropriate project from the drop down menu at the top left.
3. On the *Project* tab, open the *Compute* tab and click *Instances* category.
   The dashboard shows the instances with its name, its private and floating IP addresses, size, status, task, power state, and so on.

4. Click *Launch Instance*.

5. In the *Launch Instance* dialog box, specify the following values:
   *Details* tab

   **Instance Name**
   Assign a name to the virtual machine.

   **Availability Zone**
   By default, this value is set to the availability zone given by the cloud provider (for example, `us-west` or `apac-south`). For some cases, it could be `nova`.

   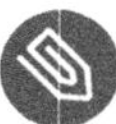
   Note

   The name you assign here becomes the initial host name of the server. If the name is longer than 63 characters, the Compute service truncates it automatically to ensure dnsmasq works correctly.

   After the server is built, if you change the server name in the API or change the host name directly, the names are not updated in the dashboard.

   Server names are not guaranteed to be unique when created so you could have two instances with the same host name.

   **Count**
   To launch multiple instances, enter a value greater than `1`. The default is `1`.

   *Source* tab

   **Instance Boot Source**
   Your options are:

   **Boot from image**
   If you choose this option, a new field for *Image Name* displays. You can select the image from the list.

   **Boot from snapshot**
   If you choose this option, a new field for *Instance Snapshot* displays. You can select the snapshot from the list.

**Boot from volume**

If you choose this option, a new field for *Volume* displays. You can select the volume from the list.

**Boot from image (creates a new volume)**

With this option, you can boot from an image and create a volume by entering the *Device Size* and *Device Name* for your volume. Click the *Delete Volume on Instance Delete* option to delete the volume on deleting the instance.

**Boot from volume snapshot (creates a new volume)**

Using this option, you can boot from a volume snapshot and create a new volume by choosing *Volume Snapshot* from a list and adding a *Device Name* for your volume. Click the *Delete Volume on Instance Delete* option to delete the volume on deleting the instance.

**Image Name**

This field changes based on your previous selection. If you have chosen to launch an instance using an image, the *Image Name* field displays. Select the image name from the dropdown list.

**Instance Snapshot**

This field changes based on your previous selection. If you have chosen to launch an instance using a snapshot, the *Instance Snapshot* field displays. Select the snapshot name from the dropdown list.

**Volume**

This field changes based on your previous selection. If you have chosen to launch an instance using a volume, the *Volume* field displays. Select the volume name from the dropdown list. If you want to delete the volume on instance delete, check the *Delete Volume on Instance Delete* option.

*Flavor* tab

**Flavor**

Specify the size of the instance to launch.

Note

The flavor is selected based on the size of the image selected for launching an instance. For example, while creating an image, if you have entered the value in the *Minimum RAM (MB)* field as 2048, then on selecting the image, the default flavor is `m1.small`.

*Networks* tab

**Selected Networks**

To add a network to the instance, click the + in the *Available* field.

*Network Ports* tab

**Ports**

Activate the ports that you want to assign to the instance.

*Security Groups* tab

**Security Groups**

Activate the security groups that you want to assign to the instance.
Security groups are a kind of cloud firewall that define which incoming network traffic is forwarded to instances.
If you have not created any security groups, you can assign only the default security group to the instance.

*Key Pair* tab

**Key Pair**

Specify a key pair.
If the image uses a static root password or a static key set (neither is recommended), you do not need to provide a key pair to launch the instance.

*Configuration* tab

**Customization Script Source**

Specify a customization script that runs after your instance launches.

*Metadata* tab

**Available Metadata**

Add Metadata items to your instance.

6. Click *Launch Instance*.

The instance starts on a compute node in the cloud.

Note

If you did not provide a key pair, security groups, or rules, users can access the instance only from inside the cloud through VNC. Even pinging the instance is not possible without an ICMP rule configured.

You can also launch an instance from the *Images* or *Volumes* category when you launch an instance from an image or a volume respectively.

When you launch an instance from an image, OpenStack creates a local copy of the image on the compute node where the instance starts.

For details on creating images, see Creating images manually (https://docs.openstack.org/image-guide/create-images-manually.html) in the *OpenStack Virtual Machine Image Guide*.

When you launch an instance from a volume, note the following steps:

- To select the volume from which to launch, launch an instance from an arbitrary image on the volume. The arbitrary image that you select does not boot. Instead, it is replaced by the image on the volume that you choose in the next steps.
  To boot a Xen image from a volume, the image you launch in must be the same type, fully virtualized or paravirtualized, as the one on the volume.

- Select the volume or volume snapshot from which to boot. Enter a device name. Enter `vda` for KVM images or `xvda` for Xen images.

### 3.4.2 Connect to your instance by using SSH

To use SSH to connect to your instance, use the downloaded keypair file.

Note

The user name is `ubuntu` for the Ubuntu cloud images on TryStack.

1. Copy the IP address for your instance.
2. Use the **ssh** command to make a secure connection to the instance. For example:

```
$ ssh -i MyKey.pem ubuntu@10.0.0.2
```

3. At the prompt, type `yes`.

It is also possible to SSH into an instance without an SSH keypair, if the administrator has enabled root password injection. For more information about root password injection, see Injecting the administrator password (https://docs.openstack.org/admin-guide/compute-admin-password-injection.html) in the *OpenStack Administrator Guide*.

### 3.4.3 Track usage for instances

You can track usage for instances for each project. You can track costs per month by showing meters like number of vCPUs, disks, RAM, and uptime for all your instances.

1. Log in to the dashboard.
2. Select the appropriate project from the drop down menu at the top left.
3. On the *Project* tab, open the *Compute* tab and click *Overview* category.
4. To query the instance usage for a month, select a month and click *Submit*.
5. To download a summary, click *Download CSV Summary*.

### 3.4.4 Create an instance snapshot

1. Log in to the dashboard.
2. Select the appropriate project from the drop down menu at the top left.
3. On the *Project* tab, open the *Compute* tab and click the *Instances* category.

4. Select the instance from which to create a snapshot.
5. In the actions column, click *Create Snapshot*.
6. In the *Create Snapshot* dialog box, enter a name for the snapshot, and click *Create Snapshot*. The *Images* category shows the instance snapshot.

To launch an instance from the snapshot, select the snapshot and click *Launch*. Proceed with launching an instance.

### 3.4.5 Manage an instance

1. Log in to the dashboard.
2. Select the appropriate project from the drop down menu at the top left.
3. On the *Project* tab, open the *Compute* tab and click *Instances* category.
4. Select an instance.
5. In the menu list in the actions column, select the state.
   You can resize or rebuild an instance. You can also choose to view the instance console log, edit instance or the security groups. Depending on the current state of the instance, you can pause, resume, suspend, soft or hard reboot, or terminate it.

## 3.5 Create and manage networks

The OpenStack Networking service provides a scalable system for managing the network connectivity within an OpenStack cloud deployment. It can easily and quickly react to changing network needs (for example, creating and assigning new IP addresses).

Networking in OpenStack is complex. This section provides the basic instructions for creating a network and a router. For detailed information about managing networks, refer to the OpenStack Administrator Guide (https://docs.openstack.org/admin-guide/networking.html) ↗.

### 3.5.1 Create a network

1. Log in to the dashboard.

2. Select the appropriate project from the drop down menu at the top left.

3. On the *Project* tab, open the *Network* tab and click *Networks* category.

4. Click *Create Network*.

5. In the *Create Network* dialog box, specify the following values.
   *Network* tab
   *Network Name*: Specify a name to identify the network.
   *Shared*: Share the network with other projects. Non admin users are not allowed to set shared option.
   *Admin State*: The state to start the network in.
   *Create Subnet*: Select this check box to create a subnet
   You do not have to specify a subnet when you create a network, but if you do not specify a subnet, the network can not be attached to an instance.
   *Subnet* tab
   *Subnet Name*: Specify a name for the subnet.
   *Network Address*: Specify the IP address for the subnet.
   *IP Version*: Select IPv4 or IPv6.
   *Gateway IP*: Specify an IP address for a specific gateway. This parameter is optional.
   *Disable Gateway*: Select this check box to disable a gateway IP address.
   *Subnet Details* tab
   *Enable DHCP*: Select this check box to enable DHCP.
   *Allocation Pools*: Specify IP address pools.
   *DNS Name Servers*: Specify a name for the DNS server.
   *Host Routes*: Specify the IP address of host routes.

6. Click *Create*.
   The dashboard shows the network on the *Networks* tab.

### 3.5.2 Create a router

1. Log in to the dashboard.

2. Select the appropriate project from the drop down menu at the top left.

3. On the *Project* tab, open the *Network* tab and click *Routers* category.

4. Click *Create Router*.

5. In the *Create Router* dialog box, specify a name for the router and *External Network*, and click *Create Router*.
   The new router is now displayed in the *Routers* tab.

6. To connect a private network to the newly created router, perform the following steps:

   a. On the *Routers* tab, click the name of the router.

   b. On the *Router Details* page, click the *Interfaces* tab, then click *Add Interface*.

   c. In the *Add Interface* dialog box, select a *Subnet*.
      Optionally, in the *Add Interface* dialog box, set an *IP Address* for the router interface for the selected subnet.
      If you choose not to set the *IP Address* value, then by default OpenStack Networking uses the first host IP address in the subnet.
      The *Router Name* and *Router ID* fields are automatically updated.

7. Click *Add Interface*.

You have successfully created the router. You can view the new topology from the *Network Topology* tab.

### 3.5.3 Create a port

Warning

Creating and managing ports requires administrator privileges. Contact an administrator before adding or changing ports.

1. Log in to the dashboard.

2. Select the appropriate project from the drop-down menu at the top left.

3. On the *Admin* tab, click *Networks* category.

4. Click on the *Network Name* of the network in which the port has to be created.

5. In the *Create Port* dialog box, specify the following values.
   *Name*: Specify name to identify the port.
   *Device ID*: Device ID attached to the port.

*Device Owner*: Device owner attached to the port.
*Binding Host*: The ID of the host where the port is allocated.
*Binding VNIC Type*: Select the VNIC type that is bound to the neutron port.

6. Click *Create Port*.
The new port is now displayed in the *Ports* list.

## 3.6 Create and manage object containers

OpenStack Object Storage (swift) is used for redundant, scalable data storage using clusters of standardized servers to store petabytes of accessible data. It is a long-term storage system for large amounts of static data which can be retrieved and updated.

OpenStack Object Storage provides a distributed, API-accessible storage platform that can be integrated directly into an application or used to store any type of file, including VM images, backups, archives, or media files. In the OpenStack dashboard, you can only manage containers and objects.

In OpenStack Object Storage, containers provide storage for objects in a manner similar to a Windows folder or Linux file directory, though they cannot be nested. An object in OpenStack consists of the file to be stored in the container and any accompanying metadata.

### 3.6.1 Create a container

1. Log in to the dashboard.
2. Select the appropriate project from the drop down menu at the top left.
3. On the *Project* tab, open the *Object Store* tab and click *Containers* category.
4. Click *Container*.
5. In the *Create Container* dialog box, enter a name for the container, and then click *Create*.

You have successfully created a container.

Note

To delete a container, click the *More* button and select *Delete Container*.

### 3.6.2 Upload an object

1. Log in to the dashboard.
2. Select the appropriate project from the drop down menu at the top left.
3. On the *Project* tab, open the *Object Store* tab and click *Containers* category.
4. Select the container in which you want to store your object.
5. Click the *Upload File* icon.
   The *Upload File To Container: <name>* dialog box appears. `<name>` is the name of the container to which you are uploading the object.
6. Enter a name for the object.
7. Browse to and select the file that you want to upload.
8. Click *Upload File*.

You have successfully uploaded an object to the container.

Note

To delete an object, click the *More button* and select *Delete Object*.

### 3.6.3 Manage an object

**To edit an object**

1. Log in to the dashboard.
2. Select the appropriate project from the drop down menu at the top left.
3. On the *Project* tab, open the *Object Store* tab and click *Containers* category.
4. Select the container in which you want to store your object.
5. Click the menu button and choose *Edit* from the dropdown list.
   The *Edit Object* dialog box is displayed.
6. Browse to and select the file that you want to upload.

7. Click *Update Object.*

Note

To delete an object, click the menu button and select *Delete Object.*

**To copy an object from one container to another**

1. Log in to the dashboard.
2. Select the appropriate project from the drop down menu at the top left.
3. On the *Project* tab, open the *Object Store* tab and click *Containers* category.
4. Select the container in which you want to store your object.
5. Click the menu button and choose *Copy* from the dropdown list.
6. In the *Copy Object* launch dialog box, enter the following values:
    - *Destination Container*: Choose the destination container from the list.
    - *Path*: Specify a path in which the new copy should be stored inside of the selected container.
    - *Destination object name*: Enter a name for the object in the new container.
7. Click *Copy Object.*

**To create a metadata-only object without a file**

You can create a new object in container without a file available and can upload the file later when it is ready. This temporary object acts a place-holder for a new object, and enables the user to share object metadata and URL info in advance.

1. Log in to the dashboard.
2. Select the appropriate project from the drop down menu at the top left.
3. On the *Project* tab, open the *Object Store* tab and click *Containers* category.
4. Select the container in which you want to store your object.
5. Click *Upload Object.*

The *Upload Object To Container:* `<name>` dialog box is displayed.
`<name>` is the name of the container to which you are uploading the object.

6. Enter a name for the object.

7. Click *Update Object.*

**To create a pseudo-folder**

Pseudo-folders are similar to folders in your desktop operating system. They are virtual collections defined by a common prefix on the object's name.

1. Log in to the dashboard.

2. Select the appropriate project from the drop down menu at the top left.

3. On the *Project* tab, open the *Object Store* tab and click *Containers* category.

4. Select the container in which you want to store your object.

5. Click *Create Pseudo-folder.*
The *Create Pseudo-Folder in Container* `<name>` dialog box is displayed. `<name>` is the name of the container to which you are uploading the object.

6. Enter a name for the pseudo-folder.
A slash (/) character is used as the delimiter for pseudo-folders in Object Storage.

7. Click *Create.*

## 3.7 Create and manage volumes

Volumes are block storage devices that you attach to instances to enable persistent storage. You can attach a volume to a running instance or detach a volume and attach it to another instance at any time. You can also create a snapshot from or delete a volume. Only administrative users can create volume types.

### 3.7.1 Create a volume

1. Log in to the dashboard.

2. Select the appropriate project from the drop down menu at the top left.

3. On the *Project* tab, open the *Compute* tab and click *Volumes* category.

4. Click *Create Volume.*
   In the dialog box that opens, enter or select the following values.
   *Volume Name*: Specify a name for the volume.
   *Description*: Optionally, provide a brief description for the volume.
   *Volume Source*: Select one of the following options:

   - No source, empty volume: Creates an empty volume. An empty volume does not contain a file system or a partition table.

   - Snapshot: If you choose this option, a new field for *Use snapshot as a source* displays. You can select the snapshot from the list.

   - Image: If you choose this option, a new field for *Use image as a source* displays. You can select the image from the list.

   - Volume: If you choose this option, a new field for *Use volume as a source* displays. You can select the volume from the list. Options to use a snapshot or a volume as the source for a volume are displayed only if there are existing snapshots or volumes.

   *Type*: Leave this field blank.
   *Size (GB)*: The size of the volume in gibibytes (GiB).
   *Availability Zone*: Select the Availability Zone from the list. By default, this value is set to the availability zone given by the cloud provider (for example, `us-west` or `apac-south`). For some cases, it could be `nova`.

5. Click *Create Volume.*

The dashboard shows the volume on the *Volumes* tab.

### 3.7.2 Attach a volume to an instance

After you create one or more volumes, you can attach them to instances. You can attach a volume to one instance at a time.

1. Log in to the dashboard.

2. Select the appropriate project from the drop down menu at the top left.

3. On the *Project* tab, open the *Compute* tab and click *Volumes* category.

4. Select the volume to add to an instance and click *Manage Attachments*.

5. In the *Manage Volume Attachments* dialog box, select an instance.

6. Enter the name of the device from which the volume is accessible by the instance.

Note

The actual device name might differ from the volume name because of hypervisor settings.

7. Click *Attach Volume*.
   The dashboard shows the instance to which the volume is now attached and the device name.

You can view the status of a volume in the Volumes tab of the dashboard. The volume is either Available or In-Use.

Now you can log in to the instance and mount, format, and use the disk.

### 3.7.3 Detach a volume from an instance

1. Log in to the dashboard.

2. Select the appropriate project from the drop down menu at the top left.

3. On the *Project* tab, open the *Compute* tab and click the *Volumes* category.

4. Select the volume and click *Manage Attachments*.

5. Click *Detach Volume* and confirm your changes.

A message indicates whether the action was successful.

### 3.7.4 Create a snapshot from a volume

1. Log in to the dashboard.

2. Select the appropriate project from the drop down menu at the top left.
3. On the *Project* tab, open the *Compute* tab and click *Volumes* category.
4. Select a volume from which to create a snapshot.
5. In the *Actions* column, click *Create Snapshot*.
6. In the dialog box that opens, enter a snapshot name and a brief description.
7. Confirm your changes.
   The dashboard shows the new volume snapshot in Volume Snapshots tab.

### 3.7.5 Edit a volume

1. Log in to the dashboard.
2. Select the appropriate project from the drop down menu at the top left.
3. On the *Project* tab, open the *Compute* tab and click *Volumes* category.
4. Select the volume that you want to edit.
5. In the *Actions* column, click *Edit Volume*.
6. In the *Edit Volume* dialog box, update the name and description of the volume.
7. Click *Edit Volume*.

**Note**

You can extend a volume by using the *Extend Volume* option available in the *More* dropdown list and entering the new value for volume size.

### 3.7.6 Delete a volume

When you delete an instance, the data in its attached volumes is not deleted.

1. Log in to the dashboard.

2. Select the appropriate project from the drop down menu at the top left.
3. On the *Project* tab, open the *Compute* tab and click *Volumes* category.
4. Select the check boxes for the volumes that you want to delete.
5. Click *Delete Volumes* and confirm your choice.
   A message indicates whether the action was successful.

## 3.8 Create and manage shares

Shares are file storage that you provide access to instances. You can allow access to a share to a running instance or deny access to a share and allow access to it to another instance at any time. You can also delete a share. You can create snapshot from a share if the driver supports it. Only administrative users can create share types.

### 3.8.1 Create a share

1. Log in to the dashboard, choose a project, and click *Shares*.
2. Click *Create Share*.
   In the dialog box that opens, enter or select the following values.
   *Share Name*: Specify a name for the share.
   *Description*: Optionally, provide a brief description for the share.
   *Share Type*: Choose a share type.
   *Size (GB)*: The size of the share in gibibytes (GiB).
   *Share Protocol*: Select NFS, CIFS, GlusterFS, or HDFS.
   *Share Network*: Choose a share network.
   *Metadata*: Enter metadata for the share creation if needed.
3. Click *Create Share*.

The dashboard shows the share on the *Shares* tab.

### 3.8.2 Delete a share

1. Log in to the dashboard, choose a project, and click *Shares*.

2. Select the check boxes for the shares that you want to delete.

3. Click *Delete Shares* and confirm your choice.
   A message indicates whether the action was successful.

### 3.8.3 Allow access

1. Log in to the dashboard, choose a project, and click *Shares*.

2. Go to the share that you want to allow access and choose *Manage Rules* from Actions.

3. Click *Add rule*.
   *Access Type*: Choose ip, user, or cert.
   *Access Level*: Choose read-write or read-only.
   *Access To*: Fill in Access To field.

4. Click *Add Rule*.
   A message indicates whether the action was successful.

### 3.8.4 Deny access

1. Log in to the dashboard, choose a project, and click *Shares*.

2. Go to the share that you want to deny access and choose *Manage Rules* from Actions.

3. Choose the rule you want to delete.

4. Click *Delete rule* and confirm your choice.
   A message indicates whether the action was successful.

### 3.8.5 Edit share metadata

1. Log in to the dashboard, choose a project, and click *Shares*.

2. Go to the share that you want to edit and choose *Edit Share Metadata* from Actions.

3. *Metadata*: To add share metadata, use key=value. To unset metadata, use key.

4. Click *Edit Share Metadata*.

A message indicates whether the action was successful.

### 3.8.6 Edit share

1. Log in to the dashboard, choose a project, and click *Shares*.
2. Go to the share that you want to edit and choose *Edit Share* from Actions.
3. *Share Name*: Enter a new share name.
4. *Description*: Enter a new description.
5. Click *Edit Share*.
   A message indicates whether the action was successful.

### 3.8.7 Extend share

1. Log in to the dashboard, choose a project, and click *Shares*.
2. Go to the share that you want to edit and choose *Extend Share* from Actions.
3. *New Size (GB)*: Enter new size.
4. Click *Extend Share*.
   A message indicates whether the action was successful.

### 3.8.8 Create share network

1. Log in to the dashboard, choose a project, click *Shares*, and click *Share Networks*.
2. Click *Create Share Network*.
   In the dialog box that opens, enter or select the following values.
   *Name*: Specify a name for the share network.
   *Description*: Optionally, provide a brief description for the share network.
   *Neutron Net*: Choose a neutron network.
   *Neutron Subnet*: Choose a neutron subnet.
3. Click *Create Share Network*.

The dashboard shows the share network on the *Share Networks* tab.

### 3.8.9 Delete a share network

1. Log in to the dashboard, choose a project, click *Shares*, and click *Share Networks*.
2. Select the check boxes for the share networks that you want to delete.
3. Click *Delete Share Networks* and confirm your choice.
   A message indicates whether the action was successful.

### 3.8.10 Edit share network

1. Log in to the dashboard, choose a project, click *Shares*, and click *Share Networks*.
2. Go to the share network that you want to edit and choose *Edit Share Network* from Actions.
3. *Name*: Enter a new share network name.
4. *Description*: Enter a new description.
5. Click *Edit Share Network*.
   A message indicates whether the action was successful.

### 3.8.11 Create security service

1. Log in to the dashboard, choose a project, click *Shares*, and click *Security Services*.
2. Click *Create Security Service*.
   In the dialog box that opens, enter or select the following values.
   *Name*: Specify a name for the security service.
   *DNS IP*: Enter the DNS IP address.
   *Server*: Enter the server name.
   *Domain*: Enter the domain name.
   *User*: Enter the user name.
   *Password*: Enter the password.
   *Confirm Password*: Enter the password again to confirm.

*Type*: Choose the type from Active Directory, LDAP, or Kerberos.
*Description*: Optionally, provide a brief description for the security service.

3. Click *Create Security Service*.

The dashboard shows the security service on the *Security Services* tab.

### 3.8.12 Delete a security service

1. Log in to the dashboard, choose a project, click *Shares*, and click *Security Services*.
2. Select the check boxes for the security services that you want to delete.
3. Click *Delete Security Services* and confirm your choice.
   A message indicates whether the action was successful.

### 3.8.13 Edit security service

1. Log in to the dashboard, choose a project, click *Shares*, and click *Security Services*.
2. Go to the security service that you want to edit and choose *Edit Security Service* from Actions.
3. *Name*: Enter a new security service name.
4. *Description*: Enter a new description.
5. Click *Edit Security Service*.
   A message indicates whether the action was successful.

## 3.9 Launch and manage stacks

OpenStack Orchestration is a service that you can use to orchestrate multiple composite cloud applications. This service supports the use of both the Amazon Web Services (AWS) CloudFormation template format through both a Query API that is compatible with CloudFormation and the native OpenStack *Heat Orchestration Template (HOT)* format through a REST API.

These flexible template languages enable application developers to describe and automate the deployment of infrastructure, services, and applications. The templates enable creation of most OpenStack resource types, such as instances, floating IP addresses, volumes, security groups, and users. Once created, the resources are referred to as stacks.

The template languages are described in the Template Guide (https://docs.openstack.org/developer/heat/template_guide/index.html) in the Heat developer documentation (http://docs.openstack.org/developer/heat/).

### 3.9.1 Launch a stack

1. Log in to the dashboard.
2. Select the appropriate project from the drop down menu at the top left.
3. On the *Project* tab, open the *Orchestration* tab and click *Stacks* category.
4. Click *Launch Stack.*
5. In the *Select Template* dialog box, specify the following values:

| | |
|---|---|
| *Template Source* | Choose the source of the template from the list. |
| *Template URL/File/Data* | Depending on the source that you select, enter the URL, browse to the file location, or directly include the template. |
| *Environment Source* | Choose the source of the environment from the list. The environment files contain additional settings for the stack. |
| *Environment File/Data* | Depending on the source that you select, browse to the file location, directly include the environment |

6. Click *Next.*

7. In the *Launch Stack* dialog box, specify the following values:

| | |
|---|---|
| *Stack Name* | Enter a name to identify the stack. |
| *Creation Timeout (minutes)* | Specify the number of minutes that can elapse before the launch of the stack times out. |
| *Rollback On Failure* | Select this check box if you want the service to roll back changes if the stack fails to launch. |
| *Password for user "demo"* | Specify the password that the default user uses when the stack is created. |
| *DBUsername* | Specify the name of the database user. |
| *LinuxDistribution* | Specify the Linux distribution that is used in the stack. |
| *DBRootPassword* | Specify the root password for the database. |
| *KeyName* | Specify the name of the key pair to use to log in to the stack. |
| *DBName* | Specify the name of the database. |
| *DBPassword* | Specify the password of the database. |
| *InstanceType* | Specify the flavor for the instance. |

8. Click *Launch* to create a stack. The *Stacks* tab shows the stack.

After the stack is created, click on the stack name to see the following details:

**Topology**

The topology of the stack.

**Overview**

The parameters and details of the stack.

**Resources**

The resources used by the stack.

**Events**

The events related to the stack.

**Template**

The template for the stack.

### 3.9.2 Manage a stack

1. Log in to the dashboard.
2. Select the appropriate project from the drop down menu at the top left.
3. On the *Project* tab, open the *Orchestration* tab and click *Stacks* category.
4. Select the stack that you want to update.
5. Click *Change Stack Template.*
6. In the *Select Template* dialog box, select the new template source or environment source.
7. Click *Next.*
   The *Update Stack Parameters* window appears.
8. Enter new values for any parameters that you want to update.
9. Click *Update.*

### 3.9.3 Delete a stack

When you delete a stack, you cannot undo this action.

1. Log in to the dashboard.
2. Select the appropriate project from the drop down menu at the top left.
3. On the *Project* tab, open the *Orchestration* tab and click *Stacks* category.
4. Select the stack that you want to delete.
5. Click *Delete Stack.*

6. In the confirmation dialog box, click *Delete Stack* to confirm the deletion.

## 3.10 Create and manage databases

The Database service provides scalable and reliable cloud provisioning functionality for both relational and non-relational database engines. Users can quickly and easily use database features without the burden of handling complex administrative tasks.

### 3.10.1 Create a database instance

**Prerequisites.** Before you create a database instance, you need to configure a default datastore and make sure you have an appropriate flavor for the type of database instance you want.

1. **Configure a default datastore.**
   Because the dashboard does not let you choose a specific datastore to use with an instance, you need to configure a default datastore. The dashboard then uses the default datastore to create the instance.

   a. Add the following line to `/etc/trove/trove.conf`:

   ```
   default_datastore = DATASTORE_NAME
   ```

   Replace `DATASTORE_NAME` with the name that the administrative user set when issuing the **`trove-manage`** command to create the datastore. You can use the trove **`datastore-list`** command to display the datastores that are available in your environment.
   For example, if your MySQL data store name is set to `mysql`, your entry would look like this:

   ```
   default_datastore = mysql
   ```

   b. Restart Database services on the controller node:

   ```
   # service trove-api restart
   # service trove-taskmanager restart
   # service trove-conductor restart
   ```

2. **Verify flavor.**
   Make sure an appropriate flavor exists for the type of database instance you want.

**Create database instance.** Once you have configured a default datastore and verified that you have an appropriate flavor, you can create a database instance.

1. Log in to the dashboard.
2. From the CURRENT PROJECT on the *Project* tab, select the appropriate project.
3. On the *Project* tab, open the *Database* tab and click *Instances* category. This lists the instances that already exist in your environment.
4. Click *Launch Instance*.
5. In the *Launch Database* dialog box, specify the following values.
   Details
   *Database Name*: Specify a name for the database instance.
   *Flavor*: Select an appropriate flavor for the instance.
   *Volume Size*: Select a volume size. Volume size is expressed in GB.
   *Initialize Databases*: Initial Database
   Optionally provide a comma separated list of databases to create, for example:
   `database1`, `database2`, `database3`
   *Initial Admin User*: Create an initial admin user. This user will have access to all the databases you create.
   *Password*: Specify a password associated with the initial admin user you just named.
   *Host*: Optionally, allow the user to connect only from this host. If you do not specify a host, this user will be allowed to connect from anywhere.
6. Click the *Launch* button. The new database instance appears in the databases list.

## 3.10.2 Backup and restore a database

You can use Database services to backup a database and store the backup artifact in the Object Storage service. Later on, if the original database is damaged, you can use the backup artifact to restore the database. The restore process creates a database instance.

This example shows you how to back up and restore a MySQL database.

### 3.10.2.1 To backup the database instance

1. Log in to the dashboard.

2. From the CURRENT PROJECT on the *Project* tab, select the appropriate project.
3. On the *Project* tab, open the *Database* tab and click *Instances* category. This displays the existing instances in your system.
4. Click *Create Backup*.
5. In the *Backup Database* dialog box, specify the following values:
   Name
   Specify a name for the backup.
   Database Instance
   Select the instance you want to back up.
6. Click *Backup*. The new backup appears in the backup list.

#### 3.10.2.2 To restore a database instance

Now assume that your original database instance is damaged and you need to restore it. You do the restore by using your backup to create a new database instance.

1. Log in to the dashboard.
2. From the CURRENT PROJECT on the *Project* tab, select the appropriate project.
3. On the *Project* tab, open the *Database* tab and click *Backups* category. This lists the available backups.
4. Check the backup you want to use and click *Restore Backup*.
5. In the *Launch Database* dialog box, specify the values you want for the new database instance.
6. Click the *Restore From Database* tab and make sure that this new instance is based on the correct backup.
7. Click *Launch*.
   The new instance appears in the database instances list.

### 3.10.3 Update a database instance

You can change various characteristics of a database instance, such as its volume size and flavor.

#### 3.10.3.1 To change the volume size of an instance

1. Log in to the dashboard.
2. From the CURRENT PROJECT on the *Project* tab, select the appropriate project.
3. On the *Project* tab, open the *Database* tab and click *Instances* category. This displays the existing instances in your system.
4. Check the instance you want to work with. In the *Actions* column, expand the drop down menu and select *Resize Volume*.
5. In the *Resize Database Volume* dialog box, fill in the *New Size* field with an integer indicating the new size you want for the instance. Express the size in GB, and note that the new size must be larger than the current size.
6. Click *Resize Database Volume*.

#### 3.10.3.2 To change the flavor of an instance

1. Log in to the dashboard.
2. From the CURRENT PROJECT on the *Project* tab, select the appropriate project.
3. On the *Project* tab, open the *Database* tab and click *Instances* category. This displays the existing instances in your system.
4. Check the instance you want to work with. In the *Actions* column, expand the drop down menu and select *Resize Instance*.
5. In the *Resize Database Instance* dialog box, expand the drop down menu in the *New Flavor* field. Select the new flavor you want for the instance.
6. Click *Resize Database Instance*.

## 3.11 View and manage load balancers v2

Load-Balancer-as-a-Service (LBaaS) enables networking to distribute incoming requests evenly among designated instances. This distribution ensures that the workload is shared predictably among instances and enables more effective use of system resources. Use one of these load-balancing methods to distribute incoming requests:

- Round robin: Rotates requests evenly between multiple instances.
- Source IP: Requests from a unique source IP address are consistently directed to the same instance.
- Least connections: Allocates requests to the instance with the least number of active connections.

As an end user, you can create and manage load balancers and related objects for users in various projects. You can also delete load balancers and related objects.

LBaaS v2 has several new concepts to understand:

**Load balancer**

The load balancer occupies a neutron network port and has an IP address assigned from a subnet.

**Listener**

Each port that listens for traffic on a particular load balancer is configured separately and tied to the load balancer. Multiple listeners can be associated with the same load balancer.

**Pool**

A pool is a group of hosts that sits behind the load balancer and serves traffic through the load balancer.

**Member**

Members are the actual IP addresses that receive traffic from the load balancer. Members are associated with pools.

**Health monitor**

Members may go offline from time to time and health monitors diverts traffic away from members that are not responding properly. Health monitors are associated with pools.

### 3.11.1 View existing load balancers

1. Log in to the OpenStack dashboard.
2. On the *Project* tab, open the *Network* tab, and click the *Load Balancers* category.
   This view shows the list of existing load balancers. To view details of any of the load balancers, click on the specific load balancer.

### 3.11.2 Create a load balancer

1. Log in to the OpenStack dashboard.
2. On the *Project* tab, open the *Network* tab, and click the *Load Balancers* category.
3. Click the *Create Load Balancer* button.
   Use the concepts described in the overview section to fill in the necessary information about the load balancer you want to create.
   Keep in mind, the health checks routinely run against each instance within a target load balancer and the result of the health check is used to determine if the instance receives new connections.

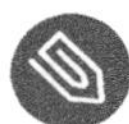

Note

A message indicates whether the action succeeded.

### 3.11.3 Delete a load balancer

- Select the load balancer you want to delete and click the *Delete Load Balancer* button.
  To be deleted successfully, a load balancer must not have any listeners or pools associated with it. The delete action is also available in the *Actions* column for the individual load balancers.

# 4 OpenStack command-line clients

## 4.1 Command-line client overview

OpenStackClient project provides a unified command-line client, which enables you to access the project API through easy-to-use commands. Also, most OpenStack project provides a command-line client for each service. For example, the Compute service provides a `nova` command-line client.

You can run the commands from the command line, or include the commands within scripts to automate tasks. If you provide OpenStack credentials, such as your user name and password, you can run these commands on any computer.

Internally, each command uses cURL command-line tools, which embed API requests. OpenStack APIs are RESTful APIs, and use the HTTP protocol. They include methods, URIs, media types, and response codes.

OpenStack APIs are open-source Python clients, and can run on Linux or Mac OS X systems. On some client commands, you can specify a debug parameter to show the underlying API request for the command. This is a good way to become familiar with the OpenStack API calls.

As a cloud end user, you can use the OpenStack Dashboard to provision your own resources within the limits set by administrators. You can modify the examples provided in this section to create other types and sizes of server instances.

### 4.1.1 Unified command-line client

You can use the unified `openstack` command (**python-openstackclient**) for the most of OpenStack services. For more information, see OpenStackClient document (https://docs.openstack.org/developer/python-openstackclient/) ↗.

### 4.1.2 Individual command-line clients

Unless the unified OpenStack Client (**python-openstackclient**) is used, the following table lists the command-line client for each OpenStack service with its package name and description.

TABLE 4.1: OPENSTACK SERVICES AND CLIENTS

| Service | Client | Package | Description |
|---|---|---|---|
| Application Catalog service | murano | python-muranoclient | Creates and manages applications. |
| Bare Metal service | ironic | python-ironicclient | manages and provisions physical machines. |
| Block Storage service | cinder | python-cinderclient | Creates and manages volumes. |
| Clustering service | senlin | python-senlinclient | Creates and manages clustering services. |
| Compute service | nova | python-novaclient | Creates and manages images, instances, and flavors. |
| Container Infrastructure Management service | magnum | python-magnumclient | Creates and manages containers. |
| Data Processing service | sahara | python-saharaclient | Creates and manages Hadoop clusters on OpenStack. |
| Database service | trove | python-troveclient | Creates and manages databases. |
| Deployment service | fuel | python-fuelclient | Plans deployments. |
| DNS service | designate | python-designateclient | Creates and manages self service authoritative DNS. |
| Image service | glance | python-glanceclient | Creates and manages images. |

| Service | Client | Package | Description |
|---|---|---|---|
| Key Manager service | barbican | python-barbicanclient | Creates and manages keys. |
| Monitoring | monasca | python-monascaclient | Monitoring solution. |
| Networking service | neutron | python-neutronclient | Configures networks for guest servers. |
| Object Storage service | swift | python-swiftclient | Gathers statistics, lists items, updates metadata, and uploads, downloads, and deletes files stored by the Object Storage service. Gains access to an Object Storage installation for ad hoc processing. |
| Orchestration service | heat | python-heatclient | Launches stacks from templates, views details of running stacks including events and resources, and updates and deletes stacks. |
| Rating service | cloudkitty | python-cloudkittyclient | Rating service. |
| Shared File Systems service | manila | python-manilaclient | Creates and manages shared file systems. |
| Telemetry service | ceilometer | python-ceilometerclient | Creates and collects measurements across OpenStack. |
| Telemetry v3 | gnocchi | python-gnocchiclient | Creates and collects measurements across OpenStack. |
| Workflow service | mistral | python-mistralclient | Workflow service for OpenStack cloud. |

## 4.2 Install the OpenStack command-line clients

Install the prerequisite software and the Python package for each OpenStack client.

### 4.2.1 Install the prerequisite software

Most Linux distributions include packaged versions of the command-line clients that you can install directly, see *Section 4.2.2.2, "Installing from packages"*.

If you need to install the source package for the command-line package, the following table lists the software needed to run the command-line clients, and provides installation instructions as needed.

TABLE 4.2: OPENSTACK COMMAND-LINE CLIENTS PREREQUISITES

| Prerequisite | Description |
| --- | --- |
| Python 2.7 or later | Supports Python 2.7, 3.4, and 3.5. |
| setuptools package | Installed by default on Mac OS X.<br>Many Linux distributions provide packages to make setuptools easy to install. Search your package manager for setuptools to find an installation package. If you cannot find one, download the setuptools package directly from Python Setuptools (https://pypi.python.org/pypi/setuptools) ↗.<br>The recommended way to install setuptools on Microsoft Windows is to follow the documentation provided on the Python Setuptools (https://pypi.python.org/pypi/setuptools) ↗ website.<br>Another option is to use the unofficial binary installer maintained by Christoph Gohlke (http://www.lfd.uci.edu/~gohlke/pythonlibs/#setuptools) ↗. |
| pip package | To install the clients on a Linux, Mac OS X, or Microsoft Windows system, use pip. It is easy to use, ensures that you get the latest version of the clients from the Python Package Index (https://pypi.python.org/) ↗, and lets you update or remove the packages later on. |

| Prerequisite | Description |
| --- | --- |
| | Since the installation process compiles source files, this requires the related Python development package for your operating system and distribution.<br>Install pip through the package manager for your system:<br>**MacOS**<br>`# easy_install pip`<br>**Microsoft Windows**<br>Ensure that the `C:\Python27\Scripts` directory is defined in the `PATH` environment variable, and use the `easy_install` command from the setuptools package:<br>`C:\>easy_install pip`<br>Another option is to use the unofficial binary installer provided by Christoph Gohlke (http://www.lfd.uci.edu/~gohlke/pythonlibs/#pip) ↗.<br>**Ubuntu or Debian**<br>`# apt install python-dev python-pip`<br>Note that extra dependencies may be required, per operating system, depending on the package being installed, such as is the case with Tempest.<br>**Red Hat Enterprise Linux, CentOS, or Fedora**<br>A packaged version enables you to use yum to install the package:<br>`# yum install python-devel python-pip`<br>There are also packaged versions of the clients available in RDO (https://www.rdoproject.org/) ↗ that enable yum to install the clients as described in *Section 4.2.2.2, "Installing from packages"*.<br>**SUSE Linux Enterprise Server** |

| Prerequisite | Description |
| --- | --- |
| | A packaged version available in the Open Build Service (https://build.opensuse.org/package/show?package=python-pip&project=Cloud:OpenStack:Master) enables you to use YaST or zypper to install the package.<br>First, add the Open Build Service repository:<br>`# zypper addrepo -f obs://Cloud:OpenStack:Mitaka/SLE_12_SP1 Mitaka`<br>Then install pip and use it to manage client installation:<br>`# zypper install python-devel python-pip`<br>There are also packaged versions of the clients available that enable zypper to install the clients as described in *Section 4.2.2.2, "Installing from packages"*.<br>**openSUSE**<br>You can install pip and use it to manage client installation:<br>`# zypper install python-devel python-pip`<br>There are also packaged versions of the clients available that enable zypper to install the clients as described in *Section 4.2.2.2, "Installing from packages"*. |

## 4.2.2 Install the OpenStack client

The following example shows the command for installing the OpenStack client with `pip`, which supports multiple services.

```
# pip install python-openstackclient
```

The following individual clients are deprecated in favor of a common client. Instead of installing and learning all these clients, we recommend installing and using the OpenStack client. You may need to install an individual project's client because coverage is not yet sufficient in the OpenStack client. If you need to install an individual client's project, replace the `PROJECT` name in this `pip install` command using the list below.

```
# pip install python-PROJECTclient
```

- `barbican` - Key Manager Service API
- `ceilometer` - Telemetry API
- `cinder` - Block Storage API and extensions
- `cloudkitty` - Rating service API
- `designate` - DNS service API
- `fuel` - Deployment service API
- `glance` - Image service API
- `gnocchi` - Telemetry API v3
- `heat` - Orchestration API
- `magnum` - Container Infrastructure Management service API
- `manila` - Shared file systems API
- `mistral` - Workflow service API
- `monasca` - Monitoring API
- `murano` - Application catalog API
- `neutron` - Networking API
- `nova` - Compute API and extensions
- `sahara` - Data Processing API
- `senlin` - Clustering service API
- `swift` - Object Storage API
- `trove` - Database service API

#### 4.2.2.1 Installing with pip

Use pip to install the OpenStack clients on a Linux, Mac OS X, or Microsoft Windows system. It is easy to use and ensures that you get the latest version of the client from the Python Package Index (https://pypi.python.org/pypi). Also, pip enables you to update or remove a package.

Install each client separately by using the following command:

- For Mac OS X or Linux:

```
# pip install python-PROJECTclient
```

- For Microsoft Windows:

```
C:\>pip install python-PROJECTclient
```

#### 4.2.2.2 Installing from packages

RDO, openSUSE, SUSE Linux Enterprise, Debian, and Ubuntu have client packages that can be installed without `pip`.

- On Red Hat Enterprise Linux, CentOS, or Fedora, use `yum` to install the clients from the packaged versions available in RDO (https://www.rdoproject.org/):

```
# yum install python-PROJECTclient
```

- For Ubuntu or Debian, use `apt-get` to install the clients from the packaged versions:

```
# apt-get install python-PROJECTclient
```

- For openSUSE, use `zypper` to install the clients from the distribution packages service:

```
# zypper install python-PROJECTclient
```

- For SUSE Linux Enterprise Server, use `zypper` to install the clients from the distribution packages in the Open Build Service. First, add the Open Build Service repository:

```
# zypper addrepo -f obs://Cloud:OpenStack:Mitaka/SLE_12_SP1 Mitaka
```

  Then you can install the packages:

```
# zypper install python-PROJECTclient
```

### 4.2.3 Upgrade or remove clients

To upgrade a client, add the `--upgrade` option to the **`pip install`** command:

```
# pip install --upgrade python-PROJECTclient
```

To remove the client, run the **`pip uninstall`** command:

```
# pip uninstall python-PROJECTclient
```

### 4.2.4 What's next

Before you can run client commands, you must create and source the `PROJECT-openrc.sh` file to set environment variables. See .

## 4.3 Discover the version number for a client

Run the following command to discover the version number for a client:

```
$ PROJECT --version
```

For example, to see the version number for the `openstack` client, run the following command:

```
$ openstack --version
openstack 3.2.0
```

## 4.4 Set environment variables using the OpenStack RC file

To set the required environment variables for the OpenStack command-line clients, you must create an environment file called an OpenStack rc file, or `openrc.sh` file. If your OpenStack installation provides it, you can download the file from the OpenStack Dashboard as an administrative user or any other user. This project-specific environment file contains the credentials that all OpenStack services use.

When you source the file, environment variables are set for your current shell. The variables enable the OpenStack client commands to communicate with the OpenStack services that run in the cloud.

Note

Defining environment variables using an environment file is not a common practice on Microsoft Windows. Environment variables are usually defined in the *Advanced › System Properties* dialog box. One method for using these scripts as-is on Windows is to install Git for Windows (https://git-for-windows.github.io/) and using Git Bash to source the environment variables and to run all CLI commands.

### 4.4.1 Download and source the OpenStack RC file

1. Log in to the dashboard and from the drop-down list select the project for which you want to download the OpenStack RC file.
2. On the *Project* tab, open the *Compute* tab and click *Access & Security*.
3. On the *API Access* tab, click *Download OpenStack RC File* and save the file. The filename will be of the form `PROJECT-openrc.sh` where `PROJECT` is the name of the project for which you downloaded the file.
4. Copy the `PROJECT-openrc.sh` file to the computer from which you want to run OpenStack commands.
   For example, copy the file to the computer from which you want to upload an image with a `glance` client command.
5. On any shell from which you want to run OpenStack commands, source the `PROJECT-openrc.sh` file for the respective project.
   In the following example, the `demo-openrc.sh` file is sourced for the demo project:

```
$ . demo-openrc.sh
```

6. When you are prompted for an OpenStack password, enter the password for the user who downloaded the `PROJECT-openrc.sh` file.

### 4.4.2 Create and source the OpenStack RC file

Alternatively, you can create the `PROJECT-openrc.sh` file from scratch, if you cannot download the file from the dashboard.

1. In a text editor, create a file named `PROJECT-openrc.sh` and add the following authentication information:

```
export OS_USERNAME=username
export OS_PASSWORD=password
export OS_TENANT_NAME=projectName
export OS_AUTH_URL=https://identityHost:portNumber/v2.0
# The following lines can be omitted
export OS_TENANT_ID=tenantIDString
export OS_REGION_NAME=regionName
export OS_CACERT=/path/to/cacertFile
```

Warning

Saving `OS_PASSWORD` in plain text may bring a security risk. You should protect the file or not save `OS_PASSWORD` into the file in the production environment.

2. On any shell from which you want to run OpenStack commands, source the `PROJECT-openrc.sh` file for the respective project. In this example, you source the `admin-openrc.sh` file for the admin project:

```
$ . admin-openrc.sh
```

Note

You are not prompted for the password with this method. The password lives in clear text format in the `PROJECT-openrc.sh` file. Restrict the permissions on this file to avoid security problems. You can also remove the `OS_PASSWORD` variable from the file, and use the `--password` parameter with OpenStack client commands instead.

Note

You must set the `OS_CACERT` environment variable when using the https protocol in the `OS_AUTH_URL` environment setting because the verification process for the TLS (HTTPS) server certificate uses the one indicated in the environment. This certificate will be used when verifying the TLS (HTTPS) server certificate.

### 4.4.3 Override environment variable values

When you run OpenStack client commands, you can override some environment variable settings by using the options that are listed at the end of the `help` output of the various client commands. For example, you can override the `OS_PASSWORD` setting in the `PROJECT-openrc.sh` file by specifying a password on a **`openstack`** command, as follows:

```
$ openstack --os-password PASSWORD server list
```

Where `PASSWORD` is your password.

A user specifies their username and password credentials to interact with OpenStack, using any client command. These credentials can be specified using various mechanisms, namely, the environment variable or command-line argument. It is not safe to specify the password using either of these methods.

For example, when you specify your password using the command-line client with the `--os-password` argument, anyone with access to your computer can view it in plain text with the `ps` field.

To avoid storing the password in plain text, you can prompt for the OpenStack password interactively.

## 4.5 Manage images

The cloud operator assigns roles to users. Roles determine who can upload and manage images. The operator might restrict image upload and management to only cloud administrators or operators.

You can upload images through the `glance` client or the Image service API. You can use the `nova` client for the image management. The latter provides mechanisms to list and delete images, set and delete image metadata, and create images of a running instance or snapshot and backup types.

After you upload an image, you cannot change it.

For details about image creation, see the Virtual Machine Image Guide (https://docs.openstack.org/image-guide/) ↗.

### 4.5.1 List or get details for images (glance)

To get a list of images and to get further details about a single image, use **openstack image list** and **openstack image show** commands.

```
$ openstack image list
+--------------------------------------+---------------------------------+--------+
| ID                                   | Name                            | Status |
+--------------------------------------+---------------------------------+--------+
| dfc1dfb0-d7bf-4fff-8994-319dd6f703d7 | cirros-0.3.2-x86_64-uec         | active |
| a3867e29-c7a1-44b0-9e7f-10db587cad20 | cirros-0.3.2-x86_64-uec-kernel  | active |
| 4b916fba-6775-4092-92df-f41df7246a6b | cirros-0.3.2-x86_64-uec-ramdisk | active |
| d07831df-edc3-4817-9881-89141f9134c3 | myCirrosImage                   | active |
+--------------------------------------+---------------------------------+--------+
```

```
$ openstack image show myCirrosImage
+------------------+------------------------------------------------------+
| Field            | Value                                                |
+------------------+------------------------------------------------------+
| checksum         | ee1eca47dc88f4879d8a229cc70a07c6                     |
| container_format | ami                                                  |
| created_at       | 2016-08-11T15:07:26Z                                 |
| disk_format      | ami                                                  |
| file             | /v2/images/d07831df-edc3-4817-9881-89141f9134c3/file |
| id               | d07831df-edc3-4817-9881-89141f9134c3                 |
| min_disk         | 0                                                    |
| min_ram          | 0                                                    |
| name             | myCirrosImage                                        |
| owner            | d88310717a8e4ebcae84ed075f82c51e                     |
| protected        | False                                                |
| schema           | /v2/schemas/image                                    |
| size             | 13287936                                             |
| status           | active                                               |
| tags             |                                                      |
| updated_at       | 2016-08-11T15:20:02Z                                 |
| virtual_size     | None                                                 |
| visibility       | private                                              |
+------------------+------------------------------------------------------+
```

When viewing a list of images, you can also use `grep` to filter the list, as follows:

```
$ openstack image list | grep 'cirros'
| dfc1dfb0-d7bf-4fff-8994-319dd6f703d7 | cirros-0.3.2-x86_64-uec         | active |
| a3867e29-c7a1-44b0-9e7f-10db587cad20 | cirros-0.3.2-x86_64-uec-kernel  | active |
| 4b916fba-6775-4092-92df-f41df7246a6b | cirros-0.3.2-x86_64-uec-ramdisk | active |
```

Note

To store location metadata for images, which enables direct file access for a client, update the `/etc/glance/glance-api.conf` file with the following statements:

- `show_multiple_locations = True`
- `filesystem_store_metadata_file = filePath`
  where filePath points to a JSON file that defines the mount point for OpenStack images on your system and a unique ID. For example:

```
[{
    "id": "2d9bb53f-70ea-4066-a68b-67960eaae673",
    "mountpoint": "/var/lib/glance/images/"
}]
```

After you restart the Image service, you can use the following syntax to view the image's location information:

```
$ openstack --os-image-api-version 2 image show imageID
```

For example, using the image ID shown above, you would issue the command as follows:

```
$ openstack --os-image-api-version 2 image show 2d9bb53f-70ea-4066-a68b-67960eaae673
```

### 4.5.2 Create or update an image (glance)

To create an image, use **`openstack image create`**:

```
$ openstack image create imageName
```

To update an image by name or ID, use **`openstack image set`**:

```
$ openstack image set imageName
```

The following list explains the optional arguments that you can use with the `create` and `set` commands to modify image properties. For more information, refer to the OpenStack Image command reference (https://docs.openstack.org/developer/python-openstackclient/command-objects/image.html) ↗.

The following example shows the command that you would use to upload a CentOS 6.3 image in qcow2 format and configure it for public access:

```
$ openstack image create --disk-format qcow2 --container-format bare \
  --public --file ./centos63.qcow2 centos63-image
```

The following example shows how to update an existing image with a properties that describe the disk bus, the CD-ROM bus, and the VIF model:

Note

When you use OpenStack with VMware vCenter Server, you need to specify the `vmware_disktype` and `vmware_adaptertype` properties with **`openstack image create`**. Also, we recommend that you set the `hypervisor_type="vmware"` property. For more information, see Images with VMware vSphere (https://docs.openstack.org/newton/config-reference/compute/hypervisor-vmware.html#images-with-vmware-vsphere) in the OpenStack Configuration Reference.

```
$ openstack image set \
    --property hw_disk_bus=scsi \
    --property hw_cdrom_bus=ide \
    --property hw_vif_model=e1000 \
    f16-x86_64-openstack-sda
```

Currently the libvirt virtualization tool determines the disk, CD-ROM, and VIF device models based on the configured hypervisor type (`libvirt_type` in `/etc/nova/nova.conf` file). For the sake of optimal performance, libvirt defaults to using virtio for both disk and VIF (NIC) models. The disadvantage of this approach is that it is not possible to run operating systems that lack virtio drivers, for example, BSD, Solaris, and older versions of Linux and Windows.

If you specify a disk or CD-ROM bus model that is not supported, see the ???. If you specify a VIF model that is not supported, the instance fails to launch. See the ???.

The valid model values depend on the `libvirt_type` setting, as shown in the following tables.

**Disk and CD-ROM bus model values**

| libvirt_type setting | Supported model values |
|---|---|
| qemu or kvm | • ide<br>• scsi<br>• virtio |
| xen | • ide<br>• xen |

**VIF model values**

| libvirt_type setting | Supported model values |
|---|---|
| qemu or kvm | • e1000<br>• ne2k_pci<br>• pcnet<br>• rtl8139<br>• virtio |
| xen | • e1000<br>• netfront<br>• ne2k_pci<br>• pcnet<br>• rtl8139 |
| vmware | • VirtualE1000<br>• VirtualPCNet32<br>• VirtualVmxnet |

Note

By default, hardware properties are retrieved from the image properties. However, if this information is not available, the `libosinfo` database provides an alternative source for these values.

If the guest operating system is not in the database, or if the use of `libosinfo` is disabled, the default system values are used.

Users can set the operating system ID or a `short-id` in image properties. For example:

```
$ openstack image set --property short-id=fedora23 \
  name-of-my-fedora-image
```

Alternatively, users can set `id` to a URL:

```
$ openstack image set \
  --property id=http://fedoraproject.org/fedora/23 \
  ID-of-my-fedora-image
```

#### 4.5.2.1 Create an image from ISO image

You can upload ISO images to the Image service (glance). You can subsequently boot an ISO image using Compute.

In the Image service, run the following command:

```
$ openstack image create ISO_IMAGE --file IMAGE.iso \
  --disk-format iso --container-format bare
```

Optionally, to confirm the upload in Image service, run:

```
$ openstack image list
```

### 4.5.3 Troubleshoot image creation

If you encounter problems in creating an image in the Image service or Compute, the following information may help you troubleshoot the creation process.

- Ensure that the version of qemu you are using is version 0.14 or later. Earlier versions of qemu result in an `unknown option -s` error message in the `/var/log/nova/nova-compute.log` file.
- Examine the `/var/log/nova/nova-api.log` and `/var/log/nova/nova-compute.log` log files for error messages.

## 4.6 Manage images using cURL

This section is intended to provide a series of commands a typical client of the API might use to create and modify an image.

These commands assume the implementation of the v2 Image API using the Identity Service for authentication and authorization. The X-Auth-Token header is used to provide the authentication token issued by the Identity Service.

The strings `$OS_IMAGE_URL` and `$OS_AUTH_TOKEN` represent variables defined in the client's environment. `$OS_IMAGE_URL` is the full path to your image service endpoint, for example, `http://example.com`. `$OS_AUTH_TOKEN` represents an auth token generated by the Identity Service, for example, `6583fb17c27b48b4b4a6033fe9cc0fe0`.

### 4.6.1 Create an image

```
$ curl -i -X POST -H "X-Auth-Token: $OS_AUTH_TOKEN" \
       -H "Content-Type: application/json" \
       -d '{"name": "Ubuntu 14.04", \
       "tags": ["ubuntu", "14.04", "trusty"]}' \
       $OS_IMAGE_URL/v2/images

HTTP/1.1 201 Created
Content-Length: 451
Content-Type: application/json; charset=UTF-8
Location: http://example.com:9292/v2/images
          /7b97f37c-899d-44e8-aaa0-543edbc4eaad
Date: Fri, 11 Mar 2016 12:25:32 GMT

{
    "id": "7b97f37c-899d-44e8-aaa0-543edbc4eaad",
    "name": "Ubuntu 14.04",
    "status": "queued",
    "visibility": "private",
```

```
    "protected": false,
    "tags": ["ubuntu", "14.04", "trusty"],
    "created_at": "2016-03-11T12:25:32Z",
    "updated_at": "2016-03-11T12:25:32Z",
    "file": "/v2/images/7b97f37c-899d-44e8-aaa0-543edbc4eaad/file",
    "self": "/v2/images/7b97f37c-899d-44e8-aaa0-543edbc4eaad",
    "schema": "/v2/schemas/image"
}
```

### 4.6.2 Update the image

```
$ curl -i -X PATCH -H "X-Auth-Token: $OS_AUTH_TOKEN" \
       -H "Content-Type: application/json" \
       -d '[{"op": "add", "path": "/login-user", "value": "root"}]' \
       $OS_IMAGE_URL/v2/images/7b97f37c-899d-44e8-aaa0-543edbc4eaad

HTTP/1.1 200 OK
Content-Length: 477
Content-Type: application/json; charset=UTF-8
Date: Fri, 11 Mar 2016 12:44:56 GMT

{
    "id": "7b97f37c-899d-44e8-aaa0-543edbc4eaad",
    "name": "Ubuntu 14.04",
    "status": "queued",
    "visibility": "private",
    "protected": false,
    "tags": ["ubuntu", "14.04", "trusty"],
    "login_user": "root",
    "created_at": "2016-03-11T12:25:32Z",
    "updated_at": "2016-03-11T12:44:56Z",
    "file": "/v2/images/7b97f37c-899d-44e8-aaa0-543edbc4eaad/file",
    "self": "/v2/images/7b97f37c-899d-44e8-aaa0-543edbc4eaad",
    "schema": "/v2/schemas/image"
}
```

### 4.6.3 Upload binary image data

```
$ curl -i -X PUT -H "X-Auth-Token: $OS_AUTH_TOKEN" \
       -H "Content-Type: application/octet-stream" \
       --data-binary @/home/glance/ubuntu-14.04.qcow2 \
       $OS_IMAGE_URL/v2/images/7b97f37c-899d-44e8-aaa0-543edbc4eaad/file
```

```
HTTP/1.1 100 Continue
HTTP/1.1 201 Created
Content-Length: 0
Date: Fri, 11 Mar 2016 12:51:02 GMT
```

### 4.6.4 Download binary image data

```
$ curl -i -X GET -H "X-Auth-Token: $OS_AUTH_TOKEN" \
       $OS_IMAGE_URL/v2/images/7b97f37c-899d-44e8-aaa0-543edbc4eaad/file

HTTP/1.1 200 OK
Content-Type: application/octet-stream
Content-Md5: 912ec803b2ce49e4a541068d495ab570
Transfer-Encoding: chunked
Date: Fri, 11 Mar 2016 12:57:41 GMT
```

### 4.6.5 Delete an image

```
$ curl -i -X DELETE -H "X-Auth-Token: $OS_AUTH_TOKEN" \
       $OS_IMAGE_URL/v2/images/7b97f37c-899d-44e8-aaa0-543edbc4eaad

HTTP/1.1 204 No Content
Content-Length: 0
Date: Fri, 11 Mar 2016 12:59:11 GMT
```

## 4.7 Manage volumes

A volume is a detachable block storage device, similar to a USB hard drive. You can attach a volume to only one instance. Use the `openstack` client commands to create and manage volumes.

### 4.7.1 Migrate a volume

As an administrator, you can migrate a volume with its data from one location to another in a manner that is transparent to users and workloads. You can migrate only detached volumes with no snapshots.

Possible use cases for data migration include:

- Bring down a physical storage device for maintenance without disrupting workloads.
- Modify the properties of a volume.
- Free up space in a thinly-provisioned back end.

Migrate a volume with the **`cinder migrate`** command, as shown in the following example:

```
$ cinder migrate --force-host-copy <True|False>
                 --lock-volume <True|False>
                 <volume> <host>
```

In this example, `--force-host-copy True` forces the generic host-based migration mechanism and bypasses any driver optimizations. `--lock-volume <True|False>` applies to the available volume. To determine whether the termination of volume migration caused by other commands. `True` locks the volume state and does not allow the migration to be aborted.

Note

If the volume has snapshots, the specified host destination cannot accept the volume. If the user is not an administrator, the migration fails.

## 4.7.2 Create a volume

This example creates a `my-new-volume` volume based on an image.

1. List images, and note the ID of the image that you want to use for your volume:

```
$ openstack image list
+--------------------------------------+---------------------------------+
| ID                                   | Name                            |
+--------------------------------------+---------------------------------+
| 8bf4dc2a-bf78-4dd1-aefa-f3347cf638c8 | cirros-0.3.4-x86_64-uec         |
| 9ff9bb2e-3a1d-4d98-acb5-b1d3225aca6c | cirros-0.3.4-x86_64-uec-kernel  |
| 4b227119-68a1-4b28-8505-f94c6ea4c6dc | cirros-0.3.4-x86_64-uec-ramdisk |
+--------------------------------------+---------------------------------+
```

2. List the availability zones, and note the ID of the availability zone in which you want to create your volume:

```
$ openstack availability zone list
```

```
+------+-----------+
| Name |   Status  |
+------+-----------+
| nova | available |
+------+-----------+
```

3. Create a volume with 8 gibibytes (GiB) of space, and specify the availability zone and image:

```
$ openstack volume create --image 8bf4dc2a-bf78-4dd1-aefa-f3347cf638c8 \
  --size 8 --availability-zone nova my-new-volume

+------------------------------+--------------------------------------+
| Property                     | Value                                |
+------------------------------+--------------------------------------+
| attachments                  | []                                   |
| availability_zone            | nova                                 |
| bootable                     | false                                |
| consistencygroup_id          | None                                 |
| created_at                   | 2016-09-23T07:52:42.000000           |
| description                  | None                                 |
| encrypted                    | False                                |
| id                           | bab4b0e0-ce3d-4d57-bf57-3c51319f5202 |
| metadata                     | {}                                   |
| multiattach                  | False                                |
| name                         | my-new-volume                        |
| os-vol-tenant-attr:tenant_id | 3f670abbe9b34ca5b81db6e7b540b8d8     |
| replication_status           | disabled                             |
| size                         | 8                                    |
| snapshot_id                  | None                                 |
| source_volid                 | None                                 |
| status                       | creating                             |
| updated_at                   | None                                 |
| user_id                      | fe19e3a9f63f4a14bd4697789247bbc5     |
| volume_type                  | lvmdriver-1                          |
+------------------------------+--------------------------------------+
```

4. To verify that your volume was created successfully, list the available volumes:

```
$ openstack volume list
+--------------------------------------+---------------+-----------+------+-------------+
| ID                                   | DisplayName   |  Status   | Size | Attached to |
+--------------------------------------+---------------+-----------+------+-------------+
| bab4b0e0-ce3d-4d57-bf57-3c51319f5202 | my-new-volume | available | 8    |             |
+--------------------------------------+---------------+-----------+------+-------------+
```

If your volume was created successfully, its status is `available`. If its status is `error`, you might have exceeded your quota.

### 4.7.3 Create a volume from specified volume type

Cinder supports these three ways to specify `volume type` during volume creation.

1. volume_type
2. cinder_img_volume_type (via glance image metadata)
3. default_volume_type (via cinder.conf)

#### 4.7.3.1 volume_type

User can specify `volume type` when creating a volume.

```
$ openstack volume create -h -f {json,shell,table,value,yaml}
                         -c COLUMN --max-width <integer>
                         --noindent --prefix PREFIX --size <size>
                         --type <volume-type> --image <image>
                         --snapshot <snapshot> --source <volume>
                         --description <description> --user <user>
                         --project <project>
                         --availability-zone <availability-zone>
                         --property <key=value>
                         <name>
```

#### 4.7.3.2 cinder_img_volume_type

If glance image has `cinder_img_volume_type` property, Cinder uses this parameter to specify `volume type` when creating a volume.

Choose glance image which has `cinder_img_volume_type` property and create a volume from the image.

```
$ openstack image list
+----------------------------------+---------------------------------+--------+
| ID                               | Name                            | Status |
+----------------------------------+---------------------------------+--------+
| 376bd633-c9c9-4c5d-a588-342f4f66 | cirros-0.3.4-x86_64-uec         | active |
| d086                             |                                 |        |
```

```
| 2c20fce7-2e68-45ee-ba8d-          | cirros-0.3.4-x86_64-uec-ramdisk | active |
| beba27a91ab5                      |                                 |        |
| a5752de4-9faf-4c47-acbc-          | cirros-0.3.4-x86_64-uec-kernel  | active |
| 78a5efa7cc6e                      |                                 |        |
+-----------------------------------+---------------------------------+--------+

$ openstack image show 376bd633-c9c9-4c5d-a588-342f4f66d086
+------------------+------------------------------------------------------+
| Field            | Value                                                |
+------------------+------------------------------------------------------+
| checksum         | eb9139e4942121f22bbc2afc0400b2a4                     |
| container_format | ami                                                  |
| created_at       | 2016-10-13T03:28:55Z                                 |
| disk_format      | ami                                                  |
| file             | /v2/images/376bd633-c9c9-4c5d-a588-342f4f66d086/file |
| id               | 376bd633-c9c9-4c5d-a588-342f4f66d086                 |
| min_disk         | 0                                                    |
| min_ram          | 0                                                    |
| name             | cirros-0.3.4-x86_64-uec                              |
| owner            | 88ba456e3a884c318394737765e0ef4d                     |
| properties       | kernel_id='a5752de4-9faf-4c47-acbc-78a5efa7cc6e',    |
|                  | ramdisk_id='2c20fce7-2e68-45ee-ba8d-beba27a91ab5'    |
| protected        | False                                                |
| schema           | /v2/schemas/image                                    |
| size             | 25165824                                             |
| status           | active                                               |
| tags             |                                                      |
| updated_at       | 2016-10-13T03:28:55Z                                 |
| virtual_size     | None                                                 |
| visibility       | public                                               |
+------------------+------------------------------------------------------+

$ openstack volume create --image 376bd633-c9c9-4c5d-a588-342f4f66d086 \
  --size 1 --availability-zone nova test
+---------------------+--------------------------------------+
| Field               | Value                                |
+---------------------+--------------------------------------+
| attachments         | []                                   |
| availability_zone   | nova                                 |
| bootable            | false                                |
| consistencygroup_id | None                                 |
| created_at          | 2016-10-13T06:29:53.688599           |
| description         | None                                 |
| encrypted           | False                                |
| id                  | e6e6a72d-cda7-442c-830f-f306ea6a03d5 |
| multiattach         | False                                |
```

```
| name                | test                                |
| properties          |                                     |
| replication_status  | disabled                            |
| size                | 1                                   |
| snapshot_id         | None                                |
| source_volid        | None                                |
| status              | creating                            |
| type                | lvmdriver-1                         |
| updated_at          | None                                |
| user_id             | 33fdc37314914796883706b33e587d51    |
+---------------------+-------------------------------------+
```

#### 4.7.3.3 default_volume_type

If above parameters are not set, Cinder uses default_volume_type which is defined in cinder.conf during volume creation.

Example cinder.conf file configuration.

```
[default]
default_volume_type = lvmdriver-1
```

### 4.7.4 Attach a volume to an instance

1. Attach your volume to a server, specifying the server ID and the volume ID:

```
$ openstack server add volume 84c6e57d-a6b1-44b6-81eb-fcb36afd31b5 \
  573e024d-5235-49ce-8332-be1576d323f8 --device /dev/vdb
```

2. Show information for your volume:

```
$ openstack volume show 573e024d-5235-49ce-8332-be1576d323f8
```

The output shows that the volume is attached to the server with ID `84c6e57d-a6b1-44b6-81eb-fcb36afd31b5`, is in the nova availability zone, and is bootable.

```
+------------------------------+-----------------------------------------------+
| Field                        | Value                                         |
+------------------------------+-----------------------------------------------+
| attachments                  | [{u'device': u'/dev/vdb',                     |
|                              |        u'server_id': u'84c6e57d-a             |
|                              |           u'id': u'573e024d-...               |
|                              |        u'volume_id': u'573e024d...            |
```

```
| availability_zone              | nova                                      |
| bootable                       | true                                      |
| consistencygroup_id            | None                                      |
| created_at                     | 2016-10-13T06:08:07.000000                |
| description                    | None                                      |
| encrypted                      | False                                     |
| id                             | 573e024d-5235-49ce-8332-be1576d323f8      |
| multiattach                    | False                                     |
| name                           | my-new-volume                             |
| os-vol-tenant-attr:tenant_id   | 7ef070d3fee24bdfae054c17ad742e28          |
| properties                     |                                           |
| replication_status             | disabled                                  |
| size                           | 8                                         |
| snapshot_id                    | None                                      |
| source_volid                   | None                                      |
| status                         | in-use                                    |
| type                           | lvmdriver-1                               |
| updated_at                     | 2016-10-13T06:08:11.000000                |
| user_id                        | 33fdc37314914796883706b33e587d51          |
| volume_image_metadata          |{u'kernel_id': u'df430cc2...,              |
|                                |        u'image_id': u'397e713c...,        |
|                                |        u'ramdisk_id': u'3cf852bd...,      |
|                                |u'image_name': u'cirros-0.3.2-x86_64-uec'} |
+--------------------------------+-------------------------------------------+
```

## 4.7.5 Resize a volume

1. To resize your volume, you must first detach it from the server. To detach the volume from your server, pass the server ID and volume ID to the following command:

```
$ openstack server remove volume 84c6e57d-a6b1-44b6-81eb-fcb36afd31b5
 573e024d-5235-49ce-8332-be1576d323f8
```

This command does not provide any output.

2. List volumes:

```
$ openstack volume list
+----------------+-----------------+-----------+------+-------------+
|       ID       |   Display Name  |  Status   | Size | Attached to |
+----------------+-----------------+-----------+------+-------------+
| 573e024d-52... |  my-new-volume  | available |  8   |             |
| bd7cf584-45... | my-bootable-vol | available |  8   |             |
+----------------+-----------------+-----------+------+-------------+
```

Note that the volume is now available.

3. Resize the volume by passing the volume ID and the new size (a value greater than the old one) as parameters:

```
$ openstack volume set 573e024d-5235-49ce-8332-be1576d323f8 --size 10
```

This command does not provide any output.

Note

When extending an LVM volume with a snapshot, the volume will be deactivated. The reactivation is automatic unless `auto_activation_volume_list` is defined in `lvm.conf`. See `lvm.conf` for more information.

### 4.7.6 Delete a volume

1. To delete your volume, you must first detach it from the server. To detach the volume from your server and check for the list of existing volumes, see steps **1** and **2** in *Section 4.7.5, "Resize a volume"*.

   Delete the volume using either the volume name or ID:

```
$ openstack volume delete my-new-volume
```

   This command does not provide any output.

2. List the volumes again, and note that the status of your volume is `deleting`:

```
$ openstack volume list
+----------------+-----------------+-----------+------+-------------+
|       ID       |   Display Name  |  Status   | Size | Attached to |
+----------------+-----------------+-----------+------+-------------+
| 573e024d-52... |  my-new-volume  |  deleting |  8   |             |
| bd7cf584-45... | my-bootable-vol | available |  8   |             |
+----------------+-----------------+-----------+------+-------------+
```

   When the volume is fully deleted, it disappears from the list of volumes:

```
$ openstack volume list
+----------------+-----------------+-----------+------+-------------+
|       ID       |   Display Name  |  Status   | Size | Attached to |
```

```
+----------------+----------------+----------+------+------------+
| bd7cf584-45... | my-bootable-vol | available |  8   |            |
+----------------+----------------+----------+------+------------+
```

### 4.7.7 Transfer a volume

You can transfer a volume from one owner to another by using the **`openstack volume transfer request create`** command. The volume donor, or original owner, creates a transfer request and sends the created transfer ID and authorization key to the volume recipient. The volume recipient, or new owner, accepts the transfer by using the ID and key.

Note

The procedure for volume transfer is intended for tenants (both the volume donor and recipient) within the same cloud.

Use cases include:

- Create a custom bootable volume or a volume with a large data set and transfer it to a customer.
- For bulk import of data to the cloud, the data ingress system creates a new Block Storage volume, copies data from the physical device, and transfers device ownership to the end user.

#### 4.7.7.1 Create a volume transfer request

1. While logged in as the volume donor, list the available volumes:

```
$ openstack volume list
+-----------------+-----------------+-----------+------+-------------+
|       ID        |   Display Name  |  Status   | Size | Attached to |
+-----------------+-----------------+-----------+------+-------------+
| 72bfce9f-cac... |       None      |   error   |  1   |             |
| a1cdace0-08e... |       None      | available |  1   |             |
+-----------------+-----------------+-----------+------+-------------+
```

2. As the volume donor, request a volume transfer authorization code for a specific volume:

```
$ openstack volume transfer request create <volume>
```

```
<volume>
   Name or ID of volume to transfer.
```

The volume must be in an `available` state or the request will be denied. If the transfer request is valid in the database (that is, it has not expired or been deleted), the volume is placed in an `awaiting-transfer` state. For example:

```
$ openstack volume transfer request create a1cdace0-08e4-4dc7-b9dc-457e9bcfe25f
```

The output shows the volume transfer ID in the `id` row and the authorization key.

```
+------------+--------------------------------------+
| Field      | Value                                |
+------------+--------------------------------------+
| auth_key   | 0a59e53630f051e2                     |
| created_at | 2016-11-03T11:49:40.346181           |
| id         | 34e29364-142b-4c7b-8d98-88f765bf176f |
| name       | None                                 |
| volume_id  | a1cdace0-08e4-4dc7-b9dc-457e9bcfe25f |
+------------+--------------------------------------+
```

Note

Optionally, you can specify a name for the transfer by using the `--name transferName` parameter.

Note

While the `auth_key` property is visible in the output of `openstack volume transfer request create VOLUME_ID`, it will not be available in subsequent `openstack volume transfer request show TRANSFER_ID` command.

3. Send the volume transfer ID and authorization key to the new owner (for example, by email).

4. View pending transfers:

```
$ openstack volume transfer request list
+--------------------------------------+--------------------------------------+------+
|                 ID                   |               Volume                 | Name |
+--------------------------------------+--------------------------------------+------+
```

```
| 6e4e9aa4-bed5-4f94-8f76-df43232f44dc | a1cdace0-08e4-4dc7-b9dc-457e9bcfe25f | None |
+--------------------------------------+--------------------------------------+------+
```

5. After the volume recipient, or new owner, accepts the transfer, you can see that the transfer is no longer available:

```
$ openstack volume transfer request list
+----+-----------+------+
| ID | Volume ID | Name |
+----+-----------+------+
+----+-----------+------+
```

### 4.7.7.2 Accept a volume transfer request

1. As the volume recipient, you must first obtain the transfer ID and authorization key from the original owner.

2. Accept the request:

```
$ openstack volume transfer request accept transferID authKey
```

For example:

```
$ openstack volume transfer request accept 6e4e9aa4-bed5-4f94-8f76-df43232f44dc
 b2c8e585cbc68a80
+-----------+--------------------------------------+
|  Property |                Value                 |
+-----------+--------------------------------------+
|     id    | 6e4e9aa4-bed5-4f94-8f76-df43232f44dc |
|    name   |                 None                 |
| volume_id | a1cdace0-08e4-4dc7-b9dc-457e9bcfe25f |
+-----------+--------------------------------------+
```

**Note**

If you do not have a sufficient quota for the transfer, the transfer is refused.

### 4.7.7.3 Delete a volume transfer

1. List available volumes and their statuses:

```
$ openstack volume list
```

```
+-----------------+-----------------+-----------------+------+-------------+
|       ID        |  Display Name   |      Status     | Size | Attached to |
+-----------------+-----------------+-----------------+------+-------------+
| 72bfce9f-cac... |       None      |      error      |  1   |             |
| a1cdace0-08e... |       None      |awaiting-transfer|  1   |             |
+-----------------+-----------------+-----------------+------+-------------+
```

2. Find the matching transfer ID:

```
$ openstack volume transfer request list
+--------------------------------------+--------------------------------------+------+
|                 ID                   |              VolumeID                | Name |
+--------------------------------------+--------------------------------------+------+
| a6da6888-7cdf-4291-9c08-8c1f22426b8a | a1cdace0-08e4-4dc7-b9dc-457e9bcfe25f | None |
+--------------------------------------+--------------------------------------+------+
```

3. Delete the volume:

```
$ openstack volume transfer request delete <transfer>
```

**<transfer>**

Name or ID of transfer to delete.

For example:

```
$ openstack volume transfer request delete a6da6888-7cdf-4291-9c08-8c1f22426b8a
```

4. Verify that transfer list is now empty and that the volume is again available for transfer:

```
$ openstack volume transfer request list
+----+-----------+------+
| ID | Volume ID | Name |
+----+-----------+------+
+----+-----------+------+
```

```
$ openstack volume list
+-----------------+-----------+--------------+------+-------------+----------
+-------------+
|       ID        |   Status  | Display Name | Size | Volume Type | Bootable | Attached
 to |
+-----------------+-----------+--------------+------+-------------+----------
+-------------+
| 72bfce9f-ca...  |   error   |     None     |  1   |     None    |  false   |
  |
| a1cdace0-08...  | available |     None     |  1   |     None    |  false   |
  |
```

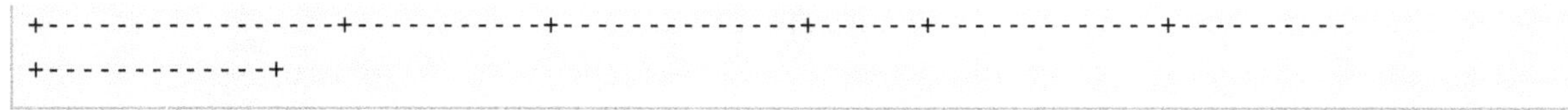
```
+---------------+---------+-------------+-----+------------+---------
+-------------+
```

## 4.7.8 Manage and unmanage a snapshot

A snapshot is a point in time version of a volume. As an administrator, you can manage and unmanage snapshots.

### 4.7.8.1 Manage a snapshot

Manage a snapshot with the **`openstack snapshot set`** command:

```
$ openstack snapshot set \
  [--name <name>] \
  [--description <description>] \
  [--property <key=value> [...] ] \
  [--state <state>] \
  <snapshot>
```

The arguments to be passed are:

`--name <name>`

New snapshot name

`--description <description>`

New snapshot description

`--property <key=value>`

Property to add or modify for this snapshot (repeat option to set multiple properties)

`--state <state>`

New snapshot state. (“available”, “error”, “creating”, “deleting”, or “error_deleting”) (admin only) (This option simply changes the state of the snapshot in the database with no regard to actual status, exercise caution when using)

`<snapshot>`

Snapshot to modify (name or ID)

```
$ openstack snapshot set my-snapshot-id
```

#### 4.7.8.2 Unmanage a snapshot

Unmanage a snapshot with the **`cinder snapshot-unmanage`** command:

```
$ cinder snapshot-unmanage SNAPSHOT
```

The arguments to be passed are:

**SNAPSHOT**

Name or ID of the snapshot to unmanage.

The following example unmanages the `my-snapshot-id` image:

```
$ cinder snapshot-unmanage my-snapshot-id
```

## 4.8 Manage shares

A share is provided by file storage. You can give access to a share to instances. To create and manage shares, you use `manila` client commands.

### 4.8.1 Create a share network

1. Create a share network.

```
$ manila share-network-create \
    --name mysharenetwork \
    --description "My Manila network" \
    --neutron-net-id dca0efc7-523d-43ef-9ded-af404a02b055 \
    --neutron-subnet-id 29ecfbd5-a9be-467e-8b4a-3415d1f82888
+-------------------+--------------------------------------+
| Property          | Value                                |
+-------------------+--------------------------------------+
| name              | mysharenetwork                       |
| segmentation_id   | None                                 |
| created_at        | 2016-03-24T14:13:02.888816           |
| neutron_subnet_id | 29ecfbd5-a9be-467e-8b4a-3415d1f82888 |
| updated_at        | None                                 |
| network_type      | None                                 |
| neutron_net_id    | dca0efc7-523d-43ef-9ded-af404a02b055 |
| ip_version        | None                                 |
| nova_net_id       | None                                 |
```

```
| cidr              | None                                 |
| project_id        | 907004508ef4447397ce6741a8f037c1     |
| id                | c895fe26-92be-4152-9e6c-f2ad230efb13 |
| description       | My Manila network                    |
+-------------------+--------------------------------------+
```

2. List share networks.

```
$ manila share-network-list
+--------------------------------------+----------------+
| id                                   | name           |
+--------------------------------------+----------------+
| c895fe26-92be-4152-9e6c-f2ad230efb13 | mysharenetwork |
+--------------------------------------+----------------+
```

### 4.8.2 Create a share

1. Create a share.

```
$ manila create NFS 1 \
    --name myshare \
    --description "My Manila share" \
    --share-network mysharenetwork \
    --share-type default
+-----------------------------+--------------------------------------+
| Property                    | Value                                |
+-----------------------------+--------------------------------------+
| status                      | creating                             |
| share_type_name             | default                              |
| description                 | My Manila share                      |
| availability_zone           | None                                 |
| share_network_id            | c895fe26-92be-4152-9e6c-f2ad230efb13 |
| share_server_id             | None                                 |
| host                        |                                      |
| access_rules_status         | active                               |
| snapshot_id                 | None                                 |
| is_public                   | False                                |
| task_state                  | None                                 |
| snapshot_support            | True                                 |
| id                          | 8d8b854b-ec32-43f1-acc0-1b2efa7c3400 |
| size                        | 1                                    |
| name                        | myshare                              |
| share_type                  | bf6ada49-990a-47c3-88bc-c0cb31d5c9bf |
| has_replicas                | False                                |
| replication_type            | None                                 |
```

```
| created_at                  | 2016-03-24T14:15:34.000000       |
| share_proto                 | NFS                              |
| consistency_group_id        | None                             |
| source_cgsnapshot_member_id | None                             |
| project_id                  | 907004508ef4447397ce6741a8f037c1 |
| metadata                    | {}                               |
+-----------------------------+----------------------------------+
```

2. Show a share.

```
$ manila show myshare
+-----------------------------
+---------------------------------------------------------------+
| Property                     | Value
     |
+-----------------------------
+---------------------------------------------------------------+
| status                       | available
     |
| share_type_name              | default
     |
| description                  | My Manila share
     |
| availability_zone            | nova
     |
| share_network_id             | c895fe26-92be-4152-9e6c-f2ad230efb13
     |
| export_locations             |
     |
|                              | path = 10.254.0.3:/share-e1c2d35e-fe67-4028-
ad7a-45f668732b1d |
|                              | preferred = False
     |
|                              | is_admin_only = False
     |
|                              | id = b6bd76ce-12a2-42a9-a30a-8a43b503867d
     |
|                              | share_instance_id = e1c2d35e-fe67-4028-ad7a-45f668732b1d
     |
|                              | path = 10.0.0.3:/share-e1c2d35e-fe67-4028-
ad7a-45f668732b1d   |
|                              | preferred = False
     |
|                              | is_admin_only = True
     |
|                              | id = 6921e862-88bc-49a5-a2df-efeed9acd583
     |
|                              | share_instance_id = e1c2d35e-fe67-4028-ad7a-45f668732b1d
     |
```

```
| share_server_id             | 2e9d2d02-883f-47b5-bb98-e053b8d1e683
    |
| host                        | nosb-devstack@london#LONDON
    |
| access_rules_status         | active
    |
| snapshot_id                 | None
    |
| is_public                   | False
    |
| task_state                  | None
    |
| snapshot_support            | True
    |
| id                          | 8d8b854b-ec32-43f1-acc0-1b2efa7c3400
    |
| size                        | 1
    |
| name                        | myshare
    |
| share_type                  | bf6ada49-990a-47c3-88bc-c0cb31d5c9bf
    |
| has_replicas                | False
    |
| replication_type            | None
    |
| created_at                  | 2016-03-24T14:15:34.000000
    |
| share_proto                 | NFS
    |
| consistency_group_id        | None
    |
| source_cgsnapshot_member_id | None
    |
| project_id                  | 907004508ef4447397ce6741a8f037c1
    |
| metadata                    | {}
    |
+-----------------------------
+--------------------------------------------------------------+
```

3. List shares.

```
$ manila list
+--------------------------------------+---------+------+-------------+-----------
+-----------+-----------------+-----------------------------+-------------------+
| ID                                   | Name    | Size | Share Proto | Status    | Is
 Public | Share Type Name | Host                        | Availability Zone |
+--------------------------------------+---------+------+-------------+-----------
+-----------+-----------------+-----------------------------+-------------------+
```

```
| 8d8b854b-ec32-43f1-acc0-1b2efa7c3400 | myshare | 1    | NFS         | available | False
    | default        | nosb-devstack@london#LONDON | nova           |
+--------------------------------------+---------+------+-------------+-----------
+-----------+---------------+-----------------------------+------------------+
```

4. List share export locations.

```
$ manila share-export-location-list myshare
+--------------------------------------
+----------------------------------------------------------------+-----------+
| ID                                   | Path
       | Preferred |
+--------------------------------------
+----------------------------------------------------------------+-----------+
| 6921e862-88bc-49a5-a2df-efeed9acd583 | 10.0.0.3:/share-e1c2d35e-fe67-4028-
ad7a-45f668732b1d   | False     |
| b6bd76ce-12a2-42a9-a30a-8a43b503867d | 10.254.0.3:/share-e1c2d35e-fe67-4028-
ad7a-45f668732b1d | False     |
+--------------------------------------
+----------------------------------------------------------------+-----------+
```

## 4.8.3 Allow read-write access

1. Allow access.

```
$ manila access-allow myshare ip 10.0.0.0/24
+--------------+--------------------------------------+
| Property     | Value                                |
+--------------+--------------------------------------+
| share_id     | 8d8b854b-ec32-43f1-acc0-1b2efa7c3400 |
| access_type  | ip                                   |
| access_to    | 10.0.0.0/24                          |
| access_level | rw                                   |
| state        | new                                  |
| id           | 0c8470ca-0d77-490c-9e71-29e1f453bf97 |
+--------------+--------------------------------------+
```

2. List access.

```
$ manila access-list myshare
+--------------------------------------+-------------+-------------+--------------
+--------+
| id                                   | access_type | access_to   | access_level | state
  |
+--------------------------------------+-------------+-------------+--------------
+--------+
```

```
| 0c8470ca-0d77-490c-9e71-29e1f453bf97 | ip          | 10.0.0.0/24 | rw           |
 active |
+--------------------------------------+-------------+-------------+-------------
+--------+
```

The access is created.

### 4.8.4 Allow read-only access

1. Allow access.

```
$ manila access-allow myshare ip 20.0.0.0/24 --access-level ro
+--------------+--------------------------------------+
| Property     | Value                                |
+--------------+--------------------------------------+
| share_id     | 8d8b854b-ec32-43f1-acc0-1b2efa7c3400 |
| access_type  | ip                                   |
| access_to    | 20.0.0.0/24                          |
| access_level | ro                                   |
| state        | new                                  |
| id           | f151ad17-654d-40ce-ba5d-98a5df67aadc |
+--------------+--------------------------------------+
```

2. List access.

```
$ manila access-list myshare
+--------------------------------------+-------------+-------------+-------------
+--------+
| id                                   | access_type | access_to   | access_level | state
  |
+--------------------------------------+-------------+-------------+-------------
+--------+
| 0c8470ca-0d77-490c-9e71-29e1f453bf97 | ip          | 10.0.0.0/24 | rw           |
 active |
| f151ad17-654d-40ce-ba5d-98a5df67aadc | ip          | 20.0.0.0/24 | ro           |
 active |
+--------------------------------------+-------------+-------------+-------------
+--------+
```

The access is created.

### 4.8.5 Deny access

1. Deny access.

```
$ manila access-deny myshare 0c8470ca-0d77-490c-9e71-29e1f453bf97
$ manila access-deny myshare f151ad17-654d-40ce-ba5d-98a5df67aadc
```

2. List access.

```
$ manila access-list myshare
+----+-------------+-----------+--------------+-------+
| id | access type | access to | access level | state |
+----+-------------+-----------+--------------+-------+
+----+-------------+-----------+--------------+-------+
```

The access is removed.

### 4.8.6 Create snapshot

1. Create a snapshot.

```
$ manila snapshot-create --name mysnapshot --description "My Manila snapshot" myshare
+-------------------+--------------------------------------+
| Property          | Value                                |
+-------------------+--------------------------------------+
| status            | creating                             |
| share_id          | 8d8b854b-ec32-43f1-acc0-1b2efa7c3400 |
| description       | My Manila snapshot                   |
| created_at        | 2016-03-24T14:39:58.232844           |
| share_proto       | NFS                                  |
| provider_location | None                                 |
| id                | e744ca47-0931-4e81-9d9f-2ead7d7c1640 |
| size              | 1                                    |
| share_size        | 1                                    |
| name              | mysnapshot                           |
+-------------------+--------------------------------------+
```

2. List snapshots.

```
$ manila snapshot-list
+--------------------------------------+--------------------------------------
+-----------+------------+------------+
| ID                                   | Share ID                             | Status
 | Name       | Share Size |
+--------------------------------------+--------------------------------------
+-----------+------------+------------+
| e744ca47-0931-4e81-9d9f-2ead7d7c1640 | 8d8b854b-ec32-43f1-acc0-1b2efa7c3400 | available
 | mysnapshot | 1          |
```

```
+----------------------------------+----------------------------------
+-----------+-----------+-----------+
```

### 4.8.7 Create share from snapshot

1. Create a share from a snapshot.

```
$ manila create NFS 1 \
    --snapshot-id e744ca47-0931-4e81-9d9f-2ead7d7c1640 \
    --share-network mysharenetwork \
    --name mysharefromsnap
+-----------------------------+--------------------------------------+
| Property                    | Value                                |
+-----------------------------+--------------------------------------+
| status                      | creating                             |
| share_type_name             | default                              |
| description                 | None                                 |
| availability_zone           | nova                                 |
| share_network_id            | c895fe26-92be-4152-9e6c-f2ad230efb13 |
| share_server_id             | None                                 |
| host                        | nosb-devstack@london#LONDON          |
| access_rules_status         | active                               |
| snapshot_id                 | e744ca47-0931-4e81-9d9f-2ead7d7c1640 |
| is_public                   | False                                |
| task_state                  | None                                 |
| snapshot_support            | True                                 |
| id                          | e73ebcd3-4764-44f0-9b42-fab5cf34a58b |
| size                        | 1                                    |
| name                        | mysharefromsnap                      |
| share_type                  | bf6ada49-990a-47c3-88bc-c0cb31d5c9bf |
| has_replicas                | False                                |
| replication_type            | None                                 |
| created_at                  | 2016-03-24T14:41:36.000000           |
| share_proto                 | NFS                                  |
| consistency_group_id        | None                                 |
| source_cgsnapshot_member_id | None                                 |
| project_id                  | 907004508ef4447397ce6741a8f037c1     |
| metadata                    | {}                                   |
+-----------------------------+--------------------------------------+
```

2. List shares.

```
$ manila list
```

```
+--------------------------------------+-----------------+------+-------------
+-----------+-----------+-----------------+----------------------------
+--------------------+
| ID                                   | Name            | Size | Share Proto | Status
 | Is Public | Share Type Name | Host                             | Availability Zone |
+--------------------------------------+-----------------+------+-------------
+-----------+-----------+-----------------+----------------------------
+--------------------+
| 8d8b854b-ec32-43f1-acc0-1b2efa7c3400 | myshare         | 1    | NFS         | available
 | False     | default         | nosb-devstack@london#LONDON | nova              |
| e73ebcd3-4764-44f0-9b42-fab5cf34a58b | mysharefromsnap | 1    | NFS         | available
 | False     | default         | nosb-devstack@london#LONDON | nova              |
+--------------------------------------+-----------------+------+-------------
+-----------+-----------+-----------------+----------------------------
+--------------------+
```

3. Show the share created from snapshot.

```
$ manila show mysharefromsnap
+------------------------------
+------------------------------------------------------------+
| Property                     | Value
     |
+------------------------------
+------------------------------------------------------------+
| status                       | available
     |
| share_type_name              | default
     |
| description                  | None
     |
| availability_zone            | nova
     |
| share_network_id             | c895fe26-92be-4152-9e6c-f2ad230efb13
     |
| export_locations             |
     |
|                              | path = 10.254.0.3:/share-4c00cb49-51d9-478e-abc1-
d1853efaf6d3 |
|                              | preferred = False
     |
|                              | is_admin_only = False
     |
|                              | id = 5419fb40-04b9-4a52-b08e-19aa1ce13a5c
     |
|                              | share_instance_id = 4c00cb49-51d9-478e-abc1-d1853efaf6d3
     |
|                              | path = 10.0.0.3:/share-4c00cb49-51d9-478e-abc1-
d1853efaf6d3   |
```

```
|                              | preferred = False
     |
|                              | is_admin_only = True
     |
|                              | id = 26f55e4c-6edc-4e55-8c55-c62b7db1aa9f
     |
|                              | share_instance_id = 4c00cb49-51d9-478e-abc1-d1853efaf6d3
     |
| share_server_id              | 2e9d2d02-883f-47b5-bb98-e053b8d1e683
     |
| host                         | nosb-devstack@london#LONDON
     |
| access_rules_status          | active
     |
| snapshot_id                  | e744ca47-0931-4e81-9d9f-2ead7d7c1640
     |
| is_public                    | False
     |
| task_state                   | None
     |
| snapshot_support             | True
     |
| id                           | e73ebcd3-4764-44f0-9b42-fab5cf34a58b
     |
| size                         | 1
     |
| name                         | mysharefromsnap
     |
| share_type                   | bf6ada49-990a-47c3-88bc-c0cb31d5c9bf
     |
| has_replicas                 | False
     |
| replication_type             | None
     |
| created_at                   | 2016-03-24T14:41:36.000000
     |
| share_proto                  | NFS
     |
| consistency_group_id         | None
     |
| source_cgsnapshot_member_id  | None
     |
| project_id                   | 907004508ef4447397ce6741a8f037c1
     |
| metadata                     | {}
     |
+------------------------------
+-----------------------------------------------------------------+
```

### 4.8.8 Delete share

1. Delete a share.

```
$ manila delete mysharefromsnap
```

2. List shares.

```
$ manila list
+--------------------------------------+-----------------+------+-------------
+-----------+------------+----------------+-----------------------------
+-------------------+
| ID                                   | Name            | Size | Share Proto | Status
 | Is Public | Share Type Name | Host                        | Availability Zone |
+--------------------------------------+-----------------+------+-------------
+-----------+------------+----------------+-----------------------------
+-------------------+
| 8d8b854b-ec32-43f1-acc0-1b2efa7c3400 | myshare         | 1    | NFS         | available
 | False     | default         | nosb-devstack@london#LONDON | nova              |
| e73ebcd3-4764-44f0-9b42-fab5cf34a58b | mysharefromsnap | 1    | NFS         | deleting
 | False     | default         | nosb-devstack@london#LONDON | nova              |
+--------------------------------------+-----------------+------+-------------
+-----------+------------+----------------+-----------------------------
+-------------------+
```

The share is being deleted.

### 4.8.9 Delete snapshot

1. List snapshots before deleting.

```
$ manila snapshot-list
+--------------------------------------+--------------------------------------
+-----------+------------+------------+
| ID                                   | Share ID                             | Status
 | Name        | Share Size |
+--------------------------------------+--------------------------------------
+-----------+------------+------------+
| e744ca47-0931-4e81-9d9f-2ead7d7c1640 | 8d8b854b-ec32-43f1-acc0-1b2efa7c3400 | available
 | mysnapshot | 1          |
+--------------------------------------+--------------------------------------
+-----------+------------+------------+
```

2. Delete a snapshot.

```
$ manila snapshot-delete mysnapshot
```

3. List snapshots after deleting.

```
$ manila snapshot-list

+----+----------+--------+------+------------+
| ID | Share ID | Status | Name | Share Size |
+----+----------+--------+------+------------+
+----+----------+--------+------+------------+
```

The snapshot is deleted.

## 4.8.10 Extend share

1. Extend share.

```
$ manila extend myshare 2
```

2. Show the share while it is being extended.

```
$ manila show myshare
+-----------------------------
+-----------------------------------------------------------------+
| Property                     | Value
     |
+-----------------------------
+-----------------------------------------------------------------+
| status                       | extending
     |
| share_type_name              | default
     |
| description                  | My Manila share
     |
| availability_zone            | nova
     |
| share_network_id             | c895fe26-92be-4152-9e6c-f2ad230efb13
     |
| export_locations             |
     |
|                              | path = 10.254.0.3:/share-e1c2d35e-fe67-4028-
ad7a-45f668732b1d |
|                              | preferred = False
     |
|                              | is_admin_only = False
     |
|                              | id = b6bd76ce-12a2-42a9-a30a-8a43b503867d
     |
```

```
|                              | share_instance_id = e1c2d35e-fe67-4028-ad7a-45f668732b1d
     |
|                              | path = 10.0.0.3:/share-e1c2d35e-fe67-4028-
ad7a-45f668732b1d    |
|                              | preferred = False
     |
|                              | is_admin_only = True
     |
|                              | id = 6921e862-88bc-49a5-a2df-efeed9acd583
     |
|                              | share_instance_id = e1c2d35e-fe67-4028-ad7a-45f668732b1d
     |
| share_server_id              | 2e9d2d02-883f-47b5-bb98-e053b8d1e683
     |
| host                         | nosb-devstack@london#LONDON
     |
| access_rules_status          | active
     |
| snapshot_id                  | None
     |
| is_public                    | False
     |
| task_state                   | None
     |
| snapshot_support             | True
     |
| id                           | 8d8b854b-ec32-43f1-acc0-1b2efa7c3400
     |
| size                         | 1
     |
| name                         | myshare
     |
| share_type                   | bf6ada49-990a-47c3-88bc-c0cb31d5c9bf
     |
| has_replicas                 | False
     |
| replication_type             | None
     |
| created_at                   | 2016-03-24T14:15:34.000000
     |
| share_proto                  | NFS
     |
| consistency_group_id         | None
     |
| source_cgsnapshot_member_id | None
     |
| project_id                   | 907004508ef4447397ce6741a8f037c1
     |
| metadata                     | {}
     |
```

```
+----------------------------
+---------------------------------------------------------+
```

3. Show the share after it is extended.

```
$ manila show myshare
+----------------------------
+---------------------------------------------------------+
| Property                     | Value
    |
+----------------------------
+---------------------------------------------------------+
| status                       | available
    |
| share_type_name              | default
    |
| description                  | My Manila share
    |
| availability_zone            | nova
    |
| share_network_id             | c895fe26-92be-4152-9e6c-f2ad230efb13
    |
| export_locations             |
    |
|                              | path = 10.254.0.3:/share-e1c2d35e-fe67-4028-
ad7a-45f668732b1d |
|                              | preferred = False
    |
|                              | is_admin_only = False
    |
|                              | id = b6bd76ce-12a2-42a9-a30a-8a43b503867d
    |
|                              | share_instance_id = e1c2d35e-fe67-4028-ad7a-45f668732b1d
    |
|                              | path = 10.0.0.3:/share-e1c2d35e-fe67-4028-
ad7a-45f668732b1d   |
|                              | preferred = False
    |
|                              | is_admin_only = True
    |
|                              | id = 6921e862-88bc-49a5-a2df-efeed9acd583
    |
|                              | share_instance_id = e1c2d35e-fe67-4028-ad7a-45f668732b1d
    |
| share_server_id              | 2e9d2d02-883f-47b5-bb98-e053b8d1e683
    |
| host                         | nosb-devstack@london#LONDON
    |
| access_rules_status          | active
    |
```

```
| snapshot_id                 | None
    |
| is_public                   | False
    |
| task_state                  | None
    |
| snapshot_support            | True
    |
| id                          | 8d8b854b-ec32-43f1-acc0-1b2efa7c3400
    |
| size                        | 2
    |
| name                        | myshare
    |
| share_type                  | bf6ada49-990a-47c3-88bc-c0cb31d5c9bf
    |
| has_replicas                | False
    |
| replication_type            | None
    |
| created_at                  | 2016-03-24T14:15:34.000000
    |
| share_proto                 | NFS
    |
| consistency_group_id        | None
    |
| source_cgsnapshot_member_id | None
    |
| project_id                  | 907004508ef4447397ce6741a8f037c1
    |
| metadata                    | {}
    |
+-----------------------------
+-------------------------------------------------------------+
```

### 4.8.11 Shrink share

1. Shrink a share.

```
$ manila shrink myshare 1
```

2. Show the share while it is being shrunk.

```
$ manila show myshare
+-----------------------------
+-------------------------------------------------------------+
```

```
| Property                    | Value
    |
+----------------------------
+-----------------------------------------------------------+
| status                      | shrinking
    |
| share_type_name             | default
    |
| description                 | My Manila share
    |
| availability_zone           | nova
    |
| share_network_id            | c895fe26-92be-4152-9e6c-f2ad230efb13
    |
| export_locations            |
    |
|                             | path = 10.254.0.3:/share-e1c2d35e-fe67-4028-
ad7a-45f668732b1d |
|                             | preferred = False
    |
|                             | is_admin_only = False
    |
|                             | id = b6bd76ce-12a2-42a9-a30a-8a43b503867d
    |
|                             | share_instance_id = e1c2d35e-fe67-4028-ad7a-45f668732b1d
    |
|                             | path = 10.0.0.3:/share-e1c2d35e-fe67-4028-
ad7a-45f668732b1d   |
|                             | preferred = False
    |
|                             | is_admin_only = True
    |
|                             | id = 6921e862-88bc-49a5-a2df-efeed9acd583
    |
|                             | share_instance_id = e1c2d35e-fe67-4028-ad7a-45f668732b1d
    |
| share_server_id             | 2e9d2d02-883f-47b5-bb98-e053b8d1e683
    |
| host                        | nosb-devstack@london#LONDON
    |
| access_rules_status         | active
    |
| snapshot_id                 | None
    |
| is_public                   | False
    |
| task_state                  | None
    |
| snapshot_support            | True
    |
```

```
| id                          | 8d8b854b-ec32-43f1-acc0-1b2efa7c3400
    |
| size                        | 2
    |
| name                        | myshare
    |
| share_type                  | bf6ada49-990a-47c3-88bc-c0cb31d5c9bf
    |
| has_replicas                | False
    |
| replication_type            | None
    |
| created_at                  | 2016-03-24T14:15:34.000000
    |
| share_proto                 | NFS
    |
| consistency_group_id        | None
    |
| source_cgsnapshot_member_id | None
    |
| project_id                  | 907004508ef4447397ce6741a8f037c1
    |
| metadata                    | {}
    |
+-----------------------------
+-----------------------------------------------------------------+
```

3. Show the share after it is being shrunk.

```
$ manila show myshare
+-----------------------------
+-----------------------------------------------------------------+
| Property                    | Value
    |
+-----------------------------
+-----------------------------------------------------------------+
| status                      | available
    |
| share_type_name             | default
    |
| description                 | My Manila share
    |
| availability_zone           | nova
    |
| share_network_id            | c895fe26-92be-4152-9e6c-f2ad230efb13
    |
| export_locations            |
    |
|                             | path = 10.254.0.3:/share-e1c2d35e-fe67-4028-
ad7a-45f668732b1d |
```

```
|                                    | preferred = False
     |
|                                    | is_admin_only = False
     |
|                                    | id = b6bd76ce-12a2-42a9-a30a-8a43b503867d
     |
|                                    | share_instance_id = e1c2d35e-fe67-4028-ad7a-45f668732b1d
     |
|                                    | path = 10.0.0.3:/share-e1c2d35e-fe67-4028-
ad7a-45f668732b1d    |
|                                    | preferred = False
     |
|                                    | is_admin_only = True
     |
|                                    | id = 6921e862-88bc-49a5-a2df-efeed9acd583
     |
|                                    | share_instance_id = e1c2d35e-fe67-4028-ad7a-45f668732b1d
     |
| share_server_id                    | 2e9d2d02-883f-47b5-bb98-e053b8d1e683
     |
| host                               | nosb-devstack@london#LONDON
     |
| access_rules_status                | active
     |
| snapshot_id                        | None
     |
| is_public                          | False
     |
| task_state                         | None
     |
| snapshot_support                   | True
     |
| id                                 | 8d8b854b-ec32-43f1-acc0-1b2efa7c3400
     |
| size                               | 1
     |
| name                               | myshare
     |
| share_type                         | bf6ada49-990a-47c3-88bc-c0cb31d5c9bf
     |
| has_replicas                       | False
     |
| replication_type                   | None
     |
| created_at                         | 2016-03-24T14:15:34.000000
     |
| share_proto                        | NFS
     |
| consistency_group_id               | None
     |
```

```
| source_cgsnapshot_member_id | None
    |
| project_id                  | 907004508ef4447397ce6741a8f037c1
    |
| metadata                    | {}
    |
+-----------------------------
+----------------------------------------------------------------+
```

## 4.9 Configure access and security for instances

When you launch a virtual machine, you can inject a *key pair*, which provides SSH access to your instance. For this to work, the image must contain the `cloud-init` package.

You can create at least one key pair for each project. You can use the key pair for multiple instances that belong to that project. If you generate a key pair with an external tool, you can import it into OpenStack.

### Note

A key pair belongs to an individual user, not to a project. To share a key pair across multiple users, each user needs to import that key pair.

If an image uses a static root password or a static key set (neither is recommended), you must not provide a key pair when you launch the instance.

A *security group* is a named collection of network access rules that are use to limit the types of traffic that have access to instances. When you launch an instance, you can assign one or more security groups to it. If you do not create security groups, new instances are automatically assigned to the default security group, unless you explicitly specify a different security group.

The associated *rules* in each security group control the traffic to instances in the group. Any incoming traffic that is not matched by a rule is denied access by default. You can add rules to or remove rules from a security group, and you can modify rules for the default and any other security group.

You can modify the rules in a security group to allow access to instances through different ports and protocols. For example, you can modify rules to allow access to instances through SSH, to ping instances, or to allow UDP traffic; for example, for a DNS server running on an instance. You specify the following parameters for rules:

- **Source of traffic.** Enable traffic to instances from either IP addresses inside the cloud from other group members or from all IP addresses.
- **Protocol.** Choose TCP for SSH, ICMP for pings, or UDP.
- **Destination port on virtual machine.** Define a port range. To open a single port only, enter the same value twice. ICMP does not support ports; instead, you enter values to define the codes and types of ICMP traffic to be allowed.

Rules are automatically enforced as soon as you create or modify them.

Note

Instances that use the default security group cannot, by default, be accessed from any IP address outside of the cloud. If you want those IP addresses to access the instances, you must modify the rules for the default security group. Additionally, security groups will automatically drop DHCP responses coming from instances.

You can also assign a floating IP address to a running instance to make it accessible from outside the cloud. See .

## 4.9.1 Add a key pair

You can generate a key pair or upload an existing public key.

1. To generate a key pair, run the following command.

```
$ openstack keypair create KEY_NAME > MY_KEY.pem
```

This command generates a key pair with the name that you specify for KEY_NAME, writes the private key to the `.pem` file that you specify, and registers the public key to the Nova database.

2. To set the permissions of the `.pem` file so that only you can read and write to it, run the following command.

```
$ chmod 600 MY_KEY.pem
```

### 4.9.2 Import a key pair

1. If you have already generated a key pair and the public key is located at `~/.ssh/id_rsa.pub`, run the following command to upload the public key.

   ```
   $ openstack keypair create --public-key ~/.ssh/id_rsa.pub KEY_NAME
   ```

   This command registers the public key at the Nova database and names the key pair the name that you specify for `KEY_NAME`.

2. To ensure that the key pair has been successfully imported, list key pairs as follows:

   ```
   $ openstack keypair list
   ```

### 4.9.3 Create and manage security groups

1. To list the security groups for the current project, including descriptions, enter the following command:

   ```
   $ openstack security group list
   ```

2. To create a security group with a specified name and description, enter the following command:

   ```
   $ openstack security group create SECURITY_GROUP_NAME --description GROUP_DESCRIPTION
   ```

3. To delete a specified group, enter the following command:

   ```
   $ openstack security group delete SECURITY_GROUP_NAME
   ```

Note

You cannot delete the default security group for a project. Also, you cannot delete a security group that is assigned to a running instance.

### 4.9.4 Create and manage security group rules

Modify security group rules with the **openstack security group rule** commands. Before you begin, source the OpenStack RC file. For details, see .

1. To list the rules for a security group, run the following command:

```
$ openstack security group rule list SECURITY_GROUP_NAME
```

2. To allow SSH access to the instances, choose one of the following options:

   - Allow access from all IP addresses, specified as IP subnet `0.0.0.0/0` in CIDR notation:

   ```
   $ openstack security group rule create SECURITY_GROUP_NAME \
         --protocol tcp --dst-port 22:22 --remote-ip 0.0.0.0/0
   ```

   - Allow access only from IP addresses from other security groups (source groups) to access the specified port:

   ```
   $ openstack security group rule create SECURITY_GROUP_NAME \
         --protocol tcp --dst-port 22:22 --remote-group SOURCE_GROUP_NAME
   ```

3. To allow pinging of the instances, choose one of the following options:

   - Allow pinging from all IP addresses, specified as IP subnet `0.0.0.0/0` in CIDR notation.

   ```
   $ openstack security group rule create --protocol icmp \
     SECURITY_GROUP_NAME
   ```

   This allows access to all codes and all types of ICMP traffic.

   - Allow only members of other security groups (source groups) to ping instances.

   ```
   $ openstack security group rule create --protocol icmp \
     --remote-group SOURCE_GROUP_NAME SECURITY_GROUP
   ```

4. To allow access through a UDP port, such as allowing access to a DNS server that runs on a VM, choose one of the following options:

   - Allow UDP access from IP addresses, specified as IP subnet `0.0.0.0/0` in CIDR notation.

```
$ openstack security group rule create --protocol udp \
  --dst-port 53:53 SECURITY_GROUP
```

- Allow only IP addresses from other security groups (source groups) to access the specified port.

```
$ openstack security group rule create --protocol udp \
  --dst-port 53:53 --remote-group SOURCE_GROUP_NAME SECURITY_GROUP
```

### 4.9.5 Delete a security group rule

To delete a security group rule, specify the ID of the rule.

```
$ openstack security group rule delete RULE_ID
```

## 4.10 Launch instances

Instances are virtual machines that run inside the cloud.

Before you can launch an instance, gather the following parameters:

- The **instance source** can be an image, snapshot, or block storage volume that contains an image or snapshot.
- A **name** for your instance.
- The **flavor** for your instance, which defines the compute, memory, and storage capacity of nova computing instances. A flavor is an available hardware configuration for a server. It defines the size of a virtual server that can be launched.
- Any **user data** files. A user data file is a special key in the metadata service that holds a file that cloud-aware applications in the guest instance can access. For example, one application that uses user data is the cloud-init (https://help.ubuntu.com/community/CloudInit) system, which is an open-source package from Ubuntu that is available on various Linux distributions and that handles early initialization of a cloud instance.

- Access and security credentials, which include one or both of the following credentials:
  - A **key pair** for your instance, which are SSH credentials that are injected into images when they are launched. For the key pair to be successfully injected, the image must contain the `cloud-init` package. Create at least one key pair for each project. If you already have generated a key pair with an external tool, you can import it into OpenStack. You can use the key pair for multiple instances that belong to that project.
  - A **security group** that defines which incoming network traffic is forwarded to instances. Security groups hold a set of firewall policies, known as *security group rules*.
- If needed, you can assign a **floating (public) IP address** to a running instance.
- You can also attach a block storage device, or **volume**, for persistent storage.

Note

Instances that use the default security group cannot, by default, be accessed from any IP address outside of the cloud. If you want those IP addresses to access the instances, you must modify the rules for the default security group.

You can also assign a floating IP address to a running instance to make it accessible from outside the cloud. See .

After you gather the parameters that you need to launch an instance, you can launch it from an or a . You can launch an instance directly from one of the available OpenStack images or from an image that you have copied to a persistent volume. The OpenStack Image service provides a pool of images that are accessible to members of different projects.

### 4.10.1 Gather parameters to launch an instance

Before you begin, source the OpenStack RC file.

1. Create a flavor.

```
$  openstack flavor create --ram 512 --disk 1 --vcpus 1 m1.tiny
```

2. List the available flavors.

```
$ openstack flavor list
```

Note the ID of the flavor that you want to use for your instance:

```
+-----+-----------+-------+------+-----------+-------+-----------+
| ID  | Name      |   RAM | Disk | Ephemeral | VCPUs | Is_Public |
+-----+-----------+-------+------+-----------+-------+-----------+
| 1   | m1.tiny   |   512 |    1 |         0 |     1 | True      |
| 2   | m1.small  |  2048 |   20 |         0 |     1 | True      |
| 3   | m1.medium |  4096 |   40 |         0 |     2 | True      |
| 4   | m1.large  |  8192 |   80 |         0 |     4 | True      |
| 5   | m1.xlarge | 16384 |  160 |         0 |     8 | True      |
+-----+-----------+-------+------+-----------+-------+-----------+
```

3. List the available images.

```
$ openstack image list
```

Note the ID of the image from which you want to boot your instance:

```
+--------------------------------------+---------------------------------+--------+
| ID                                   | Name                            | Status |
+--------------------------------------+---------------------------------+--------+
| 397e713c-b95b-4186-ad46-6126863ea0a9 | cirros-0.3.2-x86_64-uec         | active |
| df430cc2-3406-4061-b635-a51c16e488ac | cirros-0.3.2-x86_64-uec-kernel  | active |
| 3cf852bd-2332-48f4-9ae4-7d926d50945e | cirros-0.3.2-x86_64-uec-ramdisk | active |
+--------------------------------------+---------------------------------+--------+
```

You can also filter the image list by using **grep** to find a specific image, as follows:

```
$ openstack image list | grep 'kernel'

| df430cc2-3406-4061-b635-a51c16e488ac | cirros-0.3.2-x86_64-uec-kernel  | active |
```

4. List the available security groups.

```
$ openstack security group list
```

## Note

If you are an admin user, this command will list groups for all tenants.

Note the ID of the security group that you want to use for your instance:

```
+--------------------------------------+---------+------------------------
+----------------------------------+
| ID                                   | Name    | Description            | Project
                      |
+--------------------------------------+---------+------------------------
+----------------------------------+
| b0d78827-0981-45ef-8561-93aee39bbd9f | default | Default security group |
 5669caad86a04256994cdf755df4d3c1 |
| ec02e79e-83e1-48a5-86ad-14ab9a8c375f | default | Default security group |
 1eaaf6ede7a24e78859591444abf314a |
+--------------------------------------+---------+------------------------
+----------------------------------+
```

If you have not created any security groups, you can assign the instance to only the default security group.

You can view rules for a specified security group:

```
$ openstack security group rule list default
```

5. List the available key pairs, and note the key pair name that you use for SSH access.

```
$ openstack keypair list
```

### 4.10.2 Launch an instance

You can launch an instance from various sources.

#### 4.10.2.1 Launch an instance from an image

Follow the steps below to launch an instance from an image.

1. After you gather required parameters, run the following command to launch an instance. Specify the server name, flavor ID, and image ID.

```
$ openstack server create --flavor FLAVOR_ID --image IMAGE_ID --key-name KEY_NAME \
  --user-data USER_DATA_FILE --security-group SEC_GROUP_NAME --property KEY=VALUE \
  INSTANCE_NAME
```

Optionally, you can provide a key name for access control and a security group for security. You can also include metadata key and value pairs. For example, you can add a description for your server by providing the `--property description="My Server"` parameter. You can pass user data in a local file at instance launch by using the `--user-data USER-DATA-FILE` parameter.

Important

If you boot an instance with an INSTANCE_NAME greater than 63 characters, Compute truncates it automatically when turning it into a host name to ensure the correct work of dnsmasq. The corresponding warning is written into the `neutron-dnsmasq.log` file.

The following command launches the `MyCirrosServer` instance with the `m1.small` flavor (ID of `1`), `cirros-0.3.2-x86_64-uec` image (ID of `397e713c-b95b-4186-ad46-6126863ea0a9`), `default` security group, `KeyPair01` key, and a user data file called `cloudinit.file`:

```
$ openstack server create --flavor 1 --image 397e713c-b95b-4186-ad46-6126863ea0a9 \
  --security-group default --key-name KeyPair01 --user-data cloudinit.file \
  myCirrosServer
```

Depending on the parameters that you provide, the command returns a list of server properties.

```
+--------------------------------------+------------------------------------------------+
| Field                                | Value                                          |
+--------------------------------------+------------------------------------------------+
| OS-DCF:diskConfig                    | MANUAL                                         |
| OS-EXT-AZ:availability_zone          |                                                |
| OS-EXT-SRV-ATTR:host                 | None                                           |
| OS-EXT-SRV-ATTR:hypervisor_hostname  | None                                           |
| OS-EXT-SRV-ATTR:instance_name        |                                                |
| OS-EXT-STS:power_state               | NOSTATE                                        |
| OS-EXT-STS:task_state                | scheduling                                     |
| OS-EXT-STS:vm_state                  | building                                       |
| OS-SRV-USG:launched_at               | None                                           |
| OS-SRV-USG:terminated_at             | None                                           |
| accessIPv4                           |                                                |
| accessIPv6                           |                                                |
| addresses                            |                                                |
| adminPass                            | E4Ksozt4Efi8                                   |
```

```
| config_drive                        |                                          |
| created                             | 2016-11-30T14:48:05Z                     |
| flavor                              | m1.tiny                                  |
| hostId                              |                                          |
| id                                  | 89015cc9-bdf1-458a-8518-fdca2b4a5785     |
| image                               | cirros (9fef3b2d-c35d-4b61-bea8-09cc6dc41829) |
| key_name                            | KeyPair01                                |
| name                                | myCirrosServer                           |
| os-extended-volumes:volumes_attached | []                                      |
| progress                            | 0                                        |
| project_id                          | 5669caad86a04256994cdf755df4d3c1         |
| properties                          |                                          |
| security_groups                     | [{u'name': u'default'}]                  |
| status                              | BUILD                                    |
| updated                             | 2016-11-30T14:48:05Z                     |
| user_id                             | c36cec73b0e44876a4478b1e6cd749bb         |
| metadata                            | {u'KEY': u'VALUE'}                       |
+-------------------------------------+------------------------------------------+
```

A status of `BUILD` indicates that the instance has started, but is not yet online.
A status of `ACTIVE` indicates that the instance is active.

2. Copy the server ID value from the `id` field in the output. Use the ID to get server details or to delete your server.

3. Copy the administrative password value from the `adminPass` field. Use the password to log in to your server.

Note

You can also place arbitrary local files into the instance file system at creation time by using the `--file <dst-path=src-path>` option. You can store up to five files. For example, if you have a special authorized keys file named `special_authorized_keysfile` that you want to put on the instance rather than using the regular SSH key injection, you can use the `--file` option as shown in the following example.

```
$ openstack server create --image ubuntu-cloudimage --flavor 1 vm-name \
  --file /root/.ssh/authorized_keys=special_authorized_keysfile
```

4. Check if the instance is online.

```
$ openstack server list
```

The list shows the ID, name, status, and private (and if assigned, public) IP addresses for all instances in the project to which you belong:

```
+------------+--------------------+-------+-----------+------------
+----------------+-----------+
| ID         | Name               | Status | Task State | Power State | Networks
   | Image Name |
+------------+--------------------+-------+-----------+------------
+----------------+-----------+
| 84c6e57d... | myCirrosServer       | ACTIVE | None       | Running     |
 private=10.0.0.3 | cirros     |
| 8a99547e... | myInstanceFromVolume | ACTIVE | None       | Running     |
 private=10.0.0.4 | centos     |
+------------+--------------------+-------+-----------+------------
+----------------+-----------+
```

If the status for the instance is ACTIVE, the instance is online.

5. To view the available options for the **`openstack server list`** command, run the following command:

```
$ openstack help server list
```

Note

If you did not provide a key pair, security groups, or rules, you can access the instance only from inside the cloud through VNC. Even pinging the instance is not possible.

### 4.10.2.2 Launch an instance from a volume

You can boot instances from a volume instead of an image.

To complete these tasks, use these parameters on the **`openstack server create`** command:

| Task | nova boot parameter | Information |
|---|---|---|
| Boot an instance from an image and attach a non-bootable volume. | `--block-device` | *Section 4.10.2.2.1, "Boot instance from image and attach non-bootable volume"* |

| Task | nova boot parameter | Information |
| --- | --- | --- |
| Create a volume from an image and boot an instance from that volume. | `--block-device` | *Section 4.10.2.2.2, "Create volume from image and boot instance"* |
| Boot from an existing source image, volume, or snapshot. | `--block-device` | *Section 4.10.2.2.2, "Create volume from image and boot instance"* |
| Attach a swap disk to an instance. | `--swap` | *Section 4.10.2.2.3, "Attach swap or ephemeral disk to an instance"* |
| Attach an ephemeral disk to an instance. | `--ephemeral` | *Section 4.10.2.2.3, "Attach swap or ephemeral disk to an instance"* |

## Note

To attach a volume to a running instance, see *Section 4.7.4, "Attach a volume to an instance"*.

#### 4.10.2.2.1 Boot instance from image and attach non-bootable volume

Create a non-bootable volume and attach that volume to an instance that you boot from an image.

To create a non-bootable volume, do not create it from an image. The volume must be entirely empty with no partition table and no file system.

1. Create a non-bootable volume.

```
$ openstack volume create --size 8 my-volume
+---------------------+--------------------------------------+
| Field               | Value                                |
+---------------------+--------------------------------------+
| attachments         | []                                   |
| availability_zone   | nova                                 |
| bootable            | false                                |
| consistencygroup_id | None                                 |
| created_at          | 2016-11-25T10:37:08.850997           |
| description         | None                                 |
| encrypted           | False                                |
| id                  | b8f7bbec-6274-4cd7-90e7-60916a5e75d4 |
```

```
| migration_status    | None                             |
| multiattach         | False                            |
| name                | my-volume                        |
| properties          |                                  |
| replication_status  | disabled                         |
| size                | 8                                |
| snapshot_id         | None                             |
| source_volid        | None                             |
| status              | creating                         |
| type                | None                             |
| updated_at          | None                             |
| user_id             | 0678735e449149b0a42076e12dd54e28 |
+---------------------+----------------------------------+
```

2. List volumes.

```
$ openstack volume list
+--------------------------------------+--------------+-----------+------+-------------+
| ID                                   | Display Name | Status    | Size | Attached to |
+--------------------------------------+--------------+-----------+------+-------------+
| b8f7bbec-6274-4cd7-90e7-60916a5e75d4 | my-volume    | available |    8 |             |
+--------------------------------------+--------------+-----------+------+-------------+
```

3. Boot an instance from an image and attach the empty volume to the instance.

```
$ openstack server create --flavor 2 --image 98901246-af91-43d8-b5e6-a4506aa8f369 \
  --block-device source=volume,id=d620d971-
b160-4c4e-8652-2513d74e2080,dest=volume,shutdown=preserve \
  myInstanceWithVolume
+--------------------------------------+--------------------------------------------+
| Field                                | Value                                      |
+--------------------------------------+--------------------------------------------+
| OS-DCF:diskConfig                    | MANUAL                                     |
| OS-EXT-AZ:availability_zone          | nova                                       |
| OS-EXT-SRV-ATTR:host                 | -                                          |
| OS-EXT-SRV-ATTR:hypervisor_hostname  | -                                          |
| OS-EXT-SRV-ATTR:instance_name        | instance-00000004                          |
| OS-EXT-STS:power_state               | 0                                          |
| OS-EXT-STS:task_state                | scheduling                                 |
| OS-EXT-STS:vm_state                  | building                                   |
| OS-SRV-USG:launched_at               | -                                          |
| OS-SRV-USG:terminated_at             | -                                          |
| accessIPv4                           |                                            |
| accessIPv6                           |                                            |
| adminPass                            | ZaiYeC8iucgU                               |
| config_drive                         |                                            |
| created                              | 2014-05-09T16:34:50Z                       |
| flavor                               | m1.small (2)                               |
| hostId                               |                                            |
```

```
| id                                   | 1e1797f3-1662-49ff-ae8c-a77e82ee1571     |
| image                                | cirros-0.3.1-x86_64-uec (98901246-af91-... |
| key_name                             | -                                        |
| metadata                             | {}                                       |
| name                                 | myInstanceWithVolume                     |
| os-extended-volumes:volumes_attached | [{"id": "d620d971-b160-4c4e-8652-2513d7... |
| progress                             | 0                                        |
| security_groups                      | default                                  |
| status                               | BUILD                                    |
| tenant_id                            | ccef9e62b1e645df98728fb2b3076f27         |
| updated                              | 2014-05-09T16:34:51Z                     |
| user_id                              | fef060ae7bfd4024b3edb97dff59017a         |
+--------------------------------------+------------------------------------------+
```

#### 4.10.2.2.2 Create volume from image and boot instance

You can create a volume from an existing image, volume, or snapshot. This procedure shows you how to create a volume from an image, and use the volume to boot an instance.

1. List the available images.

```
$ openstack image list
+-----------------+---------------------------------+--------+
| ID              | Name                            | Status |
+-----------------+---------------------------------+--------+
| 484e05af-a14... | Fedora-x86_64-20-20131211.1-sda | active |
| 98901246-af9... | cirros-0.3.1-x86_64-uec         | active |
| b6e95589-7eb... | cirros-0.3.1-x86_64-uec-kernel  | active |
| c90893ea-e73... | cirros-0.3.1-x86_64-uec-ramdisk | active |
+-----------------+---------------------------------+--------+
```

Note the ID of the image that you want to use to create a volume.

If you want to create a volume to a specific storage backend, you need to use an image which has *cinder_img_volume_type* property. In this case, a new volume will be created as *storage_backend1* volume type.

```
$ openstack image show 98901246-af9...
+------------------+------------------------------------------------------+
| Field            | Value                                                |
+------------------+------------------------------------------------------+
| checksum         | ee1eca47dc88f4879d8a229cc70a07c6                     |
| container_format | bare                                                 |
| created_at       | 2016-10-08T14:59:05Z                                 |
| disk_format      | qcow2                                                |
| file             | /v2/images/9fef3b2d-c35d-4b61-bea8-09cc6dc41829/file |
```

```
| id               | 98901246-af9d-4b61-bea8-09cc6dc41829                 |
| min_disk         | 0                                                    |
| min_ram          | 0                                                    |
| name             | cirros-0.3.4-x86_64-uec                              |
| owner            | 8d8ef3cdf2b54c25831cbb409ad9ae86                     |
| protected        | False                                                |
| schema           | /v2/schemas/image                                    |
| size             | 13287936                                             |
| status           | active                                               |
| tags             |                                                      |
| updated_at       | 2016-10-19T09:12:52Z                                 |
| virtual_size     | None                                                 |
| visibility       | public                                               |
+------------------+------------------------------------------------------+
```

2. List the available flavors.

```
$ openstack flavor list
+-----+-----------+-------+------+-----------+-------+-----------+
| ID  | Name      |   RAM | Disk | Ephemeral | VCPUs | Is_Public |
+-----+-----------+-------+------+-----------+-------+-----------+
| 1   | m1.tiny   |   512 |    1 |         0 |     1 | True      |
| 2   | m1.small  |  2048 |   20 |         0 |     1 | True      |
| 3   | m1.medium |  4096 |   40 |         0 |     2 | True      |
| 4   | m1.large  |  8192 |   80 |         0 |     4 | True      |
| 5   | m1.xlarge | 16384 |  160 |         0 |     8 | True      |
+-----+-----------+-------+------+-----------+-------+-----------+
```

Note the ID of the flavor that you want to use to create a volume.

3. To create a bootable volume from an image and launch an instance from this volume, use the `--block-device` parameter.
For example:

```
$ openstack server create --flavor FLAVOR --block-device \
  source=SOURCE,id=ID,dest=DEST,size=SIZE,shutdown=PRESERVE,bootindex=INDEX \
  NAME
```

The parameters are:

- `--flavor` FLAVOR. The flavor ID or name.
- `--block-device`
source=SOURCE,id=ID,dest=DEST,size=SIZE,shutdown=PRESERVE,bootindex=INDEX

**source=SOURCE**

The type of object used to create the block device. Valid values are `volume`, `snapshot`, `image`, and `blank`.

**id=ID**

The ID of the source object.

**dest=DEST**

The type of the target virtual device. Valid values are `volume` and `local`.

**size=SIZE**

The size of the volume that is created.

**shutdown={preserve|remove}**

What to do with the volume when the instance is deleted. `preserve` does not delete the volume. `remove` deletes the volume.

**bootindex=INDEX**

Orders the boot disks. Use `0` to boot from this volume.

- `NAME`. The name for the server.

4. Create a bootable volume from an image. Cinder makes a volume bootable when `--image` parameter is passed.

```
$ openstack volume create --image IMAGE_ID --size SIZE_IN_GB bootable_volume
```

5. Create a VM from previously created bootable volume. The volume is not deleted when the instance is terminated.

```
$ openstack server create --flavor 2 --volume VOLUME_ID \
  --block-device source=volume,id=
$VOLUME_ID,dest=volume,size=10,shutdown=preserve,bootindex=0 \
  myInstanceFromVolume
+-------------------------------------+-------------------------------+
| Field                               | Value                         |
+-------------------------------------+-------------------------------+
| OS-EXT-STS:task_state               | scheduling                    |
| image                               | Attempt to boot from volume   |
|                                     | - no image supplied           |
| OS-EXT-STS:vm_state                 | building                      |
| OS-EXT-SRV-ATTR:instance_name       | instance-00000003             |
| OS-SRV-USG:launched_at              | None                          |
| flavor                              | m1.small                      |
```

```
| id                                   | 2e65c854-dba9-4f68-8f08-fe3... |
| security_groups                      | [{u'name': u'default'}]        |
| user_id                              | 352b37f5c89144d4ad053413926... |
| OS-DCF:diskConfig                    | MANUAL                         |
| accessIPv4                           |                                |
| accessIPv6                           |                                |
| progress                             | 0                              |
| OS-EXT-STS:power_state               | 0                              |
| OS-EXT-AZ:availability_zone          | nova                           |
| config_drive                         |                                |
| status                               | BUILD                          |
| updated                              | 2014-02-02T13:29:54Z           |
| hostId                               |                                |
| OS-EXT-SRV-ATTR:host                 | None                           |
| OS-SRV-USG:terminated_at             | None                           |
| key_name                             | None                           |
| OS-EXT-SRV-ATTR:hypervisor_hostname  | None                           |
| name                                 | myInstanceFromVolume           |
| adminPass                            | TzjqyGsRcJo9                   |
| tenant_id                            | f7ac731cc11f40efbc03a9f9e1d... |
| created                              | 2014-02-02T13:29:53Z           |
| os-extended-volumes:volumes_attached | [{"id": "2fff50ab..."}]        |
| metadata                             | {}                             |
+--------------------------------------+--------------------------------+
```

6. List volumes to see the bootable volume and its attached `myInstanceFromVolume` instance.

```
$ openstack volume list
+--------------------+----------------+--------+------
+--------------------------------+
| ID                 | Display Name   | Status | Size | Attached to
 |
+--------------------+----------------+--------+------
+--------------------------------+
| c612f739-8592-44c4- | bootable_volume | in-use |  10  | Attached to
 myInstanceFromVolume|
| b7d4-0fee2fe1da0c  |                |        |      | on /dev/vda
 |
+--------------------+----------------+--------+------
+--------------------------------+
```

#### 4.10.2.2.3 Attach swap or ephemeral disk to an instance

Use the nova `boot --swap` parameter to attach a swap disk on boot or the nova `boot --ephemeral` parameter to attach an ephemeral disk on boot. When you terminate the instance, both disks are deleted.

Boot an instance with a 512 MB swap disk and 2 GB ephemeral disk.

```
$ openstack server create --flavor FLAVOR --image IMAGE_ID --swap 512 \
--ephemeral size=2 NAME
```

Note

The flavor defines the maximum swap and ephemeral disk size. You cannot exceed these maximum values.

### 4.10.2.3 Launch an instance using ISO image

#### 4.10.2.3.1 Boot an instance from an ISO image

OpenStack supports booting instances using ISO images. But before you make such instances functional, use the **`openstack server create`** command with the following parameters to boot an instance:

```
$ openstack server create --image ubuntu-14.04.2-server-amd64.iso \
  --nic net-id = NETWORK_UUID \
  --flavor 2 INSTANCE_NAME
+--------------------------------------+--------------------------------------------+
| Field                                | Value                                      |
+--------------------------------------+--------------------------------------------+
| OS-DCF:diskConfig                    | MANUAL                                     |
| OS-EXT-AZ:availability_zone          | nova                                       |
| OS-EXT-SRV-ATTR:host                 | -                                          |
| OS-EXT-SRV-ATTR:hypervisor_hostname  | -                                          |
| OS-EXT-SRV-ATTR:instance_name        | instance-00000004                          |
| OS-EXT-STS:power_state               | 0                                          |
| OS-EXT-STS:task_state                | scheduling                                 |
| OS-EXT-STS:vm_state                  | building                                   |
| OS-SRV-USG:launched_at               | -                                          |
| OS-SRV-USG:terminated_at             | -                                          |
| accessIPv4                           |                                            |
| accessIPv6                           |                                            |
| adminPass                            | ZaiYeC8iucgU                               |
| config_drive                         |                                            |
| created                              | 2015-06-01T16:34:50Z                       |
| flavor                               | m1.small (2)                               |
| hostId                               |                                            |
| id                                   | 1e1797f3-1662-49ff-ae8c-a77e82ee1571       |
| image                                | ubuntu-14.04.2-server-amd64.iso            |
```

```
| key_name                              | -                                    |
| metadata                              | {}                                   |
| name                                  | INSTANCE_NAME                        |
| os-extended-volumes:volumes_attached | []                                   |
| progress                              | 0                                    |
| security_groups                       | default                              |
| status                                | BUILD                                |
| tenant_id                             | ccef9e62b1e645df98728fb2b3076f27     |
| updated                               | 2014-05-09T16:34:51Z                 |
| user_id                               | fef060ae7bfd4024b3edb97dff59017a     |
+--------------------------------------+--------------------------------------+
```

In this command, `ubuntu-14.04.2-server-amd64.iso` is the ISO image, and `INSTANCE_NAME` is the name of the new instance. `NETWORK_UUID` is a valid network id in your system.

Create a bootable volume for the instance to reside on after shutdown.

1. Create the volume:

```
$ openstack volume create \
  --size <SIZE_IN_GB> \
  --bootable VOLUME_NAME
```

2. Attach the instance to the volume:

```
$ openstack server add volume
  INSTANCE_NAME \
  VOLUME_NAME \
  --device /dev/vda
```

### Note

You need the Block Storage service to preserve the instance after shutdown. The `--block-device` argument, used with the legacy **`nova-boot`**, will not work with the OpenStack **`openstack server create`** command. Instead, the **`openstack volume create`** and **`openstack server add volume`** commands create persistent storage.

After the instance is successfully launched, connect to the instance using a remote console and follow the instructions to install the system as using ISO images on regular computers. When the installation is finished and system is rebooted, the instance asks you again to install the operating system, which means your instance is not usable. If you have problems with image creation, please check the Virtual Machine Image Guide (https://docs.openstack.org/image-guide/create-images-manually.html) ↗ for reference.

#### 4.10.2.3.2 Make the instances booted from ISO image functional

Now complete the following steps to make your instances created using ISO image actually functional.

1. Delete the instance using the following command.

```
$ openstack server delete INSTANCE_NAME
```

2. After you delete the instance, the system you have just installed using your ISO image remains, because the parameter `shutdown=preserve` was set, so run the following command.

```
$ openstack volume list
+--------------------------+------------------------+----------+------+-------------+
| ID                       | Display Name           | Status   | Size | Attached to |
+--------------------------+------------------------+----------+------+-------------+
| 8edd7c97-1276-47a5-9563- |dc01d873-d0f1-40b6-bfcc- | available |   10 |             |
| 1025f4264e4f             | 26a8d955a1d9-blank-vol |          |      |             |
+--------------------------+------------------------+----------+------+-------------+
```

You get a list with all the volumes in your system. In this list, you can find the volume that is attached to your ISO created instance, with the false bootable property.

3. Upload the volume to glance.

```
$ openstack image create --volume SOURCE_VOLUME IMAGE_NAME
$ openstack image list
+-------------------+------------+--------+
| ID                | Name       | Status |
+-------------------+------------+--------+
| 74303284-f802-... | IMAGE_NAME | active |
+-------------------+------------+--------+
```

The `VOLUME_UUID` is the uuid of the volume that is attached to your ISO created instance, and the `IMAGE_NAME` is the name that you give to your new image.

4. After the image is successfully uploaded, you can use the new image to boot instances. The instances launched using this image contain the system that you have just installed using the ISO image.

## 4.11 Manage instances and hosts

Instances are virtual machines that run inside the cloud on physical compute nodes. The Compute service manages instances. A host is the node on which a group of instances resides.

This section describes how to perform the different tasks involved in instance management, such as adding floating IP addresses, stopping and starting instances, and terminating instances. This section also discusses node management tasks.

### 4.11.1 Manage IP addresses

Each instance has a private, fixed IP address and can also have a public, or floating IP address. Private IP addresses are used for communication between instances, and public addresses are used for communication with networks outside the cloud, including the Internet.

When you launch an instance, it is automatically assigned a private IP address that stays the same until you explicitly terminate the instance. Rebooting an instance has no effect on the private IP address.

A pool of floating IP addresses, configured by the cloud administrator, is available in OpenStack Compute. The project quota defines the maximum number of floating IP addresses that you can allocate to the project. After you allocate a floating IP address to a project, you can:

- Associate the floating IP address with an instance of the project. Only one floating IP address can be allocated to an instance at any given time.
- Disassociate a floating IP address from an instance in the project.
- Delete a floating IP from the project which automatically deletes that IP's associations.

Use the **`openstack`** commands to manage floating IP addresses.

#### 4.11.1.1 List floating IP address information

To list all pools that provide floating IP addresses, run:

```
$ openstack floating ip pool list
+--------+
| name   |
+--------+
```

```
| public |
| test   |
+--------+
```

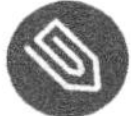

## Note

If this list is empty, the cloud administrator must configure a pool of floating IP addresses.

To list all floating IP addresses that are allocated to the current project, run:

```
$ openstack floating ip list
+--------------------------------------+---------------------+------------------+------+
| ID                                   | Floating IP Address | Fixed IP Address | Port |
+--------------------------------------+---------------------+------------------+------+
| 760963b2-779c-4a49-a50d-f073c1ca5b9e | 172.24.4.228        | None             | None |
| 89532684-13e1-4af3-bd79-f434c9920cc3 | 172.24.4.235        | None             | None |
| ea3ebc6d-a146-47cd-aaa8-35f06e1e8c3d | 172.24.4.229        | None             | None |
+--------------------------------------+---------------------+------------------+------+
```

For each floating IP address that is allocated to the current project, the command outputs the floating IP address, the ID for the instance to which the floating IP address is assigned, the associated fixed IP address, and the pool from which the floating IP address was allocated.

### 4.11.1.2 Associate floating IP addresses

You can assign a floating IP address to a project and to an instance.

1. Run the following command to allocate a floating IP address to the current project. By default, the floating IP address is allocated from the public pool. The command outputs the allocated IP address:

```
$ openstack floating ip create public
+---------------------+--------------------------------------+
| Field               | Value                                |
+---------------------+--------------------------------------+
| created_at          | 2016-11-30T15:02:05Z                 |
| description         |                                      |
| fixed_ip_address    | None                                 |
| floating_ip_address | 172.24.4.236                         |
| floating_network_id | 0bf90de6-fc0f-4dba-b80d-96670dfb331a |
| headers             |                                      |
| id                  | c70ad74b-2f64-4e60-965e-f24fc12b3194 |
```

```
| port_id              | None                                 |
| project_id           | 5669caad86a04256994cdf755df4d3c1     |
| project_id           | 5669caad86a04256994cdf755df4d3c1     |
| revision_number      | 1                                    |
| router_id            | None                                 |
| status               | DOWN                                 |
| updated_at           | 2016-11-30T15:02:05Z                 |
+---------------------+--------------------------------------+
```

2. List all project instances with which a floating IP address could be associated.

```
$ openstack server list
+---------------------+------+---------+------------+-------------+------------------
+------------+
| ID                  | Name | Status  | Task State | Power State | Networks         |
 Image Name |
+---------------------+------+---------+------------+-------------+------------------
+------------+
| d5c854f9-d3e5-4f... | VM1  | ACTIVE  | -          | Running     | private=10.0.0.3 |
 cirros     |
| 42290b01-0968-43... | VM2  | SHUTOFF | -          | Shutdown    | private=10.0.0.4 |
 centos     |
+---------------------+------+---------+------------+-------------+------------------
+------------+
```

3. Associate an IP address with an instance in the project, as follows:

```
$ openstack server add floating ip INSTANCE_NAME_OR_ID FLOATING_IP_ADDRESS
```

For example:

```
$ openstack server add floating ip VM1 172.24.4.225
```

The instance is now associated with two IP addresses:

```
$ openstack server list
+------------------+------+--------+------------+-------------
+-------------------------------+------------+
| ID               | Name | Status | Task State | Power State | Networks
     | Image Name |
+------------------+------+--------+------------+-------------
+-------------------------------+------------+
| d5c854f9-d3e5... | VM1  | ACTIVE | -          | Running     | private=10.0.0.3,
 172.24.4.225| cirros     |
| 42290b01-0968... | VM2  | SHUTOFF| -          | Shutdown    | private=10.0.0.4
     | centos     |
+------------------+------+--------+------------+-------------
+-------------------------------+------------+
```

After you associate the IP address and configure security group rules for the instance, the instance is publicly available at the floating IP address.

Note

The **openstack server** command does not allow users to associate a floating IP address with a specific fixed IP address using the optional `--fixed-address` parameter, which legacy commands required as an argument.

#### 4.11.1.3 Disassociate floating IP addresses

To disassociate a floating IP address from an instance:

```
$ openstack server remove floating ip INSTANCE_NAME_OR_ID FLOATING_IP_ADDRESS
```

To remove the floating IP address from a project:

```
$ openstack floating ip delete FLOATING_IP_ADDRESS
```

The IP address is returned to the pool of IP addresses that is available for all projects. If the IP address is still associated with a running instance, it is automatically disassociated from that instance.

### 4.11.2 Change the size of your server

Change the size of a server by changing its flavor.

1. Show information about your server, including its size, which is shown as the value of the flavor property:

```
$ openstack server show myCirrosServer
+-------------------------------------
+---------------------------------------------------------+
| Field                                | Value
         |
+-------------------------------------
+---------------------------------------------------------+
| OS-DCF:diskConfig                    | AUTO
         |
| OS-EXT-AZ:availability_zone          | nova
         |
```

```
| OS-EXT-SRV-ATTR:host                    | node-7.domain.tld
        |
| OS-EXT-SRV-ATTR:hypervisor_hostname     | node-7.domain.tld
        |
| OS-EXT-SRV-ATTR:instance_name           | instance-000000f3
        |
| OS-EXT-STS:power_state                  | 1
        |
| OS-EXT-STS:task_state                   | None
        |
| OS-EXT-STS:vm_state                     | active
        |
| OS-SRV-USG:launched_at                  | 2016-10-26T01:13:15.000000
        |
| OS-SRV-USG:terminated_at                | None
        |
| accessIPv4                              |
        |
| accessIPv6                              |
        |
| addresses                               | admin_internal_net=192.168.111.139
        |
| config_drive                            | True
        |
| created                                 | 2016-10-26T01:12:38Z
        |
| flavor                                  | m1.small (2)
        |
| hostId                                  |
 d815539ce1a8fad3d597c3438c13f1229d3a2ed66d1a75447845a2f3 |
| id                                      | 67bc9a9a-5928-47c4-852c-3631fef2a7e8
        |
| image                                   | cirros-test (dc5ec4b8-5851-4be8-98aa-
df7a9b8f538f)        |
| key_name                                | None
        |
| name                                    | myCirrosServer
        |
| os-extended-volumes:volumes_attached    | []
        |
| progress                                | 0
        |
| project_id                              | c08367f25666480f9860c6a0122dfcc4
        |
| properties                              |
        |
| security_groups                         | [{u'name': u'default'}]
        |
| status                                  | ACTIVE
        |
```

```
| updated                              | 2016-10-26T01:13:00Z
         |
| user_id                              | 0209430e30924bf9b5d8869990234e44
         |
+-------------------------------------
+-------------------------------------------------------+
```

The size (flavor) of the server is `m1.small (2)`.

2. List the available flavors with the following command:

```
$ openstack flavor list
+-----+-----------+-------+------+-----------+-------+-----------+
| ID  | Name      |   RAM | Disk | Ephemeral | VCPUs | Is_Public |
+-----+-----------+-------+------+-----------+-------+-----------+
| 1   | m1.tiny   |   512 |    1 |         0 |     1 | True      |
| 2   | m1.small  |  2048 |   20 |         0 |     1 | True      |
| 3   | m1.medium |  4096 |   40 |         0 |     2 | True      |
| 4   | m1.large  |  8192 |   80 |         0 |     4 | True      |
| 5   | m1.xlarge | 16384 |  160 |         0 |     8 | True      |
+-----+-----------+-------+------+-----------+-------+-----------+
```

3. To resize the server, use the **`openstack server resize`** command and add the server ID or name and the new flavor. For example:

```
$ openstack server resize --flavor 4 myCirrosServer
```

## Note

By default, the **`openstack server resize`** command gives the guest operating system a chance to perform a controlled shutdown before the instance is powered off and the instance is resized. The shutdown behavior is configured by the `shutdown_timeout` parameter that can be set in the `nova.conf` file. Its value stands for the overall period (in seconds) a guest operation system is allowed to complete the shutdown. The default timeout is 60 seconds. See Description of Compute configuration options (https://docs.openstack.org/newton/config-reference/compute/config-options.html) ↗ for details.

The timeout value can be overridden on a per image basis by means of `os_shutdown_timeout` that is an image metadata setting allowing different types of operating systems to specify how much time they need to shut down cleanly.

4. Show the status for your server.

```
$ openstack server list
+----------------------+----------------+--------
+---------------------------------------+
| ID                   | Name           | Status | Networks
  |
+----------------------+----------------+--------
+---------------------------------------+
| 67bc9a9a-5928-47c... | myCirrosServer | RESIZE | admin_internal_net=192.168.111.139
  |
+----------------------+----------------+--------
+---------------------------------------+
```

When the resize completes, the status becomes VERIFY_RESIZE.

5. Confirm the resize,for example:

```
$ openstack server resize --confirm 67bc9a9a-5928-47c4-852c-3631fef2a7e8
```

The server status becomes ACTIVE.

6. If the resize fails or does not work as expected, you can revert the resize. For example:

```
$ openstack server resize --revert 67bc9a9a-5928-47c4-852c-3631fef2a7e8
```

The server status becomes ACTIVE.

### 4.11.3 Stop and start an instance

Use one of the following methods to stop and start an instance.

#### 4.11.3.1 Pause and unpause an instance

To pause an instance, run the following command:

```
$ openstack server pause INSTANCE_NAME
```

This command stores the state of the VM in RAM. A paused instance continues to run in a frozen state.

To unpause an instance, run the following command:

```
$ openstack server unpause INSTANCE_NAME
```

#### 4.11.3.2 Suspend and resume an instance

To initiate a hypervisor-level suspend operation, run the following command:

```
$ openstack server suspend INSTANCE_NAME
```

To resume a suspended instance, run the following command:

```
$ openstack server resume INSTANCE_NAME
```

#### 4.11.3.3 Shelve and unshelve an instance

Shelving is useful if you have an instance that you are not using, but would like retain in your list of servers. For example, you can stop an instance at the end of a work week, and resume work again at the start of the next week. All associated data and resources are kept; however, anything still in memory is not retained. If a shelved instance is no longer needed, it can also be entirely removed.

You can run the following shelving tasks:

- Shelve an instance - Shuts down the instance, and stores it together with associated data and resources (a snapshot is taken if not volume backed). Anything in memory is lost.

```
$ openstack server shelve SERVERNAME
```

Note

By default, the **`openstack server shelve`** command gives the guest operating system a chance to perform a controlled shutdown before the instance is powered off. The shutdown behavior is configured by the `shutdown_timeout` parameter that can be set in the `nova.conf` file. Its value stands for the overall period (in seconds) a guest operation system is allowed to complete the shutdown. The default timeout is 60 seconds. See Description of Compute configuration options (https://docs.openstack.org/newton/config-reference/compute/config-options.html) for details.

The timeout value can be overridden on a per image basis by means of `os_shutdown_timeout` that is an image metadata setting allowing different types of operating systems to specify how much time they need to shut down cleanly.

- Unshelve an instance - Restores the instance.

```
$ openstack server unshelve SERVERNAME
```

- Remove a shelved instance - Removes the instance from the server; data and resource associations are deleted. If an instance is no longer needed, you can move the instance off the hypervisor in order to minimize resource usage.

```
$ nova shelve-offload SERVERNAME
```

### 4.11.4 Search for an instance using IP address

You can search for an instance using the IP address parameter, `--ip`, with the **`openstack server list`** command.

```
$ openstack server list --ip IP_ADDRESS
```

The following example shows the results of a search on `10.0.0.4`.

```
$ openstack server list --ip 10.0.0.4
+------------------+----------------------+--------+------------+-------------
+------------------+------------+
| ID               | Name                 | Status | Task State | Power State | Networks
  | Image Name |
+------------------+----------------------+--------+------------+-------------
+------------------+------------+
| 8a99547e-7385... | myInstanceFromVolume | ACTIVE | None       | Running     |
 private=10.0.0.4 | cirros     |
+------------------+----------------------+--------+------------+-------------
+------------------+------------+
```

### 4.11.5 Reboot an instance

You can soft or hard reboot a running instance. A soft reboot attempts a graceful shut down and restart of the instance. A hard reboot power cycles the instance.

By default, when you reboot an instance, it is a soft reboot.

```
$ openstack server reboot SERVER
```

To perform a hard reboot, pass the `--hard` parameter, as follows:

```
$ openstack server reboot --hard SERVER
```

It is also possible to reboot a running instance into rescue mode. For example, this operation may be required, if a filesystem of an instance becomes corrupted with prolonged use.

Note

Pause, suspend, and stop operations are not allowed when an instance is running in rescue mode, as triggering these actions causes the loss of the original instance state, and makes it impossible to unrescue the instance.

Rescue mode provides a mechanism for access, even if an image renders the instance inaccessible. By default, it starts an instance from the initial image attaching the current boot disk as a secondary one.

To perform an instance reboot into rescue mode, run the following command:

```
$ openstack server rescue SERVER
```

Note

On running the **`nova rescue`** command, an instance performs a soft shutdown first. This means that the guest operating system has a chance to perform a controlled shutdown before the instance is powered off. The shutdown behavior is configured by the `shutdown_timeout` parameter that can be set in the `nova.conf` file. Its value stands for the overall period (in seconds) a guest operation system is allowed to complete the shutdown. The default timeout is 60 seconds. See Description of Compute configuration options (https://docs.openstack.org/newton/config-reference/compute/config-options.html) for details.

The timeout value can be overridden on a per image basis by means of `os_shutdown_timeout` that is an image metadata setting allowing different types of operating systems to specify how much time they need to shut down cleanly.

To restart the instance from the normal boot disk, run the following command:

```
$ openstack server unrescue SERVER
```

If you want to rescue an instance with a specific image, rather than the default one, use the `--rescue_image_ref` parameter:

```
$ nova rescue --rescue_image_ref IMAGE_ID SERVER
```

### 4.11.6 Delete an instance

When you no longer need an instance, you can delete it.

1. List all instances:

```
$ openstack server list
+-------------+--------------------+-------+-----------+------------
+-----------------+-----------+
| ID          | Name               | Status | Task State | Power State | Networks
   | Image Name |
+-------------+--------------------+-------+-----------+------------
+-----------------+-----------+
| 84c6e57d... | myCirrosServer       | ACTIVE | None       | Running      |
 private=10.0.0.3 | cirros     |
| 8a99547e... | myInstanceFromVolume | ACTIVE | None       | Running      |
 private=10.0.0.4 | ubuntu     |
| d7efd3e4... | newServer            | ERROR  | None       | NOSTATE      |
   | centos     |
+-------------+--------------------+-------+-----------+------------
+-----------------+-----------+
```

2. Run the **`openstack server delete`** command to delete the instance. The following example shows deletion of the `newServer` instance, which is in `ERROR` state:

```
$ openstack server delete newServer
```

The command does not notify that your server was deleted.

3. To verify that the server was deleted, run the **`openstack server list`** command:

```
$ openstack server list
+-------------+--------------------+-------+-----------+------------
+-----------------+-----------+
| ID          | Name               | Status | Task State | Power State | Networks
   | Image Name |
+-------------+--------------------+-------+-----------+------------
+-----------------+-----------+
| 84c6e57d... | myCirrosServer       | ACTIVE | None       | Running      |
 private=10.0.0.3 | cirros     |
```

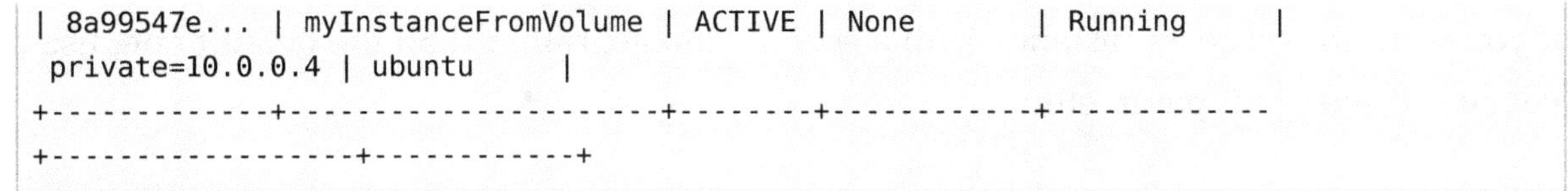

```
| 8a99547e... | myInstanceFromVolume | ACTIVE | None       | Running     |
 private=10.0.0.4 | ubuntu     |
+-------------+----------------------+--------+------------+-------------
+------------------+------------+
```

The deleted instance does not appear in the list.

### 4.11.7 Access an instance through a console

VNC or SPICE is used to view the console output of an instance, regardless of whether or not the console log has output. This allows relaying keyboard and mouse activity to and from an instance.

There are three remote console access methods commonly used with OpenStack:

**novnc**

An in-browser VNC client implemented using HTML5 Canvas and WebSockets

**spice**

A complete in-browser client solution for interaction with virtualized instances

Example:

To access an instance through a remote console, run the following command:

```
$ openstack console url show INSTANCE_NAME --novnc
```

The command returns a URL from which you can access your instance:

```
+--------+------------------------------------------------------------------------------+
| Type   | Url                                                                          |
+--------+------------------------------------------------------------------------------+
| nopvnc | http://192.168.5.96:6081/console?token=c83ae3a3-15c4-4890-8d45-aefb494a8d6c  |
+--------+------------------------------------------------------------------------------+
```

When using SPICE to view the console of an instance, a browser plugin can be used directly on the instance page, or the **`openstack console url show`** command can be used with it, as well, by returning a token-authenticated address, as in the example above.

For further information and comparisons (including security considerations), see the Security Guide (https://docs.openstack.org/security-guide/compute.html).

### 4.11.8 Manage bare-metal nodes

The bare-metal driver for OpenStack Compute manages provisioning of physical hardware by using common cloud APIs and tools such as Orchestration (Heat). The use case for this driver is for single project clouds such as a high-performance computing cluster, or for deploying OpenStack itself.

If you use the bare-metal driver, you must create a network interface and add it to a bare-metal node. Then, you can launch an instance from a bare-metal image.

You can list and delete bare-metal nodes. When you delete a node, any associated network interfaces are removed. You can list and remove network interfaces that are associated with a bare-metal node.

#### 4.11.8.1 Commands

The following commands can be used to manage bare-metal nodes.

`baremetal-interface-add`
: Adds a network interface to a bare-metal node.

`baremetal-interface-list`
: Lists network interfaces associated with a bare-metal node.

`baremetal-interface-remove`
: Removes a network interface from a bare-metal node.

`baremetal-node-create`
: Creates a bare-metal node.

`baremetal-node-delete`
: Removes a bare-metal node and any associated interfaces.

`baremetal-node-list`
: Lists available bare-metal nodes.

`baremetal-node-show`
: Shows information about a bare-metal node.

### 4.11.8.2 Create a bare-metal node

When you create a bare-metal node, your PM address, user name, and password should match the information in your hardware's BIOS/IPMI configuration.

```
$ nova baremetal-node-create --pm_address PM_ADDRESS --pm_user PM_USERNAME \
  --pm_password PM_PASSWORD $(hostname -f) 1 512 10 aa:bb:cc:dd:ee:ff
```

The following example shows the command and results from creating a node with the PM address `1.2.3.4`, the PM user name ipmi, and password `ipmi`.

```
$ nova baremetal-node-create --pm_address 1.2.3.4 --pm_user ipmi \
  --pm_password ipmi $(hostname -f) 1 512 10 aa:bb:cc:dd:ee:ff
+------------------+-------------------+
| Property         | Value             |
+------------------+-------------------+
| instance_uuid    | None              |
| pm_address       | 1.2.3.4           |
| interfaces       | []                |
| prov_vlan_id     | None              |
| cpus             | 1                 |
| memory_mb        | 512               |
| prov_mac_address | aa:bb:cc:dd:ee:ff |
| service_host     | ubuntu            |
| local_gb         | 10                |
| id               | 1                 |
| pm_user          | ipmi              |
| terminal_port    | None              |
+------------------+-------------------+
```

### 4.11.8.3 Add a network interface to the node

For each NIC on the node, you must create an interface, specifying the interface's MAC address.

```
$ nova baremetal-interface-add 1 aa:bb:cc:dd:ee:ff
+-------------+-------------------+
| Property    | Value             |
+-------------+-------------------+
| datapath_id | 0                 |
| id          | 1                 |
| port_no     | 0                 |
| address     | aa:bb:cc:dd:ee:ff |
+-------------+-------------------+
```

### 4.11.8.4 Launch an instance from a bare-metal image

A bare-metal instance is an instance created directly on a physical machine, without any virtualization layer running underneath it. Nova retains power control via IPMI. In some situations, Nova may retain network control via Neutron and OpenFlow.

```
$ openstack server create --image my-baremetal-image --flavor \
  my-baremetal-flavor test
+-----------------------------+------------------------------------+
| Property                    | Value                              |
+-----------------------------+------------------------------------+
| status                      | BUILD                              |
| id                          | cc302a8f-cd81-484b-89a8-b75eb3911b1b |
+-----------------------------+------------------------------------+

... wait for instance to become active ...
```

Note

Set the `--availability-zone` parameter to specify which zone or node to use to start the server. Separate the zone from the host name with a comma. For example:

```
$ openstack server create --availability-zone zone:HOST,NODE
```

`host` is optional for the `--availability-zone` parameter. You can simply specify `zone:,node`, still including the comma.

### 4.11.8.5 List bare-metal nodes and interfaces

Use the **`nova baremetal-node-list`** command to view all bare-metal nodes and interfaces. When a node is in use, its status includes the UUID of the instance that runs on it:

```
$ nova baremetal-node-list
+----+--------+------+-----------+---------+-------------------+------+------------
+-------------+-------------+-------------+
| ID | Host   | CPUs | Memory_MB | Disk_GB | MAC Address       | VLAN | PM Address | PM
 Username | PM Password | Terminal Port |
+----+--------+------+-----------+---------+-------------------+------+------------
+-------------+-------------+-------------+
| 1  | ubuntu | 1    | 512       | 10      | aa:bb:cc:dd:ee:ff | None | 1.2.3.4    | ipmi
  |             | None        |
+----+--------+------+-----------+---------+-------------------+------+------------
+-------------+-------------+-------------+
```

#### 4.11.8.6 Show details for a bare-metal node

Use the **`nova baremetal-node-show`** command to view the details for a bare-metal node:

```
$ nova baremetal-node-show 1
+------------------+--------------------------------------+
| Property         | Value                                |
+------------------+--------------------------------------+
| instance_uuid    | cc302a8f-cd81-484b-89a8-b75eb3911b1b |
| pm_address       | 1.2.3.4                              |
| interfaces       | [{u'datapath_id': u'0', u'id': 1,    |
|                  | u'port_no': 0,                       |
|                  | u'address': u'aa:bb:cc:dd:ee:ff'}]   |
| prov_vlan_id     | None                                 |
| cpus             | 1                                    |
| memory_mb        | 512                                  |
| prov_mac_address | aa:bb:cc:dd:ee:ff                    |
| service_host     | ubuntu                               |
| local_gb         | 10                                   |
| id               | 1                                    |
| pm_user          | ipmi                                 |
| terminal_port    | None                                 |
+------------------+--------------------------------------+
```

## 4.12 Provide user data to instances

A user data file is a special key in the metadata service that holds a file that cloud-aware applications in the guest instance can access. For example, one application that uses *user data* is the cloud-init (https://help.ubuntu.com/community/CloudInit) system, which is an open-source package from Ubuntu that is available on various Linux distributions and which handles early initialization of a cloud instance.

You can place user data in a local file and pass it through the `--user-data <user-data-file>` parameter at instance creation.

```
$ openstack server create --image ubuntu-cloudimage --flavor 1 \
  --user-data mydata.file VM_INSTANCE
```

## 4.13 Use snapshots to migrate instances

To use snapshots to migrate instances from OpenStack projects to clouds, complete these steps.

In the source project:

1. Section 4.13.1, "Create a snapshot of the instance"
2. Section 4.13.2, "Download the snapshot as an image"

In the destination project:

1. Section 4.13.3, "Import the snapshot to the new environment"
2. Section 4.13.4, "Boot a new instance from the snapshot"

**Note**

Some cloud providers allow only administrators to perform this task.

### 4.13.1 Create a snapshot of the instance

1. Shut down the source VM before you take the snapshot to ensure that all data is flushed to disk. If necessary, list the instances to view the instance name:

```
$ openstack server list
+--------------------------------------+------------+--------
+------------------------------+------------+
| ID                                   | Name       | Status | Networks
   | Image Name |
+--------------------------------------+------------+--------
+------------------------------+------------+
| c41f3074-c82a-4837-8673-fa7e9fea7e11 | myInstance | ACTIVE | private=10.0.0.3
   | cirros     |
+--------------------------------------+------------+--------
+------------------------------+------------+
```

2. Use the **`openstack server stop`** command to shut down the instance:

```
$ openstack server stop myInstance
```

3. Use the **`openstack server list`** command to confirm that the instance shows a `SHUTOFF` status:

```
$ openstack server list
+--------------------------------------+------------+---------+------------------
+------------+
```

```
| ID                                   | Name       | Status  | Networks         | Image
 Name |
+--------------------------------------+------------+---------+-----------------
+------------+
| c41f3074-c82a-4837-8673-fa7e9fea7e11 | myInstance | SHUTOFF | private=10.0.0.3 | cirros
     |
+--------------------------------------+------------+---------+-----------------
+------------+
```

4. Use the **`nova image-create`** command to take a snapshot:

```
$ nova image-create --poll myInstance myInstanceSnapshot
Instance snapshotting... 50% complete
```

5. Use the **`openstack image list`** command to check the status until the status is `active`:

```
$ openstack image list
+--------------------------------------+---------------------------------+--------+
| ID                                   | Name                            | Status |
+--------------------------------------+---------------------------------+--------+
| 657ebb01-6fae-47dc-986a-e49c4dd8c433 | cirros-0.3.2-x86_64-uec         | active |
| 72074c6d-bf52-4a56-a61c-02a17bf3819b | cirros-0.3.2-x86_64-uec-kernel  | active |
| 3c5e5f06-637b-413e-90f6-ca7ed015ec9e | cirros-0.3.2-x86_64-uec-ramdisk | active |
| f30b204e-1ce6-40e7-b8d9-b353d4d84e7d | myInstanceSnapshot              | active |
+--------------------------------------+---------------------------------+--------+
```

## 4.13.2 Download the snapshot as an image

1. Get the image ID:

```
$ openstack image list
+-------------------+-------------------+--------+
| ID                | Name              | Status |
+-------------------+-------------------+--------+
| f30b204e-1ce6...  | myInstanceSnapshot| active |
+-------------------+-------------------+--------+
```

2. Download the snapshot by using the image ID that was returned in the previous step:

```
$ glance image-download --file snapshot.raw f30b204e-1ce6-40e7-b8d9-b353d4d84e7d
```

Note

The **glance image-download** command requires the image ID and cannot use the image name. Check there is sufficient space on the destination file system for the image file.

3. Make the image available to the new environment, either through HTTP or direct upload to a machine (`scp`).

### 4.13.3 Import the snapshot to the new environment

In the new project or cloud environment, import the snapshot:

```
$ glance --os-image-api-version 1 image-create \
  --container-format bare --disk-format qcow2 --copy-from IMAGE_URL
```

### 4.13.4 Boot a new instance from the snapshot

In the new project or cloud environment, use the snapshot to create the new instance:

```
$ openstack server create --flavor m1.tiny --image myInstanceSnapshot myNewInstance
```

## 4.14 Store metadata on a configuration drive

You can configure OpenStack to write metadata to a special configuration drive that attaches to the instance when it boots. The instance can mount this drive and read files from it to get information that is normally available through the metadata service (https://docs.openstack.org/admin-guide/compute-networking-nova.html#metadata-service) ↗. This metadata is different from the user data.

One use case for using the configuration drive is to pass a networking configuration when you do not use DHCP to assign IP addresses to instances. For example, you might pass the IP address configuration for the instance through the configuration drive, which the instance can mount and access before you configure the network settings for the instance.

Any modern guest operating system that is capable of mounting an ISO 9660 or VFAT file system can use the configuration drive.

### 4.14.1 Requirements and guidelines

To use the configuration drive, you must follow the following requirements for the compute host and image.

**Compute host requirements**

- The following hypervisors support the configuration drive: libvirt, XenServer, Hyper-V, and VMware.
  Also, the Bare Metal service supports the configuration drive.

- To use configuration drive with libvirt, XenServer, or VMware, you must first install the genisoimage package on each compute host. Otherwise, instances do not boot properly.
  Use the `mkisofs_cmd` flag to set the path where you install the genisoimage program. If genisoimage is in same path as the `nova-compute` service, you do not need to set this flag.

- To use configuration drive with Hyper-V, you must set the `mkisofs_cmd` value to the full path to an `mkisofs.exe` installation. Additionally, you must set the `qemu_img_cmd` value in the `hyperv` configuration section to the full path to an **`qemu-img`** command installation.

- To use configuration drive with the Bare Metal service, you do not need to prepare anything because the Bare Metal service treats the configuration drive properly.

**Image requirements**

- An image built with a recent version of the cloud-init package can automatically access metadata passed through the configuration drive. The cloud-init package version 0.7.1 works with Ubuntu, Fedora based images (such as Red Hat Enterprise Linux) and openSUSE based images (such as SUSE Linux Enterprise Server).

- If an image does not have the cloud-init package installed, you must customize the image to run a script that mounts the configuration drive on boot, reads the data from the drive, and takes appropriate action such as adding the public key to an account. You can read more details about how data is organized on the configuration drive.

- If you use Xen with a configuration drive, use the `xenapi_disable_agent` configuration parameter to disable the agent.

**Guidelines**

- Do not rely on the presence of the EC2 metadata in the configuration drive, because this content might be removed in a future release. For example, do not rely on files in the `ec2` directory.
- When you create images that access configuration drive data and multiple directories are under the `openstack` directory, always select the highest API version by date that your consumer supports. For example, if your guest image supports the 2012-03-05, 2012-08-05, and 2013-04-13 versions, try 2013-04-13 first and fall back to a previous version if 2013-04-13 is not present.

### 4.14.2 Enable and access the configuration drive

1. To enable the configuration drive, pass the `--config-drive true` parameter to the **`openstack server create`** command.
   The following example enables the configuration drive and passes user data, two files, and two key/value metadata pairs, all of which are accessible from the configuration drive:

```
$ openstack server create --config-drive true --image my-image-name \
  --flavor 1 --key-name mykey --user-data ./my-user-data.txt \
  --file /etc/network/interfaces=/home/myuser/instance-interfaces \
  --file known_hosts=/home/myuser/.ssh/known_hosts \
  --property role=webservers --property essential=false MYINSTANCE
```

   You can also configure the Compute service to always create a configuration drive by setting the following option in the `/etc/nova/nova.conf` file:

```
force_config_drive = true
```

   Note

   If a user passes the `--config-drive true` flag to the **`nova boot`** command, an administrator cannot disable the configuration drive.

2. If your guest operating system supports accessing disk by label, you can mount the configuration drive as the `/dev/disk/by-label/configurationDriveVolumeLabel` device. In the following example, the configuration drive has the `config-2` volume label:

```
# mkdir -p /mnt/config
# mount /dev/disk/by-label/config-2 /mnt/config
```

Note

Ensure that you use at least version 0.3.1 of CirrOS for configuration drive support.

If your guest operating system does not use `udev`, the `/dev/disk/by-label` directory is not present.

You can use the **`blkid`** command to identify the block device that corresponds to the configuration drive. For example, when you boot the CirrOS image with the `m1.tiny` flavor, the device is `/dev/vdb`:

```
# blkid -t LABEL="config-2" -odevice
```

```
/dev/vdb
```

Once identified, you can mount the device:

```
# mkdir -p /mnt/config
# mount /dev/vdb /mnt/config
```

#### 4.14.2.1 Configuration drive contents

In this example, the contents of the configuration drive are as follows:

```
ec2/2009-04-04/meta-data.json
ec2/2009-04-04/user-data
ec2/latest/meta-data.json
ec2/latest/user-data
openstack/2012-08-10/meta_data.json
openstack/2012-08-10/user_data
openstack/content
openstack/content/0000
openstack/content/0001
openstack/latest/meta_data.json
openstack/latest/user_data
```

The files that appear on the configuration drive depend on the arguments that you pass to the **`openstack server create`** command.

#### 4.14.2.2 OpenStack metadata format

The following example shows the contents of the `openstack/2012-08-10/meta_data.json` and `openstack/latest/meta_data.json` files. These files are identical. The file contents are formatted for readability.

```
{
    "availability_zone": "nova",
    "files": [
        {
            "content_path": "/content/0000",
            "path": "/etc/network/interfaces"
        },
        {
            "content_path": "/content/0001",
            "path": "known_hosts"
        }
    ],
    "hostname": "test.novalocal",
    "launch_index": 0,
    "name": "test",
    "meta": {
        "role": "webservers",
        "essential": "false"
    },
    "public_keys": {
        "mykey": "ssh-rsa AAAAB3NzaC1yc2EAAAADAQABAAAAgQDBqUfVvCSez0/Wfpd8dLLgZXV9GtXQ7hnMN
+Z0OWQUyebVEHey1CXuin0uY1cAJMhUq8j98SiW+cU0sU4J3x5l2+xi1bodDm1BtFWVeLIOQINpfV1n8fKjHB
+ynPpe1F6tMDvrFGUlJs44t30BrujMXBe8Rq44cCk6wqyjATA3rQ== Generated by Nova\n"
    },
    "uuid": "83679162-1378-4288-a2d4-70e13ec132aa"
}
```

Note the effect of the `--file /etc/network/interfaces=/home/myuser/instance-interfaces` argument that was passed to the **`openstack server create`** command. The contents of this file are contained in the `openstack/content/0000` file on the configuration drive, and the path is specified as `/etc/network/interfaces` in the `meta_data.json` file.

#### 4.14.2.3 EC2 metadata format

The following example shows the contents of the `ec2/2009-04-04/meta-data.json` and the `ec2/latest/meta-data.json` files. These files are identical. The file contents are formatted to improve readability.

```
{
```

```
    "ami-id": "ami-00000001",
    "ami-launch-index": 0,
    "ami-manifest-path": "FIXME",
    "block-device-mapping": {
        "ami": "sda1",
        "ephemeral0": "sda2",
        "root": "/dev/sda1",
        "swap": "sda3"
    },
    "hostname": "test.novalocal",
    "instance-action": "none",
    "instance-id": "i-00000001",
    "instance-type": "m1.tiny",
    "kernel-id": "aki-00000002",
    "local-hostname": "test.novalocal",
    "local-ipv4": null,
    "placement": {
        "availability-zone": "nova"
    },
    "public-hostname": "test.novalocal",
    "public-ipv4": "",
    "public-keys": {
        "0": {
            "openssh-key": "ssh-rsa AAAAB3NzaC1yc2EAAAADAQABAAAAgQDBqUfVvCSez0/
Wfpd8dLLgZXV9GtXQ7hnMN+Z0OWQUyebVEHey1CXuin0uY1cAJMhUq8j98SiW
+cU0sU4J3x5l2+xi1bodDm1BtFWVeLIOQINpfV1n8fKjHB
+ynPpe1F6tMDvrFGUlJs44t30BrujMXBe8Rq44cCk6wqyjATA3rQ== Generated by Nova\n"
        }
    },
    "ramdisk-id": "ari-00000003",
    "reservation-id": "r-7lfps8wj",
    "security-groups": [
        "default"
    ]
}
```

#### 4.14.2.4 User data

The `openstack/2012-08-10/user_data`, `openstack/latest/user_data`, `ec2/2009-04-04/user-data`, and `ec2/latest/user-data` file are present only if the `--user-data` flag and the contents of the user data file are passed to the **`openstack server create`** command.

#### 4.14.2.5 Configuration drive format

The default format of the configuration drive as an ISO 9660 file system. To explicitly specify the ISO 9660 format, add the following line to the `/etc/nova/nova.conf` file:

```
config_drive_format=iso9660
```

By default, you cannot attach the configuration drive image as a CD drive instead of as a disk drive. To attach a CD drive, add the following line to the `/etc/nova/nova.conf` file:

```
config_drive_cdrom=true
```

For legacy reasons, you can configure the configuration drive to use VFAT format instead of ISO 9660. It is unlikely that you would require VFAT format because ISO 9660 is widely supported across operating systems. However, to use the VFAT format, add the following line to the `/etc/nova/nova.conf` file:

```
config_drive_format=vfat
```

If you choose VFAT, the configuration drive is 64 MB.

**Note**

In current version (Liberty) of OpenStack Compute, live migration with `config_drive` on local disk is forbidden due to the bug in libvirt of copying a read-only disk. However, if we use VFAT as the format of `config_drive`, the function of live migration works well.

## 4.15 Create and manage networks

Before you run commands, set environment variables using the OpenStack RC file (https://docs.openstack.org/user-guide/common/cli-set-environment-variables-using-openstack-rc.html)↗.

### 4.15.1 Create networks

1. List the extensions of the system:

```
$ openstack extension list -c Alias -c Name --network
+------------------------------------------+------------------------------+
```

```
| Name                                    | Alias                     |
+-----------------------------------------+---------------------------+
| Default Subnetpools                     | default-subnetpools       |
| Network IP Availability                 | network-ip-availability   |
| Auto Allocated Topology Services        | auto-allocated-topology   |
| Neutron L3 Configurable external gateway | ext-gw-mode               |
| Address scope                           | address-scope             |
| Neutron Extra Route                     | extraroute                |
+-----------------------------------------+---------------------------+
```

2. Create a network:

```
$ openstack network create net1
Created a new network:
+---------------------------+--------------------------------------+
| Field                     | Value                                |
+---------------------------+--------------------------------------+
| admin_state_up            | UP                                   |
| availability_zone_hints   |                                      |
| availability_zones        |                                      |
| created_at                | 2016-12-21T08:32:54Z                 |
| description               |                                      |
| headers                   |                                      |
| id                        | 180620e3-9eae-4ba7-9739-c5847966e1f0 |
| ipv4_address_scope        | None                                 |
| ipv6_address_scope        | None                                 |
| mtu                       | 1450                                 |
| name                      | net1                                 |
| port_security_enabled     | True                                 |
| project_id                | c961a8f6d3654657885226378ade8220     |
| provider:network_type     | vxlan                                |
| provider:physical_network | None                                 |
| provider:segmentation_id  | 14                                   |
| revision_number           | 3                                    |
| router:external           | Internal                             |
| shared                    | False                                |
| status                    | ACTIVE                               |
| subnets                   |                                      |
| tags                      | []                                   |
| updated_at                | 2016-12-21T08:32:54Z                 |
+---------------------------+--------------------------------------+
```

### Note

Some fields of the created network are invisible to non-admin users.

3. Create a network with specified provider network type.

```
$ openstack network create net2 --provider-network-type vxlan
Created a new network:
+---------------------------+--------------------------------------+
| Field                     | Value                                |
+---------------------------+--------------------------------------+
| admin_state_up            | UP                                   |
| availability_zone_hints   |                                      |
| availability_zones        |                                      |
| created_at                | 2016-12-21T08:33:34Z                 |
| description               |                                      |
| headers                   |                                      |
| id                        | c0a563d5-ef7d-46b3-b30d-6b9d4138b6cf |
| ipv4_address_scope        | None                                 |
| ipv6_address_scope        | None                                 |
| mtu                       | 1450                                 |
| name                      | net2                                 |
| port_security_enabled     | True                                 |
| project_id                | c961a8f6d3654657885226378ade8220     |
| provider:network_type     | vxlan                                |
| provider:physical_network | None                                 |
| provider:segmentation_id  | 87                                   |
| revision_number           | 3                                    |
| router:external           | Internal                             |
| shared                    | False                                |
| status                    | ACTIVE                               |
| subnets                   |                                      |
| tags                      | []                                   |
| updated_at                | 2016-12-21T08:33:34Z                 |
+---------------------------+--------------------------------------+
```

## 4.15.2 Create subnets

Create a subnet:

```
$ openstack subnet create subnet1 --network net1
  --subnet-range 192.168.2.0/24
+-------------------+--------------------------------------+
| Field             | Value                                |
+-------------------+--------------------------------------+
| allocation_pools  | 192.168.2.2-192.168.2.254            |
| cidr              | 192.168.2.0/24                       |
| created_at        | 2016-12-22T18:47:52Z                 |
| description       |                                      |
```

```
| dns_nameservers   |                                      |
| enable_dhcp       | True                                 |
| gateway_ip        | 192.168.2.1                          |
| headers           |                                      |
| host_routes       |                                      |
| id                | a394689c-f547-4834-9778-3e0bb22130dc |
| ip_version        | 4                                    |
| ipv6_address_mode | None                                 |
| ipv6_ra_mode      | None                                 |
| name              | subnet1                              |
| network_id        | 9db55b7f-e803-4e1b-9bba-6262f60b96cb |
| project_id        | e17431afc0524e0690484889a04b7fa0     |
| revision_number   | 2                                    |
| service_types     |                                      |
| subnetpool_id     | None                                 |
| updated_at        | 2016-12-22T18:47:52Z                 |
+-------------------+--------------------------------------+
```

The `subnet-create` command has the following positional and optional parameters:

- The name or ID of the network to which the subnet belongs.
  In this example, `net1` is a positional argument that specifies the network name.
- The CIDR of the subnet.
  In this example, `192.168.2.0/24` is a positional argument that specifies the CIDR.
- The subnet name, which is optional.
  In this example, `--name subnet1` specifies the name of the subnet.

For information and examples on more advanced use of neutron's `subnet` subcommand, see the OpenStack Administrator Guide (https://docs.openstack.org/admin-guide/networking-use.html#advanced-networking-operations).

## 4.15.3 Create routers

1. Create a router:

```
$ openstack router create router1
+-------------------------+--------------------------------------+
| Field                   | Value                                |
+-------------------------+--------------------------------------+
| admin_state_up          | UP                                   |
| availability_zone_hints |                                      |
| availability_zones      |                                      |
```

```
| created_at              | 2016-12-22T18:48:57Z                 |
| description             |                                      |
| distributed             | True                                 |
| external_gateway_info   | null                                 |
| flavor_id               | None                                 |
| ha                      | False                                |
| headers                 |                                      |
| id                      | e25a24ee-3458-45c7-b16e-edf49092aab7 |
| name                    | router1                              |
| project_id              | e17431afc0524e0690484889a04b7fa0     |
| revision_number         | 1                                    |
| routes                  |                                      |
| status                  | ACTIVE                               |
| updated_at              | 2016-12-22T18:48:57Z                 |
+-------------------------+--------------------------------------+
```

Take note of the unique router identifier returned, this will be required in subsequent steps.

2. Link the router to the external provider network:

```
$ openstack router set ROUTER --external-gateway NETWORK
```

Replace ROUTER with the unique identifier of the router, replace NETWORK with the unique identifier of the external provider network.

3. Link the router to the subnet:

```
$ openstack router add subnet ROUTER SUBNET
```

Replace ROUTER with the unique identifier of the router, replace SUBNET with the unique identifier of the subnet.

### 4.15.4 Create ports

1. Create a port with specified IP address:

```
$ openstack port create --network net1 --fixed-ip subnet=subnet1,ip-address=192.168.2.40
 port1
+-----------------------+---------------------------------------+
| Field                 | Value                                 |
+-----------------------+---------------------------------------+
| admin_state_up        | UP                                    |
| allowed_address_pairs |                                       |
| binding_host_id       |                                       |
| binding_profile       |                                       |
```

```
| binding_vif_details   |                                       |
| binding_vif_type      | unbound                               |
| binding_vnic_type     | normal                                |
| created_at            | 2016-12-22T18:54:43Z                  |
| description           |                                       |
| device_id             |                                       |
| device_owner          |                                       |
| extra_dhcp_opts       |                                       |
| fixed_ips             | ip_address='192.168.2.40', subnet_id='a |
|                       | 394689c-f547-4834-9778-3e0bb22130dc'  |
| headers               |                                       |
| id                    | 031ddba8-3e3f-4c3c-ae26-7776905eb24f  |
| mac_address           | fa:16:3e:df:3d:c7                     |
| name                  | port1                                 |
| network_id            | 9db55b7f-e803-4e1b-9bba-6262f60b96cb  |
| port_security_enabled | True                                  |
| project_id            | e17431afc0524e0690484889a04b7fa0      |
| revision_number       | 5                                     |
| security_groups       | 84abb9eb-dc59-40c1-802c-4e173c345b6a  |
| status                | DOWN                                  |
| updated_at            | 2016-12-22T18:54:44Z                  |
+-----------------------+---------------------------------------+
```

In the previous command, `net1` is the network name, which is a positional argument. `--fixed-ip subnet<subnet>,ip-address=192.168.2.40` is an option which specifies the port's fixed IP address we wanted.

**Note**

When creating a port, you can specify any unallocated IP in the subnet even if the address is not in a pre-defined pool of allocated IP addresses (set by your cloud provider).

2. Create a port without specified IP address:

```
$ openstack port create port2 --network net1
+-----------------------+---------------------------------------+
| Field                 | Value                                 |
+-----------------------+---------------------------------------+
| admin_state_up        | UP                                    |
| allowed_address_pairs |                                       |
| binding_host_id       |                                       |
| binding_profile       |                                       |
| binding_vif_details   |                                       |
| binding_vif_type      | unbound                               |
| binding_vnic_type     | normal                                |
```

```
| created_at            | 2016-12-22T18:56:06Z                  |
| description           |                                       |
| device_id             |                                       |
| device_owner          |                                       |
| extra_dhcp_opts       |                                       |
| fixed_ips             | ip_address='192.168.2.10', subnet_id='a |
|                       | 394689c-f547-4834-9778-3e0bb22130dc'  |
| headers               |                                       |
| id                    | eac47fcd-07ac-42dd-9993-5b36ac1f201b  |
| mac_address           | fa:16:3e:96:ae:6e                     |
| name                  | port2                                 |
| network_id            | 9db55b7f-e803-4e1b-9bba-6262f60b96cb  |
| port_security_enabled | True                                  |
| project_id            | e17431afc0524e0690484889a04b7fa0      |
| revision_number       | 5                                     |
| security_groups       | 84abb9eb-dc59-40c1-802c-4e173c345b6a  |
| status                | DOWN                                  |
| updated_at            | 2016-12-22T18:56:06Z                  |
+-----------------------+---------------------------------------+
```

Note

Note that the system allocates one IP address if you do not specify an IP address in the **`openstack port create`** command.

Note

You can specify a MAC address with `--mac-address MAC_ADDRESS`. If you specify an invalid MAC address, including `00:00:00:00:00:00` or `ff:ff:ff:ff:ff:ff`, you will get an error.

3. Query ports with specified fixed IP addresses:

```
$ neutron port-list --fixed-ips ip_address=192.168.2.2 \
  ip_address=192.168.2.40
+----------------+------+-------------------
+-------------------------------------------------+
| id             | name | mac_address       | fixed_ips
    |
+----------------+------+-------------------
+-------------------------------------------------+
| baf13412-26... |      | fa:16:3e:f6:ec:c7 | {"subnet_id"... ..."ip_address":
 "192.168.2.2"} |
```

```
| f7a08fe4-e7... |       | fa:16:3e:97:e0:fc | {"subnet_id"... ..."ip_address":
 "192.168.2.40"}|
+----------------+------+------------------
+----------------------------------------------+
```

## 4.16 Manage objects and containers

The OpenStack Object Storage service provides the `swift` client, which is a command-line interface (CLI). Use this client to list objects and containers, upload objects to containers, and download or delete objects from containers. You can also gather statistics and update metadata for accounts, containers, and objects.

This client is based on the native swift client library, `client.py`, which seamlessly re-authenticates if the current token expires during processing, retries operations multiple times, and provides a processing concurrency of 10.

### 4.16.1 Create and manage containers

- To create a container, run the following command and replace `CONTAINER` with the name of your container.

  ```
  $ swift post CONTAINER
  ```

- To list all containers, run the following command:

  ```
  $ swift list
  ```

- To check the status of containers, run the following command:

  ```
  $ swift stat
  ```

  ```
  Account: AUTH_7b5970fbe7724bf9b74c245e77c03bcg
  Containers: 2
  Objects: 3
  Bytes: 268826
  Accept-Ranges: bytes
  X-Timestamp: 1392683866.17952
  Content-Type: text/plain; charset=utf-8
  ```

  You can also use the **`swift stat`** command with the `ACCOUNT` or `CONTAINER` names as parameters.

```
$ swift stat CONTAINER
```

```
Account: AUTH_7b5970fbe7724bf9b74c245e77c03bcg
Container: storage1
Objects: 2
Bytes: 240221
Read ACL:
Write ACL:
Sync To:
Sync Key:
Accept-Ranges: bytes
X-Timestamp: 1392683866.20180
Content-Type: text/plain; charset=utf-8
```

### 4.16.2 Manage access

- Users have roles on accounts. For example, a user with the admin role has full access to all containers and objects in an account. You can set access control lists (ACLs) at the container level and support lists for read and write access, which you set with the `X-Container-Read` and `X-Container-Write` headers.
  To give a user read access, use the **`swift post`** command with the `-r` parameter. To give a user write access, use the `-w` parameter.
- The following are examples of `read` ACLs for containers:
  A request with any HTTP referer header can read container contents:

```
$ swift post CONTAINER -r ".r:*"
```

A request with any HTTP referer header can read and list container contents:

```
$ swift post CONTAINER -r ".r:*,.rlistings"
```

A list of specific HTTP referer headers permitted to read container contents:

```
$ swift post CONTAINER -r \
  ".r:openstack.example.com,.r:swift.example.com,.r:storage.example.com"
```

A list of specific HTTP referer headers denied read access:

```
$ swift post CONTAINER -r \
  ".r:*,.r:-openstack.example.com,.r:-swift.example.com,.r:-storage.example.com"
```

All users residing in project1 can read container contents:

```
$ swift post CONTAINER -r "project1:*"
```

User1 from project1 can read container contents:

```
$ swift post CONTAINER -r "project1:user1"
```

A list of specific users and projects permitted to read container contents:

```
$ swift post CONTAINER -r \
  "project1:user1,project1:user2,project3:*,project4:user1"
```

- The following are examples of `write` ACLs for containers:
  All users residing in project1 can write to the container:

```
$ swift post CONTAINER -w "project1:*"
```

User1 from project1 can write to the container:

```
$ swift post CONTAINER -w "project1:user1"
```

A list of specific users and projects permitted to write to the container:

```
$ swift post CONTAINER -w \
  "project1:user1,project1:user2,project3:*,project4:user1"
```

Note

To successfully write to a container, a user must have read privileges (in addition to write) on the container. For all aforementioned read/write ACL examples, one can replace the project/user name with project/user UUID, i.e. `<project_uuid>:<user_uuid>`. If using multiple keystone domains, UUID format is required.

### 4.16.3 Manage objects

- To upload an object to a container, run the following command:

```
$ swift upload CONTAINER OBJECT_FILENAME
```

To upload in chunks, for larger than 5GB files, run the following command:

```
$ swift upload -S CHUNK_SIZE CONTAINER OBJECT_FILENAME
```

- To check the status of the object, run the following command:

```
$ swift stat CONTAINER OBJECT_FILENAME
```

```
Account: AUTH_7b5970fbe7724bf9b74c245e77c03bcg
Container: storage1
Object: images
Content Type: application/octet-stream
Content Length: 211616
Last Modified: Tue, 18 Feb 2014 00:40:36 GMT
ETag: 82169623d55158f70a0d720f238ec3ef
Meta Orig-Filename: images.jpg
Accept-Ranges: bytes
X-Timestamp: 1392684036.33306
```

- To list the objects in a container, run the following command:

```
$ swift list CONTAINER
```

- To download an object from a container, run the following command:

```
$ swift download CONTAINER OBJECT_FILENAME
```

### 4.16.4 Environment variables required to run examples

To run the cURL command examples for the Object Storage API requests, set these environment variables:

**publicURL**

The public URL that is the HTTP endpoint from where you can access Object Storage. It includes the Object Storage API version number and your account name. For example, `https://23.253.72.207/v1/my_account`.

**token**

The authentication token for Object Storage.

To obtain these values, run the **`swift stat -v`** command.

As shown in this example, the public URL appears in the `StorageURL` field, and the token appears in the `Auth Token` field:

```
StorageURL: https://23.253.72.207/v1/my_account
Auth Token: {token}
Account: my_account
Containers: 2
Objects: 3
Bytes: 47
Meta Book: MobyDick
X-Timestamp: 1389453423.35964
X-Trans-Id: txee55498935404a2caad89-0052dd3b77
Content-Type: text/plain; charset=utf-8
Accept-Ranges: bytes
```

### 4.16.5 Object versioning

You can store multiple versions of your content so that you can recover from unintended overwrites. Object versioning is an easy way to implement version control, which you can use with any type of content.

Note

You cannot version a large-object manifest file, but the large-object manifest file can point to versioned segments.

We strongly recommend that you put non-current objects in a different container than the container where current object versions reside.

#### 4.16.5.1 To enable and use object versioning

1. To enable object versioning, ask your cloud provider to set the `allow_versions` option to `TRUE` in the container configuration file.

2. Create an `archive` container to store older versions of objects:

```
$ curl -i $publicURL/archive -X PUT -H "Content-Length: 0" -H "X-Auth-Token: $token"
```

```
HTTP/1.1 201 Created
```

```
Content-Length: 0
Content-Type: text/html; charset=UTF-8
X-Trans-Id: tx46f8c29050834d88b8d7e-0052e1859d
Date: Thu, 23 Jan 2014 21:11:57 GMT
```

3. Create a `current` container to store current versions of objects.
   Include the `X-Versions-Location` header. This header defines the container that holds the non-current versions of your objects. You must UTF-8-encode and then URL-encode the container name before you include it in the `X-Versions-Location` header. This header enables object versioning for all objects in the `current` container. Changes to objects in the `current` container automatically create non-current versions in the `archive` container.

```
$ curl -i $publicURL/current -X PUT -H "Content-Length: 0" -H \
  "X-Auth-Token: $token" -H "X-Versions-Location: archive"
```

```
HTTP/1.1 201 Created
Content-Length: 0
Content-Type: text/html; charset=UTF-8
X-Trans-Id: txb91810fb717347d09eec8-0052e18997
Date: Thu, 23 Jan 2014 21:28:55 GMT
```

4. Create the first version of an object in the `current` container:

```
$ curl -i $publicURL/current/my_object --data-binary 1 -X PUT -H \
  "Content-Length: 0" -H "X-Auth-Token: $token"
```

```
HTTP/1.1 201 Created
Last-Modified: Thu, 23 Jan 2014 21:31:22 GMT
Content-Length: 0
Etag: d41d8cd98f00b204e9800998ecf8427e
Content-Type: text/html; charset=UTF-8
X-Trans-Id: tx5992d536a4bd4fec973aa-0052e18a2a
Date: Thu, 23 Jan 2014 21:31:22 GMT
```

   Nothing is written to the non-current version container when you initially `PUT` an object in the `current` container. However, subsequent `PUT` requests that edit an object trigger the creation of a version of that object in the `archive` container.
   These non-current versions are named as follows:

```
<length><object_name><timestamp>
```

Where `length` is the 3-character, zero-padded hexadecimal character length of the object, `<object_name>` is the object name, and `<timestamp>` is the time when the object was initially created as a current version.

5. Create a second version of the object in the `current` container:

```
$ curl -i $publicURL/current/my_object --data-binary 2 -X PUT -H \
  "Content-Length: 0" -H "X-Auth-Token: $token"
```

```
HTTP/1.1 201 Created
Last-Modified: Thu, 23 Jan 2014 21:41:32 GMT
Content-Length: 0
Etag: d41d8cd98f00b204e9800998ecf8427e
Content-Type: text/html; charset=UTF-8
X-Trans-Id: tx468287ce4fc94eada96ec-0052e18c8c
Date: Thu, 23 Jan 2014 21:41:32 GMT
```

6. Issue a `GET` request to a versioned object to get the current version of the object. You do not have to do any request redirects or metadata lookups.
List older versions of the object in the `archive` container:

```
$ curl -i $publicURL/archive?prefix=009my_object -X GET -H \
  "X-Auth-Token: $token"
```

```
HTTP/1.1 200 OK
Content-Length: 30
X-Container-Object-Count: 1
Accept-Ranges: bytes
X-Timestamp: 1390513280.79684
X-Container-Bytes-Used: 0
Content-Type: text/plain; charset=utf-8
X-Trans-Id: tx9a441884997542d3a5868-0052e18d8e
Date: Thu, 23 Jan 2014 21:45:50 GMT

  009my_object/1390512682.92052
```

### Note

A `POST` request to a versioned object updates only the metadata for the object and does not create a new version of the object. New versions are created only when the content of the object changes.

7. Issue a `DELETE` request to a versioned object to remove the current version of the object and replace it with the next-most current version in the non-current container.

```
$ curl -i $publicURL/current/my_object -X DELETE -H \
  "X-Auth-Token: $token"
```

```
HTTP/1.1 204 No Content
Content-Length: 0
Content-Type: text/html; charset=UTF-8
X-Trans-Id: tx006d944e02494e229b8ee-0052e18edd
Date: Thu, 23 Jan 2014 21:51:25 GMT
```

List objects in the `archive` container to show that the archived object was moved back to the `current` container:

```
$ curl -i $publicURL/archive?prefix=009my_object -X GET -H \
  "X-Auth-Token: $token"
```

```
HTTP/1.1 204 No Content
Content-Length: 0
X-Container-Object-Count: 0
Accept-Ranges: bytes
X-Timestamp: 1390513280.79684
X-Container-Bytes-Used: 0
Content-Type: text/html; charset=UTF-8
X-Trans-Id: tx044f2a05f56f4997af737-0052e18eed
Date: Thu, 23 Jan 2014 21:51:41 GMT
```

This next-most current version carries with it any metadata last set on it. If you want to completely remove an object and you have five versions of it, you must `DELETE` it five times.

8. To disable object versioning for the `current` container, remove its `X-Versions-Location` metadata header by sending an empty key value.

```
$ curl -i $publicURL/current -X PUT -H "Content-Length: 0" -H \
  "X-Auth-Token: $token" -H "X-Versions-Location: "
```

```
  HTTP/1.1 202 Accepted
  Content-Length: 76
  Content-Type: text/html; charset=UTF-8
  X-Trans-Id: txe2476de217134549996d0-0052e19038
  Date: Thu, 23 Jan 2014 21:57:12 GMT
```

```
<html><h1>Accepted</h1><p>The request is accepted for processing.</p></html>
```

### 4.16.6 Object expiration

You can schedule Object Storage (swift) objects to expire by setting the `X-Delete-At` or `X-Delete-After` header. Once the object is deleted, swift will no longer serve the object and it will be deleted from the cluster shortly thereafter.

- Set an object to expire at an absolute time (in Unix time). You can get the current Unix time by running `date +'%s'`.

  ```
  $ swift post CONTAINER OBJECT_FILENAME -H "X-Delete-At:UNIX_TIME"
  ```

  Verify the `X-Delete-At` header has posted to the object:

  ```
  $ swift stat CONTAINER OBJECT_FILENAME
  ```

- Set an object to expire after a relative amount of time (in seconds):

  ```
  $ swift post CONTAINER OBJECT_FILENAME -H "X-Delete-After:SECONDS"
  ```

  The `X-Delete-After` header will be converted to `X-Delete-At`. Verify the `X-Delete-At` header has posted to the object:

  ```
  $ swift stat CONTAINER OBJECT_FILENAME
  ```

  If you no longer want to expire the object, you can remove the `X-Delete-At` header:

  ```
  $ swift post CONTAINER OBJECT_FILENAME -H "X-Remove-Delete-At:"
  ```

**Note**

In order for object expiration to work properly, the `swift-object-expirer` daemon will need access to all backend servers in the cluster. The daemon does not need access to the proxy-server or public network.

## 4.16.7 Serialized response formats

By default, the Object Storage API uses a `text/plain` response format. In addition, both JSON and XML data serialization response formats are supported.

### Note

To run the cURL command examples, you must export environment variables. For more information, see the section *Section 4.16.4, "Environment variables required to run examples"*.

To define the response format, use one of these methods:

| **Method** | **Description** |
|---|---|
| format= `format` query parameter | Append this parameter to the URL for a `GET` request, where `format` is `json` or `xml`. |
| `Accept` request header | Include this header in the `GET` request. The valid header values are:<br>**text/plain**<br>Plain text response format. The default.<br>**application/jsontext**<br>JSON data serialization response format.<br>**application/xml**<br>XML data serialization response format.<br>**text/xml**<br>XML data serialization response format. |

### 4.16.7.1 Example 1. JSON example with format query parameter

For example, this request uses the `format` query parameter to ask for a JSON response:

```
$ curl -i $publicURL?format=json -X GET -H "X-Auth-Token: $token"
```

```
HTTP/1.1 200 OK
Content-Length: 96
X-Account-Object-Count: 1
X-Timestamp: 1389453423.35964
```

```
X-Account-Meta-Subject: Literature
X-Account-Bytes-Used: 14
X-Account-Container-Count: 2
Content-Type: application/json; charset=utf-8
Accept-Ranges: bytes
X-Trans-Id: tx274a77a8975c4a66aeb24-0052d95365
Date: Fri, 17 Jan 2014 15:59:33 GMT
```

Object Storage lists container names with additional information in JSON format:


```
[
   {
      "count":0,
      "bytes":0,
      "name":"janeausten"
   },
   {
      "count":1,
      "bytes":14,
      "name":"marktwain"
   }
]
```


### 4.16.7.2 Example 2. XML example with Accept header

This request uses the `Accept` request header to ask for an XML response:

```
$ curl -i $publicURL -X GET -H "X-Auth-Token: $token" -H \
  "Accept: application/xml; charset=utf-8"
```

```
HTTP/1.1 200 OK
Content-Length: 263
X-Account-Object-Count: 3
X-Account-Meta-Book: MobyDick
X-Timestamp: 1389453423.35964
X-Account-Bytes-Used: 47
X-Account-Container-Count: 2
Content-Type: application/xml; charset=utf-8
Accept-Ranges: bytes
X-Trans-Id: txf0b4c9727c3e491694019-0052e03420
Date: Wed, 22 Jan 2014 21:12:00 GMT
```

Object Storage lists container names with additional information in XML format:


```
<?xml version="1.0" encoding="UTF-8"?>
```

```
<account name="AUTH_73f0aa26640f4971864919d0eb0f0880">
    <container>
        <name>janeausten</name>
        <count>2</count>
        <bytes>33</bytes>
    </container>
    <container>
        <name>marktwain</name>
        <count>1</count>
        <bytes>14</bytes>
    </container>
</account>
```

The remainder of the examples in this guide use standard, non-serialized responses. However, all `GET` requests that perform list operations accept the `format` query parameter or `Accept` request header.

### 4.16.8 Page through large lists of containers or objects

If you have a large number of containers or objects, you can use the `marker`, `limit`, and `end_marker` parameters to control how many items are returned in a list and where the list starts or ends.

- **marker**

  When you request a list of containers or objects, Object Storage returns a maximum of 10,000 names for each request. To get subsequent names, you must make another request with the `marker` parameter. Set the `marker` parameter to the name of the last item returned in the previous list. You must URL-encode the `marker` value before you send the HTTP request. Object Storage returns a maximum of 10,000 names starting after the last item returned.

- **limit**

  To return fewer than 10,000 names, use the `limit` parameter. If the number of names returned equals the specified `limit` (or 10,000 if you omit the `limit` parameter), you can assume there are more names to list. If the number of names in the list is exactly divisible by the `limit` value, the last request has no content.

- **end_marker**

  Limits the result set to names that are less than the `end_marker` parameter value. You must URL-encode the `end_marker` value before you send the HTTP request.

#### 4.16.8.1 To page through a large list of containers

Assume the following list of container names:

```
apples
bananas
kiwis
oranges
pears
```

1. Use a `limit` of two:

   ```
   # curl -i $publicURL/?limit=2 -X GET -H "X-Auth-Token: $token"
   ```

   ```
   apples
   bananas
   ```

   Because two container names are returned, there are more names to list.

2. Make another request with a `marker` parameter set to the name of the last item returned:

   ```
   # curl -i $publicURL/?limit=2&amp;marker=bananas -X GET -H \
     “X-Auth-Token: $token"
   ```

   ```
   kiwis
   oranges
   ```

   Again, two items are returned, and there might be more.

3. Make another request with a `marker` of the last item returned:

   ```
   # curl -i $publicURL/?limit=2&amp;marker=oranges -X GET -H \”
     X-Auth-Token: $token"
   ```

   ```
   pears
   ```

   You receive a one-item response, which is fewer than the `limit` number of names. This indicates that this is the end of the list.

4. Use the `end_marker` parameter to limit the result set to object names that are less than the `end_marker` parameter value:

   ```
   # curl -i $publicURL/?end_marker=oranges -X GET -H \”
    X-Auth-Token: $token"
   ```

```
apples
bananas
kiwis
```

You receive a result set of all container names before the `end-marker` value.

### 4.16.9 Pseudo-hierarchical folders and directories

Although you cannot nest directories in OpenStack Object Storage, you can simulate a hierarchical structure within a single container by adding forward slash characters (`/`) in the object name. To navigate the pseudo-directory structure, you can use the `delimiter` query parameter. This example shows you how to use pseudo-hierarchical folders and directories.

Note

In this example, the objects reside in a container called `backups`. Within that container, the objects are organized in a pseudo-directory called `photos`. The container name is not displayed in the example, but it is a part of the object URLs. For instance, the URL of the picture `me.jpg` is `https://storage.swiftdrive.com/v1/CF_xer7_343/backups/photos/me.jpg`.

#### 4.16.9.1 List pseudo-hierarchical folders request: HTTP

To display a list of all the objects in the storage container, use `GET` without a `delimiter` or `prefix`.

```
$ curl -X GET -i -H "X-Auth-Token: $token" \
 $publicurl/v1/AccountString/backups
```

The system returns status code 2xx (between 200 and 299, inclusive) and the requested list of the objects.

```
photos/animals/cats/persian.jpg
photos/animals/cats/siamese.jpg
photos/animals/dogs/corgi.jpg
photos/animals/dogs/poodle.jpg
photos/animals/dogs/terrier.jpg
photos/me.jpg
photos/plants/fern.jpg
```

```
photos/plants/rose.jpg
```

Use the delimiter parameter to limit the displayed results. To use `delimiter` with pseudo-directories, you must use the parameter slash (`/`).

```
$ curl -X GET -i -H "X-Auth-Token: $token" \
 $publicurl/v1/AccountString/backups?delimiter=/
```

The system returns status code 2xx (between 200 and 299, inclusive) and the requested matching objects. Because you use the slash, only the pseudo-directory `photos/` displays. The returned values from a slash `delimiter` query are not real objects. The value will refer to a real object if it does not end with a slash. The pseudo-directories have no content-type, rather, each pseudo-directory has its own `subdir` entry in the response of JSON and XML results. For example:


```
[
   {
     "subdir": "photos/"
   }
 ]

 [
   {
     "subdir": "photos/animals/"
   },
   {
     "hash": "b249a153f8f38b51e92916bbc6ea57ad",
     "last_modified": "2015-12-03T17:31:28.187370",
     "bytes": 2906,
     "name": "photos/me.jpg",
     "content_type": "image/jpeg"
   },
   {
     "subdir": "photos/plants/"
   }
 ]
```

```
<?xml version="1.0" encoding="UTF-8"?>
 <container name="backups">
   <subdir name="photos/">
     <name>photos/</name>
   </subdir>
 </container>

 <?xml version="1.0" encoding="UTF-8"?>
 <container name="backups">
```

```
  <subdir name="photos/animals/">
    <name>photos/animals/</name>
  </subdir>
  <object>
    <name>photos/me.jpg</name>
    <hash>b249a153f8f38b51e92916bbc6ea57ad</hash>
    <bytes>2906</bytes>
    <content_type>image/jpeg</content_type>
    <last_modified>2015-12-03T17:31:28.187370</last_modified>
  </object>
  <subdir name="photos/plants/">
    <name>photos/plants/</name>
  </subdir>
</container>
```


Use the `prefix` and `delimiter` parameters to view the objects inside a pseudo-directory, including further nested pseudo-directories.

```
$ curl -X GET -i -H "X-Auth-Token: $token" \
 $publicurl/v1/AccountString/backups?prefix=photos/&delimiter=/
```

The system returns status code 2xx (between 200 and 299, inclusive) and the objects and pseudo-directories within the top level pseudo-directory.

```
photos/animals/
photos/me.jpg
photos/plants/
```

You can create an unlimited number of nested pseudo-directories. To navigate through them, use a longer `prefix` parameter coupled with the `delimiter` parameter. In this sample output, there is a pseudo-directory called `dogs` within the pseudo-directory `animals`. To navigate directly to the files contained within `dogs`, enter the following command:

```
$ curl -X GET -i -H "X-Auth-Token: $token" \
 $publicurl/v1/AccountString/backups?prefix=photos/animals/dogs/&delimiter=/
```

The system returns status code 2xx (between 200 and 299, inclusive) and the objects and pseudo-directories within the nested pseudo-directory.

```
photos/animals/dogs/corgi.jpg
photos/animals/dogs/poodle.jpg
photos/animals/dogs/terrier.jpg
```

### 4.16.10 Discoverability

Your Object Storage system might not enable all features that this document describes. These features are:

- *Section 4.16.11, "Large objects"*
- *Section 4.16.12, "Auto-extract archive files"*
- *Section 4.16.13, "Bulk delete"*
- *Section 4.16.14, "Create static website"*

To discover which features are enabled in your Object Storage system, use the `/info` request.

To use the `/info` request, send a `GET` request using the `/info` path to the Object Store endpoint as shown in this example:

```
$ curl https://storage.example.com/info
```

This example shows a truncated response body:

```
{
   "swift":{
      "version":"1.11.0"
   },
   "staticweb":{

   },
   "tempurl":{

   }
}
```

This output shows that the Object Storage system has enabled the static website and temporary URL features.

Note

In some cases, the `/info` request will return an error. This could be because your service provider has disabled the `/info` request function, or because you are using an older version that does not support it.

### 4.16.11 Large objects

To discover whether your Object Storage system supports this feature, see Section 4.16.10, "Discoverability" or check with your service provider.

By default, the content of an object cannot be greater than 5 GB. However, you can use a number of smaller objects to construct a large object. The large object is comprised of two types of objects:

- `Segment objects` store the object content. You can divide your content into segments and upload each segment into its own segment object. Segment objects do not have any special features. You create, update, download, and delete segment objects just as you do with normal objects.

- A `manifest object` links the segment objects into one logical large object. When you download a manifest object, Object Storage concatenates and returns the contents of the segment objects in the response body. This behavior extends to the response headers returned by `GET` and `HEAD` requests. The `Content-Length` response header contains the total size of all segment objects.
  Object Storage takes the `ETag` value of each segment, concatenates them together, and returns the MD5 checksum of the result to calculate the `ETag` response header value. The manifest object types are:

  **Static large objects**

  The manifest object content is an ordered list of the names of the segment objects in JSON format. See Section 4.16.11.1, "Static large objects".

  **Dynamic large objects**

  The manifest object has no content but it has a `X-Object-Manifest` metadata header. The value of this header is `CONTAINER/PREFIX`, where `CONTAINER` is the name of the container where the segment objects are stored, and `PREFIX` is a string that all segment objects have in common. See Section 4.16.11.2, "Dynamic large objects".

#### Note

If you use a manifest object as the source of a `COPY` request, the new object is a normal, and not a segment, object. If the total size of the source segment objects exceeds 5 GB, the `COPY` request fails. However, you can make a duplicate of the manifest object and this new object can be larger than 5 GB.

#### 4.16.11.1 Static large objects

To create a static large object, divide your content into pieces and create (upload) a segment object to contain each piece.

You must record the `ETag` response header value that the `PUT` operation returns. Alternatively, you can calculate the MD5 checksum of the segment before you perform the upload and include this value in the `ETag` request header. This action ensures that the upload cannot corrupt your data.

List the name of each segment object along with its size and MD5 checksum in order.

Create a manifest object. Include the `?multipart-manifest=put` query string at the end of the manifest object name to indicate that this is a manifest object.

The body of the `PUT` request on the manifest object comprises a JSON list where each element contains these attributes:

**path**

The container and object name in the format: `CONTAINER_NAME/OBJECT_NAME`.

**etag**

The MD5 checksum of the content of the segment object. This value must match the `ETag` of that object.

**size_bytes**

The size of the segment object. This value must match the `Content-Length` of that object.

##### 4.16.11.1.1 Static large object manifest list

This example shows three segment objects. You can use several containers and the object names do not have to conform to a specific pattern, in contrast to dynamic large objects.

```
[
    {
        "path": "mycontainer/objseg1",
        "etag": "0228c7926b8b642dfb29554cd1f00963",
        "size_bytes": 1468006
    },
    {
        "path": "mycontainer/pseudodir/seg-obj2",
        "etag": "5bfc9ea51a00b790717eeb934fb77b9b",
        "size_bytes": 1572864
    },
```

```
    {
        "path": "other-container/seg-final",
        "etag": "b9c3da507d2557c1ddc51f27c54bae51",
        "size_bytes": 256
    }
]
```

The `Content-Length` request header must contain the length of the JSON content and not the length of the segment objects. However, after the `PUT` operation completes, the `Content-Length` metadata is set to the total length of all the object segments. A similar situation applies to the `ETag`. If used in the `PUT` operation, it must contain the MD5 checksum of the JSON content. The `ETag` metadata value is then set to be the MD5 checksum of the concatenated `ETag` values of the object segments. You can also set the `Content-Type` request header and custom object metadata.

When the `PUT` operation sees the `?multipart-manifest=put` query parameter, it reads the request body and verifies that each segment object exists and that the sizes and ETags match. If there is a mismatch, the `PUT` operation fails.

If everything matches, the API creates the manifest object and sets the `X-Static-Large-Object` metadata to `true` to indicate that the manifest is a static object manifest.

Normally when you perform a `GET` operation on the manifest object, the response body contains the concatenated content of the segment objects. To download the manifest list, use the `?multipart-manifest=get` query parameter. The list in the response is not formatted the same as the manifest that you originally used in the `PUT` operation.

If you use the `DELETE` operation on a manifest object, the manifest object is deleted. The segment objects are not affected. However, if you add the `?multipart-manifest=delete` query parameter, the segment objects are deleted and if all are successfully deleted, the manifest object is also deleted.

To change the manifest, use a `PUT` operation with the `?multipart-manifest=put` query parameter. This request creates a manifest object. You can also update the object metadata in the usual way.

#### 4.16.11.2 Dynamic large objects

Before you can upload objects that are larger than 5 GB, you must segment them. You upload the segment objects like you do with any other object and create a dynamic large manifest object. The manifest object tells Object Storage how to find the segment objects that comprise the large object. You can still access each segment individually, but when you retrieve the manifest object, the API concatenates the segments. You can include any number of segments in a single large object.

To ensure the download works correctly, you must upload all the object segments to the same container and prefix each object name so that the segments sort in correct concatenation order.

You also create and upload a manifest file. The manifest file is a zero-byte file with the extra `X-Object-Manifest CONTAINER/PREFIX` header. The `CONTAINER` is the container the object segments are in and `PREFIX` is the common prefix for all the segments. You must UTF-8-encode and then URL-encode the container and common prefix in the `X-Object-Manifest` header.

It is best to upload all the segments first and then create or update the manifest. With this method, the full object is not available for downloading until the upload is complete. Also, you can upload a new set of segments to a second location and update the manifest to point to this new location. During the upload of the new segments, the original manifest is still available to download the first set of segments.

#### 4.16.11.2.1 Upload segment of large object request: HTTP

```
PUT /API_VERSION/ACCOUNT/CONTAINER/OBJECT HTTP/1.1
Host: storage.example.com
X-Auth-Token: eaaafd18-0fed-4b3a-81b4-663c99ec1cbb
ETag: 8a964ee2a5e88be344f36c22562a6486
Content-Length: 1
X-Object-Meta-PIN: 1234
```

No response body is returned.

The 2``nn`` response code indicates a successful write. `nn` is a value from 00 to 99.

The `Length Required (411)` response code indicates that the request does not include a required `Content-Length` or `Content-Type` header.

The `Unprocessable Entity (422)` response code indicates that the MD5 checksum of the data written to the storage system does NOT match the optional ETag value.

You can continue to upload segments, like this example shows, before you upload the manifest.

#### 4.16.11.2.2 Upload next segment of large object request: HTTP

```
PUT /API_VERSION/ACCOUNT/CONTAINER/OBJECT HTTP/1.1
Host: storage.example.com
```

```
X-Auth-Token: eaaafd18-0fed-4b3a-81b4-663c99ec1cbb
ETag: 8a964ee2a5e88be344f36c22562a6486
Content-Length: 1
X-Object-Meta-PIN: 1234
```

Next, upload the manifest. This manifest specifies the container where the object segments reside. Note that if you upload additional segments after you create the manifest, the concatenated object becomes that much larger but you do not need to recreate the manifest file for subsequent additional segments.

#### 4.16.11.2.3 Upload manifest request: HTTP

```
PUT /API_VERSION/ACCOUNT/CONTAINER/OBJECT HTTP/1.1
Host: storage.clouddrive.com
X-Auth-Token: eaaafd18-0fed-4b3a-81b4-663c99ec1cbb
Content-Length: 0
X-Object-Meta-PIN: 1234
X-Object-Manifest: CONTAINER/PREFIX
```

#### 4.16.11.2.4 Upload manifest response: HTTP

```
[...]
```

A `GET` or `HEAD` request on the manifest returns a `Content-Type` response header value that is the same as the `Content-Type` request header value in the `PUT` request that created the manifest. To change the `Content- Type`, reissue the `PUT` request.

### 4.16.11.3 Extra transaction information

You can use the `X-Trans-Id-Extra` request header to include extra information to help you debug any errors that might occur with large object upload and other Object Storage transactions.

The Object Storage API appends the first 32 characters of the `X-Trans-Id-Extra` request header value to the transaction ID value in the generated `X-Trans-Id` response header. You must UTF-8-encode and then URL-encode the extra transaction information before you include it in the `X-Trans-Id-Extra` request header.

For example, you can include extra transaction information when you upload large objects such as images.

When you upload each segment and the manifest, include the same value in the `X-Trans-Id-Extra` request header. If an error occurs, you can find all requests that are related to the large object upload in the Object Storage logs.

You can also use `X-Trans-Id-Extra` strings to help operators debug requests that fail to receive responses. The operator can search for the extra information in the logs.

#### 4.16.11.4 Comparison of static and dynamic large objects

While static and dynamic objects have similar behavior, this table describes their differences:

| Description | Static large object | Dynamic large object |
|---|---|---|
| End-to-end integrity | Assured. The list of segments includes the MD5 checksum (`ETag`) of each segment. You cannot upload the manifest object if the `ETag` in the list differs from the uploaded segment object. If a segment is somehow lost, an attempt to download the manifest object results in an error. | Not guaranteed. The eventual consistency model means that although you have uploaded a segment object, it might not appear in the container listing until later. If you download the manifest before it appears in the container, it does not form part of the content returned in response to a `GET` request. |
| Upload order | You must upload the segment objects before upload the manifest object. | You can upload manifest and segment objects in any order. You are recommended to upload the manifest object after the segments in case a premature download of the manifest occurs. However, this is not enforced. |
| Removal or addition of segment objects | You cannot add or remove segment objects from the manifest. However, you can create a completely new | You can upload new segment objects or remove existing segments. The names must |

| Description | Static large object | Dynamic large object |
| --- | --- | --- |
| | manifest object of the same name with a different manifest list. | simply match the `PREFIX` supplied in `X-Object-Manifest`. |
| Segment object size and number | Segment objects must be at least 1 MB in size (by default). The final segment object can be any size. At most, 1000 segments are supported (by default). | Segment objects can be any size. |
| Segment object container name | The manifest list includes the container name of each object. Segment objects can be in different containers. | All segment objects must be in the same container. |
| Manifest object metadata | The object has `X-Static-Large-Object` set to `true`. You do not set this metadata directly. Instead the system sets it when you `PUT` a static manifest object. | The `X-Object-Manifest` value is the `CONTAINER/PREFIX`, which indicates where the segment objects are located. You supply this request header in the `PUT` operation. |
| Copying the manifest object | Include the `?multipart-manifest=get` query string in the `COPY` request. The new object contains the same manifest as the original. The segment objects are not copied. Instead, both the original and new manifest objects share the same set of segment objects. | The `COPY` operation does not create a manifest object. To duplicate a manifest object, use the `GET` operation to read the value of `X-Object-Manifest` and use this value in the `X-Object-Manifest` request header in a `PUT` operation. This creates a new manifest object that shares the same set of segment objects as the original manifest object. |

### 4.16.12 Auto-extract archive files

To discover whether your Object Storage system supports this feature, see *Section 4.16.10, "Discoverability"*. Alternatively, check with your service provider.

Use the auto-extract archive feature to upload a tar archive file.

The Object Storage system extracts files from the archive file and creates an object.

#### 4.16.12.1 Auto-extract archive request

To upload an archive file, make a `PUT` request. Add the `extract-archive=format` query parameter to indicate that you are uploading a tar archive file instead of normal content.

Valid values for the `format` variable are `tar`, `tar.gz`, or `tar.bz2`.

The path you specify in the `PUT` request is used for the location of the object and the prefix for the resulting object names.

In the `PUT` request, you can specify the path for:

- An account
- Optionally, a specific container
- Optionally, a specific object prefix

For example, if the first object in the tar archive is `/home/file1.txt` and you specify the `/v1/12345678912345/mybackup/castor/` path, the operation creates the `castor/home/file1.txt` object in the `mybackup` container in the `12345678912345` account.

#### 4.16.12.2 Create an archive for auto-extract

You must use the tar utility to create the tar archive file.

You can upload regular files but you cannot upload other items (for example, empty directories or symbolic links).

You must UTF-8-encode the member names.

The archive auto-extract feature supports these formats:

- The POSIX.1-1988 Ustar format.
- The GNU tar format. Includes the long name, long link, and sparse extensions.
- The POSIX.1-2001 pax format.

Use gzip or bzip2 to compress the archive.

Use the `extract-archive` query parameter to specify the format. Valid values for this parameter are `tar`, `tar.gz`, or `tar.bz2`.

#### 4.16.12.3 Auto-extract archive response

When Object Storage processes the request, it performs multiple sub-operations. Even if all sub-operations fail, the operation returns a 201 `Created` status. Some sub-operations might succeed while others fail. Examine the response body to determine the results of each auto-extract archive sub-operation.

You can set the `Accept` request header to one of these values to define the response format:

`text/plain`
: Formats response as plain text. If you omit the `Accept` header, `text/plain` is the default.

`application/json`
: Formats response as JSON.

`application/xml`
: Formats response as XML.

`text/xml`
: Formats response as XML.

The following auto-extract archive files example shows a `text/plain` response body where no failures occurred:

```
Number Files Created: 10
Errors:
```

The following auto-extract archive files example shows a `text/plain` response where some failures occurred. In this example, the Object Storage system is configured to reject certain character strings so that the 400 Bad Request error occurs for any objects that use the restricted strings.

```
Number Files Created: 8
Errors:
/v1/12345678912345/mycontainer/home/xx%3Cyy, 400 Bad Request
/v1/12345678912345/mycontainer/../image.gif, 400 Bad Request
```

The following example shows the failure response in `application/json` format.

```
{
    "Number Files Created":1,
    "Errors":[
        [
            "/v1/12345678912345/mycontainer/home/xx%3Cyy",
            "400 Bad Request"
        ],
        [
            "/v1/12345678912345/mycontainer/../image.gif",
            "400 Bad Request"
        ]
    ]
}
```

## 4.16.13 Bulk delete

To discover whether your Object Storage system supports this feature, see *Section 4.16.10, "Discoverability"*. Alternatively, check with your service provider.

With bulk delete, you can delete up to 10,000 objects or containers (configurable) in one request.

### 4.16.13.1 Bulk delete request

To perform a bulk delete operation, add the `bulk-delete` query parameter to the path of a `POST` or `DELETE` operation.

Note

The `DELETE` operation is supported for backwards compatibility.

The path is the account, such as `/v1/12345678912345`, that contains the objects and containers.

In the request body of the `POST` or `DELETE` operation, list the objects or containers to be deleted. Separate each name with a newline character. You can include a maximum of 10,000 items (configurable) in the list.

In addition, you must:

- UTF-8-encode and then URL-encode the names.
- To indicate an object, specify the container and object name as: `CONTAINER_NAME` / `OBJECT_NAME`.

- To indicate a container, specify the container name as: `CONTAINER_NAME`. Make sure that the container is empty. If it contains objects, Object Storage cannot delete the container.
- Set the `Content-Type` request header to `text/plain`.

#### 4.16.13.2 Bulk delete response

When Object Storage processes the request, it performs multiple sub-operations. Even if all sub-operations fail, the operation returns a 200 status. The bulk operation returns a response body that contains details that indicate which sub-operations have succeeded and failed. Some sub-operations might succeed while others fail. Examine the response body to determine the results of each delete sub-operation.

You can set the `Accept` request header to one of the following values to define the response format:

`text/plain`
: Formats response as plain text. If you omit the `Accept` header, `text/plain` is the default.

`application/json`
: Formats response as JSON.

`application/xml` **or** `text/xml`
: Formats response as XML.

The response body contains the following information:

- The number of files actually deleted.
- The number of not found objects.
- Errors. A list of object names and associated error statuses for the objects that failed to delete. The format depends on the value that you set in the `Accept` header.

The following bulk delete response is in `application/xml` format. In this example, the `mycontainer` container is not empty, so it cannot be deleted.

```
<delete>
    <number_deleted>2</number_deleted>
    <number_not_found>4</number_not_found>
    <errors>
        <object>
            <name>/v1/12345678912345/mycontainer</name>
```

```
            <status>409 Conflict</status>
        </object>
    </errors>
</delete>
```

### 4.16.14 Create static website

To discover whether your Object Storage system supports this feature, see *Section 4.16.10, "Discoverability"*. Alternatively, check with your service provider.

You can use your Object Storage account to create a static website. This static website is created with Static Web middleware and serves container data with a specified index file, error file resolution, and optional file listings. This mode is normally active only for anonymous requests, which provide no authentication token. To use it with authenticated requests, set the header `X-Web-Mode` to `TRUE` on the request.

The Static Web filter must be added to the pipeline in your `/etc/swift/proxy-server.conf` file below any authentication middleware. You must also add a Static Web middleware configuration section.

See the Cloud Administrator Guide for an example of the static web configuration syntax (https://docs.openstack.org/newton/config-reference/object-storage/features.html#static-web-sites).

See the Cloud Administrator Guide for a complete example of the /etc/swift/proxy-server.conf file (https://docs.openstack.org/newton/config-reference/object-storage/proxy-server.html#sample-proxy-server-configuration-file) (including static web).

Your publicly readable containers are checked for two headers, `X-Container-Meta-Web-Index` and `X-Container-Meta-Web-Error`. The `X-Container-Meta-Web-Error` header is discussed below, in the section called *Section 4.16.14.1.5, "Set error pages for static website"*.

Use `X-Container-Meta-Web-Index` to determine the index file (or default page served, such as `index.html`) for your website. When someone initially enters your site, the `index.html` file displays automatically. If you create sub-directories for your site by creating pseudo-directories in your container, the index page for each sub-directory is displayed by default. If your pseudo-directory does not have a file with the same name as your index file, visits to the sub-directory return a 404 error.

You also have the option of displaying a list of files in your pseudo-directory instead of a web page. To do this, set the `X-Container-Meta-Web-Listings` header to `TRUE`. You may add styles to your file listing by setting `X-Container-Meta-Web-Listings-CSS` to a style sheet (for example, `lists.css`).

#### 4.16.14.1 Static Web middleware through Object Storage

The following sections show how to use Static Web middleware through Object Storage.

##### 4.16.14.1.1 Make container publicly readable

Make the container publicly readable. Once the container is publicly readable, you can access your objects directly, but you must set the index file to browse the main site URL and its subdirectories.

```
$ swift post -r '.r:*,.rlistings' container
```

##### 4.16.14.1.2 Set site index file

Set the index file. In this case, `index.html` is the default file displayed when the site appears.

```
$ swift post -m 'web-index:index.html' container
```

##### 4.16.14.1.3 Enable file listing

Turn on file listing. If you do not set the index file, the URL displays a list of the objects in the container. Instructions on styling the list with a CSS follow.

```
$ swift post -m 'web-listings: true' container
```

##### 4.16.14.1.4 Enable CSS for file listing

Style the file listing using a CSS.

```
$ swift post -m 'web-listings-css:listings.css' container
```

##### 4.16.14.1.5 Set error pages for static website

You can create and set custom error pages for visitors to your website; currently, only 401 (Unauthorized) and 404 (Not Found) errors are supported. To do this, set the metadata header, `X-Container-Meta-Web-Error`.

Error pages are served with the status code pre-pended to the name of the error page you set. For instance, if you set `X-Container-Meta-Web-Error` to `error.html`, 401 errors will display the page `401error.html`. Similarly, 404 errors will display `404error.html`. You must have both of these pages created in your container when you set the `X-Container-Meta-Web-Error` metadata, or your site will display generic error pages.

You only have to set the `X-Container-Meta-Web-Error` metadata once for your entire static website.

#### 4.16.14.1.6 Set error pages for static website request

```
$ swift post -m 'web-error:error.html' container
```

Any 2`nn` response indicates success.

## 4.17 Create and manage stacks

The Orchestration service enables you to orchestrate multiple composite cloud applications. This service supports use of both the Amazon Web Services (AWS) CloudFormation template format through both a Query API that is compatible with CloudFormation and the native OpenStack *Heat Orchestration Template (HOT)* format through a REST API.

These flexible template languages enable application developers to describe and automate the deployment of infrastructure, services, and applications. The templates enable creation of most OpenStack resource types, such as instances, floating IP addresses, volumes, security groups, and users. The resources, once created, are referred to as stacks.

The template languages are described in the Template Guide (https://docs.openstack.org/developer/heat/template_guide/index.html) in the Heat developer documentation (https://docs.openstack.org/developer/heat/).

### 4.17.1 Create a stack from an example template file

- To create a stack, or template, from an example template file (https://git.openstack.org/cgit/openstack/heat-templates), run the following command:

  ```
  $ openstack stack create --template server_console.yaml \
    --parameter "image=cirros" MYSTACK
  ```

The `--parameter` values that you specify depend on the parameters that are defined in the template. If a website hosts the template file, you can also specify the URL with the `--template` parameter.

The command returns the following output:

```
+---------------------+------------------------------------------------------------------+
| Field               | Value                                                            |
+---------------------+------------------------------------------------------------------+
| id                  | 70b9feca-8f99-418e-b2f1-cc38d61b3ffb                             |
| stack_name          | MYSTACK                                                          |
| description         | The heat template is used to demo the 'console_urls' attribute |
|                     | of OS::Nova::Server.                                             |
|                     |                                                                  |
| creation_time       | 2016-06-08T09:54:15                                              |
| updated_time        | None                                                             |
| stack_status        | CREATE_IN_PROGRESS                                               |
| stack_status_reason |                                                                  |
+---------------------+------------------------------------------------------------------+
```

- You can also use the `--dry-run` option with the **`openstack stack create`** command to validate a template file without creating a stack from it.
  If validation fails, the response returns an error message.

## 4.17.2 Get information about stacks

To explore the state and history of a particular stack, you can run a number of commands.

- To see which stacks are visible to the current user, run the following command:

```
$ openstack stack list
+--------------------------------------+------------+-----------------
+---------------------+--------------+
| ID                                   | Stack Name | Stack Status    | Creation Time
   | Updated Time |
+--------------------------------------+------------+-----------------
+---------------------+--------------+
| 70b9feca-8f99-418e-b2f1-cc38d61b3ffb | MYSTACK    | CREATE_COMPLETE |
 2016-06-08T09:54:15 | None         |
+--------------------------------------+------------+-----------------
+---------------------+--------------+
```

- To show the details of a stack, run the following command:

```
$ openstack stack show MYSTACK
```

- A stack consists of a collection of resources. To list the resources and their status, run the following command:

```
$ openstack stack resource list MYSTACK
+---------------+--------------------------------------+------------------
+-----------------+---------------------+
| resource_name | physical_resource_id                 | resource_type    |
 resource_status | updated_time        |
+---------------+--------------------------------------+------------------
+-----------------+---------------------+
| server        | 1b3a7c13-42be-4999-a2a1-8fbefd00062b | OS::Nova::Server |
 CREATE_COMPLETE | 2016-06-08T09:54:15 |
+---------------+--------------------------------------+------------------
+-----------------+---------------------+
```

- To show the details for a specific resource in a stack, run the following command:

```
$ openstack stack resource show MYSTACK server
```

- Some resources have associated metadata which can change throughout the lifecycle of a resource. Show the metadata by running the following command:

```
$ openstack stack resource metadata MYSTACK server
```

- A series of events is generated during the lifecycle of a stack. To display lifecycle events, run the following command:

```
$ openstack stack event list MYSTACK
2016-06-08 09:54:15 [MYSTACK]: CREATE_IN_PROGRESS  Stack CREATE started
2016-06-08 09:54:15 [server]: CREATE_IN_PROGRESS  state changed
2016-06-08 09:54:41 [server]: CREATE_COMPLETE  state changed
2016-06-08 09:54:41 [MYSTACK]: CREATE_COMPLETE  Stack CREATE completed successfully
```

- To show the details for a particular event, run the following command:

```
$ openstack stack event show MYSTACK server EVENT
```

### 4.17.3 Update a stack

To update an existing stack from a modified template file, run a command like the following command:

```
$ openstack stack update --template server_console.yaml \
  --parameter "image=ubuntu" MYSTACK
```

```
+--------------------+----------------------------------------------------------------+
| Field              | Value                                                          |
+--------------------+----------------------------------------------------------------+
| id                 | 267a459a-a8cd-4d3e-b5a1-8c08e945764f                           |
| stack_name         | mystack                                                        |
| description        | The heat template is used to demo the 'console_urls' attribute |
|                    | of OS::Nova::Server.                                           |
|                    |                                                                |
| creation_time      | 2016-06-08T09:54:15                                            |
| updated_time       | 2016-06-08T10:41:18                                            |
| stack_status       | UPDATE_IN_PROGRESS                                             |
| stack_status_reason | Stack UPDATE started                                          |
+--------------------+----------------------------------------------------------------+
```

Some resources are updated in-place, while others are replaced with new resources.

## 4.18 Measure cloud resources

Telemetry measures cloud resources in OpenStack. It collects data related to billing. Currently, this metering service is available through only the **`ceilometer`** command-line client.

To model data, Telemetry uses the following abstractions:

### Meter

Measures a specific aspect of resource usage, such as the existence of a running instance, or ongoing performance, such as the CPU utilization for an instance. Meters exist for each type of resource. For example, a separate `cpu_util` meter exists for each instance. The lifecycle of a meter is decoupled from the existence of its related resource. The meter persists after the resource goes away.
A meter has the following attributes:

- String name
- A unit of measurement
- A type, which indicates whether values increase monotonically (cumulative), are interpreted as a change from the previous value (delta), or are stand-alone and relate only to the current duration (gauge)

### Sample

An individual data point that is associated with a specific meter. A sample has the same attributes as the associated meter, with the addition of time stamp and value attributes. The value attribute is also known as the sample `volume`.

**Statistic**

A set of data point aggregates over a time duration. (In contrast, a sample represents a single data point.) The Telemetry service employs the following aggregation functions:

- **count**. The number of samples in each period.
- **max**. The maximum number of sample volumes in each period.
- **min**. The minimum number of sample volumes in each period.
- **avg**. The average of sample volumes over each period.
- **sum**. The sum of sample volumes over each period.

**Alarm**

A set of rules that define a monitor and a current state, with edge-triggered actions associated with target states. Alarms provide user-oriented Monitoring-as-a-Service and a general purpose utility for OpenStack. Orchestration auto scaling is a typical use case. Alarms follow a tristate model of `ok`, `alarm`, and `insufficient data`. For conventional threshold-oriented alarms, a static threshold value and comparison operator govern state transitions. The comparison operator compares a selected meter statistic against an evaluation window of configurable length into the recent past.

This example uses the **`openstack`** client to create an auto-scaling stack and the **`ceilometer`** client to measure resources.

1. Create an auto-scaling stack by running the following command. The `-f` option specifies the name of the stack template file, and the `-P` option specifies the `KeyName` parameter as `heat_key`:

```
$ openstack stack create --template cfn/F17/AutoScalingCeilometer.yaml \
  --parameter "KeyName=heat_key" mystack
```

2. List the heat resources that were created:

```
$ openstack stack resource list mystack
+---------------+--------------------------------------+-----------------
+-----------------+---------------------+
| resource_name | physical_resource_id                 | resource_type    |
 resource_status | updated_time         |
+---------------+--------------------------------------+-----------------
+-----------------+---------------------+
| server        | 1b3a7c13-42be-4999-a2a1-8fbefd00062b | OS::Nova::Server |
 CREATE_COMPLETE | 2013-10-02T05:53:41Z |
```

```
| ...             | ...                                    | ...                | ...
   | ...                 |
+---------------+--------------------------------------+------------------
+-----------------+--------------------+
```

3. List the alarms that are set:

```
$ ceilometer alarm-list
+--------------------------------------+------------------------------
+------------------+---------+-----------+--------------------------------+
| Alarm ID                             | Name                          | State
 | Enabled | Continuous | Alarm condition                  |
+--------------------------------------+------------------------------
+------------------+---------+-----------+--------------------------------+
| 4f896b40-0859-460b-9c6a-b0d329814496 | as-CPUAlarmLow-i6qqgkf2fubs   | insufficient data
 | True    | False      | cpu_util &lt; 15.0 during 1x 60s |
| 75d8ecf7-afc5-4bdc-95ff-19ed9ba22920 | as-CPUAlarmHigh-sf4muyfruy5m | insufficient data
 | True    | False      | cpu_util &gt; 50.0 during 1x 60s |
+--------------------------------------+------------------------------
+------------------+---------+-----------+--------------------------------+
```

4. List the meters that are set:

```
$ ceilometer meter-list
+-------------+------------+---------+--------------------------------------
+----------------------------------+----------------------------------+
| Name          | Type        | Unit      | Resource ID                            | User ID
                       | Project ID                         |
+-------------+------------+---------+--------------------------------------
+----------------------------------+----------------------------------+
| cpu           | cumulative | ns        | 3965b41b-81b0-4386-bea5-6ec37c8841c1 |
 d1a2996d3b1f4e0e8645ba9650308011 | bf03bf32e3884d489004ac995ff7a61c |
| cpu           | cumulative | ns        | 62520a83-73c7-4084-be54-275fe770ef2c |
 d1a2996d3b1f4e0e8645ba9650308011 | bf03bf32e3884d489004ac995ff7a61c |
| cpu_util      | gauge       | %         | 3965b41b-81b0-4386-bea5-6ec37c8841c1 |
 d1a2996d3b1f4e0e8645ba9650308011 | bf03bf32e3884d489004ac995ff7a61c |
+-------------+------------+---------+--------------------------------------
+----------------------------------+----------------------------------+
```

5. List samples:

```
$ ceilometer sample-list -m cpu_util
+--------------------------------------+----------+-------+---------------+------
+---------------------+
| Resource ID                          | Name     | Type  | Volume        | Unit |
 Timestamp            |
+--------------------------------------+----------+-------+---------------+------
+---------------------+
```

```
| 3965b41b-81b0-4386-bea5-6ec37c8841c1 | cpu_util | gauge | 3.98333333333 | %     |
 2013-10-02T10:50:12 |
+--------------------------------------+----------+-------+---------------+------
+---------------------+
```

6. View statistics:

```
$ ceilometer statistics -m cpu_util
+--------+---------------------+---------------------+-------+--------------
+---------------+---------------+---------------+----------+--------------------
+---------------------+
| Period | Period Start        | Period End          | Count | Min           | Max
    | Sum           | Avg           | Duration | Duration Start      | Duration End
  |
+--------+---------------------+---------------------+-------+--------------
+---------------+---------------+---------------+----------+--------------------
+---------------------+
| 0      | 2013-10-02T10:50:12 | 2013-10-02T10:50:12 | 1     | 3.98333333333 |
 3.98333333333 | 3.98333333333 | 3.98333333333 | 0.0      | 2013-10-02T10:50:12 |
 2013-10-02T10:50:12 |
+--------+---------------------+---------------------+-------+--------------
+---------------+---------------+---------------+----------+--------------------
+---------------------+
```

## 4.19 Create and manage databases

The Database service provides scalable and reliable cloud provisioning functionality for both relational and non-relational database engines. Users can quickly and easily use database features without the burden of handling complex administrative tasks.

### 4.19.1 Create and access a database

Assume that you have installed the Database service and populated your data store with images for the type and versions of databases that you want, and that you can create and access a database.

This example shows you how to create and access a MySQL 5.5 database.

#### 4.19.1.1 Create and access a database

1. **Determine which flavor to use for your database**

When you create a database instance, you must specify a nova flavor. The flavor indicates various characteristics of the instance, such as RAM and root volume size. You will need to create or obtain new nova flavors that work for databases.

The first step is to list flavors by using the `openstack flavor list` command.

```
$ openstack flavor list
```

Now take a look at the minimum requirements for various database instances:

| Database | RAM (MB) | Disk (GB) | VCPUs |
|---|---|---|---|
| MySQL | 512 | 5 | 1 |
| Cassandra | 2048 | 5 | 1 |
| MongoDB | 1024 | 5 | 1 |
| Redis | 512 | 5 | 1 |

- If you have a custom flavor that meets the needs of the database that you want to create, proceed to *Step 2* and use that flavor.
- If your environment does not have a suitable flavor, an administrative user must create a custom flavor by using the `openstack flavor create` command.

**MySQL example.** This example creates a flavor that you can use with a MySQL database. This example has the following attributes:

- Flavor name: `mysql_minimum`
- Flavor ID: You must use an ID that is not already in use. In this example, IDs 1 through 5 are in use, so use ID `6`.
- RAM: `512`
- Root volume size in GB: `5`
- Virtual CPUs: `1`

```
$ openstack flavor create mysql-minimum --id 6 --ram 512 --disk 5 --vcpus 1
+---------------------------+--------------+
| Field                     | Value        |
```

```
+----------------------------+---------------+
| OS-FLV-DISABLED:disabled   | False         |
| OS-FLV-EXT-DATA:ephemeral  | 0             |
| disk                       | 5             |
| id                         | 6             |
| name                       | mysql-minimum |
| os-flavor-access:is_public | True          |
| properties                 |               |
| ram                        | 512           |
| rxtx_factor                | 1.0           |
| swap                       |               |
| vcpus                      | 1             |
+----------------------------+---------------+
```

2. **Create a database instance**

   This example creates a database instance with the following characteristics:

   - Name of the instance: `mysql_instance_1`
   - Database flavor: `6`

   In addition, this command specifies these options for the instance:

   - A volume size of `5` (5 GB).
   - The `myDB` database.
   - The database is based on the `mysql` data store and the `mysql-5.5` datastore_version.
   - The `userA` user with the `password` password.

```
$ trove create mysql_instance_1 6 --size 5 --databases myDB \
    --users userA:password --datastore_version mysql-5.5 \
    --datastore mysql
+-------------------
+-------------------------------------------------------------------------------------
t-----------------------------------------------------------------------------------------------------
+
|      Property      |
                                  Value
                                                |
+-------------------
+-----------------------------------------------------------------------------------------------------
+
|      created       |
                           2014-05-29T21:26:21
                                                |
```

```
|     datastore     |
        {u'version': u'mysql-5.5', u'type': u'mysql'}
                                                |
| datastore_version |
                            mysql-5.5
                                                |
|       flavor      | {u'id': u'6', u'links': [{u'href': u'https://controller:8779/
v1.0/46d0bc4fc32e4b9e8520f8fc62199f58/flavors/6', u'rel': u'self'}, {u'href': u'https://
controller:8779/flavors/6', u'rel': u'bookmark'}]} |
|         id        |
              5599dad6-731e-44df-bb60-488da3da9cfe
                                                |
|        name       |
                         mysql_instance_1
                                                |
|       status      |
                              BUILD
                                                |
|      updated      |
                       2014-05-29T21:26:21
                                                |
|       volume      |
                           {u'size': 5}
                                                |
+-------------------
+---------------------------------------------------------------------------------------
+
```

3. **Get the IP address of the database instance**

   First, use the **`trove list`** command to list all instances and their IDs:

```
$ trove list
+--------------------------------------+------------------+-----------
+-------------------+--------+-----------+------+
|                  id                  |       name       | datastore | datastore_version
 | status | flavor_id | size |
+--------------------------------------+------------------+-----------
+-------------------+--------+-----------+------+
| 5599dad6-731e-44df-bb60-488da3da9cfe | mysql_instance_1 |   mysql   |     mysql-5.5
 | BUILD  |     6     |  5   |
+--------------------------------------+------------------+-----------
+-------------------+--------+-----------+------+
```

   This command returns the instance ID of your new instance.

   You can now pass in the instance ID with the **`trove show`** command to get the IP address of the instance. In this example, replace `INSTANCE_ID` with `5599dad6-731e-44df-bb60-488da3da9cfe`.

```
$ trove show INSTANCE_ID

+-------------------+-----------------------------------+
|      Property     |               Value               |
+-------------------+-----------------------------------+
|      created      |        2014-05-29T21:26:21        |
|     datastore     |               mysql               |
| datastore_version |             mysql-5.5             |
|       flavor      |                 6                 |
|         id        | 5599dad6-731e-44df-bb60-488da3da9cfe |
|         ip        |            172.16.200.2           |
|        name       |          mysql_instance_1         |
|       status      |               BUILD               |
|      updated      |        2014-05-29T21:26:54        |
|       volume      |                 5                 |
+-------------------+-----------------------------------+
```

This command returns the IP address of the database instance.

4. **Access the new database**

   You can now access the new database you just created (myDB) by using typical database access commands. In this MySQL example, replace `IP_ADDRESS` with `172.16.200.2`.

```
$ mysql -u userA -p password -h IP_ADDRESS myDB
```

## 4.19.2 Backup and restore a database

You can use Database services to backup a database and store the backup artifact in the Object Storage service. Later on, if the original database is damaged, you can use the backup artifact to restore the database. The restore process creates a database instance.

This example shows you how to back up and restore a MySQL database.

1. **Backup the database instance**

   As background, assume that you have created a database instance with the following characteristics:

   - Name of the database instance: `guest1`
   - Flavor ID: `10`
   - Root volume size: `2`

- Databases: `db1` and `db2`
- Users: The `user1` user with the `password` password

First, get the ID of the `guest1` database instance by using the **`trove list`** command:

```
$ trove list

+--------------------------------------+--------+-----------+-------------------+--------
+-----------+------+
|                  id                  |  name  | datastore | datastore_version | status
 | flavor_id | size |
+--------------------------------------+--------+-----------+-------------------+--------
+-----------+------+
| 97b4b853-80f6-414f-ba6f-c6f455a79ae6 | guest1 |   mysql   |     mysql-5.5     | ACTIVE
 |     10    |  2   |
+--------------------------------------+--------+-----------+-------------------+--------
+-----------+------+
```

Back up the database instance by using the **`trove backup-create`** command. In this example, the backup is called `backup1`. In this example, replace `INSTANCE_ID` with `97b4b853-80f6-414f-ba6f-c6f455a79ae6`:

## Note

This command syntax pertains only to python-troveclient version 1.0.6 and later. Earlier versions require you to pass in the backup name as the first argument.

```
$ trove backup-create INSTANCE_ID backup1

+-------------+--------------------------------------+
|   Property  |                Value                 |
+-------------+--------------------------------------+
|   created   |         2014-03-18T17:09:07          |
| description |                 None                 |
|      id     | 8af30763-61fd-4aab-8fe8-57d528911138 |
| instance_id | 97b4b853-80f6-414f-ba6f-c6f455a79ae6 |
| locationRef |                 None                 |
|     name    |               backup1                |
|  parent_id  |                 None                 |
|     size    |                 None                 |
|    status   |                 NEW                  |
|   updated   |         2014-03-18T17:09:07          |
```

```
+-------------+-------------------------------------+
```

Note that the command returns both the ID of the original instance (`instance_id`) and the ID of the backup artifact (`id`).

Later on, use the **`trove backup-list`** command to get this information:

```
$ trove backup-list
+--------------------------------------+--------------------------------------+---------
+-----------+----------+--------------------+
|                  id                  |             instance_id              |  name   |
   status   | parent_id |       updated        |
+--------------------------------------+--------------------------------------+---------
+-----------+----------+--------------------+
| 8af30763-61fd-4aab-8fe8-57d528911138 | 97b4b853-80f6-414f-ba6f-c6f455a79ae6 | backup1 |
 COMPLETED |    None   | 2014-03-18T17:09:11 |
+--------------------------------------+--------------------------------------+---------
+-----------+----------+--------------------+
```

You can get additional information about the backup by using the **`trove backup-show`** command and passing in the `BACKUP_ID`, which is `8af30763-61fd-4aab-8fe8-57d528911138`.

```
$ trove backup-show BACKUP_ID

+-------------+---------------------------------------------------+
|   Property  |                     Value                         |
+-------------+---------------------------------------------------+
|   created   |              2014-03-18T17:09:07                  |
| description |                   None                            |
|      id     |                  8af...138                        |
| instance_id |                  97b...ae6                        |
| locationRef | http://10.0.0.1:.../.../8af...138.xbstream.gz.enc |
|     name    |                   backup1                         |
|  parent_id  |                   None                            |
|     size    |                   0.17                            |
|    status   |                 COMPLETED                         |
|   updated   |              2014-03-18T17:09:11                  |
+-------------+---------------------------------------------------+
```

2. **Restore a database instance**

   Now assume that your `guest1` database instance is damaged and you need to restore it. In this example, you use the **`trove create`** command to create a new database instance called `guest2`.

- You specify that the new `guest2` instance has the same flavor (`10`) and the same root volume size (`2`) as the original `guest1` instance.
- You use the `--backup` argument to indicate that this new instance is based on the backup artifact identified by `BACKUP_ID`. In this example, replace `BACKUP_ID` with `8af30763-61fd-4aab-8fe8-57d528911138`.

```
$ trove create guest2 10 --size 2 --backup BACKUP_ID

+-----------------+-------------------------------------------+
|    Property     |                   Value                   |
+-----------------+-------------------------------------------+
|     created     |           2014-03-18T17:12:03             |
|    datastore    | {u'version': u'mysql-5.5', u'type': u'mysql'}|
|datastore_version |                 mysql-5.5                 |
|     flavor      | {u'id': u'10', u'links': [{u'href': ...]}  |
|       id        |  ac7a2b35-a9b4-4ff6-beac-a1bcee86d04b     |
|      name       |                  guest2                   |
|     status      |                   BUILD                   |
|     updated     |           2014-03-18T17:12:03             |
|     volume      |               {u'size': 2}                |
+-----------------+-------------------------------------------+
```

3. **Verify backup**

Now check that the new `guest2` instance has the same characteristics as the original `guest1` instance.

Start by getting the ID of the new `guest2` instance.

```
$ trove list

+-----------+--------+-----------+-------------------+--------+-----------+------+
|     id    |  name  | datastore | datastore_version | status | flavor_id | size |
+-----------+--------+-----------+-------------------+--------+-----------+------+
| 97b...ae6 | guest1 |   mysql   |     mysql-5.5     | ACTIVE |     10    |  2   |
| ac7...04b | guest2 |   mysql   |     mysql-5.5     | ACTIVE |     10    |  2   |
+-----------+--------+-----------+-------------------+--------+-----------+------+
```

Use the **`trove show`** command to display information about the new guest2 instance. Pass in guest2's `INSTANCE_ID`, which is `ac7a2b35-a9b4-4ff6-beac-a1bcee86d04b`.

```
$ trove show INSTANCE_ID

+-------------------+--------------------------------------+
```

```
|      Property      |                Value                 |
+--------------------+--------------------------------------+
|      created       |         2014-03-18T17:12:03          |
|     datastore      |                mysql                 |
| datastore_version  |              mysql-5.5               |
|       flavor       |                  10                  |
|         id         | ac7a2b35-a9b4-4ff6-beac-a1bcee86d04b |
|         ip         |               10.0.0.3               |
|        name        |                guest2                |
|       status       |                ACTIVE                |
|      updated       |         2014-03-18T17:12:06          |
|       volume       |                  2                   |
|    volume_used     |                 0.18                 |
+--------------------+--------------------------------------+
```

Note that the data store, flavor ID, and volume size have the same values as in the original `guest1` instance.

Use the **`trove database-list`** command to check that the original databases (`db1` and `db2`) are present on the restored instance.

```
$ trove database-list INSTANCE_ID

+--------------------+
|        name        |
+--------------------+
|        db1         |
|        db2         |
| performance_schema |
|        test        |
+--------------------+
```

Use the **`trove user-list`** command to check that the original user (`user1`) is present on the restored instance.

```
$ trove user-list INSTANCE_ID

+--------+------+-----------+
|  name  | host | databases |
+--------+------+-----------+
| user1  |  %   |  db1, db2 |
+--------+------+-----------+
```

4. **Notify users**

Tell the users who were accessing the now-disabled `guest1` database instance that they can now access `guest2`. Provide them with `guest2`'s name, IP address, and any other information they might need. (You can get this information by using the **`trove show`** command.)

5. **Clean up**
   At this point, you might want to delete the disabled `guest1` instance, by using the **`trove delete`** command.

```
$ trove delete INSTANCE_ID
```

### 4.19.3 Use incremental backups

Incremental backups let you chain together a series of backups. You start with a regular backup. Then, when you want to create a subsequent incremental backup, you specify the parent backup.

Restoring a database instance from an incremental backup is the same as creating a database instance from a regular backup—the Database service handles the complexities of applying the chain of incremental backups.

This example shows you how to use incremental backups with a MySQL database.

**Assumptions.** Assume that you have created a regular backup for the following database instance:

- Instance name: `guest1`
- ID of the instance (`INSTANCE_ID`): `792a6a56-278f-4a01-9997-d997fa126370`
- ID of the regular backup artifact (`BACKUP_ID`): `6dc3a9b7-1f3e-4954-8582-3f2e4942cddd`

#### 4.19.3.1 Create and use incremental backups

1. **Create your first incremental backup**

Use the **trove backup-create** command and specify:

- The INSTANCE_ID of the database instance you are doing the incremental backup for (in this example, 792a6a56-278f-4a01-9997-d997fa126370)
- The name of the incremental backup you are creating: backup1.1
- The BACKUP_ID of the parent backup. In this case, the parent is the regular backup, with an ID of 6dc3a9b7-1f3e-4954-8582-3f2e4942cddd

```
$ trove backup-create INSTANCE_ID backup1.1  --parent BACKUP_ID

+-------------+--------------------------------------+
|  Property   |                Value                 |
+-------------+--------------------------------------+
|   created   |         2014-03-19T14:09:13          |
| description |                 None                 |
|     id      | 1d474981-a006-4f62-b25f-43d7b8a7097e |
| instance_id | 792a6a56-278f-4a01-9997-d997fa126370 |
| locationRef |                 None                 |
|    name     |              backup1.1               |
|  parent_id  | 6dc3a9b7-1f3e-4954-8582-3f2e4942cddd |
|    size     |                 None                 |
|   status    |                 NEW                  |
|   updated   |         2014-03-19T14:09:13          |
+-------------+--------------------------------------+
```

Note that this command returns both the ID of the database instance you are incrementally backing up (instance_id) and a new ID for the new incremental backup artifact you just created (id).

2. **Create your second incremental backup**
The name of your second incremental backup is backup1.2. This time, when you specify the parent, pass in the ID of the incremental backup you just created in the previous step (backup1.1). In this example, it is 1d474981-a006-4f62-b25f-43d7b8a7097e.

```
$ trove backup-create INSTANCE_ID  backup1.2  --parent BACKUP_ID

+-------------+--------------------------------------+
|  Property   |                Value                 |
+-------------+--------------------------------------+
|   created   |         2014-03-19T14:09:13          |
| description |                 None                 |
|     id      | bb84a240-668e-49b5-861e-6a98b67e7a1f |
```

```
| instance_id | 792a6a56-278f-4a01-9997-d997fa126370 |
| locationRef |                 None                 |
|     name    |              backup1.2               |
|  parent_id  | 1d474981-a006-4f62-b25f-43d7b8a7097e |
|     size    |                 None                 |
|    status   |                 NEW                  |
|   updated   |         2014-03-19T14:09:13          |
+-------------+--------------------------------------+
```

3. **Restore using incremental backups**

   Now assume that your `guest1` database instance is damaged and you need to restore it from your incremental backups. In this example, you use the **`trove create`** command to create a new database instance called `guest2`.

   To incorporate your incremental backups, you simply use the `--backup`` parameter to pass in the `BACKUP_ID` of your most recent incremental backup. The Database service handles the complexities of applying the chain of all previous incremental backups.

```
$ trove create guest2 10 --size 1 --backup BACKUP_ID

+-------------------+-----------------------------------------------------------+
|      Property     |                           Value                           |
+-------------------+-----------------------------------------------------------+
|      created      |                    2014-03-19T14:10:56                    |
|     datastore     |       {u'version': u'mysql-5.5', u'type': u'mysql'}       |
| datastore_version |                         mysql-5.5                         |
|       flavor      | {u'id': u'10', u'links':                                  |
|                   | [{u'href': u'https://10.125.1.135:8779/v1.0/              |
|                   |  626734041baa4254ae316de52a20b390/flavors/10', u'rel':    |
|                   |  u'self'}, {u'href': u'https://10.125.1.135:8779/         |
|                   |  flavors/10', u'rel': u'bookmark'}]}                      |
|         id        |            a3680953-eea9-4cf2-918b-5b8e49d7e1b3           |
|        name       |                           guest2                          |
|       status      |                           BUILD                           |
|      updated      |                    2014-03-19T14:10:56                    |
|       volume      |                       {u'size': 1}                        |
+-------------------+-----------------------------------------------------------+
```

### 4.19.4 Manage database configuration

You can manage database configuration tasks by using configuration groups. Configuration groups let you set configuration options, in bulk, on one or more databases.

This example assumes you have created a MySQL database and shows you how to use a configuration group to configure it. Although this example sets just one option on one database, you can use these same procedures to set multiple options on multiple database instances throughout your environment. This can provide significant time savings in managing your cloud.

#### 4.19.4.1 Bulk-configure a database or databases

1. **List available options**
   First, determine which configuration options you can set. Different data store versions have different configuration options.
   List the names and IDs of all available versions of the `mysql` data store:

```
$ trove datastore-version-list mysql

+--------------------------------------+-----------+
|                  id                  |    name   |
+--------------------------------------+-----------+
| eeb574ce-f49a-48b6-820d-b2959fcd38bb | mysql-5.5 |
+--------------------------------------+-----------+
```

   Pass in the data store version ID with the **`trove configuration-parameter-list`** command to get the available options:

```
$ trove configuration-parameter-list DATASTORE_VERSION_ID

+--------------------------------+---------+---------+----------------------
+------------------+
|              name              |   type  |   min   |         max          |
 restart_required |
+--------------------------------+---------+---------+----------------------
+------------------+
|    auto_increment_increment    | integer |    1    |        65535         |      False
      |
|     auto_increment_offset      | integer |    1    |        65535         |      False
      |
|           autocommit           | integer |    0    |          1           |      False
      |
|    bulk_insert_buffer_size     | integer |    0    | 18446744073709547520 |      False
      |
|      character_set_client      |  string |         |                      |      False
      |
|    character_set_connection    |  string |         |                      |      False
      |
```

```
|      character_set_database      | string |         |                      |     False
      |
|     character_set_filesystem     | string |         |                      |     False
      |
|      character_set_results       | string |         |                      |     False
      |
|       character_set_server       | string |         |                      |     False
      |
|       collation_connection       | string |         |                      |     False
      |
|        collation_database        | string |         |                      |     False
      |
|         collation_server         | string |         |                      |     False
      |
|         connect_timeout          | integer |    1    |        65535         |     False
      |
|         expire_logs_days         | integer |    1    |        65535         |     False
      |
|     innodb_buffer_pool_size      | integer |    0    |     68719476736      |      True
      |
|      innodb_file_per_table       | integer |    0    |          1           |      True
      |
| innodb_flush_log_at_trx_commit | integer |    0    |          2           |     False
      |
|      innodb_log_buffer_size      | integer | 1048576 |      4294967296      |      True
      |
|        innodb_open_files         | integer |   10    |      4294967296      |      True
      |
|    innodb_thread_concurrency     | integer |    0    |         1000         |     False
      |
|       interactive_timeout        | integer |    1    |        65535         |     False
      |
|         join_buffer_size         | integer |    0    |      4294967296      |     False
      |
|         key_buffer_size          | integer |    0    |      4294967296      |     False
      |
|           local_infile           | integer |    0    |          1           |     False
      |
|        max_allowed_packet        | integer |  1024   |      1073741824      |     False
      |
|        max_connect_errors        | integer |    1    | 18446744073709547520 |     False
      |
|         max_connections          | integer |    1    |        65535         |     False
      |
|       max_user_connections       | integer |    1    |        100000        |     False
      |
|      myisam_sort_buffer_size     | integer |    4    | 18446744073709547520 |     False
      |
|            server_id             | integer |    1    |        100000        |      True
      |
```

```
|        sort_buffer_size         | integer |  32768   | 18446744073709547520 |      False
     |
|          sync_binlog            | integer |    0     | 18446744073709547520 |      False
     |
|          wait_timeout           | integer |    1     |       31536000       |      False
     |
+--------------------------------+--------+--------+---------------------
+------------------+
```

In this example, the **`trove configuration-parameter-list`** command returns a list of options that work with MySQL 5.5.

2. **Create a configuration group**

   A configuration group contains a comma-separated list of key-value pairs. Each pair consists of a configuration option and its value.

   You can create a configuration group by using the **`trove configuration-create`** command. The general syntax for this command is:

```
$ trove configuration-create NAME VALUES --datastore DATASTORE_NAME
```

   - *NAME*. The name you want to use for this group.
   - *VALUES*. The list of key-value pairs.
   - *DATASTORE_NAME*. The name of the associated data store.

   Set *VALUES* as a JSON dictionary, for example:

```
{"myFirstKey" : "someString", "mySecondKey" : 1}
```

   This example creates a configuration group called `group1`. `group1` contains just one key and value pair, and this pair sets the `sync_binlog` option to `1`.

```
$ trove configuration-create group1 '{"sync_binlog" : 1}' --datastore mysql

+----------------------+--------------------------------------+
|       Property       |                Value                 |
+----------------------+--------------------------------------+
| datastore_version_id | eeb574ce-f49a-48b6-820d-b2959fcd38bb |
|     description      |                 None                 |
|          id          | 9a9ef3bc-079b-476a-9cbf-85aa64f898a5 |
|         name         |                group1                |
|        values        |          {"sync_binlog": 1}          |
+----------------------+--------------------------------------+
```

3. **Examine your existing configuration**

   Before you use the newly-created configuration group, look at how the `sync_binlog` option is configured on your database. Replace the following sample connection values with values that connect to your database:

```
$ mysql -u user7 -ppassword -h 172.16.200.2 myDB7
 Welcome to the MySQL monitor. Commands end with ; or \g.
 ...
 mysql> show variables like 'sync_binlog';
 +---------------+-------+
 | Variable_name | Value |
 +---------------+-------+
 | sync_binlog   | 0     |
 +---------------+-------+
```

   As you can see, the `sync_binlog` option is currently set to `0` for the `myDB7` database.

4. **Change the database configuration using a configuration group**

   You can change a database's configuration by attaching a configuration group to a database instance. You do this by using the **`trove configuration-attach`** command and passing in the ID of the database instance and the ID of the configuration group.

   Get the ID of the database instance:

```
$ trove list

+-------------+-----------------+-----------+-------------------+--------+-----------
+------+
|     id      |       name      | datastore | datastore_version | status | flavor_id |
 size |
+-------------+-----------------+-----------+-------------------+--------+-----------
+------+
| 26a265dd... | mysql_instance_7 |  mysql    |     mysql-5.5     | ACTIVE |     6     |
 5   |
+-------------+-----------------+-----------+-------------------+--------+-----------
+------+
```

   Get the ID of the configuration group:

```
$ trove configuration-list

+-------------+--------+-------------+---------------------+
|     id      |  name  | description |datastore_version_id |
+-------------+--------+-------------+---------------------+
| 9a9ef3bc... | group1 |     None    |      eeb574ce...    |
+-------------+--------+-------------+---------------------+
```

Attach the configuration group to the database instance:

Note

This command syntax pertains only to python-troveclient version 1.0.6 and later. Earlier versions require you to pass in the configuration group ID as the first argument.

```
$ trove configuration-attach DB_INSTANCE_ID CONFIG_GROUP_ID
```

5. **Re-examine the database configuration**

   Display the `sync_binlog` setting again:

```
mysql> show variables like 'sync_binlog';
+---------------+-------+
| Variable_name | Value |
+---------------+-------+
| sync_binlog   | 1     |
+---------------+-------+
```

   As you can see, the `sync_binlog` option is now set to `1`, as specified in the `group1` configuration group.

**Conclusion.** Using a configuration group to set a single option on a single database is obviously a trivial example. However, configuration groups can provide major efficiencies when you consider that:

- A configuration group can specify a large number of option values.
- You can apply a configuration group to hundreds or thousands of database instances in your environment.

Used in this way, configuration groups let you modify your database cloud configuration, on the fly, on a massive scale.

**Maintenance.** There are also a number of useful maintenance features for working with configuration groups. You can:

- Disassociate a configuration group from a database instance, using the `trove configuration-detach` command.
- Modify a configuration group on the fly, using the `trove configuration-patch` command.
- Find out what instances are using a configuration group, using the `trove configuration-instances` command.
- Delete a configuration group, using the `trove configuration-delete` command. You might want to do this if no instances use a group.

## 4.19.5 Set up database replication

You can create a replica of an existing database instance. When you make subsequent changes to the original instance, the system automatically applies those changes to the replica.

- Replicas are read-only.
- When you create a replica, do not specify the `--users` or `--databases` options.
- You can choose a smaller volume or flavor for a replica than for the original, but the replica's volume must be big enough to hold the data snapshot from the original.

This example shows you how to replicate a MySQL database instance.

### 4.19.5.1 Set up replication

1. **Get the instance ID**

   Get the ID of the original instance you want to replicate:

```
$ trove list
+-----------+-----------+----------+------------------+--------+-----------+------+
|    id     | name      | datastore | datastore_version | status | flavor_id | size |
+-----------+-----------+----------+------------------+--------+-----------+------+
| 97b...ae6 | base_1    |  mysql   |     mysql-5.5     | ACTIVE |    10     |  2   |
```

```
+-----------+-----------+----------+----------------+-------+----------+------+
```

2. **Create the replica**

   Create a new instance that will be a replica of the original instance. You do this by passing in the `--replica_of` option with the **`trove create`** command. This example creates a replica called `replica_1`. `replica_1` is a replica of the original instance, `base_1`:

```
$ trove create replica_1 6 --size=5 --datastore_version mysql-5.5 \
  --datastore mysql --replica_of ID_OF_ORIGINAL_INSTANCE
```

3. **Verify replication status**

   Pass in `replica_1`'s instance ID with the **`trove show`** command to verify that the newly created `replica_1` instance is a replica of the original `base_1`. Note that the `replica_of` property is set to the ID of `base_1`.

```
$ trove show INSTANCE_ID_OF_REPLICA_1
+-------------------+--------------------------------------+
| Property          | Value                                |
+-------------------+--------------------------------------+
| created           | 2014-09-16T11:16:49                  |
| datastore         | mysql                                |
| datastore_version | mysql-5.5                            |
| flavor            | 6                                    |
| id                | 49c6eff6-ef91-4eff-91c0-efbda7e83c38 |
| name              | replica_1                            |
| replica_of        | 97b4b853-80f6-414f-ba6f-c6f455a79ae6 |
| status            | BUILD                                |
| updated           | 2014-09-16T11:16:49                  |
| volume            | 5                                    |
+-------------------+--------------------------------------+
```

   Now pass in `base_1`'s instance ID with the **`trove show`** command to list the replica(s) associated with the original instance. Note that the `replicas` property is set to the ID of `replica_1`. If there are multiple replicas, they appear as a comma-separated list.

```
$ trove show INSTANCE_ID_OF_BASE_1
+-------------------+--------------------------------------+
| Property          | Value                                |
+-------------------+--------------------------------------+
| created           | 2014-09-16T11:04:56                  |
| datastore         | mysql                                |
| datastore_version | mysql-5.5                            |
| flavor            | 6                                    |
| id                | 97b4b853-80f6-414f-ba6f-c6f455a79ae6 |
```

```
| ip               | 172.16.200.2                         |
| name             | base_1                               |
| replicas         | 49c6eff6-ef91-4eff-91c0-efbda7e83c38 |
| status           | ACTIVE                               |
| updated          | 2014-09-16T11:05:06                  |
| volume           | 5                                    |
| volume_used      | 0.11                                 |
+------------------+--------------------------------------+
```

4. **Detach the replica**

   If the original instance goes down, you can detach the replica. The replica becomes a standalone database instance. You can then take the new standalone instance and create a new replica of that instance.

   You detach a replica using the **`trove detach-replica`** command:

   ```
   $ trove detach-replica INSTANCE_ID_OF_REPLICA
   ```

### 4.19.6 Set up database clustering

You can store data across multiple machines by setting up MongoDB sharded clusters.

Each cluster includes:

- One or more *shards*. Each shard consists of a three member replica set (three instances organized as a replica set).
- One or more *query routers*. A query router is the machine that your application actually connects to. This machine is responsible for communicating with the config server to figure out where the requested data is stored. It then accesses and returns the data from the appropriate shard(s).
- One or more *config servers*. Config servers store the metadata that links requested data with the shard that contains it.

This example shows you how to set up a MongoDB sharded cluster.

Note

**Before you begin.** Make sure that:

- The administrative user has registered a MongoDB datastore type and version.
- The administrative user has created an appropriate *Section 4.19.1, "Create and access a database"*.

### 4.19.6.1 Set up clustering

1. **Create a cluster**

   Create a cluster by using the `trove cluster-create` command. This command creates a one-shard cluster. Pass in:

   - The name of the cluster.
   - The name and version of the datastore you want to use.
   - The three instances you want to include in the replication set for the first shard. Specify each instance by using the `--instance` argument and the associated flavor ID and volume size. Use the same flavor ID and volume size for each instance. In this example, flavor `7` is a custom flavor that meets the MongoDB minimum requirements.

```
$ trove cluster-create cluster1 mongodb "2.4" \
  --instance flavor_id=7,volume=2 --instance flavor_id=7,volume=2 \
  --instance flavor_id=7,volume=2
 +-------------------+--------------------------------------+
 | Property          | Value                                |
 +-------------------+--------------------------------------+
 | created           | 2014-08-16T01:46:51                  |
 | datastore         | mongodb                              |
 | datastore_version | 2.4                                  |
 | id                | aa6ef0f5-dbef-48cd-8952-573ad881e717 |
 | name              | cluster1                             |
 | task_description  | Building the initial cluster.        |
 | task_name         | BUILDING                             |
 | updated           | 2014-08-16T01:46:51                  |
 +-------------------+--------------------------------------+
```

2. **Display cluster information**

   Display information about a cluster by using the `trove cluster-show` command. Pass in the ID of the cluster.

   The cluster ID displays when you first create a cluster. (If you need to find it later on, use the `trove cluster-list` command to list the names and IDs of all the clusters in your system.)

```
$ trove cluster-show CLUSTER_ID
 +-------------------+-----------------------------------+
 | Property          | Value                             |
 +-------------------+-----------------------------------+
 | created           | 2014-08-16T01:46:51               |
 | datastore         | mongodb                           |
 | datastore_version | 2.4                               |
 | id                | aa6ef0f5-dbef-48cd-8952-573ad881e717 |
 | ip                | 10.0.0.2                          |
 | name              | cluster1                          |
 | task_description  | No tasks for the cluster.         |
 | task_name         | NONE                              |
 | updated           | 2014-08-16T01:59:33               |
 +-------------------+-----------------------------------+
```

   Note

   **Your application connects to this IP address.** The `trove cluster-show` command displays the IP address of the query router. This is the IP address your application uses to retrieve data from the database.

3. **List cluster instances**

   List the instances in a cluster by using the `trove cluster-instances` command.

```
$ trove cluster-instances CLUSTER_ID
+--------------------------------------+----------------+-----------+------+
| ID                                   | Name           | Flavor ID | Size |
+--------------------------------------+----------------+-----------+------+
| 45532fc4-661c-4030-8ca4-18f02aa2b337 | cluster1-rs1-1 | 7         |    2 |
| 7458a98d-6f89-4dfd-bb61-5cf1dd65c121 | cluster1-rs1-2 | 7         |    2 |
| b37634fb-e33c-4846-8fe8-cf2b2c95e731 | cluster1-rs1-3 | 7         |    2 |
+--------------------------------------+----------------+-----------+------+
```

**Naming conventions for replication sets and instances.** Note that the `Name` column displays an instance name that includes the replication set name. The replication set names and instance names are automatically generated, following these rules:

- **Replication set name.** This name consists of the cluster name, followed by the string -rs*n*, where *n* is 1 for the first replication set you create, 2 for the second replication set, and so on. In this example, the cluster name is `cluster1`, and there is only one replication set, so the replication set name is `cluster1-rs1`.

- **Instance name.** This name consists of the replication set name followed by the string -*n*, where *n* is 1 for the first instance in a replication set, 2 for the second instance, and so on. In this example, the instance names are `cluster1-rs1-1`, `cluster1-rs1-2`, and `cluster1-rs1-3`.

4. **List clusters**

   List all the clusters in your system, using the **`trove cluster-list`** command.

```
$ trove cluster-list
+--------------------------------------+----------+-----------+-------------------
+-----------+
| ID                                   | Name     | Datastore | Datastore Version | Task
 Name |
+--------------------------------------+----------+-----------+-------------------
+-----------+
| aa6ef0f5-dbef-48cd-8952-573ad881e717 | cluster1 | mongodb   | 2.4               | NONE
    |
| b8829c2a-b03a-49d3-a5b1-21ec974223ee | cluster2 | mongodb   | 2.4               |
 BUILDING  |
+--------------------------------------+----------+-----------+-------------------
+-----------+
```

5. **Delete a cluster**

   Delete a cluster, using the **`trove cluster-delete`** command.

```
$ trove cluster-delete CLUSTER_ID
```

#### 4.19.6.1.1 Query routers and config servers

Each cluster includes at least one query router and one config server. Query routers and config servers count against your quota. When you delete a cluster, the system deletes the associated query router(s) and config server(s).

# 5 OpenStack Python SDK

## 5.1 Overview

OpenStack provides four different options for interacting with its APIs from Python, each targeting a slightly different user:

- OpenStack SDK
- shade
- Per-project client libraries
- Direct REST calls via keystoneauth

You should also be familiar with:

- RESTful web services
- HTTP/1.1
- JSON and data serialization formats

### 5.1.1 OpenStack SDK

The OpenStack Python Software Development Kit (SDK) (https://pypi.python.org/pypi/openstacksdk) ↗ is used to write Python automation scripts that create and manage resources in your OpenStack cloud. The SDK implements Python bindings to the OpenStack API, which enables you to perform automation tasks in Python by making calls on Python objects, rather than making REST calls directly.

New users should default to coding against the OpenStack SDK.

### 5.1.2 shade

shade (http://pypi.python.org/pypi/shade) ↗ is an abstraction library focused on hiding implementation differences between OpenStack clouds. While the OpenStack SDK presents a clean object interface to the underlying REST APIs, shade hides them if doing so is advantageous.

If you plan on running the same Python program against many OpenStack clouds, you may want to use shade - but if you need to access any features of a cloud that do not have a cloud-neutral abstraction mapping, you will be unable to do so with shade.

### 5.1.3 Per-project client libraries

Each OpenStack project produces a client library that wraps its own REST API. Unless there is no other choice for some reason, the per-project libraries should be avoided.

### 5.1.4 Direct REST calls via keystoneauth

All of OpenStack's APIs are actually REST APIs. The keystoneauth (https://docs.openstack.org/developer/keystoneauth) ↗ library provides an object that looks very much like a Session (http://docs.python-requests.org/en/master/api/#request-sessions) ↗ object from the Python requests (http://pypi.python.org/pypi/requests) ↗ library that handles all of the authentication for you. If you are more comfortable just dealing with REST or if there is a feature implemented in your cloud that has not seen support in any of the libraries yet, this option is for you.

## 5.2 Installing OpenStack SDK

Each OpenStack project has its own Python library. These libraries are bundled with the command-line clients. For example, the Python bindings for the Compute API are bundled with the python-novaclient package.

For details about how to install the clients, see .

## 5.3 Authenticate

When using the SDK, you must authenticate against an OpenStack endpoint before you can use OpenStack services. Because all projects use Keystone for authentication, the process is the same no matter which service or library you have decided to use. Each library also has more advanced and complicated ways to do things, should those be needed.

There are two basic ways to deal with your cloud config and credentials:

- Environment variables via an openrc.sh file
- clouds.yaml config file

The environment variables have been around the longest and are the form you are most likely to receive from your cloud provider. If you have one and only one cloud account, they are the most convenient way.

`clouds.yaml` is a bit newer and was designed to help folks who have more than one OpenStack cloud that they are using.

## 5.4 Create a Legacy Client Object

All of the legacy client objects can be constructed the same way - the only difference is the first argument to `make_client`. The examples will use `compute` to get a nova client, but neutron can be accessed instead by replacing `compute` with `network`.

To use the legacy `python-novaclient` with a Compute endpoint, instantiate a novaclient.v2.client.Client (https://docs.openstack.org/developer/python-novaclient/ref/v2/client.html) object using `os-client-config`:

```
import os_client_config

nova = os_client_config.make_client(
    'compute',
    auth_url='https://example.com',
    username='example-openstack-user',
    password='example-password',
    project_name='example-project-name',
    region_name='example-region-name')
```

If you desire a specific micro-version of the Nova API, you can pass that as the `version` parameter:

```
import os_client_config

nova = os_client_config.make_client(
    'compute',
    version='2.10',
    auth_url='https://example.com',
    username='example-openstack-user',
```

```
    password='example-password',
    project_name='example-project-name',
    region_name='example-region-name')
```

If you authenticate against an endpoint that uses a custom authentication back end, you must provide the name of the plugin in the `auth_type` parameter.

For instance, the Rackspace public cloud is an OpenStack deployment that has an optional custom authentication back end. While normal keystone password authentication works perfectly well, you may want to use the custom Rackspace keystoneauth API Key plugin found in rackspace-keystoneauth-plugin (https://pypi.python.org/pypi/rackspaceauth) ↗.

```
nova = os_client_config.make_client(
    'compute',
    auth_type='rackspace_apikey',
    auth_url='https://example.com',
    username='example-openstack-user',
    api_key='example-apikey',
    project_name='example-project-name',
    region_name='example-region-name')
```

## 5.5 Manage images

When working with images in the SDK, you will call both `glance` and `nova` methods.

### 5.5.1 List images

To list the available images, call the `glanceclient.v2.images.Controller.list` method:

```
import glanceclient.v2.client as glclient
glance = glclient.Client(...)
images = glance.images.list()
```

The images method returns a Python generator, as shown in the following interaction with the Python interpreter:

```
>>> images = glance.images.list()
>>> images
<generator object list at 0x105e9c2d0>
>>> list(images)
[{u'checksum': u'f8a2eeee2dc65b3d9b6e63678955bd83',
  u'container_format': u'ami',
```

```
  u'created_at': u'2013-10-20T14:28:10Z',
  u'disk_format': u'ami',
  u'file': u'/v2/images/dbc9b2db-51d7-403d-b680-3f576380b00c/file',
  u'id': u'dbc9b2db-51d7-403d-b680-3f576380b00c',
  u'kernel_id': u'c002c82e-2cfa-4952-8461-2095b69c18a6',
  u'min_disk': 0,
  u'min_ram': 0,
  u'name': u'cirros-0.3.2-x86_64-uec',
  u'protected': False,
  u'ramdisk_id': u'4c1c9b4f-3fe9-425a-a1ec-1d8fd90b4db3',
  u'schema': u'/v2/schemas/image',
  u'size': 25165824,
  u'status': u'active',
  u'tags': [],
  u'updated_at': u'2013-10-20T14:28:11Z',
  u'visibility': u'public'},
 {u'checksum': u'69c33642f44ca552ba4bb8b66ad97e85',
  u'container_format': u'ari',
  u'created_at': u'2013-10-20T14:28:09Z',
  u'disk_format': u'ari',
  u'file': u'/v2/images/4c1c9b4f-3fe9-425a-a1ec-1d8fd90b4db3/file',
  u'id': u'4c1c9b4f-3fe9-425a-a1ec-1d8fd90b4db3',
  u'min_disk': 0,
  u'min_ram': 0,
  u'name': u'cirros-0.3.2-x86_64-uec-ramdisk',
  u'protected': False,
  u'schema': u'/v2/schemas/image',
  u'size': 3714968,
  u'status': u'active',
  u'tags': [],
  u'updated_at': u'2013-10-20T14:28:10Z',
  u'visibility': u'public'},
 {u'checksum': u'c352f4e7121c6eae958bc1570324f17e',
  u'container_format': u'aki',
  u'created_at': u'2013-10-20T14:28:08Z',
  u'disk_format': u'aki',
  u'file': u'/v2/images/c002c82e-2cfa-4952-8461-2095b69c18a6/file',
  u'id': u'c002c82e-2cfa-4952-8461-2095b69c18a6',
  u'min_disk': 0,
  u'min_ram': 0,
  u'name': u'cirros-0.3.2-x86_64-uec-kernel',
  u'protected': False,
  u'schema': u'/v2/schemas/image',
  u'size': 4955792,
  u'status': u'active',
  u'tags': [],
  u'updated_at': u'2013-10-20T14:28:09Z',
```

```
  u'visibility': u'public'}]
```

### 5.5.2 Get image by ID

To retrieve an image object from its ID, call the `glanceclient.v2.images.Controller.get` method:

```
import glanceclient.v2.client as glclient
image_id = 'c002c82e-2cfa-4952-8461-2095b69c18a6'
glance = glclient.Client(...)
image = glance.images.get(image_id)
```

### 5.5.3 Get image by name

The Image service Python bindings do not support the retrieval of an image object by name. However, the Compute Python bindings enable you to get an image object by name. To get an image object by name, call the `novaclient.v2.images.ImageManager.find` method:

```
import novaclient.v2.client as nvclient
name = "cirros"
nova = nvclient.Client(...)
image = nova.images.find(name=name)
```

### 5.5.4 Upload an image

To upload an image, call the `glanceclient.v2.images.ImageManager.create` method:

```
import glanceclient.v2.client as glclient
imagefile = "/tmp/myimage.img"
glance = glclient.Client(...)
with open(imagefile) as fimage:
  glance.images.create(name="myimage", is_public=False, disk_format="qcow2",
                       container_format="bare", data=fimage)
```

## 5.6 Assign CORS headers to requests

*Cross-Origin Resource Sharing (CORS)* is a specification that defines how browsers and servers communicate across origins by using HTTP headers, such as those assigned by Object Storage API requests. The Object Storage API supports the following headers:

- Access-Control-Allow-Credentials
- Access-Control-Allow-Methods
- Access-Control-Allow-Origin
- Access-Control-Expose-Headers
- Access-Control-Max-Age
- Access-Control-Request-Headers
- Access-Control-Request-Method
- Origin

You can only assign these headers to objects. For more information, see www.w3.org/TR/access-control/ (http://www.w3.org/TR/access-control/) ↗.

This example assigns the file origin to the `Origin` header, which ensures that the file originated from a reputable source.

```
$ curl -i -X POST -H "Origin: example.com" -H "X-Auth-Token:
48e17715dfce47bb90dc2a336f63493a"
https://storage.example.com/v1/MossoCloudFS_c31366f1-9f1c-40dc-a
b92-6b3f0b5a8c45/ephotos
HTTP/1.1 204 No Content
Content-Length: 0
Content-Type: text/html; charset=UTF-8
Access-Control-Allow-Origin: example.com
Access-Control-Expose-Headers: cache-control, content-language,
content-type, expires, last-modified, pragma, etag, x-timestamp, x-trans-id
X-Trans-Id: tx979bfe26be6649c489ada-0054cba1d9ord1
Date: Fri, 30 Jan 2015 15:23:05 GMT
```

## 5.7 Schedule objects for deletion

To determine whether your Object Storage system supports this feature, see . Alternatively, check with your service provider.

Scheduling an object for deletion is helpful for managing objects that you do not want to permanently store, such as log files, recurring full backups of a dataset, or documents or images that become outdated at a specified time.

To schedule an object for deletion, include one of these headers with the `PUT` or `POST` request on the object:

**X-Delete-At**

A UNIX epoch timestamp, in integer form. For example, `1348691905` represents `Wed, 26 Sept 2012 20:38:25 GMT`. It specifies the time you want the object to expire, no longer be served, and be deleted completely from the object store.

**X-Delete-After**

An integer value which specifies the number of seconds from the time of the request to when you want to delete the object. This header is converted to a `X-Delete-At` header that is set to the sum of the `X-Delete-After` value plus the current time, in seconds.

### Note

Use EpochConverter (http://www.epochconverter.com/) to convert dates to and from epoch timestamps and for batch conversions.

Use the POST method to assign expiration headers to existing objects that you want to expire.

In this example, the `X-Delete-At` header is assigned a UNIX epoch timestamp in integer form for `Mon, 11 Jun 2012 15:38:25 GMT`.

```
$ curl -i publicURL/marktwain/goodbye -X PUT -H "X-Auth-Token: token" \
  -H "X-Delete-At: 1390581073" -H "Content-Length: 14" -H \
  "Content-Type: application/octet-stream"
```

In this example, the `X-Delete-After` header is set to 864000 seconds. The object expires after this time.

```
PUT /<api version>/<account>/<container>/<object> HTTP/1.1
Host: storage.example.com
X-Auth-Token: eaaafd18-0fed-4b3a-81b4-663c99ec1cbb
Content-Type: image/jpeg
X-Delete-After: 864000
```

## 5.8 Configure access and security for instances

When working with images in the SDK, you will call `novaclient` methods.

### 5.8.1 Add a keypair

To generate a keypair, call the novaclient.v1_1.keypairs.KeypairManager.create (http://docs.openstack.org/developer/python-novaclient/api/novaclient.v1_1.keypairs.html#novaclient.v1_1.keypairs.KeypairManager.create) ↗ method:

```
import novaclient.v2.client as nvclient
nova = nvclient.Client(...)
keypair_name = "staging"
keypair = nova.keypairs.create(name=keypair_name)
print keypair.private_key
```

The Python script output looks something like this:

```
-----BEGIN RSA PRIVATE KEY-----
MIIEowIBAAKCAQEA8XkaMqInSPfy0hMfWO+OZRtIgrQAbQkNcaNHmv2GN2G6xZlb\nuBRux5Xk/6SZ
ABaNPm1nRWm/ZDHnxCsFTcAl2LYOQXx3Cl2qKNY4r2di4G48GAkd\n7k5lDP2RgQatUM8npO0CD9PU
...
mmrceYYK08/lQ7JKLmVkdzdQKt77+v1oBBuHiykLfI6h1m77NRDw9r8cV\nzczYeoALifpjTPMkKS8
ECfDCuDn/vc9K1He8CRaJHf8AMLQLM3MN
-----END RSA PRIVATE KEY-----
```

You typically write the private key to a file to use it later. The file must be readable and writeable by only the file owner; otherwise, the SSH client will refuse to read the private key file. The safest way is to create the file with the appropriate permissions, as shown in the following example:

```
import novaclient.v2.client as nvclient
import os
nova = nvclient.Client(...)
keypair_name = "staging"
private_key_filename = "/home/alice/id-staging"
keypair = nova.keypairs.create(name=keypair_name)

# Create a file for writing that can only be read and written by
owner
fp = os.open(private_key_filename, os.O_WRONLY | os.O_CREAT, 0o600)
with os.fdopen(fp, 'w') as f:
    f.write(keypair.private_key)
```

### 5.8.2 Import a keypair

If you have already generated a keypair with the public key located at `~/.ssh/id_rsa.pub`, pass the contents of the file to the novaclient.v1_1.keypairs.KeypairManager.create (http://docs.openstack.org/developer/python-novaclient/api/novaclient.v1_1.keypairs.html#novaclient.v1_1.keypairs.KeypairManager.create) method to import the public key to Compute:

```
import novaclient.v2.client as nvclient
import os.path
with open(os.path.expanduser('~/.ssh/id_rsa.pub')) as f:
    public_key = f.read()
nova = nvclient.Client(...)
nova.keypairs.create('mykey', public_key)
```

### 5.8.3 List keypairs

To list keypairs, call the novaclient.v1_1.keypairs.KeypairManager.list (https://docs.openstack.org/developer/python-novaclient/api/novaclient.v1_1.keypairs.html#novaclient.v1_1.keypairs.KeypairManager.list) method:

```
import novaclient.v2.client as nvclient
nova = nvclient.Client(...)
keypairs = nova.keypairs.list()
```

### 5.8.4 Create and manage security groups

To list security groups for the current project, call the novaclient.v_1.security_groups.SecurityGroupManager.list (https://docs.openstack.org/developer/python-novaclient/api/novaclient.v1_1.security_groups.html#novaclient.v1_1.security_groups.SecurityGroupManager.list) method:

```
import novaclient.v2.client as nvclient
nova = nvclient.Client(...)
security_groups = nova.security_groups.list()
```

To create a security group with a specified name and description, call the novaclient.v_1.security_groups.SecurityGroupManager.create (https://docs.openstack.org/developer/python-novaclient/api/novaclient.v1_1.security_groups.html#novaclient.v1_1.security_groups.SecurityGroupManager.create) ↗ method:

```
import novaclient.v2.client as nvclient
nova = nvclient.Client(...)
nova.security_groups.create(name="web", description="Web servers")
```

To delete a security group, call the novaclient.v_1.security_groups.SecurityGroupManager.delete (https://docs.openstack.org/developer/python-novaclient/api/novaclient.v1_1.security_groups.html#novaclient.v1_1.security_groups.SecurityGroupManager.delete) ↗ method, passing either a novaclient.v1_1.security_groups.SecurityGroup (https://docs.openstack.org/developer/python-novaclient/api/novaclient.v1_1.security_groups.html#novaclient.v1_1.security_groups.SecurityGroup) ↗ object or group ID as an argument:

```
import novaclient.v2.client as nvclient
nova = nvclient.Client(...)
group = nova.security_groups.find(name="web")
nova.security_groups.delete(group)
# The following lines would also delete the group:
# nova.security_groups.delete(group.id)
# group.delete()
```

### 5.8.5 Create and manage security group rules

Access the security group rules from the `rules` attribute of a novaclient.v1_1.security_groups.SecurityGroup (http://docs.openstack.org/developer/python-novaclient/api/novaclient.v1_1.security_groups.html#novaclient.v1_1.security_groups.SecurityGroup) ↗ object:

```
import novaclient.v2.client as nvclient
nova = nvclient.Client(...)
group = nova.security_groups.find(name="web")
print group.rules
```

To add a rule to a security group, call the novaclient.v1_1.security_group_rules.SecurityGroupRuleManager.create (https://docs.openstack.org/developer/python-novaclient/api/novaclient.v1_1.security_group_rules.html#novaclient.v1_1.security_group_rules.SecurityGroupRuleManager.cre
method:

```
import novaclient.v2.client as nvclient
nova = nvclient.Client(...)
group = nova.security_groups.find(name="web")
# Add rules for ICMP, tcp/80 and tcp/443
nova.security_group_rules.create(group.id, ip_protocol="icmp",
                                 from_port=-1, to_port=-1)
nova.security_group_rules.create(group.id, ip_protocol="tcp",
                                 from_port=80, to_port=80)
nova.security_group_rules.create(group.id, ip_protocol="tcp",
                                 from_port=443, to_port=443)
```

## 5.9 Networking

To use the information in this section, you should have a general understanding of OpenStack Networking, OpenStack Compute, and the integration between the two. You should also have access to a plug-in that implements the Networking API v2.0.

### 5.9.1 Set environment variables

Make sure that you set the relevant environment variables.

As an example, see the sample shell file that sets these variables to get credentials:

```
export OS_USERNAME="admin"
export OS_PASSWORD="password"
export OS_TENANT_NAME="admin"
export OS_AUTH_URL="http://IPADDRESS/v2.0"
```

### 5.9.2 Get credentials

The examples in this section use the `get_credentials` method:

```
def get_credentials():
```

```
    d = {}
    d['username'] = os.environ['OS_USERNAME']
    d['password'] = os.environ['OS_PASSWORD']
    d['auth_url'] = os.environ['OS_AUTH_URL']
    d['tenant_name'] = os.environ['OS_TENANT_NAME']
    return d
```

This code resides in the `credentials.py` file, which all samples import.

Use the `get_credentials()` method to populate and get a dictionary:

```
credentials = get_credentials()
```

### 5.9.3 Get Nova credentials

The examples in this section use the `get_nova_credentials` method:

```
def get_nova_credentials():
    d = {}
    d['username'] = os.environ['OS_USERNAME']
    d['api_key'] = os.environ['OS_PASSWORD']
    d['auth_url'] = os.environ['OS_AUTH_URL']
    d['project_id'] = os.environ['OS_TENANT_NAME']
    return d
```

This code resides in the `credentials.py` file, which all samples import.

Use the `get_nova_credentials()` method to populate and get a dictionary:

```
nova_credentials = get_nova_credentials()
```

### 5.9.4 Print values

The examples in this section use the `print_values` and `print_values_server` methods:

```
def print_values(val, type):
    if type == 'ports':
        val_list = val['ports']
    if type == 'networks':
        val_list = val['networks']
    if type == 'routers':
        val_list = val['routers']
    for p in val_list:
        for k, v in p.items():
```

```
            print("%s : %s" % (k, v))
        print('\n')


def print_values_server(val, server_id, type):
    if type == 'ports':
        val_list = val['ports']

    if type == 'networks':
        val_list = val['networks']
    for p in val_list:
        bool = False
        for k, v in p.items():
            if k == 'device_id' and v == server_id:
                bool = True
        if bool:
            for k, v in p.items():
                print("%s : %s" % (k, v))
            print('\n')
```

This code resides in the `utils.py` file, which all samples import.

### 5.9.5 Create network

The following program creates a network:

```
#!/usr/bin/env python
from neutronclient.v2_0 import client
from credentials import get_credentials

network_name = 'sample_network'
credentials = get_credentials()
neutron = client.Client(**credentials)
try:
    body_sample = {'network': {'name': network_name,
                   'admin_state_up': True}}

    netw = neutron.create_network(body=body_sample)
    net_dict = netw['network']
    network_id = net_dict['id']
    print('Network %s created' % network_id)

    body_create_subnet = {'subnets': [{'cidr': '192.168.199.0/24',
                          'ip_version': 4, 'network_id': network_id}]}
```

```
    subnet = neutron.create_subnet(body=body_create_subnet)
    print('Created subnet %s' % subnet)
finally:
    print("Execution completed")
```

### 5.9.6 List networks

The following program lists networks:

```
#!/usr/bin/env python
from neutronclient.v2_0 import client
from credentials import get_credentials
from utils import print_values

credentials = get_credentials()
neutron = client.Client(**credentials)
netw = neutron.list_networks()

print_values(netw, 'networks')
```

For `print_values`, see *Section 5.9.4, "Print values"*.

### 5.9.7 Create ports

The following program creates a port:

```
#!/usr/bin/env python
from neutronclient.v2_0 import client
import novaclient.v2.client as nvclient
from credentials import get_credentials
from credentials import get_nova_credentials

credentials = get_nova_credentials()
nova_client = nvclient.Client(**credentials)

# Replace with server_id and network_id from your environment

server_id = '9a52795a-a70d-49a8-a5d0-5b38d78bd12d'
network_id = 'ce5d204a-93f5-43ef-bd89-3ab99ad09a9a'
server_detail = nova_client.servers.get(server_id)
print(server_detail.id)

if server_detail != None:
```

```
    credentials = get_credentials()
    neutron = client.Client(**credentials)

    body_value = {
                     "port": {
                             "admin_state_up": True,
                             "device_id": server_id,
                             "name": "port1",
                             "network_id": network_id
                      }
                 }
    response = neutron.create_port(body=body_value)
    print(response)
```

For `get_nova_credentials`, see Section 5.9.3, "Get Nova credentials".

For `get_credentials`, see Section 5.9.2, "Get credentials".

### 5.9.8 List ports

The following program lists ports:

```
#!/usr/bin/env python
from neutronclient.v2_0 import client
from credentials import get_credentials
from utils import print_values

credentials = get_credentials()
neutron = client.Client(**credentials)
ports = neutron.list_ports()
print_values(ports, 'ports')
```

For `get_credentials` see Section 5.9.2, "Get credentials".

For `print_values`, see Section 5.9.4, "Print values".

### 5.9.9 List server ports

The following program lists the ports for a server:

```
#!/usr/bin/env python
from neutronclient.v2_0 import client
import novaclient.v2.client as nvclient
from credentials import get_credentials
from credentials import get_nova_credentials
```

```
from utils import print_values_server

credentials = get_nova_credentials()
nova_client = nvclient.Client(**credentials)

# change these values according to your environment

server_id = '9a52795a-a70d-49a8-a5d0-5b38d78bd12d'
network_id = 'ce5d204a-93f5-43ef-bd89-3ab99ad09a9a'
server_detail = nova_client.servers.get(server_id)
print(server_detail.id)

if server_detail is not None:
    credentials = get_credentials()
    neutron = client.Client(**credentials)
    ports = neutron.list_ports()

    print_values_server(ports, server_id, 'ports')
    body_value = {'port': {
        'admin_state_up': True,
        'device_id': server_id,
        'name': 'port1',
        'network_id': network_id,
        }}

    response = neutron.create_port(body=body_value)
    print(response)
```

### 5.9.10 Create router and add port to subnet

This example queries OpenStack Networking to create a router and add a port to a subnet.

1. Import the following modules:

```
from neutronclient.v2_0 import client
import novaclient.v2.client as nvclient
from credentials import get_credentials
from credentials import get_nova_credentials
from utils import print_values_server
```

2. Get Nova Credentials. See :ref:'Get Nova credentials <get-nova-credentials>'.

3. Instantiate the `nova_client` client object by using the `credentials` dictionary object:

```
nova_client = nvclient.Client(**credentials)
```

4. Create a router and add a port to the subnet:

```
# Replace with network_id from your environment

network_id = '81bf592a-9e3f-4f84-a839-ae87df188dc1'

credentials = get_credentials()
neutron = client.Client(**credentials)
neutron.format = json
request = {'router': {'name': 'router name',
                      'admin_state_up': True}}

router = neutron.create_router(request)
router_id = router['router']['id']
# for example: '72cf1682-60a8-4890-b0ed-6bad7d9f5466'
router = neutron.show_router(router_id)
print(router)
body_value = {'port': {
    'admin_state_up': True,
    'device_id': router_id,
    'name': 'port1',
    'network_id': network_id,
    }}

response = neutron.create_port(body=body_value)
print(response)
print("Execution Completed")
```

#### 5.9.10.1 Create router: complete code listing example

```
#!/usr/bin/env python
from neutronclient.v2_0 import client
import novaclient.v2.client as nvclient
from credentials import get_credentials
from credentials import get_nova_credentials
from utils import print_values_server

credentials = get_nova_credentials()
nova_client = nvclient.Client(**credentials)

# Replace with network_id from your environment

network_id = '81bf592a-9e3f-4f84-a839-ae87df188dc1'
try:
    credentials = get_credentials()
```

```
    neutron = client.Client(**credentials)
    neutron.format = 'json'
    request = {'router': {'name': 'router name',
                          'admin_state_up': True}}
    router = neutron.create_router(request)
    router_id = router['router']['id']
    # for example: '72cf1682-60a8-4890-b0ed-6bad7d9f5466'
    router = neutron.show_router(router_id)
    print(router)
    body_value = {'port': {
        'admin_state_up': True,
        'device_id': router_id,
        'name': 'port1',
        'network_id': network_id,
        }}

    response = neutron.create_port(body=body_value)
    print(response)
finally:
    print("Execution completed")
```

### 5.9.11 Delete a network

This example queries OpenStack Networking to delete a network.

To delete a network:

1. Import the following modules:

```
from neutronclient.v2_0 import client
from credentials import get_credentials
```

2. Get credentials. See *Section 5.9.3, "Get Nova credentials"*.

3. Instantiate the `neutron` client object by using the `credentials` dictionary object:

```
neutron = client.Client(**credentials)
```

4. Delete the network:

```
body_sample = {'network': {'name': network_name,
               'admin_state_up': True}}

netw = neutron.create_network(body=body_sample)
net_dict = netw['network']
```

```
    network_id = net_dict['id']
    print('Network %s created' % network_id)

    body_create_subnet = {'subnets': [{'cidr': '192.168.199.0/24',
                          'ip_version': 4, 'network_id': network_id}]}

    subnet = neutron.create_subnet(body=body_create_subnet)
    print('Created subnet %s' % subnet)

    neutron.delete_network(network_id)
    print('Deleted Network %s' % network_id)

    print("Execution completed")
```

#### 5.9.11.1 Delete network: complete code listing example

```
#!/usr/bin/env python
from neutronclient.v2_0 import client
from credentials import get_credentials

network_name = 'temp_network'
credentials = get_credentials()
neutron = client.Client(**credentials)
try:
    body_sample = {'network': {'name': network_name,
                   'admin_state_up': True}}

    netw = neutron.create_network(body=body_sample)
    net_dict = netw['network']
    network_id = net_dict['id']
    print('Network %s created' % network_id)

    body_create_subnet = {'subnets': [{'cidr': '192.168.199.0/24',
                          'ip_version': 4, 'network_id': network_id}]}

    subnet = neutron.create_subnet(body=body_create_subnet)
    print('Created subnet %s' % subnet)

    neutron.delete_network(network_id)
    print('Deleted Network %s' % network_id)
finally:
    print("Execution Completed")
```

### 5.9.12 List routers

This example queries OpenStack Networking to list all routers.

1. Import the following modules:

```
from neutronclient.v2_0 import client
from credentials import get_credentials
from utils import print_values
```

2. Get credentials. See *Section 5.9.3, "Get Nova credentials"*.

3. Instantiate the `neutron` client object by using the `credentials` dictionary object:

```
neutron = client.Client(**credentials)
```

4. List the routers:

```
routers_list = neutron.list_routers(retrieve_all=True)
print_values(routers_list, 'routers')
print("Execution completed")
```

For `print_values`, see *Section 5.9.4, "Print values"*.

#### 5.9.12.1 List routers: complete code listing example

```
#!/usr/bin/env python
from neutronclient.v2_0 import client
from credentials import get_credentials
from utils import print_values

try:
    credentials = get_credentials()
    neutron = client.Client(**credentials)
    routers_list = neutron.list_routers(retrieve_all=True)
    print_values(routers_list, 'routers')
finally:
    print("Execution completed")
```

### 5.9.13 List security groups

This example queries OpenStack Networking to list security groups.

1. Import the following modules:

```
from neutronclient.v2_0 import client
from credentials import get_credentials
from utils import print_values
```

2. Get credentials. See *Section 5.9.2, "Get credentials"*.

3. Instantiate the `neutron` client object by using the `credentials` dictionary object:

```
neutron = client.Client(**credentials)
```

4. List Security groups

```
sg = neutron.list_security_groups()
print(sg)
```

#### 5.9.13.1 List security groups: complete code listing example

```
#!/usr/bin/env python
from neutronclient.v2_0 import client
from credentials import get_credentials
from utils import print_values

credentials = get_credentials()
neutron = client.Client(**credentials)
sg = neutron.list_security_groups()
print(sg)
```

Note

OpenStack Networking security groups are case-sensitive while the nova-network security groups are case-insensitive.

### 5.9.14 List subnets

This example queries OpenStack Networking to list subnets.

1. Import the following modules:

```
from neutronclient.v2_0 import client
```

```
from credentials import get_credentials
from utils import print_values
```

2. Get credentials. See :ref:'Get credentials <get-credentials>'.

3. Instantiate the `neutron` client object by using the `credentials` dictionary object:

```
neutron = client.Client(**credentials)
```

4. List subnets:

```
subnets = neutron.list_subnets()
print(subnets)
```

#### 5.9.14.1 List subnets: complete code listing example

```
#!/usr/bin/env python
from neutronclient.v2_0 import client
from credentials import get_credentials
from utils import print_values

credentials = get_credentials()
neutron = client.Client(**credentials)
subnets = neutron.list_subnets()
print(subnets)
```

## 5.10 Compute

To use the information in this section, you must be familiar with OpenStack Compute.

### 5.10.1 Set environment variables

To set up environmental variables and authenticate against Compute API endpoints, see *Section 5.3, "Authenticate"*.

### 5.10.2 Get OpenStack credentials (API v2)

This example uses the `get_nova_credentials_v2` method:

```
def get_nova_credentials_v2():
    d = {}
    d['version'] = '2'
    d['username'] = os.environ['OS_USERNAME']
    d['api_key'] = os.environ['OS_PASSWORD']
    d['auth_url'] = os.environ['OS_AUTH_URL']
    d['project_id'] = os.environ['OS_TENANT_NAME']
    return d
```

This code resides in the `credentials.py` file, which all samples import.

Use the `get_nova_credentials_v2()` method to populate and get a dictionary:

```
credentials = get_nova_credentials_v2()
```

### 5.10.3 List servers (API v2)

The following program lists servers by using the Compute API v2.

1. Import the following modules:

```
from credentials import get_nova_credentials_v2
from novaclient.client import Client
```

2. Get Nova credentials. See *Section 5.10.2, "Get OpenStack credentials (API v2)"*.

3. Instantiate the `nova_client` client object by using the `credentials` dictionary object:

```
nova_client = Client(**credentials)
```

4. List servers by calling `servers.list` on `nova_client` object:

```
print(nova_client.servers.list())
```

#### 5.10.3.1 List server code listing example

```
#!/usr/bin/env python
from credentials import get_nova_credentials_v2
```

```
from novaclient.client import Client

credentials = get_nova_credentials_v2()
nova_client = Client(**credentials)

print(nova_client.servers.list())
```

### 5.10.4 Create server (API v2)

The following program creates a server (VM) by using the Compute API v2.

1. Import the following modules:

```
import time
from credentials import get_nova_credentials_v2
from novaclient.client import Client
```

2. Get OpenStack credentials. See *Section 5.10.2, "Get OpenStack credentials (API v2)"*.

3. Instantiate the `nova_client` client object by using the `credentials` dictionary object:

```
nova_client = Client(**credentials)
```

4. Get the flavor and image to use to create a server. This code uses the `cirros` image, the `m1.tiny` flavor, and the `private` network:

```
image = nova_client.images.find(name="cirros")
flavor = nova_client.flavors.find(name="m1.tiny")
net = nova_client.networks.find(label="private")
```

5. To create the server, use the network, image, and flavor:

```
nics = [{'net-id': net.id}]
instance = nova_client.servers.create(name="vm2", image=image,
flavor=flavor, key_name="keypair-1", nics=nics)
```

6. Run the "Sleep for five seconds" command, and determine whether the server/vm was created by calling `nova_client.servers.list()`:

```
print("Sleeping for 5s after create command")
time.sleep(5)
print("List of VMs")
print(nova_client.servers.list())
```

#### 5.10.4.1 Create server code listing example

```
#!/usr/bin/env python
import time
from credentials import get_nova_credentials_v2
from novaclient.client import Client

try:
    credentials = get_nova_credentials_v2()
    nova_client = Client(**credentials)

    image = nova_client.images.find(name="cirros")
    flavor = nova_client.flavors.find(name="m1.tiny")
    net = nova_client.networks.find(label="private")
    nics = [{'net-id': net.id}]
    instance = nova_client.servers.create(name="vm2", image=image,
                                  flavor=flavor, key_name="keypair-1", nics=nics)
    print("Sleeping for 5s after create command")
    time.sleep(5)
    print("List of VMs")
    print(nova_client.servers.list())
finally:
    print("Execution Completed")
```

### 5.10.5 Delete server (API v2)

The following program deletes a server (VM) by using the Compute API v2.

1. Import the following modules:

```
import time
from credentials import get_nova_credentials_v2
from novaclient.client import Client
```

2. Get Nova credentials. See *Section 5.10.2, "Get OpenStack credentials (API v2)"*.

3. Instantiate the `nova_client` client object by using the `credentials` dictionary object:

```
nova_client = Client(**credentials)
```

4. Determine whether the `vm1` server exists:

   a. List servers: `servers_list`.

   b. Iterate over `servers_list` and compare name with `vm1`.

c. If true, set the variable name `server_exists` to `True` and break from the for loop:

```
servers_list = nova_client.servers.list()
server_del = "vm1"
server_exists = False

for s in servers_list:
    if s.name == server_del:
        print("This server %s exists" % server_del)
        server_exists = True
        break
```

5. If the server exists, run the `delete` method of the `nova_client.servers` object:

```
nova_client.servers.delete(s)
```

#### 5.10.5.1 Delete server code example

```
#!/usr/bin/env python
from credentials import get_nova_credentials_v2
from novaclient.client import Client

credentials = get_nova_credentials_v2()
nova_client = Client(**credentials)

servers_list = nova_client.servers.list()
server_del = "vm1"
server_exists = False

for s in servers_list:
    if s.name == server_del:
        print("This server %s exists" % server_del)
        server_exists = True
        break
if not server_exists:
    print("server %s does not exist" % server_del)
else:
    print("deleting server..........")
    nova_client.servers.delete(s)
    print("server %s deleted" % server_del)
```

### 5.10.6 Update server (API v2)

The following program updates the name of a server (VM) by using the Compute API v2.

1. Import the following modules:

```
from credentials import get_nova_credentials_v2
from novaclient.client import Client
from utils import print_server
```

   `print_server` is a method defined in `utils.py` and prints the server details as shown in the code listing below:

```
def print_server(server):
    print("-"*35)
    print("server id: %s" % server.id)
    print("server name: %s" % server.name)
    print("server image: %s" % server.image)
    print("server flavor: %s" % server.flavor)
    print("server key name: %s" % server.key_name)
    print("user_id: %s" % server.user_id)
    print("-"*35)
```

2. Get OpenStack Credentials. See *Section 5.10.2, "Get OpenStack credentials (API v2)"*.

3. Instantiate the `nova_client` client object by using the `credentials` dictionary object:

```
nova_client = Client(**credentials)
```

4. Get the server instance using `server_id` and print the details by calling `print_server` method:

```
server_id = '99889c8d-113f-4a7e-970c-77f1916bfe14'
server = nova_client.servers.get(server_id)
n = server.name
print_server(server)
```

5. Call `server.update` on the server object with the new value for `name` variable:

```
server.update(name = n + '1')
```

6. Get the updated instance of the server:

```
server_updated = nova_client.servers.get(server_id)
```

7. Call `print_server` again to check the update server details:

```
print_server(server_updated)
```

#### 5.10.6.1 Update server code listing example

```
#!/usr/bin/env python

from credentials import get_nova_credentials_v2
from novaclient.client import Client
from utils import print_server

credentials = get_nova_credentials_v2()
nova_client = Client(**credentials)

# Change the server_id specific to your environment

server_id = '99889c8d-113f-4a7e-970c-77f1916bfe14'
server = nova_client.servers.get(server_id)
n = server.name
print_server(server)

server.update(name=n +'1')
server_updated = nova_client.servers.get(server_id)
print_server(server_updated)
```

### 5.10.7 List flavors (API v2)

The following program lists flavors and their details by using the Compute API v2.

1. Import the following modules:

```
from credentials import get_nova_credentials_v2
from novaclient.client import Client
from utils import print_flavors
```

The `print_flavors` method is defined in `utils.py` and prints the flavor details:

```
def print_flavors(flavor_list):
    for flavor in flavor_list:
       print("-"*35)
       print("flavor id : %s" % flavor.id)
```

```
    print("flavor name : %s" % flavor.name)
    print("-"*35)
```

2. Get OpenStack credentials. *Section 5.10.2, "Get OpenStack credentials (API v2)"*.

3. Instantiate the `nova_client` client object by using the `credentials` dictionary object:

```
nova_client = Client(**credentials)
```

4. List flavors by calling `list()` on `nova_client.flavors` object:

```
flavors_list =  nova_client.flavors.list()
```

5. Print the flavor details, id and name by calling `print_flavors`:

```
print_flavors(flavors_list)
```

#### 5.10.7.1 List flavors code listing example

```
#!/usr/bin/env python

from credentials import get_nova_credentials_v2
from novaclient.client import Client
from utils import print_flavors

credentials = get_nova_credentials_v2()
nova_client = Client(**credentials)

flavors_list = nova_client.flavors.list()
print_flavors(flavors_list)
```

### 5.10.8 List floating IPs (API v2)

The following program lists the floating IPs and their details by using the Compute API v2.

1. Import the following modules:

```
from credentials import get_nova_credentials_v2
from novaclient.client import Client
from utils import print_values_ip
```

The `print_values_ip` method is defined in `utils.py` and prints the floating_ip object details:

```
def print_values_ip(ip_list):
    ip_dict_lisl = []
    for ip in ip_list:
        print("-"*35)
        print("fixed_ip : %s" % ip.fixed_ip)
        print("id : %s" % ip.id)
        print("instance_id : %s" % ip.instance_id)
        print("ip : %s" % ip.ip)
        print("pool : %s" % ip.pool)
```

2. Get OpenStack credentials. See *Section 5.10.2, "Get OpenStack credentials (API v2)"*.

3. Instantiate the `nova_client` client object by using the `credentials` dictionary object:

```
nova_client = Client(**credentials)
```

4. List floating IPs by calling `list()` on `nova_client.floating_ips` object:

```
ip_list = nova_client.floating_ips.list()
```

5. Print the floating IP object details by calling `print_values_ip`:

```
print_values_ip(ip_list)
```

#### 5.10.8.1 List floating IPs code listing example

```
#!/usr/bin/env python

from credentials import get_nova_credentials_v2
from novaclient.client import Client
from utils import print_values_ip

credentials = get_nova_credentials_v2()
nova_client = Client(**credentials)
ip_list = nova_client.floating_ips.list()
print_values_ip(ip_list)
```

### 5.10.9 List hosts (API v2)

The following program lists the hosts by using the Compute API v2.

1. Import the following modules:

```
from credentials import get_nova_credentials_v2
from novaclient.client import Client
from utils import print_hosts
```

   The `print_hosts` method is defined in `utils.py` and prints the host object details:

```
def print_hosts(host_list):
    for host in host_list:
       print("-"*35)
       print("host_name : %s" % host.host_name)
       print("service : %s" % host.service)
       print("zone : %s" % host.zone)
       print("-"*35)
```

2. Get OpenStack credentials. See *Section 5.10.2, "Get OpenStack credentials (API v2)"*.

3. Instantiate the `nova_client` client object by using the `credentials` dictionary object:

```
nova_client = Client(**credentials)
```

4. List hosts by calling `list()` on `nova_client.hosts` object:

```
host_list = nova_client.hosts.list()
```

5. Print the host object details by calling `print_hosts(host_list)`:

```
print_hosts(host_list)
```

#### 5.10.9.1 List hosts code listing example

```
#!/usr/bin/env python

from credentials import get_nova_credentials_v2
from novaclient.client import Client
from utils import print_hosts

credentials = get_nova_credentials_v2()
nova_client = Client(**credentials)
```

```
host_list = nova_client.hosts.list()

print_hosts(host_list)
```

# 6 HOT Guide

Orchestration is compatible with the CloudFormation template, but you can also write heat templates to orchestrate cloud resources.

To learn how, refer to the Template Guide (https://docs.openstack.org/developer/heat/template_guide/index.html) ↗ on the OpenStack developer documentation website.

# 7 OpenStack command-line interface cheat sheet

Here is a list of common commands for reference.

## 7.1 Identity (keystone)

List all users

```
$ openstack user list
```

List Identity service catalog

```
$ openstack catalog list
```

## 7.2 Images (glance)

List images you can access

```
$ openstack image list
```

Delete specified image

```
$ openstack image delete IMAGE
```

Describe a specific image

```
$ openstack image show IMAGE
```

Update image

```
$ openstack image set IMAGE
```

Upload kernel image

```
$ openstack image create "cirros-threepart-kernel" \
  --disk-format aki --container-format aki --public \
  --file ~/images/cirros-0.3.1~pre4-x86_64-vmlinuz
```

Upload RAM image

```
$ openstack image create "cirros-threepart-ramdisk" \
  --disk-format ari --container-format ari --public \
  --file ~/images/cirros-0.3.1~pre4-x86_64-initrd
```

Upload three-part image

```
$ openstack image create "cirros-threepart" --disk-format ami \
  --container-format ami --public \
  --property kernel_id=$KID-property ramdisk_id=$RID \
  --file ~/images/cirros-0.3.1~pre4-x86_64-blank.img
```

Register raw image

```
$ openstack image create "cirros-raw" --disk-format raw \
  --container-format bare --public \
  --file ~/images/cirros-0.3.1~pre4-x86_64-disk.img
```

## 7.3 Compute (nova)

List instances, check status of instance

```
$ openstack server list
```

List images

```
$ openstack image list
```

Create a flavor named m1.tiny

```
$ openstack flavor create --ram 512 --disk 1 --vcpus 1 m1.tiny
```

List flavors

```
$ openstack flavor list
```

Boot an instance using flavor and image names (if names are unique)

```
$ openstack server create --image IMAGE --flavor FLAVOR INSTANCE_NAME
$ openstack server create --image cirros-0.3.1-x86_64-uec --flavor m1.tiny \
  MyFirstInstance
```

Log in to the instance (from Linux)

Note

The **`ip`** command is available only on Linux. Using **`ip netns`** provides your environment a copy of the network stack with its own routes, firewall rules, and network devices for better troubleshooting.

```
# ip netns
# ip netns exec NETNS_NAME ssh USER@SERVER
# ip netns exec qdhcp-6021a3b4-8587-4f9c-8064-0103885dfba2 \
  ssh cirros@10.0.0.2
```

Note

In CirrOS, the password for user `cirros` is `cubswin:)`. For any other operating system, use SSH keys.

Log in to the instance with a public IP address (from Mac)

```
$ ssh cloud-user@128.107.37.150
```

Show details of instance

```
$ openstack server show NAME
$ openstack server show MyFirstInstance
```

View console log of instance

```
$ openstack console log show MyFirstInstance
```

Set metadata on an instance

```
$ nova meta volumeTwoImage set newmeta='my meta data'
```

Create an instance snapshot

```
$ openstack image create volumeTwoImage snapshotOfVolumeImage
$ openstack image show snapshotOfVolumeImage
```

### 7.3.1 Pause, suspend, stop, rescue, resize, rebuild, reboot an instance

Pause

```
$ openstack server pause NAME
$ openstack server pause volumeTwoImage
```

Unpause

```
$ openstack server unpause NAME
```

Suspend

```
$ openstack server suspend NAME
```

Unsuspend

```
$ openstack server resume NAME
```

Stop

```
$ openstack server stop NAME
```

Start

```
$ openstack server start NAME
```

Rescue

```
$ openstack server rescue NAME
$ openstack server rescue NAME --rescue_image_ref RESCUE_IMAGE
```

Resize

```
$ openstack server resize NAME FLAVOR
$ openstack server resize my-pem-server m1.small
$ openstack server resize --confirm my-pem-server1
```

Rebuild

```
$ openstack server rebuild NAME IMAGE
$ openstack server rebuild newtinny cirros-qcow2
```

Reboot

```
$ openstack server reboot NAME
$ openstack server reboot newtinny
```

Inject user data and files into an instance

```
$ openstack server create --user-data FILE INSTANCE
$ openstack server create --user-data userdata.txt --image cirros-qcow2 \
  --flavor m1.tiny MyUserdataInstance2
```

To validate that the file was injected, use ssh to connect to the instance, and look in `/var/lib/cloud` for the file.

Inject a keypair into an instance and access the instance with that keypair

Create keypair

```
$ openstack keypair create test > test.pem
$ chmod 600 test.pem
```

Start an instance (boot)

```
$ openstack server create --image cirros-0.3.0-x86_64 --flavor m1.small \
  --key-name test MyFirstServer
```

Use ssh to connect to the instance

```
# ip netns exec qdhcp-98f09f1e-64c4-4301-a897-5067ee6d544f \
  ssh -i test.pem cirros@10.0.0.4
```

Manage security groups

Add rules to default security group allowing ping and SSH between instances in the default security group

```
$ openstack security group rule create default \
    --remote-group default --protocol icmp
$ openstack security group rule create default \
    --remote-group default --dst-port 22
```

## 7.4 Networking (neutron)

Create network

```
$ openstack network create NETWORK_NAME
```

Create a subnet

```
$ openstack subnet create --subnet-pool SUBNET --network NETWORK SUBNET_NAME
$ openstack subnet create --subnet-pool 10.0.0.0/29 --network net1 subnet1
```

## 7.5 Block Storage (cinder)

Used to manage volumes and volume snapshots that attach to instances.

Create a new volume

```
$ openstack volume create --size SIZE_IN_GB NAME
$ openstack volume create --size 1 MyFirstVolume
```

Boot an instance and attach to volume

```
$ openstack server create --image cirros-qcow2 --flavor m1.tiny MyVolumeInstance
```

List all volumes, noticing the volume status

```
$ openstack volume list
```

Attach a volume to an instance after the instance is active, and the volume is available

```
$ openstack server add volume INSTANCE_ID VOLUME_ID
$ openstack server add volume MyVolumeInstance 573e024d-5235-49ce-8332-be1576d323f8
```

### Note

On the Xen Hypervisor it is possible to provide a specific device name instead of automatic allocation. For example:

```
$ openstack server add volume --device /dev/vdb MyVolumeInstance 573e024d..1576d323f8

This is not currently possible when using non-Xen hypervisors with OpenStack.
```

Manage volumes after login into the instance

List storage devices

```
# fdisk -l
```

Make filesystem on volume

```
# mkfs.ext3 /dev/vdb
```

Create a mountpoint

```
# mkdir /myspace
```

Mount the volume at the mountpoint

```
# mount /dev/vdb /myspace
```

Create a file on the volume

```
# touch /myspace/helloworld.txt
# ls /myspace
```

Unmount the volume

```
# umount /myspace
```

## 7.6 Object Storage (swift)

Display information for the account, container, or object

```
$ swift stat
$ swift stat ACCOUNT
$ swift stat CONTAINER
$ swift stat OBJECT
```

List containers

```
$ swift list
```

# 8 Appendix

## 8.1 Community support

The following resources are available to help you run and use OpenStack. The OpenStack community constantly improves and adds to the main features of OpenStack, but if you have any questions, do not hesitate to ask. Use the following resources to get OpenStack support and troubleshoot your installations.

### 8.1.1 Documentation

For the available OpenStack documentation, see docs.openstack.org (https://docs.openstack.org) ↗.

To provide feedback on documentation, join and use the openstack-docs@lists.openstack.org (mailto:openstack-docs@lists.openstack.org) ↗ mailing list at OpenStack Documentation Mailing List (http://lists.openstack.org/cgi-bin/mailman/listinfo/openstack-docs) ↗, join our IRC channel `#openstack-doc` on the freenode IRC network, or report a bug (https://bugs.launchpad.net/openstack-manuals/+filebug) ↗.

The following books explain how to install an OpenStack cloud and its associated components:

- Installation Tutorial for openSUSE Leap 42.2 and SUSE Linux Enterprise Server 12 SP2 (https://docs.openstack.org/newton/install-guide-obs/) ↗
- Installation Tutorial for Red Hat Enterprise Linux 7 and CentOS 7 (https://docs.openstack.org/newton/install-guide-rdo/) ↗
- Installation Tutorial for Ubuntu 16.04 (LTS) (https://docs.openstack.org/newton/install-guide-ubuntu/) ↗
- Installation Tutorial for Debian with Debconf (https://docs.openstack.org/newton/install-guide-debconf/) ↗
- Installation Tutorial for Debian (https://docs.openstack.org/newton/install-guide-debian/) ↗

The following books explain how to configure and run an OpenStack cloud:

- Architecture Design Guide (https://docs.openstack.org/arch-design/) ↗
- Administrator Guide (https://docs.openstack.org/admin-guide/) ↗

- Configuration Reference (https://docs.openstack.org/newton/config-reference/)
- Operations Guide (https://docs.openstack.org/ops/)
- Networking Guide (https://docs.openstack.org/newton/networking-guide)
- High Availability Guide (https://docs.openstack.org/ha-guide/)
- Security Guide (https://docs.openstack.org/sec/)
- Virtual Machine Image Guide (https://docs.openstack.org/image-guide/)

The following books explain how to use the OpenStack Dashboard and command-line clients:

- End User Guide (https://docs.openstack.org/user-guide/)
- Command-Line Interface Reference (https://docs.openstack.org/cli-reference/)

The following documentation provides reference and guidance information for the OpenStack APIs:

- API Guide (https://developer.openstack.org/api-guide/quick-start/)

The following guide provides how to contribute to OpenStack documentation:

- Documentation Contributor Guide (https://docs.openstack.org/contributor-guide/)

### 8.1.2 ask.openstack.org

During the set up or testing of OpenStack, you might have questions about how a specific task is completed or be in a situation where a feature does not work correctly. Use the ask.openstack.org (https://ask.openstack.org) site to ask questions and get answers. When you visit the Ask OpenStack (https://ask.openstack.org) site, scan the recently asked questions to see whether your question has already been answered. If not, ask a new question. Be sure to give a clear, concise summary in the title and provide as much detail as possible in the description. Paste in your command output or stack traces, links to screen shots, and any other information which might be useful.

### 8.1.3 OpenStack mailing lists

A great way to get answers and insights is to post your question or problematic scenario to the OpenStack mailing list. You can learn from and help others who might have similar issues. To subscribe or view the archives, go to the general OpenStack mailing list (http://lists.openstack.org/cgi-bin/mailman/listinfo/openstack) ↗. If you are interested in the other mailing lists for specific projects or development, refer to Mailing Lists (https://wiki.openstack.org/wiki/Mailing_Lists) ↗.

### 8.1.4 The OpenStack wiki

The OpenStack wiki (https://wiki.openstack.org/) ↗ contains a broad range of topics but some of the information can be difficult to find or is a few pages deep. Fortunately, the wiki search feature enables you to search by title or content. If you search for specific information, such as about networking or OpenStack Compute, you can find a large amount of relevant material. More is being added all the time, so be sure to check back often. You can find the search box in the upper-right corner of any OpenStack wiki page.

### 8.1.5 The Launchpad Bugs area

The OpenStack community values your set up and testing efforts and wants your feedback. To log a bug, you must sign up for a Launchpad account at https://launchpad.net/+login ↗. You can view existing bugs and report bugs in the Launchpad Bugs area. Use the search feature to determine whether the bug has already been reported or already been fixed. If it still seems like your bug is unreported, fill out a bug report.

Some tips:

- Give a clear, concise summary.
- Provide as much detail as possible in the description. Paste in your command output or stack traces, links to screen shots, and any other information which might be useful.
- Be sure to include the software and package versions that you are using, especially if you are using a development branch, such as, `"Kilo release" vs git commit bc79c3ecc55929bac585d04a03475b72e06a3208`.
- Any deployment-specific information is helpful, such as whether you are using Ubuntu 14.04 or are performing a multi-node installation.

The following Launchpad Bugs areas are available:

- Bugs: OpenStack Block Storage (cinder) (https://bugs.launchpad.net/cinder) ↗
- Bugs: OpenStack Compute (nova) (https://bugs.launchpad.net/nova) ↗
- Bugs: OpenStack Dashboard (horizon) (https://bugs.launchpad.net/horizon) ↗
- Bugs: OpenStack Identity (keystone) (https://bugs.launchpad.net/keystone) ↗
- Bugs: OpenStack Image service (glance) (https://bugs.launchpad.net/glance) ↗
- Bugs: OpenStack Networking (neutron) (https://bugs.launchpad.net/neutron) ↗
- Bugs: OpenStack Object Storage (swift) (https://bugs.launchpad.net/swift) ↗
- Bugs: Application catalog (murano) (https://bugs.launchpad.net/murano) ↗
- Bugs: Bare metal service (ironic) (https://bugs.launchpad.net/ironic) ↗
- Bugs: Clustering service (senlin) (https://bugs.launchpad.net/senlin) ↗
- Bugs: Container Infrastructure Management service (magnum) (https://bugs.launchpad.net/magnum) ↗
- Bugs: Data processing service (sahara) (https://bugs.launchpad.net/sahara) ↗
- Bugs: Database service (trove) (https://bugs.launchpad.net/trove) ↗
- Bugs: Deployment service (fuel) (https://bugs.launchpad.net/fuel) ↗
- Bugs: DNS service (designate) (https://bugs.launchpad.net/designate) ↗
- Bugs: Key Manager Service (barbican) (https://bugs.launchpad.net/barbican) ↗
- Bugs: Monitoring (monasca) (https://bugs.launchpad.net/monasca) ↗
- Bugs: Orchestration (heat) (https://bugs.launchpad.net/heat) ↗
- Bugs: Rating (cloudkitty) (https://bugs.launchpad.net/cloudkitty) ↗
- Bugs: Shared file systems (manila) (https://bugs.launchpad.net/manila) ↗
- Bugs: Telemetry (ceilometer) (https://bugs.launchpad.net/ceilometer) ↗
- Bugs: Telemetry v3 (gnocchi) (https://bugs.launchpad.net/gnocchi) ↗

- Bugs: Workflow service (mistral) (https://bugs.launchpad.net/mistral) ↗
- Bugs: Messaging service (zaqar) (https://bugs.launchpad.net/zaqar) ↗
- Bugs: OpenStack API Documentation (developer.openstack.org) (https://bugs.launchpad.net/openstack-api-site) ↗
- Bugs: OpenStack Documentation (docs.openstack.org) (https://bugs.launchpad.net/openstack-manuals) ↗

### 8.1.6 The OpenStack IRC channel

The OpenStack community lives in the #openstack IRC channel on the Freenode network. You can hang out, ask questions, or get immediate feedback for urgent and pressing issues. To install an IRC client or use a browser-based client, go to https://webchat.freenode.net/ (https://webchat.freenode.net) ↗. You can also use Colloquy (http://colloquy.info/) ↗ (Mac OS X), mIRC (http://www.mirc.com/) ↗ (Windows), or XChat (Linux). When you are in the IRC channel and want to share code or command output, the generally accepted method is to use a Paste Bin. The OpenStack project has one at Paste (http://paste.openstack.org) ↗. Just paste your longer amounts of text or logs in the web form and you get a URL that you can paste into the channel. The OpenStack IRC channel is `#openstack` on `irc.freenode.net`. You can find a list of all OpenStack IRC channels on the IRC page on the wiki (https://wiki.openstack.org/wiki/IRC) ↗.

### 8.1.7 Documentation feedback

To provide feedback on documentation, join and use the openstack-docs@lists.openstack.org (mailto:openstack-docs@lists.openstack.org) ↗ mailing list at OpenStack Documentation Mailing List (http://lists.openstack.org/cgi-bin/mailman/listinfo/openstack-docs) ↗, or report a bug (https://bugs.launchpad.net/openstack-manuals/+filebug) ↗.

### 8.1.8 OpenStack distribution packages

The following Linux distributions provide community-supported packages for OpenStack:

- **Debian:** https://wiki.debian.org/OpenStack ↗
- **CentOS, Fedora, and Red Hat Enterprise Linux:** https://www.rdoproject.org/ ↗

- **openSUSE and SUSE Linux Enterprise Server:** https://en.opensuse.org/Portal:OpenStack
- **Ubuntu:** https://wiki.ubuntu.com/ServerTeam/CloudArchive

# Glossary

This glossary offers a list of terms and definitions to define a vocabulary for OpenStack-related concepts.

To add to OpenStack glossary, clone the openstack/openstack-manuals repository (https://git.openstack.org/cgit/openstack/openstack-manuals) and update the source file `doc/common/glossary.rst` through the OpenStack contribution process.

## 0-9

**6to4**

A mechanism that allows IPv6 packets to be transmitted over an IPv4 network, providing a strategy for migrating to IPv6.

## A

**absolute limit**

Impassable limits for guest VMs. Settings include total RAM size, maximum number of vCPUs, and maximum disk size.

**access control list (ACL)**

A list of permissions attached to an object. An ACL specifies which users or system processes have access to objects. It also defines which operations can be performed on specified objects. Each entry in a typical ACL specifies a subject and an operation. For instance, the ACL entry `(Alice, delete)` for a file gives Alice permission to delete the file.

**access key**

Alternative term for an Amazon EC2 access key. See EC2 access key.

**account**

The Object Storage context of an account. Do not confuse with a user account from an authentication service, such as Active Directory, /etc/passwd, OpenLDAP, OpenStack Identity, and so on.

### account auditor

Checks for missing replicas and incorrect or corrupted objects in a specified Object Storage account by running queries against the back-end SQLite database.

### account database

A SQLite database that contains Object Storage accounts and related metadata and that the accounts server accesses.

### account reaper

An Object Storage worker that scans for and deletes account databases and that the account server has marked for deletion.

### account server

Lists containers in Object Storage and stores container information in the account database.

### account service

An Object Storage component that provides account services such as list, create, modify, and audit. Do not confuse with OpenStack Identity service, OpenLDAP, or similar user-account services.

### accounting

The Compute service provides accounting information through the event notification and system usage data facilities.

### Active Directory

Authentication and identity service by Microsoft, based on LDAP. Supported in OpenStack.

### active/active configuration

In a high-availability setup with an active/active configuration, several systems share the load together and if one fails, the load is distributed to the remaining systems.

### active/passive configuration

In a high-availability setup with an active/passive configuration, systems are set up to bring additional resources online to replace those that have failed.

### address pool

A group of fixed and/or floating IP addresses that are assigned to a project and can be used by or assigned to the VM instances in a project.

### Address Resolution Protocol (ARP)

The protocol by which layer-3 IP addresses are resolved into layer-2 link local addresses.

### admin API

A subset of API calls that are accessible to authorized administrators and are generally not accessible to end users or the public Internet. They can exist as a separate service (keystone) or can be a subset of another API (nova).

### admin server

In the context of the Identity service, the worker process that provides access to the admin API.

### administrator

The person responsible for installing, configuring, and managing an OpenStack cloud.

### Advanced Message Queuing Protocol (AMQP)

The open standard messaging protocol used by OpenStack components for intra-service communications, provided by RabbitMQ, Qpid, or ZeroMQ.

### Advanced RISC Machine (ARM)

Lower power consumption CPU often found in mobile and embedded devices. Supported by OpenStack.

### alert

The Compute service can send alerts through its notification system, which includes a facility to create custom notification drivers. Alerts can be sent to and displayed on the dashboard.

### allocate

The process of taking a floating IP address from the address pool so it can be associated with a fixed IP on a guest VM instance.

### Amazon Kernel Image (AKI)

Both a VM container format and disk format. Supported by Image service.

### Amazon Machine Image (AMI)

Both a VM container format and disk format. Supported by Image service.

### Amazon Ramdisk Image (ARI)

Both a VM container format and disk format. Supported by Image service.

### Anvil

A project that ports the shell script-based project named DevStack to Python.

## aodh

Part of the OpenStack *Telemetry service (telemetry)*; provides alarming functionality.

## Apache

The Apache Software Foundation supports the Apache community of open-source software projects. These projects provide software products for the public good.

## Apache License 2.0

All OpenStack core projects are provided under the terms of the Apache License 2.0 license.

## Apache Web Server

The most common web server software currently used on the Internet.

## API endpoint

The daemon, worker, or service that a client communicates with to access an API. API endpoints can provide any number of services, such as authentication, sales data, performance meters, Compute VM commands, census data, and so on.

## API extension

Custom modules that extend some OpenStack core APIs.

## API extension plug-in

Alternative term for a Networking plug-in or Networking API extension.

## API key

Alternative term for an API token.

## API server

Any node running a daemon or worker that provides an API endpoint.

## API token

Passed to API requests and used by OpenStack to verify that the client is authorized to run the requested operation.

## API version

In OpenStack, the API version for a project is part of the URL. For example, `example.com/nova/v1/foobar`.

## applet

A Java program that can be embedded into a web page.

### Application Catalog service (murano)

The project that provides an application catalog service so that users can compose and deploy composite environments on an application abstraction level while managing the application lifecycle.

### Application Programming Interface (API)

A collection of specifications used to access a service, application, or program. Includes service calls, required parameters for each call, and the expected return values.

### application server

A piece of software that makes available another piece of software over a network.

### Application Service Provider (ASP)

Companies that rent specialized applications that help businesses and organizations provide additional services with lower cost.

### arptables

Tool used for maintaining Address Resolution Protocol packet filter rules in the Linux kernel firewall modules. Used along with iptables, ebtables, and ip6tables in Compute to provide firewall services for VMs.

### associate

The process associating a Compute floating IP address with a fixed IP address.

### Asynchronous JavaScript and XML (AJAX)

A group of interrelated web development techniques used on the client-side to create asynchronous web applications. Used extensively in horizon.

### ATA over Ethernet (AoE)

A disk storage protocol tunneled within Ethernet.

### attach

The process of connecting a VIF or vNIC to a L2 network in Networking. In the context of Compute, this process connects a storage volume to an instance.

### attachment (network)

Association of an interface ID to a logical port. Plugs an interface into a port.

### auditing

Provided in Compute through the system usage data facility.

### auditor

A worker process that verifies the integrity of Object Storage objects, containers, and accounts. Auditors is the collective term for the Object Storage account auditor, container auditor, and object auditor.

### Austin

The code name for the initial release of OpenStack. The first design summit took place in Austin, Texas, US.

### auth node

Alternative term for an Object Storage authorization node.

### authentication

The process that confirms that the user, process, or client is really who they say they are through private key, secret token, password, fingerprint, or similar method.

### authentication token

A string of text provided to the client after authentication. Must be provided by the user or process in subsequent requests to the API endpoint.

### AuthN

The Identity service component that provides authentication services.

### authorization

The act of verifying that a user, process, or client is authorized to perform an action.

### authorization node

An Object Storage node that provides authorization services.

### AuthZ

The Identity component that provides high-level authorization services.

### Auto ACK

Configuration setting within RabbitMQ that enables or disables message acknowledgment. Enabled by default.

### auto declare

A Compute RabbitMQ setting that determines whether a message exchange is automatically created when the program starts.

**availability zone**

An Amazon EC2 concept of an isolated area that is used for fault tolerance. Do not confuse with an OpenStack Compute zone or cell.

**AWS CloudFormation template**

AWS CloudFormation allows Amazon Web Services (AWS) users to create and manage a collection of related resources. The Orchestration service supports a CloudFormation-compatible format (CFN).

# B

**back end**

Interactions and processes that are obfuscated from the user, such as Compute volume mount, data transmission to an iSCSI target by a daemon, or Object Storage object integrity checks.

**back-end catalog**

The storage method used by the Identity service catalog service to store and retrieve information about API endpoints that are available to the client. Examples include an SQL database, LDAP database, or KVS back end.

**back-end store**

The persistent data store used to save and retrieve information for a service, such as lists of Object Storage objects, current state of guest VMs, lists of user names, and so on. Also, the method that the Image service uses to get and store VM images. Options include Object Storage, locally mounted file system, RADOS block devices, VMware datastore, and HTTP.

**Backup, Restore, and Disaster Recovery service (freezer)**

The project that provides integrated tooling for backing up, restoring, and recovering file systems, instances, or database backups.

**bandwidth**

The amount of available data used by communication resources, such as the Internet. Represents the amount of data that is used to download things or the amount of data available to download.

### barbican

Code name of the *Key Manager service (barbican)*.

### bare

An Image service container format that indicates that no container exists for the VM image.

### Bare Metal service (ironic)

The OpenStack service that provides a service and associated libraries capable of managing and provisioning physical machines in a security-aware and fault-tolerant manner.

### base image

An OpenStack-provided image.

### Bell-LaPadula model

A security model that focuses on data confidentiality and controlled access to classified information. This model divides the entities into subjects and objects. The clearance of a subject is compared to the classification of the object to determine if the subject is authorized for the specific access mode. The clearance or classification scheme is expressed in terms of a lattice.

### Benchmark service (rally)

OpenStack project that provides a framework for performance analysis and benchmarking of individual OpenStack components as well as full production OpenStack cloud deployments.

### Bexar

A grouped release of projects related to OpenStack that came out in February of 2011. It included only Compute (nova) and Object Storage (swift). Bexar is the code name for the second release of OpenStack. The design summit took place in San Antonio, Texas, US, which is the county seat for Bexar county.

### binary

Information that consists solely of ones and zeroes, which is the language of computers.

### bit

A bit is a single digit number that is in base of 2 (either a zero or one). Bandwidth usage is measured in bits per second.

### bits per second (BPS)

The universal measurement of how quickly data is transferred from place to place.

### block device

A device that moves data in the form of blocks. These device nodes interface the devices, such as hard disks, CD-ROM drives, flash drives, and other addressable regions of memory.

### block migration

A method of VM live migration used by KVM to evacuate instances from one host to another with very little downtime during a user-initiated switchover. Does not require shared storage. Supported by Compute.

### Block Storage API

An API on a separate endpoint for attaching, detaching, and creating block storage for compute VMs.

### Block Storage service (cinder)

The OpenStack service that implement services and libraries to provide on-demand, self-service access to Block Storage resources via abstraction and automation on top of other block storage devices.

### BMC (Baseboard Management Controller)

The intelligence in the IPMI architecture, which is a specialized micro-controller that is embedded on the motherboard of a computer and acts as a server. Manages the interface between system management software and platform hardware.

### bootable disk image

A type of VM image that exists as a single, bootable file.

### Bootstrap Protocol (BOOTP)

A network protocol used by a network client to obtain an IP address from a configuration server. Provided in Compute through the dnsmasq daemon when using either the FlatDHCP manager or VLAN manager network manager.

### Border Gateway Protocol (BGP)

The Border Gateway Protocol is a dynamic routing protocol that connects autonomous systems. Considered the backbone of the Internet, this protocol connects disparate networks to form a larger network.

### browser

Any client software that enables a computer or device to access the Internet.

## builder file

Contains configuration information that Object Storage uses to reconfigure a ring or to re-create it from scratch after a serious failure.

## bursting

The practice of utilizing a secondary environment to elastically build instances on-demand when the primary environment is resource constrained.

## button class

A group of related button types within horizon. Buttons to start, stop, and suspend VMs are in one class. Buttons to associate and disassociate floating IP addresses are in another class, and so on.

## byte

Set of bits that make up a single character; there are usually 8 bits to a byte.

# C

## cache pruner

A program that keeps the Image service VM image cache at or below its configured maximum size.

## Cactus

An OpenStack grouped release of projects that came out in the spring of 2011. It included Compute (nova), Object Storage (swift), and the Image service (glance). Cactus is a city in Texas, US and is the code name for the third release of OpenStack. When OpenStack releases went from three to six months long, the code name of the release changed to match a geography nearest the previous summit.

## CALL

One of the RPC primitives used by the OpenStack message queue software. Sends a message and waits for a response.

## capability

Defines resources for a cell, including CPU, storage, and networking. Can apply to the specific services within a cell or a whole cell.

## capacity cache

A Compute back-end database table that contains the current workload, amount of free RAM, and number of VMs running on each host. Used to determine on which host a VM starts.

## capacity updater

A notification driver that monitors VM instances and updates the capacity cache as needed.

## CAST

One of the RPC primitives used by the OpenStack message queue software. Sends a message and does not wait for a response.

## catalog

A list of API endpoints that are available to a user after authentication with the Identity service.

## catalog service

An Identity service that lists API endpoints that are available to a user after authentication with the Identity service.

## ceilometer

Part of the OpenStack *Telemetry service (telemetry)*; gathers and stores metrics from other OpenStack services.

## cell

Provides logical partitioning of Compute resources in a child and parent relationship. Requests are passed from parent cells to child cells if the parent cannot provide the requested resource.

## cell forwarding

A Compute option that enables parent cells to pass resource requests to child cells if the parent cannot provide the requested resource.

## cell manager

The Compute component that contains a list of the current capabilities of each host within the cell and routes requests as appropriate.

## CentOS

A Linux distribution that is compatible with OpenStack.

### Ceph

Massively scalable distributed storage system that consists of an object store, block store, and POSIX-compatible distributed file system. Compatible with OpenStack.

### CephFS

The POSIX-compliant file system provided by Ceph.

### certificate authority (CA)

In cryptography, an entity that issues digital certificates. The digital certificate certifies the ownership of a public key by the named subject of the certificate. This enables others (relying parties) to rely upon signatures or assertions made by the private key that corresponds to the certified public key. In this model of trust relationships, a CA is a trusted third party for both the subject (owner) of the certificate and the party relying upon the certificate. CAs are characteristic of many public key infrastructure (PKI) schemes. In OpenStack, a simple certificate authority is provided by Compute for cloudpipe VPNs and VM image decryption.

### Challenge-Handshake Authentication Protocol (CHAP)

An iSCSI authentication method supported by Compute.

### chance scheduler

A scheduling method used by Compute that randomly chooses an available host from the pool.

### changes since

A Compute API parameter that downloads changes to the requested item since your last request, instead of downloading a new, fresh set of data and comparing it against the old data.

### Chef

An operating system configuration management tool supporting OpenStack deployments.

### child cell

If a requested resource such as CPU time, disk storage, or memory is not available in the parent cell, the request is forwarded to its associated child cells. If the child cell can fulfill the request, it does. Otherwise, it attempts to pass the request to any of its children.

### cinder

Codename for *Block Storage service (cinder)*.

### CirrOS

A minimal Linux distribution designed for use as a test image on clouds such as OpenStack.

### Cisco neutron plug-in

A Networking plug-in for Cisco devices and technologies, including UCS and Nexus.

### cloud architect

A person who plans, designs, and oversees the creation of clouds.

### Cloud Auditing Data Federation (CADF)

Cloud Auditing Data Federation (CADF) is a specification for audit event data. CADF is supported by OpenStack Identity.

### cloud computing

A model that enables access to a shared pool of configurable computing resources, such as networks, servers, storage, applications, and services, that can be rapidly provisioned and released with minimal management effort or service provider interaction.

### cloud controller

Collection of Compute components that represent the global state of the cloud; talks to services, such as Identity authentication, Object Storage, and node/storage workers through a queue.

### cloud controller node

A node that runs network, volume, API, scheduler, and image services. Each service may be broken out into separate nodes for scalability or availability.

### Cloud Data Management Interface (CDMI)

SINA standard that defines a RESTful API for managing objects in the cloud, currently unsupported in OpenStack.

### Cloud Infrastructure Management Interface (CIMI)

An in-progress specification for cloud management. Currently unsupported in OpenStack.

### cloud-init

A package commonly installed in VM images that performs initialization of an instance after boot using information that it retrieves from the metadata service, such as the SSH public key and user data.

### cloudadmin

One of the default roles in the Compute RBAC system. Grants complete system access.

### Cloudbase-Init

A Windows project providing guest initialization features, similar to cloud-init.

### cloudpipe

A compute service that creates VPNs on a per-project basis.

### cloudpipe image

A pre-made VM image that serves as a cloudpipe server. Essentially, OpenVPN running on Linux.

### Clustering service (senlin)

The project that implements clustering services and libraries for the management of groups of homogeneous objects exposed by other OpenStack services.

### command filter

Lists allowed commands within the Compute rootwrap facility.

### Common Internet File System (CIFS)

A file sharing protocol. It is a public or open variation of the original Server Message Block (SMB) protocol developed and used by Microsoft. Like the SMB protocol, CIFS runs at a higher level and uses the TCP/IP protocol.

### Common Libraries (oslo)

The project that produces a set of python libraries containing code shared by OpenStack projects. The APIs provided by these libraries should be high quality, stable, consistent, documented and generally applicable.

### community project

A project that is not officially endorsed by the OpenStack Foundation. If the project is successful enough, it might be elevated to an incubated project and then to a core project, or it might be merged with the main code trunk.

### compression

Reducing the size of files by special encoding, the file can be decompressed again to its original content. OpenStack supports compression at the Linux file system level but does not support compression for things such as Object Storage objects or Image service VM images.

### Compute API (Nova API)

The nova-api daemon provides access to nova services. Can communicate with other APIs, such as the Amazon EC2 API.

**compute controller**

The Compute component that chooses suitable hosts on which to start VM instances.

**compute host**

Physical host dedicated to running compute nodes.

**compute node**

A node that runs the nova-compute daemon that manages VM instances that provide a wide range of services, such as web applications and analytics.

**Compute service (nova)**

The OpenStack core project that implements services and associated libraries to provide massively-scalable, on-demand, self-service access to compute resources, including bare metal, virtual machines, and containers.

**compute worker**

The Compute component that runs on each compute node and manages the VM instance lifecycle, including run, reboot, terminate, attach/detach volumes, and so on. Provided by the nova-compute daemon.

**concatenated object**

A set of segment objects that Object Storage combines and sends to the client.

**conductor**

In Compute, conductor is the process that proxies database requests from the compute process. Using conductor improves security because compute nodes do not need direct access to the database.

**congress**

Code name for the *Governance service (congress)*.

**consistency window**

The amount of time it takes for a new Object Storage object to become accessible to all clients.

**console log**

Contains the output from a Linux VM console in Compute.

**container**

Organizes and stores objects in Object Storage. Similar to the concept of a Linux directory but cannot be nested. Alternative term for an Image service container format.

**container auditor**

Checks for missing replicas or incorrect objects in specified Object Storage containers through queries to the SQLite back-end database.

**container database**

A SQLite database that stores Object Storage containers and container metadata. The container server accesses this database.

**container format**

A wrapper used by the Image service that contains a VM image and its associated metadata, such as machine state, OS disk size, and so on.

**Container Infrastructure Management service (magnum)**

The project which provides a set of services for provisioning, scaling, and managing container orchestration engines.

**container server**

An Object Storage server that manages containers.

**container service**

The Object Storage component that provides container services, such as create, delete, list, and so on.

**content delivery network (CDN)**

A content delivery network is a specialized network that is used to distribute content to clients, typically located close to the client for increased performance.

**controller node**

Alternative term for a cloud controller node.

**core API**

Depending on context, the core API is either the OpenStack API or the main API of a specific core project, such as Compute, Networking, Image service, and so on.

**core service**

An official OpenStack service defined as core by DefCore Committee. Currently, consists of Block Storage service (cinder), Compute service (nova), Identity service (keystone), Image service (glance), Networking service (neutron), and Object Storage service (swift).

**cost**

Under the Compute distributed scheduler, this is calculated by looking at the capabilities of each host relative to the flavor of the VM instance being requested.

**credentials**

Data that is only known to or accessible by a user and used to verify that the user is who he says he is. Credentials are presented to the server during authentication. Examples include a password, secret key, digital certificate, and fingerprint.

**Cross-Origin Resource Sharing (CORS)**

A mechanism that allows many resources (for example, fonts, JavaScript) on a web page to be requested from another domain outside the domain from which the resource originated. In particular, JavaScript's AJAX calls can use the XMLHttpRequest mechanism.

**Crowbar**

An open source community project by SUSE that aims to provide all necessary services to quickly deploy and manage clouds.

**current workload**

An element of the Compute capacity cache that is calculated based on the number of build, snapshot, migrate, and resize operations currently in progress on a given host.

**customer**

Alternative term for project.

**customization module**

A user-created Python module that is loaded by horizon to change the look and feel of the dashboard.

## D

**daemon**

A process that runs in the background and waits for requests. May or may not listen on a TCP or UDP port. Do not confuse with a worker.

### Dashboard (horizon)

OpenStack project which provides an extensible, unified, web-based user interface for all OpenStack services.

### data encryption

Both Image service and Compute support encrypted virtual machine (VM) images (but not instances). In-transit data encryption is supported in OpenStack using technologies such as HTTPS, SSL, TLS, and SSH. Object Storage does not support object encryption at the application level but may support storage that uses disk encryption.

### Data loss prevention (DLP) software

Software programs used to protect sensitive information and prevent it from leaking outside a network boundary through the detection and denying of the data transportation.

### Data Processing service (sahara)

OpenStack project that provides a scalable data-processing stack and associated management interfaces.

### data store

A database engine supported by the Database service.

### database ID

A unique ID given to each replica of an Object Storage database.

### database replicator

An Object Storage component that copies changes in the account, container, and object databases to other nodes.

### Database service (trove)

An integrated project that provides scalable and reliable Cloud Database-as-a-Service functionality for both relational and non-relational database engines.

### deallocate

The process of removing the association between a floating IP address and a fixed IP address. Once this association is removed, the floating IP returns to the address pool.

### Debian

A Linux distribution that is compatible with OpenStack.

**deduplication**

The process of finding duplicate data at the disk block, file, and/or object level to minimize storage use—currently unsupported within OpenStack.

**default panel**

The default panel that is displayed when a user accesses the dashboard.

**default project**

New users are assigned to this project if no project is specified when a user is created.

**default token**

An Identity service token that is not associated with a specific project and is exchanged for a scoped token.

**delayed delete**

An option within Image service so that an image is deleted after a predefined number of seconds instead of immediately.

**delivery mode**

Setting for the Compute RabbitMQ message delivery mode; can be set to either transient or persistent.

**denial of service (DoS)**

Denial of service (DoS) is a short form for denial-of-service attack. This is a malicious attempt to prevent legitimate users from using a service.

**deprecated auth**

An option within Compute that enables administrators to create and manage users through the `nova-manage` command as opposed to using the Identity service.

**designate**

Code name for the *DNS service (designate)*.

**Desktop-as-a-Service**

A platform that provides a suite of desktop environments that users access to receive a desktop experience from any location. This may provide general use, development, or even homogeneous testing environments.

**developer**

One of the default roles in the Compute RBAC system and the default role assigned to a new user.

### device ID

Maps Object Storage partitions to physical storage devices.

### device weight

Distributes partitions proportionately across Object Storage devices based on the storage capacity of each device.

### DevStack

Community project that uses shell scripts to quickly build complete OpenStack development environments.

### DHCP agent

OpenStack Networking agent that provides DHCP services for virtual networks.

### Diablo

A grouped release of projects related to OpenStack that came out in the fall of 2011, the fourth release of OpenStack. It included Compute (nova 2011.3), Object Storage (swift 1.4.3), and the Image service (glance). Diablo is the code name for the fourth release of OpenStack. The design summit took place in the Bay Area near Santa Clara, California, US and Diablo is a nearby city.

### direct consumer

An element of the Compute RabbitMQ that comes to life when a RPC call is executed. It connects to a direct exchange through a unique exclusive queue, sends the message, and terminates.

### direct exchange

A routing table that is created within the Compute RabbitMQ during RPC calls; one is created for each RPC call that is invoked.

### direct publisher

Element of RabbitMQ that provides a response to an incoming MQ message.

### disassociate

The process of removing the association between a floating IP address and fixed IP and thus returning the floating IP address to the address pool.

### Discretionary Access Control (DAC)

Governs the ability of subjects to access objects, while enabling users to make policy decisions and assign security attributes. The traditional UNIX system of users, groups, and read-write-execute permissions is an example of DAC.

### disk encryption

The ability to encrypt data at the file system, disk partition, or whole-disk level. Supported within Compute VMs.

### disk format

The underlying format that a disk image for a VM is stored as within the Image service back-end store. For example, AMI, ISO, QCOW2, VMDK, and so on.

### dispersion

In Object Storage, tools to test and ensure dispersion of objects and containers to ensure fault tolerance.

### distributed virtual router (DVR)

Mechanism for highly available multi-host routing when using OpenStack Networking (neutron).

### Django

A web framework used extensively in horizon.

### DNS record

A record that specifies information about a particular domain and belongs to the domain.

### DNS service (designate)

OpenStack project that provides scalable, on demand, self service access to authoritative DNS services, in a technology-agnostic manner.

### dnsmasq

Daemon that provides DNS, DHCP, BOOTP, and TFTP services for virtual networks.

### domain

An Identity API v3 entity. Represents a collection of projects, groups and users that defines administrative boundaries for managing OpenStack Identity entities. On the Internet, separates a website from other sites. Often, the domain name has two or more parts that are separated by dots. For example, yahoo.com, usa.gov, harvard.edu, or mail.yahoo.com.

Also, a domain is an entity or container of all DNS-related information containing one or more records.

### Domain Name System (DNS)

A system by which Internet domain name-to-address and address-to-name resolutions are determined. DNS helps navigate the Internet by translating the IP address into an address that is easier to remember. For example, translating 111.111.111.1 into www.yahoo.com. All domains and their components, such as mail servers, utilize DNS to resolve to the appropriate locations. DNS servers are usually set up in a master-slave relationship such that failure of the master invokes the slave. DNS servers might also be clustered or replicated such that changes made to one DNS server are automatically propagated to other active servers. In Compute, the support that enables associating DNS entries with floating IP addresses, nodes, or cells so that hostnames are consistent across reboots.

### download

The transfer of data, usually in the form of files, from one computer to another.

### durable exchange

The Compute RabbitMQ message exchange that remains active when the server restarts.

### durable queue

A Compute RabbitMQ message queue that remains active when the server restarts.

### Dynamic Host Configuration Protocol (DHCP)

A network protocol that configures devices that are connected to a network so that they can communicate on that network by using the Internet Protocol (IP). The protocol is implemented in a client-server model where DHCP clients request configuration data, such as an IP address, a default route, and one or more DNS server addresses from a DHCP server. A method to automatically configure networking for a host at boot time. Provided by both Networking and Compute.

### Dynamic HyperText Markup Language (DHTML)

Pages that use HTML, JavaScript, and Cascading Style Sheets to enable users to interact with a web page or show simple animation.

# E

### east-west traffic

Network traffic between servers in the same cloud or data center. See also north-south traffic.

### EBS boot volume

An Amazon EBS storage volume that contains a bootable VM image, currently unsupported in OpenStack.

### ebtables

Filtering tool for a Linux bridging firewall, enabling filtering of network traffic passing through a Linux bridge. Used in Compute along with arptables, iptables, and ip6tables to ensure isolation of network communications.

### EC2

The Amazon commercial compute product, similar to Compute.

### EC2 access key

Used along with an EC2 secret key to access the Compute EC2 API.

### EC2 API

OpenStack supports accessing the Amazon EC2 API through Compute.

### EC2 Compatibility API

A Compute component that enables OpenStack to communicate with Amazon EC2.

### EC2 secret key

Used along with an EC2 access key when communicating with the Compute EC2 API; used to digitally sign each request.

### Elastic Block Storage (EBS)

The Amazon commercial block storage product.

### encapsulation

The practice of placing one packet type within another for the purposes of abstracting or securing data. Examples include GRE, MPLS, or IPsec.

### encryption

OpenStack supports encryption technologies such as HTTPS, SSH, SSL, TLS, digital certificates, and data encryption.

### endpoint

See API endpoint.

### endpoint registry

Alternative term for an Identity service catalog.

### endpoint template

A list of URL and port number endpoints that indicate where a service, such as Object Storage, Compute, Identity, and so on, can be accessed.

### entity

Any piece of hardware or software that wants to connect to the network services provided by Networking, the network connectivity service. An entity can make use of Networking by implementing a VIF.

### ephemeral image

A VM image that does not save changes made to its volumes and reverts them to their original state after the instance is terminated.

### ephemeral volume

Volume that does not save the changes made to it and reverts to its original state when the current user relinquishes control.

### Essex

A grouped release of projects related to OpenStack that came out in April 2012, the fifth release of OpenStack. It included Compute (nova 2012.1), Object Storage (swift 1.4.8), Image (glance), Identity (keystone), and Dashboard (horizon). Essex is the code name for the fifth release of OpenStack. The design summit took place in Boston, Massachusetts, US and Essex is a nearby city.

### ESXi

An OpenStack-supported hypervisor.

### ETag

MD5 hash of an object within Object Storage, used to ensure data integrity.

### euca2ools

A collection of command-line tools for administering VMs; most are compatible with OpenStack.

**Eucalyptus Kernel Image (EKI)**

Used along with an ERI to create an EMI.

**Eucalyptus Machine Image (EMI)**

VM image container format supported by Image service.

**Eucalyptus Ramdisk Image (ERI)**

Used along with an EKI to create an EMI.

**evacuate**

The process of migrating one or all virtual machine (VM) instances from one host to another, compatible with both shared storage live migration and block migration.

**exchange**

Alternative term for a RabbitMQ message exchange.

**exchange type**

A routing algorithm in the Compute RabbitMQ.

**exclusive queue**

Connected to by a direct consumer in RabbitMQ—Compute, the message can be consumed only by the current connection.

**extended attributes (xattr)**

File system option that enables storage of additional information beyond owner, group, permissions, modification time, and so on. The underlying Object Storage file system must support extended attributes.

**extension**

Alternative term for an API extension or plug-in. In the context of Identity service, this is a call that is specific to the implementation, such as adding support for OpenID.

**external network**

A network segment typically used for instance Internet access.

**extra specs**

Specifies additional requirements when Compute determines where to start a new instance. Examples include a minimum amount of network bandwidth or a GPU.

# F

## FakeLDAP

An easy method to create a local LDAP directory for testing Identity and Compute. Requires Redis.

## fan-out exchange

Within RabbitMQ and Compute, it is the messaging interface that is used by the scheduler service to receive capability messages from the compute, volume, and network nodes.

## federated identity

A method to establish trusts between identity providers and the OpenStack cloud.

## Fedora

A Linux distribution compatible with OpenStack.

## Fibre Channel

Storage protocol similar in concept to TCP/IP; encapsulates SCSI commands and data.

## Fibre Channel over Ethernet (FCoE)

The fibre channel protocol tunneled within Ethernet.

## fill-first scheduler

The Compute scheduling method that attempts to fill a host with VMs rather than starting new VMs on a variety of hosts.

## filter

The step in the Compute scheduling process when hosts that cannot run VMs are eliminated and not chosen.

## firewall

Used to restrict communications between hosts and/or nodes, implemented in Compute using iptables, arptables, ip6tables, and ebtables.

## FireWall-as-a-Service (FWaaS)

A Networking extension that provides perimeter firewall functionality.

## fixed IP address

An IP address that is associated with the same instance each time that instance boots, is generally not accessible to end users or the public Internet, and is used for management of the instance.

### Flat Manager

The Compute component that gives IP addresses to authorized nodes and assumes DHCP, DNS, and routing configuration and services are provided by something else.

### flat mode injection

A Compute networking method where the OS network configuration information is injected into the VM image before the instance starts.

### flat network

Virtual network type that uses neither VLANs nor tunnels to segregate project traffic. Each flat network typically requires a separate underlying physical interface defined by bridge mappings. However, a flat network can contain multiple subnets.

### FlatDHCP Manager

The Compute component that provides dnsmasq (DHCP, DNS, BOOTP, TFTP) and radvd (routing) services.

### flavor

Alternative term for a VM instance type.

### flavor ID

UUID for each Compute or Image service VM flavor or instance type.

### floating IP address

An IP address that a project can associate with a VM so that the instance has the same public IP address each time that it boots. You create a pool of floating IP addresses and assign them to instances as they are launched to maintain a consistent IP address for maintaining DNS assignment.

### Folsom

A grouped release of projects related to OpenStack that came out in the fall of 2012, the sixth release of OpenStack. It includes Compute (nova), Object Storage (swift), Identity (keystone), Networking (neutron), Image service (glance), and Volumes or Block Storage (cinder). Folsom is the code name for the sixth release of OpenStack. The design summit took place in San Francisco, California, US and Folsom is a nearby city.

### FormPost

Object Storage middleware that uploads (posts) an image through a form on a web page.

### freezer

Code name for the *Backup, Restore, and Disaster Recovery service (freezer)*.

### front end

The point where a user interacts with a service; can be an API endpoint, the dashboard, or a command-line tool.

## G

### gateway

An IP address, typically assigned to a router, that passes network traffic between different networks.

### generic receive offload (GRO)

Feature of certain network interface drivers that combines many smaller received packets into a large packet before delivery to the kernel IP stack.

### generic routing encapsulation (GRE)

Protocol that encapsulates a wide variety of network layer protocols inside virtual point-to-point links.

### glance

Codename for the *Image service (glance)*.

### glance API server

Alternative name for the *Image API*.

### glance registry

Alternative term for the Image service *image registry*.

### global endpoint template

The Identity service endpoint template that contains services available to all projects.

### GlusterFS

A file system designed to aggregate NAS hosts, compatible with OpenStack.

### gnocchi

Part of the OpenStack *Telemetry service (telemetry)*; provides an indexer and time-series database.

### golden image

A method of operating system installation where a finalized disk image is created and then used by all nodes without modification.

### Governance service (congress)

The project that provides Governance-as-a-Service across any collection of cloud services in order to monitor, enforce, and audit policy over dynamic infrastructure.

### Graphic Interchange Format (GIF)

A type of image file that is commonly used for animated images on web pages.

### Graphics Processing Unit (GPU)

Choosing a host based on the existence of a GPU is currently unsupported in OpenStack.

### Green Threads

The cooperative threading model used by Python; reduces race conditions and only context switches when specific library calls are made. Each OpenStack service is its own thread.

### Grizzly

The code name for the seventh release of OpenStack. The design summit took place in San Diego, California, US and Grizzly is an element of the state flag of California.

### Group

An Identity v3 API entity. Represents a collection of users that is owned by a specific domain.

### guest OS

An operating system instance running under the control of a hypervisor.

## H

### Hadoop

Apache Hadoop is an open source software framework that supports data-intensive distributed applications.

### Hadoop Distributed File System (HDFS)

A distributed, highly fault-tolerant file system designed to run on low-cost commodity hardware.

### handover

An object state in Object Storage where a new replica of the object is automatically created due to a drive failure.

### HAProxy

Provides a high availability load balancer and proxy server for TCP and HTTP-based applications that spreads requests across multiple servers.

### hard reboot

A type of reboot where a physical or virtual power button is pressed as opposed to a graceful, proper shutdown of the operating system.

### Havana

The code name for the eighth release of OpenStack. The design summit took place in Portland, Oregon, US and Havana is an unincorporated community in Oregon.

### health monitor

Determines whether back-end members of a VIP pool can process a request. A pool can have several health monitors associated with it. When a pool has several monitors associated with it, all monitors check each member of the pool. All monitors must declare a member to be healthy for it to stay active.

### heat

Codename for the *Orchestration service (heat)*.

### Heat Orchestration Template (HOT)

Heat input in the format native to OpenStack.

### high availability (HA)

A high availability system design approach and associated service implementation ensures that a prearranged level of operational performance will be met during a contractual measurement period. High availability systems seek to minimize system downtime and data loss.

### horizon

Codename for the *Dashboard (horizon)*.

### horizon plug-in

A plug-in for the OpenStack Dashboard (horizon).

### host

A physical computer, not a VM instance (node).

### host aggregate

A method to further subdivide availability zones into hypervisor pools, a collection of common hosts.

### Host Bus Adapter (HBA)

Device plugged into a PCI slot, such as a fibre channel or network card.

### hybrid cloud

A hybrid cloud is a composition of two or more clouds (private, community or public) that remain distinct entities but are bound together, offering the benefits of multiple deployment models. Hybrid cloud can also mean the ability to connect colocation, managed and/or dedicated services with cloud resources.

### Hyper-V

One of the hypervisors supported by OpenStack.

### hyperlink

Any kind of text that contains a link to some other site, commonly found in documents where clicking on a word or words opens up a different website.

### Hypertext Transfer Protocol (HTTP)

An application protocol for distributed, collaborative, hypermedia information systems. It is the foundation of data communication for the World Wide Web. Hypertext is structured text that uses logical links (hyperlinks) between nodes containing text. HTTP is the protocol to exchange or transfer hypertext.

### Hypertext Transfer Protocol Secure (HTTPS)

An encrypted communications protocol for secure communication over a computer network, with especially wide deployment on the Internet. Technically, it is not a protocol in and of itself; rather, it is the result of simply layering the Hypertext Transfer Protocol (HTTP) on top of the TLS or SSL protocol, thus adding the security capabilities of TLS or SSL to standard HTTP communications. Most OpenStack API endpoints and many inter-component communications support HTTPS communication.

### hypervisor

Software that arbitrates and controls VM access to the actual underlying hardware.

### hypervisor pool

A collection of hypervisors grouped together through host aggregates.

## I

### Icehouse

The code name for the ninth release of OpenStack. The design summit took place in Hong Kong and Ice House is a street in that city.

### ID number

Unique numeric ID associated with each user in Identity, conceptually similar to a Linux or LDAP UID.

### Identity API

Alternative term for the Identity service API.

### Identity back end

The source used by Identity service to retrieve user information; an OpenLDAP server, for example.

### identity provider

A directory service, which allows users to login with a user name and password. It is a typical source of authentication tokens.

### Identity service (keystone)

The project that facilitates API client authentication, service discovery, distributed multi-tenant authorization, and auditing. It provides a central directory of users mapped to the OpenStack services they can access. It also registers endpoints for OpenStack services and acts as a common authentication system.

### Identity service API

The API used to access the OpenStack Identity service provided through keystone.

**image**

A collection of files for a specific operating system (OS) that you use to create or rebuild a server. OpenStack provides pre-built images. You can also create custom images, or snapshots, from servers that you have launched. Custom images can be used for data backups or as "gold" images for additional servers.

**Image API**

The Image service API endpoint for management of VM images. Processes client requests for VMs, updates Image service metadata on the registry server, and communicates with the store adapter to upload VM images from the back-end store.

**image cache**

Used by Image service to obtain images on the local host rather than re-downloading them from the image server each time one is requested.

**image ID**

Combination of a URI and UUID used to access Image service VM images through the image API.

**image membership**

A list of projects that can access a given VM image within Image service.

**image owner**

The project who owns an Image service virtual machine image.

**image registry**

A list of VM images that are available through Image service.

**Image service (glance)**

The OpenStack service that provide services and associated libraries to store, browse, share, distribute and manage bootable disk images, other data closely associated with initializing compute resources, and metadata definitions.

**image status**

The current status of a VM image in Image service, not to be confused with the status of a running instance.

**image store**

The back-end store used by Image service to store VM images, options include Object Storage, locally mounted file system, RADOS block devices, VMware datastore, or HTTP.

### image UUID

UUID used by Image service to uniquely identify each VM image.

### incubated project

A community project may be elevated to this status and is then promoted to a core project.

### Infrastructure Optimization service (watcher)

OpenStack project that aims to provide a flexible and scalable resource optimization service for multi-tenant OpenStack-based clouds.

### Infrastructure-as-a-Service (IaaS)

IaaS is a provisioning model in which an organization outsources physical components of a data center, such as storage, hardware, servers, and networking components. A service provider owns the equipment and is responsible for housing, operating and maintaining it. The client typically pays on a per-use basis. IaaS is a model for providing cloud services.

### ingress filtering

The process of filtering incoming network traffic. Supported by Compute.

### INI format

The OpenStack configuration files use an INI format to describe options and their values. It consists of sections and key value pairs.

### injection

The process of putting a file into a virtual machine image before the instance is started.

### Input/Output Operations Per Second (IOPS)

IOPS are a common performance measurement used to benchmark computer storage devices like hard disk drives, solid state drives, and storage area networks.

### instance

A running VM, or a VM in a known state such as suspended, that can be used like a hardware server.

### instance ID

Alternative term for instance UUID.

### instance state

The current state of a guest VM image.

### instance tunnels network

A network segment used for instance traffic tunnels between compute nodes and the network node.

### instance type

Describes the parameters of the various virtual machine images that are available to users; includes parameters such as CPU, storage, and memory. Alternative term for flavor.

### instance type ID

Alternative term for a flavor ID.

### instance UUID

Unique ID assigned to each guest VM instance.

### Intelligent Platform Management Interface (IPMI)

IPMI is a standardized computer system interface used by system administrators for out-of-band management of computer systems and monitoring of their operation. In layman's terms, it is a way to manage a computer using a direct network connection, whether it is turned on or not; connecting to the hardware rather than an operating system or login shell.

### interface

A physical or virtual device that provides connectivity to another device or medium.

### interface ID

Unique ID for a Networking VIF or vNIC in the form of a UUID.

### Internet Control Message Protocol (ICMP)

A network protocol used by network devices for control messages. For example, `ping` uses ICMP to test connectivity.

### Internet protocol (IP)

Principal communications protocol in the internet protocol suite for relaying datagrams across network boundaries.

### Internet Service Provider (ISP)

Any business that provides Internet access to individuals or businesses.

### Internet Small Computer System Interface (iSCSI)

Storage protocol that encapsulates SCSI frames for transport over IP networks. Supported by Compute, Object Storage, and Image service.

## IP address

Number that is unique to every computer system on the Internet. Two versions of the Internet Protocol (IP) are in use for addresses: IPv4 and IPv6.

## IP Address Management (IPAM)

The process of automating IP address allocation, deallocation, and management. Currently provided by Compute, melange, and Networking.

## ip6tables

Tool used to set up, maintain, and inspect the tables of IPv6 packet filter rules in the Linux kernel. In OpenStack Compute, ip6tables is used along with arptables, ebtables, and iptables to create firewalls for both nodes and VMs.

## ipset

Extension to iptables that allows creation of firewall rules that match entire "sets" of IP addresses simultaneously. These sets reside in indexed data structures to increase efficiency, particularly on systems with a large quantity of rules.

## iptables

Used along with arptables and ebtables, iptables create firewalls in Compute. iptables are the tables provided by the Linux kernel firewall (implemented as different Netfilter modules) and the chains and rules it stores. Different kernel modules and programs are currently used for different protocols: iptables applies to IPv4, ip6tables to IPv6, arptables to ARP, and ebtables to Ethernet frames. Requires root privilege to manipulate.

## ironic

Codename for the *Bare Metal service (ironic)*.

## iSCSI Qualified Name (IQN)

IQN is the format most commonly used for iSCSI names, which uniquely identify nodes in an iSCSI network. All IQNs follow the pattern iqn.yyyy-mm.domain:identifier, where 'yyyy-mm' is the year and month in which the domain was registered, 'domain' is the reversed domain name of the issuing organization, and 'identifier' is an optional string which makes each IQN under the same domain unique. For example, 'iqn.2015-10.org.openstack.408ae959bce1'.

## ISO9660

One of the VM image disk formats supported by Image service.

## itsec

A default role in the Compute RBAC system that can quarantine an instance in any project.

## J

### Java

A programming language that is used to create systems that involve more than one computer by way of a network.

### JavaScript

A scripting language that is used to build web pages.

### JavaScript Object Notation (JSON)

One of the supported response formats in OpenStack.

### Jenkins

Tool used to run jobs automatically for OpenStack development.

### jumbo frame

Feature in modern Ethernet networks that supports frames up to approximately 9000 bytes.

### Juno

The code name for the tenth release of OpenStack. The design summit took place in Atlanta, Georgia, US and Juno is an unincorporated community in Georgia.

## K

### Kerberos

A network authentication protocol which works on the basis of tickets. Kerberos allows nodes communication over a non-secure network, and allows nodes to prove their identity to one another in a secure manner.

### kernel-based VM (KVM)

An OpenStack-supported hypervisor. KVM is a full virtualization solution for Linux on x86 hardware containing virtualization extensions (Intel VT or AMD-V), ARM, IBM Power, and IBM zSeries. It consists of a loadable kernel module, that provides the core virtualization infrastructure and a processor specific module.

### Key Manager service (barbican)

The project that produces a secret storage and generation system capable of providing key management for services wishing to enable encryption features.

### keystone

Codename of the *Identity service (keystone)*.

### Kickstart

A tool to automate system configuration and installation on Red Hat, Fedora, and CentOS-based Linux distributions.

### Kilo

The code name for the eleventh release of OpenStack. The design summit took place in Paris, France. Due to delays in the name selection, the release was known only as K. Because `k` is the unit symbol for kilo and the reference artifact is stored near Paris in the Pavillon de Breteuil in Sèvres, the community chose Kilo as the release name.

## L

### large object

An object within Object Storage that is larger than 5 GB.

### Launchpad

The collaboration site for OpenStack.

### Layer-2 (L2) agent

OpenStack Networking agent that provides layer-2 connectivity for virtual networks.

### Layer-2 network

Term used in the OSI network architecture for the data link layer. The data link layer is responsible for media access control, flow control and detecting and possibly correcting errors that may occur in the physical layer.

### Layer-3 (L3) agent

OpenStack Networking agent that provides layer-3 (routing) services for virtual networks.

## Layer-3 network

Term used in the OSI network architecture for the network layer. The network layer is responsible for packet forwarding including routing from one node to another.

## Liberty

The code name for the twelfth release of OpenStack. The design summit took place in Vancouver, Canada and Liberty is the name of a village in the Canadian province of Saskatchewan.

## libvirt

Virtualization API library used by OpenStack to interact with many of its supported hypervisors.

## Lightweight Directory Access Protocol (LDAP)

An application protocol for accessing and maintaining distributed directory information services over an IP network.

## Linux bridge

Software that enables multiple VMs to share a single physical NIC within Compute.

## Linux Bridge neutron plug-in

Enables a Linux bridge to understand a Networking port, interface attachment, and other abstractions.

## Linux containers (LXC)

An OpenStack-supported hypervisor.

## live migration

The ability within Compute to move running virtual machine instances from one host to another with only a small service interruption during switchover.

## load balancer

A load balancer is a logical device that belongs to a cloud account. It is used to distribute workloads between multiple back-end systems or services, based on the criteria defined as part of its configuration.

## load balancing

The process of spreading client requests between two or more nodes to improve performance and availability.

### Load-Balancer-as-a-Service (LBaaS)

Enables Networking to distribute incoming requests evenly between designated instances.

### Load-balancing service (octavia)

The project that aims to rovide scalable, on demand, self service access to load-balancer services, in technology-agnostic manner.

### Logical Volume Manager (LVM)

Provides a method of allocating space on mass-storage devices that is more flexible than conventional partitioning schemes.

## M

### magnum

Code name for the *Container Infrastructure Management service (magnum)*.

### management API

Alternative term for an admin API.

### management network

A network segment used for administration, not accessible to the public Internet.

### manager

Logical groupings of related code, such as the Block Storage volume manager or network manager.

### manifest

Used to track segments of a large object within Object Storage.

### manifest object

A special Object Storage object that contains the manifest for a large object.

### manila

Codename for OpenStack *Shared File Systems service (manila)*.

### manila-share

Responsible for managing Shared File System Service devices, specifically the back-end devices.

### maximum transmission unit (MTU)

Maximum frame or packet size for a particular network medium. Typically 1500 bytes for Ethernet networks.

### mechanism driver

A driver for the Modular Layer 2 (ML2) neutron plug-in that provides layer-2 connectivity for virtual instances. A single OpenStack installation can use multiple mechanism drivers.

### melange

Project name for OpenStack Network Information Service. To be merged with Networking.

### membership

The association between an Image service VM image and a project. Enables images to be shared with specified projects.

### membership list

A list of projects that can access a given VM image within Image service.

### memcached

A distributed memory object caching system that is used by Object Storage for caching.

### memory overcommit

The ability to start new VM instances based on the actual memory usage of a host, as opposed to basing the decision on the amount of RAM each running instance thinks it has available. Also known as RAM overcommit.

### message broker

The software package used to provide AMQP messaging capabilities within Compute. Default package is RabbitMQ.

### message bus

The main virtual communication line used by all AMQP messages for inter-cloud communications within Compute.

### message queue

Passes requests from clients to the appropriate workers and returns the output to the client after the job completes.

### Message service (zaqar)

The project that provides a messaging service that affords a variety of distributed application patterns in an efficient, scalable and highly available manner, and to create and maintain associated Python libraries and documentation.

### Meta-Data Server (MDS)

Stores CephFS metadata.

### Metadata agent

OpenStack Networking agent that provides metadata services for instances.

### migration

The process of moving a VM instance from one host to another.

### mistral

Code name for *Workflow service (mistral)*.

### Mitaka

The code name for the thirteenth release of OpenStack. The design summit took place in Tokyo, Japan. Mitaka is a city in Tokyo.

### Modular Layer 2 (ML2) neutron plug-in

Can concurrently use multiple layer-2 networking technologies, such as 802.1Q and VXLAN, in Networking.

### monasca

Codename for OpenStack *Monitoring (monasca)*.

### Monitor (LBaaS)

LBaaS feature that provides availability monitoring using the `ping` command, TCP, and HTTP/HTTPS GET.

### Monitor (Mon)

A Ceph component that communicates with external clients, checks data state and consistency, and performs quorum functions.

### Monitoring (monasca)

The OpenStack service that provides a multi-tenant, highly scalable, performant, fault-tolerant monitoring-as-a-service solution for metrics, complex event processing and logging. To build an extensible platform for advanced monitoring services that can be used by both operators and tenants to gain operational insight and visibility, ensuring availability and stability.

**multi-factor authentication**

Authentication method that uses two or more credentials, such as a password and a private key. Currently not supported in Identity.

**multi-host**

High-availability mode for legacy (nova) networking. Each compute node handles NAT and DHCP and acts as a gateway for all of the VMs on it. A networking failure on one compute node doesn't affect VMs on other compute nodes.

**multinic**

Facility in Compute that allows each virtual machine instance to have more than one VIF connected to it.

**murano**

Codename for the *Application Catalog service (murano)*.

## N

**Nebula**

Released as open source by NASA in 2010 and is the basis for Compute.

**netadmin**

One of the default roles in the Compute RBAC system. Enables the user to allocate publicly accessible IP addresses to instances and change firewall rules.

**NetApp volume driver**

Enables Compute to communicate with NetApp storage devices through the NetApp OnCommand Provisioning Manager.

**network**

A virtual network that provides connectivity between entities. For example, a collection of virtual ports that share network connectivity. In Networking terminology, a network is always a layer-2 network.

**Network Address Translation (NAT)**

Process of modifying IP address information while in transit. Supported by Compute and Networking.

**network controller**

A Compute daemon that orchestrates the network configuration of nodes, including IP addresses, VLANs, and bridging. Also manages routing for both public and private networks.

**Network File System (NFS)**

A method for making file systems available over the network. Supported by OpenStack.

**network ID**

Unique ID assigned to each network segment within Networking. Same as network UUID.

**network manager**

The Compute component that manages various network components, such as firewall rules, IP address allocation, and so on.

**network namespace**

Linux kernel feature that provides independent virtual networking instances on a single host with separate routing tables and interfaces. Similar to virtual routing and forwarding (VRF) services on physical network equipment.

**network node**

Any compute node that runs the network worker daemon.

**network segment**

Represents a virtual, isolated OSI layer-2 subnet in Networking.

**Network Service Header (NSH)**

Provides a mechanism for metadata exchange along the instantiated service path.

**Network Time Protocol (NTP)**

Method of keeping a clock for a host or node correct via communication with a trusted, accurate time source.

**network UUID**

Unique ID for a Networking network segment.

**network worker**

The `nova-network` worker daemon; provides services such as giving an IP address to a booting nova instance.

**Networking API (Neutron API)**

API used to access OpenStack Networking. Provides an extensible architecture to enable custom plug-in creation.

**Networking service (neutron)**

The OpenStack project which implements services and associated libraries to provide on-demand, scalable, and technology-agnostic network abstraction.

**neutron**

Codename for OpenStack *Networking service (neutron)*.

**neutron API**

An alternative name for *Networking API (Neutron API)*.

**neutron manager**

Enables Compute and Networking integration, which enables Networking to perform network management for guest VMs.

**neutron plug-in**

Interface within Networking that enables organizations to create custom plug-ins for advanced features, such as QoS, ACLs, or IDS.

**Newton**

The code name for the fourteenth release of OpenStack. The design summit took place in Austin, Texas, US. The release is named after "Newton House" which is located at 1013 E. Ninth St., Austin, TX. which is listed on the National Register of Historic Places.

**Nexenta volume driver**

Provides support for NexentaStor devices in Compute.

**NFV Orchestration Service (tacker)**

OpenStack service that aims to implement Network Function Virtualization (NFV) orchestration services and libraries for end-to-end life-cycle management of network services and Virtual Network Functions (VNFs).

**Nginx**

An HTTP and reverse proxy server, a mail proxy server, and a generic TCP/UDP proxy server.

### No ACK

Disables server-side message acknowledgment in the Compute RabbitMQ. Increases performance but decreases reliability.

### node

A VM instance that runs on a host.

### non-durable exchange

Message exchange that is cleared when the service restarts. Its data is not written to persistent storage.

### non-durable queue

Message queue that is cleared when the service restarts. Its data is not written to persistent storage.

### non-persistent volume

Alternative term for an ephemeral volume.

### north-south traffic

Network traffic between a user or client (north) and a server (south), or traffic into the cloud (south) and out of the cloud (north). See also east-west traffic.

### nova

Codename for OpenStack *Compute service (nova)*.

### Nova API

Alternative term for the *Compute API (Nova API)*.

### nova-network

A Compute component that manages IP address allocation, firewalls, and other network-related tasks. This is the legacy networking option and an alternative to Networking.

## O

### object

A BLOB of data held by Object Storage; can be in any format.

**object auditor**

Opens all objects for an object server and verifies the MD5 hash, size, and metadata for each object.

**object expiration**

A configurable option within Object Storage to automatically delete objects after a specified amount of time has passed or a certain date is reached.

**object hash**

Unique ID for an Object Storage object.

**object path hash**

Used by Object Storage to determine the location of an object in the ring. Maps objects to partitions.

**object replicator**

An Object Storage component that copies an object to remote partitions for fault tolerance.

**object server**

An Object Storage component that is responsible for managing objects.

**Object Storage API**

API used to access OpenStack *Object Storage service (swift)*.

**Object Storage Device (OSD)**

The Ceph storage daemon.

**Object Storage service (swift)**

The OpenStack core project that provides eventually consistent and redundant storage and retrieval of fixed digital content.

**object versioning**

Allows a user to set a flag on an *Object Storage service (swift)* container so that all objects within the container are versioned.

**Ocata**

The code name for the fifteenth release of OpenStack. The design summit will take place in Barcelona, Spain. Ocata is a beach north of Barcelona.

**Octavia**

Code name for the *Load-balancing service (octavia)*.

## Oldie

Term for an *Object Storage service (swift)* process that runs for a long time. Can indicate a hung process.

## Open Cloud Computing Interface (OCCI)

A standardized interface for managing compute, data, and network resources, currently unsupported in OpenStack.

## Open Virtualization Format (OVF)

Standard for packaging VM images. Supported in OpenStack.

## Open vSwitch

Open vSwitch is a production quality, multilayer virtual switch licensed under the open source Apache 2.0 license. It is designed to enable massive network automation through programmatic extension, while still supporting standard management interfaces and protocols (for example NetFlow, sFlow, SPAN, RSPAN, CLI, LACP, 802.1ag).

## Open vSwitch (OVS) agent

Provides an interface to the underlying Open vSwitch service for the Networking plug-in.

## Open vSwitch neutron plug-in

Provides support for Open vSwitch in Networking.

## OpenLDAP

An open source LDAP server. Supported by both Compute and Identity.

## OpenStack

OpenStack is a cloud operating system that controls large pools of compute, storage, and networking resources throughout a data center, all managed through a dashboard that gives administrators control while empowering their users to provision resources through a web interface. OpenStack is an open source project licensed under the Apache License 2.0.

## OpenStack code name

Each OpenStack release has a code name. Code names ascend in alphabetical order: Austin, Bexar, Cactus, Diablo, Essex, Folsom, Grizzly, Havana, Icehouse, Juno, Kilo, Liberty, Mitaka, Newton, Ocata, Pike, and Queens. Code names are cities or counties near where the corresponding OpenStack design summit took place. An exception, called the Waldon exception, is granted to elements of the state flag that sound especially cool. Code names are chosen by popular vote.

### openSUSE

A Linux distribution that is compatible with OpenStack.

### operator

The person responsible for planning and maintaining an OpenStack installation.

### optional service

An official OpenStack service defined as optional by DefCore Committee. Currently, consists of Dashboard (horizon), Telemetry service (Telemetry), Orchestration service (heat), Database service (trove), Bare Metal service (ironic), and so on.

### Orchestration service (heat)

The OpenStack service which orchestrates composite cloud applications using a declarative template format through an OpenStack-native REST API.

### orphan

In the context of Object Storage, this is a process that is not terminated after an upgrade, restart, or reload of the service.

### Oslo

Codename for the *Common Libraries (oslo)*.

## P

### panko

Part of the OpenStack *Telemetry service (telemetry)*; provides event storage.

### parent cell

If a requested resource, such as CPU time, disk storage, or memory, is not available in the parent cell, the request is forwarded to associated child cells.

### partition

A unit of storage within Object Storage used to store objects. It exists on top of devices and is replicated for fault tolerance.

### partition index

Contains the locations of all Object Storage partitions within the ring.

**partition shift value**

Used by Object Storage to determine which partition data should reside on.

**path MTU discovery (PMTUD)**

Mechanism in IP networks to detect end-to-end MTU and adjust packet size accordingly.

**pause**

A VM state where no changes occur (no changes in memory, network communications stop, etc); the VM is frozen but not shut down.

**PCI passthrough**

Gives guest VMs exclusive access to a PCI device. Currently supported in OpenStack Havana and later releases.

**persistent message**

A message that is stored both in memory and on disk. The message is not lost after a failure or restart.

**persistent volume**

Changes to these types of disk volumes are saved.

**personality file**

A file used to customize a Compute instance. It can be used to inject SSH keys or a specific network configuration.

**Pike**

The code name for the sixteenth release of OpenStack. The design summit will take place in Boston, Massachusetts, US. The release is named after the Massachusetts Turnpike, abbreviated commonly as the Mass Pike, which is the easternmost stretch of Interstate 90.

**Platform-as-a-Service (PaaS)**

Provides to the consumer the ability to deploy applications through a programming language or tools supported by the cloud platform provider. An example of Platform-as-a-Service is an Eclipse/Java programming platform provided with no downloads required.

**plug-in**

Software component providing the actual implementation for Networking APIs, or for Compute APIs, depending on the context.

### policy service

Component of Identity that provides a rule-management interface and a rule-based authorization engine.

### policy-based routing (PBR)

Provides a mechanism to implement packet forwarding and routing according to the policies defined by the network administrator.

### pool

A logical set of devices, such as web servers, that you group together to receive and process traffic. The load balancing function chooses which member of the pool handles the new requests or connections received on the VIP address. Each VIP has one pool.

### pool member

An application that runs on the back-end server in a load-balancing system.

### port

A virtual network port within Networking; VIFs / vNICs are connected to a port.

### port UUID

Unique ID for a Networking port.

### preseed

A tool to automate system configuration and installation on Debian-based Linux distributions.

### private image

An Image service VM image that is only available to specified projects.

### private IP address

An IP address used for management and administration, not available to the public Internet.

### private network

The Network Controller provides virtual networks to enable compute servers to interact with each other and with the public network. All machines must have a public and private network interface. A private network interface can be a flat or VLAN network interface. A flat network interface is controlled by the flat_interface with flat managers. A VLAN network interface is controlled by the `vlan_interface` option with VLAN managers.

### project

Projects represent the base unit of "ownership" in OpenStack, in that all resources in OpenStack should be owned by a specific project. In OpenStack Identity, a project must be owned by a specific domain.

### project ID

Unique ID assigned to each project by the Identity service.

### project VPN

Alternative term for a cloudpipe.

### promiscuous mode

Causes the network interface to pass all traffic it receives to the host rather than passing only the frames addressed to it.

### protected property

Generally, extra properties on an Image service image to which only cloud administrators have access. Limits which user roles can perform CRUD operations on that property. The cloud administrator can configure any image property as protected.

### provider

An administrator who has access to all hosts and instances.

### proxy node

A node that provides the Object Storage proxy service.

### proxy server

Users of Object Storage interact with the service through the proxy server, which in turn looks up the location of the requested data within the ring and returns the results to the user.

### public API

An API endpoint used for both service-to-service communication and end-user interactions.

### public image

An Image service VM image that is available to all projects.

### public IP address

An IP address that is accessible to end-users.

### public key authentication

Authentication method that uses keys rather than passwords.

## public network

The Network Controller provides virtual networks to enable compute servers to interact with each other and with the public network. All machines must have a public and private network interface. The public network interface is controlled by the `public_interface` option.

## Puppet

An operating system configuration-management tool supported by OpenStack.

## Python

Programming language used extensively in OpenStack.

# Q

## QEMU Copy On Write 2 (QCOW2)

One of the VM image disk formats supported by Image service.

## Qpid

Message queue software supported by OpenStack; an alternative to RabbitMQ.

## Quality of Service (QoS)

The ability to guarantee certain network or storage requirements to satisfy a Service Level Agreement (SLA) between an application provider and end users. Typically includes performance requirements like networking bandwidth, latency, jitter correction, and reliability as well as storage performance in Input/Output Operations Per Second (IOPS), throttling agreements, and performance expectations at peak load.

## quarantine

If Object Storage finds objects, containers, or accounts that are corrupt, they are placed in this state, are not replicated, cannot be read by clients, and a correct copy is re-replicated.

## Queens

The code name for the seventeenth release of OpenStack. The design summit will take place in Sydney, Australia. The release is named after the Queens Pound river in the South Coast region of New South Wales.

### Quick EMUlator (QEMU)

QEMU is a generic and open source machine emulator and virtualizer. One of the hypervisors supported by OpenStack, generally used for development purposes.

### quota

In Compute and Block Storage, the ability to set resource limits on a per-project basis.

## R

### RabbitMQ

The default message queue software used by OpenStack.

### Rackspace Cloud Files

Released as open source by Rackspace in 2010; the basis for Object Storage.

### RADOS Block Device (RBD)

Ceph component that enables a Linux block device to be striped over multiple distributed data stores.

### radvd

The router advertisement daemon, used by the Compute VLAN manager and FlatDHCP manager to provide routing services for VM instances.

### rally

Codename for the *Benchmark service (rally)*.

### RAM filter

The Compute setting that enables or disables RAM overcommitment.

### RAM overcommit

The ability to start new VM instances based on the actual memory usage of a host, as opposed to basing the decision on the amount of RAM each running instance thinks it has available. Also known as memory overcommit.

### rate limit

Configurable option within Object Storage to limit database writes on a per-account and/or per-container basis.

### raw

One of the VM image disk formats supported by Image service; an unstructured disk image.

### rebalance

The process of distributing Object Storage partitions across all drives in the ring; used during initial ring creation and after ring reconfiguration.

### reboot

Either a soft or hard reboot of a server. With a soft reboot, the operating system is signaled to restart, which enables a graceful shutdown of all processes. A hard reboot is the equivalent of power cycling the server. The virtualization platform should ensure that the reboot action has completed successfully, even in cases in which the underlying domain/VM is paused or halted/stopped.

### rebuild

Removes all data on the server and replaces it with the specified image. Server ID and IP addresses remain the same.

### Recon

An Object Storage component that collects meters.

### record

Belongs to a particular domain and is used to specify information about the domain. There are several types of DNS records. Each record type contains particular information used to describe the purpose of that record. Examples include mail exchange (MX) records, which specify the mail server for a particular domain; and name server (NS) records, which specify the authoritative name servers for a domain.

### record ID

A number within a database that is incremented each time a change is made. Used by Object Storage when replicating.

### Red Hat Enterprise Linux (RHEL)

A Linux distribution that is compatible with OpenStack.

### reference architecture

A recommended architecture for an OpenStack cloud.

region

A discrete OpenStack environment with dedicated API endpoints that typically shares only the Identity (keystone) with other regions.

registry

Alternative term for the Image service registry.

registry server

An Image service that provides VM image metadata information to clients.

Reliable, Autonomic Distributed Object Store

(RADOS)

A collection of components that provides object storage within Ceph. Similar to OpenStack Object Storage.

Remote Procedure Call (RPC)

The method used by the Compute RabbitMQ for intra-service communications.

replica

Provides data redundancy and fault tolerance by creating copies of Object Storage objects, accounts, and containers so that they are not lost when the underlying storage fails.

replica count

The number of replicas of the data in an Object Storage ring.

replication

The process of copying data to a separate physical device for fault tolerance and performance.

replicator

The Object Storage back-end process that creates and manages object replicas.

request ID

Unique ID assigned to each request sent to Compute.

rescue image

A special type of VM image that is booted when an instance is placed into rescue mode. Allows an administrator to mount the file systems for an instance to correct the problem.

### resize

Converts an existing server to a different flavor, which scales the server up or down. The original server is saved to enable rollback if a problem occurs. All resizes must be tested and explicitly confirmed, at which time the original server is removed.

### RESTful

A kind of web service API that uses REST, or Representational State Transfer. REST is the style of architecture for hypermedia systems that is used for the World Wide Web.

### ring

An entity that maps Object Storage data to partitions. A separate ring exists for each service, such as account, object, and container.

### ring builder

Builds and manages rings within Object Storage, assigns partitions to devices, and pushes the configuration to other storage nodes.

### role

A personality that a user assumes to perform a specific set of operations. A role includes a set of rights and privileges. A user assuming that role inherits those rights and privileges.

### Role Based Access Control (RBAC)

Provides a predefined list of actions that the user can perform, such as start or stop VMs, reset passwords, and so on. Supported in both Identity and Compute and can be configured using the dashboard.

### role ID

Alphanumeric ID assigned to each Identity service role.

### Root Cause Analysis (RCA) service (Vitrage)

OpenStack project that aims to organize, analyze and visualize OpenStack alarms and events, yield insights regarding the root cause of problems and deduce their existence before they are directly detected.

### rootwrap

A feature of Compute that allows the unprivileged "nova" user to run a specified list of commands as the Linux root user.

### round-robin scheduler

Type of Compute scheduler that evenly distributes instances among available hosts.

## router

A physical or virtual network device that passes network traffic between different networks.

## routing key

The Compute direct exchanges, fanout exchanges, and topic exchanges use this key to determine how to process a message; processing varies depending on exchange type.

## RPC driver

Modular system that allows the underlying message queue software of Compute to be changed. For example, from RabbitMQ to ZeroMQ or Qpid.

## rsync

Used by Object Storage to push object replicas.

## RXTX cap

Absolute limit on the amount of network traffic a Compute VM instance can send and receive.

## RXTX quota

Soft limit on the amount of network traffic a Compute VM instance can send and receive.

# S

## sahara

Codename for the *Data Processing service (sahara)*.

## SAML assertion

Contains information about a user as provided by the identity provider. It is an indication that a user has been authenticated.

## scheduler manager

A Compute component that determines where VM instances should start. Uses modular design to support a variety of scheduler types.

## scoped token

An Identity service API access token that is associated with a specific project.

**scrubber**

Checks for and deletes unused VMs; the component of Image service that implements delayed delete.

**secret key**

String of text known only by the user; used along with an access key to make requests to the Compute API.

**secure boot**

Process whereby the system firmware validates the authenticity of the code involved in the boot process.

**secure shell (SSH)**

Open source tool used to access remote hosts through an encrypted communications channel, SSH key injection is supported by Compute.

**security group**

A set of network traffic filtering rules that are applied to a Compute instance.

**segmented object**

An Object Storage large object that has been broken up into pieces. The re-assembled object is called a concatenated object.

**self-service**

For IaaS, ability for a regular (non-privileged) account to manage a virtual infrastructure component such as networks without involving an administrator.

**SELinux**

Linux kernel security module that provides the mechanism for supporting access control policies.

**senlin**

Code name for the *Clustering service (senlin)*.

**server**

Computer that provides explicit services to the client software running on that system, often managing a variety of computer operations. A server is a VM instance in the Compute system. Flavor and image are requisite elements when creating a server.

**server image**

Alternative term for a VM image.

### server UUID

Unique ID assigned to each guest VM instance.

### service

An OpenStack service, such as Compute, Object Storage, or Image service. Provides one or more endpoints through which users can access resources and perform operations.

### service catalog

Alternative term for the Identity service catalog.

### Service Function Chain (SFC)

For a given service, SFC is the abstracted view of the required service functions and the order in which they are to be applied.

### service ID

Unique ID assigned to each service that is available in the Identity service catalog.

### Service Level Agreement (SLA)

Contractual obligations that ensure the availability of a service.

### service project

Special project that contains all services that are listed in the catalog.

### service provider

A system that provides services to other system entities. In case of federated identity, OpenStack Identity is the service provider.

### service registration

An Identity service feature that enables services, such as Compute, to automatically register with the catalog.

### service token

An administrator-defined token used by Compute to communicate securely with the Identity service.

### session back end

The method of storage used by horizon to track client sessions, such as local memory, cookies, a database, or memcached.

## session persistence

A feature of the load-balancing service. It attempts to force subsequent connections to a service to be redirected to the same node as long as it is online.

## session storage

A horizon component that stores and tracks client session information. Implemented through the Django sessions framework.

## share

A remote, mountable file system in the context of the *Shared File Systems service (manila)*. You can mount a share to, and access a share from, several hosts by several users at a time.

## share network

An entity in the context of the *Shared File Systems service (manila)* that encapsulates interaction with the Networking service. If the driver you selected runs in the mode requiring such kind of interaction, you need to specify the share network to create a share.

## Shared File Systems API

A Shared File Systems service that provides a stable RESTful API. The service authenticates and routes requests throughout the Shared File Systems service. There is python-manilaclient to interact with the API.

## Shared File Systems service (manila)

The service that provides a set of services for management of shared file systems in a multi-tenant cloud environment, similar to how OpenStack provides block-based storage management through the OpenStack *Block Storage service (cinder)* project. With the Shared File Systems service, you can create a remote file system and mount the file system on your instances. You can also read and write data from your instances to and from your file system.

## shared IP address

An IP address that can be assigned to a VM instance within the shared IP group. Public IP addresses can be shared across multiple servers for use in various high-availability scenarios. When an IP address is shared to another server, the cloud network restrictions are modified to enable each server to listen to and respond on that IP address. You can optionally specify that the target server network configuration be modified. Shared IP addresses can be used with many standard heartbeat facilities, such as keepalive, that monitor for failure and manage IP failover.

### shared IP group

A collection of servers that can share IPs with other members of the group. Any server in a group can share one or more public IPs with any other server in the group. With the exception of the first server in a shared IP group, servers must be launched into shared IP groups. A server may be a member of only one shared IP group.

### shared storage

Block storage that is simultaneously accessible by multiple clients, for example, NFS.

### Sheepdog

Distributed block storage system for QEMU, supported by OpenStack.

### Simple Cloud Identity Management (SCIM)

Specification for managing identity in the cloud, currently unsupported by OpenStack.

### Simple Protocol for Independent Computing Environments (SPICE)

SPICE provides remote desktop access to guest virtual machines. It is an alternative to VNC. SPICE is supported by OpenStack.

### Single-root I/O Virtualization (SR-IOV)

A specification that, when implemented by a physical PCIe device, enables it to appear as multiple separate PCIe devices. This enables multiple virtualized guests to share direct access to the physical device, offering improved performance over an equivalent virtual device. Currently supported in OpenStack Havana and later releases.

### SmokeStack

Runs automated tests against the core OpenStack API; written in Rails.

### snapshot

A point-in-time copy of an OpenStack storage volume or image. Use storage volume snapshots to back up volumes. Use image snapshots to back up data, or as "gold" images for additional servers.

### soft reboot

A controlled reboot where a VM instance is properly restarted through operating system commands.

**Software Development Lifecycle Automation service (solum)**

OpenStack project that aims to make cloud services easier to consume and integrate with application development process by automating the source-to-image process, and simplifying app-centric deployment.

**Software-defined networking (SDN)**

Provides an approach for network administrators to manage computer network services through abstraction of lower-level functionality.

**SolidFire Volume Driver**

The Block Storage driver for the SolidFire iSCSI storage appliance.

**solum**

Code name for the *Software Development Lifecycle Automation service (solum)*.

**spread-first scheduler**

The Compute VM scheduling algorithm that attempts to start a new VM on the host with the least amount of load.

**SQLAlchemy**

An open source SQL toolkit for Python, used in OpenStack.

**SQLite**

A lightweight SQL database, used as the default persistent storage method in many OpenStack services.

**stack**

A set of OpenStack resources created and managed by the Orchestration service according to a given template (either an AWS CloudFormation template or a Heat Orchestration Template (HOT)).

**StackTach**

Community project that captures Compute AMQP communications; useful for debugging.

**static IP address**

Alternative term for a fixed IP address.

**StaticWeb**

WSGI middleware component of Object Storage that serves container data as a static web page.

### storage back end

The method that a service uses for persistent storage, such as iSCSI, NFS, or local disk.

### storage manager

A XenAPI component that provides a pluggable interface to support a wide variety of persistent storage back ends.

### storage manager back end

A persistent storage method supported by XenAPI, such as iSCSI or NFS.

### storage node

An Object Storage node that provides container services, account services, and object services; controls the account databases, container databases, and object storage.

### storage services

Collective name for the Object Storage object services, container services, and account services.

### strategy

Specifies the authentication source used by Image service or Identity. In the Database service, it refers to the extensions implemented for a data store.

### subdomain

A domain within a parent domain. Subdomains cannot be registered. Subdomains enable you to delegate domains. Subdomains can themselves have subdomains, so third-level, fourth-level, fifth-level, and deeper levels of nesting are possible.

### subnet

Logical subdivision of an IP network.

### SUSE Linux Enterprise Server (SLES)

A Linux distribution that is compatible with OpenStack.

### suspend

Alternative term for a paused VM instance.

### swap

Disk-based virtual memory used by operating systems to provide more memory than is actually available on the system.

**swauth**

An authentication and authorization service for Object Storage, implemented through WSGI middleware; uses Object Storage itself as the persistent backing store.

**swift**

Codename for OpenStack *Object Storage service (swift)*.

**swift All in One (SAIO)**

Creates a full Object Storage development environment within a single VM.

**swift middleware**

Collective term for Object Storage components that provide additional functionality.

**swift proxy server**

Acts as the gatekeeper to Object Storage and is responsible for authenticating the user.

**swift storage node**

A node that runs Object Storage account, container, and object services.

**sync point**

Point in time since the last container and accounts database sync among nodes within Object Storage.

**sysadmin**

One of the default roles in the Compute RBAC system. Enables a user to add other users to a project, interact with VM images that are associated with the project, and start and stop VM instances.

**system usage**

A Compute component that, along with the notification system, collects meters and usage information. This information can be used for billing.

## T

**tacker**

Code name for the *NFV Orchestration Service (tacker)*

### Telemetry service (telemetry)

The OpenStack project which collects measurements of the utilization of the physical and virtual resources comprising deployed clouds, persists this data for subsequent retrieval and analysis, and triggers actions when defined criteria are met.

### TempAuth

An authentication facility within Object Storage that enables Object Storage itself to perform authentication and authorization. Frequently used in testing and development.

### Tempest

Automated software test suite designed to run against the trunk of the OpenStack core project.

### TempURL

An Object Storage middleware component that enables creation of URLs for temporary object access.

### tenant

A group of users; used to isolate access to Compute resources. An alternative term for a project.

### Tenant API

An API that is accessible to projects.

### tenant endpoint

An Identity service API endpoint that is associated with one or more projects.

### tenant ID

An alternative term for *project ID*.

### token

An alpha-numeric string of text used to access OpenStack APIs and resources.

### token services

An Identity service component that manages and validates tokens after a user or project has been authenticated.

### tombstone

Used to mark Object Storage objects that have been deleted; ensures that the object is not updated on another node after it has been deleted.

**topic publisher**

A process that is created when a RPC call is executed; used to push the message to the topic exchange.

**Torpedo**

Community project used to run automated tests against the OpenStack API.

**transaction ID**

Unique ID assigned to each Object Storage request; used for debugging and tracing.

**transient**

Alternative term for non-durable.

**transient exchange**

Alternative term for a non-durable exchange.

**transient message**

A message that is stored in memory and is lost after the server is restarted.

**transient queue**

Alternative term for a non-durable queue.

**TripleO**

OpenStack-on-OpenStack program. The code name for the OpenStack Deployment program.

**trove**

Codename for OpenStack *Database service (trove)*.

**trusted platform module (TPM)**

Specialized microprocessor for incorporating cryptographic keys into devices for authenticating and securing a hardware platform.

## U

**Ubuntu**

A Debian-based Linux distribution.

### unscoped token

Alternative term for an Identity service default token.

### updater

Collective term for a group of Object Storage components that processes queued and failed updates for containers and objects.

### user

In OpenStack Identity, entities represent individual API consumers and are owned by a specific domain. In OpenStack Compute, a user can be associated with roles, projects, or both.

### user data

A blob of data that the user can specify when they launch an instance. The instance can access this data through the metadata service or config drive. Commonly used to pass a shell script that the instance runs on boot.

### User Mode Linux (UML)

An OpenStack-supported hypervisor.

### VIF UUID

Unique ID assigned to each Networking VIF.

### Virtual Central Processing Unit (vCPU)

Subdivides physical CPUs. Instances can then use those divisions.

### Virtual Disk Image (VDI)

One of the VM image disk formats supported by Image service.

### Virtual Extensible LAN (VXLAN)

A network virtualization technology that attempts to reduce the scalability problems associated with large cloud computing deployments. It uses a VLAN-like encapsulation technique to encapsulate Ethernet frames within UDP packets.

### Virtual Hard Disk (VHD)

One of the VM image disk formats supported by Image service.

virtual IP address (VIP)

An Internet Protocol (IP) address configured on the load balancer for use by clients connecting to a service that is load balanced. Incoming connections are distributed to back-end nodes based on the configuration of the load balancer.

virtual machine (VM)

An operating system instance that runs on top of a hypervisor. Multiple VMs can run at the same time on the same physical host.

virtual network

An L2 network segment within Networking.

Virtual Network Computing (VNC)

Open source GUI and CLI tools used for remote console access to VMs. Supported by Compute.

Virtual Network InterFace (VIF)

An interface that is plugged into a port in a Networking network. Typically a virtual network interface belonging to a VM.

virtual networking

A generic term for virtualization of network functions such as switching, routing, load balancing, and security using a combination of VMs and overlays on physical network infrastructure.

virtual port

Attachment point where a virtual interface connects to a virtual network.

virtual private network (VPN)

Provided by Compute in the form of cloudpipes, specialized instances that are used to create VPNs on a per-project basis.

virtual server

Alternative term for a VM or guest.

virtual switch (vSwitch)

Software that runs on a host or node and provides the features and functions of a hardware-based network switch.

virtual VLAN

Alternative term for a virtual network.

**VirtualBox**

An OpenStack-supported hypervisor.

**Vitrage**

Code name for the *Root Cause Analysis (RCA) service (Vitrage)*.

**VLAN manager**

A Compute component that provides dnsmasq and radvd and sets up forwarding to and from cloudpipe instances.

**VLAN network**

The Network Controller provides virtual networks to enable compute servers to interact with each other and with the public network. All machines must have a public and private network interface. A VLAN network is a private network interface, which is controlled by the `vlan_interface` option with VLAN managers.

**VM disk (VMDK)**

One of the VM image disk formats supported by Image service.

**VM image**

Alternative term for an image.

**VM Remote Control (VMRC)**

Method to access VM instance consoles using a web browser. Supported by Compute.

**VMware API**

Supports interaction with VMware products in Compute.

**VMware NSX Neutron plug-in**

Provides support for VMware NSX in Neutron.

**VNC proxy**

A Compute component that provides users access to the consoles of their VM instances through VNC or VMRC.

**volume**

Disk-based data storage generally represented as an iSCSI target with a file system that supports extended attributes; can be persistent or ephemeral.

**Volume API**

Alternative name for the Block Storage API.

**volume controller**

A Block Storage component that oversees and coordinates storage volume actions.

**volume driver**

Alternative term for a volume plug-in.

**volume ID**

Unique ID applied to each storage volume under the Block Storage control.

**volume manager**

A Block Storage component that creates, attaches, and detaches persistent storage volumes.

**volume node**

A Block Storage node that runs the cinder-volume daemon.

**volume plug-in**

Provides support for new and specialized types of back-end storage for the Block Storage volume manager.

**volume worker**

A cinder component that interacts with back-end storage to manage the creation and deletion of volumes and the creation of compute volumes, provided by the cinder-volume daemon.

**vSphere**

An OpenStack-supported hypervisor.

**Watcher**

Code name for the *Infrastructure Optimization service (watcher)*.

**weight**

Used by Object Storage devices to determine which storage devices are suitable for the job. Devices are weighted by size.

**weighted cost**

The sum of each cost used when deciding where to start a new VM instance in Compute.

### weighting

A Compute process that determines the suitability of the VM instances for a job for a particular host. For example, not enough RAM on the host, too many CPUs on the host, and so on.

### worker

A daemon that listens to a queue and carries out tasks in response to messages. For example, the cinder-volume worker manages volume creation and deletion on storage arrays.

### Workflow service (mistral)

The OpenStack service that provides a simple YAML-based language to write workflows (tasks and transition rules) and a service that allows to upload them, modify, run them at scale and in a highly available manner, manage and monitor workflow execution state and state of individual tasks.

## X

### Xen

Xen is a hypervisor using a microkernel design, providing services that allow multiple computer operating systems to execute on the same computer hardware concurrently.

### Xen API

The Xen administrative API, which is supported by Compute.

### Xen Cloud Platform (XCP)

An OpenStack-supported hypervisor.

### Xen Storage Manager Volume Driver

A Block Storage volume plug-in that enables communication with the Xen Storage Manager API.

### XenServer

An OpenStack-supported hypervisor.

### XFS

High-performance 64-bit file system created by Silicon Graphics. Excels in parallel I/O operations and data consistency.

## Z

**zaqar**

Codename for the *Message service (zaqar)*.

**ZeroMQ**

Message queue software supported by OpenStack. An alternative to RabbitMQ. Also spelled 0MQ.

**Zuul**

Tool used in OpenStack development to ensure correctly ordered testing of changes in parallel.

# FreeBSD Architecture Handbook

# FreeBSD Architecture Handbook

Revision: 51016

2017-10-01 12:11:13 by wosch.



# Abstract

Welcome to the FreeBSD Architecture Handbook. This manual is a *work in progress* and is the work of many individuals. Many sections do not yet exist and some of those that do exist need to be updated. If you are interested in helping with this project, send email to the FreeBSD documentation project mailing list.

The latest version of this document is always available from the FreeBSD World Wide Web server. It may also be downloaded in a variety of formats and compression options from the FreeBSD FTP server or one of the numerous mirror sites.

## Important

# Table of Contents

# List of Figures

# List of Tables

# List of Examples

# Part I. Kernel

# Table of Contents

# Chapter 1. Bootstrapping and Kernel Initialization

Contributed by Sergey Lyubka.
Updated and enhanced by Sergio Andrés Gómez del Real.

## 1.1. Synopsis

This chapter is an overview of the boot and system initialization processes, starting from the BIOS (firmware) POST, to the first user process creation. Since the initial steps of system startup are very architecture dependent, the IA-32 architecture is used as an example.

The FreeBSD boot process can be surprisingly complex. After control is passed from the BIOS, a considerable amount of low-level configuration must be done before the kernel can be loaded and executed. This setup must be done in a simple and flexible manner, allowing the user a great deal of customization possibilities.

## 1.2. Overview

The boot process is an extremely machine-dependent activity. Not only must code be written for every computer architecture, but there may also be multiple types of booting on the same architecture. For example, a directory listing of `/usr/src/sys/boot` reveals a great amount of architecture-dependent code. There is a directory for each of the various supported architectures. In the x86-specific `i386` directory, there are subdirectories for different boot standards like `mbr` (Master Boot Record), `gpt` (GUID Partition Table), and `efi` (Extensible Firmware Interface). Each boot standard has its own conventions and data structures. The example that follows shows booting an x86 computer from an MBR hard drive with the FreeBSD `boot0` multi-boot loader stored in the very first sector. That boot code starts the FreeBSD three-stage boot process.

The key to understanding this process is that it is a series of stages of increasing complexity. These stages are `boot1`, `boot2`, and `loader` (see boot(8) for more detail). The boot system executes each stage in sequence. The last stage, `loader`, is responsible for loading the FreeBSD kernel. Each stage is examined in the following sections.

Here is an example of the output generated by the different boot stages. Actual output may differ from machine to machine:

| FreeBSD Component | Output (may vary) |
|---|---|
| `boot0` | `F1    FreeBSD`<br>`F2    BSD`<br>`F5    Disk 2` |
| `boot2` [a] | `>>FreeBSD/i386 BOOT`<br>`Default: 1:ad(1,a)/boot/loader`<br>`boot:` |
| `loader` | `BTX loader 1.00 BTX version is 1.02`<br>`Consoles: internal video/keyboard`<br>`BIOS drive C: is disk0`<br>`BIOS 639kB/2096064kB available memory`<br><br>`FreeBSD/x86 bootstrap loader, Revision 1.1`<br>`Console internal video/keyboard`<br>`(root@snap.freebsd.org, Thu Jan 16 ↺`<br>`22:18:05 UTC 2014)`<br>`Loading /boot/defaults/loader.conf`<br>`/boot/kernel/kernel text=0xed9008 ↺`<br>`data=0x117d28+0x176650 ↺`<br>`syms=[0x8+0x137988+0x8+0x1515f8]` |

| | |
|---|---|
| kernel | `Copyright (c) 1992-2013 The FreeBSD ↺ Project. Copyright (c) 1979, 1980, 1983, 1986, ↺ 1988, 1989, 1991, 1992, 1993, 1994 The Regents of the University of ↺ California. All rights reserved. FreeBSD is a registered trademark of The ↺ FreeBSD Foundation. FreeBSD 10.0-RELEASE #0 r260789: Thu Jan ↺ 16 22:34:59 UTC 2014 root@snap.freebsd.org:/usr/obj/usr/src/ sys/GENERIC amd64 FreeBSD clang version 3.3 (tags/RELEASE_33/ final 183502) 20130610` |

[a]This prompt will appear if the user presses a key just after selecting an OS to boot at the boot0 stage.

## 1.3. The BIOS

When the computer powers on, the processor's registers are set to some predefined values. One of the registers is the *instruction pointer* register, and its value after a power on is well defined: it is a 32-bit value of 0xfffffff0 . The instruction pointer register (also known as the Program Counter) points to code to be executed by the processor. Another important register is the cr0 32-bit control register, and its value just after a reboot is 0. One of cr0's bits, the PE (Protection Enabled) bit, indicates whether the processor is running in 32-bit protected mode or 16-bit real mode. Since this bit is cleared at boot time, the processor boots in 16-bit real mode. Real mode means, among other things, that linear and physical addresses are identical. The reason for the processor not to start immediately in 32-bit protected mode is backwards compatibility. In particular, the boot process relies on the services provided by the BIOS, and the BIOS itself works in legacy, 16-bit code.

The value of 0xfffffff0 is slightly less than 4 GB, so unless the machine has 4 GB of physical memory, it cannot point to a valid memory address. The computer's hardware translates this address so that it points to a BIOS memory block.

The BIOS (Basic Input Output System) is a chip on the motherboard that has a relatively small amount of read-only memory (ROM). This memory contains various low-level routines that are specific to the hardware supplied with the motherboard. The processor will first jump to the address 0xfffffff0, which really resides in the BIOS's memory. Usually this address contains a jump instruction to the BIOS's POST routines.

The POST (Power On Self Test) is a set of routines including the memory check, system bus check, and other low-level initialization so the CPU can set up the computer properly. The important step of this stage is determining the boot device. Modern BIOS implementations permit the selection of a boot device, allowing booting from a floppy, CD-ROM, hard disk, or other devices.

The very last thing in the POST is the INT 0x19 instruction. The INT 0x19 handler reads 512 bytes from the first sector of boot device into the memory at address 0x7c00. The term *first sector* originates from hard drive architecture, where the magnetic plate is divided into a number of cylindrical tracks. Tracks are numbered, and every track is divided into a number (usually 64) of sectors. Track numbers start at 0, but sector numbers start from 1. Track 0 is the outermost on the magnetic plate, and sector 1, the first sector, has a special purpose. It is also called the MBR, or Master Boot Record. The remaining sectors on the first track are never used.

This sector is our boot-sequence starting point. As we will see, this sector contains a copy of our boot0 program. A jump is made by the BIOS to address 0x7c00 so it starts executing.

## 1.4. The Master Boot Record (boot0)

After control is received from the BIOS at memory address 0x7c00, boot0 starts executing. It is the first piece of code under FreeBSD control. The task of boot0 is quite simple: scan the partition table and let the user choose

which partition to boot from. The Partition Table is a special, standard data structure embedded in the MBR (hence embedded in `boot0`) describing the four standard PC "partitions" [1]. `boot0` resides in the filesystem as `/boot/boot0`. It is a small 512-byte file, and it is exactly what FreeBSD's installation procedure wrote to the hard disk's MBR if you chose the "bootmanager" option at installation time. Indeed, `boot0` *is* the MBR.

As mentioned previously, the `INT 0x19` instruction causes the `INT 0x19` handler to load an MBR (`boot0`) into memory at address `0x7c00`. The source file for `boot0` can be found in `sys/boot/i386/boot0/boot0.S` - which is an awesome piece of code written by Robert Nordier.

A special structure starting from offset `0x1be` in the MBR is called the *partition table*. It has four records of 16 bytes each, called *partition records*, which represent how the hard disk is partitioned, or, in FreeBSD's terminology, sliced. One byte of those 16 says whether a partition (slice) is bootable or not. Exactly one record must have that flag set, otherwise `boot0`'s code will refuse to proceed.

A partition record has the following fields:

- the 1-byte filesystem type
- the 1-byte bootable flag
- the 6 byte descriptor in CHS format
- the 8 byte descriptor in LBA format

A partition record descriptor contains information about where exactly the partition resides on the drive. Both descriptors, LBA and CHS, describe the same information, but in different ways: LBA (Logical Block Addressing) has the starting sector for the partition and the partition's length, while CHS (Cylinder Head Sector) has coordinates for the first and last sectors of the partition. The partition table ends with the special signature `0xaa55`.

The MBR must fit into 512 bytes, a single disk sector. This program uses low-level "tricks" like taking advantage of the side effects of certain instructions and reusing register values from previous operations to make the most out of the fewest possible instructions. Care must also be taken when handling the partition table, which is embedded in the MBR itself. For these reasons, be very careful when modifying `boot0.S`.

Note that the `boot0.S` source file is assembled "as is": instructions are translated one by one to binary, with no additional information (no ELF file format, for example). This kind of low-level control is achieved at link time through special control flags passed to the linker. For example, the text section of the program is set to be located at address `0x600`. In practice this means that `boot0` must be loaded to memory address `0x600` in order to function properly.

It is worth looking at the `Makefile` for `boot0` (`sys/boot/i386/boot0/Makefile`), as it defines some of the run-time behavior of `boot0`. For instance, if a terminal connected to the serial port (COM1) is used for I/O, the macro `SIO` must be defined (`-DSIO`). `-DPXE` enables boot through PXE by pressing F6. Additionally, the program defines a set of *flags* that allow further modification of its behavior. All of this is illustrated in the `Makefile`. For example, look at the linker directives which command the linker to start the text section at address `0x600`, and to build the output file "as is" (strip out any file formatting):

```
BOOT_BOOT0_ORG?=0x600
LDFLAGS=-e start -Ttext ${BOOT_BOOT0_ORG} \
-Wl,-N,-S,--oformat,binary
```

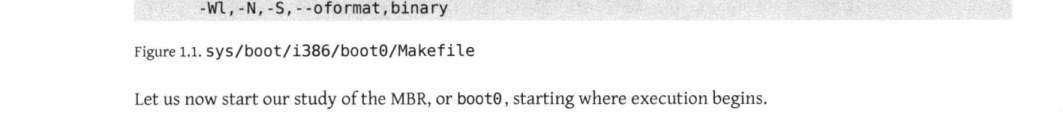

Figure 1.1. `sys/boot/i386/boot0/Makefile`

Let us now start our study of the MBR, or `boot0`, starting where execution begins.

[1] http://en.wikipedia.org/wiki/Master_boot_record

**Note**

Some modifications have been made to some instructions in favor of better exposition. For example, some macros are expanded, and some macro tests are omitted when the result of the test is known. This applies to all of the code examples shown.

```
start:
      cld   # String ops inc
      xorw %ax,%ax  # Zero
      movw %ax,%es  # Address
      movw %ax,%ds  #  data
      movw %ax,%ss  # Set up
      movw 0x7c00,%sp  #  stack
```

Figure 1.2. sys/boot/i386/boot0/boot0.S

This first block of code is the entry point of the program. It is where the BIOS transfers control. First, it makes sure that the string operations autoincrement its pointer operands (the cld instruction) [2]. Then, as it makes no assumption about the state of the segment registers, it initializes them. Finally, it sets the stack pointer register (%sp) to address 0x7c00, so we have a working stack.

The next block is responsible for the relocation and subsequent jump to the relocated code.

```
      movw $0x7c00,%si # Source
      movw $0x600,%di  # Destination
      movw $512,%cx  # Word count
      rep   # Relocate
      movsb   #  code
      movw %di,%bp  # Address variables
      movb $16,%cl  # Words to clear
      rep   # Zero
      stosb   #  them
      incb -0xe(%di)  # Set the S field to 1
      jmp main-0x7c00+0x600 # Jump to relocated code
```

Figure 1.3. sys/boot/i386/boot0/boot0.S

Because boot0 is loaded by the BIOS to address 0x7C00, it copies itself to address 0x600 and then transfers control there (recall that it was linked to execute at address 0x600). The source address, 0x7c00, is copied to register %si. The destination address, 0x600, to register %di. The number of bytes to copy, 512 (the program's size), is copied to register %cx. Next, the rep instruction repeats the instruction that follows, that is, movsb, the number of times dictated by the %cx register. The movsb instruction copies the byte pointed to by %si to the address pointed to by %di. This is repeated another 511 times. On each repetition, both the source and destination registers, %si and %di, are incremented by one. Thus, upon completion of the 512-byte copy, %di has the value 0x600+512= 0x800, and %si has the value 0x7c00+512= 0x7e00; we have thus completed the code *relocation*.

Next, the destination register %di is copied to %bp. %bp gets the value 0x800. The value 16 is copied to %cl in preparation for a new string operation (like our previous movsb). Now, stosb is executed 16 times. This instruction copies a 0 value to the address pointed to by the destination register (%di, which is 0x800), and increments it. This is repeated another 15 times, so %di ends up with value 0x810. Effectively, this clears the address range 0x800-0x80f. This range is used as a (fake) partition table for writing the MBR back to disk. Finally, the sector field for the CHS addressing of this fake partition is given the value 1 and a jump is made to the main function from the relocated code. Note that until this jump to the relocated code, any reference to an absolute address was avoided.

[2] When in doubt, we refer the reader to the official Intel manuals, which describe the exact semantics for each instruction: http://www.intel.com/content/www/us/en/processors/architectures-software-developer-manuals.html.

The following code block tests whether the drive number provided by the BIOS should be used, or the one stored in `boot0`.

```
main:
      testb $SETDRV,-69(%bp) # Set drive number?
      jnz disable_update # Yes
      testb %dl,%dl  # Drive number valid?
      js save_curdrive  # Possibly (0x80 set)
```

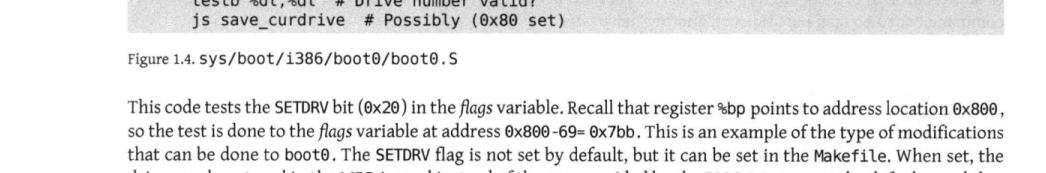

Figure 1.4. `sys/boot/i386/boot0/boot0.S`

This code tests the SETDRV bit (`0x20`) in the *flags* variable. Recall that register `%bp` points to address location `0x800`, so the test is done to the *flags* variable at address `0x800-69`= `0x7bb`. This is an example of the type of modifications that can be done to `boot0`. The SETDRV flag is not set by default, but it can be set in the `Makefile`. When set, the drive number stored in the MBR is used instead of the one provided by the BIOS. We assume the defaults, and that the BIOS provided a valid drive number, so we jump to `save_curdrive`.

The next block saves the drive number provided by the BIOS, and calls `putn` to print a new line on the screen.

```
save_curdrive:
      movb %dl, (%bp)  # Save drive number
      pushw %dx    # Also in the stack
#ifdef TEST /* test code, print internal bios drive */
      rolb $1, %dl
      movw $drive, %si
      call putkey
#endif
      callw putn  # Print a newline
```

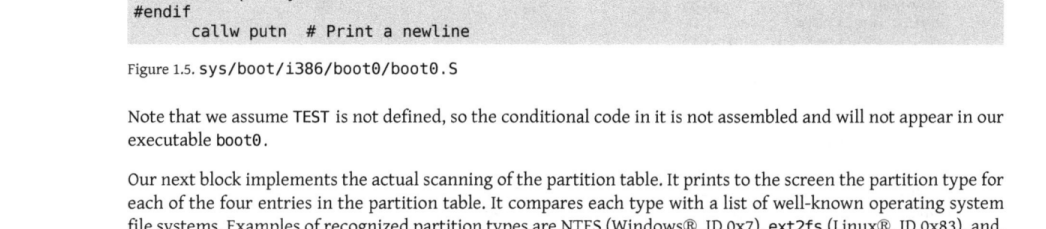

Figure 1.5. `sys/boot/i386/boot0/boot0.S`

Note that we assume TEST is not defined, so the conditional code in it is not assembled and will not appear in our executable `boot0`.

Our next block implements the actual scanning of the partition table. It prints to the screen the partition type for each of the four entries in the partition table. It compares each type with a list of well-known operating system file systems. Examples of recognized partition types are NTFS (Windows®, ID 0x7), `ext2fs` (Linux®, ID 0x83), and, of course, `ffs/ufs2` (FreeBSD, ID 0xa5). The implementation is fairly simple.

```
      movw $(partbl+0x4),%bx # Partition table (+4)
      xorw %dx,%dx   # Item number

read_entry:
      movb %ch,-0x4(%bx) # Zero active flag (ch == 0)
      btw %dx,_FLAGS(%bp) # Entry enabled?
      jnc next_entry   # No
      movb (%bx),%al  # Load type
      test %al, %al  # skip empty partition
      jz next_entry
      movw $bootable_ids,%di # Lookup tables
      movb $(TLEN+1),%cl # Number of entries
      repne   # Locate
      scasb   #  type
      addw $(TLEN-1), %di # Adjust
      movb (%di),%cl  # Partition
      addw %cx,%di  #  description
      callw putx  # Display it

next_entry:
      incw %dx    # Next item
      addb $0x10,%bl  # Next entry
      jnc read_entry  # Till done
```

Figure 1.6. `sys/boot/i386/boot0/boot0.S`

It is important to note that the active flag for each entry is cleared, so after the scanning, *no* partition entry is active in our memory copy of `boot0`. Later, the active flag will be set for the selected partition. This ensures that only one active partition exists if the user chooses to write the changes back to disk.

The next block tests for other drives. At startup, the BIOS writes the number of drives present in the computer to address `0x475`. If there are any other drives present, `boot0` prints the current drive to screen. The user may command `boot0` to scan partitions on another drive later.

```
      popw %ax    # Drive number
      subb $0x79,%al  # Does next
      cmpb 0x475,%al  #  drive exist? (from BIOS?)
      jb print_drive  # Yes
      decw %ax    # Already drive 0?
      jz print_prompt  # Yes
```

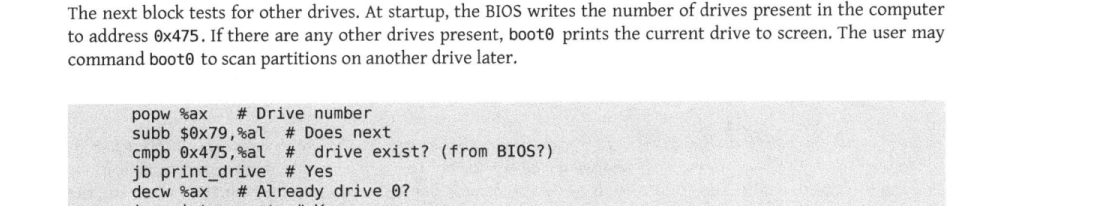

Figure 1.7. `sys/boot/i386/boot0/boot0.S`

We make the assumption that a single drive is present, so the jump to `print_drive` is not performed. We also assume nothing strange happened, so we jump to `print_prompt` .

This next block just prints out a prompt followed by the default option:

```
print_prompt:
      movw $prompt,%si  # Display
      callw putstr  #  prompt
      movb _OPT(%bp),%dl # Display
      decw %si   #  default
      callw putkey  #  key
      jmp start_input  # Skip beep
```

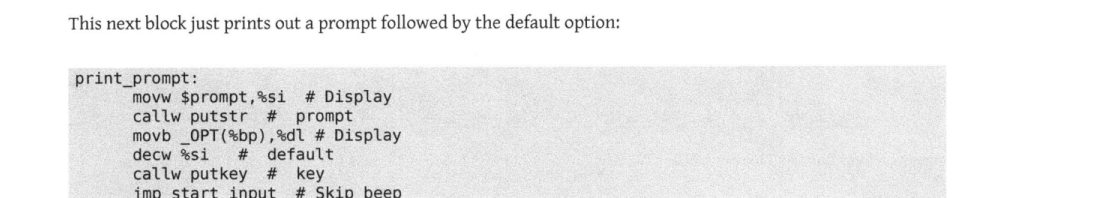

Figure 1.8. `sys/boot/i386/boot0/boot0.S`

Finally, a jump is performed to `start_input`, where the BIOS services are used to start a timer and for reading user input from the keyboard; if the timer expires, the default option will be selected:

```
start_input:
      xorb %ah,%ah  # BIOS: Get
      int $0x1a   #  system time
      movw %dx,%di  # Ticks when
      addw _TICKS(%bp),%di #  timeout
read_key:
      movb $0x1,%ah  # BIOS: Check
      int $0x16   #  for keypress
      jnz got_key  # Have input
      xorb %ah,%ah  # BIOS: int 0x1a, 00
      int $0x1a   #  get system time
      cmpw %di,%dx  # Timeout?
      jb read_key  # No
```

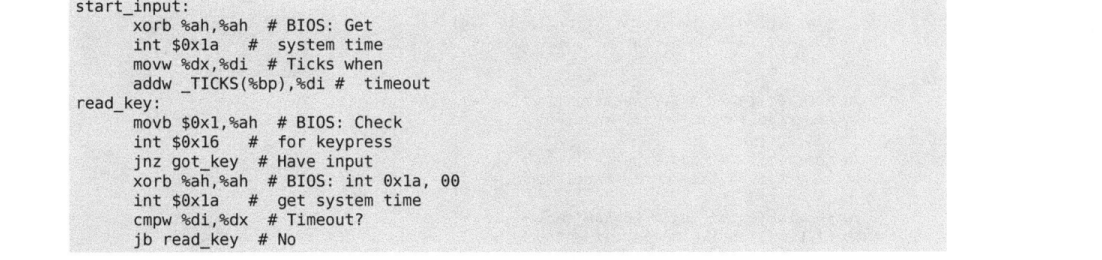

Figure 1.9. `sys/boot/i386/boot0/boot0.S`

An interrupt is requested with number `0x1a` and argument `0` in register `%ah`. The BIOS has a predefined set of services, requested by applications as software-generated interrupts through the `int` instruction and receiving arguments in registers (in this case, `%ah`). Here, particularly, we are requesting the number of clock ticks since last midnight; this value is computed by the BIOS through the RTC (Real Time Clock). This clock can be programmed to work at frequencies ranging from 2 Hz to 8192 Hz. The BIOS sets it to 18.2 Hz at startup. When the request is satisfied, a 32-bit result is returned by the BIOS in registers `%cx` and `%dx` (lower bytes in `%dx`). This result (the `%dx` part) is copied to register `%di`, and the value of the `TICKS` variable is added to `%di`. This variable resides in `boot0` at offset `_TICKS` (a negative value) from register `%bp` (which, recall, points to `0x800`). The default value of this

variable is `0xb6` (182 in decimal). Now, the idea is that `boot0` constantly requests the time from the BIOS, and when the value returned in register `%dx` is greater than the value stored in `%di`, the time is up and the default selection will be made. Since the RTC ticks 18.2 times per second, this condition will be met after 10 seconds (this default behavior can be changed in the `Makefile`). Until this time has passed, `boot0` continually asks the BIOS for any user input; this is done through `int 0x16`, argument `1` in `%ah`.

Whether a key was pressed or the time expired, subsequent code validates the selection. Based on the selection, the register `%si` is set to point to the appropriate partition entry in the partition table. This new selection overrides the previous default one. Indeed, it becomes the new default. Finally, the ACTIVE flag of the selected partition is set. If it was enabled at compile time, the in-memory version of `boot0` with these modified values is written back to the MBR on disk. We leave the details of this implementation to the reader.

We now end our study with the last code block from the `boot0` program:

```
movw $0x7c00,%bx # Address for read
movb $0x2,%ah  # Read sector
callw intx13 #  from disk
jc beep   # If error
cmpw $0xaa55,0x1fe(%bx) # Bootable?
jne beep   # No
pushw %si   # Save ptr to selected part.
callw putn  # Leave some space
popw %si   # Restore, next stage uses it
jmp *%bx   # Invoke bootstrap
```

Figure 1.10. `sys/boot/i386/boot0/boot0.S`

Recall that `%si` points to the selected partition entry. This entry tells us where the partition begins on disk. We assume, of course, that the partition selected is actually a FreeBSD slice.

> **Note**
>
> From now on, we will favor the use of the technically more accurate term "slice" rather than "partition".

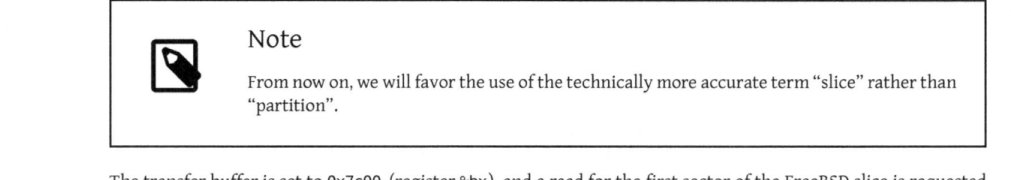

The transfer buffer is set to `0x7c00` (register `%bx`), and a read for the first sector of the FreeBSD slice is requested by calling `intx13`. We assume that everything went okay, so a jump to `beep` is not performed. In particular, the new sector read must end with the magic sequence `0xaa55`. Finally, the value at `%si` (the pointer to the selected partition table) is preserved for use by the next stage, and a jump is performed to address `0x7c00`, where execution of our next stage (the just-read block) is started.

## 1.5. `boot1` Stage

So far we have gone through the following sequence:

- The BIOS did some early hardware initialization, including the POST. The MBR (`boot0`) was loaded from absolute disk sector one to address `0x7c00`. Execution control was passed to that location.
- `boot0` relocated itself to the location it was linked to execute (`0x600`), followed by a jump to continue execution at the appropriate place. Finally, `boot0` loaded the first disk sector from the FreeBSD slice to address `0x7c00`. Execution control was passed to that location.

`boot1` is the next step in the boot-loading sequence. It is the first of three boot stages. Note that we have been dealing exclusively with disk sectors. Indeed, the BIOS loads the absolute first sector, while `boot0` loads the first sector of the FreeBSD slice. Both loads are to address `0x7c00`. We can conceptually think of these disk sectors

as containing the files boot0 and boot1, respectively, but in reality this is not entirely true for boot1. Strictly speaking, unlike boot0, boot1 is not part of the boot blocks [3]. Instead, a single, full-blown file, boot (/boot/boot ), is what ultimately is written to disk. This file is a combination of boot1, boot2 and the Boot Extender (or BTX). This single file is greater in size than a single sector (greater than 512 bytes). Fortunately, boot1 occupies *exactly* the first 512 bytes of this single file, so when boot0 loads the first sector of the FreeBSD slice (512 bytes), it is actually loading boot1 and transferring control to it.

The main task of boot1 is to load the next boot stage. This next stage is somewhat more complex. It is composed of a server called the "Boot Extender", or BTX, and a client, called boot2. As we will see, the last boot stage, loader, is also a client of the BTX server.

Let us now look in detail at what exactly is done by boot1, starting like we did for boot0, at its entry point:

```
start:
 jmp main
```

Figure 1.11. sys/boot/i386/boot2/boot1.S

The entry point at start simply jumps past a special data area to the label main, which in turn looks like this:

```
main:
      cld   # String ops inc
      xor %cx,%cx  # Zero
      mov %cx,%es  # Address
      mov %cx,%ds  #  data
      mov %cx,%ss  # Set up
      mov $start,%sp  #  stack
      mov %sp,%si  # Source
      mov $0x700,%di  # Destination
      incb %ch   # Word count
      rep   # Copy
      movsw   #  code
```

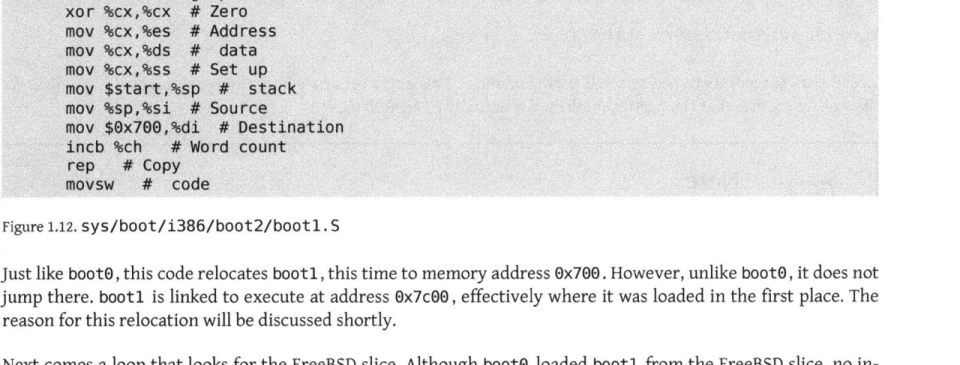

Figure 1.12. sys/boot/i386/boot2/boot1.S

Just like boot0, this code relocates boot1, this time to memory address 0x700. However, unlike boot0, it does not jump there. boot1 is linked to execute at address 0x7c00, effectively where it was loaded in the first place. The reason for this relocation will be discussed shortly.

Next comes a loop that looks for the FreeBSD slice. Although boot0 loaded boot1 from the FreeBSD slice, no information was passed to it about this [4], so boot1 must rescan the partition table to find where the FreeBSD slice starts. Therefore it rereads the MBR:

```
      mov $part4,%si  # Partition
      cmpb $0x80,%dl  # Hard drive?
      jb main.4   # No
      movb $0x1,%dh  # Block count
      callw nread  # Read MBR
```

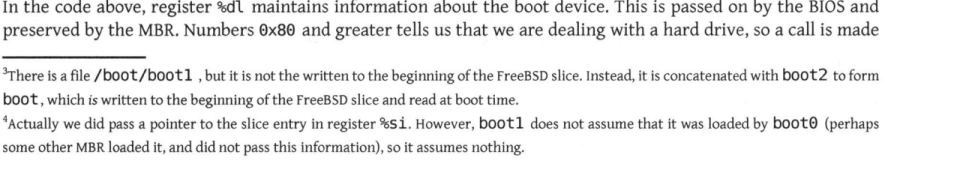

Figure 1.13. sys/boot/i386/boot2/boot1.S

In the code above, register %dl maintains information about the boot device. This is passed on by the BIOS and preserved by the MBR. Numbers 0x80 and greater tells us that we are dealing with a hard drive, so a call is made

[3] There is a file /boot/boot1 , but it is not the written to the beginning of the FreeBSD slice. Instead, it is concatenated with boot2 to form boot, which *is* written to the beginning of the FreeBSD slice and read at boot time.

[4] Actually we did pass a pointer to the slice entry in register %si. However, boot1 does not assume that it was loaded by boot0 (perhaps some other MBR loaded it, and did not pass this information), so it assumes nothing.

to `nread`, where the MBR is read. Arguments to `nread` are passed through `%si` and `%dh`. The memory address at label `part4` is copied to `%si`. This memory address holds a "fake partition" to be used by `nread`. The following is the data in the fake partition:

```
      part4:
.byte 0x80, 0x00, 0x01, 0x00
.byte 0xa5, 0xfe, 0xff, 0xff
.byte 0x00, 0x00, 0x00, 0x00
.byte 0x50, 0xc3, 0x00, 0x00
```

Figure 1.14. `sys/boot/i386/boot2/Makefile`

In particular, the LBA for this fake partition is hardcoded to zero. This is used as an argument to the BIOS for reading absolute sector one from the hard drive. Alternatively, CHS addressing could be used. In this case, the fake partition holds cylinder 0, head 0 and sector 1, which is equivalent to absolute sector one.

Let us now proceed to take a look at `nread`:

```
nread:
      mov $0x8c00,%bx  # Transfer buffer
      mov 0x8(%si),%ax  # Get
      mov 0xa(%si),%cx  #  LBA
      push %cs    # Read from
      callw xread.1  #  disk
      jnc return  # If success, return
```

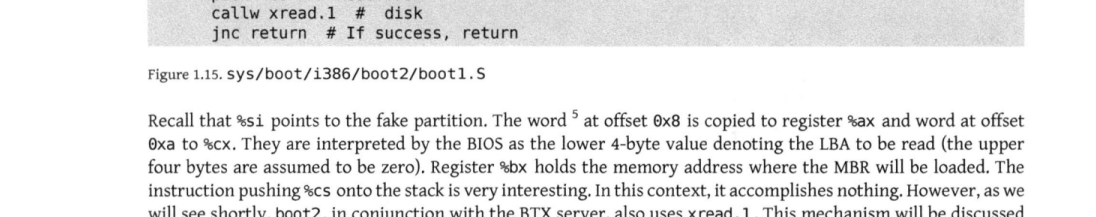

Figure 1.15. `sys/boot/i386/boot2/boot1.S`

Recall that `%si` points to the fake partition. The word [5] at offset `0x8` is copied to register `%ax` and word at offset `0xa` to `%cx`. They are interpreted by the BIOS as the lower 4-byte value denoting the LBA to be read (the upper four bytes are assumed to be zero). Register `%bx` holds the memory address where the MBR will be loaded. The instruction pushing `%cs` onto the stack is very interesting. In this context, it accomplishes nothing. However, as we will see shortly, `boot2`, in conjunction with the BTX server, also uses `xread.1`. This mechanism will be discussed in the next section.

The code at `xread.1` further calls the `read` function, which actually calls the BIOS asking for the disk sector:

```
xread.1:
 pushl $0x0  #  absolute
 push %cx  #  block
 push %ax  #  number
 push %es  # Address of
 push %bx  #  transfer buffer
 xor %ax,%ax  # Number of
 movb %dh,%al  #  blocks to
 push %ax  #  transfer
 push $0x10  # Size of packet
 mov %sp,%bp  # Packet pointer
 callw read  # Read from disk
 lea 0x10(%bp),%sp # Clear stack
 lret   # To far caller
```

Figure 1.16. `sys/boot/i386/boot2/boot1.S`

Note the long return instruction at the end of this block. This instruction pops out the `%cs` register pushed by `nread`, and returns. Finally, `nread` also returns.

With the MBR loaded to memory, the actual loop for searching the FreeBSD slice begins:

[5]In the context of 16-bit real mode, a word is 2 bytes.

```
 mov $0x1,%cx    # Two passes
main.1:
 mov $0x8dbe,%si # Partition table
 movb $0x1,%dh    # Partition
main.2:
 cmpb $0xa5,0x4(%si)  # Our partition type?
 jne main.3    # No
 jcxz main.5    # If second pass
 testb $0x80,(%si)  # Active?
 jnz main.5    # Yes
main.3:
 add $0x10,%si    # Next entry
 incb %dh    # Partition
 cmpb $0x5,%dh    # In table?
 jb main.2    # Yes
 dec %cx     # Do two
 jcxz main.1    #  passes
```

Figure 1.17. sys/boot/i386/boot2/boot1.S

If a FreeBSD slice is identified, execution continues at main.5. Note that when a FreeBSD slice is found %si points to the appropriate entry in the partition table, and %dh holds the partition number. We assume that a FreeBSD slice is found, so we continue execution at main.5:

```
main.5:
 mov %dx,0x900        # Save args
 movb $0x10,%dh        # Sector count
 callw nread        # Read disk
 mov $0x9000,%bx        # BTX
 mov 0xa(%bx),%si        # Get BTX length and set
 add %bx,%si        #  %si to start of boot2.bin
 mov $0xc000,%di        # Client page 2
 mov $0xa200,%cx        # Byte
 sub %si,%cx        #  count
 rep        # Relocate
 movsb        #  client
```

Figure 1.18. sys/boot/i386/boot2/boot1.S

Recall that at this point, register %si points to the FreeBSD slice entry in the MBR partition table, so a call to nread will effectively read sectors at the beginning of this partition. The argument passed on register %dh tells nread to read 16 disk sectors. Recall that the first 512 bytes, or the first sector of the FreeBSD slice, coincides with the boot1 program. Also recall that the file written to the beginning of the FreeBSD slice is not /boot/boot1 , but /boot/boot. Let us look at the size of these files in the filesystem:

```
-r--r--r--  1 root  wheel   512B Jan  8 00:15 /boot/boot0
-r--r--r--  1 root  wheel   512B Jan  8 00:15 /boot/boot1
-r--r--r--  1 root  wheel   7.5K Jan  8 00:15 /boot/boot2
-r--r--r--  1 root  wheel   8.0K Jan  8 00:15 /boot/boot
```

Both boot0 and boot1 are 512 bytes each, so they fit *exactly* in one disk sector. boot2 is much bigger, holding both the BTX server and the boot2 client. Finally, a file called simply boot is 512 bytes larger than boot2. This file is a concatenation of boot1 and boot2. As already noted, boot0 is the file written to the absolute first disk sector (the MBR), and boot is the file written to the first sector of the FreeBSD slice; boot1 and boot2 are *not* written to disk. The command used to concatenate boot1 and boot2 into a single boot is merely cat boot1 boot2 > boot .

So boot1 occupies exactly the first 512 bytes of boot and, because boot is written to the first sector of the FreeBSD slice, boot1 fits exactly in this first sector. Because nread reads the first 16 sectors of the FreeBSD slice, it effectively reads the entire boot file [6]. We will see more details about how boot is formed from boot1 and boot2 in the next section.

[6] 512*16=8192 bytes, exactly the size of boot

Recall that `nread` uses memory address `0x8c00` as the transfer buffer to hold the sectors read. This address is conveniently chosen. Indeed, because `boot1` belongs to the first 512 bytes, it ends up in the address range `0x8c00`-`0x8dff`. The 512 bytes that follows (range `0x8e00`-`0x8fff`) is used to store the *bsdlabel*[7].

Starting at address `0x9000` is the beginning of the BTX server, and immediately following is the `boot2` client. The BTX server acts as a kernel, and executes in protected mode in the most privileged level. In contrast, the BTX clients (`boot2`, for example), execute in user mode. We will see how this is accomplished in the next section. The code after the call to `nread` locates the beginning of `boot2` in the memory buffer, and copies it to memory address `0xc000`. This is because the BTX server arranges `boot2` to execute in a segment starting at `0xa000`. We explore this in detail in the following section.

The last code block of `boot1` enables access to memory above 1MB[8] and concludes with a jump to the starting point of the BTX server:

```
seta20:
 cli    # Disable interrupts
seta20.1:
 dec %cx    # Timeout?
 jz seta20.3  # Yes

 inb $0x64,%al  # Get status
 testb $0x2,%al  # Busy?
 jnz seta20.1  # Yes
 movb $0xd1,%al  # Command: Write
 outb %al,$0x64  #  output port
seta20.2:
 inb $0x64,%al  # Get status
 testb $0x2,%al  # Busy?
 jnz seta20.2  # Yes
 movb $0xdf,%al  # Enable
 outb %al,$0x60  #  A20
seta20.3:
 sti    # Enable interrupts
 jmp 0x9010  # Start BTX
```

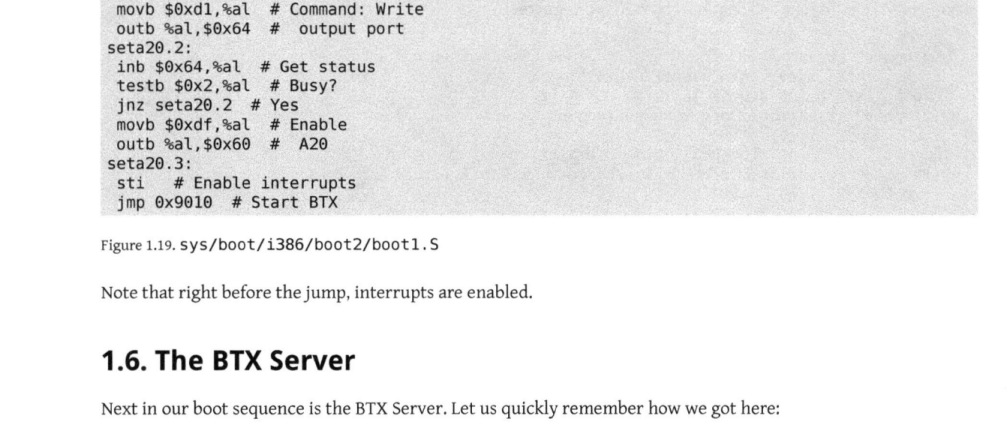

Figure 1.19. `sys/boot/i386/boot2/boot1.S`

Note that right before the jump, interrupts are enabled.

## 1.6. The BTX Server

Next in our boot sequence is the BTX Server. Let us quickly remember how we got here:

- The BIOS loads the absolute sector one (the MBR, or `boot0`), to address `0x7c00` and jumps there.
- `boot0` relocates itself to `0x600`, the address it was linked to execute, and jumps over there. It then reads the first sector of the FreeBSD slice (which consists of `boot1`) into address `0x7c00` and jumps over there.
- `boot1` loads the first 16 sectors of the FreeBSD slice into address `0x8c00`. This 16 sectors, or 8192 bytes, is the whole file `boot`. The file is a concatenation of `boot1` and `boot2`. `boot2`, in turn, contains the BTX server and the `boot2` client. Finally, a jump is made to address `0x9010`, the entry point of the BTX server.

Before studying the BTX Server in detail, let us further review how the single, all-in-one `boot` file is created. The way `boot` is built is defined in its `Makefile` (`/usr/src/sys/boot/i386/boot2/Makefile` ). Let us look at the rule that creates the `boot` file:

---

[7]Historically known as "disklabel". If you ever wondered where FreeBSD stored this information, it is in this region. See bsdlabel(8)

[8]This is necessary for legacy reasons. Interested readers should see http://en.wikipedia.org/wiki/A20_line.

```
    boot: boot1 boot2
cat boot1 boot2 > boot
```

Figure 1.20. `sys/boot/i386/boot2/Makefile`

This tells us that `boot1` and `boot2` are needed, and the rule simply concatenates them to produce a single file called `boot`. The rules for creating `boot1` are also quite simple:

```
    boot1: boot1.out
objcopy -S -O binary boot1.out boot1

    boot1.out: boot1.o
ld -e start -Ttext 0x7c00 -o boot1.out boot1.o
```

Figure 1.21. `sys/boot/i386/boot2/Makefile`

To apply the rule for creating `boot1`, `boot1.out` must be resolved. This, in turn, depends on the existence of `boot1.o`. This last file is simply the result of assembling our familiar `boot1.S`, without linking. Now, the rule for creating `boot1.out` is applied. This tells us that `boot1.o` should be linked with `start` as its entry point, and starting at address `0x7c00`. Finally, `boot1` is created from `boot1.out` applying the appropriate rule. This rule is the `objcopy` command applied to `boot1.out`. Note the flags passed to `objcopy`: `-S` tells it to strip all relocation and symbolic information; `-O binary` indicates the output format, that is, a simple, unformatted binary file.

Having `boot1`, let us take a look at how `boot2` is constructed:

```
    boot2: boot2.ld
@set -- `ls -l boot2.ld`; x=$$((7680-$$5)); \
    echo "$$x bytes available"; test $$x -ge 0
dd if=boot2.ld of=boot2 obs=7680 conv=osync

    boot2.ld: boot2.ldr boot2.bin ../btx/btx/btx
btxld -v -E 0x2000 -f bin -b ../btx/btx/btx -l boot2.ldr \
    -o boot2.ld -P 1 boot2.bin

    boot2.ldr:
dd if=/dev/zero of=boot2.ldr bs=512 count=1

    boot2.bin: boot2.out
objcopy -S -O binary boot2.out boot2.bin

    boot2.out: ../btx/lib/crt0.o boot2.o sio.o
ld -Ttext 0x2000 -o boot2.out

    boot2.o: boot2.s
${CC} ${ACFLAGS} -c boot2.s

    boot2.s: boot2.c boot2.h ${.CURDIR}/../../common/ufsread.c
${CC} ${CFLAGS} -S -o boot2.s.tmp ${.CURDIR}/boot2.c
sed -e '/align/d' -e '/nop/d' "MISSING" boot2.s.tmp > boot2.s
rm -f boot2.s.tmp

    boot2.h: boot1.out
${NM} -t d ${.ALLSRC} | awk '/([0-9])+ T xread/ \
    { x = $$1 - ORG1; \
    printf("#define XREADORG %#x\n", REL1 + x) }' \
    ORG1=`printf "%d" ${ORG1}` \
    REL1=`printf "%d" ${REL1}` > ${.TARGET}
```

Figure 1.22. `sys/boot/i386/boot2/Makefile`

The mechanism for building `boot2` is far more elaborate. Let us point out the most relevant facts. The dependency list is as follows:

```
boot2: boot2.ld
boot2.ld: boot2.ldr boot2.bin ${BTXDIR}/btx/btx
boot2.bin: boot2.out
boot2.out: ${BTXDIR}/lib/crt0.o boot2.o sio.o
boot2.o: boot2.s
boot2.s: boot2.c boot2.h ${.CURDIR}/../../common/ufsread.c
boot2.h: boot1.out
```

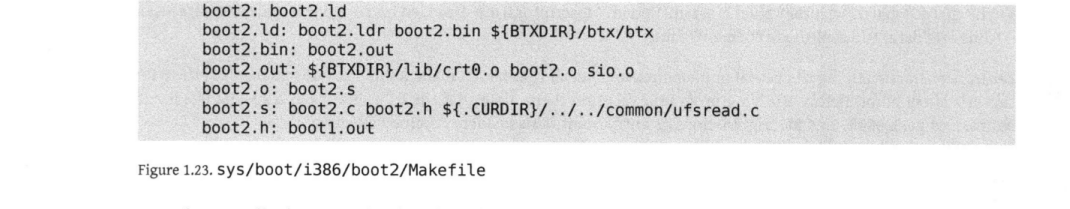

Figure 1.23. `sys/boot/i386/boot2/Makefile`

Note that initially there is no header file `boot2.h`, but its creation depends on `boot1.out`, which we already have. The rule for its creation is a bit terse, but the important thing is that the output, `boot2.h`, is something like this:

```
#define XREADORG 0x725
```

Figure 1.24. `sys/boot/i386/boot2/boot2.h`

Recall that `boot1` was relocated (i.e., copied from `0x7c00` to `0x700`). This relocation will now make sense, because as we will see, the BTX server reclaims some memory, including the space where `boot1` was originally loaded. However, the BTX server needs access to `boot1`'s `xread` function; this function, according to the output of `boot2.h`, is at location `0x725`. Indeed, the BTX server uses the `xread` function from `boot1`'s relocated code. This function is now accessible from within the `boot2` client.

We next build `boot2.s` from files `boot2.h`, `boot2.c` and `/usr/src/sys/boot/common/ufsread.c`. The rule for this is to compile the code in `boot2.c` (which includes `boot2.h` and `ufsread.c`) into assembly code. Having `boot2.s`, the next rule assembles `boot2.s`, creating the object file `boot2.o`. The next rule directs the linker to link various files (`crt0.o`, `boot2.o` and `sio.o`). Note that the output file, `boot2.out`, is linked to execute at address `0x2000`. Recall that `boot2` will be executed in user mode, within a special user segment set up by the BTX server. This segment starts at `0xa000`. Also, remember that the `boot2` portion of `boot` was copied to address `0xc000`, that is, offset `0x2000` from the start of the user segment, so `boot2` will work properly when we transfer control to it. Next, `boot2.bin` is created from `boot2.out` by stripping its symbols and format information; boot2.bin is a *raw* binary. Now, note that a file `boot2.ldr` is created as a 512-byte file full of zeros. This space is reserved for the bsdlabel.

Now that we have files `boot1`, `boot2.bin` and `boot2.ldr`, only the BTX server is missing before creating the all-in-one `boot` file. The BTX server is located in `/usr/src/sys/boot/i386/btx/btx`; it has its own `Makefile` with its own set of rules for building. The important thing to notice is that it is also compiled as a *raw* binary, and that it is linked to execute at address `0x9000`. The details can be found in `/usr/src/sys/boot/i386/btx/btx/Makefile`.

Having the files that comprise the `boot` program, the final step is to *merge* them. This is done by a special program called `btxld` (source located in `/usr/src/usr.sbin/btxld`). Some arguments to this program include the name of the output file (`boot`), its entry point (`0x2000`) and its file format (raw binary). The various files are finally merged by this utility into the file `boot`, which consists of `boot1`, `boot2`, the `bsdlabel` and the BTX server. This file, which takes exactly 16 sectors, or 8192 bytes, is what is actually written to the beginning of the FreeBSD slice during instalation. Let us now proceed to study the BTX server program.

The BTX server prepares a simple environment and switches from 16-bit real mode to 32-bit protected mode, right before passing control to the client. This includes initializing and updating the following data structures:

- Modifies the `Interrupt Vector Table (IVT)`. The IVT provides exception and interrupt handlers for Real-Mode code.
- The `Interrupt Descriptor Table (IDT)` is created. Entries are provided for processor exceptions, hardware interrupts, two system calls and V86 interface. The IDT provides exception and interrupt handlers for Protected-Mode code.
- A `Task-State Segment (TSS)` is created. This is necessary because the processor works in the *least* privileged level when executing the client (`boot2`), but in the *most* privileged level when executing the BTX server.

- The GDT (Global Descriptor Table) is set up. Entries (descriptors) are provided for supervisor code and data, user code and data, and real-mode code and data. [9]

Let us now start studying the actual implementation. Recall that `boot1` made a jump to address `0x9010`, the BTX server's entry point. Before studying program execution there, note that the BTX server has a special header at address range `0x9000-0x900f` , right before its entry point. This header is defined as follows:

```
start:       # Start of code
/*
 * BTX header.
 */
btx_hdr: .byte 0xeb    # Machine ID
   .byte 0xe    # Header size
   .ascii "BTX"    # Magic
   .byte 0x1    # Major version
   .byte 0x2    # Minor version
   .byte BTX_FLAGS    # Flags
   .word PAG_CNT-MEM_ORG>>0xc # Paging control
   .word break-start  # Text size
   .long 0x0    # Entry address
```

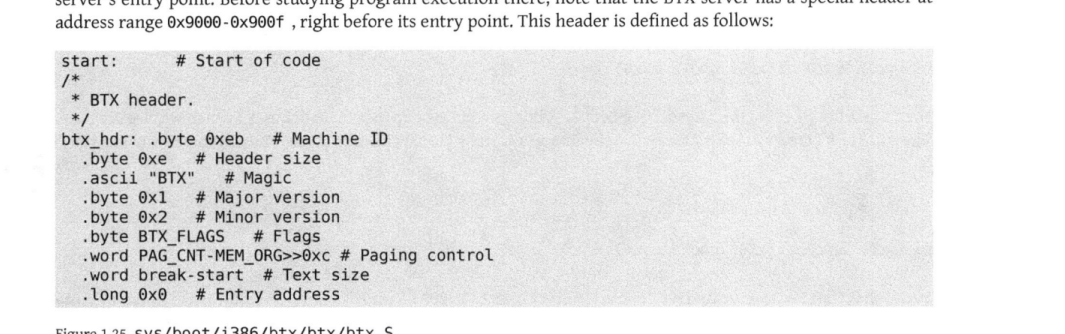

Figure 1.25. `sys/boot/i386/btx/btx/btx.S`

Note the first two bytes are `0xeb` and `0xe`. In the IA-32 architecture, these two bytes are interpreted as a relative jump past the header into the entry point, so in theory, `boot1` could jump here (address `0x9000`) instead of address `0x9010`. Note that the last field in the BTX header is a pointer to the client's (`boot2`) entry point. This field is patched at link time.

Immediately following the header is the BTX server's entry point:

```
/*
 * Initialization routine.
 */
init:  cli    # Disable interrupts
   xor %ax,%ax    # Zero/segment
   mov %ax,%ss    # Set up
   mov $0x1800,%sp  #  stack
   mov %ax,%es    # Address
   mov %ax,%ds    #  data
   pushl $0x2   # Clear
   popfl    #  flags
```

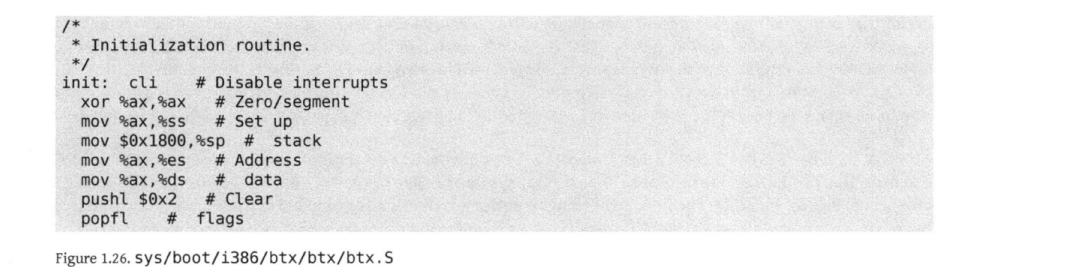

Figure 1.26. `sys/boot/i386/btx/btx/btx.S`

This code disables interrupts, sets up a working stack (starting at address `0x1800`) and clears the flags in the EFLAGS register. Note that the `popfl` instruction pops out a doubleword (4 bytes) from the stack and places it in the EFLAGS register. Because the value actually popped is 2, the EFLAGS register is effectively cleared (IA-32 requires that bit 2 of the EFLAGS register always be 1).

Our next code block clears (sets to `0`) the memory range `0x5e00-0x8fff` . This range is where the various data structures will be created:

```
/*
 * Initialize memory.
 */
   mov $0x5e00,%di  # Memory to initialize
   mov $(0x9000-0x5e00)/2,%cx # Words to zero
   rep    # Zero-fill
   stosw    #  memory
```

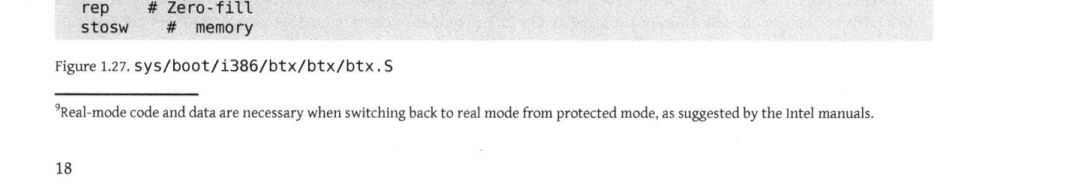

Figure 1.27. `sys/boot/i386/btx/btx/btx.S`

[9] Real-mode code and data are necessary when switching back to real mode from protected mode, as suggested by the Intel manuals.

Recall that `boot1` was originally loaded to address `0x7c00`, so, with this memory initialization, that copy effectively dissapeared. However, also recall that `boot1` was relocated to `0x700`, so *that* copy is still in memory, and the BTX server will make use of it.

Next, the real-mode IVT (Interrupt Vector Table is updated. The IVT is an array of segment/offset pairs for exception and interrupt handlers. The BIOS normally maps hardware interrupts to interrupt vectors `0x8` to `0xf` and `0x70` to `0x77` but, as will be seen, the 8259A Programmable Interrupt Controller, the chip controlling the actual mapping of hardware interrupts to interrupt vectors, is programmed to remap these interrupt vectors from `0x8-0xf` to `0x20-0x27` and from `0x70-0x77` to `0x28-0x2f`. Thus, interrupt handlers are provided for interrupt vectors `0x20-0x2f`. The reason the BIOS-provided handlers are not used directly is because they work in 16-bit real mode, but not 32-bit protected mode. Processor mode will be switched to 32-bit protected mode shortly. However, the BTX server sets up a mechanism to effectively use the handlers provided by the BIOS:

```
/*
 * Update real mode IDT for reflecting hardware interrupts.
 */
  mov $intr20,%bx    # Address first handler
  mov $0x10,%cx    # Number of handlers
  mov $0x20*4,%di    # First real mode IDT entry
init.0:  mov %bx,(%di)    # Store IP
  inc %di    # Address next
  inc %di    #  entry
  stosw    # Store CS
  add $4,%bx    # Next handler
  loop init.0    # Next IRQ
```

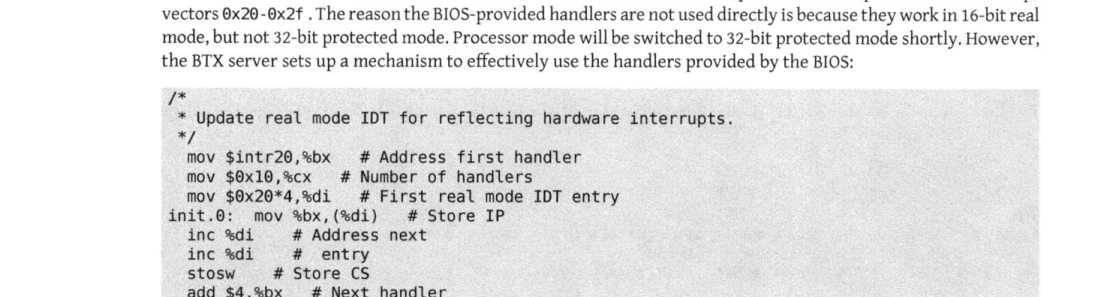

Figure 1.28. `sys/boot/i386/btx/btx/btx.S`

The next block creates the IDT (Interrupt Descriptor Table). The IDT is analogous, in protected mode, to the IVT in real mode. That is, the IDT describes the various exception and interrupt handlers used when the processor is executing in protected mode. In essence, it also consists of an array of segment/offset pairs, although the structure is somewhat more complex, because segments in protected mode are different than in real mode, and various protection mechanisms apply:

```
/*
 * Create IDT.
 */
  mov $0x5e00,%di    # IDT's address
  mov $idtctl,%si    # Control string
init.1:  lodsb    # Get entry
  cbw    #  count
  xchg %ax,%cx    #  as word
  jcxz init.4    # If done
  lodsb    # Get segment
  xchg %ax,%dx    #  P:DPL:type
  lodsw    # Get control
  xchg %ax,%bx    #  set
  lodsw    # Get handler offset
  mov $SEL_SCODE,%dh  # Segment selector
init.2:  shr %bx    # Handle this int?
  jnc init.3    # No
  mov %ax,(%di)    # Set handler offset
  mov %dh,0x2(%di)    #  and selector
  mov %dl,0x5(%di)    # Set P:DPL:type
  add $0x4,%ax    # Next handler
init.3:  lea 0x8(%di),%di  # Next entry
  loop init.2    # Till set done
  jmp init.1    # Continue
```

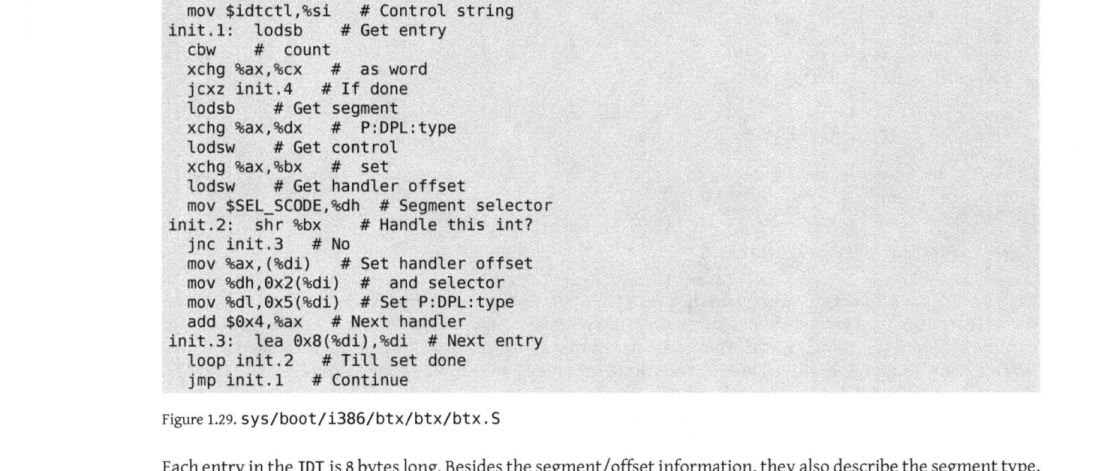

Figure 1.29. `sys/boot/i386/btx/btx/btx.S`

Each entry in the `IDT` is 8 bytes long. Besides the segment/offset information, they also describe the segment type, privilege level, and whether the segment is present in memory or not. The construction is such that interrupt

vectors from `0` to `0xf` (exceptions) are handled by function `intx00`; vector `0x10` (also an exception) is handled by `intx10`; hardware interrupts, which are later configured to start at interrupt vector `0x20` all the way to interrupt vector `0x2f`, are handled by function `intx20`. Lastly, interrupt vector `0x30`, which is used for system calls, is handled by `intx30`, and vectors `0x31` and `0x32` are handled by `intx31`. It must be noted that only descriptors for interrupt vectors `0x30`, `0x31` and `0x32` are given privilege level 3, the same privilege level as the `boot2` client, which means the client can execute a software-generated interrupt to this vectors through the `int` instruction without failing (this is the way `boot2` use the services provided by the BTX server). Also, note that *only* software-generated interrupts are protected from code executing in lesser privilege levels. Hardware-generated interrupts and processor-generated exceptions are *always* handled adequately, regardless of the actual privileges involved.

The next step is to initialize the TSS (Task-State Segment). The TSS is a hardware feature that helps the operating system or executive software implement multitasking functionality through process abstraction. The IA-32 architecture demands the creation and use of *at least* one TSS if multitasking facilities are used or different privilege levels are defined. Because the `boot2` client is executed in privilege level 3, but the BTX server does in privilege level 0, a TSS must be defined:

```
/*
 * Initialize TSS.
 */
init.4:  movb $_ESP0H,TSS_ESP0+1(%di) # Set ESP0
  movb $SEL_SDATA,TSS_SS0(%di) # Set SS0
  movb $_TSSIO,TSS_MAP(%di) # Set I/O bit map base
```

Figure 1.30. `sys/boot/i386/btx/btx/btx.S`

Note that a value is given for the Privilege Level 0 stack pointer and stack segment in the TSS. This is needed because, if an interrupt or exception is received while executing `boot2` in Privilege Level 3, a change to Privilege Level 0 is automatically performed by the processor, so a new working stack is needed. Finally, the I/O Map Base Address field of the TSS is given a value, which is a 16-bit offset from the beginning of the TSS to the I/O Permission Bitmap and the Interrupt Redirection Bitmap.

After the IDT and TSS are created, the processor is ready to switch to protected mode. This is done in the next block:

```
/*
 * Bring up the system.
 */
  mov $0x2820,%bx    # Set protected mode
  callw setpic    #  IRQ offsets
  lidt idtdesc    # Set IDT
  lgdt gdtdesc    # Set GDT
  mov %cr0,%eax    # Switch to protected
  inc %ax     #  mode
  mov %eax,%cr0   #
  ljmp $SEL_SCODE,$init.8  # To 32-bit code
  .code32
init.8:  xorl %ecx,%ecx    # Zero
  movb $SEL_SDATA,%cl  # To 32-bit
  movw %cx,%ss    #  stack
```

Figure 1.31. `sys/boot/i386/btx/btx/btx.S`

First, a call is made to `setpic` to program the 8259A PIC (Programmable Interrupt Controller). This chip is connected to multiple hardware interrupt sources. Upon receiving an interrupt from a device, it signals the processor with the appropriate interrupt vector. This can be customized so that specific interrupts are associated with specific interrupt vectors, as explained before. Next, the IDTR (Interrupt Descriptor Table Register) and GDTR (Global Descriptor Table Register) are loaded with the instructions `lidt` and `lgdt`, respectively. These registers are loaded with the base address and limit address for the IDT and GDT. The following three instructions set the Protection Enable (PE) bit of the `%cr0` register. This effectively switches the processor to 32-bit protected mode. Next, a long jump is made to `init.8` using segment selector SEL_SCODE, which selects the Supervisor Code Segment. The processor is effectively executing in CPL 0, the most privileged level, after this jump. Finally, the Supervisor

Data Segment is selected for the stack by assigning the segment selector SEL_SDATA to the `%ss` register. This data segment also has a privilege level of `0`.

Our last code block is responsible for loading the TR (Task Register) with the segment selector for the TSS we created earlier, and setting the User Mode environment before passing execution control to the `boot2` client.

```
/*
 * Launch user task.
 */
  movb $SEL_TSS,%cl  # Set task
  ltr %cx    #  register
  movl $0xa000,%edx  # User base address
  movzwl %ss:BDA_MEM,%eax  # Get free memory
  shll $0xa,%eax   # To bytes
  subl $ARGSPACE,%eax  # Less arg space
  subl %edx,%eax   # Less base
  movb $SEL_UDATA,%cl  # User data selector
  pushl %ecx   # Set SS
  pushl %eax   # Set ESP
  push $0x202   # Set flags (IF set)
  push $SEL_UCODE   # Set CS
  pushl btx_hdr+0xc  # Set EIP
  pushl %ecx   # Set GS
  pushl %ecx   # Set FS
  pushl %ecx   # Set DS
  pushl %ecx   # Set ES
  pushl %edx   # Set EAX
  movb $0x7,%cl   # Set remaining
init.9:  push $0x0   #  general
  loop init.9   #  registers
  popa    #  and initialize
  popl %es   # Initialize
  popl %ds   #  user
  popl %fs   #  segment
  popl %gs   #  registers
  iret    # To user mode
```

Figure 1.32. `sys/boot/i386/btx/btx/btx.S`

Note that the client's environment include a stack segment selector and stack pointer (registers `%ss` and `%esp`). Indeed, once the TR is loaded with the appropriate stack segment selector (instruction `ltr`), the stack pointer is calculated and pushed onto the stack along with the stack's segment selector. Next, the value `0x202` is pushed onto the stack; it is the value that the EFLAGS will get when control is passed to the client. Also, the User Mode code segment selector and the client's entry point are pushed. Recall that this entry point is patched in the BTX header at link time. Finally, segment selectors (stored in register `%ecx`) for the segment registers `%gs, %fs, %ds and %es` are pushed onto the stack, along with the value at `%edx` (`0xa000`). Keep in mind the various values that have been pushed onto the stack (they will be popped out shortly). Next, values for the remaining general purpose registers are also pushed onto the stack (note the `loop` that pushes the value `0` seven times). Now, values will be started to be popped out of the stack. First, the `popa` instruction pops out of the stack the latest seven values pushed. They are stored in the general purpose registers in order `%edi, %esi, %ebp, %ebx, %edx, %ecx, %eax` . Then, the various segment selectors pushed are popped into the various segment registers. Five values still remain on the stack. They are popped when the `iret` instruction is executed. This instruction first pops the value that was pushed from the BTX header. This value is a pointer to `boot2`'s entry point. It is placed in the register `%eip`, the instruction pointer register. Next, the segment selector for the User Code Segment is popped and copied to register `%cs`. Remember that this segment's privilege level is 3, the least privileged level. This means that we must provide values for the stack of this privilege level. This is why the processor, besides further popping the value for the EFLAGS register, does two more pops out of the stack. These values go to the stack pointer (`%esp`) and the stack segment (`%ss`). Now, execution continues at `boot0`'s entry point.

It is important to note how the User Code Segment is defined. This segment's *base address* is set to `0xa000`. This means that code memory addresses are *relative* to address 0xa000; if code being executed is fetched from address `0x2000`, the *actual* memory addressed is `0xa000+0x2000=0xc000`.

## 1.7. boot2 Stage

`boot2` defines an important structure, `struct bootinfo`. This structure is initialized by `boot2` and passed to the loader, and then further to the kernel. Some nodes of this structures are set by `boot2`, the rest by the loader. This structure, among other information, contains the kernel filename, BIOS harddisk geometry, BIOS drive number for boot device, physical memory available, `envp` pointer etc. The definition for it is:

```
/usr/include/machine/bootinfo.h:
struct bootinfo {
 u_int32_t bi_version;
 u_int32_t bi_kernelname;  /* represents a char * */
 u_int32_t bi_nfs_diskless; /* struct nfs_diskless * */
    /* End of fields that are always present. */
#define bi_endcommon bi_n_bios_used
 u_int32_t bi_n_bios_used;
 u_int32_t bi_bios_geom[N_BIOS_GEOM];
 u_int32_t bi_size;
 u_int8_t bi_memsizes_valid;
 u_int8_t bi_bios_dev;   /* bootdev BIOS unit number */
 u_int8_t bi_pad[2];
 u_int32_t bi_basemem;
 u_int32_t bi_extmem;
 u_int32_t bi_symtab;  /* struct symtab * */
 u_int32_t bi_esymtab;   /* struct symtab * */
    /* Items below only from advanced bootloader */
 u_int32_t bi_kernend;   /* end of kernel space */
 u_int32_t bi_envp;   /* environment */
 u_int32_t bi_modulep;   /* preloaded modules */
};
```

`boot2` enters into an infinite loop waiting for user input, then calls `load()`. If the user does not press anything, the loop breaks by a timeout, so `load()` will load the default file (`/boot/loader`). Functions `ino_t lookup(char *filename)` and `int xfsread(ino_t inode, void *buf, size_t nbyte)` are used to read the content of a file into memory. `/boot/loader` is an ELF binary, but where the ELF header is prepended with `a.out`'s `struct exec` structure. `load()` scans the loader's ELF header, loading the content of `/boot/loader` into memory, and passing the execution to the loader's entry:

```
sys/boot/i386/boot2/boot2.c:
    __exec((caddr_t)addr, RB_BOOTINFO | (opts & RBX_MASK),
    MAKEBOOTDEV(dev_maj[dsk.type], 0, dsk.slice, dsk.unit, dsk.part),
    0, 0, 0, VTOP(&bootinfo));
```

## 1.8. loader Stage

loader is a BTX client as well. I will not describe it here in detail, there is a comprehensive manpage written by Mike Smith, loader(8). The underlying mechanisms and BTX were discussed above.

The main task for the loader is to boot the kernel. When the kernel is loaded into memory, it is being called by the loader:

```
sys/boot/common/boot.c:
    /* Call the exec handler from the loader matching the kernel */
    module_formats[km->m_loader]->l_exec(km);
```

## 1.9. Kernel Initialization

Let us take a look at the command that links the kernel. This will help identify the exact location where the loader passes execution to the kernel. This location is the kernel's actual entry point.

```
sys/conf/Makefile.i386:
```

```
ld -elf -Bdynamic -T /usr/src/sys/conf/ldscript.i386  -export-dynamic \
-dynamic-linker /red/herring -o kernel -X locore.o \
<lots of kernel .o files>
```

A few interesting things can be seen here. First, the kernel is an ELF dynamically linked binary, but the dynamic linker for kernel is `/red/herring`, which is definitely a bogus file. Second, taking a look at the file `sys/conf/ldscript.i386` gives an idea about what ld options are used when compiling a kernel. Reading through the first few lines, the string

```
sys/conf/ldscript.i386:
ENTRY(btext)
```

says that a kernel's entry point is the symbol `btext'. This symbol is defined in `locore.s`:

```
sys/i386/i386/locore.s:
 .text
/**********************************************************************
 *
 * This is where the bootblocks start us, set the ball rolling...
 *
 */
NON_GPROF_ENTRY(btext)
```

First, the register EFLAGS is set to a predefined value of 0x00000002. Then all the segment registers are initialized:

```
sys/i386/i386/locore.s:
/* Don't trust what the BIOS gives for eflags. */
 pushl $PSL_KERNEL
 popfl

/*
 * Don't trust what the BIOS gives for %fs and %gs.  Trust the bootstrap
 * to set %cs, %ds, %es and %ss.
 */
 mov %ds, %ax
 mov %ax, %fs
 mov %ax, %gs
```

btext calls the routines `recover_bootinfo()`, `identify_cpu()`, `create_pagetables()`, which are also defined in `locore.s`. Here is a description of what they do:

| | |
|---|---|
| `recover_bootinfo` | This routine parses the parameters to the kernel passed from the bootstrap. The kernel may have been booted in 3 ways: by the loader, described above, by the old disk boot blocks, or by the old diskless boot procedure. This function determines the booting method, and stores the `struct bootinfo` structure into the kernel memory. |
| `identify_cpu` | This functions tries to find out what CPU it is running on, storing the value found in a variable `_cpu`. |
| `create_pagetables` | This function allocates and fills out a Page Table Directory at the top of the kernel memory area. |

The next steps are enabling VME, if the CPU supports it:

```
 testl $CPUID_VME, R(_cpu_feature)
 jz 1f
 movl %cr4, %eax
 orl $CR4_VME, %eax
 movl %eax, %cr4
```

Then, enabling paging:

```
/* Now enable paging */
 movl R(_IdlePTD), %eax
 movl %eax,%cr3    /* load ptd addr into mmu */
 movl %cr0,%eax    /* get control word */
 orl $CR0_PE|CR0_PG,%eax  /* enable paging */
 movl %eax,%cr0    /* and let's page NOW! */
```

The next three lines of code are because the paging was set, so the jump is needed to continue the execution in virtualized address space:

```
 pushl $begin     /* jump to high virtualized address */
 ret

/* now running relocated at KERNBASE where the system is linked to run */
begin:
```

The function `init386()` is called with a pointer to the first free physical page, after that `mi_startup()`. `init386` is an architecture dependent initialization function, and `mi_startup()` is an architecture independent one (the 'mi_' prefix stands for Machine Independent). The kernel never returns from `mi_startup()`, and by calling it, the kernel finishes booting:

```
sys/i386/i386/locore.s:
 movl physfree, %esi
 pushl %esi     /* value of first for init386(first) */
 call _init386   /* wire 386 chip for unix operation */
 call _mi_startup   /* autoconfiguration, mountroot etc */
 hlt  /* never returns to here */
```

### 1.9.1. `init386()`

`init386()` is defined in `sys/i386/i386/machdep.c` and performs low-level initialization specific to the i386 chip. The switch to protected mode was performed by the loader. The loader has created the very first task, in which the kernel continues to operate. Before looking at the code, consider the tasks the processor must complete to initialize protected mode execution:

- Initialize the kernel tunable parameters, passed from the bootstrapping program.
- Prepare the GDT.
- Prepare the IDT.
- Initialize the system console.
- Initialize the DDB, if it is compiled into kernel.
- Initialize the TSS.
- Prepare the LDT.
- Set up proc0's pcb.

`init386()` initializes the tunable parameters passed from bootstrap by setting the environment pointer (envp) and calling `init_param1()` . The envp pointer has been passed from loader in the `bootinfo` structure:

```
sys/i386/i386/machdep.c:
  kern_envp = (caddr_t)bootinfo.bi_envp + KERNBASE;

 /* Init basic tunables, hz etc */
 init_param1();
```

`init_param1()` is defined in `sys/kern/subr_param.c` . That file has a number of sysctls, and two functions, `init_param1()` and `init_param2()` , that are called from `init386()` :

```
sys/kern/subr_param.c:
 hz = HZ;
 TUNABLE_INT_FETCH("kern.hz", &hz);
```

TUNABLE_<typename>_FETCH is used to fetch the value from the environment:

```
/usr/src/sys/sys/kernel.h:
#define TUNABLE_INT_FETCH(path, var) getenv_int((path), (var))
```

Sysctl `kern.hz` is the system clock tick. Additionally, these sysctls are set by `init_param1()` : `kern.maxswzone`, `kern.maxbcache`, `kern.maxtsiz`, `kern.dfldsiz`, `kern.maxdsiz`, `kern.dflssiz`, `kern.maxssiz`, `kern.sgrowsiz`.

Then `init386()` prepares the Global Descriptors Table (GDT). Every task on an x86 is running in its own virtual address space, and this space is addressed by a segment:offset pair. Say, for instance, the current instruction to be executed by the processor lies at CS:EIP, then the linear virtual address for that instruction would be "the virtual address of code segment CS" + EIP. For convenience, segments begin at virtual address 0 and end at a 4Gb boundary. Therefore, the instruction's linear virtual address for this example would just be the value of EIP. Segment registers such as CS, DS etc are the selectors, i.e., indexes, into GDT (to be more precise, an index is not a selector itself, but the INDEX field of a selector). FreeBSD's GDT holds descriptors for 15 selectors per CPU:

```
sys/i386/i386/machdep.c:
union descriptor gdt[NGDT * MAXCPU]; /* global descriptor table */

sys/i386/include/segments.h:
/*
 * Entries in the Global Descriptor Table (GDT)
 */
#define GNULL_SEL 0 /* Null Descriptor */
#define GCODE_SEL 1 /* Kernel Code Descriptor */
#define GDATA_SEL 2 /* Kernel Data Descriptor */
#define GPRIV_SEL 3 /* SMP Per-Processor Private Data */
#define GPROC0_SEL 4 /* Task state process slot zero and up */
#define GLDT_SEL 5 /* LDT - eventually one per process */
#define GUSERLDT_SEL 6 /* User LDT */
#define GTGATE_SEL 7 /* Process task switch gate */
#define GBIOSLOWMEM_SEL 8 /* BIOS low memory access (must be entry 8) */
#define GPANIC_SEL 9 /* Task state to consider panic from */
#define GBIOSCODE32_SEL 10 /* BIOS interface (32bit Code) */
#define GBIOSCODE16_SEL 11 /* BIOS interface (16bit Code) */
#define GBIOSDATA_SEL 12 /* BIOS interface (Data) */
#define GBIOSUTIL_SEL 13 /* BIOS interface (Utility) */
#define GBIOSARGS_SEL 14 /* BIOS interface (Arguments) */
```

Note that those #defines are not selectors themselves, but just a field INDEX of a selector, so they are exactly the indices of the GDT. for example, an actual selector for the kernel code (GCODE_SEL) has the value 0x08.

The next step is to initialize the Interrupt Descriptor Table (IDT). This table is referenced by the processor when a software or hardware interrupt occurs. For example, to make a system call, user application issues the `INT 0x80` instruction. This is a software interrupt, so the processor's hardware looks up a record with index 0x80 in the IDT. This record points to the routine that handles this interrupt, in this particular case, this will be the kernel's syscall gate. The IDT may have a maximum of 256 (0x100) records. The kernel allocates NIDT records for the IDT, where NIDT is the maximum (256):

```
sys/i386/i386/machdep.c:
static struct gate_descriptor idt0[NIDT];
struct gate_descriptor *idt = &idt0[0]; /* interrupt descriptor table */
```

For each interrupt, an appropriate handler is set. The syscall gate for `INT 0x80` is set as well:

```
sys/i386/i386/machdep.c:
 setidt(0x80, &IDTVEC(int0x80_syscall),
   SDT_SYS386TGT, SEL_UPL, GSEL(GCODE_SEL, SEL_KPL));
```

So when a userland application issues the `INT 0x80` instruction, control will transfer to the function `_Xint0x80_syscall`, which is in the kernel code segment and will be executed with supervisor privileges.

Console and DDB are then initialized:

```
sys/i386/i386/machdep.c:
 cninit();
/* skipped */
#ifdef DDB
 kdb_init();
 if (boothowto & RB_KDB)
  Debugger("Boot flags requested debugger");
#endif
```

The Task State Segment is another x86 protected mode structure, the TSS is used by the hardware to store task information when a task switch occurs.

The Local Descriptors Table is used to reference userland code and data. Several selectors are defined to point to the LDT, they are the system call gates and the user code and data selectors:

```
/usr/include/machine/segments.h:
#define LSYS5CALLS_SEL 0 /* forced by intel BCS */
#define LSYS5SIGR_SEL 1
#define L43BSDCALLS_SEL 2 /* notyet */
#define LUCODE_SEL 3
#define LSOL26CALLS_SEL 4 /* Solaris >= 2.6 system call gate */
#define LUDATA_SEL 5
/* separate stack, es,fs,gs sels ? */
/* #define LPOSIXCALLS_SEL 5*/ /* notyet */
#define LBSDICALLS_SEL 16 /* BSDI system call gate */
#define NLDT  (LBSDICALLS_SEL + 1)
```

Next, proc0's Process Control Block (`struct pcb`) structure is initialized. proc0 is a `struct proc` structure that describes a kernel process. It is always present while the kernel is running, therefore it is declared as global:

```
sys/kern/kern_init.c:
    struct proc proc0;
```

The structure `struct pcb` is a part of a proc structure. It is defined in `/usr/include/machine/pcb.h` and has a process's information specific to the i386 architecture, such as registers values.

### 1.9.2. `mi_startup()`

This function performs a bubble sort of all the system initialization objects and then calls the entry of each object one by one:

```
sys/kern/init_main.c:
 for (sipp = sysinit; *sipp; sipp++) {

  /* ... skipped ... */

  /* Call function */
  (*((*sipp)->func))((*sipp)->udata);
  /* ... skipped ... */
 }
```

Although the sysinit framework is described in the Developers' Handbook, I will discuss the internals of it.

Every system initialization object (sysinit object) is created by calling a SYSINIT() macro. Let us take as example an announce sysinit object. This object prints the copyright message:

```
sys/kern/init_main.c:
static void
print_caddr_t(void *data __unused)
{
 printf("%s", (char *)data);
}
SYSINIT(announce, SI_SUB_COPYRIGHT, SI_ORDER_FIRST, print_caddr_t, copyright)
```

The subsystem ID for this object is SI_SUB_COPYRIGHT (0x0800001), which comes right after the SI_SUB_CONSOLE (0x0800000). So, the copyright message will be printed out first, just after the console initialization.

Let us take a look at what exactly the macro `SYSINIT()` does. It expands to a `C_SYSINIT()` macro. The `C_SYSINIT()` macro then expands to a static `struct sysinit` structure declaration with another `DATA_SET` macro call:

```
/usr/include/sys/kernel.h:
      #define C_SYSINIT(uniquifier, subsystem, order, func, ident) \
      static struct sysinit uniquifier ## _sys_init = { \ subsystem, \
      order, \ func, \ ident \ }; \ DATA_SET(sysinit_set,uniquifier ##
      _sys_init);

#define SYSINIT(uniquifier, subsystem, order, func, ident) \
 C_SYSINIT(uniquifier, subsystem, order,    \
 (sysinit_cfunc_t)(sysinit_nfunc_t)func, (void *)ident)
```

The `DATA_SET()` macro expands to a `MAKE_SET()` , and that macro is the point where all the sysinit magic is hidden:

```
/usr/include/linker_set.h:
#define MAKE_SET(set, sym)       \
 static void const * const __set_##set##_sym_##sym = &sym; \
 __asm(".section .set." #set ",\"aw\"");     \
 __asm(".long " #sym);       \
 __asm(".previous")
#endif
#define TEXT_SET(set, sym) MAKE_SET(set, sym)
#define DATA_SET(set, sym) MAKE_SET(set, sym)
```

In our case, the following declaration will occur:

```
static struct sysinit announce_sys_init = {
 SI_SUB_COPYRIGHT,
 SI_ORDER_FIRST,
 (sysinit_cfunc_t)(sysinit_nfunc_t)  print_caddr_t,
 (void *) copyright
};

static void const *const __set_sysinit_set_sym_announce_sys_init =
    &announce_sys_init;
__asm(".section .set.sysinit_set" ",\"aw\"");
__asm(".long " "announce_sys_init");
__asm(".previous");
```

The first `__asm` instruction will create an ELF section within the kernel's executable. This will happen at kernel link time. The section will have the name `.set.sysinit_set` . The content of this section is one 32-bit value, the address of announce_sys_init structure, and that is what the second `__asm` is. The third `__asm` instruction marks the end of a section. If a directive with the same section name occurred before, the content, i.e., the 32-bit value, will be appended to the existing section, so forming an array of 32-bit pointers.

Running objdump on a kernel binary, you may notice the presence of such small sections:

```
% objdump -h /kernel
  7 .set.cons_set 00000014  c03164c0  c03164c0  002154c0  2**2
                  CONTENTS, ALLOC, LOAD, DATA
  8 .set.kbddriver_set 00000010  c03164d4  c03164d4  002154d4  2**2
                  CONTENTS, ALLOC, LOAD, DATA
  9 .set.scrndr_set 00000024  c03164e4  c03164e4  002154e4  2**2
```

```
                 CONTENTS, ALLOC, LOAD, DATA
 10 .set.scterm_set 0000000c  c0316508  c0316508  00215508  2**2
                 CONTENTS, ALLOC, LOAD, DATA
 11 .set.sysctl_set 0000097c  c0316514  c0316514  00215514  2**2
                 CONTENTS, ALLOC, LOAD, DATA
 12 .set.sysinit_set 00000664  c0316e90  c0316e90  00215e90  2**2
                 CONTENTS, ALLOC, LOAD, DATA
```

This screen dump shows that the size of .set.sysinit_set section is 0x664 bytes, so `0x664/sizeof(void *)` sysinit objects are compiled into the kernel. The other sections such as `.set.sysctl_set` represent other linker sets.

By defining a variable of type `struct linker_set` the content of `.set.sysinit_set` section will be "collected" into that variable:

```
sys/kern/init_main.c:
      extern struct linker_set sysinit_set; /* XXX */
```

The `struct linker_set` is defined as follows:

```
/usr/include/linker_set.h:
  struct linker_set {
 int ls_length;
 void *ls_items[1];  /* really ls_length of them, trailing NULL */
};
```

The first node will be equal to the number of a sysinit objects, and the second node will be a NULL-terminated array of pointers to them.

Returning to the `mi_startup()` discussion, it is must be clear now, how the sysinit objects are being organized. The `mi_startup()` function sorts them and calls each. The very last object is the system scheduler:

```
/usr/include/sys/kernel.h:
enum sysinit_sub_id {
 SI_SUB_DUMMY   = 0x0000000, /* not executed; for linker*/
 SI_SUB_DONE   = 0x0000001, /* processed*/
 SI_SUB_CONSOLE   = 0x0800000, /* console*/
 SI_SUB_COPYRIGHT = 0x0800001, /* first use of console*/
...
 SI_SUB_RUN_SCHEDULER = 0xfffffff /* scheduler: no return*/
};
```

The system scheduler sysinit object is defined in the file `sys/vm/vm_glue.c` , and the entry point for that object is `scheduler()`. That function is actually an infinite loop, and it represents a process with PID 0, the swapper process. The proc0 structure, mentioned before, is used to describe it.

The first user process, called *init*, is created by the sysinit object `init`:

```
sys/kern/init_main.c:
static void
create_init(const void *udata __unused)
{
 int error;
 int s;

 s = splhigh();
 error = fork1(&proc0, RFFDG | RFPROC, &initproc);
 if (error)
  panic("cannot fork init: %d\n", error);
 initproc->p_flag |= P_INMEM | P_SYSTEM;
 cpu_set_fork_handler(initproc, start_init, NULL);
 remrunqueue(initproc);
 splx(s);
}
SYSINIT(init,SI_SUB_CREATE_INIT, SI_ORDER_FIRST, create_init, NULL)
```

The `create_init()` allocates a new process by calling `fork1()` , but does not mark it runnable. When this new process is scheduled for execution by the scheduler, the `start_init()` will be called. That function is defined in `init_main.c` . It tries to load and exec the `init` binary, probing `/sbin/init` first, then `/sbin/oinit` , `/sbin/init.bak` , and finally `/stand/sysinstall` :

```
sys/kern/init_main.c:
static char init_path[MAXPATHLEN] =
#ifdef INIT_PATH
    __XSTRING(INIT_PATH);
#else
    "/sbin/init:/sbin/oinit:/sbin/init.bak:/stand/sysinstall";
#endif
```

# Chapter 2. Locking Notes

*This chapter is maintained by the FreeBSD SMP Next Generation Project.*

This document outlines the locking used in the FreeBSD kernel to permit effective multi-processing within the kernel. Locking can be achieved via several means. Data structures can be protected by mutexes or lockmgr(9) locks. A few variables are protected simply by always using atomic operations to access them.

## 2.1. Mutexes

A mutex is simply a lock used to guarantee mutual exclusion. Specifically, a mutex may only be owned by one entity at a time. If another entity wishes to obtain a mutex that is already owned, it must wait until the mutex is released. In the FreeBSD kernel, mutexes are owned by processes.

Mutexes may be recursively acquired, but they are intended to be held for a short period of time. Specifically, one may not sleep while holding a mutex. If you need to hold a lock across a sleep, use a lockmgr(9) lock.

Each mutex has several properties of interest:

Variable Name
: The name of the struct mtx variable in the kernel source.

Logical Name
: The name of the mutex assigned to it by `mtx_init` . This name is displayed in KTR trace messages and witness errors and warnings and is used to distinguish mutexes in the witness code.

Type
: The type of the mutex in terms of the `MTX_*` flags. The meaning for each flag is related to its meaning as documented in mutex(9).

`MTX_DEF`
: A sleep mutex

`MTX_SPIN`
: A spin mutex

`MTX_RECURSE`
: This mutex is allowed to recurse.

Protectees
: A list of data structures or data structure members that this entry protects. For data structure members, the name will be in the form of `structure name.member name`.

Dependent Functions
: Functions that can only be called if this mutex is held.

Table 2.1. Mutex List

| Variable Name | Logical Name | Type | Protectees | Dependent Functions |
|---|---|---|---|---|
| sched_lock | "sched lock" | `MTX_SPIN` \| `MTX_RECURSE` | `_gmonparam`, `cnt.v_swtch`, `cp_time`, `curpriority`, `mtx.mtx_blocked` , `mtx.mtx_contested`, `proc.p_procq`, `proc.p_slpq`, `proc.p_sflag`, `proc.p_stat`, | `setrunqueue`, `remrunqueue`, `mi_switch` , `chooseproc`, `schedclock`, `resetpriority`, `updatepri`, `maybe_resched` , `cpu_switch` , `cpu_throw` , |

| Variable Name | Logical Name | Type | Protectees | Dependent Functions |
|---|---|---|---|---|
| | | | proc.p_estcpu, proc.p_cpticks proc.p_pctcpu, proc.p_wchan, proc.p_wmesg, proc.p_swtime, proc.p_slptime, proc.p_runtime, proc.p_uu, proc.p_su, proc.p_iu, proc.p_uticks, proc.p_sticks, proc.p_iticks, proc.p_oncpu, proc.p_lastcpu, proc.p_rqindex, proc.p_heldmtx, proc.p_blocked, proc.p_mtxname, proc.p_contested, proc.p_priority, proc.p_usrpri, proc.p_nativepri, proc.p_nice, proc.p_rtprio, pscnt, slpque, itqueuebits, itqueues, rtqueuebits, rtqueues, queuebits, queues, idqueuebits, idqueues, switchtime, switchticks | need_resched, resched_wanted, clear_resched, aston, astoff, astpending, calcru, proc_compare |
| vm86pcb_lock | "vm86pcb lock" | MTX_DEF | vm86pcb | vm86_bioscall |
| Giant | "Giant" | MTX_DEF \| MTX_RECURSE | nearly everything | lots |
| callout_lock | "callout lock" | MTX_SPIN \| MTX_RECURSE | callfree, callwheel, nextsoftcheck, proc.p_itcallout, proc.p_slpcallout, softticks, ticks | |

## 2.2. Shared Exclusive Locks

These locks provide basic reader-writer type functionality and may be held by a sleeping process. Currently they are backed by lockmgr(9).

Table 2.2. Shared Exclusive Lock List

| Variable Name | Protectees |
| --- | --- |
| allproc_lock | allproc zombproc pidhashtbl proc.p_list proc.p_hash nextpid |
| proctree_lock | proc.p_children proc.p_sibling |

## 2.3. Atomically Protected Variables

An atomically protected variable is a special variable that is not protected by an explicit lock. Instead, all data accesses to the variables use special atomic operations as described in atomic(9). Very few variables are treated this way, although other synchronization primitives such as mutexes are implemented with atomically protected variables.

- mtx.mtx_lock

# Chapter 3. Kernel Objects

Kernel Objects, or *Kobj* provides an object-oriented C programming system for the kernel. As such the data being operated on carries the description of how to operate on it. This allows operations to be added and removed from an interface at run time and without breaking binary compatibility.

## 3.1. Terminology

Object
: A set of data - data structure - data allocation.

Method
: An operation - function.

Class
: One or more methods.

Interface
: A standard set of one or more methods.

## 3.2. Kobj Operation

Kobj works by generating descriptions of methods. Each description holds a unique id as well as a default function. The description's address is used to uniquely identify the method within a class' method table.

A class is built by creating a method table associating one or more functions with method descriptions. Before use the class is compiled. The compilation allocates a cache and associates it with the class. A unique id is assigned to each method description within the method table of the class if not already done so by another referencing class compilation. For every method to be used a function is generated by script to qualify arguments and automatically reference the method description for a lookup. The generated function looks up the method by using the unique id associated with the method description as a hash into the cache associated with the object's class. If the method is not cached the generated function proceeds to use the class' table to find the method. If the method is found then the associated function within the class is used; otherwise, the default function associated with the method description is used.

These indirections can be visualized as the following:

```
object->cache<->class
```

## 3.3. Using Kobj

### 3.3.1. Structures

```
struct kobj_method
```

### 3.3.2. Functions

```
void kobj_class_compile(kobj_class_t cls);
void kobj_class_compile_static(kobj_class_t cls, kobj_ops_t ops);
void kobj_class_free(kobj_class_t cls);
kobj_t kobj_create(kobj_class_t cls, struct malloc_type *mtype, int mflags);
void kobj_init(kobj_t obj, kobj_class_t cls);
void kobj_delete(kobj_t obj, struct malloc_type *mtype);
```

### 3.3.3. Macros

```
KOBJ_CLASS_FIELDS
KOBJ_FIELDS
DEFINE_CLASS(name, methods, size)
KOBJMETHOD(NAME, FUNC)
```

### 3.3.4. Headers

```
<sys/param.h>
<sys/kobj.h>
```

### 3.3.5. Creating an Interface Template

The first step in using Kobj is to create an Interface. Creating the interface involves creating a template that the script `src/sys/kern/makeobjops.pl` can use to generate the header and code for the method declarations and method lookup functions.

Within this template the following keywords are used: `#include`, `INTERFACE`, `CODE`, `METHOD`, `STATICMETHOD` , and `DEFAULT`.

The `#include` statement and what follows it is copied verbatim to the head of the generated code file.

For example:

```
#include <sys/foo.h>
```

The `INTERFACE` keyword is used to define the interface name. This name is concatenated with each method name as [interface name]_[method name]. Its syntax is INTERFACE [interface name];.

For example:

```
INTERFACE foo;
```

The `CODE` keyword copies its arguments verbatim into the code file. Its syntax is `CODE { [whatever] };`

For example:

```
CODE {
 struct foo * foo_alloc_null(struct bar *)
 {
  return NULL;
}
};
```

The `METHOD` keyword describes a method. Its syntax is `METHOD [return type] [method name] { [object [, arguments]] };`

For example:

```
METHOD int bar {
 struct object *;
 struct foo *;
 struct bar;
};
```

The `DEFAULT` keyword may follow the `METHOD` keyword. It extends the `METHOD` key word to include the default function for method. The extended syntax is `METHOD [return type] [method name] { [object; [other arguments]] }DEFAULT [default function];`

For example:

```
METHOD int bar {
```

```
 struct object *;
 struct foo *;
 int bar;
} DEFAULT foo_hack;
```

The `STATICMETHOD` keyword is used like the `METHOD` keyword except the kobj data is not at the head of the object structure so casting to kobj_t would be incorrect. Instead `STATICMETHOD` relies on the Kobj data being referenced as 'ops'. This is also useful for calling methods directly out of a class's method table.

Other complete examples:

```
src/sys/kern/bus_if.m
src/sys/kern/device_if.m
```

### 3.3.6. Creating a Class

The second step in using Kobj is to create a class. A class consists of a name, a table of methods, and the size of objects if Kobj's object handling facilities are used. To create the class use the macro `DEFINE_CLASS()`. To create the method table create an array of kobj_method_t terminated by a NULL entry. Each non-NULL entry may be created using the macro `KOBJMETHOD()`.

For example:

```
DEFINE_CLASS(fooclass, foomethods, sizeof(struct foodata));

kobj_method_t foomethods[] = {
 KOBJMETHOD(bar_doo, foo_doo),
 KOBJMETHOD(bar_foo, foo_foo),
 { NULL, NULL}
};
```

The class must be "compiled". Depending on the state of the system at the time that the class is to be initialized a statically allocated cache, "ops table" have to be used. This can be accomplished by declaring a `struct kobj_ops` and using `kobj_class_compile_static();` otherwise, `kobj_class_compile()` should be used.

### 3.3.7. Creating an Object

The third step in using Kobj involves how to define the object. Kobj object creation routines assume that Kobj data is at the head of an object. If this in not appropriate you will have to allocate the object yourself and then use `kobj_init()` on the Kobj portion of it; otherwise, you may use `kobj_create()` to allocate and initialize the Kobj portion of the object automatically. `kobj_init()` may also be used to change the class that an object uses.

To integrate Kobj into the object you should use the macro KOBJ_FIELDS.

For example

```
struct foo_data {
 KOBJ_FIELDS;
 foo_foo;
 foo_bar;
};
```

### 3.3.8. Calling Methods

The last step in using Kobj is to simply use the generated functions to use the desired method within the object's class. This is as simple as using the interface name and the method name with a few modifications. The interface name should be concatenated with the method name using a '_' between them, all in upper case.

For example, if the interface name was foo and the method was bar then the call would be:

```
[return value = -] FOO_BAR(object [, other parameters]);
```

### 3.3.9. Cleaning Up

When an object allocated through `kobj_create()` is no longer needed `kobj_delete()` may be called on it, and when a class is no longer being used `kobj_class_free()` may be called on it.

# Chapter 4. The Jail Subsystem

Evan Sarmiento

<evms@cs.bu.edu >

On most UNIX® systems, `root` has omnipotent power. This promotes insecurity. If an attacker gained `root` on a system, he would have every function at his fingertips. In FreeBSD there are sysctls which dilute the power of `root`, in order to minimize the damage caused by an attacker. Specifically, one of these functions is called `secure levels`. Similarly, another function which is present from FreeBSD 4.0 and onward, is a utility called jail(8). Jail chroots an environment and sets certain restrictions on processes which are forked within the jail. For example, a jailed process cannot affect processes outside the jail, utilize certain system calls, or inflict any damage on the host environment.

Jail is becoming the new security model. People are running potentially vulnerable servers such as Apache, BIND, and sendmail within jails, so that if an attacker gains `root` within the jail, it is only an annoyance, and not a devastation. This article mainly focuses on the internals (source code) of jail. For information on how to set up a jail see the handbook entry on jails.

## 4.1. Architecture

Jail consists of two realms: the userland program, jail(8), and the code implemented within the kernel: the jail(2) system call and associated restrictions. I will be discussing the userland program and then how jail is implemented within the kernel.

### 4.1.1. Userland Code

The source for the userland jail is located in `/usr/src/usr.sbin/jail` , consisting of one file, `jail.c`. The program takes these arguments: the path of the jail, hostname, IP address, and the command to be executed.

#### 4.1.1.1. Data Structures

In `jail.c`, the first thing I would note is the declaration of an important structure `struct jail j;` which was included from `/usr/include/sys/jail.h` .

The definition of the `jail` structure is:

```
/usr/include/sys/jail.h :

struct jail {
        u_int32_t       version;
        char            *path;
        char            *hostname;
        u_int32_t       ip_number;
};
```

As you can see, there is an entry for each of the arguments passed to the jail(8) program, and indeed, they are set during its execution.

```
/usr/src/usr.sbin/jail/jail.c
char path[PATH_MAX];
...
if (realpath(argv[0], path) == NULL)
    err(1, "realpath: %s", argv[0]);
if (chdir(path) != 0)
    err(1, "chdir: %s", path);
memset(&j, 0, sizeof(j));
j.version = 0;
```

```
j.path = path;
j.hostname = argv[1];
```

#### 4.1.1.2. Networking

One of the arguments passed to the jail(8) program is an IP address with which the jail can be accessed over the network. jail(8) translates the IP address given into host byte order and then stores it in j (the `jail` structure).

```
/usr/src/usr.sbin/jail/jail.c  :
struct in_addr in;
...
if (inet_aton(argv[2], &in) == 0)
    errx(1, "Could not make sense of ip-number: %s", argv[2]);
j.ip_number = ntohl(in.s_addr);
```

The inet_aton(3) function "interprets the specified character string as an Internet address, placing the address into the structure provided." The `ip_number` member in the `jail` structure is set only when the IP address placed onto the `in` structure by inet_aton(3) is translated into host byte order by ntohl(3).

#### 4.1.1.3. Jailing the Process

Finally, the userland program jails the process. Jail now becomes an imprisoned process itself and then executes the command given using execv(3).

```
/usr/src/usr.sbin/jail/jail.c
i = jail(&j);
...
if (execv(argv[3], argv + 3) != 0)
    err(1, "execv: %s", argv[3]);
```

As you can see, the `jail()` function is called, and its argument is the `jail` structure which has been filled with the arguments given to the program. Finally, the program you specify is executed. I will now discuss how jail is implemented within the kernel.

### 4.1.2. Kernel Space

We will now be looking at the file `/usr/src/sys/kern/kern_jail.c` . This is the file where the jail(2) system call, appropriate sysctls, and networking functions are defined.

#### 4.1.2.1. sysctls

In `kern_jail.c` , the following sysctls are defined:

```
/usr/src/sys/kern/kern_jail.c:

int     jail_set_hostname_allowed = 1;
SYSCTL_INT(_security_jail, OID_AUTO, set_hostname_allowed, CTLFLAG_RW,
    &jail_set_hostname_allowed, 0,
    "Processes in jail can set their hostnames");

int     jail_socket_unixiproute_only = 1;
SYSCTL_INT(_security_jail, OID_AUTO, socket_unixiproute_only, CTLFLAG_RW,
    &jail_socket_unixiproute_only, 0,
    "Processes in jail are limited to creating UNIX/IPv4/route sockets only");

int     jail_sysvipc_allowed = 0;
SYSCTL_INT(_security_jail, OID_AUTO, sysvipc_allowed, CTLFLAG_RW,
    &jail_sysvipc_allowed, 0,
    "Processes in jail can use System V IPC primitives");

static int jail_enforce_statfs = 2;
SYSCTL_INT(_security_jail, OID_AUTO, enforce_statfs, CTLFLAG_RW,
```

```
    &jail_enforce_statfs, 0,
    "Processes in jail cannot see all mounted file systems");

int     jail_allow_raw_sockets = 0;
SYSCTL_INT(_security_jail, OID_AUTO, allow_raw_sockets, CTLFLAG_RW,
    &jail_allow_raw_sockets, 0,
    "Prison root can create raw sockets");

int     jail_chflags_allowed = 0;
SYSCTL_INT(_security_jail, OID_AUTO, chflags_allowed, CTLFLAG_RW,
    &jail_chflags_allowed, 0,
    "Processes in jail can alter system file flags");

int      jail_mount_allowed = 0;
SYSCTL_INT(_security_jail, OID_AUTO, mount_allowed, CTLFLAG_RW,
    &jail_mount_allowed, 0,
    "Processes in jail can mount/unmount jail-friendly file systems");
```

Each of these sysctls can be accessed by the user through the sysctl(8) program. Throughout the kernel, these specific sysctls are recognized by their name. For example, the name of the first sysctl is `security.jail.set_hostname_allowed`.

### 4.1.2.2. jail(2) System Call

Like all system calls, the jail(2) system call takes two arguments, `struct thread *td` and `struct jail_args *uap` . `td` is a pointer to the `thread` structure which describes the calling thread. In this context, `uap` is a pointer to the structure in which a pointer to the `jail` structure passed by the userland `jail.c` is contained. When I described the userland program before, you saw that the jail(2) system call was given a `jail` structure as its own argument.

```
/usr/src/sys/kern/kern_jail.c:
/*
 * struct jail_args {
 *  struct jail *jail;
 * };
 */
int
jail(struct thread *td, struct jail_args *uap)
```

Therefore, `uap->jail` can be used to access the `jail` structure which was passed to the system call. Next, the system call copies the `jail` structure into kernel space using the copyin(9) function. copyin(9) takes three arguments: the address of the data which is to be copied into kernel space, `uap->jail` , where to store it, `j` and the size of the storage. The `jail` structure pointed by `uap->jail` is copied into kernel space and is stored in another `jail` structure, `j`.

```
/usr/src/sys/kern/kern_jail.c:
error = copyin(uap->jail, &j, sizeof(j));
```

There is another important structure defined in `jail.h`. It is the `prison` structure. The `prison` structure is used exclusively within kernel space. Here is the definition of the `prison` structure.

```
/usr/include/sys/jail.h :
struct prison {
        LIST_ENTRY(prison) pr_list;                     /* (a) all prisons */
        int              pr_id;                         /* (c) prison id */
        int              pr_ref;                        /* (p) refcount */
        char             pr_path[MAXPATHLEN];           /* (c) chroot path */
        struct vnode    *pr_root;                       /* (c) vnode to rdir */
        char             pr_host[MAXHOSTNAMELEN];       /* (p) jail hostname */
        u_int32_t        pr_ip;                         /* (c) ip addr host */
        void            *pr_linux;                      /* (p) linux abi */
        int              pr_securelevel;                /* (p) securelevel */
        struct task      pr_task;                       /* (d) destroy task */
        struct mtx       pr_mtx;
      void            **pr_slots;                     /* (p) additional data */
```

```
};
```

The jail(2) system call then allocates memory for a prison structure and copies data between the jail and prison structure.

```
/usr/src/sys/kern/kern_jail.c  :
MALLOC(pr, struct prison *, sizeof(*pr), M_PRISON, M_WAITOK | M_ZERO);
...
error = copyinstr(j.path, &pr->pr_path, sizeof(pr->pr_path), 0);
if (error)
    goto e_killmtx;
...
error = copyinstr(j.hostname, &pr->pr_host, sizeof(pr->pr_host), 0);
if (error)
     goto e_dropvnref;
pr->pr_ip = j.ip_number;
```

Next, we will discuss another important system call jail_attach(2), which implements the function to put a process into the jail.

```
/usr/src/sys/kern/kern_jail.c  :
/*
 * struct jail_attach_args {
 *      int jid;
 * };
 */
int
jail_attach(struct thread *td, struct jail_attach_args *uap)
```

This system call makes the changes that can distinguish a jailed process from those unjailed ones. To understand what jail_attach(2) does for us, certain background information is needed.

On FreeBSD, each kernel visible thread is identified by its thread structure, while the processes are described by their proc structures. You can find the definitions of the thread and proc structure in /usr/include/sys/proc.h . For example, the td argument in any system call is actually a pointer to the calling thread's thread structure, as stated before. The td_proc member in the thread structure pointed by td is a pointer to the proc structure which represents the process that contains the thread represented by td. The proc structure contains members which can describe the owner's identity(p_ucred), the process resource limits(p_limit), and so on. In the ucred structure pointed by p_ucred member in the proc structure, there is a pointer to the prison structure(cr_prison ).

```
/usr/include/sys/proc.h:
struct thread {
    ...
    struct proc *td_proc;
    ...
};
struct proc {
    ...
    struct ucred *p_ucred;
    ...
};
/usr/include/sys/ucred.h
struct ucred {
    ...
    struct prison *cr_prison;
    ...
};
```

In kern_jail.c , the function jail() then calls function jail_attach() with a given jid. And jail_attach() calls function change_root() to change the root directory of the calling process. The jail_attach() then creates a new ucred structure, and attaches the newly created ucred structure to the calling process after it has successfully attached the prison structure to the ucred structure. From then on, the calling process is recognized as jailed. When the kernel routine jailed() is called in the kernel with the newly created ucred structure as its argument, it returns 1 to tell that the credential is connected with a jail. The public ancestor process of all the process forked

within the jail, is the process which runs jail(8), as it calls the jail(2) system call. When a program is executed through execve(2), it inherits the jailed property of its parent's `ucred` structure, therefore it has a jailed `ucred` structure.

```
/usr/src/sys/kern/kern_jail.c
int
jail(struct thread *td, struct jail_args *uap)
{
...
    struct jail_attach_args jaa;
...
    error = jail_attach(td, &jaa);
    if (error)
        goto e_dropprref;
...
}

int
jail_attach(struct thread *td, struct jail_attach_args *uap)
{
    struct proc *p;
    struct ucred *newcred, *oldcred;
    struct prison *pr;
...
    p = td->td_proc;
...
    pr = prison_find(uap->jid);
...
    change_root(pr->pr_root, td);
...
    newcred->cr_prison = pr;
    p->p_ucred = newcred;
...
}
```

When a process is forked from its parent process, the fork(2) system call uses `crhold()` to maintain the credential for the newly forked process. It inherently keep the newly forked child's credential consistent with its parent, so the child process is also jailed.

```
/usr/src/sys/kern/kern_fork.c  :
p2->p_ucred = crhold(td->td_ucred);
...
td2->td_ucred = crhold(p2->p_ucred);
```

## 4.2. Restrictions

Throughout the kernel there are access restrictions relating to jailed processes. Usually, these restrictions only check whether the process is jailed, and if so, returns an error. For example:

```
if (jailed(td->td_ucred))
    return (EPERM);
```

### 4.2.1. SysV IPC

System V IPC is based on messages. Processes can send each other these messages which tell them how to act. The functions which deal with messages are: msgctl(3), msgget(3), msgsnd(3) and msgrcv(3). Earlier, I mentioned that there were certain sysctls you could turn on or off in order to affect the behavior of jail. One of these sysctls was `security.jail.sysvipc_allowed`. By default, this sysctl is set to 0. If it were set to 1, it would defeat the whole purpose of having a jail; privileged users from the jail would be able to affect processes outside the jailed environment. The difference between a message and a signal is that the message only consists of the signal number.

`/usr/src/sys/kern/sysv_msg.c :`

- `msgget(key, msgflg)` : `msgget` returns (and possibly creates) a message descriptor that designates a message queue for use in other functions.
- `msgctl(msgid, cmd, buf)` : Using this function, a process can query the status of a message descriptor.
- `msgsnd(msgid, msgp, msgsz, msgflg)`: `msgsnd` sends a message to a process.
- `msgrcv(msgid, msgp, msgsz, msgtyp, msgflg)`: a process receives messages using this function

In each of the system calls corresponding to these functions, there is this conditional:

```
/usr/src/sys/kern/sysv_msg.c  :
if (!jail_sysvipc_allowed && jailed(td->td_ucred))
    return (ENOSYS);
```

Semaphore system calls allow processes to synchronize execution by doing a set of operations atomically on a set of semaphores. Basically semaphores provide another way for processes lock resources. However, process waiting on a semaphore, that is being used, will sleep until the resources are relinquished. The following semaphore system calls are blocked inside a jail: semget(2), semctl(2) and semop(2).

`/usr/src/sys/kern/sysv_sem.c :`

- `semctl(semid, semnum, cmd, ...)` : `semctl` does the specified `cmd` on the semaphore queue indicated by `semid`.
- `semget(key, nsems, flag)` : `semget` creates an array of semaphores, corresponding to `key`.

  `key and flag take on the same meaning as they do in msgget.`
- `semop(semid, array, nops)` : `semop` performs a group of operations indicated by `array`, to the set of semaphores identified by `semid`.

System V IPC allows for processes to share memory. Processes can communicate directly with each other by sharing parts of their virtual address space and then reading and writing data stored in the shared memory. These system calls are blocked within a jailed environment: shmdt(2), shmat(2), shmctl(2) and shmget(2).

`/usr/src/sys/kern/sysv_shm.c :`

- `shmctl(shmid, cmd, buf)`: `shmctl` does various control operations on the shared memory region identified by `shmid`.
- `shmget(key, size, flag)` : `shmget` accesses or creates a shared memory region of `size` bytes.
- `shmat(shmid, addr, flag)` : `shmat` attaches a shared memory region identified by `shmid` to the address space of a process.
- `shmdt(addr)`: `shmdt` detaches the shared memory region previously attached at `addr`.

### 4.2.2. Sockets

Jail treats the socket(2) system call and related lower-level socket functions in a special manner. In order to determine whether a certain socket is allowed to be created, it first checks to see if the sysctl `security.jail.socket_unixiproute_only` is set. If set, sockets are only allowed to be created if the family specified is either `PF_LOCAL`, `PF_INET` or `PF_ROUTE`. Otherwise, it returns an error.

```
/usr/src/sys/kern/uipc_socket.c  :
int
```

```
socreate(int dom, struct socket **aso, int type, int proto,
    struct ucred *cred, struct thread *td)
{
    struct protosw *prp;
...
    if (jailed(cred) && jail_socket_unixiproute_only &&
        prp->pr_domain->dom_family != PF_LOCAL &&
        prp->pr_domain->dom_family != PF_INET &&
        prp->pr_domain->dom_family != PF_ROUTE) {
        return (EPROTONOSUPPORT);
    }
...
}
```

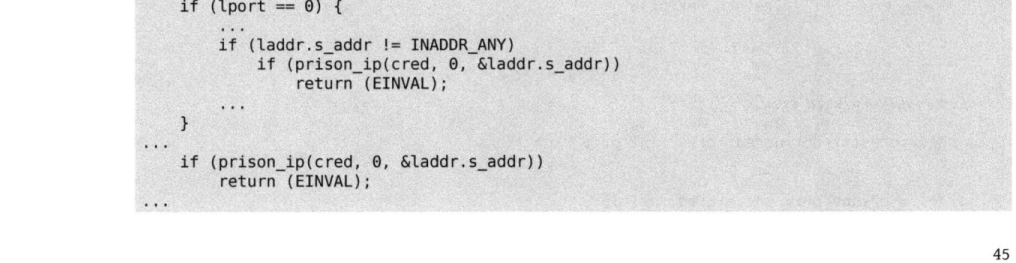

### 4.2.3. Berkeley Packet Filter

The Berkeley Packet Filter provides a raw interface to data link layers in a protocol independent fashion. BPF is now controlled by the devfs(8) whether it can be used in a jailed environment.

### 4.2.4. Protocols

There are certain protocols which are very common, such as TCP, UDP, IP and ICMP. IP and ICMP are on the same level: the network layer 2. There are certain precautions which are taken in order to prevent a jailed process from binding a protocol to a certain address only if the `nam` parameter is set. `nam` is a pointer to a `sockaddr` structure, which describes the address on which to bind the service. A more exact definition is that `sockaddr` "may be used as a template for referring to the identifying tag and length of each address". In the function `in_pcbbind_setup()`, `sin` is a pointer to a `sockaddr_in` structure, which contains the port, address, length and domain family of the socket which is to be bound. Basically, this disallows any processes from jail to be able to specify the address that does not belong to the jail in which the calling process exists.

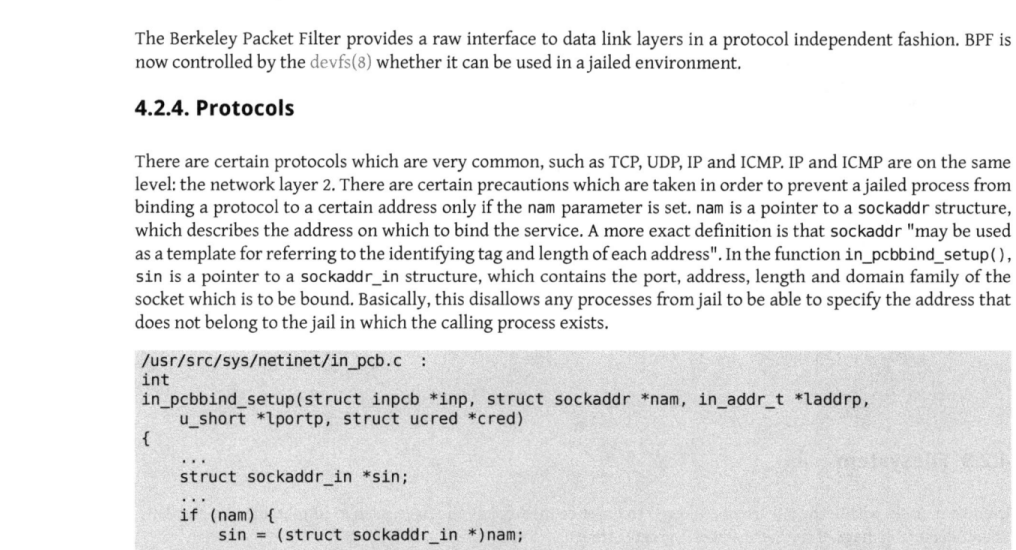

```
/usr/src/sys/netinet/in_pcb.c  :
int
in_pcbbind_setup(struct inpcb *inp, struct sockaddr *nam, in_addr_t *laddrp,
    u_short *lportp, struct ucred *cred)
{
    ...
    struct sockaddr_in *sin;
    ...
    if (nam) {
        sin = (struct sockaddr_in *)nam;
        ...
        if (sin->sin_addr.s_addr != INADDR_ANY)
            if (prison_ip(cred, 0, &sin->sin_addr.s_addr))
                return(EINVAL);
        ...
        if (lport) {
            ...
            if (prison && prison_ip(cred, 0, &sin->sin_addr.s_addr))
                return (EADDRNOTAVAIL);
            ...
        }
    }
    if (lport == 0) {
        ...
        if (laddr.s_addr != INADDR_ANY)
            if (prison_ip(cred, 0, &laddr.s_addr))
                return (EINVAL);
        ...
    }
...
    if (prison_ip(cred, 0, &laddr.s_addr))
        return (EINVAL);
...
```

```
}
```

You might be wondering what function `prison_ip()` does. `prison_ip()` is given three arguments, a pointer to the credential(represented by `cred`), any flags, and an IP address. It returns 1 if the IP address does NOT belong to the jail or 0 otherwise. As you can see from the code, if it is indeed an IP address not belonging to the jail, the protocol is not allowed to bind to that address.

```
/usr/src/sys/kern/kern_jail.c:
int
prison_ip(struct ucred *cred, int flag, u_int32_t *ip)
{
    u_int32_t tmp;

    if (!jailed(cred))
        return (0);
    if (flag)
        tmp = *ip;
    else
        tmp = ntohl(*ip);
    if (tmp == INADDR_ANY) {
        if (flag)
            *ip = cred->cr_prison->pr_ip;
        else
            *ip = htonl(cred->cr_prison->pr_ip);
        return (0);
    }
    if (tmp == INADDR_LOOPBACK) {
        if (flag)
            *ip = cred->cr_prison->pr_ip;
        else
            *ip = htonl(cred->cr_prison->pr_ip);
        return (0);
    }
    if (cred->cr_prison->pr_ip != tmp)
        return (1);
    return (0);
}
```

### 4.2.5. Filesystem

Even `root` users within the jail are not allowed to unset or modify any file flags, such as immutable, append-only, and undeleteable flags, if the securelevel is greater than 0.

```
/usr/src/sys/ufs/ufs/ufs_vnops.c:
static int
ufs_setattr(ap)
    ...
{
    ...
        if (!priv_check_cred(cred, PRIV_VFS_SYSFLAGS, 0)) {
            if (ip->i_flags
                & (SF_NOUNLINK | SF_IMMUTABLE | SF_APPEND)) {
                    error = securelevel_gt(cred, 0);
                    if (error)
                        return (error);
            }
            ...
        }
}
/usr/src/sys/kern/kern_priv.c
int
priv_check_cred(struct ucred *cred, int priv, int flags)
{
    ...
    error = prison_priv_check(cred, priv);
```

```
    if (error)
        return (error);
    ...
}
/usr/src/sys/kern/kern_jail.c
int
prison_priv_check(struct ucred *cred, int priv)
{
    ...
    switch (priv) {
    ...
    case PRIV_VFS_SYSFLAGS:
        if (jail_chflags_allowed)
            return (0);
        else
            return (EPERM);
    ...
    }
    ...
}
```

# Chapter 5. The SYSINIT Framework

SYSINIT is the framework for a generic call sort and dispatch mechanism. FreeBSD currently uses it for the dynamic initialization of the kernel. SYSINIT allows FreeBSD's kernel subsystems to be reordered, and added, removed, and replaced at kernel link time when the kernel or one of its modules is loaded without having to edit a statically ordered initialization routing and recompile the kernel. This system also allows kernel modules, currently called *KLD's*, to be separately compiled, linked, and initialized at boot time and loaded even later while the system is already running. This is accomplished using the "kernel linker" and "linker sets".

## 5.1. Terminology

Linker Set
: A linker technique in which the linker gathers statically declared data throughout a program's source files into a single contiguously addressable unit of data.

## 5.2. SYSINIT Operation

SYSINIT relies on the ability of the linker to take static data declared at multiple locations throughout a program's source and group it together as a single contiguous chunk of data. This linker technique is called a "linker set". SYSINIT uses two linker sets to maintain two data sets containing each consumer's call order, function, and a pointer to the data to pass to that function.

SYSINIT uses two priorities when ordering the functions for execution. The first priority is a subsystem ID giving an overall order for SYSINIT's dispatch of functions. Current predeclared ID's are in `<sys/kernel.h>` in the enum list `sysinit_sub_id` . The second priority used is an element order within the subsystem. Current predeclared subsystem element orders are in `<sys/kernel.h>` in the enum list `sysinit_elem_order`.

There are currently two uses for SYSINIT. Function dispatch at system startup and kernel module loads, and function dispatch at system shutdown and kernel module unload. Kernel subsystems often use system startup SYSINIT's to initialize data structures, for example the process scheduling subsystem uses a SYSINIT to initialize the run queue data structure. Device drivers should avoid using `SYSINIT()` directly. Instead drivers for real devices that are part of a bus structure should use `DRIVER_MODULE()` to provide a function that detects the device and, if it is present, initializes the device. It will do a few things specific to devices and then call `SYSINIT()` itself. For pseudo-devices, which are not part of a bus structure, use `DEV_MODULE()`.

## 5.3. Using SYSINIT

### 5.3.1. Interface

#### 5.3.1.1. Headers

```
<sys/kernel.h>
```

#### 5.3.1.2. Macros

```
SYSINIT(uniquifier, subsystem, order, func, ident)
SYSUNINIT(uniquifier, subsystem, order, func, ident)
```

### 5.3.2. Startup

The `SYSINIT()` macro creates the necessary SYSINIT data in SYSINIT's startup data set for SYSINIT to sort and dispatch a function at system startup and module load. `SYSINIT()` takes a uniquifier that SYSINIT uses to identify

the particular function dispatch data, the subsystem order, the subsystem element order, the function to call, and the data to pass the function. All functions must take a constant pointer argument.

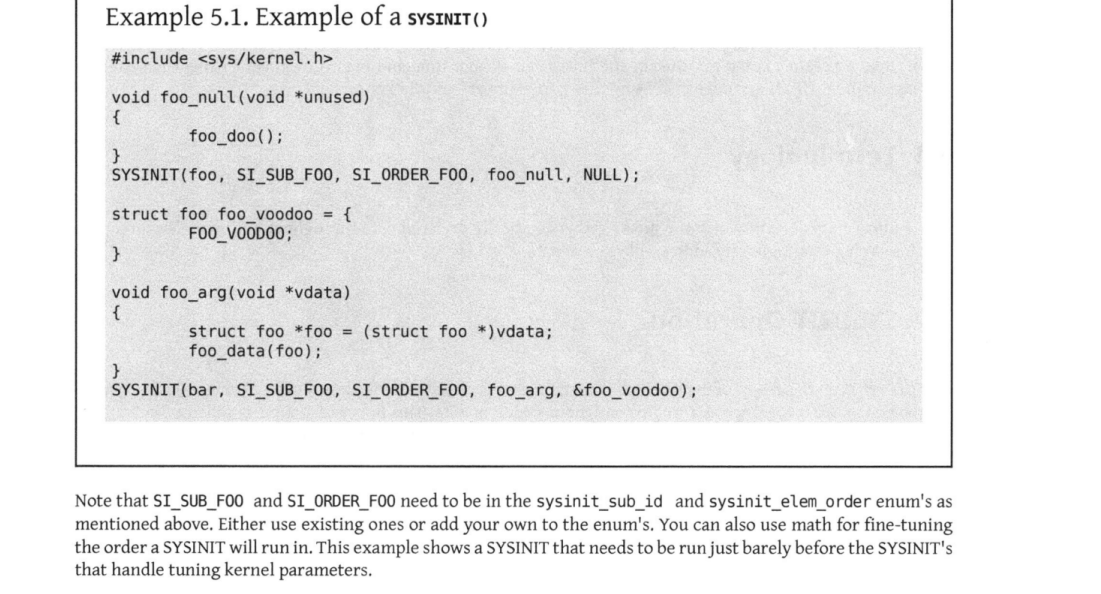

**Example 5.1. Example of a `SYSINIT()`**

```
#include <sys/kernel.h>

void foo_null(void *unused)
{
        foo_doo();
}
SYSINIT(foo, SI_SUB_FOO, SI_ORDER_FOO, foo_null, NULL);

struct foo foo_voodoo = {
        FOO_VOODOO;
}

void foo_arg(void *vdata)
{
        struct foo *foo = (struct foo *)vdata;
        foo_data(foo);
}
SYSINIT(bar, SI_SUB_FOO, SI_ORDER_FOO, foo_arg, &foo_voodoo);
```

Note that `SI_SUB_FOO` and `SI_ORDER_FOO` need to be in the `sysinit_sub_id` and `sysinit_elem_order` enum's as mentioned above. Either use existing ones or add your own to the enum's. You can also use math for fine-tuning the order a SYSINIT will run in. This example shows a SYSINIT that needs to be run just barely before the SYSINIT's that handle tuning kernel parameters.

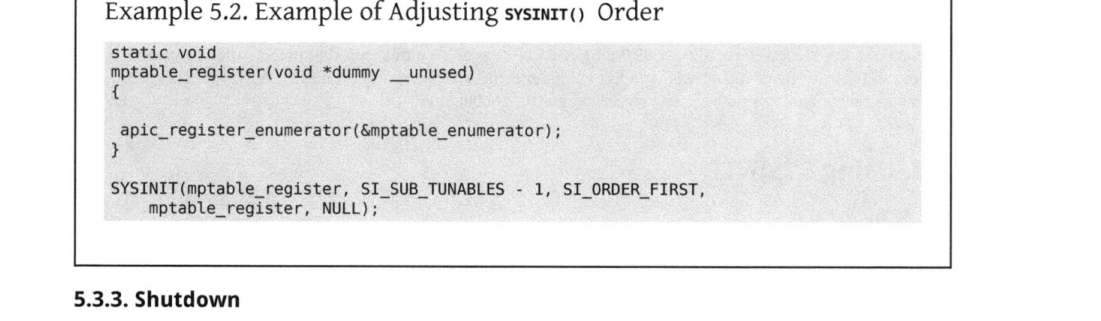

**Example 5.2. Example of Adjusting `SYSINIT()` Order**

```
static void
mptable_register(void *dummy __unused)
{

 apic_register_enumerator(&mptable_enumerator);
}

SYSINIT(mptable_register, SI_SUB_TUNABLES - 1, SI_ORDER_FIRST,
    mptable_register, NULL);
```

### 5.3.3. Shutdown

The `SYSUNINIT()` macro behaves similarly to the `SYSINIT()` macro except that it adds the SYSINIT data to SYSINIT's shutdown data set.

**Example 5.3. Example of a `SYSUNINIT()`**

```
#include <sys/kernel.h>
```

```
void foo_cleanup(void *unused)
{
        foo_kill();
}
SYSUNINIT(foobar, SI_SUB_FOO, SI_ORDER_FOO, foo_cleanup, NULL);

struct foo_stack foo_stack = {
        FOO_STACK_VOODOO;
}

void foo_flush(void *vdata)
{
}
SYSUNINIT(barfoo, SI_SUB_FOO, SI_ORDER_FOO, foo_flush, &foo_stack);
```

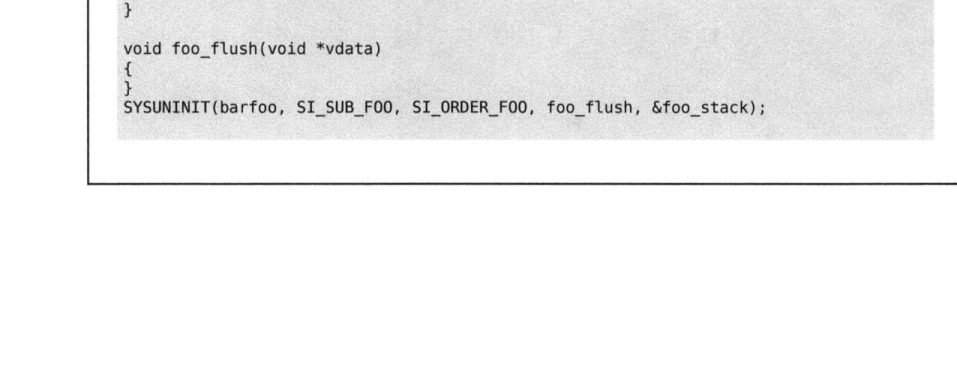

# Chapter 6. The TrustedBSD MAC Framework

Chris Costello and Robert Watson.

## 6.1. MAC Documentation Copyright



## 6.2. Synopsis

FreeBSD includes experimental support for several mandatory access control policies, as well as a framework for kernel security extensibility, the TrustedBSD MAC Framework. The MAC Framework is a pluggable access control framework, permitting new security policies to be easily linked into the kernel, loaded at boot, or loaded dynamically at run-time. The framework provides a variety of features to make it easier to implement new security policies, including the ability to easily tag security labels (such as confidentiality information) onto system objects.

This chapter introduces the MAC policy framework and provides documentation for a sample MAC policy module.

## 6.3. Introduction

The TrustedBSD MAC framework provides a mechanism to allow the compile-time or run-time extension of the kernel access control model. New system policies may be implemented as kernel modules and linked to the kernel; if multiple policy modules are present, their results will be composed. The MAC Framework provides a variety

of access control infrastructure services to assist policy writers, including support for transient and persistent policy-agnostic object security labels. This support is currently considered experimental.

This chapter provides information appropriate for developers of policy modules, as well as potential consumers of MAC-enabled environments, to learn about how the MAC Framework supports access control extension of the kernel.

## 6.4. Policy Background

Mandatory Access Control (MAC), refers to a set of access control policies that are mandatorily enforced on users by the operating system. MAC policies may be contrasted with Discretionary Access Control (DAC) protections, by which non-administrative users may (at their discretion) protect objects. In traditional UNIX systems, DAC protections include file permissions and access control lists; MAC protections include process controls preventing inter-user debugging and firewalls. A variety of MAC policies have been formulated by operating system designers and security researches, including the Multi-Level Security (MLS) confidentiality policy, the Biba integrity policy, Role-Based Access Control (RBAC), Domain and Type Enforcement (DTE), and Type Enforcement (TE). Each model bases decisions on a variety of factors, including user identity, role, and security clearance, as well as security labels on objects representing concepts such as data sensitivity and integrity.

The TrustedBSD MAC Framework is capable of supporting policy modules that implement all of these policies, as well as a broad class of system hardening policies, which may use existing security attributes, such as user and group IDs, as well as extended attributes on files, and other system properties. In addition, despite the name, the MAC Framework can also be used to implement purely discretionary policies, as policy modules are given substantial flexibility in how they authorize protections.

## 6.5. MAC Framework Kernel Architecture

The TrustedBSD MAC Framework permits kernel modules to extend the operating system security policy, as well as providing infrastructure functionality required by many access control modules. If multiple policies are simultaneously loaded, the MAC Framework will usefully (for some definition of useful) compose the results of the policies.

### 6.5.1. Kernel Elements

The MAC Framework contains a number of kernel elements:

- Framework management interfaces
- Concurrency and synchronization primitives.
- Policy registration
- Extensible security label for kernel objects
- Policy entry point composition operators
- Label management primitives
- Entry point API invoked by kernel services
- Entry point API to policy modules
- Entry points implementations (policy life cycle, object life cycle/label management, access control checks).
- Policy-agnostic label-management system calls
- `mac_syscall()` multiplex system call
- Various security policies implemented as MAC policy modules

### 6.5.2. Framework Management Interfaces

The TrustedBSD MAC Framework may be directly managed using sysctl's, loader tunables, and system calls.

In most cases, sysctl's and loader tunables of the same name modify the same parameters, and control behavior such as enforcement of protections relating to various kernel subsystems. In addition, if MAC debugging support is compiled into the kernel, several counters will be maintained tracking label allocation. It is generally advisable that per-subsystem enforcement controls not be used to control policy behavior in production environments, as they broadly impact the operation of all active policies. Instead, per-policy controls should be preferred, as they provide greater granularity and greater operational consistency for policy modules.

Loading and unloading of policy modules is performed using the system module management system calls and other system interfaces, including boot loader variables; policy modules will have the opportunity to influence load and unload events, including preventing undesired unloading of the policy.

### 6.5.3. Policy List Concurrency and Synchronization

As the set of active policies may change at run-time, and the invocation of entry points is non-atomic, synchronization is required to prevent loading or unloading of policies while an entry point invocation is in progress, freezing the set of active policies for the duration. This is accomplished by means of a framework busy count: whenever an entry point is entered, the busy count is incremented; whenever it is exited, the busy count is decremented. While the busy count is elevated, policy list changes are not permitted, and threads attempting to modify the policy list will sleep until the list is not busy. The busy count is protected by a mutex, and a condition variable is used to wake up sleepers waiting on policy list modifications. One side effect of this synchronization model is that recursion into the MAC Framework from within a policy module is permitted, although not generally used.

Various optimizations are used to reduce the overhead of the busy count, including avoiding the full cost of incrementing and decrementing if the list is empty or contains only static entries (policies that are loaded before the system starts, and cannot be unloaded). A compile-time option is also provided which prevents any change in the set of loaded policies at run-time, which eliminates the mutex locking costs associated with supporting dynamically loaded and unloaded policies as synchronization is no longer required.

As the MAC Framework is not permitted to block in some entry points, a normal sleep lock cannot be used; as a result, it is possible for the load or unload attempt to block for a substantial period of time waiting for the framework to become idle.

### 6.5.4. Label Synchronization

As kernel objects of interest may generally be accessed from more than one thread at a time, and simultaneous entry of more than one thread into the MAC Framework is permitted, security attribute storage maintained by the MAC Framework is carefully synchronized. In general, existing kernel synchronization on kernel object data is used to protect MAC Framework security labels on the object: for example, MAC labels on sockets are protected using the existing socket mutex. Likewise, semantics for concurrent access are generally identical to those of the container objects: for credentials, copy-on-write semantics are maintained for label contents as with the remainder of the credential structure. The MAC Framework asserts necessary locks on objects when invoked with an object reference. Policy authors must be aware of these synchronization semantics, as they will sometimes limit the types of accesses permitted on labels: for example, when a read-only reference to a credential is passed to a policy via an entry point, only read operations are permitted on the label state attached to the credential.

### 6.5.5. Policy Synchronization and Concurrency

Policy modules must be written to assume that many kernel threads may simultaneously enter one more policy entry points due to the parallel and preemptive nature of the FreeBSD kernel. If the policy module makes use of mutable state, this may require the use of synchronization primitives within the policy to prevent inconsistent views on that state resulting in incorrect operation of the policy. Policies will generally be able to make use of existing FreeBSD synchronization primitives for this purpose, including mutexes, sleep locks, condition variables, and counting semaphores. However, policies should be written to employ these primitives carefully, respecting

existing kernel lock orders, and recognizing that some entry points are not permitted to sleep, limiting the use of primitives in those entry points to mutexes and wakeup operations.

When policy modules call out to other kernel subsystems, they will generally need to release any in-policy locks in order to avoid violating the kernel lock order or risking lock recursion. This will maintain policy locks as leaf locks in the global lock order, helping to avoid deadlock.

### 6.5.6. Policy Registration

The MAC Framework maintains two lists of active policies: a static list, and a dynamic list. The lists differ only with regards to their locking semantics: an elevated reference count is not required to make use of the static list. When kernel modules containing MAC Framework policies are loaded, the policy module will use `SYSINIT` to invoke a registration function; when a policy module is unloaded, `SYSINIT` will likewise invoke a de-registration function. Registration may fail if a policy module is loaded more than once, if insufficient resources are available for the registration (for example, the policy might require labeling and insufficient labeling state might be available), or other policy prerequisites might not be met (some policies may only be loaded prior to boot). Likewise, de-registration may fail if a policy is flagged as not unloadable.

### 6.5.7. Entry Points

Kernel services interact with the MAC Framework in two ways: they invoke a series of APIs to notify the framework of relevant events, and they provide a policy-agnostic label structure pointer in security-relevant objects. The label pointer is maintained by the MAC Framework via label management entry points, and permits the Framework to offer a labeling service to policy modules through relatively non-invasive changes to the kernel subsystem maintaining the object. For example, label pointers have been added to processes, process credentials, sockets, pipes, vnodes, Mbufs, network interfaces, IP reassembly queues, and a variety of other security-relevant structures. Kernel services also invoke the MAC Framework when they perform important security decisions, permitting policy modules to augment those decisions based on their own criteria (possibly including data stored in security labels). Most of these security critical decisions will be explicit access control checks; however, some affect more general decision functions such as packet matching for sockets and label transition at program execution.

### 6.5.8. Policy Composition

When more than one policy module is loaded into the kernel at a time, the results of the policy modules will be composed by the framework using a composition operator. This operator is currently hard-coded, and requires that all active policies must approve a request for it to return success. As policies may return a variety of error conditions (success, access denied, object does not exist, ...), a precedence operator selects the resulting error from the set of errors returned by policies. In general, errors indicating that an object does not exist will be preferred to errors indicating that access to an object is denied. While it is not guaranteed that the resulting composition will be useful or secure, we have found that it is for many useful selections of policies. For example, traditional trusted systems often ship with two or more policies using a similar composition.

### 6.5.9. Labeling Support

As many interesting access control extensions rely on security labels on objects, the MAC Framework provides a set of policy-agnostic label management system calls covering a variety of user-exposed objects. Common label types include partition identifiers, sensitivity labels, integrity labels, compartments, domains, roles, and types. By policy agnostic, we mean that policy modules are able to completely define the semantics of meta-data associated with an object. Policy modules participate in the internalization and externalization of string-based labels provides by user applications, and can expose multiple label elements to applications if desired.

In-memory labels are stored in slab-allocated `struct label`, which consists of a fixed-length array of unions, each holding a `void *` pointer and a `long`. Policies registering for label storage will be assigned a "slot" identifier, which may be used to dereference the label storage. The semantics of the storage are left entirely up to the policy module: modules are provided with a variety of entry points associated with the kernel object life cycle, including initialization, association/creation, and destruction. Using these interfaces, it is possible to implement reference counting and other storage models. Direct access to the object structure is generally not required by policy modules

to retrieve a label, as the MAC Framework generally passes both a pointer to the object and a direct pointer to the object's label into entry points. The primary exception to this rule is the process credential, which must be manually dereferenced to access the credential label. This may change in future revisions of the MAC Framework.

Initialization entry points frequently include a sleeping disposition flag indicating whether or not an initialization is permitted to sleep; if sleeping is not permitted, a failure may be returned to cancel allocation of the label (and hence object). This may occur, for example, in the network stack during interrupt handling, where sleeping is not permitted, or while the caller holds a mutex. Due to the performance cost of maintaining labels on in-flight network packets (Mbufs), policies must specifically declare a requirement that Mbuf labels be allocated. Dynamically loaded policies making use of labels must be able to handle the case where their init function has not been called on an object, as objects may already exist when the policy is loaded. The MAC Framework guarantees that uninitialized label slots will hold a 0 or NULL value, which policies may use to detect uninitialized values. However, as allocation of Mbuf labels is conditional, policies must also be able to handle a NULL label pointer for Mbufs if they have been loaded dynamically.

In the case of file system labels, special support is provided for the persistent storage of security labels in extended attributes. Where available, extended attribute transactions are used to permit consistent compound updates of security labels on vnodes--currently this support is present only in the UFS2 file system. Policy authors may choose to implement multilabel file system object labels using one (or more) extended attributes. For efficiency reasons, the vnode label (`v_label`) is a cache of any on-disk label; policies are able to load values into the cache when the vnode is instantiated, and update the cache as needed. As a result, the extended attribute need not be directly accessed with every access control check.

Note

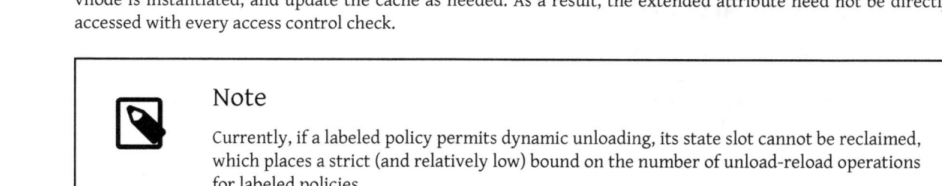

Currently, if a labeled policy permits dynamic unloading, its state slot cannot be reclaimed, which places a strict (and relatively low) bound on the number of unload-reload operations for labeled policies.

### 6.5.10. System Calls

The MAC Framework implements a number of system calls: most of these calls support the policy-agnostic label retrieval and manipulation APIs exposed to user applications.

The label management calls accept a label description structure, `struct mac`, which contains a series of MAC label elements. Each element contains a character string name, and character string value. Each policy will be given the chance to claim a particular element name, permitting policies to expose multiple independent elements if desired. Policy modules perform the internalization and externalization between kernel labels and user-provided labels via entry points, permitting a variety of semantics. Label management system calls are generally wrapped by user library functions to perform memory allocation and error handling, simplifying user applications that must manage labels.

The following MAC-related system calls are present in the FreeBSD kernel:

- `mac_get_proc()` may be used to retrieve the label of the current process.
- `mac_set_proc()` may be used to request a change in the label of the current process.
- `mac_get_fd()` may be used to retrieve the label of an object (file, socket, pipe, ...) referenced by a file descriptor.
- `mac_get_file()` may be used to retrieve the label of an object referenced by a file system path.
- `mac_set_fd()` may be used to request a change in the label of an object (file, socket, pipe, ...) referenced by a file descriptor.
- `mac_set_file()` may be used to request a change in the label of an object referenced by a file system path.

- `mac_syscall()` permits policy modules to create new system calls without modifying the system call table; it accepts a target policy name, operation number, and opaque argument for use by the policy.
- `mac_get_pid()` may be used to request the label of another process by process id.
- `mac_get_link()` is identical to `mac_get_file()` , only it will not follow a symbolic link if it is the final entry in the path, so may be used to retrieve the label on a symlink.
- `mac_set_link()` is identical to `mac_set_file()` , only it will not follow a symbolic link if it is the final entry in a path, so may be used to manipulate the label on a symlink.
- `mac_execve()` is identical to the `execve()` system call, only it also accepts a requested label to set the process label to when beginning execution of a new program. This change in label on execution is referred to as a "transition".
- `mac_get_peer()` , actually implemented via a socket option, retrieves the label of a remote peer on a socket, if available.

In addition to these system calls, the `SIOCSIGMAC` and `SIOCSIFMAC` network interface ioctls permit the labels on network interfaces to be retrieved and set.

## 6.6. MAC Policy Architecture

Security policies are either linked directly into the kernel, or compiled into loadable kernel modules that may be loaded at boot, or dynamically using the module loading system calls at runtime. Policy modules interact with the system through a set of declared entry points, providing access to a stream of system events and permitting the policy to influence access control decisions. Each policy contains a number of elements:

- Optional configuration parameters for policy.
- Centralized implementation of the policy logic and parameters.
- Optional implementation of policy life cycle events, such as initialization and destruction.
- Optional support for initializing, maintaining, and destroying labels on selected kernel objects.
- Optional support for user process inspection and modification of labels on selected objects.
- Implementation of selected access control entry points that are of interest to the policy.
- Declaration of policy identity, module entry points, and policy properties.

### 6.6.1. Policy Declaration

Modules may be declared using the `MAC_POLICY_SET()` macro, which names the policy, provides a reference to the MAC entry point vector, provides load-time flags determining how the policy framework should handle the policy, and optionally requests the allocation of label state by the framework.

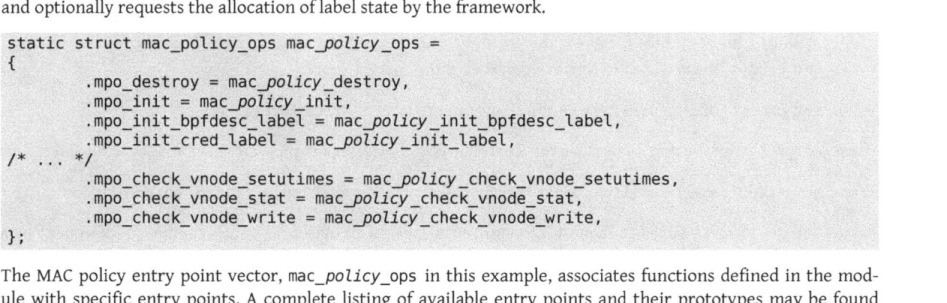

```
static struct mac_policy_ops mac_policy_ops =
{
        .mpo_destroy = mac_policy_destroy,
        .mpo_init = mac_policy_init,
        .mpo_init_bpfdesc_label = mac_policy_init_bpfdesc_label,
        .mpo_init_cred_label = mac_policy_init_label,
/* ... */
        .mpo_check_vnode_setutimes = mac_policy_check_vnode_setutimes,
        .mpo_check_vnode_stat = mac_policy_check_vnode_stat,
        .mpo_check_vnode_write = mac_policy_check_vnode_write,
};
```

The MAC policy entry point vector, `mac_policy_ops` in this example, associates functions defined in the module with specific entry points. A complete listing of available entry points and their prototypes may be found

in the MAC entry point reference section. Of specific interest during module registration are the .mpo_destroy and .mpo_init entry points. .mpo_init will be invoked once a policy is successfully registered with the module framework but prior to any other entry points becoming active. This permits the policy to perform any policy-specific allocation and initialization, such as initialization of any data or locks. .mpo_destroy will be invoked when a policy module is unloaded to permit releasing of any allocated memory and destruction of locks. Currently, these two entry points are invoked with the MAC policy list mutex held to prevent any other entry points from being invoked: this will be changed, but in the mean time, policies should be careful about what kernel primitives they invoke so as to avoid lock ordering or sleeping problems.

The policy declaration's module name field exists so that the module may be uniquely identified for the purposes of module dependencies. An appropriate string should be selected. The full string name of the policy is displayed to the user via the kernel log during load and unload events, and also exported when providing status information to userland processes.

## 6.6.2. Policy Flags

The policy declaration flags field permits the module to provide the framework with information about its capabilities at the time the module is loaded. Currently, three flags are defined:

MPC_LOADTIME_FLAG_UNLOADOK
: This flag indicates that the policy module may be unloaded. If this flag is not provided, then the policy framework will reject requests to unload the module. This flag might be used by modules that allocate label state and are unable to free that state at runtime.

MPC_LOADTIME_FLAG_NOTLATE
: This flag indicates that the policy module must be loaded and initialized early in the boot process. If the flag is specified, attempts to register the module following boot will be rejected. The flag may be used by policies that require pervasive labeling of all system objects, and cannot handle objects that have not been properly initialized by the policy.

MPC_LOADTIME_FLAG_LABELMBUFS
: This flag indicates that the policy module requires labeling of Mbufs, and that memory should always be allocated for the storage of Mbuf labels. By default, the MAC Framework will not allocate label storage for Mbufs unless at least one loaded policy has this flag set. This measurably improves network performance when policies do not require Mbuf labeling. A kernel option, `MAC_ALWAYS_LABEL_MBUF`, exists to force the MAC Framework to allocate Mbuf label storage regardless of the setting of this flag, and may be useful in some environments.

**Note**

Policies using the `MPC_LOADTIME_FLAG_LABELMBUFS` without the `MPC_LOADTIME_FLAG_NOTLATE` flag set must be able to correctly handle `NULL` Mbuf label pointers passed into entry points. This is necessary as in-flight Mbufs without label storage may persist after a policy enabling Mbuf labeling has been loaded. If a policy is loaded before the network subsystem is active (i.e., the policy is not being loaded late), then all Mbufs are guaranteed to have label storage.

## 6.6.3. Policy Entry Points

Four classes of entry points are offered to policies registered with the framework: entry points associated with the registration and management of policies, entry points denoting initialization, creation, destruction, and other life cycle events for kernel objects, events associated with access control decisions that the policy module may influence, and calls associated with the management of labels on objects. In addition, a `mac_syscall()` entry point is provided so that policies may extend the kernel interface without registering new system calls.

Policy module writers should be aware of the kernel locking strategy, as well as what object locks are available during which entry points. Writers should attempt to avoid deadlock scenarios by avoiding grabbing non-leaf locks inside of entry points, and also follow the locking protocol for object access and modification. In particular, writers should be aware that while necessary locks to access objects and their labels are generally held, sufficient locks to modify an object or its label may not be present for all entry points. Locking information for arguments is documented in the MAC framework entry point document.

Policy entry points will pass a reference to the object label along with the object itself. This permits labeled policies to be unaware of the internals of the object yet still make decisions based on the label. The exception to this is the process credential, which is assumed to be understood by policies as a first class security object in the kernel.

# 6.7. MAC Policy Entry Point Reference

## 6.7.1. General-Purpose Module Entry Points

### 6.7.1.1. `mpo_init`

```
void mpo_init(conf);

struct mac_policy_conf *conf;
```

| Parameter | Description | Locking |
|---|---|---|
| conf | MAC policy definition | |

Policy load event. The policy list mutex is held, so sleep operations cannot be performed, and calls out to other kernel subsystems must be made with caution. If potentially sleeping memory allocations are required during policy initialization, they should be made using a separate module SYSINIT().

### 6.7.1.2. `mpo_destroy`

```
void mpo_destroy(conf);

struct mac_policy_conf *conf;
```

| Parameter | Description | Locking |
|---|---|---|
| conf | MAC policy defi- | |

| Parameter | Description | Locking |
|---|---|---|
| | n-i-tion | |

Policy load event. The policy list mutex is held, so caution should be applied.

### 6.7.1.3. mpo_syscall

```
int mpo_syscall(td, call, arg);

struct thread *td;
int call;
void *arg;
```

| Parameter | Description | Locking |
|---|---|---|
| td | Calling thread | |
| call | Policy-specific syscall number | |
| arg | Pointer to syscall arguments | |

This entry point provides a policy-multiplexed system call so that policies may provide additional services to user processes without registering specific system calls. The policy name provided during registration is used to demux calls from userland, and the arguments will be forwarded to this entry point. When implementing new services, security modules should be sure to invoke appropriate access control checks from the MAC framework as needed. For example, if a policy implements an augmented signal functionality, it should call the necessary signal access control checks to invoke the MAC framework and other registered policies.

**Note**

Modules must currently perform the copyin() of the syscall data on their own.

#### 6.7.1.4. mpo_thread_userret

```
void mpo_thread_userret(td);
struct thread *td;
```

| Parameter | Description | Locking |
|---|---|---|
| td | Returning thread | |

This entry point permits policy modules to perform MAC-related events when a thread returns to user space, via a system call return, trap return, or otherwise. This is required for policies that have floating process labels, as it is not always possible to acquire the process lock at arbitrary points in the stack during system call processing; process labels might represent traditional authentication data, process history information, or other data. To employ this mechanism, intended changes to the process credential label may be stored in the `p_label` protected by a per-policy spin lock, and then set the per-thread `TDF_ASTPENDING` flag and per-process `PS_MACPENDM` flag to schedule a call to the userret entry point. From this entry point, the policy may create a replacement credential with less concern about the locking context. Policy writers are cautioned that event ordering relating to scheduling an AST and the AST being performed may be complex and interlaced in multithreaded applications.

### 6.7.2. Label Operations

#### 6.7.2.1. mpo_init_bpfdesc_label

```
void mpo_init_bpfdesc_label(label);
struct label *label;
```

| Parameter | Description | Locking |
|---|---|---|
| label | New label to apply | |

Initialize the label on a newly instantiated bpfdesc (BPF descriptor). Sleeping is permitted.

#### 6.7.2.2. mpo_init_cred_label

```
void mpo_init_cred_label(label);
struct label *label;
```

| Parameter | Description | Locking |
|---|---|---|
| label | New label | |

| Parameter | Description | Locking |
| --- | --- | --- |
| label | Label to initialize | |

Initialize the label for a newly instantiated user credential. Sleeping is permitted.

### 6.7.2.3. `mpo_init_devfsdirent_label`

```
void mpo_init_devfsdirent_label(label);

struct label *label;
```

| Parameter | Description | Locking |
| --- | --- | --- |
| label | New label to apply | |

Initialize the label on a newly instantiated devfs entry. Sleeping is permitted.

### 6.7.2.4. `mpo_init_ifnet_label`

```
void mpo_init_ifnet_label(label);

struct label *label;
```

| Parameter | Description | Locking |
| --- | --- | --- |
| label | New label to apply | |

Initialize the label on a newly instantiated network interface. Sleeping is permitted.

### 6.7.2.5. `mpo_init_ipq_label`

```
void mpo_init_ipq_label(label, flag);

struct label *label;
```

```
int flag;
```

| Parameter | Description |
|---|---|
| *label* | New label to apply |
| *flag* | Sleeping/non-sleeping malloc(9); see below |

Initialize the label on a newly instantiated IP fragment reassembly queue. The *flag* field may be one of M_WAITOK and M_NOWAIT, and should be employed to avoid performing a sleeping malloc(9) during this initialization call. IP fragment reassembly queue allocation frequently occurs in performance sensitive environments, and the implementation should be careful to avoid sleeping or long-lived operations. This entry point is permitted to fail resulting in the failure to allocate the IP fragment reassembly queue.

#### 6.7.2.6. mpo_init_mbuf_label

```
void mpo_init_mbuf_label(flag, label);

int flag;
struct label *label;
```

| Parameter | Description |
|---|---|
| *flag* | Sleeping/non-sleeping malloc(9); see below |
| *label* | Policy label to |

| Parameter | Description | Locking |
|---|---|---|
| initialize | | |

Initialize the label on a newly instantiated mbuf packet header (*mbuf*). The *flag* field may be one of M_WAITOK and M_NOWAIT, and should be employed to avoid performing a sleeping malloc(9) during this initialization call. Mbuf allocation frequently occurs in performance sensitive environments, and the implementation should be careful to avoid sleeping or long-lived operations. This entry point is permitted to fail resulting in the failure to allocate the mbuf header.

#### 6.7.2.7. mpo_init_mount_label

```
void mpo_init_mount_label(mntlabel, fslabel);

struct label *mntlabel;
struct label *fslabel;
```

| Parameter | Description | Locking |
|---|---|---|
| *mntlabel* | Policy label to be initialized for the mount itself | |
| *fslabel* | Policy label to be initialized for the file system | |

Initialize the labels on a newly instantiated mount point. Sleeping is permitted.

### 6.7.2.8. mpo_init_mount_fs_label

```
void mpo_init_mount_fs_label(label);
```

```
struct label *label;
```

| Parameter | Description |
| --- | --- |
| *label* | Label to be initialized |

Initialize the label on a newly mounted file system. Sleeping is permitted

### 6.7.2.9. mpo_init_pipe_label

```
void mpo_init_pipe_label(label);
```

```
struct label*label;
```

| Parameter | Description |
| --- | --- |
| *label* | Label to be filled in |

Initialize a label for a newly instantiated pipe. Sleeping is permitted.

### 6.7.2.10. mpo_init_socket_label

```
void mpo_init_socket_label(label, flag);
```

```
struct label *label;
int flag;
```

| Parameter | Description |
| --- | --- |
| *label* | New label to ini- |

Dek- sagip- tion ter tial- ize

flag loc(9) flags

Initialize a label for a newly instantiated socket. The *flag* field may be one of M_WAITOK and M_NOWAIT, and should be employed to avoid performing a sleeping malloc(9) during this initialization call.

### 6.7.2.11. mpo_init_socket_peer_label

```
void mpo_init_socket_peer_label(label, flag);

struct label *label;
int flag;
```

Dek- sagip- tion ter

New bel bel to ini- tial- ize

flag loc(9) flags

Initialize the peer label for a newly instantiated socket. The *flag* field may be one of M_WAITOK and M_NOWAIT, and should be employed to avoid performing a sleeping malloc(9) during this initialization call.

### 6.7.2.12. mpo_init_proc_label

```
void mpo_init_proc_label(label);

struct label *label;
```

Dek- sagip- tion ter

New bel bel to ini- tial- ize

Initialize the label for a newly instantiated process. Sleeping is permitted.

### 6.7.2.13. `mpo_init_vnode_label`

void **mpo_init_vnode_label**(*label*);

struct label **label*;

| Parameter | Description |
|---|---|
| *label* | New label to initialize |

Initialize the label on a newly instantiated vnode. Sleeping is permitted.

### 6.7.2.14. `mpo_destroy_bpfdesc_label`

void **mpo_destroy_bpfdesc_label**(*label*);

struct label **label*;

| Parameter | Description |
|---|---|
| *label* | bpfdesc label |

Destroy the label on a BPF descriptor. In this entry point a policy should free any internal storage associated with *label* so that it may be destroyed.

### 6.7.2.15. `mpo_destroy_cred_label`

void **mpo_destroy_cred_label**(*label*);

struct label **label*;

| Parameter | Description |
|---|---|
| **label** | Label being destroyed |

Destroy the label on a credential. In this entry point, a policy module should free any internal storage associated with *label* so that it may be destroyed.

#### 6.7.2.16. mpo_destroy_devfsdirent_label

```
void mpo_destroy_devfsdirent_label(label);
struct label *label;
```

| Parameter | Description | Locking |
|---|---|---|
| **label** | being destroyed | |

Destroy the label on a devfs entry. In this entry point, a policy module should free any internal storage associated with *label* so that it may be destroyed.

#### 6.7.2.17. mpo_destroy_ifnet_label

```
void mpo_destroy_ifnet_label(label);
struct label *label;
```

| Parameter | Description | Locking |
|---|---|---|
| **label** | being destroyed | |

Destroy the label on a removed interface. In this entry point, a policy module should free any internal storage associated with *label* so that it may be destroyed.

#### 6.7.2.18. mpo_destroy_ipq_label

```
void mpo_destroy_ipq_label(label);
struct label *label;
```

| Parameter | Description | Locking |
|---|---|---|
| **label** | be- | |

Deck-
isagip-
tion
ter
ing
de-
stroyed

Destroy the label on an IP fragment queue. In this entry point, a policy module should free any internal storage associated with *label* so that it may be destroyed.

#### 6.7.2.19. mpo_destroy_mbuf_label

```
void mpo_destroy_mbuf_label(label);
```

```
struct label *label;
```

Deck-
isagip-
tion
ter
**La-**
**bel**
be-
ing
de-
stroyed

Destroy the label on an mbuf header. In this entry point, a policy module should free any internal storage associated with *label* so that it may be destroyed.

#### 6.7.2.20. mpo_destroy_mount_label

```
void mpo_destroy_mount_label(label);
```

```
struct label *label;
```

Deck-
isagip-
tion
ter
Mount
point
la-
bel
be-
ing
de-
stroyed

Destroy the labels on a mount point. In this entry point, a policy module should free the internal storage associated with *mntlabel* so that they may be destroyed.

#### 6.7.2.21. mpo_destroy_mount_label

```
void mpo_destroy_mount_label(mntlabel, fslabel);
```

```
struct label *mntlabel;
struct label *fslabel;
```

| Parameter | Description | Locking |
| --- | --- | --- |
| *mntlabel* | Mount point label being destroyed | |
| *fslabel* | File system label being destroyed> | |

Destroy the labels on a mount point. In this entry point, a policy module should free the internal storage associated with *mntlabel* and *fslabel* so that they may be destroyed.

#### 6.7.2.22. mpo_destroy_socket_label

```
void mpo_destroy_socket_label(label);
```

```
struct label *label;
```

| Parameter | Description | Locking |
| --- | --- | --- |
| *label* | Socket label being destroyed | |

Destroy the label on a socket. In this entry point, a policy module should free any internal storage associated with *label* so that it may be destroyed.

#### 6.7.2.23. mpo_destroy_socket_peer_label

```
void mpo_destroy_socket_peer_label(peerlabel);
```

```
struct label *peerlabel;
```

Daek-
isagip-
tioen
ter
Soek-
eta-
peèr
la-
bel
be-
ing
de-
stroyed

Destroy the peer label on a socket. In this entry point, a policy module should free any internal storage associated with *label* so that it may be destroyed.

### 6.7.2.24. mpo_destroy_pipe_label

```
void mpo_destroy_pipe_label(label);
```

```
struct label *label;
```

Daek-
isagip-
tioen
ter
Pàpe
lael
bel

Destroy the label on a pipe. In this entry point, a policy module should free any internal storage associated with *label* so that it may be destroyed.

### 6.7.2.25. mpo_destroy_proc_label

```
void mpo_destroy_proc_label(label);
```

```
struct label *label;
```

Daek-
isagip-
tioen
ter
Paocess
lael
bel

Destroy the label on a process. In this entry point, a policy module should free any internal storage associated with *label* so that it may be destroyed.

### 6.7.2.26. mpo_destroy_vnode_label

```
void mpo_destroy_vnode_label(label);
```

```
struct label *label;
```

Pack-
ragip-
tion
ter

Pacess
lal
bel

Destroy the label on a vnode. In this entry point, a policy module should free any internal storage associated with `label` so that it may be destroyed.

### 6.7.2.27. `mpo_copy_mbuf_label`

```
void mpo_copy_mbuf_label(src, dest);

struct label *src;
struct label *dest;
```

Pack-
ragip-
tion
ter

Source
la-
bel

Dest
ti-
na-
tion
la-
bel

Copy the label information in *src* into *dest*.

### 6.7.2.28. `mpo_copy_pipe_label`

```
void mpo_copy_pipe_label(src, dest);

struct label *src;
struct label *dest;
```

Pack-
ragip-
tion
ter

Source
la-
bel

Dest
ti-
na-
tion
la-
bel

Copy the label information in *src* into *dest*.

### 6.7.2.29. mpo_copy_vnode_label

```
void mpo_copy_vnode_label(src, dest);

struct label *src;
struct label *dest;
```

| Parameter | Description |
|---|---|
| *src* | Source label |
| *dest* | Destination label |

Copy the label information in *src* into *dest*.

### 6.7.2.30. mpo_externalize_cred_label

```
int mpo_externalize_cred_label(label, element_name, sb, *claimed);

struct label *label;
char *element_name;
struct sbuf *sb;
int *claimed;
```

| Parameter | Description |
|---|---|
| *label* | Label to be externalized |
| *element_name* | Name of the policy whose |

Deck-ising-tion ter label should be externalized

Sbring buffer to be filled with a text representation of label

Shaimbd be incremented when *element_data* can be filled in.

Produce an externalized label based on the label structure passed. An externalized label consists of a text representation of the label contents that can be used with userland applications and read by the user. Currently, all policies' `externalize` entry points will be called, so the implementation should check the contents of *element_name* before attempting to fill in *sb*. If *element_name* does not match the name of your policy, simply return 0. Only return nonzero if an error occurs while externalizing the label data. Once the policy fills in *element_data*, `*claimed` should be incremented.

#### 6.7.2.31. mpo_externalize_ifnet_label

```
int mpo_externalize_ifnet_label(label, element_name, sb, *claimed);
```

```
struct label *label;
char *element_name;
struct sbuf *sb;
int *claimed;
```

| Parameter | Description |
|---|---|
| *label* | Label to be externalized |
| *element_name* | Name of the policy whose label should be externalized |
| *sb* | String buffer to be filled with a text representation of label |
| *claimed* | Should be incremented |

| Parameter | Description | Locking |
|---|---|---|
| | | ter when *element_data* can be filled in. |

Produce an externalized label based on the label structure passed. An externalized label consists of a text representation of the label contents that can be used with userland applications and read by the user. Currently, all policies' `externalize` entry points will be called, so the implementation should check the contents of *element_name* before attempting to fill in *sb*. If *element_name* does not match the name of your policy, simply return 0. Only return nonzero if an error occurs while externalizing the label data. Once the policy fills in *element_data*, `*claimed` should be incremented.

### 6.7.2.32. mpo_externalize_pipe_label

```
int mpo_externalize_pipe_label(label, element_name, sb, *claimed);

struct label *label;
char *element_name;
struct sbuf *sb;
int *claimed;
```

| Parameter | Description | Locking |
|---|---|---|
| *label* | Label to be externalized | |
| *element_name* | Name of the policy whose label should be | |

| | |
|---|---|
| sb | String buffer to be filled with a text representation of label |
| *claimed* | Should be incremented when *element_data* can be filled in. |

Produce an externalized label based on the label structure passed. An externalized label consists of a text representation of the label contents that can be used with userland applications and read by the user. Currently, all policies' `externalize` entry points will be called, so the implementation should check the contents of *`element_name`* before attempting to fill in *sb*. If *`element_name`* does not match the name of your policy, simply return `0`. Only return nonzero if an error occurs while externalizing the label data. Once the policy fills in *`element_data`*, `*claimed` should be incremented.

### 6.7.2.33. mpo_externalize_socket_label

```
int mpo_externalize_socket_label(label, element_name, sb, *claimed);

struct label *label;
char *element_name;
struct sbuf *sb;
```

```
int *claimed;
```

| Parameter | Description | Locking |
|---|---|---|
| *label* | Label to be externalized | |
| *element_name* | Name of the policy whose label should be externalized | |
| *sb* | String buffer to be filled with a text representation of label | |
| *claimed* | Should be incremented when *el-e-* | |

| Parameter | Description |
| --- | --- |
| | *ment_data* can be filled in. |

Produce an externalized label based on the label structure passed. An externalized label consists of a text representation of the label contents that can be used with userland applications and read by the user. Currently, all policies' `externalize` entry points will be called, so the implementation should check the contents of *element_name* before attempting to fill in *sb*. If *element_name* does not match the name of your policy, simply return `0`. Only return nonzero if an error occurs while externalizing the label data. Once the policy fills in *element_data*, `*claimed` should be incremented.

### 6.7.2.34. mpo_externalize_socket_peer_label

```
int mpo_externalize_socket_peer_label(label, element_name, sb, *claimed);

struct label *label;
char *element_name;
struct sbuf *sb;
int *claimed;
```

| Parameter | Description |
| --- | --- |
| `label` | Label to be externalized |
| *element_name* | Name of the policy whose label should be externalized |

| Parameter | Description | Locking |
|---|---|---|
| *sb* | String buffer to be filled with a text representation of label | |
| *claimed* | Should be incremented when *element_data* can be filled in. | |

Produce an externalized label based on the label structure passed. An externalized label consists of a text representation of the label contents that can be used with userland applications and read by the user. Currently, all policies' `externalize` entry points will be called, so the implementation should check the contents of *`element_name`* before attempting to fill in *`sb`*. If *`element_name`* does not match the name of your policy, simply return 0. Only return nonzero if an error occurs while externalizing the label data. Once the policy fills in *`element_data`*, `*claimed` should be incremented.

### 6.7.2.35. `mpo_externalize_vnode_label`

```
int mpo_externalize_vnode_label(label, element_name, sb, *claimed);

struct label *label;
char *element_name;
struct sbuf *sb;
int *claimed;
```

| Parameter | Description |
|---|---|
| **label** | Label to be externalized |
| *policy_name* | Name of the policy whose label should be externalized |
| **str** | String buffer to be filled with a text representation of label |
| *count* | Should be incremented when *element_da-* |

Parameter Description Locking

ter

*ta* can be filled in.

Produce an externalized label based on the label structure passed. An externalized label consists of a text representation of the label contents that can be used with userland applications and read by the user. Currently, all policies' `externalize` entry points will be called, so the implementation should check the contents of *`element_name`* before attempting to fill in *`sb`*. If *`element_name`* does not match the name of your policy, simply return `0`. Only return nonzero if an error occurs while externalizing the label data. Once the policy fills in *`element_data`*, `*claimed` should be incremented.

#### 6.7.2.36. `mpo_internalize_cred_label`

```
int mpo_internalize_cred_label(label, element_name, element_data, claimed);

struct label *label;
char *element_name;
char *element_data;
int *claimed;
```

Parameter Description Locking

ter

*label* Label to be filled in

*element_name* Name of the policy whose label should be internalized

*element_data* Text data to be internalized

| Parameter | Description |
|---|---|
| element_data | Data to be internalized |
| claimed | Should be incremented when data can be successfully internalized. |

Produce an internal label structure based on externalized label data in text format. Currently, all policies' `internalize` entry points are called when internalization is requested, so the implementation should compare the contents of *`element_name`* to its own name in order to be sure it should be internalizing the data in *`element_data`*. Just as in the `externalize` entry points, the entry point should return 0 if *`element_name`* does not match its own name, or when data can successfully be internalized, in which case `*claimed` should be incremented.

### 6.7.2.37. mpo_internalize_ifnet_label

```
int mpo_internalize_ifnet_label(label, element_name, element_data, claimed);

struct label *label;
char *element_name;
char *element_data;
int *claimed;
```

| Parameter | Description |
|---|---|
| label | Label to be filled in |

| Parameter | Description | Locking |
|---|---|---|
| `element_name` | Name of the policy whose label should be internalized | |
| `element_data` | Text data to be internalized | |
| `claimed` | Should be incremented when data can be successfully internalized. | |

Produce an internal label structure based on externalized label data in text format. Currently, all policies' `internalize` entry points are called when internalization is requested, so the implementation should compare the contents of *`element_name`* to its own name in order to be sure it should be internalizing the data in *`element_data`*. Just as in the `externalize` entry points, the entry point should return 0 if *`element_name`* does not match its own name, or when data can successfully be internalized, in which case `*claimed` should be incremented.

### 6.7.2.38. `mpo_internalize_pipe_label`

```
int mpo_internalize_pipe_label(label, element_name, element_data, claimed);

struct label *label;
char *element_name;
char *element_data;
int *claimed;
```

| Parameter | Description |
| --- | --- |
| *label* | Label to be filled in |
| *element_name* | Name of the policy whose label should be internalized |
| *element_data* | Text data to be internalized |
| *claimed* | Should be incremented when data can be suc- |

| Parameter | Description | Locking |
|---|---|---|
| | ter cessfully internalized. | |

Produce an internal label structure based on externalized label data in text format. Currently, all policies' `internalize` entry points are called when internalization is requested, so the implementation should compare the contents of *`element_name`* to its own name in order to be sure it should be internalizing the data in *`element_data`*. Just as in the `externalize` entry points, the entry point should return 0 if *`element_name`* does not match its own name, or when data can successfully be internalized, in which case `*claimed` should be incremented.

### 6.7.2.39. `mpo_internalize_socket_label`

```
int mpo_internalize_socket_label(label, element_name, element_data, claimed);

struct label *label;
char *element_name;
char *element_data;
int *claimed;
```

| Parameter | Description | Locking |
|---|---|---|
| ter | | |
| *label* | Label to be filled in | |
| *element_name* | Name of the policy whose label should be internalized | |
| *element_data* | Text data to be internalized | |

| Parameter | Description |
|---|---|
| *data* | to be internalized |
| *claimed* | Should be incremented when data can be successfully internalized. |

Produce an internal label structure based on externalized label data in text format. Currently, all policies' `internalize` entry points are called when internalization is requested, so the implementation should compare the contents of *`element_name`* to its own name in order to be sure it should be internalizing the data in *`element_data`*. Just as in the `externalize` entry points, the entry point should return 0 if *`element_name`* does not match its own name, or when data can successfully be internalized, in which case `*claimed` should be incremented.

### 6.7.2.40. mpo_internalize_vnode_label

```
int mpo_internalize_vnode_label(label, element_name, element_data, claimed);

struct label *label;
char *element_name;
char *element_data;
int *claimed;
```

| Parameter | Description |
|---|---|
| *label* | Label to be filled in |

| Parameter | Description | Locking |
| --- | --- | --- |
| *element_name* | Name of the policy whose label should be internalized | |
| *element_data* | Text data to be internalized | |
| *claimed* | Should be incremented when data can be successfully internalized. | |

Produce an internal label structure based on externalized label data in text format. Currently, all policies' `internalize` entry points are called when internalization is requested, so the implementation should compare the contents of *`element_name`* to its own name in order to be sure it should be internalizing the data in *`element_data`*. Just as in the `externalize` entry points, the entry point should return 0 if *`element_name`* does not match its own name, or when data can successfully be internalized, in which case `*claimed` should be incremented.

## 6.7.3. Label Events

This class of entry points is used by the MAC framework to permit policies to maintain label information on kernel objects. For each labeled kernel object of interest to a MAC policy, entry points may be registered for relevant life cycle events. All objects implement initialization, creation, and destruction hooks. Some objects will also implement relabeling, allowing user processes to change the labels on objects. Some objects will also implement object-specific events, such as label events associated with IP reassembly. A typical labeled object will have the following life cycle of entry points:

```
Label initialization          o
(object-specific wait)         \
Label creation                  o
                                 \
Relabel events,                   o--<--.
Various object-specific,          |     |
Access control events             ~-->--o
                                         \
Label destruction                         o
```

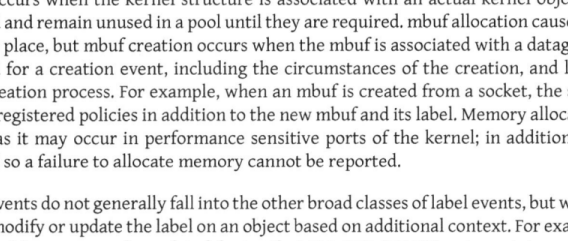

Label initialization permits policies to allocate memory and set initial values for labels without context for the use of the object. The label slot allocated to a policy will be zeroed by default, so some policies may not need to perform initialization.

Label creation occurs when the kernel structure is associated with an actual kernel object. For example, Mbufs may be allocated and remain unused in a pool until they are required. mbuf allocation causes label initialization on the mbuf to take place, but mbuf creation occurs when the mbuf is associated with a datagram. Typically, context will be provided for a creation event, including the circumstances of the creation, and labels of other relevant objects in the creation process. For example, when an mbuf is created from a socket, the socket and its label will be presented to registered policies in addition to the new mbuf and its label. Memory allocation in creation events is discouraged, as it may occur in performance sensitive ports of the kernel; in addition, creation calls are not permitted to fail so a failure to allocate memory cannot be reported.

Object specific events do not generally fall into the other broad classes of label events, but will generally provide an opportunity to modify or update the label on an object based on additional context. For example, the label on an IP fragment reassembly queue may be updated during the MAC_UPDATE_IPQ entry point as a result of the acceptance of an additional mbuf to that queue.

Access control events are discussed in detail in the following section.

Label destruction permits policies to release storage or state associated with a label during its association with an object so that the kernel data structures supporting the object may be reused or released.

In addition to labels associated with specific kernel objects, an additional class of labels exists: temporary labels. These labels are used to store update information submitted by user processes. These labels are initialized and destroyed as with other label types, but the creation event is MAC_INTERNALIZE, which accepts a user label to be converted to an in-kernel representation.

### 6.7.3.1. File System Object Labeling Event Operations

#### 6.7.3.1.1. `mpo_associate_vnode_devfs`

```
void mpo_associate_vnode_devfs(mp, fslabel, de, delabel, vp, vlabel);

struct mount *mp;
struct label *fslabel;
struct devfs_dirent *de;
struct label *delabel;
struct vnode *vp;
struct label *vlabel;
```

Pack- ing ip- tion ter

mp- vfs mount point

fs- vfs fied sys- tem la- bel (mp- >mn- t_f- s- la- bel)

de- vfs di- rec- to- ry en- try

del- la- by l la- bel as- so- ci- at- ed with de

vp- ode as- so- ci- at- ed with de

Pol- bel cy

| Parameter | Description | Locking |
|---|---|---|
| | label associated with *vp* | |

Fill in the label (*vlabel*) for a newly created devfs vnode based on the devfs directory entry passed in *de* and its label.

#### 6.7.3.1.2. `mpo_associate_vnode_extattr`

```
int mpo_associate_vnode_extattr(mp, fslabel, vp, vlabel);

struct mount *mp;
struct label *fslabel;
struct vnode *vp;
struct label *vlabel;
```

| Parameter | Description | Locking |
|---|---|---|
| *mp* | File system mount point | |
| *fslabel* | File system label | |
| *vp* | Vnode to label | |
| *vlabel* | Policy label associated with ... | |

Parameter Description Locking ter ed with *vp*

Attempt to retrieve the label for *vp* from the file system extended attributes. Upon success, the value `0` is returned. Should extended attribute retrieval not be supported, an accepted fallback is to copy *`fslabel`* into *`vlabel`*. In the event of an error, an appropriate value for `errno` should be returned.

### 6.7.3.1.3. `mpo_associate_vnode_singlelabel`

```
void mpo_associate_vnode_singlelabel(mp, fslabel, vp, vlabel);

struct mount *mp;
struct label *fslabel;
struct vnode *vp;
struct label *vlabel;
```

Parameter Description Locking ter

*mp* File system mount point

*fslabel* File system label

*vp* Vnode to label

*vlabel* Policy label associated with *vp*

On non-multilabel file systems, this entry point is called to set the policy label for *vp* based on the file system label, *`fslabel`*.

#### 6.7.3.1.4. mpo_create_devfs_device

```
void mpo_create_devfs_device(dev, devfs_dirent, label);

dev_t dev;
struct devfs_dirent *devfs_dirent;
struct label *label;
```

| Parameter | Description | Locking |
|---|---|---|
| *dev* | Device corresponding with *devfs_dirent* | |
| *devfs_dirent* | Devfs directory entry to be labeled. | |
| *label* | Label for *devfs_dirent* to be filled in. | |

Fill out the label on a devfs_dirent being created for the passed device. This call will be made when the device file system is mounted, regenerated, or a new device is made available.

#### 6.7.3.1.5. mpo_create_devfs_directory

```
void mpo_create_devfs_directory(dirname, dirnamelen, devfs_dirent, label);

char *dirname;
int dirnamelen;
```

```
struct devfs_dirent *devfs_dirent;
struct label *label;
```

| Parameter | Description | Locking |
|---|---|---|
| *dirname* | Name of directory being created | |
| *len* | Length of string *dirname* | |
| *de* | Devfs directory entry for directory being created. | |

Fill out the label on a devfs_dirent being created for the passed directory. This call will be made when the device file system is mounted, regenerated, or a new device requiring a specific directory hierarchy is made available.

### 6.7.3.1.6. `mpo_create_devfs_symlink`

```
void mpo_create_devfs_symlink(cred, mp, dd, ddlabel, de, delabel);

struct ucred *cred;
struct mount *mp;
struct devfs_dirent *dd;
struct label *ddlabel;
struct devfs_dirent *de;
struct label *delabel;
```

| Parameter | Description | Locking |
|---|---|---|
| *cred* | Subject credential | |
| *mp* | Devfs mount point | |
| *dd* | Link destination | |
| *ddlabel* | Label associated with *dd* | |
| *de* | Symlink entry | |
| *delabel* | Label associated with *de* | |

Fill in the label (*delabel*) for a newly created devfs(5) symbolic link entry.

### 6.7.3.1.7. mpo_create_vnode_extattr

```
int mpo_create_vnode_extattr(cred, mp, fslabel, dvp, dlabel, vp, vlabel, cnp);
```

```
struct ucred *cred;
struct mount *mp;
struct label *fslabel;
struct vnode *dvp;
struct label *dlabel;
struct vnode *vp;
struct label *vlabel;
```

```
struct componentname *cnp;
```

| Parameter | Description | Locking |
| --- | --- | --- |
| *cred* | Subject credential | |
| [illegible] | File system mount point | |
| *fslabel* | File system label | |
| *dvp* | Parent directory vnode | |
| *dlabel* | Label associated with *dvp* | |
| *vp* | Newly created vnode | |
| *vlabel* | Policy label associated with | |

| Parameter | Description | Locking |
| --- | --- | --- |
| | at-ed with *vp* | |
| *cnp* | Component name for *vp* | |

Write out the label for *vp* to the appropriate extended attribute. If the write succeeds, fill in *vlabel* with the label, and return 0. Otherwise, return an appropriate error.

### 6.7.3.1.8. mpo_create_mount

```
void mpo_create_mount(cred, mp, mnt, fslabel);

struct ucred *cred;
struct mount *mp;
struct label *mnt;
struct label *fslabel;
```

| Parameter | Description | Locking |
| --- | --- | --- |
| *cred* | Subject credential | |
| *mp* | Object; file system being mounted | |
| *mntlabel* | Policy label to be filled in for *mp* | |
| *fslabel* | Policy label for the file system *mp* mounts. | |

Pack- isagip- tionen ter for *mp* Fsl- la- bel label for the file system *mp* mounts.

Fill out the labels on the mount point being created by the passed subject credential. This call will be made when a new file system is mounted.

#### 6.7.3.1.9. mpo_create_root_mount

```
void mpo_create_root_mount(cred, mp, mntlabel, fslabel);

struct ucred *cred;
struct mount *mp;
struct label *mntlabel;
struct label *fslabel;
```

Pack- isagip- tionen ter

See Section 6.7.3.1.8, "mpo_create_mount".

Fill out the labels on the mount point being created by the passed subject credential. This call will be made when the root file system is mounted, after mpo_create_mount;.

#### 6.7.3.1.10. mpo_relabel_vnode

```
void mpo_relabel_vnode(cred, vp, vnodelabel, newlabel);

struct ucred *cred;
struct vnode *vp;
struct label *vnodelabel;
struct label *newlabel;
```

| Parameter | Description | Locking |
| --- | --- | --- |
| *cred* | Subject credential | |
| *vp* | vnode to relabel | |
| *vnodelabel* | Existing policy label for *vp* | |
| *newlabel* | New, possibly partial label to replace *vnodelabel* | |

Update the label on the passed vnode given the passed update vnode label and the passed subject credential.

### 6.7.3.1.11. `mpo_setlabel_vnode_extattr`

```
int mpo_setlabel_vnode_extattr(cred, vp, vlabel, intlabel);

struct ucred *cred;
struct vnode *vp;
struct label *vlabel;
struct label *intlabel;
```

| Parameter | Description | Locking |
|---|---|---|
| *cred* | Subject credential | |
| *vp* | Vnode for which the label is being written | |
| *vlabel* | Policy label associated with *vp* | |
| *intlabel* | Label to write out | |

Write out the policy from *intlabel* to an extended attribute. This is called from vop_stdcreatevnode_ea.

#### 6.7.3.1.12. mpo_update_devfsdirent

```
void mpo_update_devfsdirent(devfs_dirent, direntlabel, vp, vnodelabel);

struct devfs_dirent *devfs_dirent;
struct label *direntlabel;
struct vnode *vp;
struct label *vnodelabel;
```

| Parameter | Description | Locking |
| --- | --- | --- |
| *devfs_dirent* | Object; devfs directory entry | |
| *direntlabel* | Policy label for *devfs_dirent* to be updated. | |
| *vp* | Parent vnode | Locked |
| *vnodelabel* | Policy label for *vp* | |

Update the *devfs_dirent* label from the passed devfs vnode label. This call will be made when a devfs vnode has been successfully relabeled to commit the label change such that it lasts even if the vnode is recycled. It will also be made when a symlink is created in devfs, following a call to mac_vnode_create_from_vnode to initialize the vnode label.

### 6.7.3.2. IPC Object Labeling Event Operations

#### 6.7.3.2.1. mpo_create_mbuf_from_socket

```
void mpo_create_mbuf_from_socket(so, socketlabel, m, mbuflabel);

struct socket *so;
struct label *socketlabel;
struct mbuf *m;
struct label *mbuflabel;
```

| Parameter | Description | Locking |
|---|---|---|
| *socket* | Socket | Socket locking WIP |
| *socketlabel* | Policy label for *socket* | |
| *m* | Object; mbuf | |
| *mbuflabel* | Policy label to fill in for *m* | |

Set the label on a newly created mbuf header from the passed socket label. This call is made when a new datagram or message is generated by the socket and stored in the passed mbuf.

#### 6.7.3.2.2. `mpo_create_pipe`

```
void mpo_create_pipe(cred, pipe, pipelabel);

struct ucred *cred;
struct pipe *pipe;
struct label *pipelabel;
```

| Parameter | Description | Locking |
|---|---|---|
| *cred* | Subject credential | |
| *pipe* | Pipe | |
| *pipelabel* | | |

| Parameter | Description | Locking |
| --- | --- | --- |
| *pipe* | Policy label associated with *pipe* | |

Set the label on a newly created pipe from the passed subject credential. This call is made when a new pipe is created.

### 6.7.3.2.3. `mpo_create_socket`

```
void mpo_create_socket(cred, so, socketlabel);

struct ucred *cred;
struct socket *so;
struct label *socketlabel;
```

| Parameter | Description | Locking |
| --- | --- | --- |
| *cred* | Subject credential | Immutable |
| *so* | Object; socket to label | |
| *socketlabel* | Label to fill in for *so* | |

Set the label on a newly created socket from the passed subject credential. This call is made when a socket is created.

### 6.7.3.2.4. `mpo_create_socket_from_socket`

```
void mpo_create_socket_from_socket(oldsocket, oldsocketlabel, newsocket, new-
socketlabel);
```

```
struct socket *oldsocket;
struct label *oldsocketlabel;
struct socket *newsocket;
struct label *newsocketlabel;
```

| Parameter | Description |
|---|---|
| *oldsocket* | Listening socket |
| *oldsocketlabel* | Policy label associated with *oldsocket* |
| *newsocket* | New socket |
| *newsocketlabel* | Policy label associated with *newsocketlabel* |

Label a socket, *newsocket*, newly accept(2)ed, based on the listen(2) socket, *oldsocket*.

#### 6.7.3.2.5. `mpo_relabel_pipe`

```
void mpo_relabel_pipe(cred, pipe, oldlabel, newlabel);
```

```
struct ucred *cred;
```

```
struct pipe *pipe;
struct label *oldlabel;
struct label *newlabel;
```

| Parameter | Description | Locking |
|---|---|---|
| *cred* | Subject credential | |
| *pipe* | Pipe | |
| *oldlabel* | Current policy label associated with *pipe* | |
| *newlabel* | Policy label update to apply to *pipe* | |

Apply a new label, *newlabel*, to *pipe*.

### 6.7.3.2.6. mpo_relabel_socket

```
void mpo_relabel_socket(cred, so, oldlabel, newlabel);

struct ucred *cred;
struct socket *so;
struct label *oldlabel;
struct label *newlabel;
```

| Parameter | Description |
|---|---|
| cred | Subject credential |
| so | Object; socket |
| oldlabel | Current label for so |
| newlabel | Label update for so |

Update the label on a socket from the passed socket label update.

### 6.7.3.2.7. `mpo_set_socket_peer_from_mbuf`

```
void mpo_set_socket_peer_from_mbuf(mbuf, mbuflabel, oldlabel, newlabel);

struct mbuf *mbuf;
struct label *mbuflabel;
struct label *oldlabel;
struct label *newlabel;
```

| Parameter | Description |
|---|---|
| mbuf | First datagram received over socket |
| mbuflabel | Label for mbuf |

| Parameter | Description | Locking |
|---|---|---|
| *oldlabel* | Current label for the socket | |
| *newlabel* | Policy label to be filled out for the socket | |

Set the peer label on a stream socket from the passed mbuf label. This call will be made when the first datagram is received by the stream socket, with the exception of Unix domain sockets.

### 6.7.3.2.8. `mpo_set_socket_peer_from_socket`

```
void mpo_set_socket_peer_from_socket(oldsocket, oldsocketlabel, newsocket, newsocketpeerlabel);

struct socket *oldsocket;
struct label *oldsocketlabel;
struct socket *newsocket;
struct label *newsocketpeerlabel;
```

| Parameter | Description | Locking |
|---|---|---|
| *oldsocket* | Local socket | |
| *oldsocketlabel* | Policy label for *old-* | |

| Parameter | Description | Locking |
|---|---|---|
| *socket* | Peer socket | |
| *socketpeerlabel* | Peer label to fill in for *newsocket* | |

Set the peer label on a stream UNIX domain socket from the passed remote socket endpoint. This call will be made when the socket pair is connected, and will be made for both endpoints.

### 6.7.3.3. Network Object Labeling Event Operations

#### 6.7.3.3.1. `mpo_create_bpfdesc`

```
void mpo_create_bpfdesc(cred, bpf_d, bpflabel);

struct ucred *cred;
struct bpf_d *bpf_d;
struct label *bpflabel;
```

| Parameter | Description | Locking |
|---|---|---|
| *cred* | Subject credential | Immutable |
| *bpf_d* | Object; bpf descriptor | |
| *bpflabel* | Policy | |

Deck-
sagip-
tion
ter
la-
bel
to
be
filled
in
for
*bpf_d*

Set the label on a newly created BPF descriptor from the passed subject credential. This call will be made when a BPF device node is opened by a process with the passed subject credential.

#### 6.7.3.3.2. mpo_create_ifnet

```
void mpo_create_ifnet(ifnet, ifnetlabel);

struct ifnet *ifnet;
struct label *ifnetlabel;
```

Deck-
sagip-
tion
ter
Nfnet
work
in-
ter-
face
Pfnet-
la-
bel
la-
bel
to
fill
in
for
*ifnet*

Set the label on a newly created interface. This call may be made when a new physical interface becomes available to the system, or when a pseudo-interface is instantiated during the boot or as a result of a user action.

#### 6.7.3.3.3. mpo_create_ipq

```
void mpo_create_ipq(fragment, fragmentlabel, ipq, ipqlabel);

struct mbuf *fragment;
struct label *fragmentlabel;
struct ipq *ipq;
struct label *ipqlabel;
```

| Parameter | Description | Locking |
| --- | --- | --- |
| *fragment* | First received IP fragment | |
| *fragmentlabel* | Policy label for *fragment* | |
| *ipq* | IP reassembly queue to be labeled | |
| *ipqlabel* | Policy label to be filled in for *ipq* | |

Set the label on a newly created IP fragment reassembly queue from the mbuf header of the first received fragment.

### 6.7.3.3.4. `mpo_create_datagram_from_ipq`

void **mpo_create_create_datagram_from_ipq**(*ipq*, *ipqlabel*, *datagram*, *datagramlabel*);

```
struct ipq *ipq;
struct label *ipqlabel;
struct mbuf *datagram;
struct label *datagramlabel;
```

| Parameter | Description | Locking |
|---|---|---|
| *ipq* | IP reassembly queue | |
| *ipqlabel* | Policy label for *ipq* | |
| *datagram* | Datagram to be labeled | |
| *datagramlabel* | Policy label to be filled in for *datagramlabel* | |

Set the label on a newly reassembled IP datagram from the IP fragment reassembly queue from which it was generated.

#### 6.7.3.3.5. `mpo_create_fragment`

```
void mpo_create_fragment(datagram, datagramlabel, fragment, fragmentlabel);

struct mbuf *datagram;
struct label *datagramlabel;
struct mbuf *fragment;
struct label *fragmentlabel;
```

| Parameter | Description | Locking |
|---|---|---|
| *datagram* | Datagram | |

| Parameter | Description | Locking |
|---|---|---|
| *datagram* | Datagram | |
| *datagramlabel* | Policy label for *datagram* | |
| *fragment* | Fragment to be labeled | |
| *fragmentlabel* | Policy label to be filled in for *datagram* | |

Set the label on the mbuf header of a newly created IP fragment from the label on the mbuf header of the datagram it was generate from.

#### 6.7.3.3.6. `mpo_create_mbuf_from_mbuf`

```
void mpo_create_mbuf_from_mbuf(oldmbuf, oldmbuflabel, newmbuf, newmbuflabel);

struct mbuf *oldmbuf;
struct label *oldmbuflabel;
struct mbuf *newmbuf;
struct label *newmbuflabel;
```

| Parameter | Description | Locking |
|---|---|---|
| *oldmbuf* | Existing (source) mbuf | |
| *oldmbu-* | | |

| Parameter | Description | Locking |
|---|---|---|
| *oldmbuflabel* | Policy label for *oldmbuf* | |
| *newmbuf* | New mbuf to be labeled | |
| *newmbuflabel* | Policy label to be filled in for *newmbuf* | |

Set the label on the mbuf header of a newly created datagram from the mbuf header of an existing datagram. This call may be made in a number of situations, including when an mbuf is re-allocated for alignment purposes.

#### 6.7.3.3.7. `mpo_create_mbuf_linklayer`

```
void mpo_create_mbuf_linklayer(ifnet, ifnetlabel, mbuf, mbuflabel);

struct ifnet *ifnet;
struct label *ifnetlabel;
struct mbuf *mbuf;
struct label *mbuflabel;
```

| Parameter | Description | Locking |
|---|---|---|
| *ifnet* | Network interface | |
| *ifnetlabel* | Policy label | |

Parameter Description Locking
ter
for
*ifnet*
*mbuf* header for new datagram
*mbuflabel* label to be filled in for *mbuf*

Set the label on the mbuf header of a newly created datagram generated for the purposes of a link layer response for the passed interface. This call may be made in a number of situations, including for ARP or ND6 responses in the IPv4 and IPv6 stacks.

### 6.7.3.3.8. `mpo_create_mbuf_from_bpfdesc`

```
void mpo_create_mbuf_from_bpfdesc(bpf_d, bpflabel, mbuf, mbuflabel);

struct bpf_d *bpf_d;
struct label *bpflabel;
struct mbuf *mbuf;
struct label *mbuflabel;
```

Parameter Description Locking
ter
*bpf_d* BPF descriptor
*bpflabel* Policy label for *bpflabel*

| Parameter | Description |
|---|---|
| *mbuf* | New mbuf to be labeled |
| *mbuflabel* | Policy label to fill in for *mbuf* |

Set the label on the mbuf header of a newly created datagram generated using the passed BPF descriptor. This call is made when a write is performed to the BPF device associated with the passed BPF descriptor.

#### 6.7.3.3.9. `mpo_create_mbuf_from_ifnet`

```
void mpo_create_mbuf_from_ifnet(ifnet, ifnetlabel, mbuf, mbuflabel);

struct ifnet *ifnet;
struct label *ifnetlabel;
struct mbuf *mbuf;
struct label *mbuflabel;
```

| Parameter | Description |
|---|---|
| *ifnet* | Network interface |
| *ifnetlabel* | Policy label for *ifnetlabel* |
| *mbuf* | mbuf head- |

| Parameter | Description | Locking |
| --- | --- | --- |
| *mbuf* | mbuf header for new datagram | |
| *mbuflabel* | Policy label to be filled in for *mbuf* | |

Set the label on the mbuf header of a newly created datagram generated from the passed network interface.

### 6.7.3.3.10. `mpo_create_mbuf_multicast_encap`

```
void mpo_create_mbuf_multicast_encap(oldmbuf, oldmbuflabel, ifnet, ifnetlabel,
newmbuf, newmbuflabel);

struct mbuf *oldmbuf;
struct label *oldmbuflabel;
struct ifnet *ifnet;
struct label *ifnetlabel;
struct mbuf *newmbuf;
struct label *newmbuflabel;
```

| Parameter | Description | Locking |
| --- | --- | --- |
| *oldmbuf* | mbuf header for existing datagram | |
| *oldmbuflabel* | Policy label for | |

| | |
|---|---|
| [illegible] | [illegible] |
| *oldmbuf* | [illegible] |
| [illegible] | Network interface |
| [illegible] | Policy label for *ifnet* |
| [illegible] | [illegible] header to be labeled for new datagram |
| [illegible] | [illegible] label to be filled in for *newmbuf* |

Set the label on the mbuf header of a newly created datagram generated from the existing passed datagram when it is processed by the passed multicast encapsulation interface. This call is made when an mbuf is to be delivered using the virtual interface.

### 6.7.3.3.11. `mpo_create_mbuf_netlayer`

```
void mpo_create_mbuf_netlayer(oldmbuf, oldmbuflabel, newmbuf, newmbuflabel);

struct mbuf *oldmbuf;
struct label *oldmbuflabel;
struct mbuf *newmbuf;
struct label *newmbuflabel;
```

| Parameter | Description | Locking |
|---|---|---|
| *oldmbuf* | Received datagram | |
| *oldmbuflabel* | Policy label for *oldmbuf* | |
| *newmbuf* | Newly created datagram | |
| *newmbuflabel* | Policy label for *newmbuf* | |

Set the label on the mbuf header of a newly created datagram generated by the IP stack in response to an existing received datagram (*oldmbuf*). This call may be made in a number of situations, including when responding to ICMP request datagrams.

### 6.7.3.3.12. mpo_fragment_match

```
int mpo_fragment_match(fragment, fragmentlabel, ipq, ipqlabel);

struct mbuf *fragment;
struct label *fragmentlabel;
struct ipq *ipq;
struct label *ipqlabel;
```

| Parameter | Description | Locking |
|---|---|---|
| *fragment* | IP datagram fragment | |

| Parameter | Description | Locking |
|---|---|---|
| *fragment* | IP datagram fragment | |
| *fragmentlabel* | Policy label for *fragment* | |
| *ipq* | IP fragment reassembly queue | |
| *ipqlabel* | Policy label for *ipq* | |

Determine whether an mbuf header containing an IP datagram (*fragment*) fragment matches the label of the passed IP fragment reassembly queue (*ipq*). Return (1) for a successful match, or (0) for no match. This call is made when the IP stack attempts to find an existing fragment reassembly queue for a newly received fragment; if this fails, a new fragment reassembly queue may be instantiated for the fragment. Policies may use this entry point to prevent the reassembly of otherwise matching IP fragments if policy does not permit them to be reassembled based on the label or other information.

### 6.7.3.3.13. mpo_relabel_ifnet

```
void mpo_relabel_ifnet(cred, ifnet, ifnetlabel, newlabel);

struct ucred *cred;
struct ifnet *ifnet;
struct label *ifnetlabel;
struct label *newlabel;
```

| Parameter | Description | Locking |
|---|---|---|
| *cred* | Subject credential | |
| *ifnet* | Object; | |

| Parameter | Description | Locking |
|---|---|---|
| ifnet | Network interface | |
| ifnetlabel | Policy label for ifnet | |
| newlabel | Label update to apply to ifnet | |

Update the label of network interface, `ifnet`, based on the passed update label, *newlabel*, and the passed subject credential, *cred*.

#### 6.7.3.3.14. mpo_update_ipq

```
void mpo_update_ipq(fragment, fragmentlabel, ipq, ipqlabel);

struct mbuf *fragment;
struct label *fragmentlabel;
struct ipq *ipq;
struct label *ipqlabel;
```

| Parameter | Description | Locking |
|---|---|---|
| fragment | mbuf fragment | |
| fragmentlabel | Policy label for mbuf | |
| ipq | IP frag- | |

| Parameter | Description |
| --- | --- |
| | ment reassembly queue |
| *ipqlabel* | Policy label to be updated for *ipq* |

Update the label on an IP fragment reassembly queue (*ipq*) based on the acceptance of the passed IP fragment mbuf header (*mbuf*).

### 6.7.3.4. Process Labeling Event Operations

#### 6.7.3.4.1. mpo_create_cred

```
void mpo_create_cred(parent_cred, child_cred);

struct ucred *parent_cred;
struct ucred *child_cred;
```

| Parameter | Description |
| --- | --- |
| *parent_cred* | Parent subject credential |
| *child_cred* | Child subject credential |

Set the label of a newly created subject credential from the passed subject credential. This call will be made when crcopy(9) is invoked on a newly created struct ucred. This call should not be confused with a process forking or creation event.

#### 6.7.3.4.2. `mpo_execve_transition`

```
void mpo_execve_transition(old, new, vp, vnodelabel);

struct ucred *old;
struct ucred *new;
struct vnode *vp;
struct label *vnodelabel;
```

| Parameter | Description | Locking |
|---|---|---|
| *old* | Existing subject credential | Immutable |
| *new* | New subject credential to be labeled | |
| *vp* | File to execute | Locked |
| *vnodelabel* | Policy label for *vp* | |

Update the label of a newly created subject credential (*new*) from the passed existing subject credential (*old*) based on a label transition caused by executing the passed vnode (*vp*). This call occurs when a process executes the passed vnode and one of the policies returns a success from the `mpo_execve_will_transition` entry point. Policies may choose to implement this call simply by invoking `mpo_create_cred` and passing the two subject credentials so as not to implement a transitioning event. Policies should not leave this entry point unimplemented if they implement `mpo_create_cred`, even if they do not implement `mpo_execve_will_transition`.

#### 6.7.3.4.3. `mpo_execve_will_transition`

```
int mpo_execve_will_transition(old, vp, vnodelabel);

struct ucred *old;
```

```
struct vnode *vp;
struct label *vnodelabel;
```

| Parameter | Description | Locking |
| --- | --- | --- |
| cred | Subject credential prior to execve(2) | Immutable |
| vp | File to execute | Locked |
| vnodelabel | Policy label for vp | |

Determine whether the policy will want to perform a transition event as a result of the execution of the passed vnode by the passed subject credential. Return 1 if a transition is required, 0 if not. Even if a policy returns 0, it should behave correctly in the presence of an unexpected invocation of mpo_execve_transition, as that call may happen as a result of another policy requesting a transition.

#### 6.7.3.4.4. mpo_create_proc0

```
void mpo_create_proc0(cred);
```

```
struct ucred *cred;
```

| Parameter | Description | Locking |
| --- | --- | --- |
| cred | Subject credential to be filled in | |

Create the subject credential of process 0, the parent of all kernel processes.

#### 6.7.3.4.5. mpo_create_proc1

```
void mpo_create_proc1(cred);

struct ucred *cred;
```

| Parameter | Description | Locking |
| --- | --- | --- |
| cred | Subject credential to be filled in | |

Create the subject credential of process 1, the parent of all user processes.

#### 6.7.3.4.6. mpo_relabel_cred

```
void mpo_relabel_cred(cred, newlabel);

struct ucred *cred;
struct label *newlabel;
```

| Parameter | Description | Locking |
| --- | --- | --- |
| cred | Subject credential | |
| newlabel | label update to apply to *cred* | |

Update the label on a subject credential from the passed update label.

### 6.7.4. Access Control Checks

Access control entry points permit policy modules to influence access control decisions made by the kernel. Generally, although not always, arguments to an access control entry point will include one or more authorizing cre-

dentials, information (possibly including a label) for any other objects involved in the operation. An access control entry point may return 0 to permit the operation, or an errno(2) error value. The results of invoking the entry point across various registered policy modules will be composed as follows: if all modules permit the operation to succeed, success will be returned. If one or modules returns a failure, a failure will be returned. If more than one module returns a failure, the errno value to return to the user will be selected using the following precedence, implemented by the `error_select()` function in `kern_mac.c` :

| | |
|---|---|
| Most precedence | EDEADLK |
| | EINVAL |
| | ESRCH |
| | EACCES |
| Least precedence | EPERM |

If none of the error values returned by all modules are listed in the precedence chart then an arbitrarily selected value from the set will be returned. In general, the rules provide precedence to errors in the following order: kernel failures, invalid arguments, object not present, access not permitted, other.

#### 6.7.4.1. mpo_check_bpfdesc_receive

```
int mpo_check_bpfdesc_receive(bpf_d, bpflabel, ifnet, ifnetlabel);

struct bpf_d *bpf_d;
struct label *bpflabel;
struct ifnet *ifnet;
struct label *ifnetlabel;
```

| Parameter | Description | Locking |
|---|---|---|
| *bpf_d* | Subject; BPF descriptor | |
| *bpflabel* | Policy label for *bpf_d* | |
| *ifnet* | Object; network interface | |
| *ifnetlabel* | Policy label for *ifnet* | |

| Parameter | Description | Locking |
| --- | --- | --- |
| | label for *ifnet* | |

Determine whether the MAC framework should permit datagrams from the passed interface to be delivered to the buffers of the passed BPF descriptor. Return (0) for success, or an `errno` value for failure Suggested failure: EACCES for label mismatches, EPERM for lack of privilege.

#### 6.7.4.2. `mpo_check_kenv_dump`

```
int mpo_check_kenv_dump(cred);

struct ucred *cred;
```

| Parameter | Description | Locking |
| --- | --- | --- |
| *cred* | Subject credential | |

Determine whether the subject should be allowed to retrieve the kernel environment (see kenv(2)).

#### 6.7.4.3. `mpo_check_kenv_get`

```
int mpo_check_kenv_get(cred, name);

struct ucred *cred;
char *name;
```

| Parameter | Description | Locking |
| --- | --- | --- |
| *cred* | Subject credential | |
| *name* | Kernel environment variable name | |

Determine whether the subject should be allowed to retrieve the value of the specified kernel environment variable.

### 6.7.4.4. mpo_check_kenv_set

```
int mpo_check_kenv_set(cred, name);

struct ucred *cred;
char *name;
```

| Parameter | Description | Locking |
|---|---|---|
| *cred* | Subject credential | |
| *name* | Kernel environment variable name | |

Determine whether the subject should be allowed to set the specified kernel environment variable.

### 6.7.4.5. mpo_check_kenv_unset

```
int mpo_check_kenv_unset(cred, name);

struct ucred *cred;
char *name;
```

| Parameter | Description | Locking |
|---|---|---|
| *cred* | Subject credential | |
| *name* | Kernel environment vari- | |

| Parameter | Description | Locking |
|---|---|---|
| name | | |

(The first table shows only the word fragments "ter able name".)

Determine whether the subject should be allowed to unset the specified kernel environment variable.

### 6.7.4.6. `mpo_check_kld_load`

```
int mpo_check_kld_load(cred, vp, vlabel);

struct ucred *cred;
struct vnode *vp;
struct label *vlabel;
```

| Parameter | Description | Locking |
|---|---|---|
| *cred* | Subject credential | |
| *vp* | Kernel module vnode | |
| *vlabel* | Label associated with *vp* | |

Determine whether the subject should be allowed to load the specified module file.

### 6.7.4.7. `mpo_check_kld_stat`

```
int mpo_check_kld_stat(cred);

struct ucred *cred;
```

| Parameter | Description | Locking |
|---|---|---|
| *cred* | Subject | |

Daeck-
ssgip-
tion
ter
cre-
den-
tial

Determine whether the subject should be allowed to retrieve a list of loaded kernel module files and associated statistics.

### 6.7.4.8. mpo_check_kld_unload

```
int mpo_check_kld_unload(cred);
```

```
struct ucred *cred;
```

Daeck-
ssgip-
tion
ter
*cred* Sub-
ject
cre-
den-
tial

Determine whether the subject should be allowed to unload a kernel module.

### 6.7.4.9. mpo_check_pipe_ioctl

```
int mpo_check_pipe_ioctl(cred, pipe, pipelabel, cmd, data);
```

```
struct ucred *cred;
struct pipe *pipe;
struct label *pipelabel;
unsigned long cmd;
void *data;
```

Daeck-
ssgip-
tion
ter
*cred* Sub-
ject
cre-
den-
tial
*pipe* Pipe
*pipela-*
*bel* Pol-
cy
la-
bel
as-

Pa-ek- ra-sag rip- tion ter
so-
ci-
at-
ed
with
*pipe*
*cmd* ioctl(2)
com-
mand
*data* ioctl(2)
da-
ta

Determine whether the subject should be allowed to make the specified ioctl(2) call.

### 6.7.4.10. mpo_check_pipe_poll

```
int mpo_check_pipe_poll(cred, pipe, pipelabel);

struct ucred *cred;
struct pipe *pipe;
struct label *pipelabel;
```

Pa-ek- ra-sag rip- tion ter
*cred* Sub-
ject
cre-
den-
tial
*pipe* Pipe
*pipela-* Pol-
*bel*
cy
la-
bel
as-
so-
ci-
at-
ed
with
*pipe*

Determine whether the subject should be allowed to poll *pipe*.

### 6.7.4.11. mpo_check_pipe_read

```
int mpo_check_pipe_read(cred, pipe, pipelabel);
```

```
struct ucred *cred;
struct pipe *pipe;
struct label *pipelabel;
```

Paeck-
isagip-
tion
ter

cred
ject
cre-
den-
tial

pipe

pipela-
bel
cy
la-
bel
as-
so-
ci-
at-
ed
with
*pipe*

Determine whether the subject should be allowed read access to *pipe*.

### 6.7.4.12. mpo_check_pipe_relabel

```
int mpo_check_pipe_relabel(cred, pipe, pipelabel, newlabel);
```

```
struct ucred *cred;
struct pipe *pipe;
struct label *pipelabel;
struct label *newlabel;
```

Paeck-
isagip-
tion
ter

cred
ject
cre-
den-
tial

pipe

pipela-
bent
pol-
i-
cy
la-

Pack-ising-tion ter bel associated with *pipe*

hewla-bel update to *pipelabel*

Determine whether the subject should be allowed to relabel *pipe*.

### 6.7.4.13. `mpo_check_pipe_stat`

```
int mpo_check_pipe_stat(cred, pipe, pipelabel);

struct ucred *cred;
struct pipe *pipe;
struct label *pipelabel;
```

Pack-ising-tion ter

Subject credential

*pipe*

*pipelabel* cy label associated with *pipe*

Determine whether the subject should be allowed to retrieve statistics related to *pipe*.

### 6.7.4.14. mpo_check_pipe_write

```
int mpo_check_pipe_write(cred, pipe, pipelabel);

struct ucred *cred;
struct pipe *pipe;
struct label *pipelabel;
```

Daeck-
isagip-
tioen
ter

Sred
ject
cre-
den-
tial

pipe

pipela-
bel
cy
la-
bel
as-
so-
ci-
at-
ed
with
*pipe*

Determine whether the subject should be allowed to write to *pipe*.

### 6.7.4.15. mpo_check_socket_bind

```
int mpo_check_socket_bind(cred, socket, socketlabel, sockaddr);

struct ucred *cred;
struct socket *socket;
struct label *socketlabel;
struct sockaddr *sockaddr;
```

Daeck-
isagip-
tioen
ter

Sred
ject
cre-
den-
tial

Sock-
et
to

| Parameter | Description | Locking |
|---|---|---|
| *socketlabel* | Label for *socket* | |
| *sa* | Address of *socket* | |

### 6.7.4.16. mpo_check_socket_connect

```
int mpo_check_socket_connect(cred, socket, socketlabel, sockaddr);

struct ucred *cred;
struct socket *socket;
struct label *socketlabel;
struct sockaddr *sockaddr;
```

| Parameter | Description | Locking |
|---|---|---|
| *cred* | Subject credential | |
| *socket* | Socket to be connected | |
| *socketlabel* | Label for *socket* | |

| Parameter | Description |
|---|---|
| *socket* | Socket |
| *sockaddr* | Address of socket |

Determine whether the subject credential (*cred*) can connect the passed socket (*socket*) to the passed socket address (*sockaddr*). Return 0 for success, or an `errno` value for failure. Suggested failure: EACCES for label mismatches, EPERM for lack of privilege.

### 6.7.4.17. `mpo_check_socket_receive`

```
int mpo_check_socket_receive(cred, so, socketlabel);

struct ucred *cred;
struct socket *so;
struct label *socketlabel;
```

| Parameter | Description |
|---|---|
| *cred* | Subject credential |
| *so* | Socket |
| *socketlabel* | Policy label associated with *so* |

Determine whether the subject should be allowed to receive information from the socket *so*.

### 6.7.4.18. `mpo_check_socket_send`

```
int mpo_check_socket_send(cred, so, socketlabel);

struct ucred *cred;
struct socket *so;
```

```
struct label *socketlabel;
```

| Parameter | Description | Locking |
|---|---|---|
| *cred* | Subject credential | |
| *so* | Socket | |
| *socketlabel* | Socket label associated with *so* | |

Determine whether the subject should be allowed to send information across the socket *so*.

### 6.7.4.19. mpo_check_cred_visible

```
int mpo_check_cred_visible(u1, u2);

struct ucred *u1;
struct ucred *u2;
```

| Parameter | Description | Locking |
|---|---|---|
| *u1* | Subject credential | |
| *u2* | Object credential | |

Determine whether the subject credential *u1* can "see" other subjects with the passed subject credential *u2*. Return 0 for success, or an `errno` value for failure. Suggested failure: EACCES for label mismatches, EPERM for lack of privilege, or ESRCH to hide visibility. This call may be made in a number of situations, including inter-process status sysctl's used by `ps`, and in procfs lookups.

#### 6.7.4.20. mpo_check_socket_visible

```
int mpo_check_socket_visible(cred, socket, socketlabel);

struct ucred *cred;
struct socket *socket;
struct label *socketlabel;
```

| Parameter | Description | Locking |
|---|---|---|
| *cred* | Subject credential | |
| *socket* | Object; socket | |
| *socketlabel* | Policy label for *socket* | |

#### 6.7.4.21. mpo_check_ifnet_relabel

```
int mpo_check_ifnet_relabel(cred, ifnet, ifnetlabel, newlabel);

struct ucred *cred;
struct ifnet *ifnet;
struct label *ifnetlabel;
struct label *newlabel;
```

| Parameter | Description | Locking |
|---|---|---|
| *cred* | Subject credential | |
| *ifnet* | Object; network interface | |

| Parameter | Description | Locking |
| --- | --- | --- |
| *ifnetlabel* | Existing policy label for *ifnet* | |
| *newlabel* | Policy label update to later be applied to *ifnet* | |

Determine whether the subject credential can relabel the passed network interface to the passed label update.

#### 6.7.4.22. `mpo_check_socket_relabel`

```
int mpo_check_socket_relabel(cred, socket, socketlabel, newlabel);

struct ucred *cred;
struct socket *socket;
struct label *socketlabel;
struct label *newlabel;
```

| Parameter | Description | Locking |
| --- | --- | --- |
| *cred* | Subject credential | |
| *socket* | Object; socket | |

| Parameter | Description |
|---|---|
| *socket* | Existing policy label for *socket* |
| **newlabel** | Policy label update to later be applied to *socketlabel* |

Determine whether the subject credential can relabel the passed socket to the passed label update.

### 6.7.4.23. mpo_check_cred_relabel

```
int mpo_check_cred_relabel(cred, newlabel);

struct ucred *cred;
struct label *newlabel;
```

| Parameter | Description |
|---|---|
| *cred* | Subject credential |
| **newlabel** | Label update to |

| Parameter | Description | Locking |
|---|---|---|
| | later be applied to *cred* | |

Determine whether the subject credential can relabel itself to the passed label update.

#### 6.7.4.24. mpo_check_vnode_relabel

```
int mpo_check_vnode_relabel(cred, vp, vnodelabel, newlabel);

struct ucred *cred;
struct vnode *vp;
struct label *vnodelabel;
struct label *newlabel;
```

| Parameter | Description | Locking |
|---|---|---|
| *cred* | Subject credential | Immutable |
| *vp* | Object; vnode | Locked |
| *vnodelabel* | Existing policy label for *vp* | |
| *newlabel* | Policy label update to | |

| Parameter | Description | Locking |
|---|---|---|
| | later be applied to *vp* | |

Determine whether the subject credential can relabel the passed vnode to the passed label update.

### 6.7.4.25. mpo_check_mount_stat

```
int mpo_check_mount_stat(cred, mp, mountlabel);

struct ucred *cred;
struct mount *mp;
struct label *mountlabel;
```

| Parameter | Description | Locking |
|---|---|---|
| *cred* | Subject credential | |
| *mp* | Object; file system mount | |
| *mountlabel* | Policy label for *mp* | |

Determine whether the subject credential can see the results of a statfs performed on the file system. Return 0 for success, or an errno value for failure. Suggested failure: EACCES for label mismatches or EPERM for lack of privilege. This call may be made in a number of situations, including during invocations of statfs(2) and related calls, as well as to determine what file systems to exclude from listings of file systems, such as when getfsstat(2) is invoked.

### 6.7.4.26. mpo_check_proc_debug

```
int mpo_check_proc_debug(cred, proc);

struct ucred *cred;
```

```
struct proc *proc;
```

| Parameter | Description | Locking |
|---|---|---|
| *cred* | Subject credential | Immutable |
| *proc* | Object; process | |

Determine whether the subject credential can debug the passed process. Return 0 for success, or an errno value for failure. Suggested failure: EACCES for label mismatch, EPERM for lack of privilege, or ESRCH to hide visibility of the target. This call may be made in a number of situations, including use of the ptrace(2) and ktrace(2) APIs, as well as for some types of procfs operations.

#### 6.7.4.27. mpo_check_vnode_access

```
int mpo_check_vnode_access(cred, vp, label, flags);

struct ucred *cred;
struct vnode *vp;
struct label *label;
int flags;
```

| Parameter | Description | Locking |
|---|---|---|
| *cred* | Subject credential | |
| *vp* | Object; vnode | |
| *label* | Policy label for *vp* | |
| *flags* | access(2) flags | |

Determine how invocations of access(2) and related calls by the subject credential should return when performed on the passed vnode using the passed access flags. This should generally be implemented using the same semantics

used in mpo_check_vnode_open. Return 0 for success, or an errno value for failure. Suggested failure: EACCES for label mismatches or EPERM for lack of privilege.

### 6.7.4.28. mpo_check_vnode_chdir

```
int mpo_check_vnode_chdir(cred, dvp, dlabel);

struct ucred *cred;
struct vnode *dvp;
struct label *dlabel;
```

| Parameter | Description |
|---|---|
| cred | Subject credential |
| dvp | Object; vnode to chdir(2) into |
| dlabel | Policy label for dvp |

Determine whether the subject credential can change the process working directory to the passed vnode. Return 0 for success, or an errno value for failure. Suggested failure: EACCES for label mismatch, or EPERM for lack of privilege.

### 6.7.4.29. mpo_check_vnode_chroot

```
int mpo_check_vnode_chroot(cred, dvp, dlabel);

struct ucred *cred;
struct vnode *dvp;
struct label *dlabel;
```

| Parameter | Description |
|---|---|
| cred | Subject cre- |

| Parameter | Description | Locking |
|---|---|---|
| | [illegible]ter credential | |
| *dvp* | Directory vnode | |
| *dlabel* | Policy label associated with *dvp* | |

Determine whether the subject should be allowed to chroot(2) into the specified directory (*dvp*).

### 6.7.4.30. `mpo_check_vnode_create`

```
int mpo_check_vnode_create(cred, dvp, dlabel, cnp, vap);

struct ucred *cred;
struct vnode *dvp;
struct label *dlabel;
struct componentname *cnp;
struct vattr *vap;
```

| Parameter | Description | Locking |
|---|---|---|
| *cred* | Subject credential | |
| *dvp* | Object; vnode | |
| *dlabel* | Policy la- | |

| Parameter | Description |
|---|---|
| | Label for *dvp* |
| *cnp* | Component name for *dvp* |
| *vap* | vnode attributes for *vap* |

Determine whether the subject credential can create a vnode with the passed parent directory, passed name information, and passed attribute information. Return 0 for success, or an `errno` value for failure. Suggested failure: EACCES for label mismatch, or EPERM for lack of privilege. This call may be made in a number of situations, including as a result of calls to open(2) with O_CREAT, mkfifo(2), and others.

#### 6.7.4.31. mpo_check_vnode_delete

```
int mpo_check_vnode_delete(cred, dvp, dlabel, vp, label, cnp);

struct ucred *cred;
struct vnode *dvp;
struct label *dlabel;
struct vnode *vp;
void *label;
struct componentname *cnp;
```

| Parameter | Description |
|---|---|
| *cred* | Subject credential |
| *dvp* | Parent directory vnode |

| Parameter | Description | Locking |
| --- | --- | --- |
| *dlabel* | Policy label for *dvp* | |
| *vp* | Object; vnode to delete | |
| *label* | Policy label for *vp* | |
| *cnp* | Component name for *vp* | |

Determine whether the subject credential can delete a vnode from the passed parent directory and passed name information. Return 0 for success, or an `errno` value for failure. Suggested failure: EACCES for label mismatch, or EPERM for lack of privilege. This call may be made in a number of situations, including as a result of calls to unlink(2) and rmdir(2). Policies implementing this entry point should also implement `mpo_check_rename_to` to authorize deletion of objects as a result of being the target of a rename.

### 6.7.4.32. `mpo_check_vnode_deleteacl`

```
int mpo_check_vnode_deleteacl(cred, vp, label, type);

struct ucred *cred;
struct vnode *vp;
struct label *label;
acl_type_t type;
```

| Parameter | Description | Locking |
| --- | --- | --- |
| *cred* | Subject credential | |

| Parameter | Description | Locking |
|---|---|---|
| | Checked object; vnode | |
| | Policy label for *vp* | |
| *type* | ACL type | |

Determine whether the subject credential can delete the ACL of passed type from the passed vnode. Return 0 for success, or an `errno` value for failure. Suggested failure: EACCES for label mismatch, or EPERM for lack of privilege.

### 6.7.4.33. mpo_check_vnode_exec

```
int mpo_check_vnode_exec(cred, vp, label);

struct ucred *cred;
struct vnode *vp;
struct label *label;
```

| Parameter | Description | Locking |
|---|---|---|
| *cred* | Subject credential | |
| *vp* | Object; vnode to execute | |
| *label* | Policy label for *vp* | |

Determine whether the subject credential can execute the passed vnode. Determination of execute privilege is made separately from decisions about any transitioning event. Return 0 for success, or an `errno` value for failure. Suggested failure: EACCES for label mismatch, or EPERM for lack of privilege.

### 6.7.4.34. `mpo_check_vnode_getacl`

```
int mpo_check_vnode_getacl(cred, vp, label, type);

struct ucred *cred;
struct vnode *vp;
struct label *label;
acl_type_t type;
```

| Parameter | Description | Locking |
| --- | --- | --- |
| *cred* | Subject credential | |
| *vp* | Object; vnode | |
| *label* | Policy label for *vp* | |
| *type* | ACL type | |

Determine whether the subject credential can retrieve the ACL of passed type from the passed vnode. Return 0 for success, or an `errno` value for failure. Suggested failure: EACCES for label mismatch, or EPERM for lack of privilege.

### 6.7.4.35. `mpo_check_vnode_getextattr`

```
int mpo_check_vnode_getextattr(cred, vp, label, attrnamespace, name, uio);

struct ucred *cred;
struct vnode *vp;
struct label *label;
int attrnamespace;
const char *name;
struct uio *uio;
```

| Parameter | Description | Locking |
| --- | --- | --- |
| *cred* | Subject | |

Dack-
isagip-
tion
ter
cre-
den-
tial
Ob-
ject;
vn-
ode
Pal-
bel
cy
la-
bel
for
*vp*
Ex-
tend-
name-
space
tribute
name-
space
Name
tend-
ed
at-
tribute
name
U/io
O
struc-
ture
point-
er;
see
uio(9)

Determine whether the subject credential can retrieve the extended attribute with the passed namespace and name from the passed vnode. Policies implementing labeling using extended attributes may be interested in special handling of operations on those extended attributes. Return 0 for success, or an `errno` value for failure. Suggested failure: EACCES for label mismatch, or EPERM for lack of privilege.

### 6.7.4.36. `mpo_check_vnode_link`

```
int mpo_check_vnode_link(cred, dvp, dlabel, vp, label, cnp);

struct ucred *cred;
struct vnode *dvp;
struct label *dlabel;
struct vnode *vp;
struct label *label;
```

```
struct componentname *cnp;
```

| Parameter | Description | Locking |
| --- | --- | --- |
| *cred* | Subject credential | |
| *dvp* | Directory vnode | |
| *dlabel* | Policy label associated with *dvp* | |
| *vp* | Link destination vnode | |
| *vlabel* | Policy label associated with *vp* | |
| *cnp* | Component name for | |

| Parameter | Description | Locking |
|---|---|---|
| | the link being created | |

Determine whether the subject should be allowed to create a link to the vnode *vp* with the name specified by *cnp*.

### 6.7.4.37. mpo_check_vnode_mmap

```
int mpo_check_vnode_mmap(cred, vp, label, prot);

struct ucred *cred;
struct vnode *vp;
struct label *label;
int prot;
```

| Parameter | Description | Locking |
|---|---|---|
| *cred* | Subject credential | |
| *vp* | Vnode to map | |
| *label* | Policy label associated with *vp* | |
| *prot* | Mmap protections (see mmap(2)) | |

Determine whether the subject should be allowed to map the vnode *vp* with the protections specified in *prot*.

### 6.7.4.38. mpo_check_vnode_mmap_downgrade

```
void mpo_check_vnode_mmap_downgrade(cred, vp, label, prot);

struct ucred *cred;
struct vnode *vp;
struct label *label;
int *prot;
```

| Parameter | Description | Locking |
|---|---|---|
| *cred* | See Section 6.7.4.37, "mpo_check_vnode_mmap". | |
| *vp* | | |
| *label* | | |
| *prot* | Mmap protections to be downgraded | |

Downgrade the mmap protections based on the subject and object labels.

### 6.7.4.39. mpo_check_vnode_mprotect

```
int mpo_check_vnode_mprotect(cred, vp, label, prot);

struct ucred *cred;
struct vnode *vp;
struct label *label;
int prot;
```

| Parameter | Description | Locking |
|---|---|---|
| *cred* | Subject credential | |
| *vp* | Mapped vnode | |
| *prot* | Memory pro- | |

| Parameter | Description | Locking |
|---|---|---|
| | tec-tions | |

Determine whether the subject should be allowed to set the specified memory protections on memory mapped from the vnode *vp*.

### 6.7.4.40. `mpo_check_vnode_poll`

```
int mpo_check_vnode_poll(active_cred, file_cred, vp, label);

struct ucred *active_cred;
struct ucred *file_cred;
struct vnode *vp;
struct label *label;
```

| Parameter | Description | Locking |
|---|---|---|
| *active_cred* | Subject credential | |
| *file_cred* | Credential associated with the struct file | |
| *vp* | Polled vnode | |
| *label* | Policy label associated with *vp* | |

Determine whether the subject should be allowed to poll the vnode *vp*.

### 6.7.4.41. mpo_check_vnode_rename_from

```
int mpo_vnode_rename_from(cred, dvp, dlabel, vp, label, cnp);

struct ucred *cred;
struct vnode *dvp;
struct label *dlabel;
struct vnode *vp;
struct label *label;
struct componentname *cnp;
```

| Parameter | Description | Locking |
|---|---|---|
| *cred* | Subject credential | |
| *dvp* | Directory vnode | |
| *dlabel* | Policy label associated with *dvp* | |
| *vp* | Vnode to be renamed | |
| *label* | Policy label associat- | |

| Parameter | Description |
|---|---|
| | ed with *vp* |
| *cnp* | Component name for *vp* |

Determine whether the subject should be allowed to rename the vnode *vp* to something else.

### 6.7.4.42. mpo_check_vnode_rename_to

```
int mpo_check_vnode_rename_to(cred, dvp, dlabel, vp, label, samedir, cnp);

struct ucred *cred;
struct vnode *dvp;
struct label *dlabel;
struct vnode *vp;
struct label *label;
int samedir;
struct componentname *cnp;
```

| Parameter | Description |
|---|---|
| *cred* | Subject credential |
| *dvp* | Directory vnode |
| *dlabel* | Policy label associated with *dvp* |

| | | |
|---|---|---|
| Parameter | Description | Locking |
| vp | Overwritten vnode | |
| label | Policy label associated with vp | |
| samedir | Boolean; 1 if the source and destination directories are the same | |
| cnp | Destination component name | |

Determine whether the subject should be allowed to rename to the vnode *vp*, into the directory *dvp*, or to the name represented by *cnp*. If there is no existing file to overwrite, *vp* and `label` will be NULL.

### 6.7.4.43. `mpo_check_socket_listen`

```
int mpo_check_socket_listen(cred, socket, socketlabel);
```

```
struct ucred *cred;
```

```
struct socket *socket;
struct label *socketlabel;
```

| Parameter | Description | Locking |
|---|---|---|
| cred | Subject credential | |
| socket | Object; socket | |
| socketlabel | Policy label for socket | |

Determine whether the subject credential can listen on the passed socket. Return 0 for success, or an errno value for failure. Suggested failure: EACCES for label mismatch, or EPERM for lack of privilege.

### 6.7.4.44. mpo_check_vnode_lookup

```
int mpo_check_vnode_lookup(, , , cnp);

struct ucred *cred;
struct vnode *dvp;
struct label *dlabel;
struct componentname *cnp;
```

| Parameter | Description | Locking |
|---|---|---|
| cred | Subject credential | |
| dvp | Object; vnode | |
| dlabel | Policy label | |

| Parameter | Description | Locking |
|---|---|---|
| | label for *dvp* | |
| cnp | Component name being looked up | |

Determine whether the subject credential can perform a lookup in the passed directory vnode for the passed name. Return 0 for success, or an errno value for failure. Suggested failure: EACCES for label mismatch, or EPERM for lack of privilege.

#### 6.7.4.45. mpo_check_vnode_open

```
int mpo_check_vnode_open(cred, vp, label, acc_mode);

struct ucred *cred;
struct vnode *vp;
struct label *label;
int acc_mode;
```

| Parameter | Description | Locking |
|---|---|---|
| *cred* | Subject credential | |
| *vp* | Object; vnode | |
| *label* | Policy label for *vp* | |
| *acc_mode* | open(2) access mode | |

Determine whether the subject credential can perform an open operation on the passed vnode with the passed access mode. Return 0 for success, or an errno value for failure. Suggested failure: EACCES for label mismatch, or EPERM for lack of privilege.

### 6.7.4.46. `mpo_check_vnode_readdir`

```
int mpo_check_vnode_readdir(, , );
```

```
struct ucred *cred;
struct vnode *dvp;
struct label *dlabel;
```

| Parameter | Description | Locking |
|---|---|---|
| *cred* | Subject credential | |
| *dvp* | Object; directory vnode | |
| *dlabel* | Policy label for *dvp* | |

Determine whether the subject credential can perform a `readdir` operation on the passed directory vnode. Return 0 for success, or an `errno` value for failure. Suggested failure: EACCES for label mismatch, or EPERM for lack of privilege.

### 6.7.4.47. `mpo_check_vnode_readlink`

```
int mpo_check_vnode_readlink(cred, vp, label);
```

```
struct ucred *cred;
struct vnode *vp;
struct label *label;
```

| Parameter | Description | Locking |
|---|---|---|
| *cred* | Subject cre- | |

| Parameter | Description | Locking |
|---|---|---|
| cred | Subject credential | |
| vp | Object; vnode | |
| label | Policy label for vp | |

Determine whether the subject credential can perform a `readlink` operation on the passed symlink vnode. Return 0 for success, or an `errno` value for failure. Suggested failure: EACCES for label mismatch, or EPERM for lack of privilege. This call may be made in a number of situations, including an explicit `readlink` call by the user process, or as a result of an implicit `readlink` during a name lookup by the process.

### 6.7.4.48. mpo_check_vnode_revoke

```
int mpo_check_vnode_revoke(cred, vp, label);

struct ucred *cred;
struct vnode *vp;
struct label *label;
```

| Parameter | Description | Locking |
|---|---|---|
| cred | Subject credential | |
| vp | Object; vnode | |
| label | Policy label for vp | |

Determine whether the subject credential can revoke access to the passed vnode. Return 0 for success, or an `errno` value for failure. Suggested failure: EACCES for label mismatch, or EPERM for lack of privilege.

### 6.7.4.49. mpo_check_vnode_setacl

```
int mpo_check_vnode_setacl(cred, vp, label, type, acl);
```

```
struct ucred *cred;
struct vnode *vp;
struct label *label;
acl_type_t type;
struct acl *acl;
```

Deck-
sgip-
tion
ter

Subed
ject
cre-
den-
tial

Ob-
ject;
vn-
ode

Pol-
bel
cy
la-
bel
for
*vp*

type
type

ACL

Determine whether the subject credential can set the passed ACL of passed type on the passed vnode. Return 0 for success, or an errno value for failure. Suggested failure: EACCES for label mismatch, or EPERM for lack of privilege.

### 6.7.4.50. mpo_check_vnode_setextattr

```
int mpo_check_vnode_setextattr(cred, vp, label, attrnamespace, name, uio);
```

```
struct ucred *cred;
struct vnode *vp;
struct label *label;
int attrnamespace;
const char *name;
struct uio *uio;
```

Deck-
sgip-
tion
ter

Subed
ject

| Parameter | Description | Locking |
| --- | --- | --- |
| *cred* | Subject credential | |
| *vp* | Object; vnode | |
| *label* | Policy label for *vp* | |
| *attrnamespace* | Extended attribute namespace | |
| *name* | Extended attribute name | |
| *uio* | I/O structure pointer; see uio(9) | |

Determine whether the subject credential can set the extended attribute of passed name and passed namespace on the passed vnode. Policies implementing security labels backed into extended attributes may want to provide additional protections for those attributes. Additionally, policies should avoid making decisions based on the data referenced from *uio*, as there is a potential race condition between this check and the actual operation. The *uio* may also be `NULL` if a delete operation is being performed. Return 0 for success, or an `errno` value for failure. Suggested failure: EACCES for label mismatch, or EPERM for lack of privilege.

#### 6.7.4.51. `mpo_check_vnode_setflags`

```
int mpo_check_vnode_setflags(cred, vp, label, flags);

struct ucred *cred;
struct vnode *vp;
struct label *label;
```

```
u_long flags;
```

| Parameter | Description | Locking |
|---|---|---|
| *cred* | Subject credential | |
| *vp* | Object; vnode | |
| *label* | Policy label for *vp* | |
| *flags* | File flags; see chflags(2) | |

Determine whether the subject credential can set the passed flags on the passed vnode. Return 0 for success, or an errno value for failure. Suggested failure: EACCES for label mismatch, or EPERM for lack of privilege.

#### 6.7.4.52. mpo_check_vnode_setmode

```
int mpo_check_vnode_setmode(cred, vp, label, mode);

struct ucred *cred;
struct vnode *vp;
struct label *label;
mode_t mode;
```

| Parameter | Description | Locking |
|---|---|---|
| *cred* | Subject credential | |
| *vp* | Object; vnode | |

| Parameter | Description |
| --- | --- |
| *label* | Policy label for *vp* |
| *mode* | File mode; see chmod(2) |

Determine whether the subject credential can set the passed mode on the passed vnode. Return 0 for success, or an `errno` value for failure. Suggested failure: EACCES for label mismatch, or EPERM for lack of privilege.

### 6.7.4.53. mpo_check_vnode_setowner

```
int mpo_check_vnode_setowner(cred, vp, label, uid, gid);

struct ucred *cred;
struct vnode *vp;
struct label *label;
uid_t uid;
gid_t gid;
```

| Parameter | Description |
| --- | --- |
| *cred* | Subject credential |
| *vp* | Object; vnode |
| *label* | Policy label for *vp* |
| *uid* | User ID |
| *gid* | Group ID |

Determine whether the subject credential can set the passed uid and passed gid as file uid and file gid on the passed vnode. The IDs may be set to (-1) to request no update. Return 0 for success, or an errno value for failure. Suggested failure: EACCES for label mismatch, or EPERM for lack of privilege.

### 6.7.4.54. mpo_check_vnode_setutimes

```
int mpo_check_vnode_setutimes(, , , , );
```

```
struct ucred *cred;
struct vnode *vp;
struct label *label;
struct timespec atime;
struct timespec mtime;
```

| Parameter | Description | Locking |
|---|---|---|
| cred | Subject credential | |
| vp | Object; vp | |
| label | Policy label for vp | |
| atime | Access time; see utimes(2) | |
| mtime | Modification time; see utimes(2) | |

Determine whether the subject credential can set the passed access timestamps on the passed vnode. Return 0 for success, or an errno value for failure. Suggested failure: EACCES for label mismatch, or EPERM for lack of privilege.

### 6.7.4.55. mpo_check_proc_sched

```
int mpo_check_proc_sched(ucred, proc);
```

```
struct ucred *ucred;
struct proc *proc;
```

[illegible]ek- [illegible]ip- [illegible] ter

[illegible] ject cre- den- tial

[illegible] ject; process

Determine whether the subject credential can change the scheduling parameters of the passed process. Return 0 for success, or an `errno` value for failure. Suggested failure: EACCES for label mismatch, EPERM for lack of privilege, or ESRCH to limit visibility.

See setpriority(2) for more information.

### 6.7.4.56. mpo_check_proc_signal

```
int mpo_check_proc_signal(cred, proc, signal);

struct ucred *cred;
struct proc *proc;
int signal;
```

[illegible]ek- [illegible]ip- [illegible] ter

[illegible] ject cre- den- tial

[illegible] ject; process

[illegible] nal; see kill(2)

Determine whether the subject credential can deliver the passed signal to the passed process. Return 0 for success, or an `errno` value for failure. Suggested failure: EACCES for label mismatch, EPERM for lack of privilege, or ESRCH to limit visibility.

### 6.7.4.57. mpo_check_vnode_stat

```
int mpo_check_vnode_stat(cred, vp, label);

struct ucred *cred;
struct vnode *vp;
struct label *label;
```

| Parameter | Description | Locking |
|---|---|---|
| *cred* | Subject credential | |
| *vp* | Object; vnode | |
| *label* | Policy label for *vp* | |

Determine whether the subject credential can `stat` the passed vnode. Return 0 for success, or an `errno` value for failure. Suggested failure: EACCES for label mismatch, or EPERM for lack of privilege.

See stat(2) for more information.

#### 6.7.4.58. `mpo_check_ifnet_transmit`

```
int mpo_check_ifnet_transmit(cred, ifnet, ifnetlabel, mbuf, mbuflabel);

struct ucred *cred;
struct ifnet *ifnet;
struct label *ifnetlabel;
struct mbuf *mbuf;
struct label *mbuflabel;
```

| Parameter | Description | Locking |
|---|---|---|
| *cred* | Subject credential | |
| *ifnet* | Network interface | |
| *ifnetlabel* | Policy label | |

| Parameter | Description | Locking |
|---|---|---|
| | for *ifnet* | |
| *mbuf* | Object; mbuf to be sent | |
| *mbuflabel* | Policy label for *mbuf* | |

Determine whether the network interface can transmit the passed mbuf. Return 0 for success, or an `errno` value for failure. Suggested failure: EACCES for label mismatch, or EPERM for lack of privilege.

### 6.7.4.59. `mpo_check_socket_deliver`

```
int mpo_check_socket_deliver(cred, ifnet, ifnetlabel, mbuf, mbuflabel);

struct ucred *cred;
struct ifnet *ifnet;
struct label *ifnetlabel;
struct mbuf *mbuf;
struct label *mbuflabel;
```

| Parameter | Description | Locking |
|---|---|---|
| *cred* | Subject credential | |
| *ifnet* | Network interface | |
| *ifnetlabel* | Policy label for *ifnet* | |

| Parameter | Description | Locking |
| --- | --- | --- |
| *mbuf* | Object; mbuf to be delivered | |
| *mbuflabel* | Policy label for *mbuf* | |

Determine whether the socket may receive the datagram stored in the passed mbuf header. Return 0 for success, or an `errno` value for failure. Suggested failures: EACCES for label mismatch, or EPERM for lack of privilege.

### 6.7.4.60. `mpo_check_socket_visible`

```
int mpo_check_socket_visible(cred, so, socketlabel);

struct ucred *cred;
struct socket *so;
struct label *socketlabel;
```

| Parameter | Description | Locking |
| --- | --- | --- |
| *cred* | Subject credential | Immutable |
| *so* | Object; socket | |
| *socketlabel* | Policy label for *so* | |

Determine whether the subject credential cred can "see" the passed socket (*socket*) using system monitoring functions, such as those employed by netstat(8) and sockstat(1). Return 0 for success, or an `errno` value for failure. Suggested failure: EACCES for label mismatches, EPERM for lack of privilege, or ESRCH to hide visibility.

#### 6.7.4.61. mpo_check_system_acct

```
int mpo_check_system_acct(ucred, vp, vlabel);

struct ucred *ucred;
struct vnode *vp;
struct label *vlabel;
```

| Parameter | Description | Locking |
|---|---|---|
| ucred | Subject credential | |
| vp | Accounting file; acct(5) | |
| vlabel | Label associated with vp | |

Determine whether the subject should be allowed to enable accounting, based on its label and the label of the accounting log file.

#### 6.7.4.62. mpo_check_system_nfsd

```
int mpo_check_system_nfsd(cred);

struct ucred *cred;
```

| Parameter | Description | Locking |
|---|---|---|
| cred | Subject credential | |

Determine whether the subject should be allowed to call nfssvc(2).

#### 6.7.4.63. mpo_check_system_reboot

```
int mpo_check_system_reboot(cred, howto);
```

```
struct ucred *cred;
int howto;
```

| Parameter | Description |
|---|---|
| *cred* | Subject credential |
| *howto* | parameter from reboot(2) |

Determine whether the subject should be allowed to reboot the system in the specified manner.

### 6.7.4.64. mpo_check_system_settime

```
int mpo_check_system_settime(cred);
```

```
struct ucred *cred;
```

| Parameter | Description |
|---|---|
| *cred* | Subject credential |

Determine whether the user should be allowed to set the system clock.

### 6.7.4.65. mpo_check_system_swapon

```
int mpo_check_system_swapon(cred, vp, vlabel);
```

```
struct ucred *cred;
struct vnode *vp;
struct label *vlabel;
```

| Parameter | Description |
|---|---|
| *cred* | Subject |

| Parameter | Description | Locking |
|---|---|---|
| *cred* | Subject credential | |
| *vp* | Swap device | |
| *vplabel* | Label associated with *vp* | |

Determine whether the subject should be allowed to add *vp* as a swap device.

### 6.7.4.66. `mpo_check_system_sysctl`

```
int mpo_check_system_sysctl(cred, name, namelen, old, oldlenp, inkernel, new, newlen);

struct ucred *cred;
int *name;
u_int *namelen;
void *old;
size_t *oldlenp;
int inkernel;
void *new;
size_t newlen;
```

| Parameter | Description | Locking |
|---|---|---|
| *cred* | Subject credential | |
| *name* | See sysctl(3) | |
| *namelen* | | |
| *old* | | |
| *oldlenp* | | |
| *inkernel* | Boolean; 1 if | |

Desc- rip- tion ter called from ker- nel See sysctl(3) newlen

Determine whether the subject should be allowed to make the specified sysctl(3) transaction.

### 6.7.5. Label Management Calls

Relabel events occur when a user process has requested that the label on an object be modified. A two-phase update occurs: first, an access control check will be performed to determine if the update is both valid and permitted, and then the update itself is performed via a separate entry point. Relabel entry points typically accept the object, object label reference, and an update label submitted by the process. Memory allocation during relabel is discouraged, as relabel calls are not permitted to fail (failure should be reported earlier in the relabel check).

## 6.8. Userland Architecture

The TrustedBSD MAC Framework includes a number of policy-agnostic elements, including MAC library interfaces for abstractly managing labels, modifications to the system credential management and login libraries to support the assignment of MAC labels to users, and a set of tools to monitor and modify labels on processes, files, and network interfaces. More details on the user architecture will be added to this section in the near future.

### 6.8.1. APIs for Policy-Agnostic Label Management

The TrustedBSD MAC Framework provides a number of library and system calls permitting applications to manage MAC labels on objects using a policy-agnostic interface. This permits applications to manipulate labels for a variety of policies without being written to support specific policies. These interfaces are used by general-purpose tools such as ifconfig(8), ls(1) and ps(1) to view labels on network interfaces, files, and processes. The APIs also support MAC management tools including getfmac(8), getpmac(8), setfmac(8), setfsmac(8), and setpmac(8). The MAC APIs are documented in mac(3).

Applications handle MAC labels in two forms: an internalized form used to return and set labels on processes and objects (`mac_t`), and externalized form based on C strings appropriate for storage in configuration files, display to the user, or input from the user. Each MAC label contains a number of elements, each consisting of a name and value pair. Policy modules in the kernel bind to specific names and interpret the values in policy-specific ways. In the externalized string form, labels are represented by a comma-delimited list of name and value pairs separated by the / character. Labels may be directly converted to and from text using provided APIs; when retrieving labels from the kernel, internalized label storage must first be prepared for the desired label element set. Typically, this is done in one of two ways: using mac_prepare(3) and an arbitrary list of desired label elements, or one of the variants of the call that loads a default element set from the mac.conf(5) configuration file. Per-object defaults permit application writers to usefully display labels associated with objects without being aware of the policies present in the system.

Note

Currently, direct manipulation of label elements other than by conversion to a text string, string editing, and conversion back to an internalized label is not supported by the MAC

library. Such interfaces may be added in the future if they prove necessary for application writers.

### 6.8.2. Binding of Labels to Users

The standard user context management interface, setusercontext(3), has been modified to retrieve MAC labels associated with a user's class from login.conf(5). These labels are then set along with other user context when either `LOGIN_SETALL` is specified, or when `LOGIN_SETMAC` is explicitly specified.

Note

It is expected that, in a future version of FreeBSD, the MAC label database will be separated from the `login.conf` user class abstraction, and be maintained in a separate database. However, the setusercontext(3) API should remain the same following such a change.

## 6.9. Conclusion

The TrustedBSD MAC framework permits kernel modules to augment the system security policy in a highly integrated manner. They may do this based on existing object properties, or based on label data that is maintained with the assistance of the MAC framework. The framework is sufficiently flexible to implement a variety of policy types, including information flow security policies such as MLS and Biba, as well as policies based on existing BSD credentials or file protections. Policy authors may wish to consult this documentation as well as existing security modules when implementing a new security service.

# Chapter 7. Virtual Memory System

Contributed by Matthew Dillon.

## 7.1. Management of Physical Memory—vm_page_t

Physical memory is managed on a page-by-page basis through the vm_page_t structure. Pages of physical memory are categorized through the placement of their respective vm_page_t structures on one of several paging queues.

A page can be in a wired, active, inactive, cache, or free state. Except for the wired state, the page is typically placed in a doubly link list queue representing the state that it is in. Wired pages are not placed on any queue.

FreeBSD implements a more involved paging queue for cached and free pages in order to implement page coloring. Each of these states involves multiple queues arranged according to the size of the processor's L1 and L2 caches. When a new page needs to be allocated, FreeBSD attempts to obtain one that is reasonably well aligned from the point of view of the L1 and L2 caches relative to the VM object the page is being allocated for.

Additionally, a page may be held with a reference count or locked with a busy count. The VM system also implements an "ultimate locked" state for a page using the PG_BUSY bit in the page's flags.

In general terms, each of the paging queues operates in a LRU fashion. A page is typically placed in a wired or active state initially. When wired, the page is usually associated with a page table somewhere. The VM system ages the page by scanning pages in a more active paging queue (LRU) in order to move them to a less-active paging queue. Pages that get moved into the cache are still associated with a VM object but are candidates for immediate reuse. Pages in the free queue are truly free. FreeBSD attempts to minimize the number of pages in the free queue, but a certain minimum number of truly free pages must be maintained in order to accommodate page allocation at interrupt time.

If a process attempts to access a page that does not exist in its page table but does exist in one of the paging queues (such as the inactive or cache queues), a relatively inexpensive page reactivation fault occurs which causes the page to be reactivated. If the page does not exist in system memory at all, the process must block while the page is brought in from disk.

FreeBSD dynamically tunes its paging queues and attempts to maintain reasonable ratios of pages in the various queues as well as attempts to maintain a reasonable breakdown of clean versus dirty pages. The amount of rebalancing that occurs depends on the system's memory load. This rebalancing is implemented by the pageout daemon and involves laundering dirty pages (syncing them with their backing store), noticing when pages are activity referenced (resetting their position in the LRU queues or moving them between queues), migrating pages between queues when the queues are out of balance, and so forth. FreeBSD's VM system is willing to take a reasonable number of reactivation page faults to determine how active or how idle a page actually is. This leads to better decisions being made as to when to launder or swap-out a page.

## 7.2. The Unified Buffer Cache—vm_object_t

FreeBSD implements the idea of a generic "VM object". VM objects can be associated with backing store of various types—unbacked, swap-backed, physical device-backed, or file-backed storage. Since the filesystem uses the same VM objects to manage in-core data relating to files, the result is a unified buffer cache.

VM objects can be *shadowed*. That is, they can be stacked on top of each other. For example, you might have a swap-backed VM object stacked on top of a file-backed VM object in order to implement a MAP_PRIVATE mmap()ing. This stacking is also used to implement various sharing properties, including copy-on-write, for forked address spaces.

It should be noted that a vm_page_t can only be associated with one VM object at a time. The VM object shadowing implements the perceived sharing of the same page across multiple instances.

## 7.3. Filesystem I/O—struct buf

vnode-backed VM objects, such as file-backed objects, generally need to maintain their own clean/dirty info independent from the VM system's idea of clean/dirty. For example, when the VM system decides to synchronize a physical page to its backing store, the VM system needs to mark the page clean before the page is actually written to its backing store. Additionally, filesystems need to be able to map portions of a file or file metadata into KVM in order to operate on it.

The entities used to manage this are known as filesystem buffers, `struct buf`'s, or bp's. When a filesystem needs to operate on a portion of a VM object, it typically maps part of the object into a struct buf and then maps the pages in the struct buf into KVM. In the same manner, disk I/O is typically issued by mapping portions of objects into buffer structures and then issuing the I/O on the buffer structures. The underlying vm_page_t's are typically busied for the duration of the I/O. Filesystem buffers also have their own notion of being busy, which is useful to filesystem driver code which would rather operate on filesystem buffers instead of hard VM pages.

FreeBSD reserves a limited amount of KVM to hold mappings from struct bufs, but it should be made clear that this KVM is used solely to hold mappings and does not limit the ability to cache data. Physical data caching is strictly a function of `vm_page_t`'s, not filesystem buffers. However, since filesystem buffers are used to placehold I/O, they do inherently limit the amount of concurrent I/O possible. However, as there are usually a few thousand filesystem buffers available, this is not usually a problem.

## 7.4. Mapping Page Tables—vm_map_t, vm_entry_t

FreeBSD separates the physical page table topology from the VM system. All hard per-process page tables can be reconstructed on the fly and are usually considered throwaway. Special page tables such as those managing KVM are typically permanently preallocated. These page tables are not throwaway.

FreeBSD associates portions of vm_objects with address ranges in virtual memory through `vm_map_t` and `vm_entry_t` structures. Page tables are directly synthesized from the `vm_map_t`/`vm_entry_t`/ `vm_object_t` hierarchy. Recall that I mentioned that physical pages are only directly associated with a `vm_object`; that is not quite true. `vm_page_t`'s are also linked into page tables that they are actively associated with. One `vm_page_t` can be linked into several *pmaps*, as page tables are called. However, the hierarchical association holds, so all references to the same page in the same object reference the same `vm_page_t` and thus give us buffer cache unification across the board.

## 7.5. KVM Memory Mapping

FreeBSD uses KVM to hold various kernel structures. The single largest entity held in KVM is the filesystem buffer cache. That is, mappings relating to `struct buf` entities.

Unlike Linux, FreeBSD does *not* map all of physical memory into KVM. This means that FreeBSD can handle memory configurations up to 4G on 32 bit platforms. In fact, if the mmu were capable of it, FreeBSD could theoretically handle memory configurations up to 8TB on a 32 bit platform. However, since most 32 bit platforms are only capable of mapping 4GB of ram, this is a moot point.

KVM is managed through several mechanisms. The main mechanism used to manage KVM is the *zone allocator*. The zone allocator takes a chunk of KVM and splits it up into constant-sized blocks of memory in order to allocate a specific type of structure. You can use `vmstat -m` to get an overview of current KVM utilization broken down by zone.

## 7.6. Tuning the FreeBSD VM System

A concerted effort has been made to make the FreeBSD kernel dynamically tune itself. Typically you do not need to mess with anything beyond the `maxusers` and `NMBCLUSTERS` kernel config options. That is, kernel compilation options specified in (typically) `/usr/src/sys/i386/conf/` *`CONFIG_FILE`*. A description of all available kernel configuration options can be found in `/usr/src/sys/i386/conf/LINT` .

In a large system configuration you may wish to increase `maxusers` . Values typically range from 10 to 128. Note that raising `maxusers` too high can cause the system to overflow available KVM resulting in unpredictable operation. It is better to leave `maxusers` at some reasonable number and add other options, such as `NMBCLUSTERS`, to increase specific resources.

If your system is going to use the network heavily, you may want to increase `NMBCLUSTERS`. Typical values range from 1024 to 4096.

The `NBUF` parameter is also traditionally used to scale the system. This parameter determines the amount of KVA the system can use to map filesystem buffers for I/O. Note that this parameter has nothing whatsoever to do with the unified buffer cache! This parameter is dynamically tuned in 3.0-CURRENT and later kernels and should generally not be adjusted manually. We recommend that you *not* try to specify an `NBUF` parameter. Let the system pick it. Too small a value can result in extremely inefficient filesystem operation while too large a value can starve the page queues by causing too many pages to become wired down.

By default, FreeBSD kernels are not optimized. You can set debugging and optimization flags with the `makeoptions` directive in the kernel configuration. Note that you should not use `-g` unless you can accommodate the large (typically 7 MB+) kernels that result.

```
makeoptions        DEBUG="-g"
makeoptions        COPTFLAGS="-O -pipe"
```

Sysctl provides a way to tune kernel parameters at run-time. You typically do not need to mess with any of the sysctl variables, especially the VM related ones.

Run time VM and system tuning is relatively straightforward. First, use Soft Updates on your UFS/FFS filesystems whenever possible. `/usr/src/sys/ufs/ffs/README.softupdates` contains instructions (and restrictions) on how to configure it.

Second, configure sufficient swap. You should have a swap partition configured on each physical disk, up to four, even on your "work" disks. You should have at least 2x the swap space as you have main memory, and possibly even more if you do not have a lot of memory. You should also size your swap partition based on the maximum memory configuration you ever intend to put on the machine so you do not have to repartition your disks later on. If you want to be able to accommodate a crash dump, your first swap partition must be at least as large as main memory and `/var/crash` must have sufficient free space to hold the dump.

NFS-based swap is perfectly acceptable on 4.X or later systems, but you must be aware that the NFS server will take the brunt of the paging load.

# Chapter 8. SMPng Design Document

Written by John Baldwin and Robert Watson.

## 8.1. Introduction

This document presents the current design and implementation of the SMPng Architecture. First, the basic primitives and tools are introduced. Next, a general architecture for the FreeBSD kernel's synchronization and execution model is laid out. Then, locking strategies for specific subsystems are discussed, documenting the approaches taken to introduce fine-grained synchronization and parallelism for each subsystem. Finally, detailed implementation notes are provided to motivate design choices, and make the reader aware of important implications involving the use of specific primitives.

This document is a work-in-progress, and will be updated to reflect on-going design and implementation activities associated with the SMPng Project. Many sections currently exist only in outline form, but will be fleshed out as work proceeds. Updates or suggestions regarding the document may be directed to the document editors.

The goal of SMPng is to allow concurrency in the kernel. The kernel is basically one rather large and complex program. To make the kernel multi-threaded we use some of the same tools used to make other programs multi-threaded. These include mutexes, shared/exclusive locks, semaphores, and condition variables. For the definitions of these and other SMP-related terms, please see the Glossary section of this article.

## 8.2. Basic Tools and Locking Fundamentals

### 8.2.1. Atomic Instructions and Memory Barriers

There are several existing treatments of memory barriers and atomic instructions, so this section will not include a lot of detail. To put it simply, one can not go around reading variables without a lock if a lock is used to protect writes to that variable. This becomes obvious when you consider that memory barriers simply determine relative order of memory operations; they do not make any guarantee about timing of memory operations. That is, a memory barrier does not force the contents of a CPU's local cache or store buffer to flush. Instead, the memory barrier at lock release simply ensures that all writes to the protected data will be visible to other CPU's or devices if the write to release the lock is visible. The CPU is free to keep that data in its cache or store buffer as long as it wants. However, if another CPU performs an atomic instruction on the same datum, the first CPU must guarantee that the updated value is made visible to the second CPU along with any other operations that memory barriers may require.

For example, assuming a simple model where data is considered visible when it is in main memory (or a global cache), when an atomic instruction is triggered on one CPU, other CPU's store buffers and caches must flush any writes to that same cache line along with any pending operations behind a memory barrier.

This requires one to take special care when using an item protected by atomic instructions. For example, in the sleep mutex implementation, we have to use an `atomic_cmpset` rather than an `atomic_set` to turn on the `MTX_CONTESTED` bit. The reason is that we read the value of `mtx_lock` into a variable and then make a decision based on that read. However, the value we read may be stale, or it may change while we are making our decision. Thus, when the `atomic_set` executed, it may end up setting the bit on another value than the one we made the decision on. Thus, we have to use an `atomic_cmpset` to set the value only if the value we made the decision on is up-to-date and valid.

Finally, atomic instructions only allow one item to be updated or read. If one needs to atomically update several items, then a lock must be used instead. For example, if two counters must be read and have values that are consistent relative to each other, then those counters must be protected by a lock rather than by separate atomic instructions.

### 8.2.2. Read Locks Versus Write Locks

Read locks do not need to be as strong as write locks. Both types of locks need to ensure that the data they are accessing is not stale. However, only write access requires exclusive access. Multiple threads can safely read a value. Using different types of locks for reads and writes can be implemented in a number of ways.

First, sx locks can be used in this manner by using an exclusive lock when writing and a shared lock when reading. This method is quite straightforward.

A second method is a bit more obscure. You can protect a datum with multiple locks. Then for reading that data you simply need to have a read lock of one of the locks. However, to write to the data, you need to have a write lock of all of the locks. This can make writing rather expensive but can be useful when data is accessed in various ways. For example, the parent process pointer is protected by both the `proctree_lock` sx lock and the per-process mutex. Sometimes the proc lock is easier as we are just checking to see who a parent of a process is that we already have locked. However, other places such as `inferior` need to walk the tree of processes via parent pointers and locking each process would be prohibitive as well as a pain to guarantee that the condition you are checking remains valid for both the check and the actions taken as a result of the check.

### 8.2.3. Locking Conditions and Results

If you need a lock to check the state of a variable so that you can take an action based on the state you read, you can not just hold the lock while reading the variable and then drop the lock before you act on the value you read. Once you drop the lock, the variable can change rendering your decision invalid. Thus, you must hold the lock both while reading the variable and while performing the action as a result of the test.

## 8.3. General Architecture and Design

### 8.3.1. Interrupt Handling

Following the pattern of several other multi-threaded UNIX® kernels, FreeBSD deals with interrupt handlers by giving them their own thread context. Providing a context for interrupt handlers allows them to block on locks. To help avoid latency, however, interrupt threads run at real-time kernel priority. Thus, interrupt handlers should not execute for very long to avoid starving other kernel threads. In addition, since multiple handlers may share an interrupt thread, interrupt handlers should not sleep or use a sleepable lock to avoid starving another interrupt handler.

The interrupt threads currently in FreeBSD are referred to as heavyweight interrupt threads. They are called this because switching to an interrupt thread involves a full context switch. In the initial implementation, the kernel was not preemptive and thus interrupts that interrupted a kernel thread would have to wait until the kernel thread blocked or returned to userland before they would have an opportunity to run.

To deal with the latency problems, the kernel in FreeBSD has been made preemptive. Currently, we only preempt a kernel thread when we release a sleep mutex or when an interrupt comes in. However, the plan is to make the FreeBSD kernel fully preemptive as described below.

Not all interrupt handlers execute in a thread context. Instead, some handlers execute directly in primary interrupt context. These interrupt handlers are currently misnamed "fast" interrupt handlers since the `INTR_FAST` flag used in earlier versions of the kernel is used to mark these handlers. The only interrupts which currently use these types of interrupt handlers are clock interrupts and serial I/O device interrupts. Since these handlers do not have their own context, they may not acquire blocking locks and thus may only use spin mutexes.

Finally, there is one optional optimization that can be added in MD code called lightweight context switches. Since an interrupt thread executes in a kernel context, it can borrow the vmspace of any process. Thus, in a lightweight context switch, the switch to the interrupt thread does not switch vmspaces but borrows the vmspace of the interrupted thread. In order to ensure that the vmspace of the interrupted thread does not disappear out from under us, the interrupted thread is not allowed to execute until the interrupt thread is no longer borrowing its vmspace. This can happen when the interrupt thread either blocks or finishes. If an interrupt thread blocks, then it will use its own context when it is made runnable again. Thus, it can release the interrupted thread.

The cons of this optimization are that they are very machine specific and complex and thus only worth the effort if their is a large performance improvement. At this point it is probably too early to tell, and in fact, will probably hurt performance as almost all interrupt handlers will immediately block on Giant and require a thread fix-up when they block. Also, an alternative method of interrupt handling has been proposed by Mike Smith that works like so:

1. Each interrupt handler has two parts: a predicate which runs in primary interrupt context and a handler which runs in its own thread context.
2. If an interrupt handler has a predicate, then when an interrupt is triggered, the predicate is run. If the predicate returns true then the interrupt is assumed to be fully handled and the kernel returns from the interrupt. If the predicate returns false or there is no predicate, then the threaded handler is scheduled to run.

Fitting light weight context switches into this scheme might prove rather complicated. Since we may want to change to this scheme at some point in the future, it is probably best to defer work on light weight context switches until we have settled on the final interrupt handling architecture and determined how light weight context switches might or might not fit into it.

## 8.3.2. Kernel Preemption and Critical Sections

### 8.3.2.1. Kernel Preemption in a Nutshell

Kernel preemption is fairly simple. The basic idea is that a CPU should always be doing the highest priority work available. Well, that is the ideal at least. There are a couple of cases where the expense of achieving the ideal is not worth being perfect.

Implementing full kernel preemption is very straightforward: when you schedule a thread to be executed by putting it on a run queue, you check to see if its priority is higher than the currently executing thread. If so, you initiate a context switch to that thread.

While locks can protect most data in the case of a preemption, not all of the kernel is preemption safe. For example, if a thread holding a spin mutex preempted and the new thread attempts to grab the same spin mutex, the new thread may spin forever as the interrupted thread may never get a chance to execute. Also, some code such as the code to assign an address space number for a process during `exec` on the Alpha needs to not be preempted as it supports the actual context switch code. Preemption is disabled for these code sections by using a critical section.

### 8.3.2.2. Critical Sections

The responsibility of the critical section API is to prevent context switches inside of a critical section. With a fully preemptive kernel, every `setrunqueue` of a thread other than the current thread is a preemption point. One implementation is for `critical_enter` to set a per-thread flag that is cleared by its counterpart. If `setrunqueue` is called with this flag set, it does not preempt regardless of the priority of the new thread relative to the current thread. However, since critical sections are used in spin mutexes to prevent context switches and multiple spin mutexes can be acquired, the critical section API must support nesting. For this reason the current implementation uses a nesting count instead of a single per-thread flag.

In order to minimize latency, preemptions inside of a critical section are deferred rather than dropped. If a thread that would normally be preempted to is made runnable while the current thread is in a critical section, then a per-thread flag is set to indicate that there is a pending preemption. When the outermost critical section is exited, the flag is checked. If the flag is set, then the current thread is preempted to allow the higher priority thread to run.

Interrupts pose a problem with regards to spin mutexes. If a low-level interrupt handler needs a lock, it needs to not interrupt any code needing that lock to avoid possible data structure corruption. Currently, providing this mechanism is piggybacked onto critical section API by means of the `cpu_critical_enter` and `cpu_critical_exit` functions. Currently this API disables and re-enables interrupts on all of FreeBSD's current platforms. This approach may not be purely optimal, but it is simple to understand and simple to get right. Theoretically, this second API need only be used for spin mutexes that are used in primary interrupt context. However, to make the code simpler, it is used for all spin mutexes and even all critical sections. It may be desirable to split out the MD API

from the MI API and only use it in conjunction with the MI API in the spin mutex implementation. If this approach is taken, then the MD API likely would need a rename to show that it is a separate API.

#### 8.3.2.3. Design Tradeoffs

As mentioned earlier, a couple of trade-offs have been made to sacrifice cases where perfect preemption may not always provide the best performance.

The first trade-off is that the preemption code does not take other CPUs into account. Suppose we have a two CPU's A and B with the priority of A's thread as 4 and the priority of B's thread as 2. If CPU B makes a thread with priority 1 runnable, then in theory, we want CPU A to switch to the new thread so that we will be running the two highest priority runnable threads. However, the cost of determining which CPU to enforce a preemption on as well as actually signaling that CPU via an IPI along with the synchronization that would be required would be enormous. Thus, the current code would instead force CPU B to switch to the higher priority thread. Note that this still puts the system in a better position as CPU B is executing a thread of priority 1 rather than a thread of priority 2.

The second trade-off limits immediate kernel preemption to real-time priority kernel threads. In the simple case of preemption defined above, a thread is always preempted immediately (or as soon as a critical section is exited) if a higher priority thread is made runnable. However, many threads executing in the kernel only execute in a kernel context for a short time before either blocking or returning to userland. Thus, if the kernel preempts these threads to run another non-realtime kernel thread, the kernel may switch out the executing thread just before it is about to sleep or execute. The cache on the CPU must then adjust to the new thread. When the kernel returns to the preempted thread, it must refill all the cache information that was lost. In addition, two extra context switches are performed that could be avoided if the kernel deferred the preemption until the first thread blocked or returned to userland. Thus, by default, the preemption code will only preempt immediately if the higher priority thread is a real-time priority thread.

Turning on full kernel preemption for all kernel threads has value as a debugging aid since it exposes more race conditions. It is especially useful on UP systems were many races are hard to simulate otherwise. Thus, there is a kernel option `FULL_PREEMPTION` to enable preemption for all kernel threads that can be used for debugging purposes.

### 8.3.3. Thread Migration

Simply put, a thread migrates when it moves from one CPU to another. In a non-preemptive kernel this can only happen at well-defined points such as when calling `msleep` or returning to userland. However, in the preemptive kernel, an interrupt can force a preemption and possible migration at any time. This can have negative affects on per-CPU data since with the exception of `curthread` and `curpcb` the data can change whenever you migrate. Since you can potentially migrate at any time this renders unprotected per-CPU data access rather useless. Thus it is desirable to be able to disable migration for sections of code that need per-CPU data to be stable.

Critical sections currently prevent migration since they do not allow context switches. However, this may be too strong of a requirement to enforce in some cases since a critical section also effectively blocks interrupt threads on the current processor. As a result, another API has been provided to allow the current thread to indicate that if it preempted it should not migrate to another CPU.

This API is known as thread pinning and is provided by the scheduler. The API consists of two functions: `sched_pin` and `sched_unpin`. These functions manage a per-thread nesting count `td_pinned`. A thread is pinned when its nesting count is greater than zero and a thread starts off unpinned with a nesting count of zero. Each scheduler implementation is required to ensure that pinned threads are only executed on the CPU that they were executing on when the `sched_pin` was first called. Since the nesting count is only written to by the thread itself and is only read by other threads when the pinned thread is not executing but while `sched_lock` is held, then `td_pinned` does not need any locking. The `sched_pin` function increments the nesting count and `sched_unpin` decrements the nesting count. Note that these functions only operate on the current thread and bind the current thread to the CPU it is executing on at the time. To bind an arbitrary thread to a specific CPU, the `sched_bind` and `sched_unbind` functions should be used instead.

### 8.3.4. Callouts

The timeout kernel facility permits kernel services to register functions for execution as part of the softclock software interrupt. Events are scheduled based on a desired number of clock ticks, and callbacks to the consumer-provided function will occur at approximately the right time.

The global list of pending timeout events is protected by a global spin mutex, callout_lock; all access to the timeout list must be performed with this mutex held. When softclock is woken up, it scans the list of pending timeouts for those that should fire. In order to avoid lock order reversal, the softclock thread will release the callout_lock mutex when invoking the provided timeout callback function. If the CALLOUT_MPSAFE flag was not set during registration, then Giant will be grabbed before invoking the callout, and then released afterwards. The callout_lock mutex will be re-grabbed before proceeding. The softclock code is careful to leave the list in a consistent state while releasing the mutex. If DIAGNOSTIC is enabled, then the time taken to execute each function is measured, and a warning is generated if it exceeds a threshold.

## 8.4. Specific Locking Strategies

### 8.4.1. Credentials

struct ucred is the kernel's internal credential structure, and is generally used as the basis for process-driven access control within the kernel. BSD-derived systems use a "copy-on-write" model for credential data: multiple references may exist for a credential structure, and when a change needs to be made, the structure is duplicated, modified, and then the reference replaced. Due to wide-spread caching of the credential to implement access control on open, this results in substantial memory savings. With a move to fine-grained SMP, this model also saves substantially on locking operations by requiring that modification only occur on an unshared credential, avoiding the need for explicit synchronization when consuming a known-shared credential.

Credential structures with a single reference are considered mutable; shared credential structures must not be modified or a race condition is risked. A mutex, cr_mtxp protects the reference count of struct ucred so as to maintain consistency. Any use of the structure requires a valid reference for the duration of the use, or the structure may be released out from under the illegitimate consumer.

The struct ucred mutex is a leaf mutex and is implemented via a mutex pool for performance reasons.

Usually, credentials are used in a read-only manner for access control decisions, and in this case td_ucred is generally preferred because it requires no locking. When a process' credential is updated the proc lock must be held across the check and update operations thus avoid races. The process credential p_ucred must be used for check and update operations to prevent time-of-check, time-of-use races.

If system call invocations will perform access control after an update to the process credential, the value of td_ucred must also be refreshed to the current process value. This will prevent use of a stale credential following a change. The kernel automatically refreshes the td_ucred pointer in the thread structure from the process p_ucred whenever a process enters the kernel, permitting use of a fresh credential for kernel access control.

### 8.4.2. File Descriptors and File Descriptor Tables

Details to follow.

### 8.4.3. Jail Structures

struct prison stores administrative details pertinent to the maintenance of jails created using the jail(2) API. This includes the per-jail hostname, IP address, and related settings. This structure is reference-counted since pointers to instances of the structure are shared by many credential structures. A single mutex, pr_mtx protects read and write access to the reference count and all mutable variables inside the struct jail. Some variables are set only when the jail is created, and a valid reference to the struct prison is sufficient to read these values. The precise locking of each entry is documented via comments in sys/jail.h .

### 8.4.4. MAC Framework

The TrustedBSD MAC Framework maintains data in a variety of kernel objects, in the form of `struct label`. In general, labels in kernel objects are protected by the same lock as the remainder of the kernel object. For example, the `v_label` label in `struct vnode` is protected by the vnode lock on the vnode.

In addition to labels maintained in standard kernel objects, the MAC Framework also maintains a list of registered and active policies. The policy list is protected by a global mutex (`mac_policy_list_lock`) and a busy count (also protected by the mutex). Since many access control checks may occur in parallel, entry to the framework for a read-only access to the policy list requires holding the mutex while incrementing (and later decrementing) the busy count. The mutex need not be held for the duration of the MAC entry operation--some operations, such as label operations on file system objects--are long-lived. To modify the policy list, such as during policy registration and de-registration, the mutex must be held and the reference count must be zero, to prevent modification of the list while it is in use.

A condition variable, `mac_policy_list_not_busy`, is available to threads that need to wait for the list to become unbusy, but this condition variable must only be waited on if the caller is holding no other locks, or a lock order violation may be possible. The busy count, in effect, acts as a form of shared/exclusive lock over access to the framework: the difference is that, unlike with an sx lock, consumers waiting for the list to become unbusy may be starved, rather than permitting lock order problems with regards to the busy count and other locks that may be held on entry to (or inside) the MAC Framework.

### 8.4.5. Modules

For the module subsystem there exists a single lock that is used to protect the shared data. This lock is a shared/exclusive (SX) lock and has a good chance of needing to be acquired (shared or exclusively), therefore there are a few macros that have been added to make access to the lock more easy. These macros can be located in `sys/module.h` and are quite basic in terms of usage. The main structures protected under this lock are the `module_t` structures (when shared) and the global `modulelist_t` structure, modules. One should review the related source code in `kern/kern_module.c` to further understand the locking strategy.

### 8.4.6. Newbus Device Tree

The newbus system will have one sx lock. Readers will hold a shared (read) lock (sx_slock(9)) and writers will hold an exclusive (write) lock (sx_xlock(9)). Internal functions will not do locking at all. Externally visible ones will lock as needed. Those items that do not matter if the race is won or lost will not be locked, since they tend to be read all over the place (e.g., device_get_softc(9)). There will be relatively few changes to the newbus data structures, so a single lock should be sufficient and not impose a performance penalty.

### 8.4.7. Pipes

...

### 8.4.8. Processes and Threads

- process hierarchy

- proc locks, references

- thread-specific copies of proc entries to freeze during system calls, including td_ucred

- inter-process operations

- process groups and sessions

### 8.4.9. Scheduler

Lots of references to sched_lock and notes pointing at specific primitives and related magic elsewhere in the document.

## 8.4.10. Select and Poll

The select and poll functions permit threads to block waiting on events on file descriptors--most frequently, whether or not the file descriptors are readable or writable.

...

## 8.4.11. SIGIO

The SIGIO service permits processes to request the delivery of a SIGIO signal to its process group when the read/write status of specified file descriptors changes. At most one process or process group is permitted to register for SIGIO from any given kernel object, and that process or group is referred to as the owner. Each object supporting SIGIO registration contains pointer field that is NULL if the object is not registered, or points to a struct sigio describing the registration. This field is protected by a global mutex, sigio_lock. Callers to SIGIO maintenance functions must pass in this field "by reference" so that local register copies of the field are not made when unprotected by the lock.

One struct sigio is allocated for each registered object associated with any process or process group, and contains back-pointers to the object, owner, signal information, a credential, and the general disposition of the registration. Each process or progress group contains a list of registered struct sigio structures, p_sigiolst for processes, and pg_sigiolst for process groups. These lists are protected by the process or process group locks respectively. Most fields in each struct sigio are constant for the duration of the registration, with the exception of the sio_pgsigio field which links the struct sigio into the process or process group list. Developers implementing new kernel objects supporting SIGIO will, in general, want to avoid holding structure locks while invoking SIGIO supporting functions, such as fsetown or funsetown to avoid defining a lock order between structure locks and the global SIGIO lock. This is generally possible through use of an elevated reference count on the structure, such as reliance on a file descriptor reference to a pipe during a pipe operation.

## 8.4.12. Sysctl

The sysctl MIB service is invoked from both within the kernel and from userland applications using a system call. At least two issues are raised in locking: first, the protection of the structures maintaining the namespace, and second, interactions with kernel variables and functions that are accessed by the sysctl interface. Since sysctl permits the direct export (and modification) of kernel statistics and configuration parameters, the sysctl mechanism must become aware of appropriate locking semantics for those variables. Currently, sysctl makes use of a single global sx lock to serialize use of sysctl; however, it is assumed to operate under Giant and other protections are not provided. The remainder of this section speculates on locking and semantic changes to sysctl.

- Need to change the order of operations for sysctl's that update values from read old, copyin and copyout, write new to copyin, lock, read old and write new, unlock, copyout. Normal sysctl's that just copyout the old value and set a new value that they copyin may still be able to follow the old model. However, it may be cleaner to use the second model for all of the sysctl handlers to avoid lock operations.

- To allow for the common case, a sysctl could embed a pointer to a mutex in the SYSCTL_FOO macros and in the struct. This would work for most sysctl's. For values protected by sx locks, spin mutexes, or other locking strategies besides a single sleep mutex, SYSCTL_PROC nodes could be used to get the locking right.

## 8.4.13. Taskqueue

The taskqueue's interface has two basic locks associated with it in order to protect the related shared data. The taskqueue_queues_mutex is meant to serve as a lock to protect the taskqueue_queues TAILQ. The other mutex lock associated with this system is the one in the struct taskqueue data structure. The use of the synchronization primitive here is to protect the integrity of the data in the struct taskqueue . It should be noted that there are no separate macros to assist the user in locking down his/her own work since these locks are most likely not going to be used outside of kern/subr_taskqueue.c .

## 8.5. Implementation Notes

### 8.5.1. Sleep Queues

A sleep queue is a structure that holds the list of threads asleep on a wait channel. Each thread that is not asleep on a wait channel carries a sleep queue structure around with it. When a thread blocks on a wait channel, it donates its sleep queue structure to that wait channel. Sleep queues associated with a wait channel are stored in a hash table.

The sleep queue hash table holds sleep queues for wait channels that have at least one blocked thread. Each entry in the hash table is called a sleepqueue chain. The chain contains a linked list of sleep queues and a spin mutex. The spin mutex protects the list of sleep queues as well as the contents of the sleep queue structures on the list. Only one sleep queue is associated with a given wait channel. If multiple threads block on a wait channel than the sleep queues associated with all but the first thread are stored on a list of free sleep queues in the master sleep queue. When a thread is removed from the sleep queue it is given one of the sleep queue structures from the master queue's free list if it is not the only thread asleep on the queue. The last thread is given the master sleep queue when it is resumed. Since threads may be removed from the sleep queue in a different order than they are added, a thread may depart from a sleep queue with a different sleep queue structure than the one it arrived with.

The `sleepq_lock` function locks the spin mutex of the sleep queue chain that maps to a specific wait channel. The `sleepq_lookup` function looks in the hash table for the master sleep queue associated with a given wait channel. If no master sleep queue is found, it returns `NULL`. The `sleepq_release` function unlocks the spin mutex associated with a given wait channel.

A thread is added to a sleep queue via the `sleepq_add`. This function accepts the wait channel, a pointer to the mutex that protects the wait channel, a wait message description string, and a mask of flags. The sleep queue chain should be locked via `sleepq_lock` before this function is called. If no mutex protects the wait channel (or it is protected by Giant), then the mutex pointer argument should be `NULL`. The flags argument contains a type field that indicates the kind of sleep queue that the thread is being added to and a flag to indicate if the sleep is interruptible (`SLEEPQ_INTERRUPTIBLE`). Currently there are only two types of sleep queues: traditional sleep queues managed via the `msleep` and `wakeup` functions (`SLEEPQ_MSLEEP`) and condition variable sleep queues (`SLEEPQ_CONDVAR`). The sleep queue type and lock pointer argument are used solely for internal assertion checking. Code that calls `sleepq_add` should explicitly unlock any interlock protecting the wait channel after the associated sleepqueue chain has been locked via `sleepq_lock` and before blocking on the sleep queue via one of the waiting functions.

A timeout for a sleep is set by invoking `sleepq_set_timeout`. The function accepts the wait channel and the timeout time as a relative tick count as its arguments. If a sleep should be interrupted by arriving signals, the `sleepq_catch_signals` function should be called as well. This function accepts the wait channel as its only parameter. If there is already a signal pending for this thread, then `sleepq_catch_signals` will return a signal number; otherwise, it will return 0.

Once a thread has been added to a sleep queue, it blocks using one of the `sleepq_wait` functions. There are four wait functions depending on whether or not the caller wishes to use a timeout or have the sleep aborted by caught signals or an interrupt from the userland thread scheduler. The `sleepq_wait` function simply waits until the current thread is explicitly resumed by one of the wakeup functions. The `sleepq_timedwait` function waits until either the thread is explicitly resumed or the timeout set by an earlier call to `sleepq_set_timeout` expires. The `sleepq_wait_sig` function waits until either the thread is explicitly resumed or its sleep is aborted. The `sleepq_timedwait_sig` function waits until either the thread is explicitly resumed, the timeout set by an earlier call to `sleepq_set_timeout` expires, or the thread's sleep is aborted. All of the wait functions accept the wait channel as their first parameter. In addition, the `sleepq_timedwait_sig` function accepts a second boolean parameter to indicate if the earlier call to `sleepq_catch_signals` found a pending signal.

If the thread is explicitly resumed or is aborted by a signal, then a value of zero is returned by the wait function to indicate a successful sleep. If the thread is resumed by either a timeout or an interrupt from the userland thread scheduler then an appropriate errno value is returned instead. Note that since `sleepq_wait` can only return 0 it does not return anything and the caller should assume a successful sleep. Also, if a thread's sleep times out and is aborted simultaneously then `sleepq_timedwait_sig` will return an error indicating that a timeout occurred. If an error value of 0 is returned and either `sleepq_wait_sig` or `sleepq_timedwait_sig` was used to block, then

the function `sleepq_calc_signal_retval` should be called to check for any pending signals and calculate an appropriate return value if any are found. The signal number returned by the earlier call to `sleepq_catch_signals` should be passed as the sole argument to `sleepq_calc_signal_retval`.

Threads asleep on a wait channel are explicitly resumed by the `sleepq_broadcast` and `sleepq_signal` functions. Both functions accept the wait channel from which to resume threads, a priority to raise resumed threads to, and a flags argument to indicate which type of sleep queue is being resumed. The priority argument is treated as a minimum priority. If a thread being resumed already has a higher priority (numerically lower) than the priority argument then its priority is not adjusted. The flags argument is used for internal assertions to ensure that sleep queues are not being treated as the wrong type. For example, the condition variable functions should not resume threads on a traditional sleep queue. The `sleepq_broadcast` function resumes all threads that are blocked on the specified wait channel while `sleepq_signal` only resumes the highest priority thread blocked on the wait channel. The sleep queue chain should first be locked via the `sleepq_lock` function before calling these functions.

A sleeping thread may have its sleep interrupted by calling the `sleepq_abort` function. This function must be called with `sched_lock` held and the thread must be queued on a sleep queue. A thread may also be removed from a specific sleep queue via the `sleepq_remove` function. This function accepts both a thread and a wait channel as an argument and only awakens the thread if it is on the sleep queue for the specified wait channel. If the thread is not on a sleep queue or it is on a sleep queue for a different wait channel, then this function does nothing.

### 8.5.2. Turnstiles

- Compare/contrast with sleep queues.

- Lookup/wait/release. - Describe TDF_TSNOBLOCK race.

- Priority propagation.

### 8.5.3. Details of the Mutex Implementation

- Should we require mutexes to be owned for mtx_destroy() since we can not safely assert that they are unowned by anyone else otherwise?

#### 8.5.3.1. Spin Mutexes

- Use a critical section...

#### 8.5.3.2. Sleep Mutexes

- Describe the races with contested mutexes

- Why it is safe to read mtx_lock of a contested mutex when holding the turnstile chain lock.

### 8.5.4. Witness

- What does it do

- How does it work

## 8.6. Miscellaneous Topics

### 8.6.1. Interrupt Source and ICU Abstractions

- struct isrc

- pic drivers

### 8.6.2. Other Random Questions/Topics

- Should we pass an interlock into `sema_wait`?

- Should we have non-sleepable sx locks?

- Add some info about proper use of reference counts.

# Glossary

**atomic**
An operation is atomic if all of its effects are visible to other CPUs together when the proper access protocol is followed. In the degenerate case are atomic instructions provided directly by machine architectures. At a higher level, if several members of a structure are protected by a lock, then a set of operations are atomic if they are all performed while holding the lock without releasing the lock in between any of the operations.
See Also operation.

**block**
A thread is blocked when it is waiting on a lock, resource, or condition. Unfortunately this term is a bit overloaded as a result.
See Also sleep.

**critical section**
A section of code that is not allowed to be preempted. A critical section is entered and exited using the critical_enter(9) API.

**MD**
Machine dependent.
See Also MI.

**memory operation**
A memory operation reads and/or writes to a memory location.

**MI**
Machine independent.
See Also MD.

**operation**
See memory operation.

**primary interrupt context**
Primary interrupt context refers to the code that runs when an interrupt occurs. This code can either run an interrupt handler directly or schedule an asynchronous interrupt thread to execute the interrupt handlers for a given interrupt source.

**realtime kernel thread**
A high priority kernel thread. Currently, the only realtime priority kernel threads are interrupt threads.
See Also thread.

**sleep**
A thread is asleep when it is blocked on a condition variable or a sleep queue via `msleep` or `tsleep`.
See Also block.

**sleepable lock**
A sleepable lock is a lock that can be held by a thread which is asleep. Lockmgr locks and sx locks are currently the only sleepable locks in FreeBSD. Eventually, some sx locks such as the allproc and proctree locks may become non-sleepable locks.
See Also sleep.

**thread**
A kernel thread represented by a struct thread. Threads own locks and hold a single execution context.

**wait channel**
A kernel virtual address that threads may sleep on.

# Part II. Device Drivers

# Table of Contents

# Chapter 9. Writing FreeBSD Device Drivers

Written by Murray Stokely.
Based on intro(4) manual page by Jörg Wunsch.

## 9.1. Introduction

This chapter provides a brief introduction to writing device drivers for FreeBSD. A device in this context is a term used mostly for hardware-related stuff that belongs to the system, like disks, printers, or a graphics display with its keyboard. A device driver is the software component of the operating system that controls a specific device. There are also so-called pseudo-devices where a device driver emulates the behavior of a device in software without any particular underlying hardware. Device drivers can be compiled into the system statically or loaded on demand through the dynamic kernel linker facility `kld'.

Most devices in a UNIX®-like operating system are accessed through device-nodes, sometimes also called special files. These files are usually located under the directory `/dev` in the filesystem hierarchy.

Device drivers can roughly be broken down into two categories; character and network device drivers.

## 9.2. Dynamic Kernel Linker Facility - KLD

The kld interface allows system administrators to dynamically add and remove functionality from a running system. This allows device driver writers to load their new changes into a running kernel without constantly rebooting to test changes.

The kld interface is used through:

- `kldload` - loads a new kernel module
- `kldunload` - unloads a kernel module
- `kldstat` - lists loaded modules

Skeleton Layout of a kernel module

```
/*
 * KLD Skeleton
 * Inspired by Andrew Reiter's Daemonnews article
 */

#include <sys/types.h>
#include <sys/module.h>
#include <sys/systm.h>  /* uprintf */
#include <sys/errno.h>
#include <sys/param.h>  /* defines used in kernel.h */
#include <sys/kernel.h> /* types used in module initialization */

/*
 * Load handler that deals with the loading and unloading of a KLD.
 */

static int
skel_loader(struct module *m, int what, void *arg)
{
  int err = 0;
```

```
  switch (what) {
  case MOD_LOAD:                /* kldload */
    uprintf("Skeleton KLD loaded.\n");
    break;
  case MOD_UNLOAD:
    uprintf("Skeleton KLD unloaded.\n");
    break;
  default:
    err = EOPNOTSUPP;
    break;
  }
  return(err);
}

/* Declare this module to the rest of the kernel */

static moduledata_t skel_mod = {
  "skel",
  skel_loader,
  NULL
};

DECLARE_MODULE(skeleton, skel_mod, SI_SUB_KLD, SI_ORDER_ANY);
```

### 9.2.1. Makefile

FreeBSD provides a system makefile to simplify compiling a kernel module.

```
SRCS=skeleton.c
KMOD=skeleton

.include <bsd.kmod.mk>
```

Running make with this makefile will create a file skeleton.ko that can be loaded into the kernel by typing:

```
# kldload -v ./skeleton.ko
```

## 9.3. Character Devices

A character device driver is one that transfers data directly to and from a user process. This is the most common type of device driver and there are plenty of simple examples in the source tree.

This simple example pseudo-device remembers whatever values are written to it and can then echo them back when read.

Example 9.1. Example of a Sample Echo Pseudo-Device Driver for FreeBSD 10.X

```
/*
 * Simple Echo pseudo-device KLD
 *
 * Murray Stokely
 * Søren (Xride) Straarup
 * Eitan Adler
 */

#include <sys/types.h>
#include <sys/module.h>
#include <sys/systm.h>  /* uprintf */
#include <sys/param.h>  /* defines used in kernel.h */
```

```
#include <sys/kernel.h> /* types used in module initialization */
#include <sys/conf.h>   /* cdevsw struct */
#include <sys/uio.h>    /* uio struct */
#include <sys/malloc.h>

#define BUFFERSIZE 255

/* Function prototypes */
static d_open_t      echo_open;
static d_close_t     echo_close;
static d_read_t      echo_read;
static d_write_t     echo_write;

/* Character device entry points */
static struct cdevsw echo_cdevsw = {
 .d_version = D_VERSION,
 .d_open = echo_open,
 .d_close = echo_close,
 .d_read = echo_read,
 .d_write = echo_write,
 .d_name = "echo",
};

struct s_echo {
 char msg[BUFFERSIZE + 1];
 int len;
};

/* vars */
static struct cdev *echo_dev;
static struct s_echo *echomsg;

MALLOC_DECLARE(M_ECHOBUF);
MALLOC_DEFINE(M_ECHOBUF, "echobuffer", "buffer for echo module");

/*
 * This function is called by the kld[un]load(2) system calls to
 * determine what actions to take when a module is loaded or unloaded.
 */
static int
echo_loader(struct module *m __unused, int what, void *arg __unused)
{
 int error = 0;

 switch (what) {
 case MOD_LOAD:                /* kldload */
  error = make_dev_p(MAKEDEV_CHECKNAME | MAKEDEV_WAITOK,
      &echo_dev,
      &echo_cdevsw,
      0,
      UID_ROOT,
      GID_WHEEL,
      0600,
      "echo");
  if (error != 0)
   break;

  echomsg = malloc(sizeof(*echomsg), M_ECHOBUF, M_WAITOK |
      M_ZERO);
  printf("Echo device loaded.\n");
  break;
 case MOD_UNLOAD:
  destroy_dev(echo_dev);
  free(echomsg, M_ECHOBUF);
  printf("Echo device unloaded.\n");
  break;
```

```
 default:
  error = EOPNOTSUPP;
  break;
 }
 return (error);
}

static int
echo_open(struct cdev *dev __unused, int oflags __unused, int devtype __unused,
    struct thread *td __unused)
{
 int error = 0;

 uprintf("Opened device \"echo\" successfully.\n");
 return (error);
}

static int
echo_close(struct cdev *dev __unused, int fflag __unused, int devtype __unused,
    struct thread *td __unused)
{

 uprintf("Closing device \"echo\".\n");
 return (0);
}

/*
 * The read function just takes the buf that was saved via
 * echo_write() and returns it to userland for accessing.
 * uio(9)
 */
static int
echo_read(struct cdev *dev __unused, struct uio *uio, int ioflag __unused)
{
 size_t amt;
 int error;

 /*
  * How big is this read operation?  Either as big as the user wants,
  * or as big as the remaining data.  Note that the 'len' does not
  * include the trailing null character.
  */
 amt = MIN(uio->uio_resid, uio->uio_offset >= echomsg->len + 1 ? 0 :
     echomsg->len + 1 - uio->uio_offset);

 if ((error = uiomove(echomsg->msg, amt, uio)) != 0)
  uprintf("uiomove failed!\n");

 return (error);
}

/*
 * echo_write takes in a character string and saves it
 * to buf for later accessing.
 */
static int
echo_write(struct cdev *dev __unused, struct uio *uio, int ioflag __unused)
{
 size_t amt;
 int error;

 /*
  * We either write from the beginning or are appending -- do
  * not allow random access.
  */
 if (uio->uio_offset != 0 && (uio->uio_offset != echomsg->len))
```

```
        return (EINVAL);

    /* This is a new message, reset length */
    if (uio->uio_offset == 0)
        echomsg->len = 0;

    /* Copy the string in from user memory to kernel memory */
    amt = MIN(uio->uio_resid, (BUFFERSIZE - echomsg->len));

    error = uiomove(echomsg->msg + uio->uio_offset, amt, uio);

    /* Now we need to null terminate and record the length */
    echomsg->len = uio->uio_offset;
    echomsg->msg[echomsg->len] = 0;

    if (error != 0)
        uprintf("Write failed: bad address!\n");
    return (error);
}

DEV_MODULE(echo, echo_loader, NULL);
```

With this driver loaded try:

```
# echo -n "Test Data" > /dev/echo
# cat /dev/echo
Opened device "echo" successfully.
Test Data
Closing device "echo".
```

Real hardware devices are described in the next chapter.

## 9.4. Block Devices (Are Gone)

Other UNIX® systems may support a second type of disk device known as block devices. Block devices are disk devices for which the kernel provides caching. This caching makes block-devices almost unusable, or at least dangerously unreliable. The caching will reorder the sequence of write operations, depriving the application of the ability to know the exact disk contents at any one instant in time.

This makes predictable and reliable crash recovery of on-disk data structures (filesystems, databases, etc.) impossible. Since writes may be delayed, there is no way the kernel can report to the application which particular write operation encountered a write error, this further compounds the consistency problem.

For this reason, no serious applications rely on block devices, and in fact, almost all applications which access disks directly take great pains to specify that character (or "raw") devices should always be used. Because the implementation of the aliasing of each disk (partition) to two devices with different semantics significantly complicated the relevant kernel code FreeBSD dropped support for cached disk devices as part of the modernization of the disk I/O infrastructure.

## 9.5. Network Drivers

Drivers for network devices do not use device nodes in order to be accessed. Their selection is based on other decisions made inside the kernel and instead of calling open(), use of a network device is generally introduced by using the system call socket(2).

For more information see ifnet(9), the source of the loopback device, and Bill Paul's network drivers.

# Chapter 10. ISA Device Drivers

Written by Sergey Babkin.
Modifications for Handbook made by Murray Stokely, Valentino Vaschetto and Wylie Stilwell.

## 10.1. Synopsis

This chapter introduces the issues relevant to writing a driver for an ISA device. The pseudo-code presented here is rather detailed and reminiscent of the real code but is still only pseudo-code. It avoids the details irrelevant to the subject of the discussion. The real-life examples can be found in the source code of real drivers. In particular the drivers `ep` and `aha` are good sources of information.

## 10.2. Basic Information

A typical ISA driver would need the following include files:

```
#include <sys/module.h>
#include <sys/bus.h>
#include <machine/bus.h>
#include <machine/resource.h>
#include <sys/rman.h>

#include <isa/isavar.h>
#include <isa/pnpvar.h>
```

They describe the things specific to the ISA and generic bus subsystem.

The bus subsystem is implemented in an object-oriented fashion, its main structures are accessed by associated method functions.

The list of bus methods implemented by an ISA driver is like one for any other bus. For a hypothetical driver named "xxx" they would be:

- `static void xxx_isa_identify (driver_t *, device_t);` Normally used for bus drivers, not device drivers. But for ISA devices this method may have special use: if the device provides some device-specific (non-PnP) way to auto-detect devices this routine may implement it.
- `static int xxx_isa_probe (device_t dev);` Probe for a device at a known (or PnP) location. This routine can also accommodate device-specific auto-detection of parameters for partially configured devices.
- `static int xxx_isa_attach (device_t dev);` Attach and initialize device.
- `static int xxx_isa_detach (device_t dev);` Detach device before unloading the driver module.
- `static int xxx_isa_shutdown (device_t dev);` Execute shutdown of the device before system shutdown.
- `static int xxx_isa_suspend (device_t dev);` Suspend the device before the system goes to the power-save state. May also abort transition to the power-save state.
- `static int xxx_isa_resume (device_t dev);` Resume the device activity after return from power-save state.

`xxx_isa_probe()` and `xxx_isa_attach()` are mandatory, the rest of the routines are optional, depending on the device's needs.

The driver is linked to the system with the following set of descriptions.

```
    /* table of supported bus methods */
```

```
static device_method_t xxx_isa_methods[] = {
    /* list all the bus method functions supported by the driver */
    /* omit the unsupported methods */
    DEVMETHOD(device_identify,  xxx_isa_identify),
    DEVMETHOD(device_probe,     xxx_isa_probe),
    DEVMETHOD(device_attach,    xxx_isa_attach),
    DEVMETHOD(device_detach,    xxx_isa_detach),
    DEVMETHOD(device_shutdown,  xxx_isa_shutdown),
    DEVMETHOD(device_suspend,   xxx_isa_suspend),
    DEVMETHOD(device_resume,    xxx_isa_resume),

DEVMETHOD_END
};

static driver_t xxx_isa_driver = {
    "xxx",
    xxx_isa_methods,
    sizeof(struct xxx_softc),
};


static devclass_t xxx_devclass;

DRIVER_MODULE(xxx, isa, xxx_isa_driver, xxx_devclass,
    load_function, load_argument);
```

Here struct `xxx_softc` is a device-specific structure that contains private driver data and descriptors for the driver's resources. The bus code automatically allocates one softc descriptor per device as needed.

If the driver is implemented as a loadable module then `load_function()` is called to do driver-specific initialization or clean-up when the driver is loaded or unloaded and load_argument is passed as one of its arguments. If the driver does not support dynamic loading (in other words it must always be linked into the kernel) then these values should be set to 0 and the last definition would look like:

```
DRIVER_MODULE(xxx, isa, xxx_isa_driver,
      xxx_devclass, 0, 0);
```

If the driver is for a device which supports PnP then a table of supported PnP IDs must be defined. The table consists of a list of PnP IDs supported by this driver and human-readable descriptions of the hardware types and models having these IDs. It looks like:

```
static struct isa_pnp_id xxx_pnp_ids[] = {
    /* a line for each supported PnP ID */
    { 0x12345678,   "Our device model 1234A" },
    { 0x12345679,   "Our device model 1234B" },
    { 0,        NULL }, /* end of table */
};
```

If the driver does not support PnP devices it still needs an empty PnP ID table, like:

```
static struct isa_pnp_id xxx_pnp_ids[] = {
    { 0,        NULL }, /* end of table */
};
```

## 10.3. `device_t` Pointer

`device_t` is the pointer type for the device structure. Here we consider only the methods interesting from the device driver writer's standpoint. The methods to manipulate values in the device structure are:

- `device_t device_get_parent(dev)` Get the parent bus of a device.

- `driver_t device_get_driver(dev)` Get pointer to its driver structure.
- `char *device_get_name(dev)` Get the driver name, such as "xxx" for our example.
- `int device_get_unit(dev)` Get the unit number (units are numbered from 0 for the devices associated with each driver).
- `char *device_get_nameunit(dev)` Get the device name including the unit number, such as "xxx0", "xxx1" and so on.
- `char *device_get_desc(dev)` Get the device description. Normally it describes the exact model of device in human-readable form.
- `device_set_desc(dev, desc)` Set the description. This makes the device description point to the string desc which may not be deallocated or changed after that.
- `device_set_desc_copy(dev, desc)` Set the description. The description is copied into an internal dynamically allocated buffer, so the string desc may be changed afterwards without adverse effects.
- `void *device_get_softc(dev)` Get pointer to the device descriptor (struct `xxx_softc` ) associated with this device.
- `u_int32_t device_get_flags(dev)` Get the flags specified for the device in the configuration file.

A convenience function `device_printf(dev, fmt, ...)` may be used to print the messages from the device driver. It automatically prepends the unitname and colon to the message.

The device_t methods are implemented in the file `kern/bus_subr.c`.

## 10.4. Configuration File and the Order of Identifying and Probing During Auto-Configuration

The ISA devices are described in the kernel configuration file like:

```
device xxx0 at isa? port 0x300 irq 10 drq 5
       iomem 0xd0000 flags 0x1 sensitive
```

The values of port, IRQ and so on are converted to the resource values associated with the device. They are optional, depending on the device's needs and abilities for auto-configuration. For example, some devices do not need DRQ at all and some allow the driver to read the IRQ setting from the device configuration ports. If a machine has multiple ISA buses the exact bus may be specified in the configuration line, like `isa0` or `isa1`, otherwise the device would be searched for on all the ISA buses.

`sensitive` is a resource requesting that this device must be probed before all non-sensitive devices. It is supported but does not seem to be used in any current driver.

For legacy ISA devices in many cases the drivers are still able to detect the configuration parameters. But each device to be configured in the system must have a config line. If two devices of some type are installed in the system but there is only one configuration line for the corresponding driver, ie:

```
device xxx0 at isa?
```

then only one device will be configured.

But for the devices supporting automatic identification by the means of Plug-n-Play or some proprietary protocol one configuration line is enough to configure all the devices in the system, like the one above or just simply:

```
device xxx at isa?
```

If a driver supports both auto-identified and legacy devices and both kinds are installed at once in one machine then it is enough to describe in the config file the legacy devices only. The auto-identified devices will be added automatically.

When an ISA bus is auto-configured the events happen as follows:

All the drivers' identify routines (including the PnP identify routine which identifies all the PnP devices) are called in random order. As they identify the devices they add them to the list on the ISA bus. Normally the drivers' identify routines associate their drivers with the new devices. The PnP identify routine does not know about the other drivers yet so it does not associate any with the new devices it adds.

The PnP devices are put to sleep using the PnP protocol to prevent them from being probed as legacy devices.

The probe routines of non-PnP devices marked as `sensitive` are called. If probe for a device went successfully, the attach routine is called for it.

The probe and attach routines of all non-PNP devices are called likewise.

The PnP devices are brought back from the sleep state and assigned the resources they request: I/O and memory address ranges, IRQs and DRQs, all of them not conflicting with the attached legacy devices.

Then for each PnP device the probe routines of all the present ISA drivers are called. The first one that claims the device gets attached. It is possible that multiple drivers would claim the device with different priority; in this case, the highest-priority driver wins. The probe routines must call `ISA_PNP_PROBE()` to compare the actual PnP ID with the list of the IDs supported by the driver and if the ID is not in the table return failure. That means that absolutely every driver, even the ones not supporting any PnP devices must call `ISA_PNP_PROBE()`, at least with an empty PnP ID table to return failure on unknown PnP devices.

The probe routine returns a positive value (the error code) on error, zero or negative value on success.

The negative return values are used when a PnP device supports multiple interfaces. For example, an older compatibility interface and a newer advanced interface which are supported by different drivers. Then both drivers would detect the device. The driver which returns a higher value in the probe routine takes precedence (in other words, the driver returning 0 has highest precedence, returning -1 is next, returning -2 is after it and so on). In result the devices which support only the old interface will be handled by the old driver (which should return -1 from the probe routine) while the devices supporting the new interface as well will be handled by the new driver (which should return 0 from the probe routine). If multiple drivers return the same value then the one called first wins. So if a driver returns value 0 it may be sure that it won the priority arbitration.

The device-specific identify routines can also assign not a driver but a class of drivers to the device. Then all the drivers in the class are probed for this device, like the case with PnP. This feature is not implemented in any existing driver and is not considered further in this document.

Because the PnP devices are disabled when probing the legacy devices they will not be attached twice (once as legacy and once as PnP). But in case of device-dependent identify routines it is the responsibility of the driver to make sure that the same device will not be attached by the driver twice: once as legacy user-configured and once as auto-identified.

Another practical consequence for the auto-identified devices (both PnP and device-specific) is that the flags can not be passed to them from the kernel configuration file. So they must either not use the flags at all or use the flags from the device unit 0 for all the auto-identified devices or use the sysctl interface instead of flags.

Other unusual configurations may be accommodated by accessing the configuration resources directly with functions of families `resource_query_*()` and `resource_*_value()`. Their implementations are located in `kern/subr_bus.c`. The old IDE disk driver `i386/isa/wd.c` contains examples of such use. But the standard means of configuration must always be preferred. Leave parsing the configuration resources to the bus configuration code.

## 10.5. Resources

The information that a user enters into the kernel configuration file is processed and passed to the kernel as configuration resources. This information is parsed by the bus configuration code and transformed into a value of structure device_t and the bus resources associated with it. The drivers may access the configuration resources directly using functions `resource_*` for more complex cases of configuration. However, generally this is neither needed nor recommended, so this issue is not discussed further here.

The bus resources are associated with each device. They are identified by type and number within the type. For the ISA bus the following types are defined:

- *SYS_RES_IRQ* - interrupt number
- *SYS_RES_DRQ* - ISA DMA channel number
- *SYS_RES_MEMORY* - range of device memory mapped into the system memory space
- *SYS_RES_IOPORT* - range of device I/O registers

The enumeration within types starts from 0, so if a device has two memory regions it would have resources of type `SYS_RES_MEMORY` numbered 0 and 1. The resource type has nothing to do with the C language type, all the resource values have the C language type `unsigned long` and must be cast as necessary. The resource numbers do not have to be contiguous, although for ISA they normally would be. The permitted resource numbers for ISA devices are:

```
IRQ: 0-1
DRQ: 0-1
MEMORY: 0-3
IOPORT: 0-7
```

All the resources are represented as ranges, with a start value and count. For IRQ and DRQ resources the count would normally be equal to 1. The values for memory refer to the physical addresses.

Three types of activities can be performed on resources:

- set/get
- allocate/release
- activate/deactivate

Setting sets the range used by the resource. Allocation reserves the requested range that no other driver would be able to reserve it (and checking that no other driver reserved this range already). Activation makes the resource accessible to the driver by doing whatever is necessary for that (for example, for memory it would be mapping into the kernel virtual address space).

The functions to manipulate resources are:

- `int bus_set_resource(device_t dev, int type, int rid, u_long start, u_long count)`

  Set a range for a resource. Returns 0 if successful, error code otherwise. Normally, this function will return an error only if one of `type`, `rid`, `start` or `count` has a value that falls out of the permitted range.

  - dev - driver's device
  - type - type of resource, SYS_RES_*
  - rid - resource number (ID) within type

  - start, count - resource range

- `int bus_get_resource(device_t dev, int type, int rid, u_long *startp, u_long *countp)`

  Get the range of resource. Returns 0 if successful, error code if the resource is not defined yet.

- `u_long bus_get_resource_start(device_t dev, int type, int rid) u_long bus_get_resource_count (device_t dev, int type, int rid)`

  Convenience functions to get only the start or count. Return 0 in case of error, so if the resource start has 0 among the legitimate values it would be impossible to tell if the value is 0 or an error occurred. Luckily, no ISA resources for add-on drivers may have a start value equal to 0.

- `void bus_delete_resource(device_t dev, int type, int rid)`

  Delete a resource, make it undefined.

- `struct resource * bus_alloc_resource(device_t dev, int type, int *rid, u_long start, u_long end, u_long count, u_int flags)`

  Allocate a resource as a range of count values not allocated by anyone else, somewhere between start and end. Alas, alignment is not supported. If the resource was not set yet it is automatically created. The special values of start 0 and end ~0 (all ones) means that the fixed values previously set by `bus_set_resource()` must be used instead: start and count as themselves and end=(start+count), in this case if the resource was not defined before then an error is returned. Although rid is passed by reference it is not set anywhere by the resource allocation code of the ISA bus. (The other buses may use a different approach and modify it).

Flags are a bitmap, the flags interesting for the caller are:

- *RF_ACTIVE* - causes the resource to be automatically activated after allocation.
- *RF_SHAREABLE* - resource may be shared at the same time by multiple drivers.
- *RF_TIMESHARE* - resource may be time-shared by multiple drivers, i.e., allocated at the same time by many but activated only by one at any given moment of time.
- Returns 0 on error. The allocated values may be obtained from the returned handle using methods `rhand_*()` .
- `int bus_release_resource(device_t dev, int type, int rid, struct resource *r)`
- Release the resource, r is the handle returned by `bus_alloc_resource()`. Returns 0 on success, error code otherwise.
- `int bus_activate_resource(device_t dev, int type, int rid, struct resource *r)  int bus_deactivate_resource(device_t dev, int type, int rid, struct resource *r)`
- Activate or deactivate resource. Return 0 on success, error code otherwise. If the resource is time-shared and currently activated by another driver then `EBUSY` is returned.
- `int bus_setup_intr(device_t dev, struct resource *r, int flags, driver_intr_t *handler, void *arg, void **cookiep) int bus_teardown_intr(device_t dev, struct resource *r, void *cookie)`
- Associate or de-associate the interrupt handler with a device. Return 0 on success, error code otherwise.
- r - the activated resource handler describing the IRQ

  flags - the interrupt priority level, one of:

  - `INTR_TYPE_TTY` - terminals and other likewise character-type devices. To mask them use `spltty()`.

- `(INTR_TYPE_TTY | INTR_TYPE_FAST)` - terminal type devices with small input buffer, critical to the data loss on input (such as the old-fashioned serial ports). To mask them use `spltty()`.
- `INTR_TYPE_BIO` - block-type devices, except those on the CAM controllers. To mask them use `splbio()` .
- `INTR_TYPE_CAM` - CAM (Common Access Method) bus controllers. To mask them use `splcam()` .
- `INTR_TYPE_NET` - network interface controllers. To mask them use `splimp()` .
- `INTR_TYPE_MISC` - miscellaneous devices. There is no other way to mask them than by `splhigh()` which masks all interrupts.

When an interrupt handler executes all the other interrupts matching its priority level will be masked. The only exception is the MISC level for which no other interrupts are masked and which is not masked by any other interrupt.

- *handler* - pointer to the handler function, the type driver_intr_t is defined as `void driver_intr_t(void *)`
- *arg* - the argument passed to the handler to identify this particular device. It is cast from void* to any real type by the handler. The old convention for the ISA interrupt handlers was to use the unit number as argument, the new (recommended) convention is using a pointer to the device softc structure.
- *cookie[p]* - the value received from `setup()` is used to identify the handler when passed to `teardown()`

A number of methods are defined to operate on the resource handlers (struct resource *). Those of interest to the device driver writers are:

- `u_long rman_get_start(r) u_long rman_get_end(r)` Get the start and end of allocated resource range.
- `void *rman_get_virtual(r)` Get the virtual address of activated memory resource.

## 10.6. Bus Memory Mapping

In many cases data is exchanged between the driver and the device through the memory. Two variants are possible:

(a) memory is located on the device card

(b) memory is the main memory of the computer

In case (a) the driver always copies the data back and forth between the on-card memory and the main memory as necessary. To map the on-card memory into the kernel virtual address space the physical address and length of the on-card memory must be defined as a `SYS_RES_MEMORY` resource. That resource can then be allocated and activated, and its virtual address obtained using `rman_get_virtual()`. The older drivers used the function `pmap_mapdev()` for this purpose, which should not be used directly any more. Now it is one of the internal steps of resource activation.

Most of the ISA cards will have their memory configured for physical location somewhere in range 640KB-1MB. Some of the ISA cards require larger memory ranges which should be placed somewhere under 16MB (because of the 24-bit address limitation on the ISA bus). In that case if the machine has more memory than the start address of the device memory (in other words, they overlap) a memory hole must be configured at the address range used by devices. Many BIOSes allow configuration of a memory hole of 1MB starting at 14MB or 15MB. FreeBSD can handle the memory holes properly if the BIOS reports them properly (this feature may be broken on old BIOSes).

In case (b) just the address of the data is sent to the device, and the device uses DMA to actually access the data in the main memory. Two limitations are present: First, ISA cards can only access memory below 16MB. Second, the contiguous pages in virtual address space may not be contiguous in physical address space, so the device may have to do scatter/gather operations. The bus subsystem provides ready solutions for some of these problems, the rest has to be done by the drivers themselves.

Two structures are used for DMA memory allocation, `bus_dma_tag_t` and `bus_dmamap_t`. Tag describes the properties required for the DMA memory. Map represents a memory block allocated according to these properties. Multiple maps may be associated with the same tag.

Tags are organized into a tree-like hierarchy with inheritance of the properties. A child tag inherits all the requirements of its parent tag, and may make them more strict but never more loose.

Normally one top-level tag (with no parent) is created for each device unit. If multiple memory areas with different requirements are needed for each device then a tag for each of them may be created as a child of the parent tag.

The tags can be used to create a map in two ways.

First, a chunk of contiguous memory conformant with the tag requirements may be allocated (and later may be freed). This is normally used to allocate relatively long-living areas of memory for communication with the device. Loading of such memory into a map is trivial: it is always considered as one chunk in the appropriate physical memory range.

Second, an arbitrary area of virtual memory may be loaded into a map. Each page of this memory will be checked for conformance to the map requirement. If it conforms then it is left at its original location. If it is not then a fresh conformant "bounce page" is allocated and used as intermediate storage. When writing the data from the non-conformant original pages they will be copied to their bounce pages first and then transferred from the bounce pages to the device. When reading the data would go from the device to the bounce pages and then copied to their non-conformant original pages. The process of copying between the original and bounce pages is called synchronization. This is normally used on a per-transfer basis: buffer for each transfer would be loaded, transfer done and buffer unloaded.

The functions working on the DMA memory are:

- `int bus_dma_tag_create(bus_dma_tag_t parent, bus_size_t alignment, bus_size_t boundary, bus_addr_t lowaddr, bus_addr_t highaddr, bus_dma_filter_t *filter, void *filterarg, bus_size_t maxsize, int nsegments, bus_size_t maxsegsz, int flags, bus_dma_tag_t *dmat)`

  Create a new tag. Returns 0 on success, the error code otherwise.

  - *parent* - parent tag, or NULL to create a top-level tag.
  - *alignment* - required physical alignment of the memory area to be allocated for this tag. Use value 1 for "no specific alignment". Applies only to the future `bus_dmamem_alloc()` but not `bus_dmamap_create()` calls.
  - *boundary* - physical address boundary that must not be crossed when allocating the memory. Use value 0 for "no boundary". Applies only to the future `bus_dmamem_alloc()` but not `bus_dmamap_create()` calls. Must be power of 2. If the memory is planned to be used in non-cascaded DMA mode (i.e., the DMA addresses will be supplied not by the device itself but by the ISA DMA controller) then the boundary must be no larger than 64KB (64*1024) due to the limitations of the DMA hardware.
  - *lowaddr, highaddr* - the names are slightly misleading; these values are used to limit the permitted range of physical addresses used to allocate the memory. The exact meaning varies depending on the planned future use:

    - For `bus_dmamem_alloc()` all the addresses from 0 to lowaddr-1 are considered permitted, the higher ones are forbidden.
    - For `bus_dmamap_create()` all the addresses outside the inclusive range [lowaddr; highaddr] are considered accessible. The addresses of pages inside the range are passed to the filter function which decides if they are accessible. If no filter function is supplied then all the range is considered unaccessible.
    - For the ISA devices the normal values (with no filter function) are:

      lowaddr = BUS_SPACE_MAXADDR_24BIT

  highaddr = BUS_SPACE_MAXADDR

  - *filter, filterarg* - the filter function and its argument. If NULL is passed for filter then the whole range [lowaddr, highaddr] is considered unaccessible when doing `bus_dmamap_create()`. Otherwise the physical address of each attempted page in range [lowaddr; highaddr] is passed to the filter function which decides if it is accessible. The prototype of the filter function is: `int filterfunc(void *arg, bus_addr_t paddr)`. It must return 0 if the page is accessible, non-zero otherwise.
  - *maxsize* - the maximal size of memory (in bytes) that may be allocated through this tag. In case it is difficult to estimate or could be arbitrarily big, the value for ISA devices would be `BUS_SPACE_MAXSIZE_24BIT`.
  - *nsegments* - maximal number of scatter-gather segments supported by the device. If unrestricted then the value `BUS_SPACE_UNRESTRICTED` should be used. This value is recommended for the parent tags, the actual restrictions would then be specified for the descendant tags. Tags with nsegments equal to `BUS_SPACE_UNRESTRICTED` may not be used to actually load maps, they may be used only as parent tags. The practical limit for nsegments seems to be about 250-300, higher values will cause kernel stack overflow (the hardware can not normally support that many scatter-gather buffers anyway).
  - *maxsegsz* - maximal size of a scatter-gather segment supported by the device. The maximal value for ISA device would be `BUS_SPACE_MAXSIZE_24BIT`.
  - *flags* - a bitmap of flags. The only interesting flags are:
    - *BUS_DMA_ALLOCNOW* - requests to allocate all the potentially needed bounce pages when creating the tag.
    - *BUS_DMA_ISA* - mysterious flag used only on Alpha machines. It is not defined for the i386 machines. Probably it should be used by all the ISA drivers for Alpha machines but it looks like there are no such drivers yet.
  - *dmat* - pointer to the storage for the new tag to be returned.

- `int bus_dma_tag_destroy(bus_dma_tag_t dmat)`

  Destroy a tag. Returns 0 on success, the error code otherwise.

  dmat - the tag to be destroyed.

- `int bus_dmamem_alloc(bus_dma_tag_t dmat, void** vaddr, int flags, bus_dmamap_t *mapp)`

  Allocate an area of contiguous memory described by the tag. The size of memory to be allocated is tag's maxsize. Returns 0 on success, the error code otherwise. The result still has to be loaded by `bus_dmamap_load()` before being used to get the physical address of the memory.

  - *dmat* - the tag
  - *vaddr* - pointer to the storage for the kernel virtual address of the allocated area to be returned.
  - flags - a bitmap of flags. The only interesting flag is:
    - *BUS_DMA_NOWAIT* - if the memory is not immediately available return the error. If this flag is not set then the routine is allowed to sleep until the memory becomes available.
  - *mapp* - pointer to the storage for the new map to be returned.

- `void bus_dmamem_free(bus_dma_tag_t dmat, void *vaddr, bus_dmamap_t map)`

  Free the memory allocated by `bus_dmamem_alloc()`. At present, freeing of the memory allocated with ISA restrictions is not implemented. Because of this the recommended model of use is to keep and re-use the allocated areas for as long as possible. Do not lightly free some area and then shortly allocate it again. That does not mean that `bus_dmamem_free()` should not be used at all: hopefully it will be properly implemented soon.

  - *dmat* - the tag
  - *vaddr* - the kernel virtual address of the memory
  - *map* - the map of the memory (as returned from `bus_dmamem_alloc()`)

- `int bus_dmamap_create(bus_dma_tag_t dmat, int flags, bus_dmamap_t *mapp)`

  Create a map for the tag, to be used in `bus_dmamap_load()` later. Returns 0 on success, the error code otherwise.

  - *dmat* - the tag
  - *flags* - theoretically, a bit map of flags. But no flags are defined yet, so at present it will be always 0.
  - *mapp* - pointer to the storage for the new map to be returned

- `int bus_dmamap_destroy(bus_dma_tag_t dmat, bus_dmamap_t map)`

  Destroy a map. Returns 0 on success, the error code otherwise.

  - dmat - the tag to which the map is associated
  - map - the map to be destroyed

- `int bus_dmamap_load(bus_dma_tag_t dmat, bus_dmamap_t map, void *buf, bus_size_t buflen, bus_dmamap_callback_t *callback, void *callback_arg, int flags)`

  Load a buffer into the map (the map must be previously created by `bus_dmamap_create()` or `bus_dmamem_alloc()`). All the pages of the buffer are checked for conformance to the tag requirements and for those not conformant the bounce pages are allocated. An array of physical segment descriptors is built and passed to the callback routine. This callback routine is then expected to handle it in some way. The number of bounce buffers in the system is limited, so if the bounce buffers are needed but not immediately available the request will be queued and the callback will be called when the bounce buffers will become available. Returns 0 if the callback was executed immediately or EINPROGRESS if the request was queued for future execution. In the latter case the synchronization with queued callback routine is the responsibility of the driver.

  - *dmat* - the tag
  - *map* - the map
  - *buf* - kernel virtual address of the buffer
  - *buflen* - length of the buffer
  - *callback*, `callback_arg` - the callback function and its argument

  The prototype of callback function is:

  ```
  void callback(void *arg, bus_dma_segment_t *seg, int nseg, int error)
  ```

  - *arg* - the same as callback_arg passed to `bus_dmamap_load()`
  - *seg* - array of the segment descriptors
  - *nseg* - number of descriptors in array
  - *error* - indication of the segment number overflow: if it is set to EFBIG then the buffer did not fit into the maximal number of segments permitted by the tag. In this case only the permitted number of descriptors will be in the array. Handling of this situation is up to the driver: depending on the desired semantics it can either consider this an error or split the buffer in two and handle the second part separately

Each entry in the segments array contains the fields:

  - *ds_addr* - physical bus address of the segment
  - *ds_len* - length of the segment

- `void bus_dmamap_unload(bus_dma_tag_t dmat, bus_dmamap_t map)`

  unload the map.

  - *dmat* - tag
  - *map* - loaded map

- `void bus_dmamap_sync (bus_dma_tag_t dmat, bus_dmamap_t map, bus_dmasync_op_t op)`

  Synchronise a loaded buffer with its bounce pages before and after physical transfer to or from device. This is the function that does all the necessary copying of data between the original buffer and its mapped version. The buffers must be synchronized both before and after doing the transfer.

  - *dmat* - tag
  - *map* - loaded map
  - *op* - type of synchronization operation to perform:
  - `BUS_DMASYNC_PREREAD` - before reading from device into buffer
  - `BUS_DMASYNC_POSTREAD` - after reading from device into buffer
  - `BUS_DMASYNC_PREWRITE` - before writing the buffer to device
  - `BUS_DMASYNC_POSTWRITE` - after writing the buffer to device

As of now PREREAD and POSTWRITE are null operations but that may change in the future, so they must not be ignored in the driver. Synchronization is not needed for the memory obtained from `bus_dmamem_alloc()`.

Before calling the callback function from `bus_dmamap_load()` the segment array is stored in the stack. And it gets pre-allocated for the maximal number of segments allowed by the tag. Because of this the practical limit for the number of segments on i386 architecture is about 250-300 (the kernel stack is 4KB minus the size of the user structure, size of a segment array entry is 8 bytes, and some space must be left). Because the array is allocated based on the maximal number this value must not be set higher than really needed. Fortunately, for most of hardware the maximal supported number of segments is much lower. But if the driver wants to handle buffers with a very large number of scatter-gather segments it should do that in portions: load part of the buffer, transfer it to the device, load next part of the buffer, and so on.

Another practical consequence is that the number of segments may limit the size of the buffer. If all the pages in the buffer happen to be physically non-contiguous then the maximal supported buffer size for that fragmented case would be (nsegments * page_size). For example, if a maximal number of 10 segments is supported then on i386 maximal guaranteed supported buffer size would be 40K. If a higher size is desired then special tricks should be used in the driver.

If the hardware does not support scatter-gather at all or the driver wants to support some buffer size even if it is heavily fragmented then the solution is to allocate a contiguous buffer in the driver and use it as intermediate storage if the original buffer does not fit.

Below are the typical call sequences when using a map depend on the use of the map. The characters -> are used to show the flow of time.

For a buffer which stays practically fixed during all the time between attachment and detachment of a device:

bus_dmamem_alloc -> bus_dmamap_load -> ...use buffer... -> -> bus_dmamap_unload -> bus_dmamem_free

For a buffer that changes frequently and is passed from outside the driver:

```
bus_dmamap_create ->
-> bus_dmamap_load -> bus_dmamap_sync(PRE...) -> do transfer ->
-> bus_dmamap_sync(POST...) -> bus_dmamap_unload ->
...
-> bus_dmamap_load -> bus_dmamap_sync(PRE...) -> do transfer ->
-> bus_dmamap_sync(POST...) -> bus_dmamap_unload ->
-> bus_dmamap_destroy
```

When loading a map created by `bus_dmamem_alloc()` the passed address and size of the buffer must be the same as used in `bus_dmamem_alloc()`. In this case it is guaranteed that the whole buffer will be mapped as one segment (so the callback may be based on this assumption) and the request will be executed immediately (EINPROGRESS will never be returned). All the callback needs to do in this case is to save the physical address.

A typical example would be:

```
  static void
alloc_callback(void *arg, bus_dma_segment_t *seg, int nseg, int error)
{
  *(bus_addr_t *)arg = seg[0].ds_addr;
}

  ...
  int error;
  struct somedata {
    ....
  };
  struct somedata *vsomedata; /* virtual address */
  bus_addr_t psomedata; /* physical bus-relative address */
  bus_dma_tag_t tag_somedata;
  bus_dmamap_t map_somedata;
  ...

  error=bus_dma_tag_create(parent_tag, alignment,
   boundary, lowaddr, highaddr, /*filter*/ NULL, /*filterarg*/ NULL,
   /*maxsize*/ sizeof(struct somedata), /*nsegments*/ 1,
   /*maxsegsz*/ sizeof(struct somedata), /*flags*/ 0,
   &tag_somedata);
  if(error)
  return error;

  error = bus_dmamem_alloc(tag_somedata, &vsomedata, /* flags*/ 0,
     &map_somedata);
  if(error)
     return error;

  bus_dmamap_load(tag_somedata, map_somedata, (void *)vsomedata,
     sizeof (struct somedata), alloc_callback,
     (void *) &psomedata, /*flags*/0);
```

Looks a bit long and complicated but that is the way to do it. The practical consequence is: if multiple memory areas are allocated always together it would be a really good idea to combine them all into one structure and allocate as one (if the alignment and boundary limitations permit).

When loading an arbitrary buffer into the map created by `bus_dmamap_create()` special measures must be taken to synchronize with the callback in case it would be delayed. The code would look like:

```
  {
   int s;
   int error;

   s = splsoftvm();
```

```
        error = bus_dmamap_load(
            dmat,
            dmamap,
            buffer_ptr,
            buffer_len,
            callback,
            /*callback_arg*/ buffer_descriptor,
            /*flags*/0);
        if (error == EINPROGRESS) {
            /*
             * Do whatever is needed to ensure synchronization
             * with callback. Callback is guaranteed not to be started
             * until we do splx() or tsleep().
             */
           }
        splx(s);
    }
```

Two possible approaches for the processing of requests are:

1. If requests are completed by marking them explicitly as done (such as the CAM requests) then it would be simpler to put all the further processing into the callback driver which would mark the request when it is done. Then not much extra synchronization is needed. For the flow control reasons it may be a good idea to freeze the request queue until this request gets completed.

2. If requests are completed when the function returns (such as classic read or write requests on character devices) then a synchronization flag should be set in the buffer descriptor and `tsleep()` called. Later when the callback gets called it will do its processing and check this synchronization flag. If it is set then the callback should issue a wakeup. In this approach the callback function could either do all the needed processing (just like the previous case) or simply save the segments array in the buffer descriptor. Then after callback completes the calling function could use this saved segments array and do all the processing.

## 10.7. DMA

The Direct Memory Access (DMA) is implemented in the ISA bus through the DMA controller (actually, two of them but that is an irrelevant detail). To make the early ISA devices simple and cheap the logic of the bus control and address generation was concentrated in the DMA controller. Fortunately, FreeBSD provides a set of functions that mostly hide the annoying details of the DMA controller from the device drivers.

The simplest case is for the fairly intelligent devices. Like the bus master devices on PCI they can generate the bus cycles and memory addresses all by themselves. The only thing they really need from the DMA controller is bus arbitration. So for this purpose they pretend to be cascaded slave DMA controllers. And the only thing needed from the system DMA controller is to enable the cascaded mode on a DMA channel by calling the following function when attaching the driver:

```
void isa_dmacascade(int channel_number)
```

All the further activity is done by programming the device. When detaching the driver no DMA-related functions need to be called.

For the simpler devices things get more complicated. The functions used are:

- `int isa_dma_acquire(int chanel_number)`

  Reserve a DMA channel. Returns 0 on success or EBUSY if the channel was already reserved by this or a different driver. Most of the ISA devices are not able to share DMA channels anyway, so normally this function is called when attaching a device. This reservation was made redundant by the modern interface of bus resources but still must be used in addition to the latter. If not used then later, other DMA routines will panic.

- `int isa_dma_release(int chanel_number)`

  Release a previously reserved DMA channel. No transfers must be in progress when the channel is released (in addition the device must not try to initiate transfer after the channel is released).

- `void isa_dmainit(int chan, u_int bouncebufsize)`

  Allocate a bounce buffer for use with the specified channel. The requested size of the buffer can not exceed 64KB. This bounce buffer will be automatically used later if a transfer buffer happens to be not physically contiguous or outside of the memory accessible by the ISA bus or crossing the 64KB boundary. If the transfers will be always done from buffers which conform to these conditions (such as those allocated by `bus_dmamem_alloc()` with proper limitations) then `isa_dmainit()` does not have to be called. But it is quite convenient to transfer arbitrary data using the DMA controller. The bounce buffer will automatically care of the scatter-gather issues.

  - *chan* - channel number
  - *bouncebufsize* - size of the bounce buffer in bytes

- `void isa_dmastart(int flags, caddr_t addr, u_int nbytes, int chan)`

  Prepare to start a DMA transfer. This function must be called to set up the DMA controller before actually starting transfer on the device. It checks that the buffer is contiguous and falls into the ISA memory range, if not then the bounce buffer is automatically used. If bounce buffer is required but not set up by `isa_dmainit()` or too small for the requested transfer size then the system will panic. In case of a write request with bounce buffer the data will be automatically copied to the bounce buffer.

- flags - a bitmask determining the type of operation to be done. The direction bits B_READ and B_WRITE are mutually exclusive.

  - B_READ - read from the ISA bus into memory
  - B_WRITE - write from the memory to the ISA bus
  - B_RAW - if set then the DMA controller will remember the buffer and after the end of transfer will automatically re-initialize itself to repeat transfer of the same buffer again (of course, the driver may change the data in the buffer before initiating another transfer in the device). If not set then the parameters will work only for one transfer, and `isa_dmastart()` will have to be called again before initiating the next transfer. Using B_RAW makes sense only if the bounce buffer is not used.

- addr - virtual address of the buffer

- nbytes - length of the buffer. Must be less or equal to 64KB. Length of 0 is not allowed: the DMA controller will understand it as 64KB while the kernel code will understand it as 0 and that would cause unpredictable effects. For channels number 4 and higher the length must be even because these channels transfer 2 bytes at a time. In case of an odd length the last byte will not be transferred.

- chan - channel number

- `void isa_dmadone(int flags, caddr_t addr, int nbytes, int chan)`

  Synchronize the memory after device reports that transfer is done. If that was a read operation with a bounce buffer then the data will be copied from the bounce buffer to the original buffer. Arguments are the same as for `isa_dmastart()`. Flag B_RAW is permitted but it does not affect `isa_dmadone()` in any way.

- `int isa_dmastatus(int channel_number)`

  Returns the number of bytes left in the current transfer to be transferred. In case the flag B_READ was set in `isa_dmastart()` the number returned will never be equal to zero. At the end of transfer it will be automatically reset back to the length of buffer. The normal use is to check the number of bytes left after the device signals that the transfer is completed. If the number of bytes is not 0 then something probably went wrong with that transfer.

- `int isa_dmastop(int channel_number)`

  Aborts the current transfer and returns the number of bytes left untransferred.

## 10.8. xxx_isa_probe

This function probes if a device is present. If the driver supports auto-detection of some part of device configuration (such as interrupt vector or memory address) this auto-detection must be done in this routine.

As for any other bus, if the device cannot be detected or is detected but failed the self-test or some other problem happened then it returns a positive value of error. The value ENXIO must be returned if the device is not present. Other error values may mean other conditions. Zero or negative values mean success. Most of the drivers return zero as success.

The negative return values are used when a PnP device supports multiple interfaces. For example, an older compatibility interface and a newer advanced interface which are supported by different drivers. Then both drivers would detect the device. The driver which returns a higher value in the probe routine takes precedence (in other words, the driver returning 0 has highest precedence, one returning -1 is next, one returning -2 is after it and so on). In result the devices which support only the old interface will be handled by the old driver (which should return -1 from the probe routine) while the devices supporting the new interface as well will be handled by the new driver (which should return 0 from the probe routine).

The device descriptor struct xxx_softc is allocated by the system before calling the probe routine. If the probe routine returns an error the descriptor will be automatically deallocated by the system. So if a probing error occurs the driver must make sure that all the resources it used during probe are deallocated and that nothing keeps the descriptor from being safely deallocated. If the probe completes successfully the descriptor will be preserved by the system and later passed to the routine `xxx_isa_attach()`. If a driver returns a negative value it can not be sure that it will have the highest priority and its attach routine will be called. So in this case it also must release all the resources before returning and if necessary allocate them again in the attach routine. When `xxx_isa_probe()` returns 0 releasing the resources before returning is also a good idea and a well-behaved driver should do so. But in cases where there is some problem with releasing the resources the driver is allowed to keep resources between returning 0 from the probe routine and execution of the attach routine.

A typical probe routine starts with getting the device descriptor and unit:

```
struct xxx_softc *sc = device_get_softc(dev);
 int unit = device_get_unit(dev);
 int pnperror;
 int error = 0;

 sc->dev = dev; /* link it back */
 sc->unit = unit;
```

Then check for the PnP devices. The check is carried out by a table containing the list of PnP IDs supported by this driver and human-readable descriptions of the device models corresponding to these IDs.

```
pnperror=ISA_PNP_PROBE(device_get_parent(dev), dev,
xxx_pnp_ids); if(pnperror == ENXIO) return ENXIO;
```

The logic of ISA_PNP_PROBE is the following: If this card (device unit) was not detected as PnP then ENOENT will be returned. If it was detected as PnP but its detected ID does not match any of the IDs in the table then ENXIO is returned. Finally, if it has PnP support and it matches on of the IDs in the table, 0 is returned and the appropriate description from the table is set by `device_set_desc()`.

If a driver supports only PnP devices then the condition would look like:

```
 if(pnperror != 0)
```

```
        return pnperror;
```

No special treatment is required for the drivers which do not support PnP because they pass an empty PnP ID table and will always get ENXIO if called on a PnP card.

The probe routine normally needs at least some minimal set of resources, such as I/O port number to find the card and probe it. Depending on the hardware the driver may be able to discover the other necessary resources automatically. The PnP devices have all the resources pre-set by the PnP subsystem, so the driver does not need to discover them by itself.

Typically the minimal information required to get access to the device is the I/O port number. Then some devices allow to get the rest of information from the device configuration registers (though not all devices do that). So first we try to get the port start value:

```
sc->port0 = bus_get_resource_start(dev,
       SYS_RES_IOPORT, 0 /*rid*/); if(sc->port0 == 0) return ENXIO;
```

The base port address is saved in the structure softc for future use. If it will be used very often then calling the resource function each time would be prohibitively slow. If we do not get a port we just return an error. Some device drivers can instead be clever and try to probe all the possible ports, like this:

```
/* table of all possible base I/O port addresses for this device */
static struct xxx_allports {
    u_short port; /* port address */
    short used; /* flag: if this port is already used by some unit */
} xxx_allports = {
    { 0x300, 0 },
    { 0x320, 0 },
    { 0x340, 0 },
    { 0, 0 } /* end of table */
};

...
int port, i;
...

port =  bus_get_resource_start(dev, SYS_RES_IOPORT, 0 /*rid*/);
if(port !=0 ) {
    for(i=0; xxx_allports[i].port!=0; i++) {
        if(xxx_allports[i].used || xxx_allports[i].port != port)
            continue;

        /* found it */
        xxx_allports[i].used = 1;
        /* do probe on a known port */
        return xxx_really_probe(dev, port);
    }
    return ENXIO; /* port is unknown or already used */
}

/* we get here only if we need to guess the port */
for(i=0; xxx_allports[i].port!=0; i++) {
    if(xxx_allports[i].used)
        continue;

    /* mark as used - even if we find nothing at this port
     * at least we won't probe it in future
     */
     xxx_allports[i].used = 1;

    error = xxx_really_probe(dev, xxx_allports[i].port);
    if(error == 0) /* found a device at that port */
```

```
                return 0;
        }
        /* probed all possible addresses, none worked */
        return ENXIO;
```

Of course, normally the driver's `identify()` routine should be used for such things. But there may be one valid reason why it may be better to be done in `probe()` : if this probe would drive some other sensitive device crazy. The probe routines are ordered with consideration of the `sensitive` flag: the sensitive devices get probed first and the rest of the devices later. But the `identify()` routines are called before any probes, so they show no respect to the sensitive devices and may upset them.

Now, after we got the starting port we need to set the port count (except for PnP devices) because the kernel does not have this information in the configuration file.

```
        if(pnperror /* only for non-PnP devices */
        && bus_set_resource(dev, SYS_RES_IOPORT, 0, sc->port0,
        XXX_PORT_COUNT)<0)
            return ENXIO;
```

Finally allocate and activate a piece of port address space (special values of start and end mean "use those we set by `bus_set_resource()`"):

```
        sc->port0_rid = 0;
        sc->port0_r = bus_alloc_resource(dev, SYS_RES_IOPORT,
        &sc->port0_rid,
            /*start*/ 0, /*end*/ ~0, /*count*/ 0, RF_ACTIVE);

        if(sc->port0_r == NULL)
            return ENXIO;
```

Now having access to the port-mapped registers we can poke the device in some way and check if it reacts like it is expected to. If it does not then there is probably some other device or no device at all at this address.

Normally drivers do not set up the interrupt handlers until the attach routine. Instead they do probes in the polling mode using the `DELAY()` function for timeout. The probe routine must never hang forever, all the waits for the device must be done with timeouts. If the device does not respond within the time it is probably broken or misconfigured and the driver must return error. When determining the timeout interval give the device some extra time to be on the safe side: although `DELAY()` is supposed to delay for the same amount of time on any machine it has some margin of error, depending on the exact CPU.

If the probe routine really wants to check that the interrupts really work it may configure and probe the interrupts too. But that is not recommended.

```
        /* implemented in some very device-specific way */
        if(error = xxx_probe_ports(sc))
            goto bad; /* will deallocate the resources before returning */
```

The function `xxx_probe_ports()` may also set the device description depending on the exact model of device it discovers. But if there is only one supported device model this can be as well done in a hardcoded way. Of course, for the PnP devices the PnP support sets the description from the table automatically.

```
        if(pnperror)
            device_set_desc(dev, "Our device model 1234");
```

Then the probe routine should either discover the ranges of all the resources by reading the device configuration registers or make sure that they were set explicitly by the user. We will consider it with an example of on-board

memory. The probe routine should be as non-intrusive as possible, so allocation and check of functionality of the rest of resources (besides the ports) would be better left to the attach routine.

The memory address may be specified in the kernel configuration file or on some devices it may be pre-configured in non-volatile configuration registers. If both sources are available and different, which one should be used? Probably if the user bothered to set the address explicitly in the kernel configuration file they know what they are doing and this one should take precedence. An example of implementation could be:

```
/* try to find out the config address first */
sc->mem0_p = bus_get_resource_start(dev, SYS_RES_MEMORY, 0 /*rid*/);
if(sc->mem0_p == 0) { /* nope, not specified by user */
    sc->mem0_p = xxx_read_mem0_from_device_config(sc);


if(sc->mem0_p == 0)
        /* can't get it from device config registers either */
        goto bad;
} else {
    if(xxx_set_mem0_address_on_device(sc) < 0)
        goto bad; /* device does not support that address */
}

/* just like the port, set the memory size,
 * for some devices the memory size would not be constant
 * but should be read from the device configuration registers instead
 * to accommodate different models of devices. Another option would
 * be to let the user set the memory size as "msize" configuration
 * resource which will be automatically handled by the ISA bus.
 */
 if(pnperror) { /* only for non-PnP devices */
    sc->mem0_size = bus_get_resource_count(dev, SYS_RES_MEMORY, 0 /*rid*/);
    if(sc->mem0_size == 0) /* not specified by user */
        sc->mem0_size = xxx_read_mem0_size_from_device_config(sc);

    if(sc->mem0_size == 0) {
        /* suppose this is a very old model of device without
         * auto-configuration features and the user gave no preference,
         * so assume the minimalistic case
         * (of course, the real value will vary with the driver)
         */
        sc->mem0_size = 8*1024;
    }

    if(xxx_set_mem0_size_on_device(sc) < 0)
        goto bad; /* device does not support that size */

    if(bus_set_resource(dev, SYS_RES_MEMORY, /*rid*/0,
            sc->mem0_p, sc->mem0_size)<0)
        goto bad;
} else {
    sc->mem0_size = bus_get_resource_count(dev, SYS_RES_MEMORY, 0 /*rid*/);
}
```

Resources for IRQ and DRQ are easy to check by analogy.

If all went well then release all the resources and return success.

```
xxx_free_resources(sc);
return 0;
```

Finally, handle the troublesome situations. All the resources should be deallocated before returning. We make use of the fact that before the structure softc is passed to us it gets zeroed out, so we can find out if some resource was allocated: then its descriptor is non-zero.

```
bad:
```

```
        xxx_free_resources(sc);
        if(error)
              return error;
        else /* exact error is unknown */
            return ENXIO;
```

That would be all for the probe routine. Freeing of resources is done from multiple places, so it is moved to a function which may look like:

```
static void
           xxx_free_resources(sc)
              struct xxx_softc *sc;
          {
              /* check every resource and free if not zero */

              /* interrupt handler */
              if(sc->intr_r) {
                  bus_teardown_intr(sc->dev, sc->intr_r, sc->intr_cookie);
                  bus_release_resource(sc->dev, SYS_RES_IRQ, sc->intr_rid,
                      sc->intr_r);
                  sc->intr_r = 0;
              }

              /* all kinds of memory maps we could have allocated */
              if(sc->data_p) {
                  bus_dmamap_unload(sc->data_tag, sc->data_map);
                  sc->data_p = 0;
              }
               if(sc->data) { /* sc->data_map may be legitimately equal to 0 */
                  /* the map will also be freed */
                  bus_dmamem_free(sc->data_tag, sc->data, sc->data_map);
                  sc->data = 0;
              }
              if(sc->data_tag) {
                  bus_dma_tag_destroy(sc->data_tag);
                  sc->data_tag = 0;
              }

              ... free other maps and tags if we have them ...

              if(sc->parent_tag) {
                  bus_dma_tag_destroy(sc->parent_tag);
                  sc->parent_tag = 0;
              }

              /* release all the bus resources */
              if(sc->mem0_r) {
                  bus_release_resource(sc->dev, SYS_RES_MEMORY, sc->mem0_rid,
                      sc->mem0_r);
                  sc->mem0_r = 0;
              }
              ...
              if(sc->port0_r) {
                  bus_release_resource(sc->dev, SYS_RES_IOPORT, sc->port0_rid,
                      sc->port0_r);
                  sc->port0_r = 0;
              }
          }
```

## 10.9. xxx_isa_attach

The attach routine actually connects the driver to the system if the probe routine returned success and the system had chosen to attach that driver. If the probe routine returned 0 then the attach routine may expect to receive the

device structure softc intact, as it was set by the probe routine. Also if the probe routine returns 0 it may expect that the attach routine for this device shall be called at some point in the future. If the probe routine returns a negative value then the driver may make none of these assumptions.

The attach routine returns 0 if it completed successfully or error code otherwise.

The attach routine starts just like the probe routine, with getting some frequently used data into more accessible variables.

```
struct xxx_softc *sc = device_get_softc(dev);
int unit = device_get_unit(dev);
int error = 0;
```

Then allocate and activate all the necessary resources. Because normally the port range will be released before returning from probe, it has to be allocated again. We expect that the probe routine had properly set all the resource ranges, as well as saved them in the structure softc. If the probe routine had left some resource allocated then it does not need to be allocated again (which would be considered an error).

```
sc->port0_rid = 0;
sc->port0_r = bus_alloc_resource(dev, SYS_RES_IOPORT,  &sc->port0_rid,
    /*start*/ 0, /*end*/ ~0, /*count*/ 0, RF_ACTIVE);

if(sc->port0_r == NULL)
     return ENXIO;

/* on-board memory */
sc->mem0_rid = 0;
sc->mem0_r = bus_alloc_resource(dev, SYS_RES_MEMORY,  &sc->mem0_rid,
    /*start*/ 0, /*end*/ ~0, /*count*/ 0, RF_ACTIVE);

if(sc->mem0_r == NULL)
      goto bad;

/* get its virtual address */
sc->mem0_v = rman_get_virtual(sc->mem0_r);
```

The DMA request channel (DRQ) is allocated likewise. To initialize it use functions of the isa_dma*() family. For example:

```
isa_dmacascade(sc->drq0);
```

The interrupt request line (IRQ) is a bit special. Besides allocation the driver's interrupt handler should be associated with it. Historically in the old ISA drivers the argument passed by the system to the interrupt handler was the device unit number. But in modern drivers the convention suggests passing the pointer to structure softc. The important reason is that when the structures softc are allocated dynamically then getting the unit number from softc is easy while getting softc from the unit number is difficult. Also this convention makes the drivers for different buses look more uniform and allows them to share the code: each bus gets its own probe, attach, detach and other bus-specific routines while the bulk of the driver code may be shared among them.

```
sc->intr_rid = 0;
sc->intr_r = bus_alloc_resource(dev, SYS_RES_MEMORY,  &sc->intr_rid,
      /*start*/ 0, /*end*/ ~0, /*count*/ 0, RF_ACTIVE);

if(sc->intr_r == NULL)
    goto bad;

/*
 * XXX_INTR_TYPE is supposed to be defined depending on the type of
 * the driver, for example as INTR_TYPE_CAM for a CAM driver
 */
error = bus_setup_intr(dev, sc->intr_r, XXX_INTR_TYPE,
    (driver_intr_t *) xxx_intr, (void *) sc, &sc->intr_cookie);
```

```
        if(error)
            goto bad;
```

If the device needs to make DMA to the main memory then this memory should be allocated like described before:

```
        error=bus_dma_tag_create(NULL, /*alignment*/ 4,
            /*boundary*/ 0, /*lowaddr*/ BUS_SPACE_MAXADDR_24BIT,
            /*highaddr*/ BUS_SPACE_MAXADDR, /*filter*/ NULL, /*filterarg*/ NULL,
            /*maxsize*/ BUS_SPACE_MAXSIZE_24BIT,
            /*nsegments*/ BUS_SPACE_UNRESTRICTED,
            /*maxsegsz*/ BUS_SPACE_MAXSIZE_24BIT, /*flags*/ 0,
            &sc->parent_tag);
        if(error)
            goto bad;

        /* many things get inherited from the parent tag
         * sc->data is supposed to point to the structure with the shared data,
         * for example for a ring buffer it could be:
         * struct {
         *   u_short rd_pos;
         *   u_short wr_pos;
         *   char    bf[XXX_RING_BUFFER_SIZE]
         * } *data;
         */
        error=bus_dma_tag_create(sc->parent_tag, 1,
            0, BUS_SPACE_MAXADDR, 0, /*filter*/ NULL, /*filterarg*/ NULL,
            /*maxsize*/ sizeof(* sc->data), /*nsegments*/ 1,
            /*maxsegsz*/ sizeof(* sc->data), /*flags*/ 0,
            &sc->data_tag);
        if(error)
            goto bad;

        error = bus_dmamem_alloc(sc->data_tag, &sc->data, /* flags*/ 0,
            &sc->data_map);
        if(error)
             goto bad;

        /* xxx_alloc_callback() just saves the physical address at
         * the pointer passed as its argument, in this case &sc->data_p.
         * See details in the section on bus memory mapping.
         * It can be implemented like:
         *
         * static void
         * xxx_alloc_callback(void *arg, bus_dma_segment_t *seg,
         *     int nseg, int error)
         * {
         *    *(bus_addr_t *)arg = seg[0].ds_addr;
         * }
         */
        bus_dmamap_load(sc->data_tag, sc->data_map, (void *)sc->data,
            sizeof (* sc->data), xxx_alloc_callback, (void *) &sc->data_p,
            /*flags*/0);
```

After all the necessary resources are allocated the device should be initialized. The initialization may include testing that all the expected features are functional.

```
        if(xxx_initialize(sc) < 0)
             goto bad;
```

The bus subsystem will automatically print on the console the device description set by probe. But if the driver wants to print some extra information about the device it may do so, for example:

```
      device_printf(dev, "has on-card FIFO buffer of %d bytes\n", sc->fifosize);
```

If the initialization routine experiences any problems then printing messages about them before returning error is also recommended.

The final step of the attach routine is attaching the device to its functional subsystem in the kernel. The exact way to do it depends on the type of the driver: a character device, a block device, a network device, a CAM SCSI bus device and so on.

If all went well then return success.

```
error = xxx_attach_subsystem(sc);
if(error)
    goto bad;

return 0;
```

Finally, handle the troublesome situations. All the resources should be deallocated before returning an error. We make use of the fact that before the structure softc is passed to us it gets zeroed out, so we can find out if some resource was allocated: then its descriptor is non-zero.

```
bad:

xxx_free_resources(sc);
if(error)
    return error;
else /* exact error is unknown */
    return ENXIO;
```

That would be all for the attach routine.

## 10.10. xxx_isa_detach

If this function is present in the driver and the driver is compiled as a loadable module then the driver gets the ability to be unloaded. This is an important feature if the hardware supports hot plug. But the ISA bus does not support hot plug, so this feature is not particularly important for the ISA devices. The ability to unload a driver may be useful when debugging it, but in many cases installation of the new version of the driver would be required only after the old version somehow wedges the system and a reboot will be needed anyway, so the efforts spent on writing the detach routine may not be worth it. Another argument that unloading would allow upgrading the drivers on a production machine seems to be mostly theoretical. Installing a new version of a driver is a dangerous operation which should never be performed on a production machine (and which is not permitted when the system is running in secure mode). Still, the detach routine may be provided for the sake of completeness.

The detach routine returns 0 if the driver was successfully detached or the error code otherwise.

The logic of detach is a mirror of the attach. The first thing to do is to detach the driver from its kernel subsystem. If the device is currently open then the driver has two choices: refuse to be detached or forcibly close and proceed with detach. The choice used depends on the ability of the particular kernel subsystem to do a forced close and on the preferences of the driver's author. Generally the forced close seems to be the preferred alternative.

```
struct xxx_softc *sc = device_get_softc(dev);
int error;

error = xxx_detach_subsystem(sc);
if(error)
    return error;
```

Next the driver may want to reset the hardware to some consistent state. That includes stopping any ongoing transfers, disabling the DMA channels and interrupts to avoid memory corruption by the device. For most of the drivers this is exactly what the shutdown routine does, so if it is included in the driver we can just call it.

```
xxx_isa_shutdown(dev);
```

And finally release all the resources and return success.

```
        xxx_free_resources(sc);
        return 0;
```

## 10.11. xxx_isa_shutdown

This routine is called when the system is about to be shut down. It is expected to bring the hardware to some consistent state. For most of the ISA devices no special action is required, so the function is not really necessary because the device will be re-initialized on reboot anyway. But some devices have to be shut down with a special procedure, to make sure that they will be properly detected after soft reboot (this is especially true for many devices with proprietary identification protocols). In any case disabling DMA and interrupts in the device registers and stopping any ongoing transfers is a good idea. The exact action depends on the hardware, so we do not consider it here in any detail.

## 10.12. xxx_intr

The interrupt handler is called when an interrupt is received which may be from this particular device. The ISA bus does not support interrupt sharing (except in some special cases) so in practice if the interrupt handler is called then the interrupt almost for sure came from its device. Still, the interrupt handler must poll the device registers and make sure that the interrupt was generated by its device. If not it should just return.

The old convention for the ISA drivers was getting the device unit number as an argument. This is obsolete, and the new drivers receive whatever argument was specified for them in the attach routine when calling `bus_setup_intr()`. By the new convention it should be the pointer to the structure softc. So the interrupt handler commonly starts as:

```
        static void
        xxx_intr(struct xxx_softc *sc)
        {
```

It runs at the interrupt priority level specified by the interrupt type parameter of `bus_setup_intr()`. That means that all the other interrupts of the same type as well as all the software interrupts are disabled.

To avoid races it is commonly written as a loop:

```
        while(xxx_interrupt_pending(sc)) {
            xxx_process_interrupt(sc);
            xxx_acknowledge_interrupt(sc);
        }
```

The interrupt handler has to acknowledge interrupt to the device only but not to the interrupt controller, the system takes care of the latter.

# Chapter 11. PCI Devices

This chapter will talk about the FreeBSD mechanisms for writing a device driver for a device on a PCI bus.

## 11.1. Probe and Attach

Information here about how the PCI bus code iterates through the unattached devices and see if a newly loaded kld will attach to any of them.

### 11.1.1. Sample Driver Source (`mypci.c`)

```
/*
 * Simple KLD to play with the PCI functions.
 *
 * Murray Stokely
 */

#include <sys/param.h>  /* defines used in kernel.h */
#include <sys/module.h>
#include <sys/systm.h>
#include <sys/errno.h>
#include <sys/kernel.h>  /* types used in module initialization */
#include <sys/conf.h>  /* cdevsw struct */
#include <sys/uio.h>  /* uio struct */
#include <sys/malloc.h>
#include <sys/bus.h>  /* structs, prototypes for pci bus stuff and DEVMETHOD macros! */

#include <machine/bus.h>
#include <sys/rman.h>
#include <machine/resource.h>

#include <dev/pci/pcivar.h> /* For pci_get macros! */
#include <dev/pci/pcireg.h>

/* The softc holds our per-instance data. */
struct mypci_softc {
 device_t my_dev;
 struct cdev *my_cdev;
};

/* Function prototypes */
static d_open_t  mypci_open;
static d_close_t mypci_close;
static d_read_t  mypci_read;
static d_write_t mypci_write;

/* Character device entry points */

static struct cdevsw mypci_cdevsw = {
 .d_version = D_VERSION,
 .d_open = mypci_open,
 .d_close = mypci_close,
 .d_read = mypci_read,
 .d_write = mypci_write,
 .d_name = "mypci",
};

/*
 * In the cdevsw routines, we find our softc by using the si_drv1 member
 * of struct cdev.  We set this variable to point to our softc in our
 * attach routine when we create the /dev entry.
 */
```

```
int
mypci_open(struct cdev *dev, int oflags, int devtype, struct thread *td)
{
 struct mypci_softc *sc;

 /* Look up our softc. */
 sc = dev->si_drv1;
 device_printf(sc->my_dev, "Opened successfully.\n");
 return (0);
}

int
mypci_close(struct cdev *dev, int fflag, int devtype, struct thread *td)
{
 struct mypci_softc *sc;

 /* Look up our softc. */
 sc = dev->si_drv1;
 device_printf(sc->my_dev, "Closed.\n");
 return (0);
}

int
mypci_read(struct cdev *dev, struct uio *uio, int ioflag)
{
 struct mypci_softc *sc;

 /* Look up our softc. */
 sc = dev->si_drv1;
 device_printf(sc->my_dev, "Asked to read %d bytes.\n", uio->uio_resid);
 return (0);
}

int
mypci_write(struct cdev *dev, struct uio *uio, int ioflag)
{
 struct mypci_softc *sc;

 /* Look up our softc. */
 sc = dev->si_drv1;
 device_printf(sc->my_dev, "Asked to write %d bytes.\n", uio->uio_resid);
 return (0);
}

/* PCI Support Functions */

/*
 * Compare the device ID of this device against the IDs that this driver
 * supports.  If there is a match, set the description and return success.
 */
static int
mypci_probe(device_t dev)
{

 device_printf(dev, "MyPCI Probe\nVendor ID : 0x%x\nDevice ID : 0x%x\n",
     pci_get_vendor(dev), pci_get_device(dev));

 if (pci_get_vendor(dev) == 0x11c1) {
  printf("We've got the Winmodem, probe successful!\n");
  device_set_desc(dev, "WinModem");
  return (BUS_PROBE_DEFAULT);
 }
 return (ENXIO);
}
```

```
/* Attach function is only called if the probe is successful. */

static int
mypci_attach(device_t dev)
{
 struct mypci_softc *sc;

 printf("MyPCI Attach for : deviceID : 0x%x\n", pci_get_devid(dev));

 /* Look up our softc and initialize its fields. */
 sc = device_get_softc(dev);
 sc->my_dev = dev;

 /*
  * Create a /dev entry for this device.  The kernel will assign us
  * a major number automatically.  We use the unit number of this
  * device as the minor number and name the character device
  * "mypci<unit>".
  */
 sc->my_cdev = make_dev(&mypci_cdevsw, device_get_unit(dev),
     UID_ROOT, GID_WHEEL, 0600, "mypci%u", device_get_unit(dev));
 sc->my_cdev->si_drv1 = sc;
 printf("Mypci device loaded.\n");
 return (0);
}

/* Detach device. */

static int
mypci_detach(device_t dev)
{
 struct mypci_softc *sc;

 /* Teardown the state in our softc created in our attach routine. */
 sc = device_get_softc(dev);
 destroy_dev(sc->my_cdev);
 printf("Mypci detach!\n");
 return (0);
}

/* Called during system shutdown after sync. */

static int
mypci_shutdown(device_t dev)
{

 printf("Mypci shutdown!\n");
 return (0);
}

/*
 * Device suspend routine.
 */
static int
mypci_suspend(device_t dev)
{

 printf("Mypci suspend!\n");
 return (0);
}

/*
 * Device resume routine.
 */
static int
mypci_resume(device_t dev)
```

```
{
 printf("Mypci resume!\n");
 return (0);
}

static device_method_t mypci_methods[] = {
 /* Device interface */
 DEVMETHOD(device_probe,  mypci_probe),
 DEVMETHOD(device_attach, mypci_attach),
 DEVMETHOD(device_detach, mypci_detach),
 DEVMETHOD(device_shutdown, mypci_shutdown),
 DEVMETHOD(device_suspend, mypci_suspend),
 DEVMETHOD(device_resume, mypci_resume),

 DEVMETHOD_END
};

static devclass_t mypci_devclass;

DEFINE_CLASS_0(mypci, mypci_driver, mypci_methods, sizeof(struct mypci_softc));
DRIVER_MODULE(mypci, pci, mypci_driver, mypci_devclass, 0, 0);
```

### 11.1.2. Makefile for Sample Driver

```
# Makefile for mypci driver

KMOD= mypci
SRCS= mypci.c
SRCS+= device_if.h bus_if.h pci_if.h

.include <bsd.kmod.mk>
```

If you place the above source file and `Makefile` into a directory, you may run `make` to compile the sample driver. Additionally, you may run `make load` to load the driver into the currently running kernel and `make unload` to unload the driver after it is loaded.

### 11.1.3. Additional Resources

- PCI Special Interest Group
- PCI System Architecture, Fourth Edition by Tom Shanley, et al.

## 11.2. Bus Resources

FreeBSD provides an object-oriented mechanism for requesting resources from a parent bus. Almost all devices will be a child member of some sort of bus (PCI, ISA, USB, SCSI, etc) and these devices need to acquire resources from their parent bus (such as memory segments, interrupt lines, or DMA channels).

### 11.2.1. Base Address Registers

To do anything particularly useful with a PCI device you will need to obtain the *Base Address Registers* (BARs) from the PCI Configuration space. The PCI-specific details of obtaining the BAR are abstracted in the `bus_alloc_resource()` function.

For example, a typical driver might have something similar to this in the `attach()` function:

```
    sc->bar0id = PCIR_BAR(0);
    sc->bar0res = bus_alloc_resource(dev, SYS_RES_MEMORY, &sc->bar0id,
      0, ~0, 1, RF_ACTIVE);
    if (sc->bar0res == NULL) {
```

```
        printf("Memory allocation of PCI base register 0 failed!\n");
        error = ENXIO;
        goto fail1;
    }

    sc->bar1id = PCIR_BAR(1);
    sc->bar1res = bus_alloc_resource(dev, SYS_RES_MEMORY, &sc->bar1id,
      0, ~0, 1, RF_ACTIVE);
    if (sc->bar1res == NULL) {
        printf("Memory allocation of PCI base register 1 failed!\n");
        error =  ENXIO;
        goto fail2;
    }
    sc->bar0_bt = rman_get_bustag(sc->bar0res);
    sc->bar0_bh = rman_get_bushandle(sc->bar0res);
    sc->bar1_bt = rman_get_bustag(sc->bar1res);
    sc->bar1_bh = rman_get_bushandle(sc->bar1res);
```

Handles for each base address register are kept in the `softc` structure so that they can be used to write to the device later.

These handles can then be used to read or write from the device registers with the `bus_space_*` functions. For example, a driver might contain a shorthand function to read from a board specific register like this:

```
uint16_t
board_read(struct ni_softc *sc, uint16_t address)
{
    return bus_space_read_2(sc->bar1_bt, sc->bar1_bh, address);
}
```

Similarly, one could write to the registers with:

```
void
board_write(struct ni_softc *sc, uint16_t address, uint16_t value)
{
    bus_space_write_2(sc->bar1_bt, sc->bar1_bh, address, value);
}
```

These functions exist in 8bit, 16bit, and 32bit versions and you should use `bus_space_{read|write}_{1|2|4}` accordingly.

Note

In FreeBSD 7.0 and later, you can use the `bus_*` functions instead of `bus_space_*` . The `bus_*` functions take a struct resource * pointer instead of a bus tag and handle. Thus, you could drop the bus tag and bus handle members from the `softc` and rewrite the `board_read()` function as:

```
uint16_t
board_read(struct ni_softc *sc, uint16_t address)
{
 return (bus_read(sc->bar1res, address));
}
```

### 11.2.2. Interrupts

Interrupts are allocated from the object-oriented bus code in a way similar to the memory resources. First an IRQ resource must be allocated from the parent bus, and then the interrupt handler must be set up to deal with this IRQ.

Again, a sample from a device `attach()` function says more than words.

```
/* Get the IRQ resource */

    sc->irqid = 0x0;
    sc->irqres = bus_alloc_resource(dev, SYS_RES_IRQ, &(sc->irqid),
      0, ~0, 1, RF_SHAREABLE | RF_ACTIVE);
    if (sc->irqres == NULL) {
 printf("IRQ allocation failed!\n");
 error = ENXIO;
 goto fail3;
    }

    /* Now we should set up the interrupt handler */

    error = bus_setup_intr(dev, sc->irqres, INTR_TYPE_MISC,
      my_handler, sc, &(sc->handler));
    if (error) {
 printf("Couldn't set up irq\n");
 goto fail4;
    }
```

Some care must be taken in the detach routine of the driver. You must quiesce the device's interrupt stream, and remove the interrupt handler. Once bus_teardown_intr() has returned, you know that your interrupt handler will no longer be called and that all threads that might have been executing this interrupt handler have returned. Since this function can sleep, you must not hold any mutexes when calling this function.

### 11.2.3. DMA

This section is obsolete, and present only for historical reasons. The proper methods for dealing with these issues is to use the bus_space_dma*() functions instead. This paragraph can be removed when this section is updated to reflect that usage. However, at the moment, the API is in a bit of flux, so once that settles down, it would be good to update this section to reflect that.

On the PC, peripherals that want to do bus-mastering DMA must deal with physical addresses. This is a problem since FreeBSD uses virtual memory and deals almost exclusively with virtual addresses. Fortunately, there is a function, vtophys() to help.

```
#include <vm/vm.h>
#include <vm/pmap.h>

#define vtophys(virtual_address) (...)
```

The solution is a bit different on the alpha however, and what we really want is a function called vtobus().

```
#if defined(__alpha__)
#define vtobus(va)      alpha_XXX_dmamap((vm_offset_t)va)
#else
#define vtobus(va)      vtophys(va)
#endif
```

### 11.2.4. Deallocating Resources

It is very important to deallocate all of the resources that were allocated during attach(). Care must be taken to deallocate the correct stuff even on a failure condition so that the system will remain usable while your driver dies.

# Chapter 12. Common Access Method SCSI Controllers

Written by Sergey Babkin.
Modifications for Handbook made by Murray Stokely.

## 12.1. Synopsis

This document assumes that the reader has a general understanding of device drivers in FreeBSD and of the SCSI protocol. Much of the information in this document was extracted from the drivers:

- ncr (`/sys/pci/ncr.c` ) by Wolfgang Stanglmeier and Stefan Esser
- sym (`/sys/dev/sym/sym_hipd.c` ) by Gerard Roudier
- aic7xxx (`/sys/dev/aic7xxx/aic7xxx.c` ) by Justin T. Gibbs

and from the CAM code itself (by Justin T. Gibbs, see `/sys/cam/*` ). When some solution looked the most logical and was essentially verbatim extracted from the code by Justin T. Gibbs, I marked it as "recommended".

The document is illustrated with examples in pseudo-code. Although sometimes the examples have many details and look like real code, it is still pseudo-code. It was written to demonstrate the concepts in an understandable way. For a real driver other approaches may be more modular and efficient. It also abstracts from the hardware details, as well as issues that would cloud the demonstrated concepts or that are supposed to be described in the other chapters of the developers handbook. Such details are commonly shown as calls to functions with descriptive names, comments or pseudo-statements. Fortunately real life full-size examples with all the details can be found in the real drivers.

## 12.2. General Architecture

CAM stands for Common Access Method. It is a generic way to address the I/O buses in a SCSI-like way. This allows a separation of the generic device drivers from the drivers controlling the I/O bus: for example the disk driver becomes able to control disks on both SCSI, IDE, and/or any other bus so the disk driver portion does not have to be rewritten (or copied and modified) for every new I/O bus. Thus the two most important active entities are:

- *Peripheral Modules* - a driver for peripheral devices (disk, tape, CD-ROM, etc.)
- *SCSI Interface Modules* (SIM) - a Host Bus Adapter drivers for connecting to an I/O bus such as SCSI or IDE.

A peripheral driver receives requests from the OS, converts them to a sequence of SCSI commands and passes these SCSI commands to a SCSI Interface Module. The SCSI Interface Module is responsible for passing these commands to the actual hardware (or if the actual hardware is not SCSI but, for example, IDE then also converting the SCSI commands to the native commands of the hardware).

Because we are interested in writing a SCSI adapter driver here, from this point on we will consider everything from the SIM standpoint.

A typical SIM driver needs to include the following CAM-related header files:

```
#include <cam/cam.h>
#include <cam/cam_ccb.h>
#include <cam/cam_sim.h>
#include <cam/cam_xpt_sim.h>
#include <cam/cam_debug.h>
```

```
#include <cam/scsi/scsi_all.h>
```

The first thing each SIM driver must do is register itself with the CAM subsystem. This is done during the driver's `xxx_attach()` function (here and further xxx_ is used to denote the unique driver name prefix). The `xxx_attach()` function itself is called by the system bus auto-configuration code which we do not describe here.

This is achieved in multiple steps: first it is necessary to allocate the queue of requests associated with this SIM:

```
    struct cam_devq *devq;

    if(( devq = cam_simq_alloc(SIZE) )==NULL) {
        error; /* some code to handle the error */
    }
```

Here `SIZE` is the size of the queue to be allocated, maximal number of requests it could contain. It is the number of requests that the SIM driver can handle in parallel on one SCSI card. Commonly it can be calculated as:

```
SIZE = NUMBER_OF_SUPPORTED_TARGETS * MAX_SIMULTANEOUS_COMMANDS_PER_TARGET
```

Next we create a descriptor of our SIM:

```
    struct cam_sim *sim;

    if(( sim = cam_sim_alloc(action_func, poll_func, driver_name,
            softc, unit, mtx, max_dev_transactions,
            max_tagged_dev_transactions, devq) )==NULL) {
        cam_simq_free(devq);
        error; /* some code to handle the error */
    }
```

Note that if we are not able to create a SIM descriptor we free the `devq` also because we can do nothing else with it and we want to conserve memory.

If a SCSI card has multiple SCSI buses on it then each bus requires its own `cam_sim` structure.

An interesting question is what to do if a SCSI card has more than one SCSI bus, do we need one `devq` structure per card or per SCSI bus? The answer given in the comments to the CAM code is: either way, as the driver's author prefers.

The arguments are:

- `action_func` - pointer to the driver's `xxx_action` function.

  `static void` **`xxx_action`** `(`*`struct cam_sim *sim, union ccb *ccb`*`);`

  *`struct cam_sim *sim, , union ccb *ccb ;`*

- `poll_func` - pointer to the driver's `xxx_poll()`

  `static void` **`xxx_poll`** `(`*`struct cam_sim *sim`*`);`

  *`struct cam_sim *sim ;`*

- driver_name - the name of the actual driver, such as “ncr” or “wds”.

- `softc` - pointer to the driver's internal descriptor for this SCSI card. This pointer will be used by the driver in future to get private data.

- unit - the controller unit number, for example for controller “mps0” this number will be 0

- mtx - Lock associated with this SIM. For SIMs that don't know about locking, pass in Giant. For SIMs that do, pass in the lock used to guard this SIM's data structures. This lock will be held when xxx_action and xxx_poll are called.

- max_dev_transactions - maximal number of simultaneous transactions per SCSI target in the non-tagged mode. This value will be almost universally equal to 1, with possible exceptions only for the non-SCSI cards. Also the drivers that hope to take advantage by preparing one transaction while another one is executed may set it to 2 but this does not seem to be worth the complexity.

- max_tagged_dev_transactions - the same thing, but in the tagged mode. Tags are the SCSI way to initiate multiple transactions on a device: each transaction is assigned a unique tag and the transaction is sent to the device. When the device completes some transaction it sends back the result together with the tag so that the SCSI adapter (and the driver) can tell which transaction was completed. This argument is also known as the maximal tag depth. It depends on the abilities of the SCSI adapter.

Finally we register the SCSI buses associated with our SCSI adapter:

```
if(xpt_bus_register(sim, softc, bus_number) != CAM_SUCCESS) {
    cam_sim_free(sim, /*free_devq*/ TRUE);
    error; /* some code to handle the error */
}
```

If there is one devq structure per SCSI bus (i.e., we consider a card with multiple buses as multiple cards with one bus each) then the bus number will always be 0, otherwise each bus on the SCSI card should be get a distinct number. Each bus needs its own separate structure cam_sim.

After that our controller is completely hooked to the CAM system. The value of devq can be discarded now: sim will be passed as an argument in all further calls from CAM and devq can be derived from it.

CAM provides the framework for such asynchronous events. Some events originate from the lower levels (the SIM drivers), some events originate from the peripheral drivers, some events originate from the CAM subsystem itself. Any driver can register callbacks for some types of the asynchronous events, so that it would be notified if these events occur.

A typical example of such an event is a device reset. Each transaction and event identifies the devices to which it applies by the means of "path". The target-specific events normally occur during a transaction with this device. So the path from that transaction may be re-used to report this event (this is safe because the event path is copied in the event reporting routine but not deallocated nor passed anywhere further). Also it is safe to allocate paths dynamically at any time including the interrupt routines, although that incurs certain overhead, and a possible problem with this approach is that there may be no free memory at that time. For a bus reset event we need to define a wildcard path including all devices on the bus. So we can create the path for the future bus reset events in advance and avoid problems with the future memory shortage:

```
struct cam_path *path;

if(xpt_create_path(&path, /*periph*/NULL,
            cam_sim_path(sim), CAM_TARGET_WILDCARD,
            CAM_LUN_WILDCARD) != CAM_REQ_CMP) {
    xpt_bus_deregister(cam_sim_path(sim));
    cam_sim_free(sim, /*free_devq*/TRUE);
    error; /* some code to handle the error */
}

softc->wpath = path;
softc->sim = sim;
```

As you can see the path includes:

- ID of the peripheral driver (NULL here because we have none)

- ID of the SIM driver (cam_sim_path(sim) )

- SCSI target number of the device (CAM_TARGET_WILDCARD means "all devices")

- SCSI LUN number of the subdevice (CAM_LUN_WILDCARD means "all LUNs")

If the driver can not allocate this path it will not be able to work normally, so in that case we dismantle that SCSI bus.

And we save the path pointer in the `softc` structure for future use. After that we save the value of sim (or we can also discard it on the exit from `xxx_probe()` if we wish).

That is all for a minimalistic initialization. To do things right there is one more issue left.

For a SIM driver there is one particularly interesting event: when a target device is considered lost. In this case resetting the SCSI negotiations with this device may be a good idea. So we register a callback for this event with CAM. The request is passed to CAM by requesting CAM action on a CAM control block for this type of request:

```
struct ccb_setasync csa;

xpt_setup_ccb(&csa.ccb_h, path, /*priority*/5);
csa.ccb_h.func_code = XPT_SASYNC_CB;
csa.event_enable = AC_LOST_DEVICE;
csa.callback = xxx_async;
csa.callback_arg = sim;
xpt_action((union ccb *)&csa);
```

Now we take a look at the `xxx_action()` and `xxx_poll()` driver entry points.

`static void` **`xxx_action`** *`(struct cam_sim *sim, union ccb *ccb)`*`;`

*`struct cam_sim *sim, , union ccb *ccb ;`*

Do some action on request of the CAM subsystem. Sim describes the SIM for the request, CCB is the request itself. CCB stands for "CAM Control Block". It is a union of many specific instances, each describing arguments for some type of transactions. All of these instances share the CCB header where the common part of arguments is stored.

CAM supports the SCSI controllers working in both initiator ("normal") mode and target (simulating a SCSI device) mode. Here we only consider the part relevant to the initiator mode.

There are a few function and macros (in other words, methods) defined to access the public data in the struct sim:

- `cam_sim_path(sim)` - the path ID (see above)
- `cam_sim_name(sim)` - the name of the sim
- `cam_sim_softc(sim)` - the pointer to the softc (driver private data) structure
- `cam_sim_unit(sim)` - the unit number
- `cam_sim_bus(sim)` - the bus ID

To identify the device, `xxx_action()` can get the unit number and pointer to its structure softc using these functions.

The type of request is stored in `ccb->ccb_h.func_code` . So generally `xxx_action()` consists of a big switch:

```
struct xxx_softc *softc = (struct xxx_softc *) cam_sim_softc(sim);
struct ccb_hdr *ccb_h = &ccb->ccb_h;
int unit = cam_sim_unit(sim);
int bus = cam_sim_bus(sim);

switch(ccb_h->func_code) {
case ...:
    ...
default:
    ccb_h->status = CAM_REQ_INVALID;
    xpt_done(ccb);
    break;
}
```

As can be seen from the default case (if an unknown command was received) the return code of the command is set into `ccb->ccb_h.status` and the completed CCB is returned back to CAM by calling `xpt_done(ccb)`.

`xpt_done()` does not have to be called from `xxx_action()`: For example an I/O request may be enqueued inside the SIM driver and/or its SCSI controller. Then when the device would post an interrupt signaling that the processing of this request is complete `xpt_done()` may be called from the interrupt handling routine.

Actually, the CCB status is not only assigned as a return code but a CCB has some status all the time. Before CCB is passed to the `xxx_action()` routine it gets the status CCB_REQ_INPROG meaning that it is in progress. There are a surprising number of status values defined in `/sys/cam/cam.h` which should be able to represent the status of a request in great detail. More interesting yet, the status is in fact a "bitwise or" of an enumerated status value (the lower 6 bits) and possible additional flag-like bits (the upper bits). The enumerated values will be discussed later in more detail. The summary of them can be found in the Errors Summary section. The possible status flags are:

- *CAM_DEV_QFRZN* - if the SIM driver gets a serious error (for example, the device does not respond to the selection or breaks the SCSI protocol) when processing a CCB it should freeze the request queue by calling `xpt_freeze_simq()`, return the other enqueued but not processed yet CCBs for this device back to the CAM queue, then set this flag for the troublesome CCB and call `xpt_done()`. This flag causes the CAM subsystem to unfreeze the queue after it handles the error.

- *CAM_AUTOSNS_VALID* - if the device returned an error condition and the flag CAM_DIS_AUTOSENSE is not set in CCB the SIM driver must execute the REQUEST SENSE command automatically to extract the sense (extended error information) data from the device. If this attempt was successful the sense data should be saved in the CCB and this flag set.

- *CAM_RELEASE_SIMQ* - like CAM_DEV_QFRZN but used in case there is some problem (or resource shortage) with the SCSI controller itself. Then all the future requests to the controller should be stopped by `xpt_freeze_simq()`. The controller queue will be restarted after the SIM driver overcomes the shortage and informs CAM by returning some CCB with this flag set.

- *CAM_SIM_QUEUED* - when SIM puts a CCB into its request queue this flag should be set (and removed when this CCB gets dequeued before being returned back to CAM). This flag is not used anywhere in the CAM code now, so its purpose is purely diagnostic.

- *CAM_QOS_VALID* - The QOS data is now valid.

The function `xxx_action()` is not allowed to sleep, so all the synchronization for resource access must be done using SIM or device queue freezing. Besides the aforementioned flags the CAM subsystem provides functions `xpt_release_simq()` and `xpt_release_devq()` to unfreeze the queues directly, without passing a CCB to CAM.

The CCB header contains the following fields:

- *path* - path ID for the request

- *target_id* - target device ID for the request

- *target_lun* - LUN ID of the target device

- *timeout* - timeout interval for this command, in milliseconds

- *timeout_ch* - a convenience place for the SIM driver to store the timeout handle (the CAM subsystem itself does not make any assumptions about it)

- *flags* - various bits of information about the request spriv_ptr0, spriv_ptr1 - fields reserved for private use by the SIM driver (such as linking to the SIM queues or SIM private control blocks); actually, they exist as unions: spriv_ptr0 and spriv_ptr1 have the type (void *), spriv_field0 and spriv_field1 have the type unsigned long, sim_priv.entries[0].bytes and sim_priv.entries[1].bytes are byte arrays of the size consistent with the other incarnations of the union and sim_priv.bytes is one array, twice bigger.

The recommended way of using the SIM private fields of CCB is to define some meaningful names for them and use these meaningful names in the driver, like:

```
#define ccb_some_meaningful_name    sim_priv.entries[0].bytes
#define ccb_hcb spriv_ptr1 /* for hardware control block */
```

The most common initiator mode requests are:

- *XPT_SCSI_IO* - execute an I/O transaction

  The instance "struct ccb_scsiio csio" of the union ccb is used to transfer the arguments. They are:

  - *cdb_io* - pointer to the SCSI command buffer or the buffer itself
  - *cdb_len* - SCSI command length
  - *data_ptr* - pointer to the data buffer (gets a bit complicated if scatter/gather is used)
  - *dxfer_len* - length of the data to transfer
  - *sglist_cnt* - counter of the scatter/gather segments
  - *scsi_status* - place to return the SCSI status
  - *sense_data* - buffer for the SCSI sense information if the command returns an error (the SIM driver is supposed to run the REQUEST SENSE command automatically in this case if the CCB flag CAM_DIS_AUTOSENSE is not set)
  - *sense_len* - the length of that buffer (if it happens to be higher than size of sense_data the SIM driver must silently assume the smaller value) resid, sense_resid - if the transfer of data or SCSI sense returned an error these are the returned counters of the residual (not transferred) data. They do not seem to be especially meaningful, so in a case when they are difficult to compute (say, counting bytes in the SCSI controller's FIFO buffer) an approximate value will do as well. For a successfully completed transfer they must be set to zero.
  - *tag_action* - the kind of tag to use:
    - CAM_TAG_ACTION_NONE - do not use tags for this transaction
    - MSG_SIMPLE_Q_TAG, MSG_HEAD_OF_Q_TAG, MSG_ORDERED_Q_TAG - value equal to the appropriate tag message (see /sys/cam/scsi/scsi_message.h); this gives only the tag type, the SIM driver must assign the tag value itself

  The general logic of handling this request is the following:

  The first thing to do is to check for possible races, to make sure that the command did not get aborted when it was sitting in the queue:

```
    struct ccb_scsiio *csio = &ccb->csio;

    if ((ccb_h->status & CAM_STATUS_MASK) != CAM_REQ_INPROG) {
        xpt_done(ccb);
        return;
    }
```

  Also we check that the device is supported at all by our controller:

```
    if(ccb_h->target_id > OUR_MAX_SUPPORTED_TARGET_ID
    || cch_h->target_id == OUR_SCSI_CONTROLLERS_OWN_ID) {
        ccb_h->status = CAM_TID_INVALID;
        xpt_done(ccb);
        return;
    }
    if(ccb_h->target_lun > OUR_MAX_SUPPORTED_LUN) {
```

```
        ccb_h->status = CAM_LUN_INVALID;
        xpt_done(ccb);
        return;
    }
```

Then allocate whatever data structures (such as card-dependent hardware control block) we need to process this request. If we can not then freeze the SIM queue and remember that we have a pending operation, return the CCB back and ask CAM to re-queue it. Later when the resources become available the SIM queue must be unfrozen by returning a ccb with the `CAM_SIMQ_RELEASE` bit set in its status. Otherwise, if all went well, link the CCB with the hardware control block (HCB) and mark it as queued.

```
    struct xxx_hcb *hcb = allocate_hcb(softc, unit, bus);

    if(hcb == NULL) {
        softc->flags |= RESOURCE_SHORTAGE;
        xpt_freeze_simq(sim, /*count*/1);
        ccb_h->status = CAM_REQUEUE_REQ;
        xpt_done(ccb);
        return;
    }

    hcb->ccb = ccb; ccb_h->ccb_hcb = (void *)hcb;
    ccb_h->status |= CAM_SIM_QUEUED;
```

Extract the target data from CCB into the hardware control block. Check if we are asked to assign a tag and if yes then generate an unique tag and build the SCSI tag messages. The SIM driver is also responsible for negotiations with the devices to set the maximal mutually supported bus width, synchronous rate and offset.

```
    hcb->target = ccb_h->target_id; hcb->lun = ccb_h->target_lun;
    generate_identify_message(hcb);
    if( ccb_h->tag_action != CAM_TAG_ACTION_NONE )
        generate_unique_tag_message(hcb, ccb_h->tag_action);
    if( !target_negotiated(hcb) )
        generate_negotiation_messages(hcb);
```

Then set up the SCSI command. The command storage may be specified in the CCB in many interesting ways, specified by the CCB flags. The command buffer can be contained in CCB or pointed to, in the latter case the pointer may be physical or virtual. Since the hardware commonly needs physical address we always convert the address to the physical one, typically using the busdma API.

In case if a physical address is requested it is OK to return the CCB with the status CAM_REQ_INVALID, the current drivers do that. If necessary a physical address can be also converted or mapped back to a virtual address but with big pain, so we do not do that.

```
    if(ccb_h->flags & CAM_CDB_POINTER) {
        /* CDB is a pointer */
        if(!(ccb_h->flags & CAM_CDB_PHYS)) {
            /* CDB pointer is virtual */
            hcb->cmd = vtobus(csio->cdb_io.cdb_ptr);
        } else {
            /* CDB pointer is physical */
            hcb->cmd = csio->cdb_io.cdb_ptr -;
        }
    } else {
        /* CDB is in the ccb (buffer) */
        hcb->cmd = vtobus(csio->cdb_io.cdb_bytes);
    }
    hcb->cmdlen = csio->cdb_len;
```

Now it is time to set up the data. Again, the data storage may be specified in the CCB in many interesting ways, specified by the CCB flags. First we get the direction of the data transfer. The simplest case is if there is no data to transfer:

```
int dir = (ccb_h->flags & CAM_DIR_MASK);

if (dir == CAM_DIR_NONE)
    goto end_data;
```

Then we check if the data is in one chunk or in a scatter-gather list, and the addresses are physical or virtual. The SCSI controller may be able to handle only a limited number of chunks of limited length. If the request hits this limitation we return an error. We use a special function to return the CCB to handle in one place the HCB resource shortages. The functions to add chunks are driver-dependent, and here we leave them without detailed implementation. See description of the SCSI command (CDB) handling for the details on the address-translation issues. If some variation is too difficult or impossible to implement with a particular card it is OK to return the status CAM_REQ_INVALID. Actually, it seems like the scatter-gather ability is not used anywhere in the CAM code now. But at least the case for a single non-scattered virtual buffer must be implemented, it is actively used by CAM.

```
int rv;

initialize_hcb_for_data(hcb);

if((!(ccb_h->flags & CAM_SCATTER_VALID)) {
    /* single buffer */
    if(!(ccb_h->flags & CAM_DATA_PHYS)) {
        rv = add_virtual_chunk(hcb, csio->data_ptr, csio->dxfer_len, dir);
        }
    } else {
        rv = add_physical_chunk(hcb, csio->data_ptr, csio->dxfer_len, dir);
    }
} else {
    int i;
    struct bus_dma_segment *segs;
    segs = (struct bus_dma_segment *)csio->data_ptr;

    if ((ccb_h->flags & CAM_SG_LIST_PHYS) != 0) {
        /* The SG list pointer is physical */
        rv = setup_hcb_for_physical_sg_list(hcb, segs, csio->sglist_cnt);
    } else if (!(ccb_h->flags & CAM_DATA_PHYS)) {
        /* SG buffer pointers are virtual */
        for (i = 0; i < csio->sglist_cnt; i++) {
            rv = add_virtual_chunk(hcb, segs[i].ds_addr,
                segs[i].ds_len, dir);
            if (rv != CAM_REQ_CMP)
                break;
        }
    } else {
        /* SG buffer pointers are physical */
        for (i = 0; i < csio->sglist_cnt; i++) {
            rv = add_physical_chunk(hcb, segs[i].ds_addr,
                segs[i].ds_len, dir);
            if (rv != CAM_REQ_CMP)
                break;
        }
    }
}
if(rv != CAM_REQ_CMP) {
    /* we expect that add_*_chunk() functions return CAM_REQ_CMP
     * if they added a chunk successfully, CAM_REQ_TOO_BIG if
     * the request is too big (too many bytes or too many chunks),
     * CAM_REQ_INVALID in case of other troubles
     */
    free_hcb_and_ccb_done(hcb, ccb, rv);
    return;
}
end_data:
```

If disconnection is disabled for this CCB we pass this information to the hcb:

```
if(ccb_h->flags & CAM_DIS_DISCONNECT)
    hcb_disable_disconnect(hcb);
```

If the controller is able to run REQUEST SENSE command all by itself then the value of the flag CAM_DIS_AUTOSENSE should also be passed to it, to prevent automatic REQUEST SENSE if the CAM subsystem does not want it.

The only thing left is to set up the timeout, pass our hcb to the hardware and return, the rest will be done by the interrupt handler (or timeout handler).

```
ccb_h->timeout_ch = timeout(xxx_timeout, (caddr_t) hcb,
    (ccb_h->timeout * hz) / 1000); /* convert milliseconds to ticks */
put_hcb_into_hardware_queue(hcb);
return;
```

And here is a possible implementation of the function returning CCB:

```
static void
free_hcb_and_ccb_done(struct xxx_hcb *hcb, union ccb *ccb, u_int32_t status)
{
    struct xxx_softc *softc = hcb->softc;

    ccb->ccb_h.ccb_hcb = 0;
    if(hcb != NULL) {
        untimeout(xxx_timeout, (caddr_t) hcb, ccb->ccb_h.timeout_ch);
        /* we're about to free a hcb, so the shortage has ended */
        if(softc->flags & RESOURCE_SHORTAGE)  {
            softc->flags &= ~RESOURCE_SHORTAGE;
            status |= CAM_RELEASE_SIMQ;
        }
        free_hcb(hcb); /* also removes hcb from any internal lists */
    }
    ccb->ccb_h.status = status |
        (ccb->ccb_h.status & ~(CAM_STATUS_MASK|CAM_SIM_QUEUED));
    xpt_done(ccb);
}
```

- *XPT_RESET_DEV* - send the SCSI "BUS DEVICE RESET" message to a device

  There is no data transferred in CCB except the header and the most interesting argument of it is target_id. Depending on the controller hardware a hardware control block just like for the XPT_SCSI_IO request may be constructed (see XPT_SCSI_IO request description) and sent to the controller or the SCSI controller may be immediately programmed to send this RESET message to the device or this request may be just not supported (and return the status CAM_REQ_INVALID). Also on completion of the request all the disconnected transactions for this target must be aborted (probably in the interrupt routine).

  Also all the current negotiations for the target are lost on reset, so they might be cleaned too. Or they clearing may be deferred, because anyway the target would request re-negotiation on the next transaction.

- *XPT_RESET_BUS* - send the RESET signal to the SCSI bus

  No arguments are passed in the CCB, the only interesting argument is the SCSI bus indicated by the struct sim pointer.

  A minimalistic implementation would forget the SCSI negotiations for all the devices on the bus and return the status CAM_REQ_CMP.

The proper implementation would in addition actually reset the SCSI bus (possible also reset the SCSI controller) and mark all the CCBs being processed, both those in the hardware queue and those being disconnected, as done with the status CAM_SCSI_BUS_RESET. Like:

```
int targ, lun;
struct xxx_hcb *h, *hh;
struct ccb_trans_settings neg;
struct cam_path *path;

/* The SCSI bus reset may take a long time, in this case its completion
 * should be checked by interrupt or timeout. But for simplicity
 * we assume here that it is really fast.
 */
reset_scsi_bus(softc);

/* drop all enqueued CCBs */
for(h = softc->first_queued_hcb; h != NULL; h = hh) {
    hh = h->next;
    free_hcb_and_ccb_done(h, h->ccb, CAM_SCSI_BUS_RESET);
}

/* the clean values of negotiations to report */
neg.bus_width = 8;
neg.sync_period = neg.sync_offset = 0;
neg.valid = (CCB_TRANS_BUS_WIDTH_VALID
    | CCB_TRANS_SYNC_RATE_VALID | CCB_TRANS_SYNC_OFFSET_VALID);

/* drop all disconnected CCBs and clean negotiations  */
for(targ=0; targ <= OUR_MAX_SUPPORTED_TARGET; targ++) {
    clean_negotiations(softc, targ);

    /* report the event if possible */
    if(xpt_create_path(&path, /*periph*/NULL,
            cam_sim_path(sim), targ,
            CAM_LUN_WILDCARD) == CAM_REQ_CMP) {
        xpt_async(AC_TRANSFER_NEG, path, &neg);
        xpt_free_path(path);
    }

    for(lun=0; lun <= OUR_MAX_SUPPORTED_LUN; lun++)
        for(h = softc->first_discon_hcb[targ][lun]; h != NULL; h = hh) {
            hh=h->next;
            free_hcb_and_ccb_done(h, h->ccb, CAM_SCSI_BUS_RESET);
        }
}

ccb->ccb_h.status = CAM_REQ_CMP;
xpt_done(ccb);

/* report the event */
xpt_async(AC_BUS_RESET, softc->wpath, NULL);
return;
```

Implementing the SCSI bus reset as a function may be a good idea because it would be re-used by the timeout function as a last resort if the things go wrong.

- *XPT_ABORT* - abort the specified CCB

The arguments are transferred in the instance "struct ccb_abort cab" of the union ccb. The only argument field in it is:

*abort_ccb* - pointer to the CCB to be aborted

If the abort is not supported just return the status CAM_UA_ABORT. This is also the easy way to minimally implement this call, return CAM_UA_ABORT in any case.

The hard way is to implement this request honestly. First check that abort applies to a SCSI transaction:

```
struct ccb *abort_ccb;
abort_ccb = ccb->cab.abort_ccb;

if(abort_ccb->ccb_h.func_code != XPT_SCSI_IO) {
    ccb->ccb_h.status = CAM_UA_ABORT;
    xpt_done(ccb);
    return;
}
```

Then it is necessary to find this CCB in our queue. This can be done by walking the list of all our hardware control blocks in search for one associated with this CCB:

```
struct xxx_hcb *hcb, *h;

hcb = NULL;

/* We assume that softc->first_hcb is the head of the list of all
 * HCBs associated with this bus, including those enqueued for
 * processing, being processed by hardware and disconnected ones.
 */
for(h = softc->first_hcb; h != NULL; h = h->next) {
    if(h->ccb == abort_ccb) {
        hcb = h;
        break;
    }
}

if(hcb == NULL) {
    /* no such CCB in our queue */
    ccb->ccb_h.status = CAM_PATH_INVALID;
    xpt_done(ccb);
    return;
}

hcb=found_hcb;
```

Now we look at the current processing status of the HCB. It may be either sitting in the queue waiting to be sent to the SCSI bus, being transferred right now, or disconnected and waiting for the result of the command, or actually completed by hardware but not yet marked as done by software. To make sure that we do not get in any races with hardware we mark the HCB as being aborted, so that if this HCB is about to be sent to the SCSI bus the SCSI controller will see this flag and skip it.

```
int hstatus;

/* shown as a function, in case special action is needed to make
 * this flag visible to hardware
 */
set_hcb_flags(hcb, HCB_BEING_ABORTED);

abort_again:

hstatus = get_hcb_status(hcb);
switch(hstatus) {
case HCB_SITTING_IN_QUEUE:
    remove_hcb_from_hardware_queue(hcb);
    /* FALLTHROUGH */
case HCB_COMPLETED:
    /* this is an easy case */
    free_hcb_and_ccb_done(hcb, abort_ccb, CAM_REQ_ABORTED);
```

```
        break;
```

If the CCB is being transferred right now we would like to signal to the SCSI controller in some hardware-dependent way that we want to abort the current transfer. The SCSI controller would set the SCSI ATTENTION signal and when the target responds to it send an ABORT message. We also reset the timeout to make sure that the target is not sleeping forever. If the command would not get aborted in some reasonable time like 10 seconds the timeout routine would go ahead and reset the whole SCSI bus. Because the command will be aborted in some reasonable time we can just return the abort request now as successfully completed, and mark the aborted CCB as aborted (but not mark it as done yet).

```
    case HCB_BEING_TRANSFERRED:
        untimeout(xxx_timeout, (caddr_t) hcb, abort_ccb->ccb_h.timeout_ch);
        abort_ccb->ccb_h.timeout_ch =
            timeout(xxx_timeout, (caddr_t) hcb, 10 * hz);
        abort_ccb->ccb_h.status = CAM_REQ_ABORTED;
        /* ask the controller to abort that HCB, then generate
         * an interrupt and stop
         */
        if(signal_hardware_to_abort_hcb_and_stop(hcb) < 0) {
            /* oops, we missed the race with hardware, this transaction
             * got off the bus before we aborted it, try again */
            goto abort_again;
        }

        break;
```

If the CCB is in the list of disconnected then set it up as an abort request and re-queue it at the front of hardware queue. Reset the timeout and report the abort request to be completed.

```
    case HCB_DISCONNECTED:
        untimeout(xxx_timeout, (caddr_t) hcb, abort_ccb->ccb_h.timeout_ch);
        abort_ccb->ccb_h.timeout_ch =
            timeout(xxx_timeout, (caddr_t) hcb, 10 * hz);
        put_abort_message_into_hcb(hcb);
        put_hcb_at_the_front_of_hardware_queue(hcb);
        break;
    }
    ccb->ccb_h.status = CAM_REQ_CMP;
    xpt_done(ccb);
    return;
```

That is all for the ABORT request, although there is one more issue. Because the ABORT message cleans all the ongoing transactions on a LUN we have to mark all the other active transactions on this LUN as aborted. That should be done in the interrupt routine, after the transaction gets aborted.

Implementing the CCB abort as a function may be quite a good idea, this function can be re-used if an I/O transaction times out. The only difference would be that the timed out transaction would return the status CAM_CMD_TIMEOUT for the timed out request. Then the case XPT_ABORT would be small, like that:

```
    case XPT_ABORT:
        struct ccb *abort_ccb;
        abort_ccb = ccb->cab.abort_ccb;

        if(abort_ccb->ccb_h.func_code != XPT_SCSI_IO) {
            ccb->ccb_h.status = CAM_UA_ABORT;
            xpt_done(ccb);
            return;
        }
        if(xxx_abort_ccb(abort_ccb, CAM_REQ_ABORTED) < 0)
            /* no such CCB in our queue */
            ccb->ccb_h.status = CAM_PATH_INVALID;
        else
            ccb->ccb_h.status = CAM_REQ_CMP;
        xpt_done(ccb);
```

```
        return;
```

- *XPT_SET_TRAN_SETTINGS* - explicitly set values of SCSI transfer settings

  The arguments are transferred in the instance "struct ccb_trans_setting cts" of the union ccb:

  - *valid* - a bitmask showing which settings should be updated:
  - *CCB_TRANS_SYNC_RATE_VALID* - synchronous transfer rate
  - *CCB_TRANS_SYNC_OFFSET_VALID* - synchronous offset
  - *CCB_TRANS_BUS_WIDTH_VALID* - bus width
  - *CCB_TRANS_DISC_VALID* - set enable/disable disconnection
  - *CCB_TRANS_TQ_VALID* - set enable/disable tagged queuing
  - *flags* - consists of two parts, binary arguments and identification of sub-operations. The binary arguments are:
    - *CCB_TRANS_DISC_ENB* - enable disconnection
    - *CCB_TRANS_TAG_ENB* - enable tagged queuing
  - the sub-operations are:
    - *CCB_TRANS_CURRENT_SETTINGS* - change the current negotiations
    - *CCB_TRANS_USER_SETTINGS* - remember the desired user values sync_period, sync_offset - self-explanatory, if sync_offset==0 then the asynchronous mode is requested bus_width - bus width, in bits (not bytes)

  Two sets of negotiated parameters are supported, the user settings and the current settings. The user settings are not really used much in the SIM drivers, this is mostly just a piece of memory where the upper levels can store (and later recall) its ideas about the parameters. Setting the user parameters does not cause re-negotiation of the transfer rates. But when the SCSI controller does a negotiation it must never set the values higher than the user parameters, so it is essentially the top boundary.

  The current settings are, as the name says, current. Changing them means that the parameters must be re-negotiated on the next transfer. Again, these "new current settings" are not supposed to be forced on the device, just they are used as the initial step of negotiations. Also they must be limited by actual capabilities of the SCSI controller: for example, if the SCSI controller has 8-bit bus and the request asks to set 16-bit wide transfers this parameter must be silently truncated to 8-bit transfers before sending it to the device.

  One caveat is that the bus width and synchronous parameters are per target while the disconnection and tag enabling parameters are per lun.

  The recommended implementation is to keep 3 sets of negotiated (bus width and synchronous transfer) parameters:

  - *user* - the user set, as above
  - *current* - those actually in effect
  - *goal* - those requested by setting of the "current" parameters

  The code looks like:

```
    struct ccb_trans_settings *cts;
    int targ, lun;
    int flags;
```

```
cts = &ccb->cts;
targ = ccb_h->target_id;
lun = ccb_h->target_lun;
flags = cts->flags;
if(flags & CCB_TRANS_USER_SETTINGS) {
    if(flags & CCB_TRANS_SYNC_RATE_VALID)
        softc->user_sync_period[targ] = cts->sync_period;
    if(flags & CCB_TRANS_SYNC_OFFSET_VALID)
        softc->user_sync_offset[targ] = cts->sync_offset;
    if(flags & CCB_TRANS_BUS_WIDTH_VALID)
        softc->user_bus_width[targ] = cts->bus_width;

    if(flags & CCB_TRANS_DISC_VALID) {
        softc->user_tflags[targ][lun] &= ~CCB_TRANS_DISC_ENB;
        softc->user_tflags[targ][lun] |= flags & CCB_TRANS_DISC_ENB;
    }
    if(flags & CCB_TRANS_TQ_VALID) {
        softc->user_tflags[targ][lun] &= ~CCB_TRANS_TQ_ENB;
        softc->user_tflags[targ][lun] |= flags & CCB_TRANS_TQ_ENB;
    }
}
if(flags & CCB_TRANS_CURRENT_SETTINGS) {
    if(flags & CCB_TRANS_SYNC_RATE_VALID)
        softc->goal_sync_period[targ] =
            max(cts->sync_period, OUR_MIN_SUPPORTED_PERIOD);
    if(flags & CCB_TRANS_SYNC_OFFSET_VALID)
        softc->goal_sync_offset[targ] =
            min(cts->sync_offset, OUR_MAX_SUPPORTED_OFFSET);
    if(flags & CCB_TRANS_BUS_WIDTH_VALID)
        softc->goal_bus_width[targ] = min(cts->bus_width, OUR_BUS_WIDTH);

    if(flags & CCB_TRANS_DISC_VALID) {
        softc->current_tflags[targ][lun] &= ~CCB_TRANS_DISC_ENB;
        softc->current_tflags[targ][lun] |= flags & CCB_TRANS_DISC_ENB;
    }
    if(flags & CCB_TRANS_TQ_VALID) {
        softc->current_tflags[targ][lun] &= ~CCB_TRANS_TQ_ENB;
        softc->current_tflags[targ][lun] |= flags & CCB_TRANS_TQ_ENB;
    }
}
ccb->ccb_h.status = CAM_REQ_CMP;
xpt_done(ccb);
return;
```

Then when the next I/O request will be processed it will check if it has to re-negotiate, for example by calling the function target_negotiated(hcb). It can be implemented like this:

```
int
target_negotiated(struct xxx_hcb *hcb)
{
    struct softc *softc = hcb->softc;
    int targ = hcb->targ;

    if( softc->current_sync_period[targ] != softc->goal_sync_period[targ]
    || softc->current_sync_offset[targ] != softc->goal_sync_offset[targ]
    || softc->current_bus_width[targ] != softc->goal_bus_width[targ] )
        return 0; /* FALSE */
    else
        return 1; /* TRUE */
}
```

After the values are re-negotiated the resulting values must be assigned to both current and goal parameters, so for future I/O transactions the current and goal parameters would be the same and `target_negotiated()` would return TRUE. When the card is initialized (in `xxx_attach()`) the current negotiation values must be initialized

to narrow asynchronous mode, the goal and current values must be initialized to the maximal values supported by controller.

*XPT_GET_TRAN_SETTINGS* - get values of SCSI transfer settings

This operations is the reverse of XPT_SET_TRAN_SETTINGS. Fill up the CCB instance "struct ccb_trans_setting cts" with data as requested by the flags CCB_TRANS_CURRENT_SETTINGS or CCB_TRANS_USER_SETTINGS (if both are set then the existing drivers return the current settings). Set all the bits in the valid field.

*XPT_CALC_GEOMETRY* - calculate logical (BIOS) geometry of the disk

The arguments are transferred in the instance "struct ccb_calc_geometry ccg" of the union ccb:

- *block_size* - input, block (A.K.A sector) size in bytes
- *volume_size* - input, volume size in bytes
- *cylinders* - output, logical cylinders
- *heads* - output, logical heads
- *secs_per_track* - output, logical sectors per track

If the returned geometry differs much enough from what the SCSI controller BIOS thinks and a disk on this SCSI controller is used as bootable the system may not be able to boot. The typical calculation example taken from the aic7xxx driver is:

```
struct    ccb_calc_geometry *ccg;
u_int32_t size_mb;
u_int32_t secs_per_cylinder;
int   extended;

ccg = &ccb->ccg;
size_mb = ccg->volume_size
    / ((1024L * 1024L) / ccg->block_size);
extended = check_cards_EEPROM_for_extended_geometry(softc);

if (size_mb > 1024 && extended) {
    ccg->heads = 255;
    ccg->secs_per_track = 63;
} else {
    ccg->heads = 64;
    ccg->secs_per_track = 32;
}
secs_per_cylinder = ccg->heads * ccg->secs_per_track;
ccg->cylinders = ccg->volume_size / secs_per_cylinder;
ccb->ccb_h.status = CAM_REQ_CMP;
xpt_done(ccb);
return;
```

This gives the general idea, the exact calculation depends on the quirks of the particular BIOS. If BIOS provides no way set the "extended translation" flag in EEPROM this flag should normally be assumed equal to 1. Other popular geometries are:

```
128 heads, 63 sectors - Symbios controllers
16 heads, 63 sectors - old controllers
```

Some system BIOSes and SCSI BIOSes fight with each other with variable success, for example a combination of Symbios 875/895 SCSI and Phoenix BIOS can give geometry 128/63 after power up and 255/63 after a hard reset or soft reboot.

- *XPT_PATH_INQ* - path inquiry, in other words get the SIM driver and SCSI controller (also known as HBA - Host Bus Adapter) properties

  The properties are returned in the instance “struct ccb_pathinq cpi” of the union ccb:

  - version_num - the SIM driver version number, now all drivers use 1
  - hba_inquiry - bitmask of features supported by the controller:
  - PI_MDP_ABLE - supports MDP message (something from SCSI3?)
  - PI_WIDE_32 - supports 32 bit wide SCSI
  - PI_WIDE_16 - supports 16 bit wide SCSI
  - PI_SDTR_ABLE - can negotiate synchronous transfer rate
  - PI_LINKED_CDB - supports linked commands
  - PI_TAG_ABLE - supports tagged commands
  - PI_SOFT_RST - supports soft reset alternative (hard reset and soft reset are mutually exclusive within a SCSI bus)
  - target_sprt - flags for target mode support, 0 if unsupported
  - hba_misc - miscellaneous controller features:
  - PIM_SCANHILO - bus scans from high ID to low ID
  - PIM_NOREMOVE - removable devices not included in scan
  - PIM_NOINITIATOR - initiator role not supported
  - PIM_NOBUSRESET - user has disabled initial BUS RESET
  - hba_eng_cnt - mysterious HBA engine count, something related to compression, now is always set to 0
  - vuhba_flags - vendor-unique flags, unused now
  - max_target - maximal supported target ID (7 for 8-bit bus, 15 for 16-bit bus, 127 for Fibre Channel)
  - max_lun - maximal supported LUN ID (7 for older SCSI controllers, 63 for newer ones)
  - async_flags - bitmask of installed Async handler, unused now
  - hpath_id - highest Path ID in the subsystem, unused now
  - unit_number - the controller unit number, cam_sim_unit(sim)
  - bus_id - the bus number, cam_sim_bus(sim)
  - initiator_id - the SCSI ID of the controller itself
  - base_transfer_speed - nominal transfer speed in KB/s for asynchronous narrow transfers, equals to 3300 for SCSI
  - sim_vid - SIM driver's vendor id, a zero-terminated string of maximal length SIM_IDLEN including the terminating zero

- hba_vid - SCSI controller's vendor id, a zero-terminated string of maximal length HBA_IDLEN including the terminating zero
- dev_name - device driver name, a zero-terminated string of maximal length DEV_IDLEN including the terminating zero, equal to cam_sim_name(sim)

The recommended way of setting the string fields is using strncpy, like:

```
    strncpy(cpi->dev_name, cam_sim_name(sim), DEV_IDLEN);
```

After setting the values set the status to CAM_REQ_CMP and mark the CCB as done.

## 12.3. Polling

`static void` **`xxx_poll`** `(`*`struct cam_sim *sim`*`);`

*`struct cam_sim *sim ;`*

The poll function is used to simulate the interrupts when the interrupt subsystem is not functioning (for example, when the system has crashed and is creating the system dump). The CAM subsystem sets the proper interrupt level before calling the poll routine. So all it needs to do is to call the interrupt routine (or the other way around, the poll routine may be doing the real action and the interrupt routine would just call the poll routine). Why bother about a separate function then? Because of different calling conventions. The `xxx_poll` routine gets the struct cam_sim pointer as its argument when the PCI interrupt routine by common convention gets pointer to the struct `xxx_softc` and the ISA interrupt routine gets just the device unit number. So the poll routine would normally look as:

```
static void
xxx_poll(struct cam_sim *sim)
{
    xxx_intr((struct xxx_softc *)cam_sim_softc(sim)); /* for PCI device */
}
```

or

```
static void
xxx_poll(struct cam_sim *sim)
{
    xxx_intr(cam_sim_unit(sim)); /* for ISA device */
}
```

## 12.4. Asynchronous Events

If an asynchronous event callback has been set up then the callback function should be defined.

```
static void
ahc_async(void *callback_arg, u_int32_t code, struct cam_path *path, void *arg)
```

- callback_arg - the value supplied when registering the callback
- code - identifies the type of event
- path - identifies the devices to which the event applies
- arg - event-specific argument

Implementation for a single type of event, AC_LOST_DEVICE, looks like:

```
    struct xxx_softc *softc;
```

```
struct cam_sim *sim;
int targ;
struct ccb_trans_settings neg;

sim = (struct cam_sim *)callback_arg;
softc = (struct xxx_softc *)cam_sim_softc(sim);
switch (code) {
case AC_LOST_DEVICE:
    targ = xpt_path_target_id(path);
    if(targ <= OUR_MAX_SUPPORTED_TARGET) {
        clean_negotiations(softc, targ);
        /* send indication to CAM */
        neg.bus_width = 8;
        neg.sync_period = neg.sync_offset = 0;
        neg.valid = (CCB_TRANS_BUS_WIDTH_VALID
            | CCB_TRANS_SYNC_RATE_VALID | CCB_TRANS_SYNC_OFFSET_VALID);
        xpt_async(AC_TRANSFER_NEG, path, &neg);
    }
    break;
default:
    break;
}
```

## 12.5. Interrupts

The exact type of the interrupt routine depends on the type of the peripheral bus (PCI, ISA and so on) to which the SCSI controller is connected.

The interrupt routines of the SIM drivers run at the interrupt level splcam. So `splcam()` should be used in the driver to synchronize activity between the interrupt routine and the rest of the driver (for a multiprocessor-aware driver things get yet more interesting but we ignore this case here). The pseudo-code in this document happily ignores the problems of synchronization. The real code must not ignore them. A simple-minded approach is to set `splcam()` on the entry to the other routines and reset it on return thus protecting them by one big critical section. To make sure that the interrupt level will be always restored a wrapper function can be defined, like:

```
static void
xxx_action(struct cam_sim *sim, union ccb *ccb)
{
    int s;
    s = splcam();
    xxx_action1(sim, ccb);
    splx(s);
}

static void
xxx_action1(struct cam_sim *sim, union ccb *ccb)
{
    ... process the request ...
}
```

This approach is simple and robust but the problem with it is that interrupts may get blocked for a relatively long time and this would negatively affect the system's performance. On the other hand the functions of the `spl()` family have rather high overhead, so vast amount of tiny critical sections may not be good either.

The conditions handled by the interrupt routine and the details depend very much on the hardware. We consider the set of "typical" conditions.

First, we check if a SCSI reset was encountered on the bus (probably caused by another SCSI controller on the same SCSI bus). If so we drop all the enqueued and disconnected requests, report the events and re-initialize our SCSI controller. It is important that during this initialization the controller will not issue another reset or else two controllers on the same SCSI bus could ping-pong resets forever. The case of fatal controller error/hang could be

handled in the same place, but it will probably need also sending RESET signal to the SCSI bus to reset the status of the connections with the SCSI devices.

```
    int fatal=0;
    struct ccb_trans_settings neg;
    struct cam_path *path;

    if( detected_scsi_reset(softc)
    || (fatal = detected_fatal_controller_error(softc)) ) {
        int targ, lun;
        struct xxx_hcb *h, *hh;

        /* drop all enqueued CCBs */
        for(h = softc->first_queued_hcb; h != NULL; h = hh) {
            hh = h->next;
            free_hcb_and_ccb_done(h, h->ccb, CAM_SCSI_BUS_RESET);
        }

        /* the clean values of negotiations to report */
        neg.bus_width = 8;
        neg.sync_period = neg.sync_offset = 0;
        neg.valid = (CCB_TRANS_BUS_WIDTH_VALID
            | CCB_TRANS_SYNC_RATE_VALID | CCB_TRANS_SYNC_OFFSET_VALID);

        /* drop all disconnected CCBs and clean negotiations  */
        for(targ=0; targ <= OUR_MAX_SUPPORTED_TARGET; targ++) {
            clean_negotiations(softc, targ);

            /* report the event if possible */
            if(xpt_create_path(&path, /*periph*/NULL,
                    cam_sim_path(sim), targ,
                    CAM_LUN_WILDCARD) == CAM_REQ_CMP) {
                xpt_async(AC_TRANSFER_NEG, path, &neg);
                xpt_free_path(path);
            }

            for(lun=0; lun <= OUR_MAX_SUPPORTED_LUN; lun++)
                for(h = softc->first_discon_hcb[targ][lun]; h != NULL; h = hh) {
                    hh=h->next;
                    if(fatal)
                        free_hcb_and_ccb_done(h, h->ccb, CAM_UNREC_HBA_ERROR);
                    else
                        free_hcb_and_ccb_done(h, h->ccb, CAM_SCSI_BUS_RESET);
                }
        }

        /* report the event */
        xpt_async(AC_BUS_RESET, softc->wpath, NULL);

        /* re-initialization may take a lot of time, in such case
         * its completion should be signaled by another interrupt or
         * checked on timeout - but for simplicity we assume here that
         * it is really fast
         */
        if(!fatal) {
            reinitialize_controller_without_scsi_reset(softc);
        } else {
            reinitialize_controller_with_scsi_reset(softc);
        }
        schedule_next_hcb(softc);
        return;
    }
```

If interrupt is not caused by a controller-wide condition then probably something has happened to the current hardware control block. Depending on the hardware there may be other non-HCB-related events, we just do not consider them here. Then we analyze what happened to this HCB:

```
    struct xxx_hcb *hcb, *h, *hh;
    int hcb_status, scsi_status;
    int ccb_status;
    int targ;
    int lun_to_freeze;

    hcb = get_current_hcb(softc);
    if(hcb == NULL) {
        /* either stray interrupt or something went very wrong
         * or this is something hardware-dependent
         */
        handle as necessary;
        return;
    }

    targ = hcb->target;
    hcb_status = get_status_of_current_hcb(softc);
```

First we check if the HCB has completed and if so we check the returned SCSI status.

```
    if(hcb_status == COMPLETED) {
        scsi_status = get_completion_status(hcb);
```

Then look if this status is related to the REQUEST SENSE command and if so handle it in a simple way.

```
        if(hcb->flags & DOING_AUTOSENSE) {
            if(scsi_status == GOOD) { /* autosense was successful */
                hcb->ccb->ccb_h.status |= CAM_AUTOSNS_VALID;
                free_hcb_and_ccb_done(hcb, hcb->ccb, CAM_SCSI_STATUS_ERROR);
            } else {
        autosense_failed:
                free_hcb_and_ccb_done(hcb, hcb->ccb, CAM_AUTOSENSE_FAIL);
            }
            schedule_next_hcb(softc);
            return;
        }
```

Else the command itself has completed, pay more attention to details. If auto-sense is not disabled for this CCB and the command has failed with sense data then run REQUEST SENSE command to receive that data.

```
        hcb->ccb->csio.scsi_status = scsi_status;
        calculate_residue(hcb);

        if( (hcb->ccb->ccb_h.flags & CAM_DIS_AUTOSENSE)==0
        && ( scsi_status == CHECK_CONDITION
                || scsi_status == COMMAND_TERMINATED) ) {
            /* start auto-SENSE */
            hcb->flags |= DOING_AUTOSENSE;
            setup_autosense_command_in_hcb(hcb);
            restart_current_hcb(softc);
            return;
        }
        if(scsi_status == GOOD)
            free_hcb_and_ccb_done(hcb, hcb->ccb, CAM_REQ_CMP);
        else
            free_hcb_and_ccb_done(hcb, hcb->ccb, CAM_SCSI_STATUS_ERROR);
        schedule_next_hcb(softc);
        return;
    }
```

One typical thing would be negotiation events: negotiation messages received from a SCSI target (in answer to our negotiation attempt or by target's initiative) or the target is unable to negotiate (rejects our negotiation messages or does not answer them).

```
    switch(hcb_status) {
    case TARGET_REJECTED_WIDE_NEG:
```

```
        /* revert to 8-bit bus */
        softc->current_bus_width[targ] = softc->goal_bus_width[targ] = 8;
        /* report the event */
        neg.bus_width = 8;
        neg.valid = CCB_TRANS_BUS_WIDTH_VALID;
        xpt_async(AC_TRANSFER_NEG, hcb->ccb.ccb_h.path_id, &neg);
        continue_current_hcb(softc);
        return;
    case TARGET_ANSWERED_WIDE_NEG:
        {
            int wd;

            wd = get_target_bus_width_request(softc);
            if(wd <= softc->goal_bus_width[targ]) {
                /* answer is acceptable */
                softc->current_bus_width[targ] =
                softc->goal_bus_width[targ] = neg.bus_width = wd;

                /* report the event */
                neg.valid = CCB_TRANS_BUS_WIDTH_VALID;
                xpt_async(AC_TRANSFER_NEG, hcb->ccb.ccb_h.path_id, &neg);
            } else {
                prepare_reject_message(hcb);
            }
        }
        continue_current_hcb(softc);
        return;
    case TARGET_REQUESTED_WIDE_NEG:
        {
            int wd;

            wd = get_target_bus_width_request(softc);
            wd = min (wd, OUR_BUS_WIDTH);
            wd = min (wd, softc->user_bus_width[targ]);

            if(wd != softc->current_bus_width[targ]) {
                /* the bus width has changed */
                softc->current_bus_width[targ] =
                softc->goal_bus_width[targ] = neg.bus_width = wd;

                /* report the event */
                neg.valid = CCB_TRANS_BUS_WIDTH_VALID;
                xpt_async(AC_TRANSFER_NEG, hcb->ccb.ccb_h.path_id, &neg);
            }
            prepare_width_nego_rsponse(hcb, wd);
        }
        continue_current_hcb(softc);
        return;
    }
```

Then we handle any errors that could have happened during auto-sense in the same simple-minded way as before. Otherwise we look closer at the details again.

```
    if(hcb->flags & DOING_AUTOSENSE)
        goto autosense_failed;

    switch(hcb_status) {
```

The next event we consider is unexpected disconnect. Which is considered normal after an ABORT or BUS DEVICE RESET message and abnormal in other cases.

```
    case UNEXPECTED_DISCONNECT:
        if(requested_abort(hcb)) {
            /* abort affects all commands on that target+LUN, so
             * mark all disconnected HCBs on that target+LUN as aborted too
             */
```

```
            for(h = softc->first_discon_hcb[hcb->target][hcb->lun];
                    h != NULL; h = hh) {
                hh=h->next;
                free_hcb_and_ccb_done(h, h->ccb, CAM_REQ_ABORTED);
            }
            ccb_status = CAM_REQ_ABORTED;
        } else if(requested_bus_device_reset(hcb)) {
            int lun;

            /* reset affects all commands on that target, so
             * mark all disconnected HCBs on that target+LUN as reset
             */

            for(lun=0; lun <= OUR_MAX_SUPPORTED_LUN; lun++)
                for(h = softc->first_discon_hcb[hcb->target][lun];
                        h != NULL; h = hh) {
                    hh=h->next;
                    free_hcb_and_ccb_done(h, h->ccb, CAM_SCSI_BUS_RESET);
                }

            /* send event */
            xpt_async(AC_SENT_BDR, hcb->ccb->ccb_h.path_id, NULL);

            /* this was the CAM_RESET_DEV request itself, it is completed */
            ccb_status = CAM_REQ_CMP;
        } else {
            calculate_residue(hcb);
            ccb_status = CAM_UNEXP_BUSFREE;
            /* request the further code to freeze the queue */
            hcb->ccb->ccb_h.status |= CAM_DEV_QFRZN;
            lun_to_freeze = hcb->lun;
        }
        break;
```

If the target refuses to accept tags we notify CAM about that and return back all commands for this LUN:

```
    case TAGS_REJECTED:
        /* report the event */
        neg.flags = 0 & ~CCB_TRANS_TAG_ENB;
        neg.valid = CCB_TRANS_TQ_VALID;
        xpt_async(AC_TRANSFER_NEG, hcb->ccb.ccb_h.path_id, &neg);

        ccb_status = CAM_MSG_REJECT_REC;
        /* request the further code to freeze the queue */
        hcb->ccb->ccb_h.status |= CAM_DEV_QFRZN;
        lun_to_freeze = hcb->lun;
        break;
```

Then we check a number of other conditions, with processing basically limited to setting the CCB status:

```
    case SELECTION_TIMEOUT:
        ccb_status = CAM_SEL_TIMEOUT;
        /* request the further code to freeze the queue */
        hcb->ccb->ccb_h.status |= CAM_DEV_QFRZN;
        lun_to_freeze = CAM_LUN_WILDCARD;
        break;
    case PARITY_ERROR:
        ccb_status = CAM_UNCOR_PARITY;
        break;
    case DATA_OVERRUN:
    case ODD_WIDE_TRANSFER:
        ccb_status = CAM_DATA_RUN_ERR;
        break;
    default:
        /* all other errors are handled in a generic way */
        ccb_status = CAM_REQ_CMP_ERR;
        /* request the further code to freeze the queue */
```

```
        hcb->ccb->ccb_h.status |= CAM_DEV_QFRZN;
        lun_to_freeze = CAM_LUN_WILDCARD;
        break;
    }
```

Then we check if the error was serious enough to freeze the input queue until it gets proceeded and do so if it is:

```
    if(hcb->ccb->ccb_h.status & CAM_DEV_QFRZN) {
        /* freeze the queue */
        xpt_freeze_devq(ccb->ccb_h.path, /*count*/1);

        /* re-queue all commands for this target/LUN back to CAM */

        for(h = softc->first_queued_hcb; h != NULL; h = hh) {
            hh = h->next;

            if(targ == h->targ
            && (lun_to_freeze == CAM_LUN_WILDCARD || lun_to_freeze == h->lun) )
                free_hcb_and_ccb_done(h, h->ccb, CAM_REQUEUE_REQ);
        }
    }
    free_hcb_and_ccb_done(hcb, hcb->ccb, ccb_status);
    schedule_next_hcb(softc);
    return;
```

This concludes the generic interrupt handling although specific controllers may require some additions.

## 12.6. Errors Summary

When executing an I/O request many things may go wrong. The reason of error can be reported in the CCB status with great detail. Examples of use are spread throughout this document. For completeness here is the summary of recommended responses for the typical error conditions:

- *CAM_RESRC_UNAVAIL* - some resource is temporarily unavailable and the SIM driver cannot generate an event when it will become available. An example of this resource would be some intra-controller hardware resource for which the controller does not generate an interrupt when it becomes available.
- *CAM_UNCOR_PARITY* - unrecovered parity error occurred
- *CAM_DATA_RUN_ERR* - data overrun or unexpected data phase (going in other direction than specified in CAM_DIR_MASK) or odd transfer length for wide transfer
- *CAM_SEL_TIMEOUT* - selection timeout occurred (target does not respond)
- *CAM_CMD_TIMEOUT* - command timeout occurred (the timeout function ran)
- *CAM_SCSI_STATUS_ERROR* - the device returned error
- *CAM_AUTOSENSE_FAIL* - the device returned error and the REQUEST SENSE COMMAND failed
- *CAM_MSG_REJECT_REC* - MESSAGE REJECT message was received
- *CAM_SCSI_BUS_RESET* - received SCSI bus reset
- *CAM_REQ_CMP_ERR* - "impossible" SCSI phase occurred or something else as weird or just a generic error if further detail is not available
- *CAM_UNEXP_BUSFREE* - unexpected disconnect occurred
- *CAM_BDR_SENT* - BUS DEVICE RESET message was sent to the target

- *CAM_UNREC_HBA_ERROR* - unrecoverable Host Bus Adapter Error
- *CAM_REQ_TOO_BIG* - the request was too large for this controller
- *CAM_REQUEUE_REQ* - this request should be re-queued to preserve transaction ordering. This typically occurs when the SIM recognizes an error that should freeze the queue and must place other queued requests for the target at the sim level back into the XPT queue. Typical cases of such errors are selection timeouts, command timeouts and other like conditions. In such cases the troublesome command returns the status indicating the error, the and the other commands which have not be sent to the bus yet get re-queued.
- *CAM_LUN_INVALID* - the LUN ID in the request is not supported by the SCSI controller
- *CAM_TID_INVALID* - the target ID in the request is not supported by the SCSI controller

## 12.7. Timeout Handling

When the timeout for an HCB expires that request should be aborted, just like with an XPT_ABORT request. The only difference is that the returned status of aborted request should be CAM_CMD_TIMEOUT instead of CAM_REQ_ABORTED (that is why implementation of the abort better be done as a function). But there is one more possible problem: what if the abort request itself will get stuck? In this case the SCSI bus should be reset, just like with an XPT_RESET_BUS request (and the idea about implementing it as a function called from both places applies here too). Also we should reset the whole SCSI bus if a device reset request got stuck. So after all the timeout function would look like:

```
static void
xxx_timeout(void *arg)
{
    struct xxx_hcb *hcb = (struct xxx_hcb *)arg;
    struct xxx_softc *softc;
    struct ccb_hdr *ccb_h;

    softc = hcb->softc;
    ccb_h = &hcb->ccb->ccb_h;

    if(hcb->flags & HCB_BEING_ABORTED
    || ccb_h->func_code == XPT_RESET_DEV) {
        xxx_reset_bus(softc);
    } else {
        xxx_abort_ccb(hcb->ccb, CAM_CMD_TIMEOUT);
    }
}
```

When we abort a request all the other disconnected requests to the same target/LUN get aborted too. So there appears a question, should we return them with status CAM_REQ_ABORTED or CAM_CMD_TIMEOUT? The current drivers use CAM_CMD_TIMEOUT. This seems logical because if one request got timed out then probably something really bad is happening to the device, so if they would not be disturbed they would time out by themselves.

# Chapter 13. USB Devices

Written by Nick Hibma.
Modifications for Handbook made by Murray Stokely.

## 13.1. Introduction

The Universal Serial Bus (USB) is a new way of attaching devices to personal computers. The bus architecture features two-way communication and has been developed as a response to devices becoming smarter and requiring more interaction with the host. USB support is included in all current PC chipsets and is therefore available in all recently built PCs. Apple's introduction of the USB-only iMac has been a major incentive for hardware manufacturers to produce USB versions of their devices. The future PC specifications specify that all legacy connectors on PCs should be replaced by one or more USB connectors, providing generic plug and play capabilities. Support for USB hardware was available at a very early stage in NetBSD and was developed by Lennart Augustsson for the NetBSD project. The code has been ported to FreeBSD and we are currently maintaining a shared code base. For the implementation of the USB subsystem a number of features of USB are important.

*Lennart Augustsson has done most of the implementation of the USB support for the NetBSD project. Many thanks for this incredible amount of work. Many thanks also to Ardy and Dirk for their comments and proofreading of this paper.*

- Devices connect to ports on the computer directly or on devices called hubs, forming a treelike device structure.
- The devices can be connected and disconnected at run time.
- Devices can suspend themselves and trigger resumes of the host system
- As the devices can be powered from the bus, the host software has to keep track of power budgets for each hub.
- Different quality of service requirements by the different device types together with the maximum of 126 devices that can be connected to the same bus, require proper scheduling of transfers on the shared bus to take full advantage of the 12Mbps bandwidth available. (over 400Mbps with USB 2.0)
- Devices are intelligent and contain easily accessible information about themselves

The development of drivers for the USB subsystem and devices connected to it is supported by the specifications that have been developed and will be developed. These specifications are publicly available from the USB home pages. Apple has been very strong in pushing for standards based drivers, by making drivers for the generic classes available in their operating system MacOS and discouraging the use of separate drivers for each new device. This chapter tries to collate essential information for a basic understanding of the USB 2.0 implementation stack in FreeBSD/NetBSD. It is recommended however to read it together with the relevant 2.0 specifications and other developer resources:

- USB 2.0 Specification (http://www.usb.org/developers/docs/usb20_docs/)
- Universal Host Controller Interface (UHCI) Specification (ftp://ftp.netbsd.org/pub/NetBSD/misc/blymn/uhci11d.pdf)
- Open Host Controller Interface (OHCI) Specification(ftp://ftp.compaq.com/pub/supportinformation/papers/hcir1_0a.pdf)
- Developer section of USB home page (http://www.usb.org/developers/)

### 13.1.1. Structure of the USB Stack

The USB support in FreeBSD can be split into three layers. The lowest layer contains the host controller driver, providing a generic interface to the hardware and its scheduling facilities. It supports initialisation of the hardware, scheduling of transfers and handling of completed and/or failed transfers. Each host controller driver implements

a virtual hub providing hardware independent access to the registers controlling the root ports on the back of the machine.

The middle layer handles the device connection and disconnection, basic initialisation of the device, driver selection, the communication channels (pipes) and does resource management. This services layer also controls the default pipes and the device requests transferred over them.

The top layer contains the individual drivers supporting specific (classes of) devices. These drivers implement the protocol that is used over the pipes other than the default pipe. They also implement additional functionality to make the device available to other parts of the kernel or userland. They use the USB driver interface (USBDI) exposed by the services layer.

## 13.2. Host Controllers

The host controller (HC) controls the transmission of packets on the bus. Frames of 1 millisecond are used. At the start of each frame the host controller generates a Start of Frame (SOF) packet.

The SOF packet is used to synchronise to the start of the frame and to keep track of the frame number. Within each frame packets are transferred, either from host to device (out) or from device to host (in). Transfers are always initiated by the host (polled transfers). Therefore there can only be one host per USB bus. Each transfer of a packet has a status stage in which the recipient of the data can return either ACK (acknowledge reception), NAK (retry), STALL (error condition) or nothing (garbled data stage, device not available or disconnected). Section 8.5 of the USB 2.0 Specification explains the details of packets in more detail. Four different types of transfers can occur on a USB bus: control, bulk, interrupt and isochronous. The types of transfers and their characteristics are described below.

Large transfers between the device on the USB bus and the device driver are split up into multiple packets by the host controller or the HC driver.

Device requests (control transfers) to the default endpoints are special. They consist of two or three phases: SETUP, DATA (optional) and STATUS. The set-up packet is sent to the device. If there is a data phase, the direction of the data packet(s) is given in the set-up packet. The direction in the status phase is the opposite of the direction during the data phase, or IN if there was no data phase. The host controller hardware also provides registers with the current status of the root ports and the changes that have occurred since the last reset of the status change register. Access to these registers is provided through a virtualised hub as suggested in the USB specification. The virtual hub must comply with the hub device class given in chapter 11 of that specification. It must provide a default pipe through which device requests can be sent to it. It returns the standard andhub class specific set of descriptors. It should also provide an interrupt pipe that reports changes happening at its ports. There are currently two specifications for host controllers available: Universal Host Controller Interface (UHCI) from Intel and Open Host Controller Interface (OHCI) from Compaq, Microsoft, and National Semiconductor. The UHCI specification has been designed to reduce hardware complexity by requiring the host controller driver to supply a complete schedule of the transfers for each frame. OHCI type controllers are much more independent by providing a more abstract interface doing a lot of work themselves.

### 13.2.1. UHCI

The UHCI host controller maintains a framelist with 1024 pointers to per frame data structures. It understands two different data types: transfer descriptors (TD) and queue heads (QH). Each TD represents a packet to be communicated to or from a device endpoint. QHs are a means to groupTDs (and QHs) together.

Each transfer consists of one or more packets. The UHCI driver splits large transfers into multiple packets. For every transfer, apart from isochronous transfers, a QH is allocated. For every type of transfer these QHs are collected at a QH for that type. Isochronous transfers have to be executed first because of the fixed latency requirement and are directly referred to by the pointer in the framelist. The last isochronous TD refers to the QH for interrupt transfers for that frame. All QHs for interrupt transfers point at the QH for control transfers, which in turn points at the QH for bulk transfers. The following diagram gives a graphical overview of this:

This results in the following schedule being run in each frame. After fetching the pointer for the current frame from the framelist the controller first executes the TDs for all the isochronous packets in that frame. The last of these TDs refers to the QH for the interrupt transfers for thatframe. The host controller will then descend from that QH to the QHs for the individual interrupt transfers. After finishing that queue, the QH for the interrupt transfers will refer the controller to the QH for all control transfers. It will execute all the subqueues scheduled there, followed by all the transfers queued at the bulk QH. To facilitate the handling of finished or failed transfers different types of interrupts are generated by the hardware at the end of each frame. In the last TD for a transfer the Interrupt-On Completion bit is set by the HC driver to flag an interrupt when the transfer has completed. An error interrupt is flagged if a TD reaches its maximum error count. If the short packet detect bit is set in a TD and less than the set packet length is transferred this interrupt is flagged to notify the controller driver of the completed transfer. It is the host controller driver's task to find out which transfer has completed or produced an error. When called the interrupt service routine will locate all the finished transfers and call their callbacks.

Refer to the UHCI Specification for a more elaborate description.

### 13.2.2. OHCI

Programming an OHCI host controller is much simpler. The controller assumes that a set of endpoints is available, and is aware of scheduling priorities and the ordering of the types of transfers in a frame. The main data structure used by the host controller is the endpoint descriptor (ED) to which a queue of transfer descriptors (TDs) is attached. The ED contains the maximum packet size allowed for an endpoint and the controller hardware does the splitting into packets. The pointers to the data buffers are updated after each transfer and when the start and end pointer are equal, the TD is retired to the done-queue. The four types of endpoints (interrupt, isochronous, control, and bulk) have their own queues. Control and bulk endpoints are queued each at their own queue. Interrupt EDs are queued in a tree, with the level in the tree defining the frequency at which they run.

The schedule being run by the host controller in each frame looks as follows. The controller will first run the non-periodic control and bulk queues, up to a time limit set by the HC driver. Then the interrupt transfers for that frame number are run, by using the lower five bits of the frame number as an index into level 0 of the tree of interrupts EDs. At the end of this tree the isochronous EDs are connected and these are traversed subsequently. The isochronous TDs contain the frame number of the first frame the transfer should be run in. After all the periodic transfers have been run, the control and bulk queues are traversed again. Periodically the interrupt service routine is called to process the done queue and call the callbacks for each transfer and reschedule interrupt and isochronous endpoints.

See the UHCI Specification for a more elaborate description. The middle layer provides access to the device in a controlled way and maintains resources in use by the different drivers and the services layer. The layer takes care of the following aspects:

- The device configuration information
- The pipes to communicate with a device
- Probing and attaching and detaching form a device.

## 13.3. USB Device Information

### 13.3.1. Device Configuration Information

Each device provides different levels of configuration information. Each device has one or more configurations, of which one is selected during probe/attach. A configuration provides power and bandwidth requirements. Within each configuration there can be multiple interfaces. A device interface is a collection of endpoints. For example USB speakers can have an interface for the audio data (Audio Class) and an interface for the knobs, dials and buttons (HID Class). All interfaces in a configuration are active at the same time and can be attached to by different drivers. Each interface can have alternates, providing different quality of service parameters. In for example cameras this is used to provide different frame sizes and numbers of frames per second.

Within each interface, 0 or more endpoints can be specified. Endpoints are the unidirectional access points for communicating with a device. They provide buffers to temporarily store incoming or outgoing data from the device. Each endpoint has a unique address within a configuration, the endpoint's number plus its direction. The default endpoint, endpoint 0, is not part of any interface and available in all configurations. It is managed by the services layer and not directly available to device drivers.

This hierarchical configuration information is described in the device by a standard set of descriptors (see section 9.6 of the USB specification). They can be requested through the Get Descriptor Request. The services layer caches these descriptors to avoid unnecessary transfers on the USB bus. Access to the descriptors is provided through function calls.

- Device descriptors: General information about the device, like Vendor, Product and Revision Id, supported device class, subclass and protocol if applicable, maximum packet size for the default endpoint, etc.
- Configuration descriptors: The number of interfaces in this configuration, suspend and resume functionality supported and power requirements.
- Interface descriptors: interface class, subclass and protocol if applicable, number of alternate settings for the interface and the number of endpoints.
- Endpoint descriptors: Endpoint address, direction and type, maximum packet size supported and polling frequency if type is interrupt endpoint. There is no descriptor for the default endpoint (endpoint 0) and it is never counted in an interface descriptor.
- String descriptors: In the other descriptors string indices are supplied for some fields.These can be used to retrieve descriptive strings, possibly in multiple languages.

Class specifications can add their own descriptor types that are available through the GetDescriptor Request.

Pipes Communication to end points on a device flows through so-called pipes. Drivers submit transfers to endpoints to a pipe and provide a callback to be called on completion or failure of the transfer (asynchronous transfers) or wait for completion (synchronous transfer). Transfers to an endpoint are serialised in the pipe. A transfer can either complete, fail or time-out (if a time-out has been set). There are two types of time-outs for transfers. Time-outs can happen due to time-out on the USBbus (milliseconds). These time-outs are seen as failures and can be due to disconnection of the device. A second form of time-out is implemented in software and is triggered when a transfer does not complete within a specified amount of time (seconds). These are caused by a device acknowledging negatively (NAK) the transferred packets. The cause for this is the device not being ready to receive data, buffer under- or overrun or protocol errors.

If a transfer over a pipe is larger than the maximum packet size specified in the associated endpoint descriptor, the host controller (OHCI) or the HC driver (UHCI) will split the transfer into packets of maximum packet size, with the last packet possibly smaller than the maximum packet size.

Sometimes it is not a problem for a device to return less data than requested. For example abulk-in-transfer to a modem might request 200 bytes of data, but the modem has only 5 bytes available at that time. The driver can set the short packet (SPD) flag. It allows the host controller to accept a packet even if the amount of data transferred is less than requested. This flag is only valid for in-transfers, as the amount of data to be sent to a device is always known beforehand. If an unrecoverable error occurs in a device during a transfer the pipe is stalled. Before any more data is accepted or sent the driver needs to resolve the cause of the stall and clear the endpoint stall condition through send the clear endpoint halt device request over the default pipe. The default endpoint should never stall.

There are four different types of endpoints and corresponding pipes: - Control pipe / default pipe: There is one control pipe per device, connected to the default endpoint (endpoint 0). The pipe carries the device requests and associated data. The difference between transfers over the default pipe and other pipes is that the protocol for the transfers is described in the USB specification. These requests are used to reset and configure the device. A basic set of commands that must be supported by each device is provided in chapter 9 of the USB specification. The commands supported on this pipe can be extended by a device class specification to support additional functionality.

- Bulk pipe: This is the USB equivalent to a raw transmission medium.

- Interrupt pipe: The host sends a request for data to the device and if the device has nothing to send, it will NAK the data packet. Interrupt transfers are scheduled at a frequency specified when creating the pipe.
- Isochronous pipe: These pipes are intended for isochronous data, for example video or audio streams, with fixed latency, but no guaranteed delivery. Some support for pipes of this type is available in the current implementation. Packets in control, bulk and interrupt transfers are retried if an error occurs during transmission or the device acknowledges the packet negatively (NAK) due to for example lack of buffer space to store the incoming data. Isochronous packets are however not retried in case of failed delivery or NAK of a packet as this might violate the timing constraints.

The availability of the necessary bandwidth is calculated during the creation of the pipe. Transfers are scheduled within frames of 1 millisecond. The bandwidth allocation within a frame is prescribed by the USB specification, section 5.6 [ 2]. Isochronous and interrupt transfers are allowed to consume up to 90% of the bandwidth within a frame. Packets for control and bulk transfers are scheduled after all isochronous and interrupt packets and will consume all the remaining bandwidth.

More information on scheduling of transfers and bandwidth reclamation can be found in chapter 5 of the USB specification, section 1.3 of the UHCI specification, and section 3.4.2 of the OHCI specification.

## 13.4. Device Probe and Attach

After the notification by the hub that a new device has been connected, the service layer switches on the port, providing the device with 100 mA of current. At this point the device is in its default state and listening to device address 0. The services layer will proceed to retrieve the various descriptors through the default pipe. After that it will send a Set Address request to move the device away from the default device address (address 0). Multiple device drivers might be able to support the device. For example a modem driver might be able to support an ISDN TA through the AT compatibility interface. A driver for that specific model of the ISDN adapter might however be able to provide much better support for this device. To support this flexibility, the probes return priorities indicating their level of support. Support for a specific revision of a product ranks the highest and the generic driver the lowest priority. It might also be that multiple drivers could attach to one device if there are multiple interfaces within one configuration. Each driver only needs to support a subset of the interfaces.

The probing for a driver for a newly attached device checks first for device specific drivers. If not found, the probe code iterates over all supported configurations until a driver attaches in a configuration. To support devices with multiple drivers on different interfaces, the probe iterates over all interfaces in a configuration that have not yet been claimed by a driver. Configurations that exceed the power budget for the hub are ignored. During attach the driver should initialise the device to its proper state, but not reset it, as this will make the device disconnect itself from the bus and restart the probing process for it. To avoid consuming unnecessary bandwidth should not claim the interrupt pipe at attach time, but should postpone allocating the pipe until the file is opened and the data is actually used. When the file is closed the pipe should be closed again, even though the device might still be attached.

### 13.4.1. Device Disconnect and Detach

A device driver should expect to receive errors during any transaction with the device. The design of USB supports and encourages the disconnection of devices at any point in time. Drivers should make sure that they do the right thing when the device disappears.

Furthermore a device that has been disconnected and reconnected will not be reattached at the same device instance. This might change in the future when more devices support serial numbers (see the device descriptor) or other means of defining an identity for a device have been developed.

The disconnection of a device is signaled by a hub in the interrupt packet delivered to the hub driver. The status change information indicates which port has seen a connection change. The device detach method for all device drivers for the device connected on that port are called and the structures cleaned up. If the port status indicates

that in the mean time a device has been connected to that port, the procedure for probing and attaching the device will be started. A device reset will produce a disconnect-connect sequence on the hub and will be handled as described above.

## 13.5. USB Drivers Protocol Information

The protocol used over pipes other than the default pipe is undefined by the USB specification. Information on this can be found from various sources. The most accurate source is the developer's section on the USB home pages. From these pages, a growing number of deviceclass specifications are available. These specifications specify what a compliant device should look like from a driver perspective, basic functionality it needs to provide and the protocol that is to be used over the communication channels. The USB specification includes the description of the Hub Class. A class specification for Human Interface Devices (HID) has been created to cater for keyboards, tablets, bar-code readers, buttons, knobs, switches, etc. A third example is the class specification for mass storage devices. For a full list of device classes see the developers section on the USB home pages.

For many devices the protocol information has not yet been published however. Information on the protocol being used might be available from the company making the device. Some companies will require you to sign a Non - Disclosure Agreement (NDA) before giving you the specifications. This in most cases precludes making the driver open source.

Another good source of information is the Linux driver sources, as a number of companies have started to provide drivers for Linux for their devices. It is always a good idea to contact the authors of those drivers for their source of information.

Example: Human Interface Devices The specification for the Human Interface Devices like keyboards, mice, tablets, buttons, dials,etc. is referred to in other device class specifications and is used in many devices.

For example audio speakers provide endpoints to the digital to analogue converters and possibly an extra pipe for a microphone. They also provide a HID endpoint in a separate interface for the buttons and dials on the front of the device. The same is true for the monitor control class. It is straightforward to build support for these interfaces through the available kernel and userland libraries together with the HID class driver or the generic driver. Another device that serves as an example for interfaces within one configuration driven by different device drivers is a cheap keyboard with built-in legacy mouse port. To avoid having the cost of including the hardware for a USB hub in the device, manufacturers combined the mouse data received from the PS/2 port on the back of the keyboard and the key presses from the keyboard into two separate interfaces in the same configuration. The mouse and keyboard drivers each attach to the appropriate interface and allocate the pipes to the two independent endpoints.

Example: Firmware download Many devices that have been developed are based on a general purpose processor with an additional USB core added to it. Because the development of drivers and firmware for USB devices is still very new, many devices require the downloading of the firmware after they have been connected.

The procedure followed is straightforward. The device identifies itself through a vendor and product Id. The first driver probes and attaches to it and downloads the firmware into it. After that the device soft resets itself and the driver is detached. After a short pause the device announces its presence on the bus. The device will have changed its vendor/product/revision Id to reflect the fact that it has been supplied with firmware and as a consequence a second driver will probe it and attach to it.

An example of these types of devices is the ActiveWire I/O board, based on the EZ-USB chip. For this chip a generic firmware downloader is available. The firmware downloaded into the ActiveWire board changes the revision Id. It will then perform a soft reset of the USB part of the EZ-USB chip to disconnect from the USB bus and again reconnect.

Example: Mass Storage Devices Support for mass storage devices is mainly built around existing protocols. The Iomega USB Zipdrive is based on the SCSI version of their drive. The SCSI commands and status messages are wrapped in blocks and transferred over the bulk pipes to and from the device, emulating a SCSI controller over the USB wire. ATAPI and UFI commands are supported in a similar fashion.

The Mass Storage Specification supports 2 different types of wrapping of the command block.The initial attempt was based on sending the command and status through the default pipe and using bulk transfers for the data to be moved between the host and the device. Based on experience a second approach was designed that was based on wrapping the command and status blocks and sending them over the bulk out and in endpoint. The specification specifies exactly what has to happen when and what has to be done in case an error condition is encountered. The biggest challenge when writing drivers for these devices is to fit USB based protocol into the existing support for mass storage devices. CAM provides hooks to do this in a fairly straight forward way. ATAPI is less simple as historically the IDE interface has never had many different appearances.

The support for the USB floppy from Y-E Data is again less straightforward as a new command set has been designed.

# Chapter 14. Newbus

Written by Jeroen Ruigrok van der Werven (asmodai) and Hiten Pandya.

*Special thanks to Matthew N. Dodd, Warner Losh, Bill Paul, Doug Rabson, Mike Smith, Peter Wemm and Scott Long.*

This chapter explains the Newbus device framework in detail.

## 14.1. Device Drivers

### 14.1.1. Purpose of a Device Driver

A device driver is a software component which provides the interface between the kernel's generic view of a peripheral (e.g., disk, network adapter) and the actual implementation of the peripheral. The *device driver interface (DDI)* is the defined interface between the kernel and the device driver component.

### 14.1.2. Types of Device Drivers

There used to be days in UNIX®, and thus FreeBSD, in which there were four types of devices defined:

- block device drivers
- character device drivers
- network device drivers
- pseudo-device drivers

*Block devices* performed in a way that used fixed size blocks [of data]. This type of driver depended on the so-called *buffer cache*, which had cached accessed blocks of data in a dedicated part of memory. Often this buffer cache was based on write-behind, which meant that when data was modified in memory it got synced to disk whenever the system did its periodical disk flushing, thus optimizing writes.

### 14.1.3. Character Devices

However, in the versions of FreeBSD 4.0 and onward the distinction between block and character devices became non-existent.

## 14.2. Overview of Newbus

*Newbus* is the implementation of a new bus architecture based on abstraction layers which saw its introduction in FreeBSD 3.0 when the Alpha port was imported into the source tree. It was not until 4.0 before it became the default system to use for device drivers. Its goals are to provide a more object-oriented means of interconnecting the various busses and devices which a host system provides to the *Operating System*.

Its main features include amongst others:

- dynamic attaching
- easy modularization of drivers
- pseudo-busses

One of the most prominent changes is the migration from the flat and ad-hoc system to a device tree layout.

At the top level resides the *"root"* device which is the parent to hang all other devices on. For each architecture, there is typically a single child of "root" which has such things as *host-to-PCI bridges*, etc. attached to it. For x86, this "root" device is the *"nexus"* device. For Alpha, various different models of Alpha have different top-level devices corresponding to the different hardware chipsets, including *lca*, *apecs*, *cia* and *tsunami*.

A device in the Newbus context represents a single hardware entity in the system. For instance each PCI device is represented by a Newbus device. Any device in the system can have children; a device which has children is often called a *"bus"*. Examples of common busses in the system are ISA and PCI, which manage lists of devices attached to ISA and PCI busses respectively.

Often, a connection between different kinds of bus is represented by a *"bridge"* device, which normally has one child for the attached bus. An example of this is a *PCI-to-PCI bridge* which is represented by a device `pcibN` on the parent PCI bus and has a child `pciN` for the attached bus. This layout simplifies the implementation of the PCI bus tree, allowing common code to be used for both top-level and bridged busses.

Each device in the Newbus architecture asks its parent to map its resources. The parent then asks its own parent until the nexus is reached. So, basically the nexus is the only part of the Newbus system which knows about all resources.

## Tip

An ISA device might want to map its IO port at `0x230`, so it asks its parent, in this case the ISA bus. The ISA bus hands it over to the PCI-to-ISA bridge which in its turn asks the PCI bus, which reaches the host-to-PCI bridge and finally the nexus. The beauty of this transition upwards is that there is room to translate the requests. For example, the `0x230` IO port request might become memory-mapped at `0xb0000230` on a MIPS box by the PCI bridge.

Resource allocation can be controlled at any place in the device tree. For instance on many Alpha platforms, ISA interrupts are managed separately from PCI interrupts and resource allocations for ISA interrupts are managed by the Alpha's ISA bus device. On IA-32, ISA and PCI interrupts are both managed by the top-level nexus device. For both ports, memory and port address space is managed by a single entity - nexus for IA-32 and the relevant chipset driver on Alpha (e.g., CIA or tsunami).

In order to normalize access to memory and port mapped resources, Newbus integrates the `bus_space` APIs from NetBSD. These provide a single API to replace inb/outb and direct memory reads/writes. The advantage of this is that a single driver can easily use either memory-mapped registers or port-mapped registers (some hardware supports both).

This support is integrated into the resource allocation mechanism. When a resource is allocated, a driver can retrieve the associated `bus_space_tag_t` and `bus_space_handle_t` from the resource.

Newbus also allows for definitions of interface methods in files dedicated to this purpose. These are the `.m` files that are found under the `src/sys` hierarchy.

The core of the Newbus system is an extensible "object-based programming" model. Each device in the system has a table of methods which it supports. The system and other devices uses those methods to control the device and request services. The different methods supported by a device are defined by a number of "interfaces". An "interface" is simply a group of related methods which can be implemented by a device.

In the Newbus system, the methods for a device are provided by the various device drivers in the system. When a device is attached to a driver during *auto-configuration*, it uses the method table declared by the driver. A device can later *detach* from its driver and *re-attach* to a new driver with a new method table. This allows dynamic replacement of drivers which can be useful for driver development.

The interfaces are described by an interface definition language similar to the language used to define vnode operations for file systems. The interface would be stored in a methods file (which would normally be named `foo_if.m`).

### Example 14.1. Newbus Methods

```
    # Foo subsystem/driver (a comment...)

  INTERFACE foo

METHOD int doit {
 device_t dev;
};

# DEFAULT is the method that will be used, if a method was not
# provided via: DEVMETHOD()

METHOD void doit_to_child {
 device_t dev;
 driver_t child;
} DEFAULT doit_generic_to_child;
```

When this interface is compiled, it generates a header file "`foo_if.h`" which contains function declarations:

```
    int FOO_DOIT(device_t dev);
    int FOO_DOIT_TO_CHILD(device_t dev, device_t child);
```

A source file, "`foo_if.c`" is also created to accompany the automatically generated header file; it contains implementations of those functions which look up the location of the relevant functions in the object's method table and call that function.

The system defines two main interfaces. The first fundamental interface is called *"device"* and includes methods which are relevant to all devices. Methods in the *"device"* interface include *"probe"*, *"attach"* and *"detach"* to control detection of hardware and *"shutdown"*, *"suspend"* and *"resume"* for critical event notification.

The second, more complex interface is *"bus"*. This interface contains methods suitable for devices which have children, including methods to access bus specific per-device information [1], event notification (*child_detached*, *driver_added*) and resource management (*alloc_resource*, *activate_resource*, *deactivate_resource*, *release_resource*).

Many methods in the "bus" interface are performing services for some child of the bus device. These methods would normally use the first two arguments to specify the bus providing the service and the child device which is requesting the service. To simplify driver code, many of these methods have accessor functions which lookup the parent and call a method on the parent. For instance the method `BUS_TEARDOWN_INTR(device_t dev, device_t child, ...)` can be called using the function `bus_teardown_intr(device_t child, ...)`.

Some bus types in the system define additional interfaces to provide access to bus-specific functionality. For instance, the PCI bus driver defines the "pci" interface which has two methods *read_config* and *write_config* for accessing the configuration registers of a PCI device.

## 14.3. Newbus API

As the Newbus API is huge, this section makes some effort at documenting it. More information to come in the next revision of this document.

[1] bus_generic_read_ivar(9) and bus_generic_write_ivar(9)

## 14.3.1. Important Locations in the Source Hierarchy

`src/sys/[arch]/[arch]` - Kernel code for a specific machine architecture resides in this directory. For example, the `i386` architecture, or the `SPARC64` architecture.

`src/sys/dev/[bus]` - device support for a specific `[bus]` resides in this directory.

`src/sys/dev/pci` - PCI bus support code resides in this directory.

`src/sys/[isa|pci]` - PCI/ISA device drivers reside in this directory. The PCI/ISA bus support code used to exist in this directory in FreeBSD version `4.0`.

## 14.3.2. Important Structures and Type Definitions

`devclass_t` - This is a type definition of a pointer to a `struct devclass`.

`device_method_t` - This is the same as `kobj_method_t` (see `src/sys/kobj.h`).

`device_t` - This is a type definition of a pointer to a `struct device`. `device_t` represents a device in the system. It is a kernel object. See `src/sys/sys/bus_private.h` for implementation details.

`driver_t` - This is a type definition which references `struct driver`. The `driver` struct is a class of the `device` kernel object; it also holds data private to the driver.

```
 struct driver {
KOBJ_CLASS_FIELDS;
void *priv;    /* driver private data */
 };
```

Figure 14.1. *driver_t* Implementation

A `device_state_t` type, which is an enumeration, `device_state`. It contains the possible states of a Newbus device before and after the autoconfiguration process.

```
 /*
  * src/sys/sys/bus.h
  */
 typedef enum device_state {
DS_NOTPRESENT, /* not probed or probe failed */
DS_ALIVE,   /* probe succeeded */
DS_ATTACHED, /* attach method called */
DS_BUSY    /* device is open */
 } device_state_t;
```

Figure 14.2. Device States *device_state_t*

# Chapter 15. Sound Subsystem

Contributed by Jean-Francois Dockes.

## 15.1. Introduction

The FreeBSD sound subsystem cleanly separates generic sound handling issues from device-specific ones. This makes it easier to add support for new hardware.

The pcm(4) framework is the central piece of the sound subsystem. It mainly implements the following elements:

- A system call interface (read, write, ioctls) to digitized sound and mixer functions. The ioctl command set is compatible with the legacy *OSS* or *Voxware* interface, allowing common multimedia applications to be ported without modification.
- Common code for processing sound data (format conversions, virtual channels).
- A uniform software interface to hardware-specific audio interface modules.
- Additional support for some common hardware interfaces (ac97), or shared hardware-specific code (ex: ISA DMA routines).

The support for specific sound cards is implemented by hardware-specific drivers, which provide channel and mixer interfaces to plug into the generic `pcm` code.

In this chapter, the term `pcm` will refer to the central, common part of the sound driver, as opposed to the hardware-specific modules.

The prospective driver writer will of course want to start from an existing module and use the code as the ultimate reference. But, while the sound code is nice and clean, it is also mostly devoid of comments. This document tries to give an overview of the framework interface and answer some questions that may arise while adapting the existing code.

As an alternative, or in addition to starting from a working example, you can find a commented driver template at https://people.FreeBSD.org/~cg/template.c

## 15.2. Files

All the relevant code lives in `/usr/src/sys/dev/sound/` , except for the public ioctl interface definitions, found in `/usr/src/sys/sys/soundcard.h`

Under `/usr/src/sys/dev/sound/` , the `pcm/` directory holds the central code, while the `pci/`, `isa/` and `usb/` directories have the drivers for PCI and ISA boards, and for USB audio devices.

## 15.3. Probing, Attaching, etc.

Sound drivers probe and attach in almost the same way as any hardware driver module. You might want to look at the ISA or PCI specific sections of the handbook for more information.

However, sound drivers differ in some ways:

- They declare themselves as `pcm` class devices, with a `struct snddev_info` device private structure:

```
        static driver_t xxx_driver = {
            "pcm",
```

```
        xxx_methods,
        sizeof(struct snddev_info)
};

DRIVER_MODULE(snd_xxxpci, pci, xxx_driver, pcm_devclass, 0, 0);
MODULE_DEPEND(snd_xxxpci, snd_pcm, PCM_MINVER, PCM_PREFVER,PCM_MAXVER);
```

Most sound drivers need to store additional private information about their device. A private data structure is usually allocated in the attach routine. Its address is passed to pcm by the calls to `pcm_register()` and `mixer_init()`. pcm later passes back this address as a parameter in calls to the sound driver interfaces.

- The sound driver attach routine should declare its MIXER or AC97 interface to pcm by calling `mixer_init()`. For a MIXER interface, this causes in turn a call to `xxxmixer_init()`.
- The sound driver attach routine declares its general CHANNEL configuration to pcm by calling `pcm_register(dev, sc, nplay, nrec)` , where `sc` is the address for the device data structure, used in further calls from pcm, and `nplay` and `nrec` are the number of play and record channels.
- The sound driver attach routine declares each of its channel objects by calls to `pcm_addchan()`. This sets up the channel glue in pcm and causes in turn a call to `xxxchannel_init()`.
- The sound driver detach routine should call `pcm_unregister()` before releasing its resources.

There are two possible methods to handle non-PnP devices:

- Use a `device_identify()` method (example: `sound/isa/es1888.c` ). The `device_identify()` method probes for the hardware at known addresses and, if it finds a supported device, creates a new pcm device which is then passed to probe/attach.
- Use a custom kernel configuration with appropriate hints for pcm devices (example: `sound/isa/mss.c` ).

pcm drivers should implement `device_suspend`, `device_resume` and `device_shutdown` routines, so that power management and module unloading function correctly.

## 15.4. Interfaces

The interface between the pcm core and the sound drivers is defined in terms of kernel objects.

There are two main interfaces that a sound driver will usually provide: *CHANNEL* and either *MIXER* or *AC97*.

The *AC97* interface is a very small hardware access (register read/write) interface, implemented by drivers for hardware with an AC97 codec. In this case, the actual MIXER interface is provided by the shared AC97 code in pcm.

### 15.4.1. The CHANNEL Interface

#### 15.4.1.1. Common Notes for Function Parameters

Sound drivers usually have a private data structure to describe their device, and one structure for each play and record data channel that it supports.

For all CHANNEL interface functions, the first parameter is an opaque pointer.

The second parameter is a pointer to the private channel data structure, except for `channel_init()` which has a pointer to the private device structure (and returns the channel pointer for further use by pcm).

#### 15.4.1.2. Overview of Data Transfer Operations

For sound data transfers, the pcm core and the sound drivers communicate through a shared memory area, described by a `struct snd_dbuf`.

struct snd_dbuf is private to pcm, and sound drivers obtain values of interest by calls to accessor functions (sndbuf_getxxx()).

The shared memory area has a size of sndbuf_getsize() and is divided into fixed size blocks of sndbuf_getblksz() bytes.

When playing, the general transfer mechanism is as follows (reverse the idea for recording):

- pcm initially fills up the buffer, then calls the sound driver's xxxchannel_trigger() function with a parameter of PCMTRIG_START.
- The sound driver then arranges to repeatedly transfer the whole memory area (sndbuf_getbuf(), sndbuf_getsize()) to the device, in blocks of sndbuf_getblksz() bytes. It calls back the chn_intr() pcm function for each transferred block (this will typically happen at interrupt time).
- chn_intr() arranges to copy new data to the area that was transferred to the device (now free), and make appropriate updates to the snd_dbuf structure.

### 15.4.1.3. channel_init

xxxchannel_init() is called to initialize each of the play or record channels. The calls are initiated from the sound driver attach routine. (See the probe and attach section).

```
static void *
xxxchannel_init(kobj_t obj, void *data,
   struct snd_dbuf *b, struct pcm_channel *c, int dir)❶
{
    struct xxx_info *sc = data;
    struct xxx_chinfo *ch;
     ...
    return ch;❷
}
```

❶ b is the address for the channel struct snd_dbuf. It should be initialized in the function by calling sndbuf_alloc(). The buffer size to use is normally a small multiple of the 'typical' unit transfer size for your device.

c is the pcm channel control structure pointer. This is an opaque object. The function should store it in the local channel structure, to be used in later calls to pcm (ie: chn_intr(c)).

dir indicates the channel direction (PCMDIR_PLAY or PCMDIR_REC ).

❷ The function should return a pointer to the private area used to control this channel. This will be passed as a parameter to other channel interface calls.

### 15.4.1.4. channel_setformat

xxxchannel_setformat() should set up the hardware for the specified channel for the specified sound format.

```
static int
xxxchannel_setformat(kobj_t obj, void *data, u_int32_t format)❶
{
    struct xxx_chinfo *ch = data;
     ...
    return 0;
}
```

❶ format is specified as an AFMT_XXX value (soundcard.h).

### 15.4.1.5. channel_setspeed

xxxchannel_setspeed() sets up the channel hardware for the specified sampling speed, and returns the possibly adjusted speed.

```
static int
xxxchannel_setspeed(kobj_t obj, void *data, u_int32_t speed)
{
    struct xxx_chinfo *ch = data;
     ...
    return speed;
}
```

### 15.4.1.6. channel_setblocksize

`xxxchannel_setblocksize()` sets the block size, which is the size of unit transactions between `pcm` and the sound driver, and between the sound driver and the device. Typically, this would be the number of bytes transferred before an interrupt occurs. During a transfer, the sound driver should call `pcm`'s `chn_intr()` every time this size has been transferred.

Most sound drivers only take note of the block size here, to be used when an actual transfer will be started.

```
static int
xxxchannel_setblocksize(kobj_t obj, void *data, u_int32_t blocksize)
{
    struct xxx_chinfo *ch = data;
     ...
    return blocksize;❶
}
```

❶ The function returns the possibly adjusted block size. In case the block size is indeed changed, `sndbuf_resize()` should be called to adjust the buffer.

### 15.4.1.7. channel_trigger

`xxxchannel_trigger()` is called by `pcm` to control data transfer operations in the driver.

```
static int
xxxchannel_trigger(kobj_t obj, void *data, int go)❶
{
    struct xxx_chinfo *ch = data;
     ...
    return 0;
}
```

❶ go defines the action for the current call. The possible values are:

- `PCMTRIG_START`: the driver should start a data transfer from or to the channel buffer. If needed, the buffer base and size can be retrieved through `sndbuf_getbuf()` and `sndbuf_getsize()`.
- `PCMTRIG_EMLDMAWR` / `PCMTRIG_EMLDMARD`: this tells the driver that the input or output buffer may have been updated. Most drivers just ignore these calls.
- `PCMTRIG_STOP` / `PCMTRIG_ABORT` : the driver should stop the current transfer.

**Note**

If the driver uses ISA DMA, `sndbuf_isadma()` should be called before performing actions on the device, and will take care of the DMA chip side of things.

### 15.4.1.8. channel_getptr

`xxxchannel_getptr()` returns the current offset in the transfer buffer. This will typically be called by `chn_intr()`, and this is how `pcm` knows where it can transfer new data.

#### 15.4.1.9. channel_free

xxxchannel_free() is called to free up channel resources, for example when the driver is unloaded, and should be implemented if the channel data structures are dynamically allocated or if sndbuf_alloc() was not used for buffer allocation.

#### 15.4.1.10. channel_getcaps

```
struct pcmchan_caps *
xxxchannel_getcaps(kobj_t obj, void *data)
{
    return &xxx_caps;❶
}
```

❶ The routine returns a pointer to a (usually statically-defined) pcmchan_caps structure (defined in sound/pcm/channel.h. The structure holds the minimum and maximum sampling frequencies, and the accepted sound formats. Look at any sound driver for an example.

#### 15.4.1.11. More Functions

channel_reset(), channel_resetdone(), and channel_notify() are for special purposes and should not be implemented in a driver without discussing it on the FreeBSD multimedia mailing list.

channel_setdir() is deprecated.

### 15.4.2. The MIXER Interface

#### 15.4.2.1. mixer_init

xxxmixer_init() initializes the hardware and tells pcm what mixer devices are available for playing and recording

```
static int
xxxmixer_init(struct snd_mixer *m)
{
    struct xxx_info   *sc = mix_getdevinfo(m);
    u_int32_t v;

    [Initialize hardware]

    [Set appropriate bits in v for play mixers]❶
    mix_setdevs(m, v);
    [Set appropriate bits in v for record mixers]
    mix_setrecdevs(m, v)

    return 0;
}
```

❶ Set bits in an integer value and call mix_setdevs() and mix_setrecdevs() to tell pcm what devices exist.

Mixer bits definitions can be found in soundcard.h (SOUND_MASK_XXX values and SOUND_MIXER_XXX bit shifts).

#### 15.4.2.2. mixer_set

xxxmixer_set() sets the volume level for one mixer device.

```
static int
xxxmixer_set(struct snd_mixer *m, unsigned dev,
                 unsigned left, unsigned right)❶
{
    struct sc_info *sc = mix_getdevinfo(m);
    [set volume level]
    return left | (right << 8);❷
}
```

❶ The device is specified as a SOUND_MIXER_XXX value

The volume values are specified in range [0-100]. A value of zero should mute the device.

❷ As the hardware levels probably will not match the input scale, and some rounding will occur, the routine returns the actual level values (in range 0-100) as shown.

### 15.4.2.3. mixer_setrecsrc

`xxxmixer_setrecsrc()` sets the recording source device.

```
static int
xxxmixer_setrecsrc(struct snd_mixer *m, u_int32_t src)❶
{
    struct xxx_info *sc = mix_getdevinfo(m);

    [look for non zero bit(s) in src, set up hardware]

    [update src to reflect actual action]
    return src;❷
}
```

❶ The desired recording devices are specified as a bit field

❷ The actual devices set for recording are returned. Some drivers can only set one device for recording. The function should return -1 if an error occurs.

### 15.4.2.4. mixer_uninit, mixer_reinit

`xxxmixer_uninit()` should ensure that all sound is muted and if possible mixer hardware should be powered down

`xxxmixer_reinit()` should ensure that the mixer hardware is powered up and any settings not controlled by `mixer_set()` or `mixer_setrecsrc()` are restored.

## 15.4.3. The AC97 Interface

The *AC97* interface is implemented by drivers with an AC97 codec. It only has three methods:

- `xxxac97_init()` returns the number of ac97 codecs found.
- `ac97_read()` and `ac97_write()` read or write a specified register.

The *AC97* interface is used by the AC97 code in `pcm` to perform higher level operations. Look at `sound/pci/maestro3.c` or many others under `sound/pci/` for an example.

# Chapter 16. PC Card

This chapter will talk about the FreeBSD mechanisms for writing a device driver for a PC Card or CardBus device. However, at present it just documents how to add a new device to an existing pccard driver.

## 16.1. Adding a Device

Device drivers know what devices they support. There is a table of supported devices in the kernel that drivers use to attach to a device.

### 16.1.1. Overview

PC Cards are identified in one of two ways, both based on the *Card Information Structure* (CIS) stored on the card. The first method is to use numeric manufacturer and product numbers. The second method is to use the human readable strings that are also contained in the CIS. The PC Card bus uses a centralized database and some macros to facilitate a design pattern to help the driver writer match devices to his driver.

Original equipment manufacturers (OEMs) often develop a reference design for a PC Card product, then sell this design to other companies to market. Those companies refine the design, market the product to their target audience or geographic area, and put their own name plate onto the card. The refinements to the physical card are typically very minor, if any changes are made at all. To strengthen their brand, these vendors place their company name in the human readable strings in the CIS space, but leave the manufacturer and product IDs unchanged.

Because of this practice, FreeBSD drivers usually rely on numeric IDs for device identification. Using numeric IDs and a centralized database complicates adding IDs and support for cards to the system. One must carefully check to see who really made the card, especially when it appears that the vendor who made the card might already have a different manufacturer ID listed in the central database. Linksys, D-Link, and NetGear are a number of US manufacturers of LAN hardware that often sell the same design. These same designs can be sold in Japan under names such as Buffalo and Corega. Often, these devices will all have the same manufacturer and product IDs.

The PC Card bus code keeps a central database of card information, but not which driver is associated with them, in `/sys/dev/pccard/pccarddevs` . It also provides a set of macros that allow one to easily construct simple entries in the table the driver uses to claim devices.

Finally, some really low end devices do not contain manufacturer identification at all. These devices must be detected by matching the human readable CIS strings. While it would be nice if we did not need this method as a fallback, it is necessary for some very low end CD-ROM players and Ethernet cards. This method should generally be avoided, but a number of devices are listed in this section because they were added prior to the recognition of the OEM nature of the PC Card business. When adding new devices, prefer using the numeric method.

### 16.1.2. Format of pccarddevs

There are four sections in the `pccarddevs` files. The first section lists the manufacturer numbers for vendors that use them. This section is sorted in numerical order. The next section has all of the products that are used by these vendors, along with their product ID numbers and a description string. The description string typically is not used (instead we set the device's description based on the human readable CIS, even if we match on the numeric version). These two sections are then repeated for devices that use the string matching method. Finally, C-style comments enclosed in `/*` and `*/` characters are allowed anywhere in the file.

The first section of the file contains the vendor IDs. Please keep this list sorted in numeric order. Also, please coordinate changes to this file because we share it with NetBSD to help facilitate a common clearing house for this information. For example, here are the first few vendor IDs:

```
vendor FUJITSU   0x0004  Fujitsu Corporation
vendor NETGEAR_2  0x000b  Netgear
```

```
vendor PANASONIC  0x0032 Matsushita Electric Industrial Co.
vendor SANDISK    0x0045 Sandisk Corporation
```

Chances are very good that the `NETGEAR_2` entry is really an OEM that NETGEAR purchased cards from and the author of support for those cards was unaware at the time that Netgear was using someone else's ID. These entries are fairly straightforward. The vendor keyword denotes the kind of line that this is, followed by the name of the vendor. This name will be repeated later in `pccarddevs`, as well as used in the driver's match tables, so keep it short and a valid C identifier. A numeric ID in hex identifies the manufacturer. Do not add IDs of the form `0xffffffff` or `0xffff` because these are reserved IDs (the former is "no ID set" while the latter is sometimes seen in extremely poor quality cards to try to indicate "none"). Finally there is a string description of the company that makes the card. This string is not used in FreeBSD for anything but commentary purposes.

The second section of the file contains the products. As shown in this example, the format is similar to the vendor lines:

```
/* Allied Telesis K.K. */
product ALLIEDTELESIS LA_PCM 0x0002 Allied Telesis LA-PCM

/* Archos */
product ARCHOS ARC_ATAPI 0x0043 MiniCD
```

The `product` keyword is followed by the vendor name, repeated from above. This is followed by the product name, which is used by the driver and should be a valid C identifier, but may also start with a number. As with the vendors, the hex product ID for this card follows the same convention for `0xffffffff` and `0xffff`. Finally, there is a string description of the device itself. This string typically is not used in FreeBSD, since FreeBSD's pccard bus driver will construct a string from the human readable CIS entries, but it can be used in the rare cases where this is somehow insufficient. The products are in alphabetical order by manufacturer, then numerical order by product ID. They have a C comment before each manufacturer's entries and there is a blank line between entries.

The third section is like the previous vendor section, but with all of the manufacturer numeric IDs set to `-1`, meaning "match anything found" in the FreeBSD pccard bus code. Since these are C identifiers, their names must be unique. Otherwise the format is identical to the first section of the file.

The final section contains the entries for those cards that must be identified by string entries. This section's format is a little different from the generic section:

```
product ADDTRON AWP100  { "Addtron", "AWP-100&spWireless&spPCMCIA", "Version&sp01.02", ↺
NULL }
product ALLIEDTELESIS WR211PCM { "Allied&spTelesis&spK.K.", "WR211PCM", NULL, NULL } ↺
Allied Telesis WR211PCM
```

The familiar `product` keyword is followed by the vendor name and the card name, just as in the second section of the file. Here the format deviates from that used earlier. There is a {} grouping, followed by a number of strings. These strings correspond to the vendor, product, and extra information that is defined in a CIS_INFO tuple. These strings are filtered by the program that generates `pccarddevs.h` to replace &sp with a real space. NULL strings mean that the corresponding part of the entry should be ignored. The example shown here contains a bad entry. It should not contain the version number unless that is critical for the operation of the card. Sometimes vendors will have many different versions of the card in the field that all work, in which case that information only makes it harder for someone with a similar card to use it with FreeBSD. Sometimes it is necessary when a vendor wishes to sell many different parts under the same brand due to market considerations (availability, price, and so forth). Then it can be critical to disambiguating the card in those rare cases where the vendor kept the same manufacturer/product pair. Regular expression matching is not available at this time.

## 16.1.3. Sample Probe Routine

To understand how to add a device to the list of supported devices, one must understand the probe and/or match routines that many drivers have. It is complicated a little in FreeBSD 5.x because there is a compatibility layer for OLDCARD present as well. Since only the window-dressing is different, an idealized version will be presented here.

```
static const struct pccard_product wi_pccard_products[] = {
 PCMCIA_CARD(3COM, 3CRWE737A, 0),
 PCMCIA_CARD(BUFFALO, WLI_PCM_S11, 0),
 PCMCIA_CARD(BUFFALO, WLI_CF_S11G, 0),
 PCMCIA_CARD(TDK, LAK_CD011WL, 0),
 { NULL }
};

static int
wi_pccard_probe(dev)
 device_t dev;
{
 const struct pccard_product *pp;

 if ((pp = pccard_product_lookup(dev, wi_pccard_products,
     sizeof(wi_pccard_products[0]), NULL)) != NULL) {
  if (pp->pp_name != NULL)
   device_set_desc(dev, pp->pp_name);
  return (0);
 }
 return (ENXIO);
}
```

Here we have a simple pccard probe routine that matches a few devices. As stated above, the name may vary (if it is not `foo_pccard_probe()` it will be `foo_pccard_match()`). The function `pccard_product_lookup()` is a generalized function that walks the table and returns a pointer to the first entry that it matches. Some drivers may use this mechanism to convey additional information about some cards to the rest of the driver, so there may be some variance in the table. The only requirement is that each row of the table must have a `struct pccard_product` as the first element.

Looking at the table `wi_pccard_products`, one notices that all the entries are of the form `PCMCIA_CARD(`*`foo`*`, `*`bar`*`, `*`baz`*`)`. The *`foo`* part is the manufacturer ID from `pccarddevs`. The *`bar`* part is the product ID. *`baz`* is the expected function number for this card. Many pccards can have multiple functions, and some way to disambiguate function 1 from function 0 is needed. You may see `PCMCIA_CARD_D`, which includes the device description from `pccarddevs`. You may also see `PCMCIA_CARD2` and `PCMCIA_CARD2_D` which are used when you need to match both CIS strings and manufacturer numbers, in the "use the default description" and "take the description from pccarddevs" flavors.

### 16.1.4. Putting it All Together

To add a new device, one must first obtain the identification information from the device. The easiest way to do this is to insert the device into a PC Card or CF slot and issue `devinfo -v`. Sample output:

```
        cbb1 pnpinfo vendor=0x104c device=0xac51 subvendor=0x1265 subdevice=0x0300 ↺
class=0x060700 at slot=10 function=1
          cardbus1
          pccard1
            unknown pnpinfo manufacturer=0x026f product=0x030c cisvendor="BUFFALO" ↺
cisproduct="WLI2-CF-S11" function_type=6 at function=0
```

`manufacturer` and `product` are the numeric IDs for this product, while `cisvendor` and `cisproduct` are the product description strings from the CIS.

Since we first want to prefer the numeric option, first try to construct an entry based on that. The above card has been slightly fictionalized for the purpose of this example. The vendor is BUFFALO, which we see already has an entry:

```
vendor BUFFALO   0x026f BUFFALO (Melco Corporation)
```

But there is no entry for this particular card. Instead we find:

```
/* BUFFALO */
product BUFFALO WLI_PCM_S11 0x0305 BUFFALO AirStation 11Mbps WLAN
product BUFFALO LPC_CF_CLT 0x0307 BUFFALO LPC-CF-CLT
```

```
product BUFFALO LPC3_CLT 0x030a BUFFALO LPC3-CLT Ethernet Adapter
product BUFFALO WLI_CF_S11G 0x030b BUFFALO AirStation 11Mbps CF WLAN
```

To add the device, we can just add this entry to pccarddevs:

```
product BUFFALO WLI2_CF_S11G 0x030c BUFFALO AirStation ultra 802.11b CF
```

Once these steps are complete, the card can be added to the driver. That is a simple operation of adding one line:

```
static const struct pccard_product wi_pccard_products[] = {
 PCMCIA_CARD(3COM, 3CRWE737A, 0),
 PCMCIA_CARD(BUFFALO, WLI_PCM_S11, 0),
 PCMCIA_CARD(BUFFALO, WLI_CF_S11G, 0),
+ PCMCIA_CARD(BUFFALO, WLI_CF2_S11G, 0),
 PCMCIA_CARD(TDK, LAK_CD011WL, 0),
 { NULL }
};
```

Note that I have included a '+' in the line before the line that I added, but that is simply to highlight the line. Do not add it to the actual driver. Once you have added the line, you can recompile your kernel or module and test it. If the device is recognized and works, please submit a patch. If it does not work, please figure out what is needed to make it work and submit a patch. If the device is not recognized at all, you have done something wrong and should recheck each step.

If you are a FreeBSD src committer, and everything appears to be working, then you can commit the changes to the tree. However, there are some minor tricky things to be considered. pccarddevs must be committed to the tree first. Then pccarddevs.h must be regenerated and committed as a second step, ensuring that the right $FreeBSD$ tag is in the latter file. Finally, commit the additions to the driver.

## 16.1.5. Submitting a New Device

Please do not send entries for new devices to the author directly. Instead, submit them as a PR and send the author the PR number for his records. This ensures that entries are not lost. When submitting a PR, it is unnecessary to include the pccardevs.h diffs in the patch, since those will be regenerated. It is necessary to include a description of the device, as well as the patches to the client driver. If you do not know the name, use OEM99 as the name, and the author will adjust OEM99 accordingly after investigation. Committers should not commit OEM99, but instead find the highest OEM entry and commit one more than that.

# Part III. Appendices

# Table of Contents

# Bibliography

[1] Marshall Kirk McKusick, Keith Bostic, Michael J Karels, and John S Quarterman. Copyright © 1996 Addison-Wesley Publishing Company, Inc.. 0-201-54979-4. Addison-Wesley Publishing Company, Inc.. *The Design and Implementation of the 4.4 BSD Operating System*. 1-2.

# Index

## N



## O



## P



## R



## S



## T



## U



## V



## W

www.ingramcontent.com/pod-product-compliance
Lightning Source LLC
Chambersburg PA
CBHW082116070326
40690CB00049B/3318

www.ingramcontent.com/pod-product-compliance
Lightning Source LLC
Chambersburg PA
CBHW062058050326
40690CB00016B/3141
* 9 7 8 1 6 8 0 9 2 1 6 8 7 *